VINO

VINO

The Wines and Winemakers
of Italy

BURTON ANDERSON

An Atlantic Monthly Press Book
LITTLE, BROWN AND COMPANY • BOSTON • TORONTO

FIRST EDITION

Library of Congress Cataloging in Publication Data

Anderson, Burton.
  Vino, the wines and winemakers of Italy.

  "An Atlantic Monthly Press book."
  Includes index.
  1. Wine and wine making — Italy. I. Title.
TP559.I8A57   641.2'22'0945   80–19133
ISBN 0–316–03948–9

The maps for this book were drawn by Angelo Cattaneo.
Photographs on pages 242, 249, 256, 299, and 305 are re-
produced through the courtesy of *Italian Wines & Spirits*.
The photograph on page 309 is by Aldo Bartoccioni. All other
photographs are by the author.

ATLANTIC–LITTLE, BROWN BOOKS
ARE PUBLISHED BY
LITTLE, BROWN AND COMPANY
IN ASSOCIATION WITH
THE ATLANTIC MONTHLY PRESS

MV
Published simultaneously in Canada
by Little, Brown & Company (Canada) Limited

PRINTED IN THE UNITED STATES OF AMERICA

For Nancy, Gaia,
and Benjamin

CONTENTS

VINO

THE ITINERARY

From Mont Blanc to Pantelleria

THIS journey in quest of the wines of Italy has physical points of departure and arrival, though they are mere expedients, for in literature even the pursuit of an infinitude has to have a beginning and an end. Mont Blanc in the Alps and the isle of Pantelleria off the coast of Tunisia are real places, but they could just as well be considered symbols in the context of this work, extremities of a world whose exploration might begin anywhere at any time but once begun is endless. If you follow the course of this journey with map in hand, you will find that it often strays off main routes onto byways. These back roads through a land of vines more abundant and diversified than any other on earth are not always clearly charted. But the rewards for those who follow them are wines whose virtues can only be enhanced by the challenge of discovering their sources.

The route winds down the length of the peninsula and out across the Mediterranean to Sardinia and Sicily, crisscrossing all twenty regions of an ancient land whose majesty prevails despite strains thrust upon it by a people's sometimes painful striving for modernity. Along the way, the landscape changes with dramatic abruptness, from mountains to valleys, from gentle hills to rolling plains and rugged seacoasts, vineyards claiming a share of space nearly everywhere a vine can put its roots down.

More than just a trip, this book represents a continuing adventure in which time plays a greater role than distance, for it began in 1959 when I first entered Italy at the Brenner Pass and drove down the old route through Bolzano and Trento to Verona, passing more vineyards in an afternoon, it seemed, than I had seen before in my lifetime. I have traveled many wine roads since, in Italy and elsewhere, yet my most vivid impression of the sort of place wine comes from is still of those vineyards of the Adige valley, climbing from the stony banks of the river to as far up the mountainsides as a man with a hoe would dare to scramble.

In those days much Italian wine was sold in unlabeled flasks with hand-woven straw bases, crudely hewn corks forced into their necks just far enough so they could be pulled out again without using a corkscrew. The wine, well, with due allowance for my youthful lack of discretion, was usually decent and often very good. And even when it was a trifle rough, one was consoled by the low price and the inevitable spoken assurance of the seller that it was not only *locale* but *genuino*.

But that was long ago, before the trans-Europe superhighway cut the driving time between the Brenner Pass and Verona to two hours, before the flask gave way to less colorful containers, before wines that are not only "local" and "genuine" but unlabeled and unclassified became the object of wistful quests by writers and nostalgia buffs. It must have been the era that Professors M. A. Amerine and V. D. Singleton had in mind when they wrote in *Wine: An Introduction for Americans,* first published in 1965:

Thus, in summary, the wines of Italy are made from small vineyard holdings in mountainous areas in promiscuous culture, and the many untrained winemakers use rather primitive techniques. The wines do not enjoy sufficient distribution among critical consumers either inside or outside Italy to force an improvement in the quality. The average Italian consumer is not critical of the quality of his wines.

Indeed, times have changed. Since 1963, when laws were decreed to control name and origin, Italy has made greater progress in defining and improving its premium wines than has any other nation, with a subsequent impact on the entire scope of wine production that has been truly revolutionary.

By 1980, more than 200 zones had met *denominazione di origine controllata* standards for their wines of "particular reputation and worth." The regulations, known by their initials as DOC, resemble the *appellation contrôlée* laws of France, and in some respects even go beyond them. Four wines — first Barolo and Barbaresco, then Vino Nobile di Montepulciano and Brunello di Montalcino — have been designated for an even more elite category, *denominazione di origine controllata e garantita* (DOCG), reserved for certain wines of special status produced under conditions of guaranteed quality.

The rules have helped to create a climate of trust that, in turn, has encouraged producers throughout Italy to make premium wines to be sold by the bottle at premium prices. Although DOC wines represent only about 12 percent of Italian production, that portion looks significant in light of an average volume of more than 7 billion liters a year, largest of any nation.

Throughout the DOC era, with its focus on quality, growth has continued in the rest of the industry, with its emphasis on quantity. Most wine consumed by Italians at the rate of nearly 100 liters a year is of the mass variety, and most wine shipped abroad at the rate of about 1.5 billion liters annually is too. But lately even large-scale production of wine has improved so markedly in Italy that the attitude so aptly described by Hugh Johnson in *The World Atlas of Wine* (1971) — "Yet what is at the same time amiable and maddening about her is her age-old insouciance about it all" — is rapidly becoming just a memory.

Italy produces more than a fifth of the world's wine and accounts for nearly a third of the world's total exports. Production has been increasing slowly while the percentage of the citizenry that derives income primarily from grapes and wine has been decreasing rapidly. This change is due directly to the subsidized consolidation of winemaking in cooperatives and to the conversion of most of the nation's vineyards from promiscuous culture (land shared by vines and other crops) to specialized culture. Since 1956, the number of *cantine sociali* has increased from 264 to more than 800. By 1980, these cooperatives accounted for more than 40 percent of national production, though they have the plant capacity to produce more than half the nation's wine. Staffed by trained experts, some cooperatives compete successfully in the quality field, though many others have not lived up to expectations either qualitatively or financially.

Italy has numerous institutions that provide training in viticulture and oenology, several at university level. The graduates, some employed by wineries, some working independently, have been injecting fresh ideas into a craft that has flourished in their homeland for as long as history has been recorded. In the last decade, Italians have made tradition-shattering advancements in winemaking techniques, adapting new concepts, sometimes of foreign origin, to the special conditions of their climate, soil, and vines to make better use of those raw materials, the grapes, whose overall quality is unsurpassed anywhere.

Italy still has a way to go, but remarkable improvements have been recorded, particularly in the style of transmitting grapes into wines that are brighter and more harmoniously composed than before. In this sense, white wines have probably benefited most. A decade ago many were vinified and aged (according to prevailing Italian tastes) into wines that could be somewhat oxidized and off balance; today many show admirable equilibrium in fruit and acids with resulting fresher and livelier flavors than before (and Italian tastes have been changing with them).

A trend toward "new wines," predominately red, gained momentum through the late 1970s. Producers in many regions were busy creating their own versions of, and markets for, these *vini novelli* whose inspiration can be traced directly to France's Beaujolais *nouveau*. By generating quick capital and enabling wineries to clear their stocks in a matter of weeks instead of months or years, they have provided a boost to an industry that has quickly learned the meaning of a relatively new term in the winemakers' vocabulary: *marketing*. These new wines, enthusiastically received by Italian consumers, also have been finding markets abroad.

Still, it would be an error and an injustice to credit innovation alone with the current high level of winemaking in Italy. The core of excellence has been there all along; many individuals have always set their standards above any that could be imposed by law. In every era Italy has boasted winemakers of skill and integrity. If at certain points in time their methods seemed outmoded when compared to those current in other nations, the dedication of these men and women has remained exemplary. Today there seem to be more such winemakers at work than ever before, equipped not only with the techniques but, perhaps even more important, the desire to carry their wines to the forefront of international prestige.

The Predicament of Image

Talk of a Renaissance or at least a Risorgimento of Italian wine seems neither premature nor exaggerated within Italy, though the magnitude of the revival has yet to manifest itself fully abroad. The key stimulus to recent improvement has been the changing attitude in Italy toward wine, the increasing demand for quality that is by no means confined to the middle range. The market for elite, estate-bottled, relatively costly wine has increased at a startling rate in Italy in recent years, to such an extent that few of the truly great bottles leave the country.

Interest in wine nationwide has now reached striking dimensions.

Scores of periodicals are devoted primarily to wines and spirits, and dozens of books and catalogues on the subject have appeared in recent years. Wine roads have been institutionalized through production zones in many regions. Numerous *enoteche,* wine libraries that double as tasting centers, have been set up through both public and private funds to boost national, regional, or local products. As an indication of the scope of Italian production, more than a thousand producers present bottles annually at Vinitaly in Verona and Bibe in Genoa, the most important of Italy's many wine fairs.

Shops in Milan, Rome, Bari, Palermo, and even small towns, now carry wines from far afield. Wine clubs offer their selections through the mail. Some restaurants have well-stocked cellars where not long ago the choice of wines was confined to either *rosso* or *bianco.* Many places that serve wine employ a professional steward, who is likely to be a member of the increasingly active Associazione Italiana Sommeliers.

But despite this flourish, the fact remains that most non-Italians have never tasted a great Italian wine; some may even doubt that such a thing exists. Italians know better, of course, but so far they could be accused of keeping their finest wines to themselves.

The problem is not lack of exports. Italy is the chief supplier of wine to many countries, including France (its leading customer), West Germany, the United States, and Canada. An impressive increase in sales of DOC wines in the United States, Britain, and Canada, along with steady growth in other countries, cannot hide the fact that the principal earner of foreign currency is unclassified wine, much of it *vino da taglio* that finds its way into vats in the south of France. Vineyards of Apulia, Sicily, Sardinia, and other southern regions provide most of this blending wine in two basic types. One is potent and usually red; it gives a needed spike to the average Frenchman's quota of *vin ordinaire.* The other is rather neutral in aroma and flavor, usually white; it fits nicely into the formulas for vermouths. *Vino da taglio* was the issue in the so-called wine war between France and Italy that flared at intervals through the 1970s.

Blending wine is only one facet of a larger, more complex, predicament of image that has haunted Italian wine for decades and, even now that it is the world's number one best-seller, prevents it from winning its fair share of critical acclaim. The word *vino* still evokes smiles, winks, memories of lighthearted liquids that were worth the price if for no other reason than that the flasks they came in made nifty candleholders. Image builders have faced an uphill task in trying to suppress the shady, if colorful, tales that grew around Italian wines during the years of abuse and neglect.

It is admittedly difficult to ponder things Italian without a touch of levity, for after all one of the nation's perpetual assets has been its ability to laugh at itself. Still, the era of the comic approach to Italian wine is over, or ought to be. No wonder Italian winemakers anticipate the day when they may enjoy the last laugh.

In the meantime, serious work remains to be done, as much in the marketplace as in the vineyards. The world's wine drinkers do not now associate Italy with the sort of greatness worthy of the inflated prices that are routine for so many wines of France, Germany, and California. How do you convince an American, for instance, that a Barbaresco *riserva* at $6 or $7 a bottle may be equal to a *premier cru* of the Haut-Médoc at $30 or $35? Only Brunello di Montalcino of Tuscany has come onto the U.S. market in the price range of the great Bordeaux and Burgundys, but Brunello alone has not been enough to convince the experts.

Bordeaux owes its greatness in part to its foreign market, originally English, which has served as a continuing stimulus to widespread production of fine wine. On the other hand, the demand for the great wines of Italy until recently was largely limited to regional clienteles, as often as not relatives of the winemaker or friends of the family. So those growers who lacked independent means tended to make wine as a passionate sideline while farming or holding down a job somewhere else. Many small-scale winemakers lacked the vineyard space, the cellar facilities, or the assured market to devote their time entirely to wine.

The heightening of domestic demand has claimed most of the finest wines almost as soon as they go into bottle. Hence little has been available for export despite increasing signals of interest coming in from abroad. However, some winemakers have passed up certain sales in Italy, even accepting lower profits than warranted, in the hope of gaining international recognition. Others have let their overseas aspirations be frustrated by visions of bureaucratic red tape and fears that their wine would be improperly dealt with by shippers and foreign importers.

Even if trade barriers in fine Italian wine are more imagined than real, they are breaking down only gradually. Foreign buyers and Italian shippers have had little trouble doing business in the mass market, where satisfactory earnings have been realized by many Italian companies, often on small profit margins. Italy enjoys a clear advantage over all other nations in its capacity to produce healthy, ripe grapes in enormous quantity, thanks to favorable climatic conditions throughout the country. Italian wineries have been able to turn out sound, wholesome wine on a large scale and sell it at reasonable price. Foreign markets have further encouraged the seemingly endless production of such good wines as Soave, Bardolino, Frascati, Lambrusco, Verdicchio, young Chianti, and many more wines that are rarely considered great but provide the consumer with good value.

Low cost has often worked in favor of the Italians with their seemingly uncanny knack for providing good quality at more reasonable prices than those of equivalent wines from other nations. But there is a difference between reasonable and just plain cheap. The tactics of price cutting and flooding the market with bargain wine sold at less than cost, as engaged in by some Italian firms lately to undercut competitors, have probably done more than anything else to harm the good name of Italian wine abroad. Whatever the short-term gains of such practices, in the long run they are likely to prove self-defeating.

In the elite bracket there has been a marked reluctance by non-Italian buyers to commit themselves. A factor working against the Italians is that many foreign professionals have had their palates educated in the English tradition toward Bordeaux and Burgundy in red wines, and Burgundy and the Rhine in whites. As a result, wines of Italy and some other nations, wines that are truly distinguished but "different," have had trouble establishing themselves with taste leaders.

In the United States, Italian wines enjoyed a boom in sales through the 1970s that was little short of spectacular. In 1979, Americans drank more than eleven times as much Italian wine as they had in 1970 and they also drank more than three times as much Italian wine as they did French. The 163 million liters of Italian table wine imported in 1979 represented about 55 percent of the total for foreign wines on the U.S. market and about 10 percent of all wine consumed in the United States. But the Italian conquest was not in the high-quality field. About 80 percent of the wine sold consisted of five popular types, and Lambrusco alone accounted for more than 50 percent of sales. Only in 1979 did the Italians finally surpass the French in earnings on the U.S. market, but that signified that the average bottle of Italian wine cost about a third the price of a French bottle.

In the United Kingdom, sales of Italian table wines also increased more than tenfold between 1970 and 1979, but France maintained its solid lead as a supplier of bottled wines. More than half the Italian wine sold was DOC, though the field in Britain too was dominated by popular brands.

Still, the outlook is not as bleak as it might appear for exports of fine Italian wine. Extensive vine plantings in Italy in the late 1960s and early 1970s, and advanced techniques of winemaking, are steadily increasing production of superior quality wine, although there has never been a shortage of good wine for export. Some judicious importers and merchants in the United States and Britain have acquired exceptional Italian wines, sometimes after traveling to the cellars to get them. But Italians themselves will need to educate foreign consumers more effectively about special quality and value if they expect to gain their justified share of the world market for great wine.

Great Expectations

As the Renaissance gathers momentum, claims have been made about Italy's "natural preeminence" in the world of wine by promoters who hark back to the days when the ancient Greeks called the country Enotria, the land of wine. The challenge is there, and many Italian winemakers are meeting it gallantly, but the ultimate status of Italian wine relies on a sustained effort in the vineyards and wineries to realize the nation's eminent potentiality.

This text, then, scrutinizes an era of profound change and great expectations. Yet, for all we know, today's vineyard could be tomorrow's corn patch or the site of next year's plastics factory, because winemaking is a tenuous sort of occupation that, especially at the highest levels, demands more labor and skill than most modern persons are willing or able to put into it. Wine, the most artistic of agricultural products, reflects most tellingly the nature of its producer. So, as I survey the wines of these twenty regions, I have kept the human element foremost in my mind.

Italy's topography does not lend itself to convenient partition into cohesive units, as various emperors, popes, politicians, and conquerors have learned the hard way over two and a half millennia. The nation has been unified after a fashion for more than a century, but many of its citizens still place precious little faith in any group larger than the family. Each of the twenty richly diverse regions has its own character, customs, and quirks; any semblance of uniformity in the national fiber will probably turn out to be as ephemeral as a federal cabinet. Italy is not a nation of conformists.

(A region — the Veneto, Tuscany, Sicily, for example — is roughly equivalent to an American state in terms of autonomous rights and powers. Within each region are provinces — Verona, Siena, Catania, for example — administered from the city that gives the province its name.)

Though Italy is not large, by American standards anyway, no other country can match the immensity of its historical impact on the course of Western civilization, its artistic and scientific achievements, or its contributions to the good things in life. Wine is one of those good things, an important one at that, an integral part of the Italian spirit and temperament, past and present.

To write about Italian wine with a sense of intimacy required a measure of selectivity that was sometimes painful and not always fair, for so many of the wines, the people, and the places described here have the scope to merit more intensive appraisal.

Consider, for example, that the Veneto in an area smaller than New Jersey annually produced almost three-quarters as much wine as did the entire United States in the mid-1970s, with a similar range of quality and a comparable variety of types and styles. Or consider that Piedmont (with 37 DOC classifications, including Barolo, Barbaresco, Asti Spumante, and Gattinara) and Tuscany (whose 15 DOCs include Chianti, Brunello di Montalcino, and Vino Nobile di Montepulciano), rank only sixth and seventh among Italian regions in average volume of production. And yet, despite this glorious outpouring, many fine wines made in these and other regions remain relatively obscure, hundreds of wines of every description, tacitly defying the curious to come and discover them.

This is a record of one such quest — aided by literature that sometimes helped and sometimes hindered — a continuing adventure of a writer and wine enthusiast who in years of traveling in Europe's wine zones came to realize that the preeminence accorded French and German wine by its admirers in the English-speaking world was neither innate nor imperative. Today that alleged superiority is not so clearcut to anyone with a discriminating palate, not because the French and Germans have faltered (on the contrary, they are more able than ever), but because now, at last, Italians have begun to catch up, perfecting methods of cultivating vines and vinifying grapes grown under exceptionally favorable conditions of climate and terrain (as Californians on a smaller scale did before them).

Although loose references are often made to northern Italy and southern Italy, especially for the purpose of pointing out contrasts, Italians themselves most often split the country three ways for surveys and statistical purposes. Thus we learn that the north (Valle d'Aosta, Piedmont, Liguria, Lombardy, Trentino–Alto Adige, the Veneto, Friuli–Venezia Giulia, and Emilia-Romagna) produces about 55 percent of DOC wine; the center (Tuscany, Umbria, the Marches, Latium, the Abruzzi, and Molise) accounts for another 32 percent; and the south (Campania, Apulia, Basilicata, Calabria, Sardinia, and Sicily) turns out only about 13 percent. It should be noted, however, that this pattern is rapidly changing.

The contrasts are still apparent, but it is no longer true that the north — heavily populated, industrially advanced, and relatively wealthy as it is — has a monopoly on quality wine. True, the north and north-central regions have more solid recent traditions with established markets in Italy and abroad. Most of what are currently considered the great wines of Italy come from points north of Rome. But anyone who thinks that south of Rome this tour is all downhill will be in for some surprises.

Take Sicily, much of whose territory lies parallel to northernmost Africa. Long an anonymous supplier of blending wines to other places, the island in less than two decades has been transformed into a model of vinicultural progress under programs carried out by regional, federal, and European institutions. Similar achievements have been made in Apulia and Sardinia and other regions north and south.

In each of these regions, large and small, the story of wine and all that goes with it is as boundless as time itself. Within the limits of a volume I have taken an admiring look at the land, the traditions, the legends, the food, and, above all, the wines of today and the people who make them. The long and eventful history of Italian wine provides a touch of color here and there, though the focus is steadfast on the present. It had to be. Even putting together the material on the current status of each region was akin to trying to fit the pieces of twenty jigsaw puzzles into one coherent picture.

In a field as subjective as wine, I submit no unique capacity for objectivity. I have tried to be fair and rational in my judgments, to take into account the conditions that underly each wine's individuality —

from sunlight to soil, from vine to vat, from bottle to glass. But in dealing with so many variables, my conclusions and somebody else's could never be quite the same. My primary criterion in determining a wine's worth, and thus for discussing it here, is quality. However, other factors have been considered: commercial prominence, for example, or some trait of the wine that is out of the ordinary.

Listings of wines and producers are neither all-inclusive nor conclusive. Rather, these citations reflect my experiences of recent years. The appraisals, most of them personal but some based on reliable sources, have not been directly influenced by any of the publications I have been connected with during the preparation of this book, their publishers, editors, writers, or advertisers. Nor were the wine producers or other persons interviewed selected solely on the basis of competence. The subjects were determined partly by chance, partly through a conscious effort to illustrate the multiplicity of personalities, attitudes, conditions, styles, and levels of success behind Italian wine today, an attempt to add a human ingredient to the contents of all those labeled and sealed bottles.

Other wines and winemakers deserve mention, for in every corner of Italy there is always some oenological treasure to uncover. That a worthy producer or a good wine is not cited should not be taken as a slight or condemnation. It could be that I did not know of it, or had not had a chance to try it.

Many wines described should be available at shops in importing nations; others might not be obtainable even after a trek through the vineyards to reach their source. But whether they are marketed with brand names in lots of a million bottles or more or sold in limited quantity by their artisan makers in bottles or demijohns, they may have a certain validity that allows them to take their place in the vast spectrum of special Italian wines. In that case, whenever I could manage, I have tried to give them their due.

This book is an introduction, a guide, and an homage to the most exciting wine nation on earth, an ancient land of eternal promise. Inevitably, it leaves much to be discussed and discovered. But I hope what follows transmits enough of the feel and the flavor of Italy's wine country so that even if you never make the journey you might share in the spirit of adventure.

THE LAWS
AND THE LABELS

Realizing the Impossible

I TALY produces more types of wine than any other nation, so many that nobody has ever successfully documented them all. Professors Giovanni Dalmasso and Italo Cosmo years ago completed a monumental study of the nation's wine grape varieties in a five-volume work (the fifth was the index) entitled *Principali vitigni da vino coltivati in Italia*. More recently, Gianni Bonacina listed 3,811 more or less individually identified wines with concise descriptions in a three-volume paperback encyclopedia entitled *Lo stivale in bottiglia* (*The Boot in Bottle*). But even he missed some. Others have estimated the total at from about 2,000 to nearly 5,000. Ultimately, it depends on how you count them.

If the numbers seem staggering, consider the nomenclature, the labyrinth of names of grape varieties, places, people, historical events, legend, lore, and pure poetic fancy that Italian wines go under. How do you begin to make distinctions when you can turn to the index of one reliable reference (Riccardo Di Corato's *2214 vini d'Italia*) and find 56 entries beginning with "Bar —"? A few names are recognizable to anyone familiar with Italian wines — Barbaresco, Barbera, Bardolino, Barolo, for instance — but others are decidedly unfamiliar, even to experts. And yet each entry stands for a wine that in some way can be differentiated from others. Di Corato lists 26 wines called Barbera, and that barely begins to review the range that derives in whole or in part from that vine of Piedmontese origin that is now planted in most if not all the regions of Italy. A dark grape used chiefly for dry red wine, Barbera is also converted into white and rosé, still and sparkling, sweet and semisweet wines. And Barbera is not the extreme example; Di Corato lists 58 entries under Pinot and 67 under Moscato.

Italian wines, if infinitely complex, are endlessly fascinating, a national heritage that can be displayed only fragmentarily in museums or studied superficially in libraries. The experience of seeing, smelling, tasting is the only way to come to know them intimately, to appreciate their personalities, their styles, their uniqueness.

Sorting through the multitude is a pleasure for most. For a few it can also be an obligation, a laborious one at that. Consider the task of determining which zones and which wines qualify for DOC and now for other categories prescribed by law. Passed by chance in a rush of parliamentary legislation in 1963, the *denominazione di origine* laws have carried Italian wine from disgrace to respectability. Much of the force behind this continuing transformation has been provided by Paolo Desana, a tough former senator from Piedmont who believes that the politics of Italian wine is the art of realizing the impossible. As head of the 29-member national DOC committee almost since its inception, Desana has demonstrated that you can get things done on an official level in Italy by replacing under-the-table deals with aboveboard accountability, favoritism with pragmatism, do-nothingism with drive. For that alone, he should be considered a national hero.

The Wine Laws

Four official categories of Italian wine have been determined under national and European Economic Community policies. Only two were fully in effect by 1980: *denominazione di origine controllata* and *vini da tavola*. The others — *denominazione di origine controllata e garantita* and *vini tipici* — were being implemented gradually, hindered by administrative delays.

Denominazione di Origine Controllata (DOC)

DOC has been the pillar of the Italian wine laws, a vast program of control that applies from cultivation through production and sales. Although more than two hundred zones have been delimited, DOC is a select category that applied to only about 12 percent of national production through 1979. The choices have not been universally applauded, of course, but even producers in districts so far excluded should admire the integrity shown in carrying out the program. The DOC committee has been charged by the Common Market with bringing the portion of national wine production covered by DOC (and DOCG) to about 20 percent eventually, to correspond with the percentage of *appellation contrôlée* wines of France. The candidates for DOC increase, but Desana and his committee, which works under the Ministry of Agriculture and Forests, have chosen to progress with deliberate caution because the challenges of selection and control are formidable.

The conferment of DOC follows a painstaking process usually initiated by producers in a zone through their consortiums and supported by regional, provincial, and local official bodies and interested parties who help present the case. An established tradition of quality wine is an important consideration, though some zones have succeeded by presenting evidence of a recently achieved level of competence and future possibility. Once approved by the DOC committee and confirmed by presidential decree, each vineyard in the zone must be approved by inspectors of the agricultural directorates, then registered in a public ledger.

After qualifying, each grower must declare the quantity of grapes harvested each year in each of his vineyards. If the amount exceeds a maximum permitted yield prescribed by DOC regulations, his entire crop is invalidated. If the cultivator is not also the winemaker, authenticated documents of sale must be provided to the agricultural directorates and antifraud authorities who are responsible for verifying the process of turning grapes into wine and selling it. In all cases, a set limit on the weight of grapes converted into wine (usually 70 percent or less) must be observed.

DOC on a label means that the wine was made under specified conditions of terrain and exposure from determined amounts of clearly defined grape varieties, vinified with respect to procedures determined by tradition, whether historic or recent. DOC verifies that its authenticity and basic character have been subject to control. Although such control can never be perfect, Italian authorities have strived to enforce the rules. In that respect, DOC has been much more effective than its many early opponents anticipated. DOC indicates quality but does not ultimately affirm it; a wine's class also relies on the talent and motivation of its producer and the inherent advantages, however subtle, of soil and climate.

Each DOC is a geographical entity, a delimited zone identified by an appellation that may refer to the type of wine or the oenological name of the territory covered or both. An example of an oenological name is Chianti; though it derived from a portion of what is now called Chianti Classico, the term has since been applied to the wine of seven separate DOC zones, each also identified geographically. The possible variations are confusing. Some zones are large, some small. Some cover the approved vineyards of an entire region or province, others the territory of a small community. Sometimes the name of the wine and the DOC zone are synonymous (Barolo, Soave, Marsala). Sometimes a type of wine is made in more than one zone (Barbera, Moscato, Merlot). Sometimes a zone will have more than one wine covered by its discipline (Alto Adige has 16 types, Collio Goriziano 11, Torgiano 2). Sometimes a single wine can be vinified into several possible types or styles (dry, semisweet, sweet, still, or sparkling, for example). In just over 200 DOC zones some 450 distinct wines or types of wine are made.

DOC wines automatically belong in the Common Market category of VQPRD (*Vin de qualité produit en régions déterminées*) or "Quality wine produced in specific regions."

Denominazione di Origine Controllata e Garantita (DOCG)

DOCG is an unprecedented endeavor to guarantee the quality of elite DOC wines. As it takes effect, producers in the zones designated may voluntarily subject their wines to most rigid measures of control and, if the wine is approved, each bottle will carry a government seal of quality. The program has been stalled for years, partly because of bureaucratic idleness, partly because of doubts about the program's eventual efficacy demonstrated by the apathy of certain producers toward participation. The four wines originally designated — Barolo, Barbaresco, Vino Nobile di Montepulciano, and Brunello di Montalcino — were to be followed by Chianti and Albana di Romagna.

It is difficult to speculate on how many wines will be classified as DOCG, because the program's future depends heavily on the success of the early choices. Chianti, because it is produced in such great quantity in such a vast territory, was expected to be the real test of the effectiveness of DOCG.

Vini Tipici

The Common Market recently approved this category for Italy as the equivalent of the French *vins de pays* and the German *Landwein*. The term *vini tipici* refers to wines representative of specific areas and specific grapes that bear the right to cite the information on the label. Designed to be the category beneath DOC with less stringent regulations and controls, it caused some initial confusion in Italy about how to apply a program that had not really been planned on beforehand. When the *vini tipici* program is fully implemented, the number of recognized wines of quality will greatly increase because they too will be classified VQPRD.

Vini da Tavola

This is the catchall category that applied to all non-DOC wines before the term *vini tipici* was introduced; it still applies to most. Two levels of this so-called table wine are allowed for: that with a geographical indication (Pinot Grigio delle Tre Venezie is a popular example) and that labeled simply *vino da tavola*. One might imagine that this latter was invariably of the lowest grade, though curiously enough some of the greatest wines of Italy must carry the description. One reason for this discrepancy is that many special and rare wines originate outside delimited zones. Another is that some producers within DOC zones, for reasons of pride or convenience, have chosen not to comply with DOC.

Inadequacies and Injustices

The current categorization of Italian wine, though sound in principle and generally beneficial, does involve inadequacies and injustices. No rule can declare a DOCG superior per se to a DOC, or a DOC superior to a *vino da tavola*. Some special wines labeled *vino da tavola* are undeniably superior to the majority of DOC wines.

Consider Sassicaia, a Cabernet Sauvignon from a section of Tuscany that does not officially acknowledge Cabernet's existence. Or consider Costozza Cabernet from the Veneto, which qualifies in every respect as Colli Berici DOC; however, its producer sees no point in participating in the program. Or consider the Riesling Renano (Johannisberg Riesling) made by Mario Schiopetto in Friuli–Venezia Giulia's Collio Goriziano, a DOC zone that recognizes Riesling Italico but not Riesling Renano. Or consider the Bricco Manzoni made by Valentino Migliorini at Monforte d'Alba in Piedmont from grape varieties each of which alone could make DOC wine (Barolo and Barbera d'Alba) but combined cannot qualify. Or consider the Tignanello of Marchesi Antinori in Tuscany, the vines of which grow in the Chianti Classico zone but which, because the wine excludes the prescribed white grapes and includes an inadmissible 10 percent of Cabernet Sauvignon with the permitted Sangiovese and Canaiolo, could not be sold as Chianti even if Marchesi Antinori wanted it to be (they do not).

Each of these splendid wines, like many others of similar merit, can stand on its own, proudly, even with the degrading description *vino da tavola* prominent on its label. In each case, the reputation is established. But for other excellent but less noted wines, that inaccurate and unfair term can mislead the consumer and underestimate the wine's true value.

Recent Italian wine policy has clearly favored the large and well organized over the small and artisanal, which helps explain why some 40 percent of Italian production is controlled by cooperative wineries and much of the rest is in the hands of large-scale private firms. In other places and under more propitious circumstances the wines of some estates that now make what is considered *vino da tavola* might be classified as outstanding growths or something equally indicative of exceptional merit. That sort of recognition takes not only time but motivations based on historical, political, economic, and, above all, qualitative factors that Italy has not begun to consider seriously, at least not at official levels. So while France continues by ministerial decree to sanction many of its greatest wines as *crus* of various heights of illustriousness, Italy, for the foreseeable future at least, will go on stigmatizing some of its finest wines as *vino da tavola*.

The Common Market forbids use of the term *cru* on labels of all but French wine. That policy, now several years old and in this case most reasonable, squelched a widespread if unauthorized and disjointed effort to establish ratings of vineyards in Italy based on proven quality and prestige of the wines they produce. The Italian *cru* concept reflected worthy motives even if the tactics employed were often somewhat obtuse and use of the term *cru* was clearly inappropriate. Various groups and individuals — wine producers and consortiums, journalists, commercial interests — continue to favor vineyard rating systems in Italy, particularly in established zones such as Barolo and Chianti, where over the years certain plots of land have tended to produce better wines than others. Rating is a tricky business, more subjective than objective, with pitfalls lying all along the way. Official direction would help to sort out the speculators from the serious interests, but so far there has been no sign of approval from high places. Apparently the Italian government feels that DOCG is the ultimate classification. But DOCG, whatever its strong points, could never apply to all of Italy's great wines.

The Politics of Sugar

Although much grumbling has been heard over Italy's chronic ineffectiveness in influencing Common Market wine policy (an area where France and West Germany succeed admirably), most Italian winemakers seem to accept the rules as a necessary form of protection and control. But one earlier Common Market policy remains an explosively controversial point. This is the forbiddance in Italy of chaptalization (addition of sugar to the musts of the newly pressed grapes before fermentation to increase alcohol content), a practice permitted routinely in many other wine-producing nations. However, stronger wine or wine concentrates made by reducing musts to a syrup rich in natural sugar are permitted in many DOC and most non-DOC wines for the same purpose. These concentrates, most of which are made in southerly regions, are allowed in some (but not all) DOC wines up to a maximum of 5 to 15 percent. In some cases they must be made from DOC grapes from the zone of origin. Many winemakers, particularly in the north, where a boost in alcohol is more often needed, argue that stronger wine and concentrates alter the character of a fine wine but that chaptalization is imperceptible in the flavor and aroma.

A widespread myth has it that Italy's fine climate obviates the need to differentiate between vintages. Nonsense. A sunny but mountainous land subject to abrupt shifts in wind and weather, Italy has an extraordinary variety of meteorological conditions. Within each zone, distinct microclimates are determined by altitude, exposure, and position. Most years, it is true, there is no need to add anything to a well-made Italian wine. But in those not altogether rare cool seasons when natural sugars in the grapes are insufficient, the additives increase strength, allowing the wine to last longer and cope with the strains of transportation. Many winemakers who refuse to use the legally permitted concentrates chaptalize secretly in poor years. They know that even though such violations carry penalties, the risks are slight; the addition of certain types of sucrose to wine is virtually impossible to detect under chemical analysis.

Responsible producers use sugar and concentrates minimally, and only as a last resort. Some would not use them under any circumstances. A few Italian winemakers are dedicated to making "organically pure wine," avoiding the use of chemicals in fertilizers, sprays, or to control phases of the winemaking process. In these days when even the feeblest harvests can be transmitted into at least passable wine, it takes extraordinary courage to remain a purist.

Most Italian firms that export use advanced techniques to clarify and stabilize their wines, particularly dry whites. But some producers shun any form of what they consider tampering, and instead rely on elemental racking and barrel aging to settle their wines naturally. Unstabilized wine can be vulnerable to poor handling. Too much cold can make it cloudy and unattractive and too much heat or motion can spoil not only its looks but its flavor. Therefore, more Italian producers now stabilize, though sometimes with great reluctance, for the practice inhibits a wine's ability to age gracefully in bottle, a process Italian oenophiles still regard with utmost reverence. Old wines aged naturally inevitably throw a deposit, so their bottles should be stood upright at least a few hours before serving.

Reading the Labels

Italian wine labels are funds of information, much of it now required by law. Recent Common Market standards for all categories of wine limit terminology on the main label to pertinent data. For bottles imported into the United States, further basic information in English is required. This means that those elaborate and often wordy labels resulting from a wine-maker's irrepressible desire to share his feelings about a subject close to his heart are now severely limited.

Most requirements for labels on exported wine are self-explanatory: basic identification of producer, bottler or brand, importer, denomination of the wine (with a description of type), container size, and alcoholic content by volume. Common Market rules have further standardized the format, limiting the usable terms and even specifying where words, figures, and illustrations are to be positioned on the label.

The change of labels has been accompanied by a standardization of container sizes, a move prompted at least in part by U.S. regulations. The standard Italian wine bottle for export now contains 75 centiliters instead of the former 72. The other permitted container sizes for the United States are 3 liters, 1.5 liters, 1 liter, 37.5 centiliters (the half-bottle), 18.7 centiliters, and 10 centiliters. Some DOC rules limit bottle sizes to no more than the standard 75-centiliter bottle. These volumes are expressed in metric terms in accordance with the conversion of the U.S. and British systems. One advantage of all this is that those large containers and flasks that previously came in a range of odd sizes are now a recognizable "honest measure."

The recent rules have inhibited the fanciful labeling of the past, but the artistry remains. Italian wine labels are still unsurpassed for color and imaginative design. Secondary labels are permitted as a forum for the producer to express a message to the consumer, to tell about the wine, the estate, the vineyards, the history or the legend, providing, of course, that the information is justified. Some Italian terminology is helpful to know in reading labels and literature about Italian wine. Here are some common examples:

★ The approved way of referring to estate-bottled wines is *imbottigliato dal produttore all'origine* (bottled by the producer at the source) or *imbottigliato dal viticoltore* (by the cultivator). Other terms that may follow *imbottigliato* include *dalla cantina sociale* or *dalla cooperativa* (cooperative wineries) or *dai produttori riuniti* (an organization of united cooperatives). *Imbottigliato nella zona di produzione* (in the production zone) indicates that the wine was not estate-bottled.

★ Terms for wineries and estates include *castello* (castle), *villa* (manor), *azienda agraria, azienda agricola, tenimento, podere, fattoria, tenuta* (all meaning farm or agricultural holding), *cantina* or *cantine* (winery or cellars), *stabilimento* (firm).

★ Terms used in winemaking include *uva* (grape), *vite* (vine) *vigna, vigneto* (vineyard), *vitigno* (grape variety), *coltivatore, vignaiuolo* (cultivator), *viticoltura* (vine cultivation), *fermentazione naturale* (natural fermentation), *vinificazione* (vinification), *enologia* (oenology), *enologo, enotecnico* (oenologist, wine technician), *invecchiamento* (aging).

★ *Annata* and *vendemmia* refer to year of vintage. Some aged DOC wines may be called *vecchio* (old), *riserva* (reserve), or *riserva speciale* (special reserve) in reference to specific lengths of aging in barrel and bottle. *Stravecchio* (very old) is permitted on labels of very few wines.

★ *Classico* in a DOC wine means that the vineyards lie within the historic heartland of the production zone. *Superiore* means the wine met an elevated set of standards of production, alcohol content, and aging defined for its making.

★ Descriptive words include *rosso* (red), *bianco* (white), *rosato* (rosé), *secco* (very dry), *asciutto* (dry), *amabile, abboccato, semi-secco, cannellino, pastoso* (medium sweet, though the degrees of residual sugars vary from wine to wine), *dolce* (sweet), *passito* (sweet wine made from grapes semidried before pressing), *liquoroso* (dessert wine fortified with alcohol).

The lexicon is endless; these are but a few familiar and for the most part elementary terms.

Seals of producers' associations, though winemakers are not required to belong to such groups, provide added assurance of discipline in wine-making. They usually appear near the bottle's neck and should include a number, the name of the *consorzio*, and its symbol. Chianti Classico, for example, is symbolized by a *gallo nero* (black rooster). The consortiums sometimes enforce regulations and impose standards even more demanding than DOC norms.

Some wine producers go to extra trouble and expense to convey messages to consumers, adding supplementary labels to tell how to store and serve the wine or to discuss its virtues or to describe how it was made and aged. If often enlightening and entertaining, they can create a clutter. I once counted seven labels attached to a bottle.

One way to remember Italian wines as you drink them is to check a map and see where they came from. Or save the labels and make notes. Or, better yet, visit Italy and meet their makers. Many of these people, like their wines, are truly unforgettable.

Mt. BLANC

BLANC
DE MORGEX

ENFER
D'ARVIER

MALVOISIE
DE NUS

CHAMBAVE

DORA BALTEA

Aosta

DONNAZ

VALLE D' AOSTA

PROVINCE

AOSTA

POPULATION

110,000

AREA

1,260 square miles

AVERAGE WINE PRODUCTION

3.5 million liters

DOC WINES

Donnaz, Enfer d'Arvier

OTHER WINES

*Aymaville · Blanc de La Salle · Blanc de Morgex · Chambave Rouge ·
Crême du Vien du Nus · Gamay · La Colline de Sarre et Chesallet ·
La Sabla · Le Vin du Conseil · Malvoisie de Nus · Malvoisie du
Prieuré de Montfleury · Montouvert · Passito di Chambave · Petit
Rouge · Réserve du Prieur Grenache · St. Pierre · Torrette*

French Names, Vaguely Italian Styles

I TALY's historic lack of access to neighboring lands only seemed to
heighten its allure. Whether they came to tour, to trade, or to conquer, foreigners rarely let the Alps stand in the way of their Italian
destinations. Since Roman times the roads of Valle d'Aosta have led
back and forth across the mountains into France and Switzerland over
passes that tested human fortitude.

Times are no longer so trying. From France, Valle d'Aosta is a convenient drive through the Mont Blanc tunnel, which merely draws the
curtain on one country and, twelve kilometers later, opens it on the other.
If wine is the object, France's is a hard act to follow. But Valle d'Aosta,
tiniest of Italy's twenty regions, is a fitting place to make the connection.

The people, who speak a well-blended patois to each other, seem
equally at ease in French or Italian when dealing with outsiders. They
take obvious delight in being considered somewhat foreign to each culture, a distinction that in these days of mass tourism has exploitable
advantages. Thus, to the French their region seems very Italian, and to
Italians from points south it provides a taste of France without involving
the fuss of crossing the border.

The wines, naturally enough, reflect this cultural ambivalence. Their
names more often than not are French; their styles tend, in a vague sort
of way, toward Italian. Viniculture has been practiced on the mountain
slopes since Aosta was the Roman colony of Augusta Praetoria, controlling the St. Bernard Pass. Some vines were planted by monks in the
Middle Ages, but there seems to be no modern consensus about where
they came from. Local lore traces Petit Rouge and Gros Vien to French
vineyards while indicating a relationship between Blanc de Valdigne
and the Riesling grape of the Rhine. But, as in other cultural buffer
zones, conditions have changed so often that accounts of viticultural
evolution remain sketchy and confused.

Whatever the vines' background, the wines of this remote corner are
as distinctively endowed as any in Italy. Though they range from deli-

cate whites to rather powerful reds, a strain of related character runs through the best of them, evincing the rugged terrain they come from and the pains taken in their making.

The traveler arriving from France need not waste time before tasting them. Just down the road from the tunnel's mouth, at Entrèves de Courmayeur, the Maison de Filippo serves local wine and food in an irresistibly rustic mountain setting. The restaurant, owned by Filippo Garin, is a family operation in the Italian tradition. Garin's wife, Esterina, runs the kitchen and his son, Leo, the dining room while he gives his attention to the house wines.

If Garin's red Torrette from 1961 could be judged solely by the nose, it would rank among the most esteemed of wines, for it was as fragrant as fresh mountain flowers. With age its flavor, though smooth and elegant, becomes increasingly austere. A recent vintage drawn directly from the barrel tasted as full of fruit as a *cru* Beaujolais but was relatively short on aroma. Torrette from several different vintages showed this pattern of developing bouquet and fading flavor, unique in my experience.

"They say it has to do with the intensity of heat on the grapes," said Filippo Garin, a man not given to erudite explanations. "At ten o'clock at night in the summer you can still feel the heat rising from the stones in the vineyard. But there are so many reasons. If only we could ask Mother Nature."

Garin's modesty, however becoming, is not to be taken literally. His experience in winemaking covers almost half a century, and although he proceeds in a time-proven manner, he is not at all as naïve about modern methods as he would have you believe. His vineyards, some 30 kilometers from the restaurant, include about 4 acres of mainly Petit Rouge vines on south-facing slopes overlooking the Château St. Pierre, the Valle d'Aosta's most handsome fortress castle. In good years, Garin produces about 10,000 bottles of Torrette, not enough even to supply the restaurant. But he supplements his stocks with a good selection of the region's bottles, plus red and white of notable class for carafe wines.

The restaurant's rustic chalet interior of wood, stone, and whitewashed plaster achieves its warm look from a clutter of heavy antique furniture, carvings, and copper cooking ware hanging on the walls. Hearty local dishes dominate the menu, though refined preparations — trout with almonds, filet of venison, *canard à l'orange* — can be ordered in advance. Quantities are designed for outdoorsmen, such as hikers and skiers, but only a full-time lumberjack could make his way through all the food offered. A dozen or more antipasti are crowded onto each table on platters — cooked and air-dried hams, salami, vegetable and meat salads, chunks of fresh white goat cheeses served with pungent herbs and sauces. Then come thick Valdostana vegetable soup, grilled steaks of mountain-grazed beef, fondue, game stews with cornmeal polenta, more cheeses, and desserts of both Italian and French inspiration.

In winter, when Entrèves and Courmayeur are hosts to skiers of many nations, an easygoing multilingual camaraderie prevails at the Maison de Filippo. Before venturing back out into the cold, the custom is to pass the *grolla,* a hand-carved, covered wooden bowl with six or eight teapot-like spouts protruding from its sides. Filled with coffee "corrected" with Filippo Garin's own grappa, the *grolla* is relayed around the table for warming sips.

Morgex: An Epic Struggle

After a meal of Maison de Filippo dimensions fresh air is advisable, and the vineyards at nearby Morgex offer plenty of that. The producers of Blanc de Morgex and the neighboring Blanc de La Salle have proclaimed their vineyards to be the highest in Europe, at altitudes ranging from 2,500 to 3,400 feet above sea level. From some angles the low pergolas on which the vines are trained seem to be set into the snow of Mont Blanc's southern face, whose massiveness gives the illusion of being so close you could reach out and touch it.

The late Don Alexandre Bougeat, the village priest, was credited with resurrecting the vines of Morgex one by one over three decades after more than six centuries of constant cultivation had left them enfeebled and unproductive. The pros and cons of the Church's historic dominance of the Italian peoples can be debated ad infinitum, but there is no denying the blessings the clergy has bestowed on their vineyards. As a modern example, Don Alexandre Bougeat's work achieved epic proportions, culminating in a wine considered by those cognoscenti who managed to acquire it to be among the nation's most deservedly exalted.

Its legend was no doubt enhanced by visions of the heroic priest, struggling against odds and elements that most Italians would write off as hopeless, nurturing his fragile shoots to productivity with one eye always on the weather. For if spring frosts or hail had not destroyed the fruit after budding, there was the looming threat that autumn frosts would freeze the unripened grapes on the vine. But Don Alexandre prevailed, building to a yield that in some fine years reached several thousand bottles. The wine, sold to benefit his parish, was worthy of his efforts. His death in 1972, however, prompted fears that Blanc de Morgex would once again lapse into decline.

So with no great expectations I went looking for those former parishioners and friends reported to be trying to follow in the late priest's footsteps. By chance among the first I found was Alberto Vevey, a telephone linesman by trade and an optimist by nature, who heads the Association Viticulteurs, the largest group of growers. He assured me that Blanc de Morgex was holding its own and, through the more diligent efforts planned by the 42 members of his association, would soon regain the status it had had under Don Alexandre Bougeat, and with a wider base of production.

Blanc de Morgex may never be made in much greater quantity than its present 40,000 to 60,000 liters annually. The 42 growers in Vevey's group produced from a recent vintage only about 15,000 bottles that they judged to be of commercial value. The Blanc de Valdigne vines are among the few varieties of Europe immune to phylloxera and, therefore, not grafted to American root stock. They thrive in only two small zones, of which the higher usually produces superior grapes. Attempts to place them elsewhere in the valley have failed; unlike most vines they do better in the soft, fertile soil found in the mountain meadows above Morgex and neighboring La Salle than in the stony terrain that dominates the landscape.

No producer of Blanc de Morgex can afford to devote his time entirely to winemaking because plots are small and yields are ridiculously low, even in good years. Plans for a cooperative have been put aside by the Association Viticulteurs because, as Vevey put it, growers fear that pooling their grapes would result in wine of compromised quality. Instead, they are working to stimulate improvement by individuals to bring quality to such a level that Blanc de Morgex cannot be denied DOC status.

In this sphere, Vevey serves as a model. In a small tasting room in the cellar of his home at Villair, above Morgex, he opened a bottle of his latest vintage. I had never tried a wine made by Don Alexandre Bougeat, but descriptions of it I have read would apply to Vevey's wine as well: "Pale green-gold, dry, extremely delicate, but balanced and complete in flavor, with a hint of herbs in its subtle bouquet; an aristocrat to be appreciated at cellar temperature, never too cold." Vevey has won awards for his wine, including a citation from the Turin newspaper *Stampa Sera* for the best white of the Valle d'Aosta one year.

"Blanc de Morgex is a legend, and none of us here would wish it otherwise," said Vevey, "but we want our wine judged for its present quality, not just its legendary virtues."

Vevey's aspirations are not overstated, but after trying wines from several other producers I found myself hoping that his will soon be more widely emulated, for Blanc de Morgex is difficult to make, even under the best of conditions. It tends to be low in alcohol and acidic, and it can easily become cloudy or sour when the phases of its production are not skillfully coordinated.

Another group of Blanc de Morgex growers, Piccoli Viticultori, sells its wine to CE.DI.VI., a Piedmont bottling operation, for distribution by Marchesi Villadoria, the Piedmontese firm. That wine, which is fresh, light, and crisp, is now being exported in limited quantity.

At the neighboring village of La Salle, growers call their association Les Riboteurs, from the French *ribot,* for drinking spree. Made from Blanc de Valdigne grapes grown at comparable altitudes, their wine is essentially the same as that of Morgex, with a reputation for more consistent quality.

Arvier: The Fires of Hell

Every town along the Dora Baltea River, which flows from Mont Blanc through the Valle d'Aosta, has a wine or two of its own. After La Salle the first of more than local significance is grown at Arvier, where Enfer d'Arvier shares with Donnaz the honor of being the region's only DOC wines.

Enfer d'Arvier, like Garin's Torrette, is made from Petit Rouge grapes. Although the vineyards are just 8 kilometers apart, there are marked differences in the wines. In contrast with Torrette's finesse, Enfer is often rough and assertive with sharp flavor when young. Its vineyard area, ideally exposed to the south and sheltered from winds by an enclosure of rock walls, is known as the hottest of the area: hence the name Enfer (Inferno) and labels depicting the fires of hell licking at grape clusters. Despite the heat, the permitted yield from Arvier's stony slopes is the lowest of any DOC red wine of Italy — 3,500 liters per hectare, fewer than 1,500 liters or 2,000 standard bottles from an acre — of which the alcohol must be at least 11.5°.

Albino Thomain, a grower and wine merchant in Arvier, explained that the heat causes the tiny grapes to develop thick skins whose heavy pigmentation can give the wine excessive color. To tone it down, Thomain has tried drawing the wine off the skins and stalks early in the fermentation. His latest vintages showed promise but, as he readily admitted, there is room for improvement.

There seems to be no lack of zeal, however. Arvier growers recently bulldozed away most of the terraces that had held the vines for centuries, then planted new cuttings in rows on the resultant steep incline. This will permit a greater concentration of vines and at least some machine cultivation. But any proof of benefit to the wine is still a few years away.

Although the neighboring villages of Aymaville, Sarre, and St. Pierre do not have classified vineyards, the best wines there often surpass Enfer d'Arvier in class. Garin's Torrette is not alone among St. Pierre's good wines. At Aymaville Antonio Charrère makes La Sabla, a red from Petit Rouge that has been winning praise. At Sarre, Ottavio Valet has successfully mixed Petit Rouge with the French Gamay in a wine called La Colline de Sarre et Chesallet.

Perhaps the rarest of the region's wines is made at Montouvert above the village of Villeneuve by a few persons who do not advertise their product. Montouvert is an *Eiswein* made by a German method in which the grapes (in this case the sweet Moscato) are pressed into wine after they freeze on the vine. It supposedly makes a pleasant dessert wine. But when I asked a grocer at Villeneuve where I might try some, he told me he had no idea. "Those people up there keep it to themselves," he said.

Aosta: Heavenly Whites

Valle d'Aosta's land mass appears to be about 90 percent uninhabitable. Even the lower portions of the valley, where the majority of the 110,000 inhabitants cluster, is not an easy place to make a living, at any rate not off the land. Tourism and industry have expanded as sources of income while agriculture as a livelihood has shown an alarming decline. Recent annual wine production has been about 3.5 million liters; consumption, however, is 135 liters per capita, highest in Italy, meaning that more than 10 million liters a year must be brought in from outside. Bulk wines are simply not practical in such rugged country.

Piedmont, of which Valle d'Aosta was a province until 1945, when it became an autonomous region, supplies most of the table wine, predominately Barbera. In turn, the Piedmontese provide a market for Valle d'Aosta's finer wines, often including them in regional competition and listings. But the special Valle d'Aosta wines warrant separate consideration, for elsewhere in Italy there are none quite like them.

In the vinicultural department of the Regional Agricultural School at Aosta, the emphasis is decidedly on quality wines. Students learn to some extent by doing, and they could have no more patient or dedicated teacher than the Reverend Joseph Vaudan, director of the school and canon of the Great St. Bernard Pass. At least seven wines are produced for sale under the name of the school's vineyards: Vignoble de Prieuré de Montfleury. Vaudan considers the dry white Vin du Conseil, made from the Petite Arvine grape, as the school's outstanding wine. Its most remarkable trait is an unmistakable scent of pear, which some attribute to the proximity of an orchard. Of the other school wines, which include Gamay, Merlot, and Pinots, two other whites come closest to approaching the heavenly status of Le Vin du Conseil: the semisweet Malvoisie and the sweet Réserve du Prieur Grenache.

Nus: Buried Hopes

The nearly universal trend toward dry white wines has not been as stifling to dessert wines in the Valle d'Aosta as elsewhere. Among the sweet survivors none is more highly regarded than Malvoisie de Nus, another wine that owes its precarious existence to the clergy. Don Augusto Pramotton is the latest in a line of village priests at the Church of Sant'Ilario in Nus who have directed part of their devotion to the parish vineyards. But Don Augusto, who comes from a family of winemakers, suffers the physical pains of advancing years and a moral anguish caused by a project, recently completed, that supplanted half the vineyards with an addition to the church graveyard.

"In their hearts people want to do what's right, but so often they end up doing something harmful," said Don Augusto, relating the cemetery episode in his residence before mass one winter afternoon. "Obviously, we need places to bury the dead, but in this valley blessed little space remains where a vine can put its roots down."

Don Augusto's tones rose readily to the lofty pitch of those singsong voices that echo through the empty spaces of Italian country churches, but his sad blue eyes revealed the depths of feelings that ranged from intensely bitter to hopelessly resigned.

"There was a battle, and I lost. So now a wine that was scarce before is almost nonexistent." Don Augusto, wearing two heavy sweaters, priestly black trousers, sandals over wool stockings, and a blue beret pulled down almost to his eyebrows, held his palms upward in a gesture of despair.

"I can't sell you a bottle. I can't even give you a bottle. All the Malvoisie I make is reserved in advance. Some of them buy it because it's a collector's item. I wish I could keep it for people who truly care about wine. Well, I know that would not be honest."

Although the Malvoisie of the Valle d'Aosta bears the French name for Malvasia or Malmsey, the vines actually seem to be in the Pinot family, according to Luigi Veronelli, Italy's most diligent wine chronicler and critic, in his *Catalogo Bolaffi dei vini d'Italia*. Malvoisie is vinified *forzato*, from the must of semidried grapes put through a prolonged fermentation of forty to fifty days in a sealed vat. Afterward it ages in oaken barrels for two to three years before being bottled. Don Augusto recalled opening a bottle fifty years old on the fiftieth anniversary of a neighboring priest's church and finding it to be "sublime."

"It would be a sin to let this wine die out," said Don Augusto. "I only wish more people could try it."

As consolation he provided me with a bottle of Crème du Vien de Nus, a red wine from vines he planted after assuming his post in 1942. Even from the medium vintage of 1974, it was deep and rich in both color and taste, and would undoubtedly become truly elegant after two or three years more of aging. The Crème is made from selected grapes of three varieties, Vien de Nus (a native vine), Petit Rouge, and Merlot. As for the Malvoisie de Nus, I have a bottle of the 1977 on reserve. It ought to be available any year now.

Chambave's Winemaker-Croupier

The neighboring town of Chambave also has a famous and hard-to-acquire sweet wine: Passito di Chambave, from the Moscato grape. A wine, like Malvoisie de Nus, of almost limitless aging potential, Passito is made in a different way, from grapes semidried after the harvest, fermented, and put through a brief settling phase before bottling. The Passito is light golden; the Malvoisie picks up a deep amber color from the wood.

From its chief producer, Ezio Voyat, Passito di Chambave is one of Italy's most expensive white wines. Even so, if you want any, you must get your order in early. Voyat moonlights as head croupier at the casino in St. Vincent, leaving his days free to work in the vineyards.

Voyat produces Chambave Rouge, considered by some to be the finest red of the Valle d'Aosta. Made from a unique mixture of Gros Vien and the popular Piedmontese varieties of Dolcetto and Barbera, it has the dual distinction of being very good when bottled, after two to three years in barrel, and becoming even better after moderate aging. Chambave Rouge has none of the initial hardness of the classically big wines of Piedmont, Barolo and Barbaresco, but at its peak it approaches their qualities of richness and depth. Of course, a Barolo from an exceptional vintage might be good for fifty years, while a Chambave Rouge should not be expected to stand up for more than ten years, or at the most fifteen. Yet Chambave Rouge is as expensive as most Barolo its age; at this level, wine is never cheap.

As the Dora Baltea River approaches Piedmont, its valley broadens, affording more space for vines. The wines from the few flat places in the Valle d'Aosta are rarely as interesting as those from the hillsides that seem to draw their special strength of character from the stones.

Donnaz, the last important wine of the Valle d'Aosta on the route south, is so closely related to its Piedmontese neighbor Carema that the two DOC wines are regularly lumped together descriptively. Donnaz will be discussed with Carema in the following chapter. Indeed they share distinctive traits as members of the family of Nebbiolo vines whose grapes render the noblest wines of Piedmont.

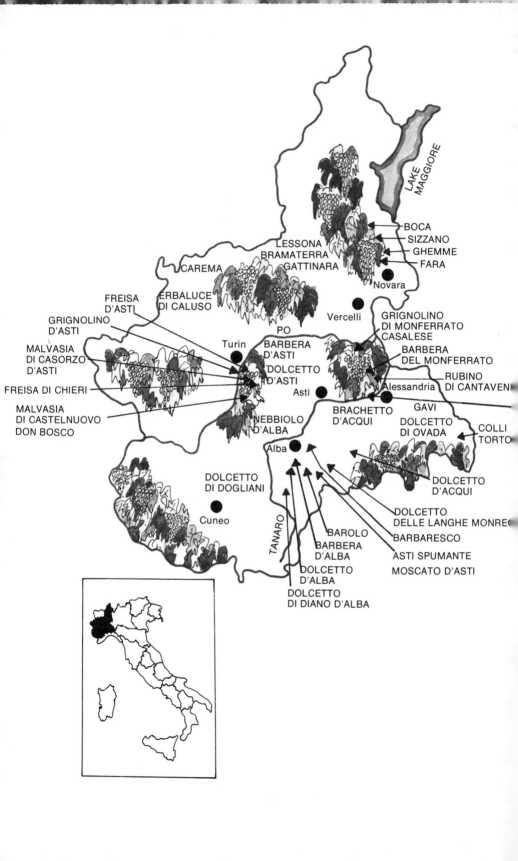

LAKE MAGGIORE

BOCA
SIZZANO
GHEMME
FARA

LESSONA
BRAMATERRA
GATTINARA

CAREMA

Novara

ERBALUCE
DI CALUSO

FREISA
D'ASTI

GRIGNOLINO
D'ASTI

Vercelli

GRIGNOLINO
DI MONFERRATO
CASALESE

PO

MALVASIA
DI CASORZO
D'ASTI

Turin

BARBERA
D'ASTI

BARBERA
DEL MONFERRATO

DOLCETTO
D'ASTI

FREISA DI CHIERI

RUBINO
DI CANTAVEN

Asti

Alessandria

MALVASIA
DI CASTELNUOVO
DON BOSCO

GAVI

BRACHETTO
D'ACQUI

DOLCETTO
DI OVADA

COLLI
TORTO

NEBBIOLO
D'ALBA

Alba

DOLCETTO
D'ACQUI

DOLCETTO
DI DOGLIANI

Cuneo

DOLCETTO
DELLE LANGHE MONRE

TANARO

BARBARESCO

BAROLO
BARBERA
D'ALBA

ASTI SPUMANTE

MOSCATO D'ASTI

DOLCETTO
D'ALBA

DOLCETTO
DI DIANO D'ALBA

PIEDMONT

PROVINCES

TURIN, Alessandria, Asti, Cuneo, Novara, Vercelli

POPULATION

4,435,000

AREA

9,187 square miles

ESE
ALTO MONFERRATO

AVERAGE WINE PRODUCTION

500 million liters

DOC WINES

Asti Spumante · Barbaresco · Barbera d'Alba · Barbera d'Asti · Barbera del Monferrato · Barolo · Boca · Brachetto d'Acqui · Bramaterra · Carema · Colli Tortonesi (Barbera, Cortese) · Cortese di Gavi · Cortese dell'Alto Monferrato · Dolcetto d'Acqui · Dolcetto d'Alba · Dolcetto d'Asti · Dolcetto di Diano d'Alba · Dolcetto di Dogliani · Dolcetto delle Langhe Monregalesi · Dolcetto di Ovada · Erbaluce di Caluso (Passito, Liquoroso) · Fara · Freisa d'Asti · Freisa di Chieri · Gattinara · Ghemme · Grignolino d'Asti · Grignolino del Monferrato Casalese · Lessona · Malvasia di Casorzo d'Asti · Malvasia di Castelnuovo Don Bosco · Moscato d'Asti · Moscato Naturale d'Asti · Nebbiolo d'Alba · Rubino di Cantavenna · Sizzano

OTHER WINES

Arneis · Barengo · Bianco dei Roeri · Bonarda · Brachetto d'Asti · Bricco del Drago · Bricco Manzoni · Caramino · Castello di Gabiano · Favorita · Greco · Moscato di Strevi · Orbello · Piccone · Pinot Spumante · Riesling · Santa Maria Rossa · Spanna · Vinòt

A Taste for the Extraordinary

THOSE who uphold Piedmont as Italy's leading region for quality wines presuppose a taste for the uncommon, though perhaps *extraordinary* is a better word. Ours — for I am indeed a believer — is not an easy position to defend, even if we resort to the ultimate ploy of "try them and see." To be candid, the first Barolo I tried overwhelmed me; as I recall, it took four or five experiences before I saw the light. And even now I approach that wine with a healthy measure of caution, for it is not to be taken casually. Nor is Barbaresco, nor several other wines from the Nebbiolo grape, presuming you start at the top.

Even if you start at a less lofty level, you will be in respectable company, because when it comes to wine the Piedmontese put up with very little nonsense. Their tastes run to robust, often complex, assertive reds, the quantity field dominated by Barbera, the people's wine, though there is nothing particularly common about it either. Though Piedmont has more DOC zones — thirty-six — than any other region, it produces less than half the volume of Emilia-Romagna or the Veneto. Red wine accounts for most of the production; only Asti Spumante, Cortese, and Erbaluce di Caluso are prominent among the whites.

Piedmontese, more than any other Italians except possibly Tuscans, have stuck with their traditional vines and wines through phylloxera, war, and less conspicuous calamities. Improved types of vines and new technology have tempted some to change their styles, though such change is rarely dramatic. Piedmont, with its borders on France and Switzerland and its dynamic capital, Turin, is one of the wealthiest and most industrially advanced regions. Still, city and country life sometimes seem ages apart. But backwardness is hardly a valid interpretation of the reluctance to vinicultural change. Pride and the unrelenting taste for the extraordinary come nearer the mark.

More than a grain of truth can be found in the remark of an authority in another part of Italy: "When it comes to wine, the Piedmontese are strict racists. If it isn't from Piedmont — or possibly Bordeaux — it isn't worth drinking."

Barolo: The Old School and the New

Paolo Cordero di Montezemolo pushed down on the levers of a tarnished brass corkscrew, eased the cork from a bottle of his 1971 Barolo, and poured the wine gently into two large tumblers. Lighting a candle on his desk, he lifted his glass and peered at the wine against the candlelight, swished it around, and sniffed.

"It's not warm enough," he said. "It needs air. But you'll get the idea. *Salute!*"

On my arrival in the hilltop town of La Morra one July morning a few years ago, a man at the laundry a few doors down the Via XX Settembre directed me to the Marchese Cordero di Montezemolo compound, telling me to push open the heavy arched wooden door and "just shout."

Three boys at play in the courtyard took care of the shouting, and within moments I was greeted amiably by a man of about sixty, wearing, despite the wilting heat, white shirt, tie, and tweed jacket of the nonchalant cut favored by certain members of the landed gentry in Italy.

"I'm Cordero," he said, extending his hand. I asked if I could buy some Barolo, specifying the 1971.

"Of course," he said. "The 1971 is all I have available in bottle now. An exceptional vintage, as you know. It's from the last barrel. The best one. And, frankly, it's expensive. But come and try some."

Leaving the courtyard, where the boys had returned to play and half a dozen women sat knitting and chatting in a shady corner, we passed into his office through a studio where draftsman's easels stood. Cordero, an industrial designer, had done projects for the Fiat automobile factory in Turin. He did not say which he considered his primary career, making Barolo or designing automotive systems, but I gathered that he applied his sense of precision masterfully to each. On a label on the back of each bottle he lists to the square meter the size of each vineyard plot he owns or rents on the slopes of a hill called Monfalletto.

"*Salute!*" I said, taking a first sip. The wine was at cellar temperature, slightly cooler than the air in Cordero's shuttered office, about the way the French like a young Burgundy.

Paolo Cordero di Montezemolo

"Warm your glass over the candle," Cordero advised. "The heat brings out the flavor."

It was opening up: a powerful wine of extraordinary depth. My enthusiasm was answered by an expression of regret from Cordero that such mundane laws as supply and demand now applied to dealings in Barolo.

"It's 8,500 lire a bottle," he said, as though he could hardly believe it himself. "But understand now, you don't have to buy any. There are other Barolos available at half the price, less even." He unselfishly suggested the names of other producers in La Morra and neighboring towns.

His warning was not exaggerated. At the day's exchange rate, 8,500 lire was more than $10, much more than any Barolo of recent vintage I knew of at that time. I took two bottles anyway.

"You don't have to store it long," he said. "My Barolo can be drunk young."

Under DOC rules, Barolo is made from the Michet, Lampia, or Rosé subvarieties of the Nebbiolo grape grown in approved vineyards within a delimited zone of about 25,000 acres southwest of the city of Alba in the province of Cuneo. The name comes from the small town of Barolo, where it first gained recognition, but its DOC zone includes the communities of Roddi, Verduno, Grinzane, Diano d'Alba, La Morra, Castiglione Falletto, Serralunga d'Alba, and Monforte d'Alba.

Most vineyards on the moorlike Langhe hills are worked by hand. DOC standards for Barolo are demanding: a maximum yield of 5,600 liters a hectare (about 2,200 liters from an acre), though growers seldom realize anywhere near that much, and a minimum alcohol content of 13°. At least three years' aging in barrel and bottle are required before the wine can be called Barolo. (It could be sold earlier as Nebbiolo *vino da tavola*.) After four years' aging it qualifies as *riserva*, after five as *riserva speciale*. DOC also permits a Barolo Chinato whose name comes from *china* (chinchona), a bitter Peruvian bark. When a tonic made from this *china* is steeped in Barolo it makes a drink much appreciated locally for its healthful virtues. A superb *amaro*, it is good either before or after a meal. Sad to say, it is nearly impossible to find in commerce now.

Cordero, who produced about twenty-seven thousand bottles from the 1971 vintage, does not make reserve Barolo, insisting his wine is ready to drink after four or five years instead of the customary six to eight. His techniques are similar to those advanced by research in California in the 1960s and developed almost concurrently by French oenologists, notably in Burgundy. Cordero's Barolo is fermented with the skins at a controlled temperature for about a week (other winemakers draw the musts off the skins after as little as three days), instead of the traditional two to three weeks. Barrel aging is kept to the three-year minimum. In theory, this makes red wine somewhat lighter in body, fruitier in flavor, and, supposedly, more appealing to contemporary tastes, but it also tends to diminish the propensity for aging.

"In America, maybe, but not here," said Violante Sobrero when I asked his opinion of the new method as we toured his small cellar at Castiglione Falletto. "There's one way to make Barolo, the traditional way — complete fermentation and long aging in wood. There are no shortcuts."

Sobrero, a ruggedly built fellow of about Cordero's age, revealed an independent, even stubborn, frame of mind of the sort often evident in those men of the soil who do all their work themselves. He wore blue work trousers drawn tight at the waist by a tattered leather belt, and his neatly pressed shirt showed fading stains from a recent vintage or two. His 1971 Barolo, of which he made only seven thousand bottles, cost slightly more than one-third that of Cordero's. Sobrero, whose wines carry the name Filippo Sobrero & Figli, also makes Dolcetto, a lesser red wine for everyday consumption in Piedmont, where Barolo is kept for special occasions, even by those who produce it.

Ironically, Sobrero's Barolo seemed nearer its prime than did Cordero's, softer and more harmonious, with a more pronounced scent of wood. When I remarked on this, Sobrero expressed only limited agreement. He explained that the 1971s were so high in alcohol (up to 15 percent) and acids (more than 7 parts per 1,000) that they seemed to balance their tannin early. "But they still have a long way to go," he said. "Wait till the 1980s."

Sobrero's reference to tannin touched upon the crux of the controversy. In a young wine, too much tannic acid — which is derived from the grape skins, seeds, and stems during fermentation — imparts an astringent, slightly bitter, aspect, reminiscent of unsweetened tea. With age, it lends itself to the complex structure of red wines, precipitating a light deposit after serving out its role as a preserver of the other elements.

"Without that tannin, without that wood, Barolo isn't Barolo," Sobrero insisted. "This quick business sounds like propaganda to me. It helps to sell the wine sooner."

Standing on the terrace beneath his neat white-plaster house, Sobrero pointed out his vines in the patchwork of green plots of the Conca, a valley that in size and shape resembled the interior of a large volcano. With a sweep of his hand toward Monfalletto, where Cordero's vineyards lie, he smiled, deepening the creases in his sunburned face.

"Don't get me wrong about Cordero. I respect him," Sobrero said. "As to the wines, that's for you to judge. But I'll bet Cordero's 1971 will improve right into the 1980s, just as mine will. It's the nature of the grape."

Contrasts between the old school and the new in Barolo are not as sharp as they might appear. Excellent wines are made by each, their quality evidently more dependent on the nature of the grape and the skill of the winemaker than on the methods used.

Fresh Ideas

Renato Ratti, one of the more accomplished and articulate of the Langhe's small-scale winemakers, has played a conspicuous role in promoting the new methods, though he might argue that they are not so much innovative or avant-garde as economically and scientifically functional. His position seems to be that it would be senseless to ignore the wealth of practical knowledge about viticulture and oenology developed in Italy and other nations in recent years. He and others like him see no disloyalty in applying fresh ideas to their métier. Indeed, just the opposite: in their view they are strengthening an already strong tradition.

Ratti has served as president of the consortiums of Barolo and Barbaresco, as well as Asti Spumante. And he has been a leader in the nationwide movement to advance the concept of what was formerly called *cru* by some, though, as mentioned earlier, the term no longer can be used for Italian wines. Certainly the strongest evidence in favor of a vineyard classification system in Italy exists right here in the Alba zone. Appropriately, Ratti has encouraged producers in his consortiums to vinify their wines vineyard by vineyard and call attention to the fact on the label. They have also been urged to cite the number of bottles in each reserve and to number each bottle individually. So, in a sense, producers here are already presenting the wines of their best vineyards with the highest set of credentials possible short of official classification.

Ratti, who has assembled a small wine museum in the desanctified Abbey of the Annunziata next to his estate, has written books about wine and appears frequently in public to discuss them. Tall and dignified, he can give the impression initially of being reserved, even a bit severe, but once expounding his theories of winemaking he loosens up, occasionally injecting a touch of ironic humor into his otherwise scholarly discourses.

He makes several wines to be drunk young (*da pronta beva*, as they say here), among the freshest red varietals of Piedmont. Some of his Nebbiolo, from the same grape as Barolo, is ready to drink in the spring after the harvest, remarkably balanced for so young a wine. Ratti uses the method for some Barbera and Dolcetto as well, successfully contradicting the widely accepted notion in Piedmont that these wines begin to approach their primes only with two or three years or more of age.

Ratti's 1971 Barolo from the Marcenasco vineyard hardly fits the category of *da pronta beva*, because it underwent three years of barrel aging. By 1975 it was an outstanding Barolo, showing roundness, depth, smoothness, and more complete aroma and flavor than some of the finer Barolos from 1961 and 1964, both of which were rated outstanding vintages. But it remained to be seen if the 1971 Marcenasco would hold up for decades as some Barolo from previous great years has done.

"Age will mellow it a bit," said Ratti. "It comes down to a question of taste. To me, it's close to its prime, but it wouldn't be a mistake to keep some bottles around for a while."

Ratti's philosophy has been given added plausibility by a series of substandard vintages through the 1970s. Though 1971 and 1978 were great years and 1970, 1974, and 1979 excellent for Barolo, 1973, 1975, 1976, and 1977 were weak vintages and 1972 was such a disaster that all Barolo was declassified. In the poor years Ratti and others favor shortening the required aging for Barolo and Barbaresco and making simpler, lighter wines — though still of DOC standards — to be sold sooner and at lower cost. He believes this could be accomplished through modifications in existing DOC rules, though the process of altering them is inevitably complex and drawn out.

The chief problem seems to be in what to call the wine from subpar years. Considerable opposition has been voiced to calling it Barolo (yet the reputations of some fabled French châteaux have survived despite the occasionally dreadful vintage wines issued under their names). Until this matter is sorted out it would be wise to pay close attention to vintage charts and to select Barolo from the good to great years. Wines from the weak years do not always stand up admirably through the required long barrel aging. Of the vintages available now, 1974 was a fine and abundant harvest whose wines should be rounding into top form in the early 1980s; 1971 was generally superb, though 1970 was nearly its equal and can provide better buys; and 1967 and 1964 should still be very drinkable. Perhaps the finest Barolo in three decades, the 1978 crop, will emerge between 1982 and 1985 and should make for outstanding drinking from the late 1980s until (in some cases, at least) the turn of the century.

The "Crisis" of Short Supply

Somewhere between the old and new school is Elvio Cogno, whose Barolo Marcarini from the vineyards of Brunate and La Serra is consistently among the best and most sought-out Barolo. When I stopped at his cellars in La Morra not long ago, he told me that because of a "crisis" the entire stock of Barolo — some 30,000 bottles annually — plus Barbera and Dolcetto had been sold, and that he had not even been able to supply a dealer in Milan who had bought regularly from him for years. Such crises have hit other outstanding producers as well.

Aldo Conterno, whose approach seems to combine the best of the old and the new in his Barolo, just shook his head when I asked if he had any 1971 Barolo left in 1979. "I don't even have any '74," he said apologetically. "I'm afraid you'll have to wait for the '78."

Conterno, whose attractively situated new white winery is surrounded by vineyards acknowledged as exceptional for Barolo, offered a Chinato as *aperitivo*, though he did not have enough of that left to sell either. "Barolo sales slowed down for a while," he said, "but after the run of poor vintages everybody suddenly wanted to buy bottles from the best vintages to put away. What little I have left I'll drink myself."

Conterno is a practitioner of what he calls "rational cultivation" (apparently another way of saying do-it-yourself), long fermentation on the skins, and plenty of bottle age after the wine comes out of barrel. He even buries bottles in sand to maintain an even temperature. Raised in a winemaking family (his brother Giacomo is also a noted producer), Conterno follows a policy of moderation in his techniques. "I'm not inclined to go overboard either way," he answered when asked to evaluate the two schools of thought. "In the good years I make more Barolo and in the poor years more Nebbiolo. Each year you have to evaluate the grapes you have to work with and what you expect to achieve with them. You don't want to exaggerate aging but you don't want to make Barolo into Beaujolais either."

With much of the good vintage Barolo from small producers already sold, most exportation has been carried out by larger producers such as Arturo Bersano, Calissano, Alberto Contratto, Luigi Einaudi, Fontanafredda, Kiola, Marchesi di Barolo, the Terre del Barolo cooperative, Marchesi Villadoria, and Valfieri. But *larger* should not be taken to mean *large*, because Barolo is one wine that defies mass production. About 6 million bottles of Barolo are produced each year; many single wineries in other places surpass that total. And only about 1 million bottles are exported, a drop in the bucket compared with shipments of Lambrusco, Chianti, and the Verona wines.

Some relatively small-scale Barolo producers have shipped cases abroad in recent years: Ratti, Cordero, Cogno-Marcarini, Ceretto, Aldo Conterno, Giacomo Conterno, Bruno Giacosa, Giuseppe Mascarello, Valentino Migliorini, Fratelli Oddero, Alfredo Prunotto, and Pio Cesare among them. But their wine could never be widely available. Barolo travels exceedingly well, but so far Piedmontese wine drinkers have given the great bottles precious little chance to prove it.

Several larger firms are now vinifying Barolo vineyard by vineyard from good vintages. Fontanafredda marked its centennial year in 1978 by offering six individually labeled vintage Barolos each from distinct plots of land at Serralunga d'Alba and all on the property that once belonged to Italy's first king, Victor Emmanuel II of Savoy, who acquired the estate of his lover and later morganatic wife who was known as "la Bela Rusin" (dialect for "la bella Rosina"). Fontanafredda, like others, planned to continue this more costly method when the vintage warrants it.

Livio Testa, Fontanafredda's young technical director, said he did not view the practice as competitive with small-scale producers. "There's room for everybody in the Barolo market," he said. "We Piedmontese have a nasty habit of competing against each other when we should be cooperating in affirming Barolo as one of the world's great wines."

Barolo's classified vineyards are not being used to maximum capacity, so there is some possibility of expanded production, although the decision to plant Nebbiolo for Barolo instead of grapes for a less imposing wine that can be sold much sooner is not always an attractive one to growers. For the moment there is little sign of any significant increase in production. If foreigners want to increase their share of the market, they will have to get their bids in early.

Time-Proven Techniques

Most independent producers in the Langhe, where tiny, often scattered holdings prevail, follow traditional methods of making Barolo. Some, like Sobrero, criticize the new concepts; others seem only vaguely aware that they exist. Individualists all, the small producers of Barolo practice their craft (some call it art, others science) with a dedication that at times approaches fanaticism.

Luigi Pira of the village of Barolo states on his label: *"Lavorazione artigianale — Pigiatura a piedi"* (Artisan labor — Crushing by foot). Castello Verduno boasts not only that the property once belonged to His Majesty the King of Italy but that it was the sole provider of wine to the expedition led by the Duke of the Abruzzi to the North Pole in 1899. Many labels on the back of the bottle give detailed information, some suggesting that the wine be opened many hours ahead of time and served at as much as 22° C (72° F), a bit warm for some tastes. If you polled them, the majority of producers would probably agree that their six- to eight-year-old Barolo needed maturing and that anything made more than ten years earlier would be in the drinkable stages.

If the methods employed are not invariably the latest, they are based on time-proven techniques. And the Barolo producers' consortium, to which most belong, provides expert assistance to insure that winemakers meet high standards. The traditionalists might be encouraged to learn that the trend in Burgundy and Bordeaux is once again toward longer fermentation and more durable wine after years of experimentation. But some growers in Barolo seem blissfully impervious to trends even in the next valley, let alone the next country.

The following listing recommends producers whose Barolo has rated 16 or higher on a scale of 20 in tastings in recent years. It includes most names in the established elite plus some small-scale producers whose wines are not widely available but are worth seeking out by visitors to the Barolo zone. Many are available at the Enoteca Regionale at Grinzane Cavour. The producer's name is followed by the location of the winery and, in parentheses, the vineyard if specified on the label:

★ Fratelli Barale, Barolo
★ Giacomo Borgogno & Figli, Barolo
★ Serio & Battista Borgogno, Barolo
★ Cantina della Porta Rossa, Diano d'Alba
★ Casa Vinicola Ceretto, Alba (Grignöré, Zonchetta)
★ Castello di Verduno, Verduno
★ Fratelli Cavalotto, Castiglione Falletto (Bricco Boschis)
★ Cogno-Marcarini, La Morra (Brunate, La Serra)
★ Aldo Conterno, Monforte d'Alba (Granbussia)
★ Giacomo Conterno, Monforte d'Alba
★ Alberto Contratto, Canelli
★ Paolo Cordero di Montezemolo, La Morra (Monfalletto)
★ Lorenzo Denegri, La Morra
★ Marchese Fracassi di Torre Rossano, Nazzole
★ Franco-Fiorina, Alba
★ Fontanafredda, Serralunga d'Alba (La Rosa)
★ Fontana Severio, Castiglione Falletto
★ Bruno Giacosa, Neive (Vigna Rionda di Serralunga d'Alba)
★ Fratelli Giacosa di Leone, Neive
★ Angelo Germano & Figli, Barolo

★ Giulio Mascarello, Barolo (Canubbi)
★ Giuseppe Mascarello & Figlio, Monchiero (Bussia Soprana di Monforte d'Alba)
★ Giuseppe Massolino & Figli, Serralunga d'Alba
★ Valentino Migliorini, Monforte d'Alba
★ Fratelli Oddero, La Morra
★ Luigi Oddero & Figlio, Monforte d'Alba
★ Pio Cesare, Alba
★ E. Pira & Figli, Barolo
★ Alfredo Prunotto, Alba (Bussia di Monforte d'Alba)
★ Teobaldo Prandi & Figlio, Barolo
★ Renato Ratti, Abbazia dell'Annunziata, La Morra (Marcenasco)
★ Francesco Rinaldi & Figli, Barolo
★ Giuseppe Rinaldi, Barolo
★ Filippo Sobrero & Figli, Castiglione Falletto
★ Tenuta Carretta, Piobesi d'Alba
★ Tenuta Montanello, Castiglione Falletto
★ Terre del Barolo (a cooperative), Castiglione Falletto
★ Giovanni Veglio, Diano d'Alba
★ Vezza, Santa Vittoria d'Alba (Cascina Bruni di Serralunga d'Alba)
★ Vietti, Castiglione Falletto (Vigneto Rocche)

Whatever the differences in attitudes and methods of its producers, Barolo stands as an exemplar of excellence, a position shared by its neighbor and acknowledged peer, Babaresco. Although growers in several regions of Italy make red wine that may equal or, in certain years, surpass Barolo and Barbaresco, no single zone of wine production can match these two for consistent class. Their designation as the first DOCG wines attests to their status.

Barolo and Barbaresco are made from the same subvarieties of the Nebbiolo grape under almost identical conditions, yet there are subtle differences between them. Their growers' consortiums have been unified, though each maintains its own set of standards and symbol: Barolo a lion and Barbaresco the town tower of Barbaresco. Barolo ("King of wines and wine of kings") is often described as powerful, intense, robust, yes, even masculine; Barbaresco as seductive, more delicate, smoother, thus, of course, feminine. Such sexist discrimination is largely fantasy. Barolo is generally grown at slightly greater altitudes, has a higher minimum alcoholic content (13° to 12.5° for Barbaresco) and must age a year longer under DOC rules. But only the most experienced palate could invariably tell one from the other.

Basically they are both hard, even harsh, when young, growing rounder and softer with bottle age. Rich in extract and glycerol, they are classically big wines in which the aroma of violets and raspberries with a hint of tar is often noted. Their youthful rich ruby color takes on garnet tones with orange reflections after several years, then tends toward dense auburn with great age. Bottles should be chambered before serving, and, if not opened a couple of hours ahead of time, the wine will benefit from decantation with care to avoid pouring the sediment.

Barbaresco tends to develop more quickly than Barolo and perhaps for that reason is most often recommended to novices as the first of the two to try. For people whose palates are attuned to wines from Cabernet, Pinot, and Merlot grapes, Barolo and Barbaresco might take some getting used to. They are what the Italians call wines of *arrivo*, to be arrived at after experiences with less imposing wines, for they can be extraordinarily complex. Oenophiles who know them well consider them among the most consistently rewarding red wines of Europe.

Piedmontese Cooking at a Country Inn

Piedmont's food has been acclaimed almost as widely as its wine. The Piedmontese, who display an overwhelming preference for red over white, will drink their favorite Barbera or Dolcetto with just about anything. Still, to my taste at least, two of the region's most famous dishes go better with white wine — or no wine at all — than with red. They are *bagna caöda*, whose name, "hot bath," derives from the boiling sauce of olive oil, anchovies, garlic, seasonings, and butter into which raw vegetables are dipped, and *fonduta*, the Italian version of cheese fondue.

Piedmontese restaurant food is invariably good, and sometimes brilliant, for example at Armando Rosa d'Oro in San Gillio, the Villa Sassi and the Tuscan Al Gatto Nero in Turin, Pinocchio in Borgomanero, and da Guido, in Costigliole d'Asti, where Guido and Lidia Alciati's inspired cooking has won nationwide praise though they serve only fifteen to twenty diners at a time and then only those who reserve well ahead of time. The region's fine wines can also be matched admirably with non-Piedmontese cooking. Valentino Migliorini, a young restaurateur from Caorso in Emilia-Romagna, bought vineyards in Monforte d'Alba a few years ago and has since become such a dedicated winemaker that he spends more time in his vineyards than in his fine restaurant.

The art of matching Piedmontese food and wine is rarely performed with more traditional good taste than at a country inn at Monforte d'Alba, Il Giardino di Felicin. There, in the spacious dining room with a view across the vineyards to the Maritime Alps, Giorgio Rocca provides a sage selection of Piedmont's fine wine. The dishes, prepared by Rocca, his wife Rosina, and his elderly but energetic father Felicin, are designed to follow the customary progression of wines through the meal, opening with light, fresh reds and working up to well-aged Barolo or Barbaresco.

Antipasto is copious, consisting of at least five portions, more if the Roccas have had an inspired day in the kitchen. Choices might include local *prosciutto*, salami, pâtés, *carne cruda* (tender strips of raw veal marinated in a sort of vinaigrette), green asparagus with butter and Parmesan, or a salad of wild mushrooms called *porcini*, whose firm white flesh has a flavor remindful of the earthen odor a meadow gives off after a late summer rain. With these the Roccas serve their own Dolcetto or Barbera from the most recent vintage, purple and full of fruit and altogether too conducive to quaffing with bites of the meter-long *grissini*, crisp breadsticks that are plopped across the table as the meal begins. With luck a glassful of Dolcetto will remain to accompany the *maltagliatei* or *tajerin*, hand-cut ribbons of pasta mixed with butter and coarse-grated Parmesan and topped with razor-thin shavings of *tartufi*, pale yellow truffles, the nearly priceless early autumn delicacy of the Alba zone.

At that point Rocca will permit a respite to taste and discuss the merits of the Barolo or Barbaresco that will go with the main course. That may be game, if it is the season, or kid braised in red wine, or roast guinea hen, all prepared with that Italian genius for using herbs and natural flavorings to elevate a flavor without destroying its essence. Creamy *fontina*, pungent goat cheese, or a chunk of *grana*, as most Italians call Parmesan, bring the wine to its optimum.

Discretion would dictate stopping there, except that desserts are just possibly what Rocca does best. His crème caramel, from a base of fresh sweet cream, is so uncommonly delicious that customers who did not really want dessert in the first place have been known to order a second. His impromptu concoctions can be equally memorable, such as a zabaglione he whipped up one time, substituting very old Barolo Chinato for the regulation Marsala, and served with a scoop of home-made vanilla ice cream melting in the steaming mass.

Some Italian chefs consider the French-originated *Guide Michelin* to Italy stingy in light of the fact that its maximum rating for a restaurant is two stars, where in France it is three. But Giorgio Rocca seems serenely content with the single star the *Guide* awards him, pointing out with a devil-may-care shrug that if he had the two stars his cooking merits, he might have to worry constantly about pleasing a more critical clientele.

French chefs, groomed in a fiercely competitive system where such symbols as stars and crowned roosters are tickets to fame and fortune, would doubtless gasp in disbelief at Rocca's nonchalance. There is no question that French restaurant cooking at the star level is more dazzlingly innovative than Italian, but the splendors of *haute cuisine* carry a rather stiff price.

A Frenchman, a Parisian jewelry designer dining at the next table one evening not long ago, mused over the virtues of Il Giardino di Felicin. "I'd forgotten," he said, "that meals like this were created anymore. Each dish was of an honest product simply but beautifully prepared. The wines, superb. I have not tasted many Bordeaux to equal that Barbaresco. And the chef, my God, such talent, and he enjoys himself."

When truffles are included, Rocca's meals are not cheap. But, we agreed, the price in terms of quality would be hard to match anywhere in Europe these days. Wines are an outstanding part of the bargain.

A Rustic Order in the Vineyards

During the half-hour drive north from Monforte to Barbaresco, vines are never out of sight, except for a moment or two while traversing the marketing center of Alba when buildings block the view of the surrounding hills. From Alba, climbing out of the Tanaro River valley, the road curves past high points that provide glimpses to the southeast across a landscape that warrants description as a sea of vines. The southern Monferrato hills, wave after wave, roll on as far as the eye can see, their pattern of green broken only by the pastels of dwellings, fronts lined with wooden balustrades, elongated forms that at a distance from a moving car appear to float on the hillsides like longboats riding out a storm.

Most vineyards here are not of the textbook variety. The vine rows are too close together for tractors to pass through and the hand-cut wooden poles that support the wires that in turn support the heavy new growth lean here and there, haphazardly it seems, rustic remnants of an unmechanized past. They are not nearly so neat as those new vineyards one sees elsewhere with their concrete columns stretching wires straight as arrows, trim vine rows interspaced by wide plowed furrows, the picture of symmetry. No, it might appear to the untrained eye that growers here spend their summers sitting in the shade. Then, as the harvest approaches and the grapes turn purple, even the untrained eye will note that the clusters hang just a foot or two above the clay soil, the foliage above absorbing the autumn sun, the way the books say they should. Order out of chaos? Hardly. "That's the way we've always done it" is the inevitable explanation, the tone implicitly demanding, "Is there any better way?"

Barbaresco: No Need to Advertise

The Barbaresco zone reaches the outskirts of Alba and surrounds the villages of Neive and Treiso as well as Barbaresco. As in Barolo, much of the wine is made by growers with small holdings and sold directly to consumers from their cellars. But, unlike in many other wine zones, the largest producers in terms of volume are also among the most respected and emulated winemakers. The two biggest wineries in Barbaresco contrast sharply in concept and style, but in their separate ways serve as models to an industry that, despite surface appearances to the contrary, is in the midst of thorough transition.

Produttori di Barbaresco, a cooperative of 48 growers who pool the products of their land and labor and share the profits, has an output of about 200,000 bottles of Barbaresco and Nebbiolo in a normal year. Gaja, a family-owned enterprise produces some 150,000 bottles of Barbaresco annually, along with 60,000 to 70,000 bottles of other wines. The two wineries have headquarters less than a block apart from each other on the quiet main road of Barbaresco, the Produttori in a modern brick building opposite the church, Gaja almost invisible behind a high whitewashed wall. Unimposing signs on each discreetly illustrate that in Barbaresco there is no need to advertise.

Although many Italians will argue otherwise, cooperatives have undoubtedly helped to upgrade the general quality level of wines. Still, their benefits have been offset to some extent by a loss of identity among growers in a nation where great emphasis is placed on individual creativity. Pride does not seem to have suffered at Produttori di Barbaresco, but then, the members have more to work with than others; between them they possess some of the most valuable vineyards of Italy.

The original wooden vats are still in use in the part of the cellar where the Produttori began their operation in the early 1960s, but little else has been retained from the formative years. As membership grew, the plant was expanded. Glass-lined concrete vats were installed, then modern grape processors and presses, a pumping system, more oaken barrels, bottling and labeling machines, an analytic laboratory. Today, the full-time director, Franco Giordano, and a university-trained oenologist, Roberto Macaluso, run a sophisticated operation that makes a comfortable profit by selling some of the region's best wines at truly moderate prices.

In very good years — 1967, 1970, 1971, 1974, and 1978, for example — grapes from choice vineyards are separated to become either *riserva* or *riserva speciale,* meaning they must age either three or four years in barrel followed by at least a year in bottle before being sold. The most prestigious plot, Rabayà, is a vineyard just outside the town owned in parcels by four members. The 1971 Rabayà went on sale in 1977 and was judged to have been among the elite wines made in Piedmont from that exceptional year.

The Produttori plan to expand gradually their line of wines from special vineyards to about a dozen. Most of their other production is labeled as Barbaresco DOC, some reserve, some not, invariably of good quality. There is also a Nebbiolo, a less expensive wine from the same grapes that go into Barbaresco. The winery makes a judgment each fall on which proportion of the harvest meets Barbaresco standards. That which does not goes into Nebbiolo.

Opponents of consolidation voice the often justified lament that large wineries tend to standardize wines for mass taste, whatever that is, creating products that meet regulations for name and origin, but lack any other distinction. The cellarmaster at Produttori, while allowing that many cooperatives have fallen into that pattern, insists that their role should be just the opposite.

"We can give all the care to a vineyard, to harvesting, to making wine, that any small producer can," he said. "In a sense, more even, because experts can supervise each step. Not many small growers are expert in all aspects of winemaking, you know.

"As for mass production, well, it simply isn't practiced here. *Cru* and *riserva* wines are made vineyard by vineyard, barrel by barrel. As much as possible we try to make the other wines by vineyard as well. When we mix grapes, we're not thinking of mass tastes. We try to make the best wine we can with what we have."

An air of communal confidence pervades the Produttori winery, even among the hired help. Among growers it appears that any loss of ego suffered by not having one's name alone on the label is compensated for by the superior production facilities and guarantees of financial security provided by the group operation. The owners of the special vineyards at least have their last names given on labels.

"Here the whole is greater than the sum of its parts," the cellarmaster said. "I doubt that anyone feels he could make better wine if he were doing it on his own."

The Gaja Principle

Angelo Gaja, who heads the family firm now in its fifth generation, couples his passion for viniculture with an adroit sense of business, qualities that have made him one of the most successful and admired winemakers in Italy. Gaja's remarkable Barbarescos warrant the elevated reputation, but he maintains excellence through a line of wines ranging from reserve Barbaresco made under the *cru* concept to lesser varietals to Vinòt, a red from Nebbiolo grapes frankly modeled after Beaujolais *nouveau*.

Gaja has benefited immeasurably from a decision made in 1961 to cut back production, a move that went against the trend of the times and also against what competing firms must have considered better judgment. Previously, the Gaja family made more of the same wines they do now plus Barolo, which was considered among the best available at the time. But to do so they needed to rent land and buy grapes from other growers. Finding themselves increasingly preoccupied with quantity, they decided to sell all but 50 hectares (124 acres) of their finest vineyards in and around Barbaresco and to put their emphasis exclusively on personally controlled quality production.

About 70 percent of Gaja's production from Nebbiolo grapes in a vintage year goes into Barbaresco, most of it nonreserve to be sold after at least two years of aging. A few thousand bottles from choice grapes are made into a *riserva* called Infernot, in which fermentation and aging are carried out in the traditional manner. Vinòt production has increased gradually since its inception in 1975 as Italy's first respectable *vino novello*.

Vinòt, which is to be sold and consumed by the end of the year of harvest, represents a rather recent marketing concept in Italy, but it is

Angelo Gaja

not a gimmick nor is it unique. Guido Rivella, Gaja's young oenologist, explained that Gaja was the first winery in Italy to use carbonic maceration, the fermentation process that has been used widely in France, chiefly in Beaujolais and parts of Burgundy, to bring wine to a fragrant, fruity peak of drinkability sooner, sometimes within weeks of the harvest. The success of Vinòt prompted other wineries in Italy to follow suit with their own versions of *vino novello*, though rarely as successfully. These new wines enable producers to generate capital by clearing their stocks within months instead of years. But new wine is by no means a new idea in Italy, where the most recent pressings often appear on country tables straight from the vat at almost the moment they finish fermenting.

The Vinòt experiment is a natural extension of the Gaja principle that most of Piedmont's popular wines are better young than old. So most of the firm's varietals — Nebbiolo, Dolcetto, Barbera, Freisa — are bottled and sold after carbonic maceration and light fermentation and the standard racking, fining, and filtration. Most are on the market six months to a year after the harvest. Supple, smooth, and fruity, these wines to my palate are usually more satisfying than the aged versions, many of which tend to lose their balance after more than two years in bottle.

Barbaresco is, of course, a different story. Gaja and Rivella put their skills together in making it, particularly their two most prestigious Barbarescos known as Sorì San Lorenzo and Sorì Tildin. Sorì in Piedmontese dialect refers to southern exposure, a characteristic of the best vineyards. Gaja has always preferred that term to cru, not because of any disrespect for the French, to whom Piedmontese winemakers may owe more than many are prepared to acknowledge, but rather as homage to tradition. For, clearly, any ideas or techniques imported by the Piedmontese have been used to enhance, not to supplant, their own ways of doing things. Gaja makes no secret of his admiration for the French, their techniques, their sense of quality, or their prices, all of which he feels he can match. He should know, because he sells one of their greatest wines through an exclusive concession in Italy to distribute the production of the Société Civile de la Romanée-Conti.

Gaja is a disciple of carbonic maceration, known in Italy as macerazione carbonica, under which uncrushed grapes are macerated in closed stainless steel vats and the musts are then drawn off and fermented under temperature control. Ideally wine made that way retains more of the essence of the fruit because the grapes are placed whole in the vats to macerate under the pressure of their self-created carbonic acid gases. Then the wine undergoes both its primary and secondary (or malolactic) fermentation virtually simultaneously, resulting in fruitier, more fragrant, more acidic and less tannic wine than normal. Gaja even used it experimentally in his two Sorì wines with what he called gratifying results, but he has decided to employ more traditional methods for the time being and use the carbonic maceration for the younger wines.

Sorì Tildin is a three-acre plot from which choice grapes are picked late, after the vine leaves begin to fall but before noble rot sets in (about the middle of November most years). The wine is soft, rich, perfumed, ready to drink after aging three years, part of the time in small barrels of Slavonian oak for maximum contact with wood. Sorì Tildin classifies as dry, but it has more natural glycerol than most dry reds, giving it a mouth-filling richness that is hard to forget. In vintage years, about 4,000 bottles of Sorì Tildin are made, all allotted in advance to retailers in Italy who set their prices above the vineyard figure. The 1971s were selling at more than $20 a bottle in Rome and Milan by 1980, though they were almost impossible to find.

Sorì San Lorenzo is made in even smaller lots (of about 2,500 bottles a year) from that two-acre vineyard's choicest, individually selected grapes, which are picked toward the end of the normal harvest. The wine is a bit drier, more classically structured than the Sorì Tildin, and, judging by its price, is held in even greater esteem. Sorì San Lorenzo is sold directly by Gaja, who is not only reluctant to quote a price but seems about as willing to part with a bottle as an artist would be with his favorite painting.

The choicest Barbaresco, as well as some of the old Barolo, is kept in a special section of the cantina known as the Infernot, along with what amounts to a fortune in bottles from great vintages dating back over a century. None of that wine is for sale.

"Those bottles are kept for special occasions, for friends, as curiosities," Gaja said. There was no need to add that Gaja did not need the money. The personal-control formula has paid off handsomely here, not only in profits but in personal satisfaction.

The Case for "Égalité"

Angelo Gaja is not alone in his conviction that his wine can stand comparison with the greats of France. Although Barolo and Barbaresco prices have been held comfortably below the inflated and occasionally outlandish levels of the French elite, there is a growing conviction in the Alba area that the gap is far too great. Why should an outstanding Barbaresco made and aged with similar costs of labor, equipment, and storage, and all the personal skill, attention, and passion of any wine of France, sell for half or a third or a fifth the price of a château bottling of the same year from the Côte de Nuits or Pauillac? Even considering the long-established reputations — not to mention the worldwide cult of snobbishness — attached to the great growths of France, the feeling in

Alba is that nothing can justify the current differential. Some producers in the area (and elsewhere) are convinced that holding the line on prices abroad is self-destructive. Money talks, so the saying goes, and all it is saying in this case is that the best Barbaresco is not half as good as the best Bordeaux.

If you want to argue this point, the man to corner is Bruno Ceretto, who with his oenologist brother Marcello stands behind several of the outstanding wines of Alba, including a Barbaresco from the property of Bricco Asili that would probably rank as *hors classe* if the Italians had ever succeeded in stratifying their growths.

"I don't want to outshine the French. I just want to sit down at the same table with them," said Bruno Ceretto, a flush of anger coloring his light complexion. "What we need is a little more *égalité* and *fraternité* in the European wine community. Look at it this way. We Italians buy the finest wines France has to offer, Bordeaux, Burgundy, more Champagne than any other country, never mind the price. Meanwhile, what do the French buy from us? Blending wine from Apulia, pizza wine like Lambrusco. They turn up their noses at our quality products even though they could be drinking better wine for their money if they'd ever get over the vainglorious attitude that Italian wines are intrinsically inferior to theirs.

"We make magnificent wines here, surely among the greatest on earth," he continued, "and I say that with no qualms whatsoever. I'm happy to see great French wines served in our better restaurants. But my ambition is to have Ceretto wines on the lists of the great restaurants of Paris. Until that day comes, until there's some equilibrium in the international price structure, I don't think we Italian winemakers who care can feel we've realized our potential in this field."

Casa Vinicola Ceretto, with cellars in Barbaresco and Castiglione Falletto, is a medium-sized operation that produces Barbaresco and Barolo as well as the other wines of Alba. Ceretto also distills the pressings left over from the wines to make different types of grappa, which rank with the finest of Piedmont.

The most prestigious Ceretto wines are products of the family's own vineyards. Other leading wineries in the zone work mainly with purchased grapes, although their cultivation is carefully controlled and certain guarantees are understood between producer and grower. Two such wineries worthy of special attention for their traditional quality and progressive approach to oenology and marketing are Pio Cesare of Alba, run by Giuseppe Boffa and his son Pio, and Alfredo Prunotto, owned by Giuseppe Colla and Carlo Filiberti. Their Barolo and Barbaresco is consistently ranked with the finest.

The village of Neive is a center of quality production, home of several small but significant wineries that excel in Barbaresco from the surrounding vineyards. Don Giuseppe Cogno, the village priest, supervises a winemaking operation for church benefit under the name Parroco del Neive. The wines — Barbaresco, Barbera, and others, including an excellent Moscato d'Asti — are carried by some of Italy's better shops and restaurants. The Barbaresco made vineyard by vineyard in good vintages is exceptional, worthy of all the glory that has been showered on this gifted winemaker-priest. The vineyards have been used for parochial benefit for more than two centuries. Needless to say, the old Church of Ss. Pietro e Paolo is in impeccable repair.

The town castle serves as headquarters for another thriving small winery with a big name: Azienda Agricola Cantina del Castello di Neive. A French oenologist, Louis Oudart, was summoned to Piedmont in the 1850s by Count Camillo di Cavour, the leading political force behind the Risorgimento and the nation's first prime minister, to run the count's cellars at Grinzane. Oudart was credited with introducing techniques of vinification and aging of red wines that were subsequently adopted in Piedmont and elsewhere. In later years, Oudart established himself at the Castello di Neive, where he made a wine that won a gold medal at the London Exposition of 1862. Today the castle and its winemaking facilities look much the way they must have in Oudart's day. Despite much evidence of modernization, the wine made there is still worthy of international honors. The 1971 Riserva Santo Stefano, of which only 4,250 bottles were produced, is an opulent Barbaresco of great distinction, among the outstanding red wines made in Piedmont in that fine vintage.

Bruno Giacosa, another winemaker in Neive, personally produces and bottles a little bit of nearly everything the Alba area has to offer in wine and grappa, all of it first class. A few cases even make it into export channels. Bruno Giacosa's 1970 Barolo and Barbaresco, from an excellent vintage largely forgotten in the great year that followed, were equal to the 1971s at lower prices. As for the 1971 Barolo, it was judged the best by a clear margin of 29 from that vintage rated by the magazine *Dove*

Vai? and based on a tasting conducted by the National Association of Wine Tasters and the Italian Association of Oenologists in 1979.

The following listing of recommended Barbaresco is based on the same criteria as the earlier list of Barolo:

★ Azienda Agricola Moccagatta di Mario Minuto & Figli, Barbaresco
★ Alfredo Bianco, Barbaresco (Cascina Morassino)
★ Cantina della Porta Rossa, Diano d'Alba
★ Castello di Neive, Neive (Riserva Santo Stefano)
★ Casa Vinicola Ceretto, Alba (Montefico, Bricco Asili)
★ Franco-Fiorina, Alba
★ Paolo de Forville, Barbaresco
★ Angelo Gaja, Barbaresco (Sorì San Lorenzo, Sorì Tildin, Infernot)
★ Bruno Giacosa, Neive (Vigneto Santo Stefano, Asili di Barbaresco, Montefico di Barbaresco)
★ Fratelli Giacosa di Leone, Neive
★ Giovannini Moresco, Treiso (Podere del Pajorè)
★ Fratelli Oddero, La Morra
★ Paglieri di Alfredo e Giovanni Roagna, Barbaresco (Pajè, Asili)
★ Parroco di Neive, Neive
★ Pasquero-Elia Secondo, Neive (Sorì d' Paytin)
★ Pio Cesare, Alba
★ Produttori di Barbaresco, Barbaresco (Rabayà, Moccagatta)
★ Alfredo Prunotto, Alba (Montestefano)
★ Francesco Rinaldi & Figli, Barolo
★ Tenuta Cisa Asinari dei Marchesi di Gresy, Barbaresco (La Martinenga)
★ Vietti, Castiglione Falletto (Masseria)

Nebbiolo, though in theory not as grand a wine as Barolo and Barbaresco, can still be a worthy representative of the grape that ennobles it. Some producers make it their primary wine, particularly those in the Nebbiolo d'Alba DOC zone that lies mostly to the north of the Tanaro River but also extends south of it into parts of the Barolo and Barbaresco districts. Other producers make a Nebbiolo when they feel their grapes are not up to Barolo or Barbaresco standards. Such progressive oenologists as Renato Ratti and Angelo Gaja have been experimenting with Nebbiolo as young wine, even a *pronta beva* type, that can be delightfully refreshing within months after the harvest.

To qualify as DOC, Nebbiolo d'Alba must have 12° alcohol and be aged at least a year in wood. It can be made into *amabile* and *spumante* versions, both popular locally, or into the classically dry *secco,* which is capable of medium-long aging. Among the many good Nebbiolo d'Alba wines on the market, that of the Antica Casa Vinicola Scarpa at Nizza Monferrato stands out. From vineyards at Vezza d'Alba and Corneliano d'Alba, Scarpa vinifies the grapes into soft, warm, full-bodied wines, extraordinarily round and smooth on the palate. At less than half the price of Barolo and Barbaresco, Scarpa's Nebbiolo can achieve a level of drinkability in three years that some of its so-called big brothers will never arrive at.

Scarpa has also been producing since 1974 a wine called Rouchet from a rare vine of that name still found in some vineyards in the highest reaches of the hills around Castagnole Monferrato. Only 2,710 bottles were produced from the 1978 vintage. Rouchet's magnificence is singular even if its style is reminiscent of the Scarpa Nebbiolo in its full, soft richness of aroma and flavor. It is such a rarity, however, that none of the major catalogues of Italian wines even cite it.

Asti: A Propensity for Bubbles

From Neive the road to Asti winds leisurely for a few more kilometers through the vineyards of Barbaresco before plunging back into the Tanaro River valley, where it picks up traffic through a stretch flanked by concrete, steel, and glass edifices that house industry, not the least of which hereabouts is wine. Fast-paced for a city of 80,000, Asti suffers from the growing pains of the urban sprawl that has extended at an alarming rate from its rather staid and prosperous-looking historic center. But if Asti is no longer a picture-book wine town, its Spumante is not exactly quaint either.

In the middle of the last century, some 150 years after Dom Perignon discovered how to make Champagne, it occurred to some Piedmontese of pioneer spirit that Italians might appreciate bubbly wine as much as the French did. As it turned out, they liked it even better, and the pioneers, led by Carlo Gancia, a vermouth maker, could scarcely turn it out fast enough. The Italians over the years have perfected methods of converting the Moscato Bianco, sweet Muscat, grape into sparkling wine by adopting the charmat method of fermentation in sealed vats under pressure in place of the time-consuming *méthode champenoise* with its innumerable twists and turns of each bottle by skilled hands. Asti Spumante (*spumante* is, literally, foaming) and the slightly sweeter Moscato d'Asti have grown in popularity both in Italy and abroad. The industry has spilled over from Asti to Canelli, 30 kilometers away. Large vermouth firms control a major portion of its production, which surpasses 40 million bottles a year.

For years Asti Spumante was saddled with the image of "the poor man's Champagne." Alexis Lichine once described it as "sometimes sickly sweet" and Cyril Ray allowed that it was "generally considered too sweet for the more sophisticated English tastes." But, in its own way, it often succeeds where other sparkling wines fail. It has a worldwide following among admirers of sweet apéritifs, and it is much better suited than a dry sparkling wine to fruit or dessert. The trend in recent years has been toward a more delicately sweet Asti Spumante than before, with a lightness and freshness that were not always so prominent when Lichine and Ray made their assessments.

For years Asti was sold in Italy and abroad at prices that did not accurately reflect the careful cultivation of its rather delicate vines or the costly technology behind its production. Even the charmat method is complex; its perfection is a recent achievement in Piedmont, made largely through the efforts of the dozen or so large firms that control most production.

The current process involves a light pressing of the grapes by horizontal presses, followed by clarification, filtration, vinification, stabilization, pasteurization, and bottling, all of which require sophisticated and expensive equipment — centrifuges, refrigerated and pressurized fermentation vats known as *autoclave,* isobaric bottling systems that maintain counterpressure between the tank and the bottle, and more.

The trick is to keep the wine's natural sweetness throughout the process by maintaining a degree of residual sugars, because if the wine is fermented out to dryness it loses the Moscato bouquet that gives Asti its distinction. Only a few producers make Asti by the *méthode champenoise* — Contratto's is a fine example — because maintaining the sweetness is painstakingly difficult. The sweetness in Champagne is due to the addition of the so-called *liqueur d'expédition* at the end, a relatively simple process.

Under DOC regulations, Asti Spumante must have at least 12° alcohol by volume (but only 7.5 to 9° developed, meaning that the remaining sugar has not been transformed into alcohol). Moscato d'Asti must have at least 11.5° alcohol, and Moscato Naturale d'Asti, a still wine, 10.5°.

Oddly enough, a tenfold increase in the price of Moscato Bianco grapes between the 1974 and 1978 vintages (in 1977 the Asti grapes were the most expensive of Italy) probably did more good than harm by forcing numerous "cheap" producers and imitators out of business. Asti is one wine that clearly benefits from large-scale production techniques. Indeed, only when a certain volume is reached can the cost of production be maintained. And to the credit of its major producers, Asti prices have not risen in proportion to the costs of grapes or winery modernization.

Asti has nonetheless gone from being a cheap wine to being an expensive one, though the dip in sales due to price rises in 1978 seemed to have straightened itself out by 1980. The Asti Spumante consortium, directed by Renato Ratti, has been successfully upgrading Asti's status by controlling quality standards and encouraging a more uniform price system among producers. The demand for this rather unusual sparkling wine is once again growing, though production is approaching its limits. Moscato vines for DOC Asti must grow in sunny and well-drained vineyards with limestone and clay soil. The vines simply will not produce satisfactorily anywhere else.

Production of the base Moscato Naturale d'Asti reached a peak of 36 million liters in 1977 and 32 million liters in 1978, making it by far the most prominent DOC wine of Piedmont (well ahead of the 20 million liter average of Barbera d'Asti). Indeed, Moscato Naturale d'Asti accounts for about 97 percent of the region's DOC white wine. Not all this still Moscato Naturale is converted into Asti Spumante. In fact, the lighter and fruitier Moscato d'Asti and still Moscato were gaining favor with a certain elite of Italian wine drinkers as an after-dinner drink.

Americans have shown a fondness for *spumante,* drinking far more of it in 1976, 1977, and 1978 than they did Champagne. This was no doubt due in part to lower price, but also to American taste for lightly sweet sparkling wines. Fontanafredda makes fine Asti. Spumante from Bersano, Kiola, Riccadonna, Cinzano, Martini & Rossi, Gancia, Cora, and the Cantina Sociale di Canelli, all exported, are highly regarded as well. Though not an Asti, the good Moscato di Strevi of Bruzzone is being imported by House of Banfi in the United States.

The vanguard of big producers, by no means in Piedmont alone, has been moving into dry sparkling wines, often from the various Pinot and

Chardonnay grapes, but also from such varieties as Prosecco, Riesling, and Verdicchio. In most recent years Italy has been the leading importer of French Champagne, so the Piedmontese have been actively building their share of that market. Among the admirable versions of Piedmontese *méthode champenoise* wine are Fontanafredda's Contessa Rosa, Contratto's Brut, Carlo Gancia's Riserva Brut, Cinzano's Principe di Piemonte, Calissano's Duca d'Alba, and Riccadonna's President Brut. Others are emerging at prices generally well below those of Champagne. In their special ways, some are comparable to Champagne, though they are not easily mistakable by experts for the original.

Contratto, Cinzano, Fontanafredda, Gancia, and Calissano belong to the Istituto Spumante Italiano Metodo Champenois, a group of ten producers campaigning for recognition of their products in a special category of what they prefer to call *metodo classico* sparkling wine. (Other members are Ferrari and Équipe 5 of Trentino, Carpené Malvolti of the Veneto, Marchesi Antinori of Tuscany, and the La Versa cooperative of Lombardy.) With their well-publicized code of standards and shrewd promotion, they have been moving ahead smartly on the Italian market while stepping up exportation gradually. Their regulations now call for all wine to be made only from Pinot and Chardonnay grapes and labeled by vintage and that it be bottle fermented by the Champagne method.

This trend toward drier *spumante* has also put on the market a number of quite acceptable wines made by the charmat method from Pinot, Moscato, and other grapes. The sweet, sparkling, and cheap Lacrima Christi is known abroad, and even some Cold Duck for the U.S. market originates in Piedmont, but I have not noticed either being sold in Italy. They fall into the category of what Italians call *fantasia* wines, whose names and contents are being subjected to greater surveillance these days.

The Italian propensity for bubbly wine is not limited to white. Most popular red wines of Piedmont have a sparkling counterpart, naturally fermented as a rule, usually dry, but sometimes sweet. Brachetto, a varietal, is rather sweet but robust enough that some natives drink it with salami, sausages, and soup. Most is consumed locally, though enough is made to warrant one DOC classification, Brachetto d'Acqui, and expectations of another, Brachetto d'Asti.

Malvasia di Casorzo d'Asti and Malvasia di Castelnuovo Don Bosco, both from the Malvasia Rossa grape, have much in common with Brachetto. Usually sweetish, often sparkling or *frizzante*, they tend to be lighter in color than Brachetto. Made in the hills between Turin and Asti, they have both been granted DOC status. The name Malvasia usually applies to light grapes of the Malmsey or Malvoisie family; Malvasia Rossa is apparently unrelated.

Barbera and Dolcetto: Loyal Proletarians

If a popularity contest were held among the wines of northwestern Italy — the most prosperous, most sophisticated, most wine-oriented section of the country — Barbera would win hands down. Estimates are that at least half the red wine of Piedmont is "la Barbera," affectionately referred to in the feminine gender, a status reserved for it alone. Some scholarly types insist on calling it il Barbera, masculine as all wine is supposed to be, but on its home grounds, the Monferrato hills, the "la" is there to stay. Perhaps Arturo Marescalchi, a scholar himself, captured Barbera's character when he wrote: "It has the body and strength of a male and the lovableness of a female."

Barbera is not only the predominant wine of northwestern Italy; its vine may be the nation's most widely diffused. DOC wines called Barbera are made in Piedmont, Lombardy, and Emilia-Romagna, and Barbera grapes either dominate or figure in the formulas of numerous other wines, both DOC and not, in nearly every region of Italy. The Barbera grape is widely appreciated as a blender because of its natural generosity and adaptability. It is converted into so many styles of wine, both on its own and in mixtures, that it is difficult to keep track of them all. Consider what Gianni Bonacina, author of *Lo stivale in bottiglia*, had to say about it:

You know, I once had an urge to collect bottles of Barbera, not only Piedmontese, but also Lombard, Emilian, Sardinian, Campanian, Venetian, Friulian, and Ligurian, just as long as it was Barbera. Then, after surpassing the mark of 600 diverse types, I abandoned the undertaking, because I realized that I'd need a huge cellar just for Barbera.

Do you have any idea of the confusion to the poor consumer who is not an expert or born in a Barbera area? Anyhow, the vine is a strong one that renders a valid wine grape, and to this end many experiments are under way with it even beyond Piedmont and Lombardy, which are regions of vocation. . . . Still, too many ignoble pretenders have turned up on the market as

Barbera, and not only at the level of everyday table wine. Therefore, keep an eye on the production zone and the producer's name, and for the rest nothing is more valuable than personal experience.

In Piedmont, Barbera is most often made into dry table wine to be drunk fairly young, but there are those who age it long in barrel and bottle and after a decade or so laud it in terms usually associated with the likes of Barolo and Barbaresco. I have yet to taste an aged Barbera of that class. But when served young, as it often is in the good restaurants and *trattorie* that abound in the hills of Asti, Alba, and Alessandria, Barbera can show considerable charm. The native custom of aging it baffles some outsiders, who find it gritty and poorly balanced after several years of age and murky and insipid after many years.

Barbera comes in many types and styles. Sometimes it is deep ruby in color, sometimes inky purple, sometimes bright red, sometimes garnet, sometimes rosé, and sometimes even white. It may be sweet, semisweet, sparkling, *frizzante*. In some places and in some years it comes out nearly as weak as tea and in others it can hit you with all the power of, as they say, *un pugno nello stomaco,* a punch in the gut.

Barbera seems to have been around a long time (its etymology has been traced to the family variously referred to as Barbero, Barberi, Barberis, and so on, in the thirteenth century). But it really came into its own in this century only after phylloxera forced vine varieties to undergo a traumatically rapid evolution and Barbera emerged as one of the fittest.

Barbera vines have been planted throughout Italy and carried overseas to many lands, notably California. In *Massee's Guide to the Wines of America,* William Massee wrote: "Barbera is one of the best grapes of the Piedmont, and does even better in Napa or Sonoma, where it produces a full, fruity wine with a pleasing sharpness that is the best of the Italianesque wines of California." He would get an argument on that point in Piedmont, but it must be acknowledged that Italian Barbera has not yet been as effectively distributed in the United States and other nations as have some other popular Italian wines.

Because of its relatively recent diffusion, Barbera has not been burdened with the confusing synonyms, homonyms, and pseudonyms that some other varieties have. Basically, wherever it grows it is called Barbera, though often with an appendage to indicate special traits of the vine or grape in various types of climate and soil.

The principal zones of Barbera production remain Asti, Monferrato, and Alba. Piedmontese dispute which is superior; it might be said diplomatically that some excellent Barbera is made in each zone but that character and quality vary sharply between one locale and another, between one winemaker and the next. Within the limits of the DOC disciplines (and outside them), producers manage to express a myriad of styles.

Barbera d'Asti, from the provinces of Asti and Alessandria, must have at least 12.5° alcohol and be aged two years. The *superiore* requires 13° and three years of age. Robust and full, it tends to be well rounded, rather soft, and fruity.

Barbera d'Alba, which covers much the same territory as Barolo, Barbaresco, and Nebbiolo d'Alba combined, must have 12° alcohol and two years of age, the *superiore* 13° and three years. It tends to be somewhat sharper in flavor and aroma with a hint of tannin, and some say it has a bit more body than the Barbera d'Asti.

Barbera del Monferrato overlaps much of the Asti zone and extends widely through the province of Alessandria to the east. It is usually lighter, livelier wine than the others, often with less alcohol, fresher flavor, and occasionally a tickle of fizz. The basic wine has no specific aging requirement but must have 12° alcohol, the *superiore* 12.5° and two years of aging. Barbera del Monferrato may be mixed with 10 to 15 percent Freisa, Grignolino, or Dolcetto grapes. The Asti and Alba Barberas are both pure varietals.

Two other DOC wines of Piedmont are based on Barbera. Rubino di Cantavenna, from a small zone in the province of Alessandria, is similar to Barbera di Monferrato in structure, with Barbera at 75 to 90 percent and Freisa and/or Grignolino making up the difference. A wine of 11.5° minimum, it requires no specific aging. Barbera dei Colli Tortonesi, from around the town of Tortona in the province of Alessandria, may be either a 100 percent varietal or include Freisa, Bonarda Piemontese, or Dolcetto at up to 15 percent. It must have 12° alcohol; when it has 12.5° and two years of age it may be called *superiore*. Still another Barbera wine, Castello di Gabiano from the Monferrato hills, is a candidate for DOC.

Much Barbera sold in Italy is not DOC. The tendency these days is to make it light and fresh: *da pronta beva*. Sweet and semisweet Barbera remain popular in parts of Piedmont. By using special vinification techniques, some winemakers also make rosé and white Barbera, though neither enjoys widespread popularity.

In the final analysis, Barbera — red, dry, generous, solid, dependable, and feminine — remains the everyday wine of Piedmont par excellence, a role it shares with Dolcetto, the region's second most popular wine. At its best, it is smooth, opulent, adaptable to a wide range of dishes (even *bagna caöda* and *fonduta,* some say) because it can be so remarkably easy to drink. I have heard it described as a loyal proletarian, but from the cellars of some, it can rise to aristocratic levels.

Barbera has been gaining acceptance abroad lately, but I shall not attempt to single out the better producers among the thousands who sell the wine, primarily in Italy. A good Barbera should not be difficult to find outside Italy at any store well stocked in Italian wines, because many shippers of Piedmontese wines now include it in their export lines. Its price should be low enough to permit comparative tasting.

Dolcetto, the other loyal proletarian of Piedmont, has advocates for aging as well. Their arguments are largely ignored, however, for the overwhelming bulk of Dolcetto of 11° to 11.5° alcohol is consumed within a year or two. In the seven DOC zones — Acqui, Alba, Asti, Diano d'Alba, Ovada, Dogliani, and Langhe Monregalesi — no aging is required, though one year is called for in the *superiore* versions of 12° to 12.5° alcohol.

Dolcetto tends to be more supple than Barbera, with a faint undertone of bitterness that pleasantly offsets its otherwise fresh and lively flavor. In the Langhe hills, where it reaches its most auspicious levels, it often serves as an opener when a bigger wine is to follow. But it also holds up nicely through a meal. Dolcetto has been exported increasingly to the United States, where it seems to have captured the fancy of admirers of classical Piedmontese reds. From the 1978 vintage it became as big and robust a wine as Nebbiolo with the advantage of being drinkable sooner. Some producers of Barolo and Barbaresco began exporting Dolcetto of the Alba area from the 1978 and 1979 vintages.

The name Dolcetto indicates sweetness, because the Dolcetto grape is unusually luscious when mature. And, indeed, years ago Dolcetto often was a sweet wine, as were other reds of Piedmont, including Barolo, vinified to retain some residual sugar. But today nearly all Dolcetto is dry, and occasionally *frizzante*. It is well worth getting to know, for its character is uniquely Piedmontese.

Grignolino and Freisa: A Struggle for Survival

Two vines that once flourished in Piedmont, Grignolino and Freisa, are in a state of decline, their places gradually being taken over by heartier varieties that bring greater yields. Much as traditionalists lament their demise, economic factors have been decisive in most vineyards. Neither vine faces extinction because some determined growers have seen fit to continue working them, even though their colleagues long since wrote them off as relics.

Freisa, which is most prominent around Asti and the town of Chieri just east of Turin, where it has DOC status, was never a wine of great importance. But in the days when tastes were determined somewhat by the limited choices available, its pronounced astringency and acidity were highly appreciated by some. Sweet and sparkling Freisas were also prominent then, and a few producers still make them that way. A few have even found an export market for this unusual wine.

Grignolino, on the other hand, was once a major wine, served regularly at the royal table when the House of Savoy ruled Italy. Its delicacy and light color provided a welcome contrast to the robustness of other Piedmontese reds. It was further reputed to have medicinal value, most notably as relief for a common ailment of the old days: excessive consumption.

Among the Grignolino made in Piedmont today, few are true to tradition, apparently because current tastes in red wine run to fuller and fruitier flavors. Some producers vinify them to have more body and color than before in good wines of about 11° alcohol that have a loyal following locally and to a moderate degree elsewhere in Italy and abroad. Grignolino is classified in two zones — Asti and Monferrato — though it is made in scattered other parts of the region as well.

When true to type, Grignolino is austerely dry with a pronounced acidity and a delicate freshness in bouquet and flavor. Although best when drunk young, it is not to be taken lightly. Its past was too illustrious and its future is too equivocal for that. Perhaps the most highly regarded Grignolino is made in limited quantity at a small estate owned by Paolo Biggio, a lawyer, below the village of Migliandolo in the province of Asti. Two other fine traditional Grignolinos are made by Livio Pavese at Treville Monferrato and by the Castello di Lignano at Frassinello Monferrato.

Grignolino may be the most special wine of all to Piedmontese who recall less commercialized eras of winemaking. Some speak emotionally of the wine they drank then, of its unique attributes as a product of times when, to them anyway, tastes and values were more precious and refined.

Piedmontese winemakers generally avoid much mixing of grape varieties, though the practice can bring out unexpected character in the types used. Mario Capuzzo at Castagnole Monferrato combines Barbera and Grignolino in a wine he calls Santa Maria Rossa. Luciano de Giacomi at San Rocco Seno d'Elvio, near Alba, combines some Nebbiolo with the dominant Dolcetto in a wine called Bricco del Drago. Valentino Migliorini mixes Nebbiolo and Barbera in Bricco Manzoni at his Podere Manzoni at Monforte d'Alba. Because they are made from mixtures, these outstanding wines must be labeled *vino da tavola,* though to find their peers one would need to return to the aristocratic thoroughbreds of the Nebbiolo family.

Carema and Donnaz: An Ethereal Quality

Piedmont's mountains, the Alps on the north and west, the Apennines rising in the south, resemble in relief a horseshoe inside which the Po and its tributaries have carved out a basin that affords benign conditions for viticulture. The region suffers neither extreme heat nor cold; its major vineyards lie high enough to catch refreshing summer breezes, low enough to benefit from insulating mists of autumn. The steepness of the Langhe and Monferrato hills provides natural drainage for the rather heavy clay and gravel soil.

Vines thrive almost everywhere in Piedmont, from high in the Alpine foothills to the outskirts of Turin. The zones of greatest predilection are Alba and Asti. But a third zone, split inconveniently into two unequal sectors some 50 kilometers apart, is also of special interest because the Nebbiolo grape is turned into wines there that can on occasion rival Barolo and Barbaresco.

Nebbiolo is not a shiftless sort of vine like Barbera that can take root almost anywhere. In fact, after innumerable attempts to establish it elsewhere in Italy and abroad, there are only three places it can call home. One is, of course, around Alba; another is the Alpine indentation of northern Lombardy known as the Valtellina; the third is the split zone of northern Piedmont just cited that includes Carema on the west, Gattinara on the east. (Mario Soldati, an author in his seventies who has taken some time to rediscover "genuine" wines and tell about them in three entertaining volumes entitled *Vino a Vino,* writes that a good Nebbiolo has been made experimentally in the hills near Syracuse, Sicily, by a man he calls "The Sheriff." Most wine lovers have yet to try that one.)

Carema is either the last town in Piedmont or the first, depending on whether you are traveling north or south along the Dora Baltea River valley. But whichever way you are going, from the Turin–Mont Blanc *autostrada* Carema's aged structures do not stand out against the rocky terraces that engulf the town. In these mountainside vineyards, some at more than 2,500 feet above sea level, the Nebbiolo vine is put to its severest tests. In most years, with some fine weather and more than a little luck, it passes with distinction. The town's winemakers, like their neighbors at Donnaz in Valle d'Aosta who labor under equally trying conditions, refer to the Nebbiolo grape in dialect as Picotener or Pugnet. The vines are trained over low trellises, with additional support improvised as needed to give the foliage and fruit maximum exposure not only to the sun's direct rays but, more important, to the heat reflecting off underlying boulders.

The wines of Carema and Donnaz, though usually lighter in body and shorter-lived than Barolo or Barbaresco, can have reminiscent strength of character plus an ethereal quality that legend attributes to rocky terrain and rarefied air. DOC requirements of four years' aging, at least two in wood, and a minimum alcohol content of 12° are prohibitive to some growers, who opt to sell their wine as simpler stuff. As a rule Carema and Donnaz are to drink soon after bottling; they rarely improve after five or six years.

Luigi Ferrando turns out two special vineyard Caremas and a Donnaz. His high standards are often equaled by two cooperatives, Cantina Produttori Nebbiolo di Carema and Caves Cooperatives de Donnaz. Prices for wines from good vintages may approach the levels of some Barolo. But if effort seeks a just reward, Carema and Donnaz are worth every lire.

The enclave of Carema and Donnaz is separated by Alpine foothills from the other zone of Nebbiolo vines, centered in Gattinara in the uppermost reaches of the Po Valley.

Novara and Vercelli: A Multiplicity of Styles

Nebbiolo wines from the hills north of Vercelli and Novara are as a rule well made; some show splendid class, comparable to Barolo and Barbaresco, and extraordinary capacity for aging. Seven DOC classifications all bear place names: Gattinara, Ghemme, Boca, Sizzano, Fara, Lessona, and Bramaterra. Some excellent non-DOC wines are called Spanna, whose name is the local term for the Nebbiolo grape. Among the dozens of other wines made locally, the best invariably contain some Nebbiolo. They may take their names from vineyards, ancestors, historical figures, symbols, myth, fantasy. In a sense such complexity is apt, for growers here demonstrate a multiplicity of attitudes and styles in their approach to winemaking.

Gattinara has the greatest reputation. It is often cited as one of Italy's premier red wines, especially in Milan and Switzerland, where much of it is consumed. But little Gattinara in commerce is worthy of a great name. In fact, the quality of some supposedly lesser wines from these subalpine hills often surpasses that of Gattinara.

There are exceptions, though, among them the Gattinara of Luigi Dessilani & Figli, a most elegant wine that is now being exported to the United States in limited amounts. Luigi Dessilani, robust and spirited though he is approaching ninety, and his young assistant, Enzo Lucca, both know that you cannot make great wine unless you have great grapes. That explains why they still cultivate most of their own vines, using an outdated method that has them trained onto poles jutting from a base like the struts on a half-opened umbrella. The result is vines that are not only uniquely picturesque but outstandingly healthy.

"You don't work close to those vines with machines," said "Nonno" (Grandpa) Dessilani, holding up his thick hands to show off calluses conditioned by decades of labor. "I still hoe," he said proudly. "Keeps me in shape. But the young people don't want to work like that. No, they just want to use their heads enough to make some money and be treated like *signori*."

Nonno Dessilani, a loden hat perched jauntily on his head as he mused over the changing fortunes of winemaking through world wars, depressions, dictatorships, and other manner of strife and hard times, laughed about it all. "I wouldn't trade my life for anybody's," he said, "and I'm still having a wonderful time."

He put his arm around the shoulder of Enzo Lucca, the botanist-oenologist, who would soon join the family by marrying Dessilani's

Enzo Lucca (left) and Luigi Dessilani

granddaughter. "Enzo here gives me hope," he said. "He's a traditional-ist, too, but he's smarter than I ever was. He's figuring out how to grow grapes best using new methods, because machine cultivation is an in-evitability now. And when it comes to making wine, well, I thought I knew all the tricks, but now I know there were a few I didn't."

Together they make wine from grapes grown in their own 25 hec-tares of vineyards along with some purchased from neighboring culti-vators who meet their standards. The Dessilani line includes most of the area's DOC wines, plus Spanna, Barbera, and another unclassified gem called Caramino, from vineyards on the land around the Caramino castle outside Fara once owned by a relative of the Savoys.

"An American journalist called Caramino one of the best wines in the world," said Lucca in his modest manner. "And he might be right. It can be even better than Gattinara." The Dessilani wines are exported to the United States by Neil Empson of Milan, a New Zealander who has been searching out some of Italy's finest wines and exporting them as one of the few negotiants in Italy working in the French manner.

Another Gattinara in the noble tradition is Monsecco, made by the Conti Ravizza. The name Monsecco is a commutation of *mon vin sec,* a term that evokes the Savoyard roots of Piedmontese nobility and the peculiar but by no means cacophonous mingling of Italian and French in the regional dialects. Indeed, Monsecco's tone resembles that of some French wines, with the full-flavored elegance of, say, a good Hermitage to be sensed in a well-aged bottle. Made in very limited quantity and sold with numbered labels, Monsecco from certain vintages is among the most expensive wines of Piedmont.

Other sound Gattinaras are available from, among others, Mario Antoniolo, Giancarlo Travaglini, Agostino Brugo, Antonio Vallana, and Lorenzo Bertolo. There are signs that the producers' consortium has been encouraging more estate bottling, perhaps in response to the lament voiced by some experts that this wine has not generally been living up to its extraordinary potential. Further proof of this capacity was an unlabeled bottle of red wine from a certain Signor Valdoi, who sold his unclassified Gattinara by the demijohn a few years ago. That wine, from 1967, could take its place among the great wines of Piedmont had Valdoi not somehow managed to remain anonymous.

Spanna, despite its lack of DOC credentials, is often a better wine and almost invariably a better value than the regulated Gattinara. This is because of the self-discipline practiced by some of its leading growers, most conspicuously Antonio Vallana & Figlio.

Vallana creates Spannas with extraordinary life spans, wines that must be considered outstanding among Italy's fine reds. Bernardo Vallana, latest member of his family to run the firm at Maggiora, owns vineyards in several communities and carefully selects other types of wine from other growers to be bottled at his cantina. Each Spanna is his own and each has a special designation: Podere Tre Torri di Traversagna, Cantina del Camino, Campi Raudii, Cinque Castelli, Castello di Montalbano, each with a personality and history. In addition, in some years Vallana bottles his wine with the date prominent on the label, indicating a Spanna of particular class and durability. Although some vineyards are somewhat superior to others, the relative quality of the wine varies according to vintage. In 1961, Tre Torri di Traversagna was exceptional; in 1971, Campi Raudii stood out.

While concerning himself with the intricacies of his operation, Vallana still finds time to devote to the study of wine in all its aspects. After apologizing for his "lack of education," reference to the fact that he was too busy working as a youth to attend college, he talked about the vinicultural history of the Novara area. He traced events from their Roman origins to the present with emphasis on his family's role, starting in the eighteenth century, when one of his ancestors ran the cellars of the Bishop of Novara. As we toured the vineyards, he mentioned, with a smile, that his theories and practices did not always coincide with those taught at school.

"For instance, I know, as my great-grandfather knew, that if a vine is to spread its roots out fully and evenly it needs a roomy bed to lie in," he said. "In hill country that means terraces, not rows of vines on steep inclines. Young people tell me terraces aren't practical anymore with the cost of labor rising. I know that. I build them anyway."

Vallana's cellars are spacious and intricately equipped, a laboratory where the modern technician in his intellect consorts with the alchemist, the poet, the traditionalist in his soul. Even if he had the same batches of grapes to work with, no other winemaker would end up with wines quite like his, for Vallana guides each vatful through its critical stages, relying as much on intuition as on his finely honed sense of taste to decide when the moment is right to progress from one step to the next.

"*Vini di altri tempi,*" he defines his Spannas. Aged at least two years in wood, longer still in bottle, their traits indeed recall wines of other times, their breeding, substance, and longevity showing no compromise whatever with conceptions of mass consumerism. And yet, they are produced in ample quantity and sold at prices to match any wine of their class.

Vallana's labels have illustrations that fall somewhere between neoclassicism and high camp, but, like other things about the man, defy not only imitation but precise description. Spanna Campi Raudii shows a statue of a Roman chariot, horse, and driver, set against a stone arch; Spanna Cantina del Camino, a fireplace in a medieval castle; Greco, a white wine, an exotic Grecian urn between Doric columns; and so on through a dozen more, the Spannas, a Boca, a Barbera, and an everyday but hardly common red called Bucciarossa. He recently began making a Gattinara from his holding at Castel San Lorenzo.

Vallana's subcellars contain Spanna of the last half-century, concrete bins with hundreds of bottles lying on their sides from such special years as 1927, 1938, 1955, and the vintage that may be the greatest of recent times, 1961. These, too, are bargains for their age. A 1931, its ruby color still brilliant against a dim basement lamp, was available not long ago for $35.

Ghemme and Sizzano are the only other widely distributed wines of the Novara hills; occasional bottles find their way onto the export market. Ghemme consists of at least 60 percent Nebbiolo mixed with Vespolina and Bonarda grapes and must be aged four years before sale. Sizzano must contain at least 40 percent Nebbiolo mixed with the same varieties and be aged three years. Gattinara and the better Spannas contain from 90 to 100 percent Nebbiolo. Gattinara must be aged four years, though Spanna has no set requirements. All the DOC wines from Nebbiolo here must contain at least 12° alcohol.

Boca and Fara, wines of sturdy character, are not made in great enough quantity yet to achieve widespread recognition. There is room for expansion in their zones, however, so there may be more of these DOC wines available before long. Boca must contain from 45 to 70 percent Nebbiolo, Fara from 30 to 50 percent. Both need three years' aging.

Though Gattinara is noted as the most refined, the other wines are generous and are generally better buys. A bottle of 1964 Ghemme from Agostino Brugo was on par with fine Gattinara and decidedly more robust after its first twelve years. But it could not be expected to show as well after another twelve.

Total production of Nebbiolo-based wines in the Novara and Vercelli hills is estimated at less than 2 million bottles annually, but the volume is increasing. If growers could consolidate their interests to come up with a single broad appellation and subcategories for each type, they might generate more impact on the Italian market for fine wines. They seem unlikely to do so in the near future. Individual status counts for more here than community pride.

Lessona, from the province of Vercelli, is not widely available either, but its name is well known among Italian connoisseurs. It gained DOC status in 1977 chiefly thanks to the merits of its originators and leading growers, the Sella family. Descendants of some of the more illustrious statesmen, financiers, and industrialists of the region, the Sellas trace their holdings at Lessona to 1671, when the first vineyard was acquired through a banking transaction. Even then the wines were recognized as among the finest of that special row of hills rising from the Po Valley between Biella and the Ticino River, flowing out of Lake Maggiore.

One branch of the family, represented by Venanzio Sella and his son Fabrizio, now makes the wine, while others handle such varying interests as banks and woolen factories. Their Lessona is made from at least 75 percent Spanna and the rest Vespolina and Bonarda grapes from vines in the Tenuta San Sebastiano allo Zoppo, which lies directly in front of the family manor somewhat in the style of a French château. The soil is porphyritic — that is, containing rather large crystals in a mass of fine texture — a factor that the Sellas, like Vallana and others, consider the greatest difference between their wines and those of Barolo and Barbaresco, whose vines grow in more chalky clay.

Venanzio Sella had made Lessona the traditional way into a tannic, robust, long-lived wine that from certain vintages developed extraordinary finesse. But Venanzio's son Fabrizio has been diminishing the tannin through modern vinification techniques, so vintages from 1974 on are softer wines that as a rule mature earlier. This has created some amiable friction between the generations, with Venanzio still insisting that true arbiters of taste appreciate tannin and Fabrizio pointing out that the modern palate demands softer and fruitier wines. Lessona must have at least 12° alcohol and be aged two years in barrels.

The Sellas also make Piccone, a less imposing wine that is nonetheless very good, and they have reasserted historical claims to a wine called Bramaterra, which is grown in the hills between Lessona and Gattinara in a clearing surrounded by a subalpine forest. Bramaterra, from 50 to 70 percent Nebbiolo and the rest Bonarda, Vespolina, and Croatina, gained DOC status in 1978, though not without some preliminary bickering among its growers. The Sellas have documents showing that their family had holdings in Bramaterra in the last century, where they originated the wine. But another producer, Luigi Perazzi of Roasio Santa Maria, has also made claims to giving the wine its name. What matters, of course, is the quality of the wine, and that is excellent from both: deep ruby with sound body and depth, though with less aging potential than Piedmont's biggest wines.

Fabrizio Sella has begun using grapes from his Bramaterra vineyards to make Orbello, a pleasantly soft and fruity wine to drink within two to five years. The Sellas began exporting some Lessona in 1978 with expectations of following up with limited shipments of Bramaterra, Piccone, and Orbello.

Among other unclassified wines in the Novara-Vercelli zone is Barengo, a red dominated by the Bonarda grape. A white Barengo has both dry and sweet versions. Dozens of other good, little-known wines, mainly red but sometimes white or rosé, are also made nearby.

The Whites: Few and Far Between

The Piedmontese have relegated still white wines almost to the status of oblivion. Except for Asti Spumante and Moscato, which do not seem to be taken all that seriously by native epicures, the only white wines made in quantity are Cortese, from the southeastern reaches of the region, and Erbaluce di Caluso, from the northwest.

The dry Erbaluce di Caluso and its sweet versions, Passito and Passito Liquoroso di Caluso, are DOC wines from the Erbaluce vine grown in an area just northeast of Turin in the low hills near Ivrea, centered around the town of Caluso. Erbaluce is a delicate wine of 11° alcohol, most agreeable in its first year or two, though the Piedmontese often keep it around longer, a practice that does nothing for it at all. It goes nicely with fish *risotto,* the rice of the large-grained sort harvested in the adjacent Po lowlands. Fresh brook trout from nearby mountain streams, when available, complements Erbaluce's flinty flavor.

The Passito and Passito Liquoroso are made from selected grape clusters, hung in well-ventilated attics for up to six months to collect beneficial yeasts while they wither. They are then pressed into rich, velvet-textured, golden-amber wines that must be aged for five years and can age for twenty years or more. The Passito of at least 13.5° alcohol is primarily a dessert wine, though it is also reputed to enhance the creamy pungency of Gorgonzola and other strong cheeses. For deep thinkers with a sweet tooth, the Passito Liquoroso of 16° stands alone as *vino da meditazione.*

The agricultural school at Caluso, Istituto Professionale di Stato per l'Agricoltura Carlo Ubertini, is credited with propagating over the last century the high standards for winemaking practiced here. The school sells fine Erbaluce and Passito under its own name. Other reputable growers, most of whom make both dry and sweet wines, include Dr. Corrado Gnavi, Renato Bianco, Casa Vinicola Orsolani, and Cantina Cazzulo.

The Cortese vine, cultivated in a zone south and east of the city of Alessandria, produces light and dry white wines that are most noteworthy from the community of Gavi. Elsewhere, Cortese is an uncomplex wine with a pleasantly acidic bite that has been finding growing favor in the seafood restaurants of northern Italy. Low in alcohol (10° to 11° usually), it is traditionally drunk with dispatch because age does nothing for it. Cortese, the cultivation of which is spreading through the hills of southern Piedmont and Lombardy, is one of many Italian whites that have clearly benefited from modern winemaking techniques. In the past it had a tendency to oxidize or sour if transported or kept around more than a few months. But these days many producers offer Cortese that retains the clean, dry qualities and the sharpness that sets it off so well with fish. Some Cortese is now being exported, following a recent upsurge in production, particularly in the Gavi zone, where new investments have been made by Italian and foreign interests, including the American House of Banfi. The activity seems to confirm the conviction that Cortese is a rising star among Italian white wines.

In Gavi, DOC wines may be called either Cortese di Gavi or simply Gavi. These whites, which may also be made *frizzante* or *spumante*, have been winning wide acclaim. A Gavi dei Gavi from the estate of La Scolca, owned by Federica Soldati, costs as much as some of the region's great reds and is often ranked among the nation's finest wines of any color. As the most refined and generous of Cortese wines, it has evident attributes to back its name, though like that of other products of Piedmont its character, though exquisite, is not ordinary and it takes a certain amount of getting used to. Other esteemed Gavis include Rovereto di Gavi from Nicola Bergaglio, Raggio from Marchese Edilio Raggio d'Azeglio, Tenuta La Giustiniana from Paola Olivari Pastorino, Monterotondo from Maria Fugazza Busch, Castello di Tassarolo from the Marchesi Spinola, and Tenuta San Pietro.

The Cortese grape is used in numerous other white wines, three of which have DOC status: Cortese dell'Alto Monferrato, Colli Tortonesi Bianco (from the town of Tortona), and Oltrepò Pavese Cortese from neighboring Lombardy.

Arneis, from a native vine "rediscovered" not long ago near Alba, makes such a light, elegantly dry wine that several producers, most notably Bruno Giacosa and Vietti, created special networks of grape suppliers and are now offering it for sale. Tenuta Carretta at Piobesi d'Alba makes an excellent Bianco dei Roeri from half Arneis and half Nebbiolo vinified off the skins. Favorita, another native white from Alba, is not so fine as Arneis but is nonetheless worth the effort behind its survival.

Pinots, Rieslings, other still white wines, and rosés remain strangers in Piedmont, though when available they can be remarkably good. In

Barolo country, Fontanafredda makes a Pinot Bianco that bears a striking resemblance to good Mâcons and Beaujolais Blancs made in France from the same variety. A large firm, owned by the Monte dei Paschi di Siena bank, Fontanafredda seems to be setting an enviable pace, stepping up production of white wines, especially sparkling, of consistent good quality. Some stirrings of interest have appeared among other growers, perhaps because white wines represent a growing market internationally. But the Piedmontese continue to down their reds with imperturbable contentment, not about to let outsiders interfere with their drinking habits.

Big Money in Vermouth

In economic terms, vermouth dominates Piedmont's wine industry. It is by far the biggest export item among Italian alcoholic beverages (more than 110 million liters are shipped abroad most years). And, because vermouth is more expensive than most wines, it is easily the biggest earner of foreign currency. The majority of Italy's large vermouth firms are centered in Piedmont — in Turin, Asti, and Canelli. Some have used their profits to stimulate production of wine, chiefly Asti Spumante, and many exporters have built up lines that include premium wines.

But, strictly speaking, vermouth is not wine. Although anything labeled as vermouth in Italy must contain at least 70 percent wine, its origin is no longer likely to be Piedmontese. In the old days, which began some two centuries ago when vermouths were regarded as elixirs, local Moscato wines were often part of the secret and intricate blends that included herbs, spices, roots, bitters, grains, or fruits, among other natural flavorings. Today the medicinal values of vermouth are largely discounted. If the ingredients are still complex and top secret, there is no hiding the fact that most of the wine incorporated originates at points south. Cheaper and more plentiful than Moscato, those wines are less sweet and flavorful, but more alcoholic, therefore ideal for the dry white vermouths prevalent on the market in Britain, the leading buyer, and the United States.

Italians often consume dark-colored vermouths and related aromatic concoctions neat, as *aperitivo*, sometimes adding ice cubes and soda with a shaving of lemon peel, especially in hot weather. Americans have long favored the drier, lighter vermouths designed to be dribbled discreetly into overpowering cocktails. But some dark, bittersweet brands have caught on lately in the United States, indicating, perhaps, new-found appreciation of the light sort of apéritif that prepares the palate for the taste of dinner wine.

The Vintages

Wines from Nebbiolo Grapes of Piedmont–Valle d'Aosta

	Barolo	Barbaresco	Novara-Vercelli Hills	Donnaz-Carema
1979	Excellent	Excellent	Excellent	Excellent
1978	Great, scarce	Great, scarce	Excellent, scarce	Great
1977	Fair	Poor	Poor	—
1976	Uneven, some very good	Uneven, some very good	Excellent	Good
1975	Fair	Fair	Good	Good
1974	Excellent	Excellent	Excellent, some great	Excellent
1973	Fair	Fair	Excellent	Good
1972	—	—	Good, but limited	Fair
1971	Great	Great	Good to excellent	Excellent
1970	Excellent	Excellent	Excellent	Excellent
1969	Good	Good	Good	(Most wine previous to 1970 would now be past its prime.)
1968	Good	Good	Spotty, some superb	
1967	Excellent	Good	Good, limited	
1966	Poor	—	—	
1965	Excellent	Good	Poor	
1964	Excellent	Exceptional	Exceptional	
1963	Fair	—	—	

	Barolo	Barbaresco	Novara-Vercelli Hills	Donnaz-Carema
1962	Excellent	Excellent	Very good	
1961	Exceptional	Excellent	Good to exceptional	
1960	Poor	—	Uneven, some good	
	(Some earlier vintages from which wine should still be drinkable: 1958, 1957, 1952, 1951, 1947, 1945)	(Some earlier vintages from which wine should still be drinkable: 1958, 1957, 1952, 1951, 1945)	(Some earlier vintages from which wine should still be drinkable: 1957, 1956, 1952, 1950, 1947, 1946, 1945)	

Four Other Representative Wines

	Barbera d'Asti	Dolcetto d'Alba	Grignolino d'Asti	Erbaluce di Caluso
1979	Excellent	Excellent	Excellent	Excellent
1978	Great, scarce	Great, scarce	Great, scarce	Excellent
1977	Poor	Fair	Poor	Fair
1976	Good	Good, but uneven	Good	Excellent
1975	Fair	Fair	Poor	Good
1974	Good	Good	Good	Good
1973	Good	Fair	Good	Fair
1972	Poor	Fair	Poor	Fair
1971	Good	Excellent	Excellent	Excellent
1970	Good	Good	Good	Excellent
1969	Good	Poor	Good	—

VERMENTINO

PIGATO

ROSSESE
DI DOLCEACQUA

Imperia

Savona

Genoa

CINQUETERRE

La S

LIGURIA

PROVINCES

GENOA, Imperia, La Spezia, Savona

POPULATION

1,880,000

AREA

2,098 square miles

AVERAGE WINE PRODUCTION

42 million liters

DOC WINES

Cinqueterre (Sciacchetrà) · Rossese di Dolceacqua

OTHER WINES

Barbarossa · Barbera · Buzzeto di Quiliano · Campochiesa · Colli di
Luni · Coronata · Dolcetto · Linero · Lumassina · Massarda ·
Piematone · Pigato · Polcevera · Rossese di Campochiesa ·
Vermentino

A Touch of Baroque

DESCENDING from the Apennines and Piedmont, where the Gothic forms of central Europe prevail, the towns of Liguria come into view against the Mediterranean as silhouettes in baroque. Popularly known as the Italian Riviera, Liguria stretches along the Ligurian Sea from the French border to Tuscany, a sliver of coastline whose cartographic outline resembles the new moon. Its axis is Genoa, the nation's largest seaport. Its inhabitants' life-style reveals that they have absorbed more of the ways of their maritime trading partners than of their landlocked neighbors across the mountains.

The baroque touch carries over into attitudes as well. The Piedmontese take their wines rather seriously; the Ligurians often take theirs with a hint of fancy. Liguria is less than twice the size of the Valle d'Aosta, but its wine output, though declining, is ten times greater. White wine dominates, appropriately enough, because the staple of the region's diet is fish, and the demand in summer when tourists crowd the seaside resorts is for beverages on the cool and light side. But Liguria's most notable wine, unquestionably, is red.

Rossese di Dolceacqua comes from vineyards on the rocky slopes of the narrow valleys behind the resorts of Ventimiglia and Bordighera, just across the border from Provence. Reputedly a favorite of Napoleon, it remained inexplicably obscure until recently when singled out for DOC and praised by influential critics. These attentions have accorded it some vogue. Its heightened reputation is deserved. Even the unlabeled Rossese sold in Dolceacqua, the zone's namesake and epicenter, is an uncommonly attractive table wine with the sort of forthright goodness that demands to be noticed. Its color varies from deep to bright ruby, depending on the vineyard and the vintage. Although it is not as a rule a wine to lay down, at least a dozen growers sell bottles that hold up admirably for five to ten years. Foremost among them is the mayor of Perinaldo.

Emilio Croesi's Extraordinary Dimensions

A quiet hill town whose population has declined from 1,500 to 750 since the war, Perinaldo might seem a hopelessly limited setting for a man of scope to function in. But Emilio Croesi, the mayor, does not feel cramped by his surroundings. At sixty, his body resembles in its lines those of a bear, and his other dimensions likewise defy measure by ordinary standards. Meeting him, you sense immediately that he is not just another politician.

Two powerful hands grasped mine. Bright eyes, honest smile, warm words, Croesi welcomed me to his home as though I were a nephew returning from a foreign land. Wine was opened, a 1970 Rossese from an unlabeled bottle. Signora Croesi, whose serenity posed a counterpoint to her husband's manifest dynamism, set out a platter of *sott'olio* — tomatoes, peppers, artichoke hearts, onions from their garden, wild mushrooms from the woods, all preserved in oil pressed by stone from their own olives. And we sat down to *merenda,* the nourishment that sustains country people between meals.

Croesi led the discussion from wine to sports, politics, agriculture, economics, war and peace, and the human condition, speaking with the natural grace of one who knows each topic intimately. He talked of his youth, of leaving Perinaldo to become a cycling champion, and later a tennis pro at Monaco, where he helped the late King Gustav of Sweden improve his game. World War II cut short his athletic career. He joined the Partisan guerrillas, was captured and tortured by the Nazis, and returned to Perinaldo in 1945 a bitter young man minus eighteen teeth.

"The hate disappeared quickly," he recalled, "when I got back to work in the vineyards."

As mayor, Croesi has grown in stature as Perinaldo's population diminished, its young people moving to the cities to seek work in industry and commerce. He runs the town with integrity, compassion, and solid support, some due to the fact that Perinaldo's budget has always been in the black, a rarity for an Italian community of any size these days.

"People have asked me why I never ran for regional or national office," he said. "Well, there's an easy answer to that. I'm happy in Perinaldo."

His reasons go beyond any desire to remain a big fish in a small pond. Agriculture is chief among them. He says he draws strength and inspiration from working the soil, and he laments that ever fewer people seem to share his sentiments.

Emilio Croesi

"It's insane," he said. "Italy, with its magnificent climate for growing things, with a wealth of good, honest people who know how to work the land, but with a federal structure that can't offer them incentives to stay on it. So the land is idle and we Italians import produce we used to be famous for abroad. Meantime the cities are full of young people out of jobs. You don't have to dig very deep to find the roots of crime and other economic and social problems everybody talks about these days.

"We need industry, of course we do, but we also need a balanced economic program and a sense of human purpose. They're trying to industrialize agriculture, but it isn't working, because you can't mechanize man."

Croesi filled my plate with food, my glass with wine.

"With a little honest effort we could all have these products of our own hands," he said. "Taste them. You don't get good things like that from a can."

It was true. You could dine in the Continent's finest restaurants and never equal the essential flavor of the simple food arrayed on the Croesi's plastic-topped kitchen table. You could spend twenty times as much as the list price for his and not taste a wine as eminently satisfying as Emilio Croesi's Rossese, which had left a coating of purple on the inside of its heavy brown bottle.

"We call it the magic bottle," Croesi said, "because it always looks full."

In fact, it was almost empty, but there was a touch of magic in the wine. Its components, taken individually, would seem to lack finesse, but taken together, like brush strokes in a Van Gogh landscape, they expressed the quintessence of an environment. One should ask no more of a wine, or a landscape, than that.

That the other Rossese I tried did not equal Emilio Croesi's is not to belittle the skills of their makers; several are worthy of wider recognition. But Rossese di Dolceacqua is not produced in great quantity. Crespi, the largest producer, exports some bottles, but most remain to be sought out by visitors to the Riviera, where its status among wine, red or white, is elite.

Rossese di Dolceacqua must have 12° alcohol, the *superiore* version 13° and a year of barrel age. Producers' names to look for include Solamito e Garoscio, Pippo Viale, Rubino Balestra e Tornatore, Enzo Guglielmi, and Antonio Orrigo. The Rossese grape is cultivated in several neighboring zones as well. Around Albenga, the Rossese di Campochiesa from the Cantine Calleri equals most Rossese di Dolceacqua.

Several other red and rosé wines are made in western Liguria. Dolcetto is common, particularly in the back country around the town of Pornassio. Barbarossa, a native Ligurian vine, makes both red and rosé. Both are served young and cool as accompaniment to almost any antipasto, including *frutta di mare*, fruit of the sea, a plate of raw or lightly poached shellfish.

White Wine and Pesto

Many of the pleasant white wines produced along the Ligurian coast demand no more than to be called *bianco locale*. If a place name is mentioned, it indicates that somebody has paid attention to where they came from, but it provides no assurance of either their origin or their worth. The only other wine besides Rossese di Dolceacqua with DOC status is Cinqueterre (and its sweet Sciacchetrà), the storied white from the opposite end of the region.

There are finer whites in Liguria than Cinqueterre. Two of particular note, Pigato and Vermentino, both aspire to DOC. They are grown west of Genoa, most prominently in the hills behind Albenga, between San Remo and Savona. Though they are distinct varietals, they have some similarity as crisp, dry, pale-gold wines that go down very smoothly with fish. Of the two, Pigato is capable of attaining a higher aesthetic level, though only marginally, due to a bit more substance and elegance than Vermentino. Both should be drunk fairly young. Bottles are now sold elsewhere in the region, and occasionally outside it. Cantine Calleri makes both wines. Its Fiore di Pigato is considered by some to be the best white of Liguria. Castello di Conscente and Fratelli Pozzo, both at Cisano sul Neva, make very good Pigato as well.

Special notice should also be given to white wines from Campochiesa in the province of Savona and to Massarda and Piematone, both from the Bordighera area. In the hills around Savona a number of growers have initiated a group effort to sell an exquisite and fragile white known as Buzzetto di Quiliano. That wine, sold only in the villages centered around Quiliano, should be drunk up soon after it goes on sale at Eastertime, for it is not made to last. In the province of Genoa, two white wines have achieved enough prominence to be bottled and sold outside the region. They are Coronata and Polcevera, but they too are delicate and should be drunk within a year of harvest.

Simple white wines are required with *pesto,* Liguria's glorious green sauce used to top off pasta or flavor minestrone. Traditionally pounded with mortar and pestle (but now often put through a blender), the combination of fresh basil leaves, pine nuts, garlic, Parmesan cheese, and green *vergine* olive oil will obfuscate the subtleties of any fine wine, though some say that Lumassina from Finale Ligure has the acidic bite to stand up to it. Otherwise, a *bianco locale,* possibly even mixed with bubbly mineral water, as the natives sometimes do, will serve to freshen the palate between mouthfuls.

East of Savona toward Genoa the space available for agriculture dwindles, but even amidst the urban clutter the odd vineyard can be spotted. Wines made there might not matter in the least to those of us who will never taste them, but to the people who maintain the vines they are not only a badge of privilege but a mark of perseverance, for Genoa has not been kind to its countryside.

Wedged majestically between mountain and sea, the city maintains a certain dignified pluck while choking pathetically on the fumes of its unavoidable excesses. The port long ago reached its limits for comfortable human and industrial cohabitation, and has since spilled over into adjacent valleys and climbed almost inaccessible hills to claim a bit more space to build on. Genoa still attracts tourists, but some push on through the city these days seeking a quiet place to resume breathing deeply.

At Rapallo, where the air is clear once again, vineyards share the extensive terraces on the lower reaches of the mountainsides. Villages, farmhouses, villas, and monasteries, their pastels gleaming in the reflection of sun off sea, punctuate the lush, green landscape. From here to La Spezia the scenery is magnificent, even if taken in glimpses from the roads and railways that have gained access through a network of tunnels.

From vines around Rapallo, Lavagna, Sestri Levante, and smaller seaside resorts, the wines, both red and white, are usually satisfying if rarely memorable. They are the sort to be drunk on the spot, though some visitors, apparently charmed by special moments beside the sea, tote them off in bottles as souvenirs.

Cinqueterre with a Grain of Salt

Cinqueterre has long been Liguria's leading collector's item. A visit to its isolated growing area is all the evidence needed to know why. Stony terraces dominate the precipitous terrain around the five fishing villages (the five lands) of Monterosso, Vernazza, Corniglia, Manarola, and Riomaggiore. The vineyards in some places are just out of range of the spray from crashing Mediterranean breakers, and legend states that some of them can be reached only by boat. When I asked for verification of that story I was told that it was largely romantic fancy. Well, anyway, the five lands are worth a visit for the scenery as much as for the wine. Getting there is not so easy, however; all the towns are reachable by boat or train, but only Monterosso, Manarola, and Riomaggiore have roads to them.

DOC enforcement has done away with imitations of Cinqueterre, a wine that, had it not been for the folklore, would not have warranted imitation in the first place. That is not to malign it. The dry version, made from Bosco, Albarola, and Vermentino grapes, is a perfectly acceptable table wine of about 11° alcohol when well made, coming across with good balance between acid and fruit, neither of which is pronounced. Its lightness goes well with fish, which are brought in fresh each morning by each village's fleet and sold at the marketplaces. Specialties are grilled giant shrimp called *gamberoni*, mussels, and *dateri*, clams pried from their hiding places in the rocks. They are delicious when sautéed lightly in olive oil and herbs.

Giuliano Corvara makes a fine Cinqueterre, but his limited stocks are available only at his home along one of Manarola's narrow, winding walkways. Luigi Veronelli writes that he has not found a bottle of Cinqueterre on the market worthy of inclusion in his catalogue. Judging from the several bottles I have come across, I can understand why. Cinqueterre's charms should be enjoyed against a backdrop of its legendary vineyards and the sea.

Sciacchetrà, the sweet Cinqueterre, is made from the same grapes, which in this case are dried before pressing. It must have 13.5° alcohol and age a year in barrel. Rarer and more expensive than the dry wine, a Sciacchetrà was served by the glass at the Bar-Ristorante Aristide in Manarola. Made by a local cooperative, it was more suitable as an *aperitivo* than a dessert wine, because it was only slightly sweet with a pleasing measure of fruit and even a hint of salt in its flavor.

Colli di Luni: Following the General's Lead

A few kilometers inland from the port of La Spezia the Apennines rise to such impressive heights that they are known as the Alpe Apuane, and indeed they resemble the Alps in their majesty. In the Colli di Luni, the well-protected foothills along the Magra River, in an area where Etruscans once had vineyards, the activities of a few growers indicate a potential for fine wine equal to that of any other part of Liguria.

One man, the late Giorgio Tognoni, led the way there until his death in 1978. Tognoni was unique, a retired general, blind since World War I, who let his senses of smell and taste guide his winemaking decisions. He brought in some grape varieties foreign to the region to make red and white wines of splendid class.

From Piedmont came the vines for a Barbera di Linero that is rarely matched for quality in its native Asti. Linero Rosso is made from Sangiovese (Chianti's mainstay), Ligurian Vermentino Nero, and Piedmontese Nebbiolo, which is rarely mixed with other grapes at home. It also contains a smattering of Cabernet and Merlot, perhaps to give it an international flavor. Linero Bianco, made chiefly of the Ligurian Vermentino with Malvasia and the Tuscan Trebbiano added, is a luxuriously smooth wine whose amber hue matches the color of Cognac but whose flavor gives no hint of maderization. Dry and fresh-flavored, it has character to equal the region's finest whites.

It was too early to tell if the general's death would signal a decline in the wines of Linero. But his example seemed to have survived. If other winemakers in the area around Castelnuovo Magra, Santo Stefano Magra, and Sarzana show less creative genius than did the late General Tognoni, some at least seem to share his dedication. Their wines, now sold locally, may soon find a wider market.

The Vintages

	Rossese di Dolceacqua	Ligurian Whites
1979	Excellent	Excellent
1978	Excellent, scarce	Excellent
1977	Fair	Poor to fair
1976	Uneven, some good	Uneven
1975	Excellent	Good to excellent
1974	Good	Good
1973	Excellent	Fair to good
1972	Poor	(Any older than
1971	Good	1973 not recommended,
1970	Exceptional	except for sweet wines.)
1969	Good	
1968	Good	
1967	Excellent	
1966	Excellent (Some bottles from 1964, a great vintage, should still be drinkable.)	

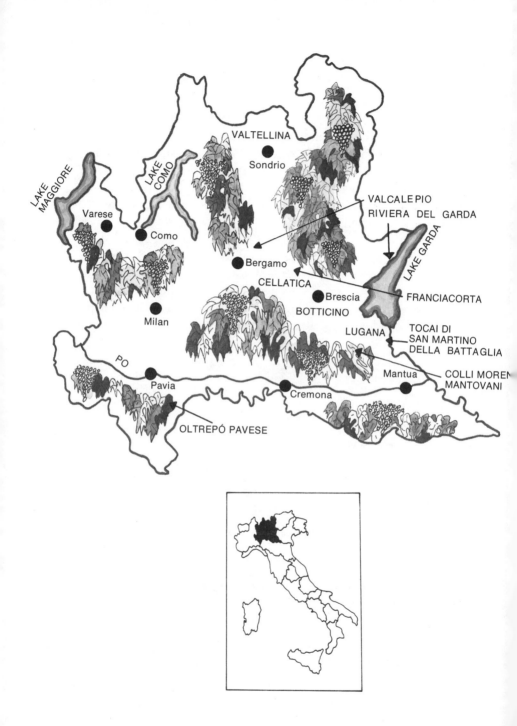

VALTELLINA

Sondrio

LAKE
MAGGIORE

LAKE
COMO

Varese

Como

VALCALEPIO

RIVIERA DEL GARDA

LAKE GARDA

Bergamo

CELLATICA

Milan

Brescia

BOTTICINO

FRANCIACORTA

LUGANA

TOCAI DI
SAN MARTINO
DELLA BATTAGLIA

PO

Mantua

COLLI MOREN
MANTOVANI

Pavia

Cremona

OLTREPÓ PAVESE

LOMBARDY

PROVINCES

MILAN, Bergamo, Brescia, Como, Cremona, Mantua, Pavia, Sondrio, Varese

POPULATION

8,450,000

AREA

9,190 square miles

AVERAGE WINE PRODUCTION

220 million liters

DOC WINES

Botticino · Cellatica · Colli Morenici Mantovani del Garda (Bianco, Chiaretto, Rosato, Rubino) · Franciacorta (Pinot, Rosso) · Lugana · Oltrepò Pavese (Barbacarlo, Barbera, Bonarda, Buttafuoco, Cortese, Moscato, Pinot, Riesling, Rosso, Sangue di Giuda) · Riviera del Garda (Chiaretto, Rosso) · Tocai di San Martino della Battaglia · Valcalepio (Bianco, Rosso) · Valtellina (Sfursat or Sforzato) · Valtellina Superiore (Grumello, Inferno, Sassella, Valgella)

OTHER WINES

Angera · Capriano del Colle · Castel Chiuro · Clastidio · Colli dei Frati · Groppello della Valtenesi · Lambrusco Mantovano · Le Fracce · Malvasia · Montevecchia · Müller Thurgau · Perla Villa · Rosso di Bellagio · San Colombano al Lambro

Oltrepò Pavese: Conspicuously Underrated

CROSSING the Apennines once again, this time due north from Genoa, you soon reach a point that is virtually a junction of four regions: Liguria, Piedmont, Emilia-Romagna, and Lombardy. To the east looms a final wave of gently rounded hills, dominating the vast plain where the Ticino River meets the Po. The wine from those inclines goes under the name Oltrepò Pavese, in reference to the position across the Po from the city of Pavia.

The territory was once contested by the powerful families of Malaspina, Sforza, and Visconti, whose castles, now often in ruins, still top the highest points. It was also long an adjunct of Piedmont, which explains continuing allusions to it as Antico Piemonte. Though reminders of glorious wines of the past are often pronounced, the surviving tradition of quality has emerged here only in the last century, during which time the wines of Oltrepò Pavese have been carried proudly under the colors of Lombardy.

The region's major wine production is split between two sectors: the Oltrepò Pavese in the southwest and the lake country to the northeast, a subalpine area that includes numerous DOC zones in the provinces of Bergamo, Brescia, and Sondrio. Although Lombardy's reputation for quality has been overshadowed by its neighbors to the west (Piedmont) and east (the Veneto and Trentino–Alto Adige), the region's finer wines merit greater esteem than they have so far received. Those of the Oltrepò Pavese are conspicuously underrated.

The Oltrepò, as it is often called, is the region's most productive DOC zone (some 16 million liters a year), yet the name is not as widely known as it ought to be, even within Lombardy, perhaps because the types of wine made here are so many and varied. It covers a large area of exclusively hill vineyards of unsurpassed repute among northern Italian *spumante* producers for the Pinot grapes used in the rapidly expanding production of dry sparkling wines. Unfortunately, not all the good *spumante* made from Oltrepò Pinot cites the source on the label.

Still, the cultivators and winemakers of the Oltrepò have been doing rather well financially by judiciously exploiting natural factors working in their favor. Their primary benefit is growing conditions, the mild climate, the availability of hillside vineyards of manageable size, the relative ease with which the sloping terrain can be worked. Cultivators have been able to grow grapes and, if they choose to, make wine in adequate quantity as their main source of income, thanks also to the proximity of markets.

Through their consortium they have regularly taken part in cooperative ventures, such as improvements in vines and winemaking techniques, and promotion and sales of Oltrepò wines as a unit. Their association, reorganized in 1977, has been among the most progressive of Italy. So far, however, only a limited amount of Oltrepò wine has been shipped abroad.

The advent of DOC brought a measure of uniformity to the wines of Oltrepò Pavese, where in the middle of the last century 260 different varieties of vines were cultivated. Today the number is a fraction of that, but still enough to be confusing. The DOC wines come in ten basic types with variations in color and style. Six varietals are included: the red Barbera and Bonarda, the white Riesling (both Renano and Italico), Cortese, and Moscato, and Pinot (which curiously enough allows for red wine from Pinot Nero and rosé and white from Pinot Nero and Pinot Grigio). The Pinots, Rieslings, and Moscato may also be made into *spumante*. There is also a recognized Rosso Oltrepò Pavese from varying portions of Barbera, Croatina, and Uva Rara grapes. And three Oltrepò wines, all red and from the same basic grapes as the Rosso with Barbera dominant, have special appellations: Buttafuoco, Barbacarlo, and Sangue di Giuda. They must have at least 12° alcohol and some aging (eighteen months for Barbacarlo, five months for the others). The other Oltrepò DOC wines have minimum alcohol levels of either 11° or 11.5° and no required aging.

Some producers in the zone remain outside DOC jurisdiction and sell their wine under their own or other names but never with Oltrepò Pavese on the label. This, of course, compounds an already perplexing situation for consumers. Many cultivators and winemakers belong to the consortium. Their labels will bear its emblem — an elf in a red Santa Claus outfit, who appears to have just stolen a bottle — along with a number and the words "Consorzio Vini DOC Oltrepò Pavese."

Seven cooperatives in the zone include 5,000 members. They have the capacity to process more than 50 million liters of wine a year, obviously only a small part of it DOC. The many small independent producers and private firms often market their wines with estate or brand names. You would need a catalogue to keep track of them all.

For all the signs of cooperation here, lively intramural competition persists over who makes the best wine. Outsiders would be well advised to stay out of the argument, because the number of candidates in all categories could run into the hundreds, and few people can claim to have tasted them all. But one white wine stands out in my mind as I ponder the multitude: Clastidium Gran Riserva, made by the Angelo Ballabio winery at Casteggio.

I discovered this wine in 1974 when I opened a bottle from the 1964 vintage, expecting it to be well past its prime. Astonishingly, it was crisp, clean, fresh, with an opulent bouquet; its color was as pale as a young wine's and its texture was as velvety as any I have tasted in a Pinot white wine anywhere. It was, strictly speaking, neither dry nor sweet, but nicely in between, with the sort of character that demands to be appreciated on its own.

Giovanni Ballabio, son of the founder, ran the winery until his death in 1975. His other wines showed nearly equal grace. The *spumante,* from Pinot Nero and Grigio, are often ranked among the finer *méthode champenoise* wines of Italy. Clastidio Rosso, from Barbera, Uva Rara, and Croatina, is a robust accompaniment to roast meat, cheese, and game. Clastidio Rosato, from the same grapes as the red, is uncommonly balanced and flavorful.

The Ballabio vineyards and cantina at Casteggio, which was the Roman town of Clastidium, were taken over in 1977 by five local businessmen with little experience in winemaking. Combining the Ballabio vineyards with the nearby Balestriere estate, which they also own, they expect to bring total production to about 400,000 bottles annually, all to be sold under the Angelo Ballabio name. The owners, who are leaving the winemaking to a qualified oenologist, Marco Bellani, and the old cellarmaster, Aldo Piaggi, were confident they could uphold the Ballabio tradition.

Frecciarossa: Inspired by Lafite

The most famous name in Oltrepò Pavese is Frecciarossa (Red Arrow), whose wines only recently have been included in DOC. Dr. Giorgio

Odero, who owns the Frecciarossa estate, resolved more than fifty years ago to make wine as well as the French did. He took his degree in oenology at Montpellier University in southern France, then worked in and observed the operations of some of the most prestigious châteaux of the Médoc. Returning to his family's vast property above Casteggio, he installed a vineyard of the "exact dimensions and capacities of Lafite."

His emulation of the French was ultimately more in spirit than in letter, for he planted mainly vines of local origin and adapted his French-educated skills to Lombardy's natural conditions. But his unique background shone through; he succeeded in making wines that earned not only wide recognition but quickly became the envy of his neighbors.

By 1931, nine years after planting, Odero had obtained Italy's nineteenth export license for wine. He shipped several cases to the United States and England, where the wine was readily acclaimed. Those two nations have remained his best foreign customers. His first labels were written entirely in English, a language he learned as a boy. But later he dubbed his wines Grand Cru (a deep, rich red), St. George (which could be described as either a light ruby red or a hearty rosé), and La Vigne Blanche (a dry, subtle white with a hint of almond in its flavor).

Odero once requested a separate DOC for Frecciarossa but was denied it because the name applies to a single-owner property. More recently he decided to participate in Oltrepò Pavese DOC, which has meant that the grandiose foreign names have been replaced by mundane colors. So Grand Cru, his finest wine from Croatina, Uva Rara, and Barbera, became simply Rosso. St. George, from the same grapes vinified briefly with their skins, became Rosso Rubino. And La Vigne Blanche, from Pinot Nero and Riesling Renano and Italico, became Bianco.

At one time nearly all Odero's wine was exported, but today more than half is sold in Italy. His influence on other Oltrepò Pavese winemakers was enormous, but it took a while for the few others who have done so, such as his now-deceased friends Angelo and Giovanni Ballabio, to catch up with him. Many more are still trying.

Odero, in his seventies, no longer takes as active a role in production as he would like to. A gentleman of impeccable manners and sharp intellect, Odero sat at his desk in the study of his elegant red villa and quietly reminisced in three languages over a career in wine that he described as "a great satisfaction."

He told of visits to New York, where the 21 Club, which carries his wine, created a special section for storing it in the cellar; of the Fascist era, when Mussolini banned the use of foreign terms on labels, and how he showed his defiance by wording them in Latin; of his apprenticeship in France and of pioneering prestige wines in the Oltrepò Pavese.

A butler, whose uniform included a fine-striped Philip Morris jacket and white gloves, served one of the last vintages of La Vigne Blanche in crystal with hors d'oeuvres as the conversation shifted from the past to the present.

"The status of Oltrepò Pavese wine has never been greater," said Odero, "but some young people seem to take their success casually. They ask, 'Who needs the consortium? My wine stands on its own merits.' Well, maybe so. But if they suppose that they can sit back and watch things get even better, they may be in for surprises."

Odero knows about wine standing on its own merits, for his has done so for decades. He believes Frecciarossa deserved an appellation of its own, and though he sees some imperfections in DOC, he finally decided it was best to take part. But all along he has played a leading role in the consortium, proudly carrying its symbol on his labels.

"No matter how well you make wine, there is always something to learn from your colleagues," he said. "I hope this idea isn't forgotten now that the old guard is changing."

Buttafuoco: "Vino d'Autore"

The Alberici estate at Castana has little in common with Lafite, except that the Buttafuoco made there is about as distinguished as a wine can be. That is not to elevate it to some lofty position in the wine world, for its makers do not seem to have those aspirations, even though their wine at a contest in 1976 was judged to be the best of Lombardy.

Casa Alberici would not have been discernible from the other big farmhouses along the narrow lane that winds up the hillside from Broni had it not been for a large, crudely lettered sign on the fence outside, announcing: "QUI BUTTAFUOCO." Usually that sort of advertising makes me want to keep driving, but I had tasted Buttafuoco before. Of all the wines of the Oltrepò Pavese, this may be the most identifiable as a *vino d'autore*.

The author, or authors in this case, are Cavaliere Ufficiale Bianchina Alberici, who kept her family name, and her husband, Cavaliere Ufficiale Natalino de Simoni. The titles were granted by the state for agricultural excellence. She, in the full bloom of middle age, has been described, aptly, as a phenomenon, a burly dynamo of a woman making her presence felt in a man's world; he, considerably older, is spirited and canny, still able to put in long hours in the vineyards. The Buttafuoco they produce on a few acres of steep, terraced land is generous and deep in the best rustic tradition. When it is young, its bold measure of fruit is set off by a hint of bitter almond and the faintest sort of fizz, which vanishes within moments after the wine is poured. With age it softens to the point that some vintages evoke comparisons with much older Barolo.

Bianchina Alberici maintains that there is no secret to Buttafuoco's goodness unless, as she says, "hard work and artisan practices" have been forgotten. The grapes are Uva Rara, Croatina, and Barbera fermented the long way and kept in ancient wooden barrels for two years before being bottled. Maximum production is 40,000 bottles a year, most of which go to shops and restaurants. But they keep a few to sell directly. They give their phone number on the label with an invitation to "visit the century-old cantina."

The name Buttafuoco refers in dialect to "sparking like fire," the idea being that the wine is too lively to hold long in the mouth. DOC status was granted under Oltrepò Pavese to the Albericis and a very few neighbors who share the name. Two vaguely similar red wines made near Broni have also been classified: Barbacarlo and Sangue di Giuda.

From Wild Fizz to Quiet Dispositions

Sangue di Giuda (Judas' Blood) has one of those melodramatic names like Lacrima Christi (Tear of Christ) that are hard to take seriously. As made by Luigi Valenti, it fizzes wildly when poured, but on the palate his Sangue di Giuda is nothing to joke about. A "caressable" wine, as some of its admirers insist, it has, like many Oltrepò Pavese wines red and white, a taste of almonds and a freshness that lingers.

Barbacarlo shares with Buttafuoco the virtue of being good either young or moderately aged. Lino Maga, whose family estate at Broni is believed to have the oldest continuing operation in the district, makes his wine "by hand" as his forebears did. His Barbacarlo may show a trace of bubbles, but it is more complex than Sangue di Giuda and deserves its ranking among the elite wines of the Oltrepò Pavese.

Several other wines with quieter dispositions rate prominently among the zone's reds. The good ones invariably bear the stamp of their makers, so any attempt at categorical description would be futile. Here are a few worth seeking out:

★ Rosso della Madonna Isabella, made by Giulio Venco at Casteggio. Complex, tannic, elegant stuff that sometimes needs ten years to round into peak form.

★ Le Fracce del Pavone, made by Fernando Bussolera at Mairano di Casteggio. Full-bodied, dry, lovely aroma and big flavor that are ideally suited to game.

★ Gaggiarone Amaro, made by Giacomo Agnes at Rovescala. Ample, well-structured stuff, which, as its name suggests, has a pronounced bitterness that is very attractive. Improves for a dozen years.

★ Mombrione, made by the Cavazzana winery at Casteggio. Flowery aroma and delicate rounded flavor make it a fine accompaniment to that superb luncheon dish, *vitello tonnato,* thin slices of veal covered with a tuna-flavored cream sauce.

★ 4 Castagni Rosso, made by Roberto Girani at Cadelazzi di Torrazza Coste. Bold, spicy, and full of personality, it will keep well for a decade.

★ Il Frater, made by Tullio Bellani at Casteggio. Balanced, soft, full in its bouquet, it is good to drink within three to six years.

★ Rubino di Scagno, one of three wines made from Barbera, Uva Rara, and Croatina grapes at the estate of Conte dal Pozzo at Rocca de' Giorgi (Rosso and Rosato are the others). A bright, medium-bodied wine, well suited to poultry dishes.

★ Canneto Amaro, as made by Francesco Quaquarini and the Fratelli Giorgi, among others, at Canneto Pavese. A wine that some drink young and others prefer aged; in both cases it should be served at cellar temperature and will show the familiar bitter aftertaste.

★ Monsupello, as made by Carlo Boatti at Torricella Verzate. Robust, smooth, well-composed wine, pleasant with roast veal and fowl. Among the most elegant of Oltrepò reds.

★ Monteceresino Rosso, as made by Azienda Agricola Montagna from vineyards at Santa Giulietta. Dry with a hint of sweetness, light and well balanced. The same winery makes a refreshing rosé called Monteceresino Rosa.

★ Ca' Longa, as made by the Brega family at San Damiano al Colle. It has the body and tannin to improve over a decade to an elegant austerity that stands out with beef stews and game.

★ Barbera, as made by Enrico Orlandi at Scazzolino di Rovescala. A smooth, robust wine that may be among the best made anywhere from this ubiquitous varietal.

★ Bonarda, as made by Edmondo Tronconi at Rovescala. Deep, rich, velvety, it has a slightly bitter undertone, and ages well.

★ Pinot Nero, as made by the Cantina Sociale di Santa Maria della Versa. Fine, bubbly, refreshing, it is best served cool, like a rosé. It comes from an admirable cooperative.

★ Pinot Nero, as made by the Dezza family at Montecalvo Versiggia. A warm, soft, round, balanced wine that gains from moderate aging.

A Predilection for White

A respectable school of thought in the Oltrepò Pavese holds that the earth here has even more predilection for vines whose grapes make white wines than vines whose grapes make red. Winemakers who make both are understandably noncommittal on this point, but the increasing amount of vineyard space given over to white wine production might speak for itself.

The old standbys, Moscato, Malvasia, and Cortese, are often over-shadowed now by Pinot, Chardonnay, Riesling, and Müller Thurgau, which have gained prominence only in the last two decades. Indications are that the splendid Clastidium Gran Riserva of Angelo Ballabio may soon be rivaled by wines from producers who are still learning how to work confidently with the new methods for whites. Outstanding Rieslings are now made by producers already noted for their red wines: La Madonna Isabella, 4 Castagni, Tullio Bellani, Conte dal Pozzo, and the cooperative at Santa Maria della Versa. That same cooperative makes a satisfying *spumante* of the Champagne type from Pinot grapes, along with a sweet Moscato. Other good sparkling wines include Pinot della Rocca from the Tenuta Conti Giorgi di Vistarino, distributed by Gancia, Santa Maria Brut from Pietro Achilli, and the light and fragrant Moscato of Franco Visconti.

Müller Thurgau, the Swiss hybrid of Riesling and Sylvaner vines, becomes a fine, zesty wine here that is best drunk within months after its vinification. It has been sharing increasing attention with Rieslings and Pinots.

Pinot and Chardonnay grapes grown in the Oltrepò lately have been fetching prices among the nation's highest. Producers from Lombardy, Piedmont, and other regions use them to make *spumante,* often by the

Champagne method, on what must be the fastest growing sector of Italy's premium wine market.

Noble Taste at Il Casale

In the verdant hills around the village of Santa Maria della Versa, rural order has lost ground lately to the slapdash of advancing scrub. Farm folk have been dropping out in increasing numbers to face the challenges of urban life; but whatever the social implications of their exodus, they left the countryside behind in a state of appealing rusticity. Il Casale is the estate of Conte Vittorio de' Micheli Vitturi, who bucked the local trend and gave up his former interests to return to the land. His estate is splendid: a five-hundred-year-old grange amidst vineyards where promise still holds the upper hand over neglect.

Conte de' Micheli is obviously a man of noble tastes. At one end of the elongated structure of Il Casale he maintains a small *hostaria* offering hearty country fare and wines made by another nobleman, Duca Antonio Denari, who is head of the Cantina Sociale of Santa Maria della Versa, the Oltrepò consortium, and an organization of Lombardian wine producers as well.

The Hostaria Il Casale evokes the days when the fastest way to travel was by horse-drawn carriage. Generous soups, stews, and piquant cold cuts on slabs of bread freshly baked in a wood-fired oven complement the grandeur of the Duke's wines. There is a delicate, pale, very dry Riesling, or a Pinot Gris of amber-rose color, whose silky dry qualities are best tasted with only a light chilling. The Rosso del Roccolo, from the 1971 vintage, is as impressive a red as I have tasted in the Oltrepò Pavese. If it concedes anything to the great reds of Piedmont it is life span, for it reaches its top form in three to five years and may begin to fade after eight. Otherwise Rosso del Roccolo shows, in its special way, similar class and distinction.

Cucina Classica in Voghera

In this section of the Po Valley you would have to go out of your way to find a mediocre wine or an unsatisfactory meal, because local tastes would not endure the source of either for long. At Voghera, a small city where life moves at a comfortably bourgeois tempo, a sojourn at the Albergo Reale d'Italia is like a visit to the Italy of Victor Emmanuel III.

Emilio Torti, proprietor and chef, has undoubtedly kept it that way on purpose; the venerable decor is an appropriate setting for his *cucina classica*, the unadorned artistry of which many young chefs would be wise to rediscover.

Torti's menu and wine list do not change much from year to year, though there are seasonal variations in the food. He has borrowed a few things from neighboring regions — *trenette col pesto* from Liguria, Parma ham and cheese from Emilia-Romagna, two or three wines from Piedmont, the latter apparently as a sop to guests who refuse to believe that local wines are often as good and cheaper. Among the many admirably prepared dishes, perhaps the most revelatory to a visitor from a country with an Anglo-Saxon heritage is boiled meat. *Bollito misto* — simmered beef, veal, hen, *zampone* (pigs-feet sausage), and tongue immersed in a broth in the well of a steam trolley — might not sound like the sort of creation to fire the imagination. But with a dab of *salsa verde* (finely chopped parsley, garlic, and anchovy in olive oil) it becomes interesting; with *mostarda di frutta* (candied fruit in a syrup heavily laden with dry mustard) it becomes exotic. Whatever its effect on the taste buds, anyone who fancies himself a gastronome should try the combination of *bollito* and *mostarda* at least once.

Brio in San Colombano

North of the Po, just beyond the periphery of greater Milan, the winemakers of San Colombano al Lambro labor with no apparent fear that their vineyards could some day be swallowed up by what is referred to euphemistically as progress. Although growing conditions on the gentle rises around the town seem less favorable than in the Oltrepò Pavese, there is little noticeable difference in standards. What the wines of San Colombano al Lambro lack in finesse, they make up for in brio — and not just because so many of them sparkle. Even the still wines are lively.

The most prominent red wines are made from Bonarda and Merlot grapes, sometimes mixed with small amounts of other varieties. The whites come from Pinots, Rieslings, and the less familiar Tocai and Verdea grapes. Three wineries have built reputations that are more than local: Angelo Cesari, who makes a fine Bonarda; the Pietrasanta firm, which sells several wines under the name Podere Costa Regina; and Enrico Riccardi, who alludes to his wines unabashedly as "Nectar of the Saints."

Other wines from the Polesine flatlands around Milan are usually less distinctive than those of San Colombano. Vines throughout the Po Valley from Pavia to the Adriatic yield stupefying quantities of grapes that are often made into simple wines to refresh workers in the hot fields, or to wash down a heavy meal. *"Basta che non fa male la testa,"* as they say. "It's enough that they don't give you a headache."

Milan, Broker and Patron

As banker, broker, and consumer, Milan plays an elemental role in the marketing of Italian wines. A city almost invariably depicted as business-like, of broad streets, square blocks, and some buildings tall enough to be called *grattacieli* (skyscrapers), Milan stands unchallenged as the capital of Italian commerce and industry. The textbook Milanese expects to work hard and be paid for it, a factor behind his image as efficient, sober-minded, rich, and even a bit ruthless. But to give him his due, the modern Milanese is remarkably free of the sort of local or regional jingoism one witnesses elsewhere in Italy, perhaps because the chances are better than fifty-fifty that he was born somewhere other than Milan.

His tastes are cosmopolitan; his choice of food and wine is wide-ranging and judicious; he demands, and gets, the best products available from the soil and the sea. Thus, with the freshest fish or the choicest cut of meat, the Milanese will drink a Pinot Grigio from Friuli–Venezia Giulia or a Riesling from the Oltrepò, a Barolo or a Gattinara from Piedmont, or a favorite little Barbera, Valpolicella, or Chianti. Though Milan has no wine it can truly call its own, it serves as a wise and magnanimous patron of many wines from many places.

A number of the city's wine shops are called *enoteca*, precisely because they purport to offer library-like selections from Italy and abroad. The Enoteca Solci has a particularly impressive array of wines available. The Boccondivino restaurant provides a setting for sampling not only the wines but the cheeses of Italy and personnel to advise expertly on which goes with which.

Milan boasts some of the finest and most elegant restaurants of the peninsula — Giannino and Gualtiero Marchesi for two — plus a great range of eating places offering well-chosen and inventive dishes from many regions. The *trattoria Toscana* is a fixture in many Milan neighborhoods, though the eclectic Milanese have compelled most to offer a menu with more than the tasty but not terribly imaginative food of

Tuscany. "Far out" might best describe the food at Emilio oste in Milano, a basement *spaghetteria* that has captured the imagination of the city's gastronomic elite. There owner-chef Emilio Regonaschi, who has been described as a mad genius, creates sauces based on bananas, violets, or marine algae, among other unlikely sources, to dress his spaghetti. He serves each with an unerring sense of just which wine will go with it.

The time-honored specialties of Milanese cooking are *cotoletta alla milanese* and *ossobuco*, usually served with the saffron-colored *risotto alla milanese*. But it is not always easy to find these flavors of what is left of old Milan. The Antica Trattoria della Pesa provides an authentically dated setting, and at Gran San Bernardo-da Alfredo, Alfredo Valli prepares the traditional dishes very well indeed.

Northern Lombardy: A Tranquil Aspect

That Lombardy is Italy's most populous and industrialized region is not everywhere apparent within its bounds. Northern Lombardy is a land of lakes and mountains, scenic country that takes kindly to vines. The lakes retain a tranquil aspect even if the villas that serve as summer retreats for Milanese, Swiss, and Germans have claimed most of the space along shorelines where vineyards and pastures once prevailed.

The area that stretches from Lake Maggiore on the west to Lake Garda on the east and scales the Alps on the north to a lofty frontier with Switzerland, has a measure of geographical cohesion. It has even been said that wines here — fairly evenly distributed among red, white and rosé — have a common bond, a bright, fresh, frank quality about them, that is appealingly free of complexity. Any such observations should be stated with caution; as elsewhere, wine is not only its maker's pride and joy but proof of his individuality.

Only the wines of the Valtellina are well known abroad. These sturdy reds from the Nebbiolo grape have sterling reputations in Switzerland; many are now sold in the United States and Britain as well. Red and pink wines called Riviera del Garda from the western shore of Lake Garda have proved so popular with vacationers that they, too, have fashioned a market outside Lombardy. Two notable whites, Lugana and Pinot di Franciacorta (particularly its sparkling version), are earning the sort of praise elsewhere that they have long enjoyed close to home.

But most wine from northern Lombardy does not need to travel far to be appreciated. Some perfectly lovely wines made in the area around lakes Maggiore, Varese, and Como never make it into bottle. They are served by the carafe in restaurants and bars, or toted off in demijohns by city dwellers who like to boast of a *vino quotidiano* that draws from friends compliments for their good taste.

Some such wines have neither specific names nor reliable notations available about their origins; others enjoy enough prestige to have achieved at least tentative identity. At the town of Angera on Lake Maggiore tasty red wines made from Bonarda, Barbera, and Nebbiolo grapes may be called either Angera or Rocca Rosso. A Rosso di Bellagio, from the Como resort, contains Malbec, Pinot Nero, Cabernet, and Merlot. The red and white wines of Montevecchia, near Como, are well enough known to occasionally show up in labeled bottles in Milan. The white is from Biancame, Pinot, and Riesling, the red from Barbera, Nebbiolo, and Merlot. Equally imaginative mixtures of old and new, native and foreign varieties have been reported hereabouts in either red or rosé wines on the light side or white wines of rather high color. They are usually very good, occasionally superb, and there is rarely anything bizarre about their flavor.

Foreign vines, chiefly French, were brought into Lombardy and the Veneto in the last century and again around the time of the First World War, after vineyards were ravished by phylloxera. Some varieties have adapted themselves so well to the environment that the young generation of winemakers in northern Italy does not think of them as foreign. And, indeed, whatever their names, their character is by now uniquely Italian.

East of Milan toward Bergamo, wines begin to show enough consistency in their makeup to rate classification. Valcalepio, with red and white wines, was among the most recent districts to gain DOC recognition. The Cantina Sociale Bergamasca at San Paolo d'Argon makes a dry white from Pinot Bianco and Grigio and a red from Merlot, Cabernet, and Marzemino, that requires 12° alcohol and two years' aging, both promising enough to indicate that wine of real interest will be forthcoming under the Valcalepio name.

The Champagne Style of Franciacorta

Around Cortefranca, a town south of Lake Iseo, winemaking traditions have been solidly established. The hills north of Cortefranca are known as Franciacorta, the result of a centuries-old play on words. The DOC wines are registered as Franciacorta, a name emerging among the region's proudest.

The Pinot grapes are employed in a still white of distinction and Champagne-style wines of true eminence. The firm of Guido Berlucchi makes four sparkling wines by the *méthode champenoise:* Pinot di Franciacorta brut; a delicate Grand Cremant; a full-blossomed pink Max Rosé; and an exquisitely dry Pinot di Franciacorta *pas dosé.* The Berlucchi winery, directed by Franco Ziliani, who learned his techniques in Champagne, leads in sales of *champenoise* wines in Italy with some 500,000 bottles a year. Berlucchi wines approach good Champagnes in style if not in price.

Franciacorta Rosso, of Cabernet Franc, Barbera, Nebbiolo, and Merlot grapes, is a red of about 11° alcohol that can be very attractive when served cool. Rosso di Borgonato from Fratelli Berlucchi and Rosso di San Michele from Nobili Barboglio de' Gaioncelli are light and fine. The Rosso of Barone Monti della Corte is also distinguished. Giacomo Ragnoli uses the Tuscan *governo* method to induce a refermentation that gives his Rosso a tantalizing liveliness. Though not a big wine, it is formidably good. It should be drunk within two or three years to be fully appreciated.

Brescia's "Local" Wines

The citizens of Brescia have a widespread assortment of wines that they refer to, more or less justifiably, as "local." The wines of Franciacorta qualify; even more immediate examples are Cellatica and Botticino, red DOC wines from hills just outside the city. Cellatica, from a small zone around the town of that name, uses Schiava Gentile as its main grape, with Barbera and Marzemino (here called Berzamino) in slightly smaller amounts. Botticino, which also takes its name from a town, is dominated by Barbera, with smaller measures of Marzemino, Schiava Gentile, and Sangiovese included.

Botticino is considered the bigger of the two. With 12° minimum of alcohol and 10 months of barrel aging, it can improve considerably after a few years in bottle, when it makes a good accompaniment to roasts. Cellatica is more versatile, lighter in color and alcohol (11.5° minimum), and because of its fresher aspect is best served young at cellar temperature. Botticino tends toward a robust warmth — as made by Giacomo

Giossi and Pietro Bracchi — with more than a hint of caramel-like sweetness. Cellatica is slightly drier and because of the prominence of the Schiava grape has a light bitter taste. Tenuta Santella, made by the Fratelli Tonoli, is a respected name in Cellatica.

Wines from Lombardy's shores of Lake Garda are also in Brescia's province. DOC classifications there include Riviera del Garda, both Rosso and Chiaretto (rosé), and the white Lugana and Tocai di San Martino della Battaglia. These wines, which have been growing in stature, can often equal the more famous Verona wines from vineyards in the Veneto. In fact, the DOC zones of both Lugana and Tocai di San Martino della Battaglia extend into Verona province.

Riviera del Garda, a vast district, covers the entire eastern shore of the lake from just outside Riva on the north to Sirmione on the south, reaching back into the hills and valleys. The name, now well known in Italy, has also gained recognition abroad, particularly in northern Europe and the United States. The wines, both Rosso and Chiaretto, are above all light and refreshing, but that should not be taken to mean they lack character. The red can show an unexpected range of nuance before it begins to fade after two or three years. The Chiaretto, which should be consumed even sooner, has depth for a pink wine.

Both types are made from a mixture of Groppello, Sangiovese, Barbera, and Marzemino grapes. The Chiaretto is drawn off the skins early in the fermentation and bottled after a short settling period in the vats. The Rosso, fermented longer on the skins, rests in barrels a few months before being bottled. If it has 12° or more alcohol it can be labeled as *superiore* after a year of aging. A few cooperatives and large firms — Bertani, Bolla, Folonari, and Lamberti among them — bottle Riviera del Garda wines on a fairly large scale. Theirs can be sound and competitively priced.

Good Riviera del Garda wines are also available from smaller producers in the zone, among them Azienda Agricola M. Mor, Franco & Valerio Bottarelli, Colombaro, Frassine, Redaelli de Zinis, and Bertanzi.

A Groppello della Valtenesi from the town of Puegnago is very similar to the reds of the Riviera del Garda zone surrounding it. Producers there requested a separate DOC, but had not been granted it by 1980. Two worthy producers of Groppello della Valtenesi are Fratelli Comincioli and Fulvio Leali.

Still another zone of Brescia province has won initial approval for DOC. Capriano del Colle Rosso and Bianco are produced in a small zone around the towns of Capriano del Colle and Poncavale in the low hills just south of Brescia. The red is from Sangiovese, Marzemino, Barbera, and a bit of Merlot and the hybrid Incrocio Terzi 1. The white is from Trebbiano, known here as Capriano del Colle-Trebbiano.

Lugana, White from the Flatlands

Lugana, a particularly graceful white wine, goes well with lake fish or antipasto, though it has the capacity to be most enjoyable on its own. Made from the Trebbiano di Lugana grape, it is one of the few high-quality white wines I know of whose vines thrive in flat country. Its vineyards are centered around the towns of Lugana, Peschiera, and Desenzano, many of them on what once must have been the bottom of the southern end of Lake Garda.

Several growers make Lugana admirably well, rarely better than the Fratelli Fraccaroli at Peschiera. Theirs is a light golden wine, dry but substantial, with distinct undertones that include the flavor of nuts and, though I hesitate to say it, licorice. They go together well, though, especially when set off by the firm, pink flesh of a lake trout grilled over the coals at the family restaurant. The Fraccaroli vineyards and restaurant (whose unpretentious building was originally constructed as a filling station) are the enterprises of a close-knit farm family succeeding on the strength of its members' industriousness, good sense, and integrity.

Francesco Fraccaroli, short and wiry with courtly manners, calloused hands, and a shy smile, makes the wine with his brother Giuseppe. They are sticklers for purity at all stages of production.

"When people ask me how we make such good wine, the first thing I tell them is manure," said Francesco. "That's the key to healthy vines. Cow manure, specifically, and well aged. Anything else, at least in Lugana, will result in inferior grapes. There's much more to it than that, as you know, but natural fertilization is the essential that I'm afraid too many cultivators neglect nowadays."

The Fraccaroli brothers make about 100,000 bottles of Lugana a year at their Cascina Berra Vecchia, which is actually in the province of Verona. The Fraccarolis were among the first small-scale producers to export their wine to the United States.

Other reliable producers are Franco Visconti (whose Lugana is an outstanding example of the modern style), Vittorio Zenegaglia, Azienda

Francesco (left) and Giuseppe Fraccaroli

Agricola Ambrosi, Podere Co' de Fer, Fratelli Zenato, Salvalai, and Pietro Dal Cero. Dal Cero, whose passion and talents seem limited only by economic factors, has not confined his work to Lugana. In his cantina, a converted barn, we tasted from the vat a Merlot rosé, extremely pale in color with a persistent flint-dry quality balanced by a delicate taste of fruit — a unique experiment locally that he had good reason to be pleased with. He had not then decided whether to bottle and sell it in the future or to keep it for private consumption.

Dal Cero's Rosso dei Frati, a fresh, well-rounded *frizzante* red from Sangiovese, Groppello, Merlot, and Corvina grapes, would surely win over even the most devoted fan of Lambrusco. But the few thousand bottles he turns out each year are not about to cut into that market.

Lugana's vineyards have been expanded lately to meet growing demand for the wine in Italy, with some left over to ship abroad. Bottlers of Veronese wines — Bardolino, Valpolicella, and Soave — now often include Lugana in their export line. Best drunk within a year or two,

Lugana is so well suited to being sipped on a lakeside terrace while admiring the view up the length of Garda toward the Alps, that it seems a shame somehow to send it anywhere else.

The Tocai from the nearby village of San Martino della Battaglia is less well known than Lugana, but it has a liveliness that can make it equally enjoyable. The Tocai Friulano grape (no relation to the Hungarian Tokay) is a native of Friuli–Venezia Giulia, where it makes wines of a nobility rarely realized elsewhere. The Tocai of San Martino is no exception, but when made with the gifted touch shown by Ercole Romano at Stefanona, there is reason to believe that one day it will escape its current state of obscurity.

From the plains around nearby Mantua, fizzy red Lambrusco Mantovano is made, non-DOC wine that can nonetheless equal in quality some better-known Lambrusco from the DOC zones of neighboring Emilia.

Wines from the adjacent DOC zone in Mantua province, known as Colli Morenici Mantovani del Garda, have maintained a low profile. The Bianco of Garganega, Trebbiano di Soave, and other varieties resembles Soave in style. The Rubino, Rosato, and Chiaretto (which is slightly stronger than the Rosato) are all made from Rondinella, Rossanella, and Negrara Trentina grapes and bear a similarity to wines from the Brescia and Verona areas. The Colli Morenici wines, from what has been described as an "amphitheater of hills opening toward Lake Garda," are plentiful, but none enjoys a wide reputation.

Valtellina: Nebbiolo by Still Another Name

The Adda River tumbles down from its glacial source high in the Rhaetian Alps to Tirano, beside the Swiss border, where it broadens and flows through Sondrio into Lake Como. Its path is the Valtellina, whose lower slopes along the river's right bank face south, basking in reflections of sun off water. For 25 kilometers or so between Tirano and Sondrio nearly all accessible sections of the gravelly terrain are under vine, Nebbiolo at that, although here the grape is called Chiavennasca. The wines from this mountain setting bear a family resemblance to those of Donnaz and Carema, but they rarely reach the proportions of the big Nebbiolo wines made in gentler climes of Piedmont. Barolo, Barbaresco, Spanna, and Gattinara.

The Valtellina, with its tidy stone-walled terraces, resembles certain wine-producing sectors of Switzerland; and, indeed, the Swiss behave as if they own the wines made there. Well, why not? Some do. Swiss proprietors of Italian vineyards within 10 kilometers of the border have a special dispensation to bring their wine — or grapes — home duty-free. Their fellow countrymen buy Valtellina wines with such fervor that precious little remains for the rest of the world.

The best known wines, all red, are Sassella, Inferno, Grumello, and Valgella, each defined geographically in the general category of Valtellina *superiore*. They must contain 95 percent or more of Chiavennasca grapes and have at least 12° alcohol. A simpler category, Valtellina DOC, includes reds made throughout the zone of at least 70 percent Chiavennasca mixed with Pinot Nero, Merlot, Rossola, Pignola, and Brugnola; minimum alcohol content is 11°. Sforzato, or Sfursat in dialect, whose name refers to a special vinification process which uses semidried grapes to bring the alcohol up to at least 14.5°, is also a DOC wine.

Of the four *superiore* types, Sassella is sometimes cited as the finest, followed closely by Inferno. The four have much in common, however, so experienced buyers often depend more on the producer's reputation or the vintage than on geographical designation. They are said to be more individualistic when young than after aging. Enologica Valtellinese, which makes all four with exemplary consistency, exports some wine to the United States and Britain. Other reliable wineries, most of whom export, are Casa Vinicola Tona, Casa Vinicola Nera, Fratelli Bettini, Aldo Rainoldi, Franco Balgera, and Fratelli Triacca. Two important wineries here, Nino Negri and Arturo Pelizzatti, have been part of the Winefood group, which has an interest in a number of Italian firms.

Essentially, Sassella, Inferno, Grumello, and Valgella share the characteristic Nebbiolo hardness when they go into bottle after two to three years in cask. With a further three to six years, depending on the vintage, they begin to open up, their aromas often more impressive initially than their flavors. At their peak, anywhere from six to twelve years, seldom more, they become mellow and round with a color tending toward rust. If they rarely reach the class of great Barolo, they rarely reach Barolo's price range either. A Sassella, for example, may be one of the best values in Nebbiolo as a well-aged wine worthy of a special occasion. The Swiss adore Valtellina wines with game, particularly venison.

Most producers have a special wine of slightly superior quality made in small lots, and not often covered by DOC. Tona's is Perla Villa. Nino

Negri makes Fracia and Castel Chiuro, the latter both red and white. The white, a lovely wine, comes from Pinot and Riesling grapes. Pelizzatti offers a Riserva della Casa.

To my taste, the finest Valtellina wine is Sfursat. Made from grapes partly dried on mats for two months after the harvest, it becomes a richer and more powerful wine than the others. Its warm and generous traits are enhanced by mountain cheeses. Sfursat has neither the elegance nor complexity of the greatest Barolos and Barbarescos, but in a way it can be as satisfying to drink. Tona's Sforzato of the 1970 vintage was superb seven years later; it may be even better after another seven years in the cellar.

The Vintages

Oltrepò Pavese

	Red wines	White wines
1979	Excellent	Excellent
1978	Excellent, scarce	Exceptional
1977	Good to excellent	Good to excellent
1976	Good to excellent	Excellent
1975	Uneven, some exceptional	Fair
1974	Good to excellent	Good
1973	Fair to good	Good
1972	Poor	Poor
1971	Great	Good
1970	Good to excellent	Good
1969	Excellent	

Brescia Wines

	Pinot di Franciacorta	Botticino, Cellatica	Riviera del Garda	Lugana, Tocai di San Martino
1979	Good	Excellent	Excellent	Excellent
1978	Excellent	Excellent	Excellent	Excellent
1977	Good	Good	Good	Good
1976	Good	Fair	Fair	Fair
1975	Good	Fair to good	Fair	Fair
1974	Good	Good	Good	Excellent
1973	Good	Good	Good	Good
1972	Fair	Good	Good	Very good
1971	Fair	Fair to good	Fair	Good
1970	Excellent	Good to excellent	Good	Good

Valtellina Reds: Sassella, Inferno, Valgella, Grumello, Sfursat

1979	Great
1978	Very good, scarce
1977	Poor
1976	Uneven, some good
1975	Good
1974	Fair
1973	Good
1972	Fair
1971	Excellent
1970	Excellent
1969	Excellent
1968	Fair
1967	Great
1966	Fair
1965	Poor
1964	Great, long-lived

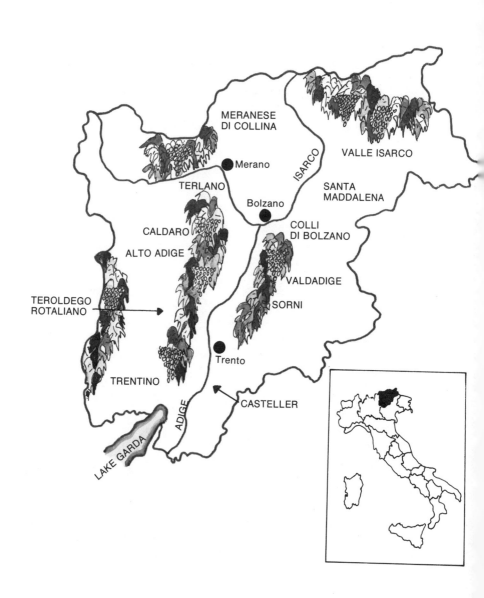

MERANESE
DI COLLINA

VALLE ISARCO

Merano

TERLANO

ISARCO

SANTA
MADDALENA

Bolzano

CALDARO

COLLI
DI BOLZANO

ALTO ADIGE

VALDADIGE

TEROLDEGO
ROTALIANO

SORNI

Trento

TRENTINO

CASTELLER

ADIGE

LAKE GARDA

TRENTINO-ALTO ADIGE

PROVINCES

TRENTO, Bolzano

POPULATION

800,000

AREA

5,252 square miles

AVERAGE WINE PRODUCTION

150 million liters

DOC WINES

Alto Adige/Südtiroler (Cabernet, Gewürztraminer, Lagrein, Malvasia, Merlot, Moscato Giallo, Moscato Rosa, Müller Thurgau, Pinot Bianco, Pinot Grigio, Pinot Nero, Rheinriesling, Riesling Italico, Sauvignon, Schiava, Sylvaner) · Casteller · Colli di Bolzano/Bozner Leiten · Lago di Caldaro/Kalterersee · Meranese di Collina/Meraner Hügel · Santa Maddalena/St. Magdalener · Sorni (Bianco, Rosso, Rosato) · Terlano/Terlaner · Teroldego Rotaliano · Trentino (Cabernet, Lagrein, Marzemino, Merlot, Moscato, Pinot Bianco, Pinot Nero, Riesling, Traminer Aromatico, Vin Santo) · Valdadige/Etschtaler (Rosso, Bianco) · Valle Isarco/Eisarcktaler (Gewürztraminer, Müller Thurgau, Pinot Grigio, Sylvaner, Veltliner)

OTHER WINES

Castel San Michele · .Castelsegonzano · De Vite · Foianeghe · Geierberg · Gran Spumante · Grauvernatsch Groppello · Kolbenhof · Mori Vecio · 4 Vicariati · Sandbichler · San Zeno · Schiava di Faedo · Torggeltropfen

Viva la Differenza!

TRENTINO–ALTO ADIGE, whose compound name reflects a history of division and duplicity, still exhibits symptoms of a split personality. But in some regards — winemaking, for one — its record is enviably stable.

The northern sector is the province of Bolzano (or Bozen); its Italian name is Alto Adige, though it is probably better known to the world as the Süd Tirol or South Tyrol. Wines there go under such names as Ruländer, Gewürztraminer, Torggeltropfen, and Grauvernatsch, from such producers as Hofstätter, Kettmeir, Schloss Kehlburg, and Kellereigenossenschaft Nals. The southern sector, Trentino, is the province of Trento (Trent), where the names of the wines and their makers have a familiar Italian ring to them.

The Trentino–Alto Adige union has never been all that compatible. Trentino, historically Italian in language and culture, was incorporated into the South Tyrol during Austrian domination. Then both provinces bounced back into Italy after World War I as Venezia Tridentina, one of the Tre Venezie — along with the Veneto and Friuli–Venezia Giulia — which at one time were in the domain of the Venetian Republics. In 1947, Italy designated Trentino–Alto Adige as one of its original autonomous regions, the soothing terms of which have been implemented gradually, and never to everyone's satisfaction.

Until quite recently, hostile feelings between the peoples of these contrasting cultures frequently flared into violence. But in these days of détente, the ethnic groups coexist, no longer letting their differences interfere with the pursuit of happiness and prosperity. In winemaking, cooperation has led to regionwide standards that, by some measures, are the highest in Italy. This has not come about through compromise. Producers in each sector consider their wines to be special; by mutual consent, their guiding principle seems to be *Viva la differenza!*

Trentino–Alto Adige ranks first among Italy's regions in the proportion of DOC wines produced (about 50 percent of the total) and in the proportion of wine in all categories shipped abroad (close to 35 percent most years). Larger regions far surpass its total yield of about 150 million liters a year because Trentino–Alto Adige's vineyard areas, hemmed in by the Alps, are strictly limited. But nowhere is space used with more industriousness and thrift.

The region's DOC classifications, however, are not as methodical as one might expect. In Alto Adige the breakdown is so complex that it tends not only to confuse consumers but, in some cases, to discourage producers from making DOC wines. To compound matters, many wines have both Italian and German names and producers are free to use either language on the label.

In Trentino the pattern is more or less comprehensible. Three zones – Teroldego Rotaliano, Casteller, and Sorni – have individual status. All other DOC wines have been grouped under the name Trentino and defined by type: Cabernet, Lagrein, Marzemino, Merlot, Moscato, Pinot Bianco, Pinot Nero, Riesling, Traminer Aromatico (Gewürztraminer), Vin Santo.

In Alto Adige four red wines – Colli di Bolzano (Bozner Leiten), Lago di Caldaro (Kalterersee), Meranese di Collina (Meraner Hügel), Santa Maddalena (St. Magdalener) – have individual classifications. Three zones that overlap in places have various types of wine grouped under them. They are:

★ Alto Adige (Südtiroler), a general classification with sixteen types – Cabernet, Gewürztraminer, Lagrein, Malvasia, Merlot, Moscato Giallo, Moscato Rosa, Müller Thurgau, Pinot Bianco, Pinot Grigio, Pinot Nero, Rheinriesling, Riesling Italico, Sauvignon, Schiava, Sylvaner.

★ Terlano (Terlaner) with six types – Pinot Bianco, Riesling Italico, Riesling Renano, Sauvignon, Sylvaner, Terlano.

★ Valle Isarco (Eisarcktaler) with five types – Gewürztraminer, Müller Thurgau, Pinot Grigio, Sylvaner, Veltliner.

Then there is Valdadige (Etschtaler), with Bianco and Rosso, in a zone that follows the Adige River through both provinces and on into the Veneto. The Casteller zone of Trentino also extends into the Veneto. And the Caldaro zone extends from Alto Adige into Trentino.

Each area, to be sure, has distinct factors to consider, such as soil, altitude, and tradition. But these differences are apparent only to persons intimately acquainted with the wines. It might help consumers to identify them if all qualified wines of Bolzano province were labeled Alto Adige DOC followed by zone and type: Valle Isarco Sylvaner or Terlaner Gewürztraminer, for example. Though the wording might be cumbersome, the labels would thus include the particulars so understandably important to growers. However, authorities have shown no inclination to unify or simplify the classifications, which, it must be remembered, took them years to decide upon.

Foreign Echoes in the Süd Tirol

As you drive in from the west, from the Valtellina if the Tonale Pass is not closed by snow, the first vineyards worth noting along the road to Bolzano are at Caldés in the upper Val di Non. There, Groppello grapes make a light red mountain wine that is entirely apropos with the hearty fare served in the tidy *Weinstuben* of roadside inns. A few kilometers farther along, after one has wound down from the Mendel Pass through countless hairpin curves, the jagged citadels of the Dolomites come into view beyond Bolzano as the pine forest yields to the first vineyards of Lago di Caldaro.

The Italian name for this rosy-complexioned red wine has an outlandish ring to it here, a foreign echo in a landscape that, save for the stupefying sweep of vines, could have been lifted straight from the Salzkammergut. So let us call Lago di Caldaro Kalterersee, as most people who drink it do.

Kalterersee has never been a wine to rhapsodize over, though some of the tourists who venture south across the Alps to drink it in sight of the pretty lake it is named after seem blissfully incognizant of that. Even with *classico superiore* and *Auslese* touted on its labels, it fails to rise above its station, which remains, to put it tritely, wetting the whistle and whetting the appetite. Although produced in abundance (some 25 million liters a year), so much Kalterersee is shipped north to its admirers across the Brenner Pass that many Italians who dwell south of Verona have never heard its name in either language.

As made by the firms of G. Kettmeir, J. Hofstätter, and the Cantina Sociale di Termeno (under the name Schloss Rechtenthal), it achieves respectability as a balanced and fruity red wine of 10.5 to 12 percent alcohol that keeps nicely for three or four years. Served cool, like rosé, it goes admirably with hot sausages, *Knödel* (dumplings), and *Kraut*, famously with *Speck* (succulent smoke-cured bacon), sliced into chunks and distributed over a layer of freshly churned butter on a slab of rye bread. Made from a combination of the Schiava grapes (Vernatsch in German) that dominate Alto Adige reds, Kalterersee is one of those uncommon wines of any color that really seem to quench thirst.

Santa Maddalena: Living Down a Legend

If Kalterersee is Alto Adige's most popular wine, Santa Maddalena, in a sense, is its most famous, though its name now lacks the luster it once had.

In 1941, Mussolini's cadre in Rome proclaimed Santa Maddalena one of Italy's three great wines (along with Barolo and Barbaresco), a puzzling gesture that for a time enhanced the wine's reputation, but over the years has tended to demean it. For, while there was scant dissent, if any, about the choice of the two Piedmontese reds, there was widespread disapproval of Santa Maddalena. As a consequence, this supple, fragrant, unassuming red wine bears even to this day the stigma of Fascist over-zealousness and vanity. Underrated* and undervalued, it deserves a bit more goodwill and support than it has been getting.

Santa Maddalena (St. Magdalener in German) comes from the hills on the northern edge of Balzano, some of its *classico* vineyards a stone's throw from the city limits. Its grape composition, like Kalterersee's, is dominated by Schiava, but Santa Maddalena is more elegant and complex, a wine of at least 11.5° alcohol to reckon with after three to six years — rarely more — of aging. Kellereigenossenschaft St. Magdalena at St. Justina u. Leitach and the Cantina Sociale di Terlano both make excellent versions. Also recommended are bottles from Weingut Schloss Schwanburg, Klosterkellerei Muri-Gries, Josef Brigl, G. Kettmeir, J. Hofstätter, Alois Lageder, Castel Rametz, and Weingut Eberlehof.

Meranese di Collina (Meraner Hügel) made in the hills around the handsome Alpine city of Merano, is another DOC wine from Schiava grapes. It receives less attention than the other two "historic" wines of Alto Adige. As made by the Cantina Sociale di Merano, Meranese di Collina compares to good Kalterersee — a light red wine of about 11° alcohol.

---

* Except by the Swiss, who still rate Santa Maddalena and Barolo as the only Italian wines with the right on import to be marked "Extra class."

DOC? Only When Convenient

Given the random order of the remaining five DOC districts of Alto Adige, any attempt to progress geographically from one to the other and make distinctions about the wines of each would lead to a prohibitive series of detours and backtrackings, if not to total bewilderment. To keep track of the wines originating in any of the zones would be impossible. Some firms — Kettmeir, Hofstätter, Castel Rametz, and Schloss Schwanburg, notably — buy grapes from various sources and make numerous varieties and types of wine from them that may or may not qualify as DOC. These wineries consider their reputations for integrity to be the prime assurance of quality.

J. Hofstätter, one of the region's largest privately owned wineries, produces fourteen types of wine in its imposing complex of towered, steep-roofed *Bauernhof* buildings in the village of Tramin (Termeno), home of the Traminer vine. *Gewürz* (spicy) was prefixed to the name as the vines were dispersed in the Rhine and Moselle, where they sometimes make richer, more distinguished wines than they do at home. The Italians call Gewürztraminer Traminer Aromatico, and indeed as it is made by Hofstätter, its outstanding trait is its full aroma.

Paolo Foradori, assistant to the firm's director, Konrad Oberhofer, is a tall, easygoing native of Trentino province who "married in" to the Hofstätter family enterprise. "Otherwise," he said with a wink, "we all speak German here." Foradori, an oenologist, takes a hand in the winemaking, although with some 3 million liters to process, much of it from grapes selected and vinified by vineyard, the workload at harvest time is divided among specialists. Hofstätter maintains 80 acres of its own vines while drawing from a network of about 200 regular suppliers of grapes. Some 80 percent of the firm's wine is exported, chiefly to West Germany, Austria, and Switzerland, though Foradori said some orders had been received from the United States. (The excellent Kettmeir winery is established on the American and British markets.)

Hofstätter and Kettmeir, like most medium-large wineries in Alto Adige, do not have an industrial look or atmosphere about them, and their wines certainly do not have mass-produced tastes. They are made with expertise, honesty, and more than a little pride. Hofstätter complies with DOC requirements only when convenient, as Foradori explains it, because "DOC helps sell wines south of Trento, but our business is overwhelmingly north of Bolzano. If the market changed, I imagine we'd make more effort to comply. But even if we made more DOC wines, the quality wouldn't be any better than it is now."

Hofstätter's white wines are Gewürztraminer, Rheinriesling, Weissburgunder (Pinot Bianco), Ruländer (Pinot Grigio), and de Vite, from a curious cross of Riesling and Trollinger, an offshoot of the Schiava vine. A wine to be drunk very young, de Vite has so much personality that it tastes good with asparagus, a food that compromises the flavor of most other wines.

The Hofstätter reds are Kalterersee, Santa Maddalena, Cabernet, Merlot, Blauburgunder (Pinot Nero), and the native Lagrein in both Dunkel ("dark" red) and Kretzer (rosé). Grauvernatsch, made from the Schiava Grigia grape, is another, a typical wine of the area, rather better than most Kalterersee. Along the same lines, but superior still, is Kolbenhof, made from a mixture of Schiava grapes grown at the premier vineyard on a hillside overlooking the winery. Though light and fruity, Kolbenhof is endowed with considerable grace.

Foradori, echoing the views of many other producers, adamantly opposed rules requiring non-DOC wines to be labeled as *vino da tavola.* "*Vino da tavola* has a common sound to it," he complained, "and who the hell gives those politicians in Rome and Brussels the power to call our wines common?"

There is nothing common either about the wine of Antonio von Elzenbaum, a grower in Tramin who works on a smaller scale. His Gewürztraminer may be the finest of the province, if not the nation: a pale golden-green wine that epitomizes the soft, luscious, perfumed qualities rendered by the proudest of the native vines.

Among imported varieties, Pinot Nero, or Blauburgunder, makes a generous, lightly tannic wine that in certain years can be aged as long as any red in Bolzano province. One of the finest comes from the Centro Sperimentale e Forestale at Laimburg, an experimental station that, like many government-supported institutions in Italy, sells products to the public. A number of good wines are made there by a young oenologist named Hans Ferzer.

Heinrich Lun, whose vineyards lie close to Bolzano, makes an excellent Sandbichler Rot, deeper and richer than most red wines of Alto Adige. Though I am not sure of the formula, it tastes as if it is made chiefly of Schiava grapes, for the closest wine to it would be a superior Santa Maddalena.

Bolzano's *"Gemütlich"* Lagrein

Bolzano, a thriving city of 105,000 inhabitants, is not only a cultural and financial center, but a wine town. Vineyards are spotted through the suburban hills and valleys along the Adige and Isarco rivers, which join west of the city. From the northeast come the whites of the Isarco valley, from the northwest the whites of Terlano. From the west and southwest come Kalterersee and other wines — red, white, and pink — of less renown. Santa Maddalena's hills lie just to the north. The nearby Colli di Bolzano provide still more red from Schiava. And around Gries, at the city's western threshold, are the vineyards of Lagrein, the wine that lies closest — literally and figuratively — to Bolzano's heart.

Lagrein has been implanted elsewhere, but the wine rarely equals that made from the gnarled, knotty vines in the sandy plain of Gries, where it has steadily yielded terrain to truck gardens, service stations, warehouses, and factories. Although less Lagrein is made now than in years past, it is not in danger of disappearing. The citizens of Bolzano, whatever their linguistic background, would never permit it; for their Lagrein (I have seen the Italian version, Lagrina, written but never heard it spoken) is too *gemütlich* or, as the case may be, *simpatico* for that.

The brothers of the Benedictine order of Muri-Gries have held out against land speculation, retaining their vineyards and orchards as Bolzano's inexorable expansion transformed Gries from a peaceful hamlet to a borough of its urban complex.

In the Benedictine Klosterkellerei, high-vaulted cellars reached via the barren marble-floored halls of the cloister, Lagrein rests a couple of years in immense oaken casks before being bottled and sold. I had, quite frankly, expected to come upon a scene of rosy-cheeked monks in brown habits and sandals checking the progress of each barrel, but there was to be none of that. Instead, I found blue-outfitted workmen stacking plastic cases of empty bottles, and inside the *Buro* two men in nonclerical attire were occupied with ledgers and adding machines.

"No, no, the monks don't make the wine here," one of them explained, "just Padre Gregor, the abbot. He's the administrator."

Padre Gregor appeared moments later, a diminutive figure in flowing black habit, with close-cropped white hair and a face full of creases deepened by an almost perpetual smile. The Swiss-born abbot spoke hesitant Italian in a tiny, guttural voice, concluding most phrases with

Padre Gregor

a nervous chuckle. "I just don't have the ear for it," he confessed, "even after all these years here."

In forty years in Gries he has, however, developed a highly regarded palate. He makes the decisions on harvesting, fermentation, and aging of the order's Lagrein, Dunkel and Kretzer, along with six other wines: Santa Maddalena, a red Malvasia, Riesling, Gewürztraminer, and the white and gray Pinots, called in German Weissburgunder and Ruländer.

The Lagreins, particularly the Dunkel, are generally conceded to be Alto Adige's finest of the type; no other wines of the order, good as they are, can quite match them. Though they fall into the Alto Adige DOC category, the Lagreins of Gries are given special dispensation to be known as Lagrein di Gries or Grieser Lagrein. The Dunkel, a rich ruby color, is smooth and mouth-filling, its elements gaining harmony and composure after two or three years in bottle. It goes well with roasts or grilled pork chops, which often are served in northern Italy with polenta, the cornmeal mush made light and fluffy by an arm-wearying stir with a wooden paddle in a copper pot heated over a wood fire. The Kretzer is drier, livelier, a rosé of hearty disposition that makes a solid companion to a whole range of dishes.

Padre Gregor has become a bit of a celebrity in the Bolzano area, though you would never guess it from his modest demeanor or self-effacing words. Other winemakers insist that the Lagrein has reached new heights since he took charge. Though the abbot tries to give all credit to the *Padreterno,* the consensus is that without Padre Gregor's inspiration the Klosterkellerei's might be just another good Lagrein.

The Benedictines make a neat profit from their 75 acres of land, producing with additional purchased grapes about a million liters of wine a year. About a third of that is Lagrein. The monastery also deals in apples, another of the region's major crops. Their wine has found a growing market in Italy to add to the customary exports to Switzerland, Germany, and Austria. Padre Gregor is amenable to selling it elsewhere as well.

"Even in America," he said, chuckling at what to him must have seemed an extraordinarily cosmopolitan thought.

A Taste of Central Europe

Bolzano's progressive bustle and ethnic integration (more than half its citizens are Italian-speaking) contrasts with the languor and insularity that give the countryside its ageless, central European charm. Thin-faced old men sporting loden hats, blue canvas aprons protecting their work clothes, shuffle along the roadsides with herds of cattle. Ruddy-complexioned women, some with blonde hair braided and coiled at the back of their heads, wear dirndls as they gather flowers or wild greens in lush, green pastures. Nestled here and there amidst the rolling meadows and woods, a *Gasthaus* with a name like Goldener Hirsch or Dolomiten will have a sign pointing to it advertising *"Zimmer frei"* or *"Warme und kalte Speisen. Eigenbauwein."* Schoolchildren greet you with *"Grüss Gott,"* or simply *"Grüssti"* if they think they have seen you before.

Landowners, thus the winemakers, of the South Tyrol are overwhelmingly German-speaking. North of Bolzano, whether you follow the Isarco valley or the Adige, white wines become more prominent, although overall they comprise less than a quarter of Alto Adige's production. Their names are almost invariably German, with Italian given (if the wines are bottled and labeled) in the manner of an afterthought.

The village of Terlan (Terlano), northwest of Bolzano on the banks of the Adige, lies at the center of a zone whose white wines bear a resemblance to those of the Rhine and Moselle. The six DOC varietals are all whites, known in German as Weissburgunder, Rheinriesling, Welschriesling, Sylvaner, Sauvignon, and Terlaner, the latter made chiefly of grapes from that native vine.

Not all wines made from grapes purchased in the zone are labeled as Terlan, but among those that are several are worth noting: the light, vivacious Terlaner of G. Kettmeir; the crisply fruity Rheinriesling of the Klosterkellerei Muri-Gries; the balanced, fragrant Sauvignon of the Cantina Sociale di Terlano; the sharp, refreshing Sylvaner of Schloss Schwanburg.

Schloss Schwanburg, in the community of Nals, is another sophisticated winery with both variety and quality to offer. One of its better wines is Geierberg, a red from Schiava grapes. Another large firm, Castel Rametz or Schloss Rametz, run by Alberto Crastan above Merano, makes a formidable line of wines from grapes gathered at many locations. Its Weissburgunder showed the clean, fresh, fruit-acid balance that a fine white Pinot should have.

A small but valid cooperative, the Kellereigenossenschaft Nals (or Cantina Sociale di Nalles), includes 26 growers who between them produce about 150,000 bottles of various wines each year. A wine called simply Rosato Secco dell'Alto Adige was judged to be the best Italian wine entered in 1976 at the world wine competition in Ljubljana, Yugoslavia.

The wines of the Isarco valley, between Bolzano and Bressanone (Brixen), have not achieved widespread recognition, although those from the Abbazia Novacella, one of the world's loveliest wineries, have given a touch of luster to the name. The abbey (known as Chorherrenstift Neustift in German) is a Gothic complex of monastic quarters, chapel, fortress, farm buildings, winery, gardens, vineyards, orchards, and pastures, no doubt constructed over decades in an era when architects thought more about form than function. The setting calls for a warm spring day with blossoms, birds singing, a picnic lunch, perhaps, and the time to sit and wonder if man, with all his other achievements, will ever again equal the aesthetic sense shown by the people who put this place together.

Then again, even if the abbey's wines are not the region's undisputed finest, they are undoubtedly better than those made back in the seventeenth century, so some progress has been made. The Sylvaner has a tantalizing bit of spice to it that is very satisfying, and the Blauburgunder, Gewürztraminer, and Ruländer are all above-average wines. The abbey also makes a Torggeltropfen, an astringently dry white of delicate aroma that goes superbly with fresh brook trout.

Valle Isarco's DOC wines are all white: Gewürztraminer, Ruländer, Sylvaner, Müller Thurgau, and Veltliner, the latter a sturdy if rarely inspiring wine not often found outside this area. The hearty Müller Thurgau vine begins to show its stuff when grown in vineyards more than 2,000 feet above sea level. Most whites from the Isarco valley are for local consumption. They sometimes show a marked acidity, and they do not often surpass their required minimum alcohol content of 10.5 to 11 percent.

North of Bressanone, the quest for fine wine reaches a cul-de-sac; the valleys that meander upward to the Austrian and Swiss borders are better suited to winter sports or livestock grazing than grape cultivation. But before turning back toward Bolzano and Trento, anyone with the appetite may want to take on one of Italy's great gastronomic feats: getting through the *piatto elefante* at the Albergo Elefante in Bressanone. An enormous platter that includes many of the region's specialties, it makes a meal that is never to be forgotten.

Teroldego, an Aristocrat in Trentino

As the Adige enters Trentino from the north, its valley broadens at Mezzocorona into an alluvial plain where fruit trees and vines cover the space between mountains like a wall-to-wall carpet. Apple orchards dominate most of the plain, but around Mezzolombardo and San Michele all'Adige, grapevines claim their share of the land. The scenery here is not as rustically pretty as it was up north, but the wines lose nothing in comparison. In fact, Teroldego Rotaliano in certain years from certain vineyards is considered the finest wine of the region; and it has plenty of local competition.

Although the mountains give the feeling of altitude, the plain where Teroldego grows is only about seven hundred feet above sea level, meaning it has the potential for a long, hot growing season that can give grapes the sugar and pigmentation to make a big red wine. It does not work out that way every year, but the Teroldego grape is flexible; in medium years it makes wine of medium strength, body, and color that can still be a delight to drink.

Teroldego's historic growing area is called the Campo Rotaliano, flat land split into individual holdings flanking the Noce River between Mezzocorona, Mezzolombardo, and Grumo. The vines are trained onto *pergole trentine,* inverted L-shaped supports that extend the new growth toward the south three to four feet above the earth, a system that exposes the foliage to the sun and, even more important in flat country, to both horizontal and vertical movements of air.

The Azienda Agricola Barone de Cles is the leading name in Teroldego. It is run by two brothers of a noble family noted for winemaking since the fourteenth century, when vines were planted around the castle at Cles in the Val di Non. The brothers, Leonardo, of medium build and intense manner, and Michele, hefty and easygoing, have plunged themselves into viniculture with a passion that would have ruffled the finery of some of their forebears, who surely hired such work done. The two modern barons put on their old clothes and do as much of the labor as they can manage, especially at key points during the vinification when their skill counts most. Even when they are not physically involved, they are likely to be talking or thinking about wine, for along about the mid-1960s they seem to have caught the "bug" that impels certain practitioners of various arts and crafts to strive for perfection.

They came as close as could reasonably be expected with the 1971 vintage from a plot called Maso Scari, one of their two holdings. (The other is Maso Ischia.) That wine, according to Leonardo de Cles, has been compared more than once to Bordeaux, most notably to a Château Pétrus. We drank it in crystal chalices in the drawing room of their palazzo in Mezzolombardo in 1977, and whoever made the Pétrus analogy knows his Pomerol.

"Of course," Michele de Cles explained, "this was a case where everything clicked. We had a dry, hot summer. We harvested at the right moment, using the choicest grapes. We had the feeling that the wine was exceptional by the time it was in the fermenting vats, so the only thing to do was let it take its natural course, to express itself. For uniformity, we aged it in one barrel, Number 13. We haven't had a wine like it before or since."

After bottling in November, 1973, they took some to Asti, where it won a gold medal at a national competition for DOC wine. Yet, as we drank it years later, it was beautiful, no question about it, but not completely ready. Velvety, even somewhat fat, which is not typical of Teroldego, but sturdily structured with 13 percent alcohol, still tannic, mellowing elegantly, it promised still greater things. The brothers were not in accord about when it would reach its prime; one said before 1980, the other said after. By 1977 there were only a few bottles of the original 6,000 left in the cellars, and the barons were in no rush to sell them, even at quadruple the usual price for their Teroldego.

In normal years they make about 60,000 bottles of Teroldego Rotaliano from Maso Scari and Maso Ischia. (*Maso* in Trentino is directly related to *mas*, the Provençal term for a country estate, but the connection is mysterious because *maso* is seldom used elsewhere in Italy.) The barons also make excellent Lagrein, Merlot, and Pinot Bianco and Grigio, which qualify as Trentino DOC and sell at reasonable prices. The 1973 through 1979 Teroldegos from both plots were good; the Maso Scari from 1974 and 1979 were excellent, but not in the class with the 1971.

"You hope for a wine like the Maso Scari 1971 every year," said Michele de Cles. "But if you're lucky, you might get one like it once in a decade. If you're not lucky, it might be once in a lifetime."

Barone de Cles cannot take all the credit for Teroldego's good name. Mario Soldati, in *Vino a Vino*, praised the Teroldego Granato of Pierfranco Donati, so called because of its garnet color, and the Teroldego Rosato of the Fratelli Dorigati, a rosé that Soldati found "more velvety, lighter, more irresistible: above all more perfumed" than the red. The Catalogo Bolaffi gives its maximum three-star rating only to the Teroldego made by Roberto Zeni at Grumo.

The Vines of Trentino: Freedom of Choice

At San Michele all'Adige, on the edge of Teroldego's plain, the Istituto Agrario Provinciale has been a factor behind the unsurpassed regionwide standards of winemaking. Because it is considered — along with Conegliano in the Veneto and Alba in Piedmont — one of Italy's leading schools and research centers for viniculture, its influence is widely felt. Its reputation has been enhanced by the wines it makes and sells to the public from the campus vineyards and cellars. The nine types, all moderately priced, are Riesling, Traminer, Pinot Bianco, Moscato Rosa (a sweet rosé), Pinot Nero, Teroldego, Cabernet, Merlot, and Castel San Michele. The latter, a red made from Cabernet and Merlot, may be the most impressive. Deep, full-bodied, tannic, Castel San Michele, like a fine Bordeaux, needs six to ten years to arrive at peak form.

Trento's wine, Casteller, light and tasty, pale red or rosé, bears a resemblance to some of those inconsequential but good little wines from up around Bolzano. That is no coincidence, for its main grapes are Schiava, though it also contains Lambrusco and Merlot. Although it has DOC status, Casteller is rarely shipped outside the zone that stretches south from Trento to the Veneto. Historically, it has been the carafe wine of a city whose people insist on maintaining standards, old-fashioned as they seem, of discreet good taste.

Trentino's newest DOC zone, approved in 1978, is Sorni in Bianco, Rosso, and Rosato, from vineyards near the town of Lavis and San Michele all'Adige. The white, from Nosiola grapes, is fresh and versatile, especially good with fish. The red, from Lagrein, Schiava, and Teroldego, is dry and richly perfumed, a wine to drink young and slightly cool. The rosé is similar, though lighter and fresher. The Cantina Sociale Lavis-Sorni-Salorno makes these and other local wines well and in amounts adequate to boost the Sorni name on Italian markets.

In Trentino, the names and language are overwhelmingly Italian, but some older people still refer to "Italy" as a place that lies somewhere to the south. One reason might be that they have been forced to change allegiances so often they have lost faith in national government. It is not surprising that people here tend to think of themselves first as citizens of Trentino–Alto Adige and only secondarily as Italians. Living as they do along one of the major north–south arteries of Europe, they have been habitually exposed to foreign ideas and have had access to foreign things. The grapevines, particularly in Trentino, reflect their freedom of choice.

Ten types of wine, with variations, fall into the category of Trentino DOC. They are the red Cabernet, Lagrein, Marzemino, Merlot, and Pinot Nero, and the white Moscato, Pinot (Bianco, Grigio, and Chardonnay — which is technically not a Pinot but is usually listed as one), Riesling, Traminer, and Vin Santo (a sweet wine made from the native Nosiola grape). The breakdown is too intricate to describe in detail, but the basic plan is broad enough and logical enough that Trentino DOC seems to have a head start toward becoming a significant appellation. Certainly the potential is there, some of it already realized. But the program is still relatively new, and some growers have shown a reluctance to participate. As a result, some wines that could be DOC are not.

Marzemino is a native vine, whose wine is most distinguished, from Conte Bossi Fedrigotti at Rovereto. Its vines are not as prolific as Teroldego's, nor do they make as big a wine, but in some years Marzemino can be equally impressive, with a bitter-almond aspect in both aroma and flavor adding to its character. Other good producers are I. Baldo & Figli at Pomarolo, Italo Pedrotti at Nomi, and Leonello Letrari at Nogaredo.

Merlot, in most of Trentino–Alto Adige, is a soft, attractive wine, good to drink from two to six years after harvest. Cabernet, especially in Trentino, can become a wine of real importance that may improve for ten years or more. The Cabernet San Leonardo made by Marchese Anselmo Guerrieri Gonzaga at Borghetto all'Adige is an outstanding example of how well Bordeaux's vines do in Italy. The Marquis combines Cabernet Franc and Cabernet Sauvignon grapes in a wine of noble mien that continues to show its class for hours after a bottle has been opened. Cabernet San Leonardo had been a leading value among truly fine red wine capable of aging, though inflation has gradually forced its price upward. Fratelli Pisoni at Pergolese, Conte Bossi Fedrigotti, and Fratelli Endrizzi at San Michele all'Adige also turn out very good Cabernet.

Conte Bossi Fedrigotti mixes Cabernet Franc and Cabernet Sauvignon with Merlot to make Foianeghe Rosso, which vies with Cabernet San Leonardo for honors as the finest Bordeaux-style wine of Trentino. Foianeghe is more robust but perhaps not as elegant as San Leonardo. Both are superb wines, about equal in price. San Zeno, from the same grapes as Foianeghe but with Merlot dominant, is produced by a cooperative, La Vinicola Sociale, at Aldeno. If not so fine as Foianeghe or Cabernet San Leonardo, its price is lower. A promising operation, La Vinicola Sociale has introduced several other good wines as well.

Mori Vecio includes Merlot and Cabernet Franc, though Lagariavini, its sole producer, will not reveal the precise mixture. The name Mori Vecio has a double significance. Its grapes are grown in a place called Mori and the wine is for aging, thus Vecio (for *vecchio*, old). But it is also supposed to mean *morire vecchio* (to die old), presumably the result of making a steady diet of it.

Lagariavini of Volano, with a production of some 3 million bottles a year, is the largest independent winery in Trentino. It exports to the United States and elsewhere. The region's largest producer is Càvit, a confederation of cooperatives from all over Trentino. Càvit's quality standards are relatively high and its prices relatively low, which explains why it has moved strongly onto the premium market in northern Italy with a vast assortment of wine. Càvit's 4 Vicariati, another Merlot and Cabernet combination, is an outstanding cooperative product.

Fratelli Endrizzi, a small operation, makes a plush Pinot Nero that seems to hit its stride after two or three years. A subtler, longer-lived Pinot Nero is sold under the name Castelsegonzano. It is made by the Cantina Baroni a Prato at Segonzano in the hills northeast of Trento.

The Lagrein made by Barone de Cles from Maso Scari approaches the quality of the Dunkel of Padre Gregor at Gries. Otherwise, though there seems to be plenty of it around, Trentino Lagrein does not often match the Gries standard.

Red wines overshadow whites in Trentino, except in the prestige category of Champagne types, where two firms — Ferrari and Équipe 5 — turn out some of Italy's finest *spumante* from Pinot grapes. Among the still whites, those of the Istituto Agrario Provinciale stand out. The Cantina Sociale Lavis-Sorni-Salorno, at the center of a zone where Pinot grapes for *spumante* are grown, make a fine, dry Pinot from a mixture of Bianco, Grigio, and Chardonnay. A Müller Thurgau made by Fiorentino Sandri at his Azienda Agricola Pojer & Sandri at Faedo is an excellent representative of that high-altitude grape. Sandri's Schiava di Faedo, a rosé, is equally impressive. Remo Calovi, also at Faedo, makes a Müller Thurgau that rivals Sandri's in class.

Moscato is a grapy dessert wine with exceptional aroma. Conte Bossi Fedrigotti, Fratelli Pedrotti, and Fratelli Endrizzi are recommended producers. Vin Santo, made from dried Nosiola grapes, is a richer, denser sweet wine than Moscato; it can improve for twenty years or more in bottle after five years of aging in barrel. A fine version of it is made by the Cantina di Toblino Sarche, near the lake of Toblino, just west of Trento. Most of Italy's "holy wine" comes from Tuscany and central Italy, where it is usually made from Malvasia and Trebbiano grapes. The Trentino Vin Santo is similarly strong (14° to 17° alcohol), with a golden-amber color and rich, smooth texture.

Ferrari, the Champagne of Italian Spumante

One of the endearing traits of the Italian character is its festive spirit, the aptitude, even when times are hard, for finding a reason to celebrate. Italy has an exorbitant number of feast days, but most Italians do not need an official excuse to express their *gioia di vivere*. Sunday, for instance, is reason enough to assemble family and friends for hours to eat good food, make stimulating conversation, and, of course, drink the best wines that Papa can afford. Despite recurring reports in recent years of impending economic disaster, many Italian papas manage to afford rather expensive stuff. Italians habitually drink more genuine Champagne than do any people but the French.

Those Italians whose Champagne tastes are tempered by a sense of patriotism (or thrift) have their own fine wines to choose from, such as the Pinots of Guido Berlucchi in Franciacorta, Contratto and Fontana-fredda in Piedmont, and Angelo Ballabio in the Oltrepò Pavese. But Ferrari of Trento remains the most respected name in Italian sparkling wine.

The firm, founded by Giulio Ferrari in 1902 and sold to the Lunelli family in 1952, calls its wines Gran Spumante, with the notation *"méthode champenoise."* Of all the replicas, this wine may come closest to matching the taste of Champagne.

Ferrari learned to make sparkling wine in France and Germany, then brought in vine cuttings from Champagne to implant in the stony-chalky soil around Lavis, north of Trento, at altitudes between 1,500 and 2,300 feet — high enough to approximate the climate of north-central France. He not only mastered the system, but showed an uncanny sense of the nuances of Champagne as he built his reputation. When other Italians decided to copy Champagne, they had to go only as far as Trento to get the cuttings and witness the work of a man whose style was so true that Ferrari wines won top awards in their class in French competition.

Today, Ferrari production is 300,000 bottles a year in six types: Brut, Nature (a still white), Brut Rosé, Riserva (vintage), Demi-Sec, and an innovation, Brut de Bruts (Blanc de Blancs, meaning it consists entirely of Chardonnay grapes). The firm, run by Gino and Mauro Lunelli, general manager and chief winemaker respectively, grows most of its own grapes — predominately Chardonnay with some Pinot Nero — on thirty acres. It buys more grapes from local growers only on condition that their vines can be inspected and controlled regularly. The Lunelli brothers have resisted temptations to expand production in their new plant at Ravina. Instead they have kept each phase of the Champagne process, from *tirage* to *remuage* to *dégorgement,* in the hands of their own experts. They cite the similarity in their operation and those of medium-sized cultivator-producers of Champagne, such as Bonnaire-Rodhain at Cramant, whose Blanc de Blancs is among the finest made. Ferrari's wines, unavoidably, cost almost as much.

Ferrari Gran Spumante Riserva is noted for its breed, dryness, and *perlage*, the minute and persistent bubbles that distinguish great vintage Champagne. It is served regularly at presidential dinners and receptions at the Quirinale Palace in Rome. Enzo Ferrari, the grand old man of Italian automobile racing, is said to have been flattered when asked if he owned the company. He had to admit he did not, of course, but he always added that he was one of its leading customers.

Équipe 5, an association of five independent producers, turns out 50,000 bottles of *méthode champenoise* a year. From a base of 55 percent Pinot Nero and 45 percent Chardonnay in their brut version, they make a fuller, rounder *spumante* than Ferrari's. Équipe 5 has a following in Trentino that has proclaimed its superiority. To my taste, though, it is not so true to type as Ferrari, but it is a very sound wine and in its own way is equally enjoyable. Càvit makes a Pinot Brut Spumante that is not quite in the league with Ferrari and Équipe 5, though it will do in a pinch for it costs less.

The Vintages

Alto Adige

	Red Wines	White Wines
1979	Great	Great
1978	Exceptional, scarce	Exceptional, scarce
1977	Good to excellent	Good to excellent
1976	Good	Good
1975	Excellent	Good
1974	Good to excellent	Excellent
1973	Good	Uneven, some excellent
1972	Good	Uneven, some good
1971	Excellent	Good to excellent

	Red Wines	White Wines
1970	Fair	Excellent
1969	Excellent, some great	
1968	Good to excellent	

Trentino Red Wines

	Teroldego	Marzemino	Cabernet
1979	Excellent	Excellent	Excellent
1978	Good	Good	Good
1977	Good	Good	Good
1976	Good	Good	Good
1975	Good	Excellent	Good
1974	Very good	Good	Fair
1973	Good	Fair	Fair
1972	Fair	Fair	Fair
1971	Excellent, some great	Excellent	Excellent
1970	Good	Excellent	Great
1969	Excellent	Great	Great
1968	Fair	Poor	Fair
1967	Good	Poor	Good
1966	Good	Excellent	Good
1965	—	Fair	—
1964	Great	Fair	Great

Trentino White Wines

	Pinot, still and spumante	Others
1979	Great	Excellent
1978	Exceptional	Excellent
1977	Excellent	Good to excellent
1976	Excellent	Good
1975	Good	Excellent
1974	Excellent	Very good
1973	Good	Fair to good

	Pinot, still and spumante	Others
1972	Good	Uneven, some good
1971	Excellent	Uneven, some excellent
1970	Excellent	Good

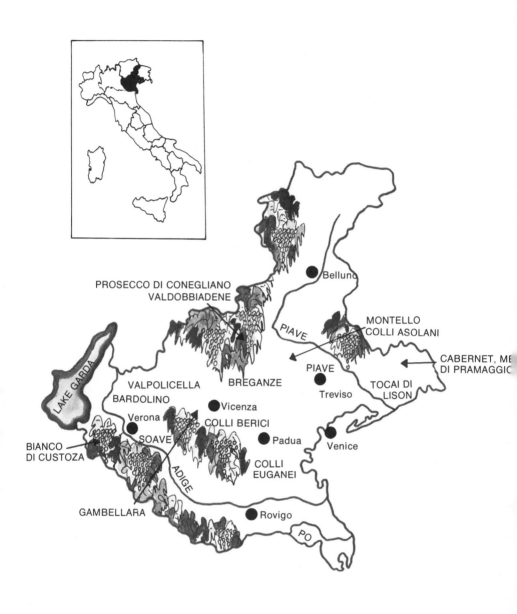

PROSECCO DI CONEGLIANO
VALDOBBIADENE

Belluno

MONTELLO
COLLI ASOLANI

PIAVE

CABERNET, ME
DI PRAMAGGIC

PIAVE

BREGANZE

Treviso

TOCAI DI
LISON

LAKE GARDA

VALPOLICELLA
BARDOLINO

Vicenza

COLLI BERICI

Verona

SOAVE

Padua

Venice

BIANCO
DI CUSTOZA

ADIGE

COLLI
EUGANEI

GAMBELLARA

Rovigo

PO

THE VENETO

PROVINCES

VENICE, Belluno, Padua, Rovigo, Treviso, Verona, Vicenza

POPULATION

4,100,000

AREA

7,098 square miles

AVERAGE WINE PRODUCTION

1 billion liters

DOC WINES

Bardolino (Chiaretto) · Bianco di Custoza · Breganze (Bianco, Cabernet, Pinot Bianco, Pinot Nero, Rosso, Vespaiolo) · Cabernet di Pramaggiore · Colli Berici (Cabernet, Garganega, Merlot, Pinot Bianco, Sauvignon, Tocai, Tocai Rosso) · Colli Euganei (Bianco, Cabernet, Merlot, Moscato, Rosso, Tocai) · Gambellara (Recioto di Gambellara, Vin Santo di Gambellara) · Merlot di Pramaggiore · Montello–Colli Asolani (Cabernet, Merlot, Prosecco) · Piave (Cabernet, Merlot, Tocai, Verduzzo) · Prosecco di Conegliano-Valdobbiadene (Superiore di Cartizze) · Soave (Recioto di Soave) · Tocai di Lison · Valpolicella (Recioto della Valpolicella, Recioto della Valpolicella Amarone, Valpolicella-Valpantena)

OTHER WINES

Cabernet Manzoni (I.M.2,15) · Clinton · Costozza · Durello · FOL · I.M.6,0,13 · Malbec · Masianco · Pinot Bianco · Pinot Grigio · Pinot Nero · Pinot Spumante · Quarto Vecchio · Raboso · Riesling · Rustico · Torcolato · Venegazzù · Verdiso

Plenty of Everything

THE Veneto is Italy's most modern and complete wine region. Its vineyards yield not only great quantities of premium wine but an enormous volume of wine for mass consumption. Three of its wines — Soave, Bardolino, and Valpolicella — are known throughout the world. A few others, not nearly so renowned, are considered great. But Venice's region, above all, is distinguished for its range and diversity.

There is plenty of everything here: hill wines, valley wines, red, white, pink, and amber wines, still or bubbly, dry or sweet, from more varieties of vines — both domestic and foreign — than can be found in any other region of Italy.

Several reasons exist for this diversity. The ravages of phylloxera and war, for example, played roles in the introduction of French, German, and American vines. Perhaps just as important, though, has been the demand for variety in wines from the region's aristocracy — the nobility, traders, and merchants of Venice and other cities — which, from the time of the Venetian Republics, has been respected not only for its wealth and democratic sense of government, but for its civilized taste. This, as anyone who has visited Venezia la Serenissima will have noted, includes a penchant for the exotic. It also includes, if less saliently, an appreciation of the simple and natural things that abound in the soft fertility of the countryside. Every possessor of a villa, however elegant its surroundings, has devoted some space to vines and other things that grow.

The Veneto, with its "Italian wine capital," Conegliano, has led the nation in research and innovation. Its wine industry has been modernized to a degree that it resembles California's in concepts of production and marketing, though rapid expansion recently has put the American state well ahead of the Veneto in volume. Among Italian regions, the Veneto ranks second to Emilia-Romagna in average quantity, but in some years, such as 1972 and 1977, has surpassed it in output. The Veneto's wineries set the standard toward which others throughout Italy are progressing. Though some doubt exists about whether that direction is invariably the right one, by now the trend is irreversible.

Discriminating consumers in Italy and abroad shun wines produced en masse with little or no authentication provided about their origins. But not everyone can afford to be choosy about his wine these days. Such wine, often sold in large bottles with metal caps, has found a receptive market in Italy as well as in Germany, other European countries, and the United States, where it is considered "jug wine."

Not that all the Veneto's wines are produced en masse and sold in outsize containers. Far from it. The region produces and exports more DOC wine by volume than any other. The Veneto boasts some magnificent wines made with the artisan touch. And many large firms go to commendable lengths to provide wines that are not only authentic but good, and in some cases even of exceptional quality. The Veneto's most encouraging influence on Italian production has been in its premium wines made on a large scale.

The well-organized and profitable wine operations here have attracted outside capital. At one point Winefood, the Swiss-based holding company that became a major financial force in Italian wine in the last decade, controlled Folonari, Lamberti, and Maschio, three of the largest firms dealing with the Veneto's wine. Despite a scandal that led to financial losses in the late 1970s, the Winefood empire was holding together and at last report still controlled more than twenty Italian wine and food enterprises. Numerous firms based in other parts of Italy or abroad have also invested in the production and marketing of the Veneto's wines, most notably the popular Veronese trio.

This trend was bucked recently by Zonin, a large Veneto-based producer-bottler-shipper of mainly table wines. Zonin bought up 800 acres of land at Barboursville, Virginia, and planted Cabernet Sauvignon, Pinot Noir, Riesling, and Chardonnay grapes with plans for putting some bottles on the U.S. market in the early 1980s. Zonin, one of Europe's largest wineries, with a growing exportation of DOC and non-DOC Italian wines to the United States, thus gave an unexpected boost to Virginia's new wine industry. The move was the most prominent direct Italian investment in American wine to date, though Italian immigrants individually played a major role in developing America's wine industry.

Verona's Wines: Good and Abundant

South along the Adige River from Trentino, the Alps taper off to foothills and the valleys broaden. To the west, toward Lake Garda, lie the vineyards of Bardolino; to the east, above Verona, those of Valpolicella; and still farther east, those of Soave. These are the Verona wines, the three that have assumed a standing among foreigners as perhaps the most typical of Italy today. As such, they have contributed only moderately to Italy's image as a great wine nation, because Bardolino, Valpolicella, and Soave are rarely categorized as great. But they have played a major part in giving Italian wines their reputation as good, abundant, and reasonably priced; from a consumer's perspective, there is a great deal to admire in that.

From the Brenner-Verona *autostrada*, Bardolino's Classico zone can be seen just north of the Affi turnoff, in the hills between the Adige and Lake Garda. Bardolino, a pretty lakeside town, is the axis of the historic growing area that includes the towns of Affi, Costermano, Garda, Lazise, and Cavaion. The broader Bardolino zone includes Torri del Benaco, Ricoli, Castelnuovo, Peschiera, and Sommacampagna.

Bardolino, both red and Chiaretto (or rosé), is most adaptable with food. It comes from Corvina (at 50 to 65 percent), Rondinella, Molinara, and Negrara grapes vinified to render light-bodied, refreshing wines to be drunk young. Under DOC rules, Bardolino must have 10.5° alcohol, the *superiore*, aged fifteen months, at least 11.5°. The red, of a brilliant ruby color, goes with most any pasta or risotto, antipasto, or meat dish, especially highly flavored or piquant stews with a base of poultry or veal. Chiaretto, bright cherry pink, is a luncheon wine suitable with fish or salads, or pleasant for casual summer sipping. Some producers have also been making a *novello* version to be consumed within months of the harvest, so far the only "new wine" among Italy's DOCs.

Bardolino and its neighboring towns, blissfully quiet in the cold months, become crowded resorts in summer. The zone is noted for good restaurants — notably Aurora and Speranza–da Attilio in Bardolino and Da Remigio al Bellavista at Costermano — which usually serve wines from their own vineyards or purchased from small wineries. A not particularly well-kept secret is that the "real" Bardolino from the smaller vineyards is reserved for home consumption. Another secret of good Bardolino is knowing how and when to serve it. The practice is red at room temperature in winter, cellar temperature in summer; Chiaretto at cellar temperature in winter, refrigerated in summer. Although youthful freshness is the key to the goodness of both, some red from fine vintages is put away for two or more years to mellow into wine of some depth. Such wine rarely leaves the area.

In Bardolino, the distinction *superiore* indicates a bit more depth, but "Classico" is not necessarily a mark of higher quality. Much Bardolino sold abroad is produced by large firms from purchased grapes, skillfully made by oenologists who seek a consistent standard year after year. That is not an easy goal to achieve, and each producer has his own degree of success. But collectively the makers of Bardolino — and Valpolicella and Soave — have earned their reputation for reliability. Their wines are widely appreciated as accompaniment to the overseas version of an Italian meal (which is, as anyone who has visited Italy knows, rarely of the proportions of the home version).

Among reliable exporters of Bardolino are Bertani, Bolla, Lamberti, Masi, Montresor, Pasqua, Santi, and Fratelli Tedeschi. Bottles from some producers with excellent local reputations are also worth watching for: Ca' Furia, Colle dei Cipressi, Innocente Campostrini, Rosino Ferri, Girasole, Gianni Lonardi, Umberto Peretti, Fratelli Poggi, Luigi Rossi, Taborro, Le Tende, Tre Colline, and Aldo Zanon.

Valpolicella and Recioto: Sunlight and Soul

Valpolicella at its best has more to it than does Bardolino, a bit more color, depth, sturdiness, and durability, though it is made from almost the same combination of grapes: Corvina at 55 to 70 percent, Rondinella at 25 to 30 percent, and Molinara at up to 15 percent. Its yield of grapes per hectare is slightly lower than that allowed for Bardolino, and the minimum alcohol content is slightly higher: 12° for *superiore,* which is aged a year, and 11° for the regular version. The same standards apply to Valpolicella-Valpantena, from the valley to the east of the Classico zone. Valpolicella, especially the Classico and *superiore,* can be an excellent wine, though rarely a big one. To make up for that, some producers also make Recioto, one of the biggest red wines anywhere.

Recioto is so called because its grapes come from the ears, the *recie* (from *orecchie*), those at the upper perimeter of each cluster that receive the most sun. They are semi-dried to concentrate their sugars, then pressed into musts that can make either sweet and sometimes sparkling Recioto or, when all the sugar is converted to alcohol in the vinification, the dry Recioto Amarone, one of Italy's most distinguished red wines. Deeply colored, strong (from 13° to 17° alcohol), velvety, full of character, good Amarone goes well with a rich meal or a strong cheese, though some are so dignified they demand only an hour or two of breathing to stand all alone — and in a class by themselves.

Parts of the Valpolicella and Valpantena zones overlook Verona, a comfortably middle-sized city with a well-preserved ancient center known to the world as the setting of *Romeo and Juliet*. Verona and its hills still have a romantic look about them: urban palaces and rural villas set amidst gardens surrounded by stone walls beyond which lie orchards and vineyards. Although wine is an important factor in the local economy, even on the scale practiced here the industry does not mar the beauty of the countryside.

The hills of Valpolicella rise rather sharply from the Adige valley and Verona to high woodlands. Grouped on the slopes between 600 and 1,600 feet are hundreds of vineyards of various size, their density particularly noticeable around Negrar, Marano, and Fumane in the Classico zone, and near Grezzana in the Valpantena. East of there, the zone coincides with that of Soave.

Some dispute whether Valpantena is distinctive enough to warrant its special denomination. But its quality, like that of the others, depends at least as much on who makes the wine as on where it comes from. And although much Valpolicella and Valpolicella-Valpantena are turned out on a grand scale, there are individuals around who make their wine with an encouraging measure of personal pride and enthusiasm.

One is Maria Marta Galli Bortoletto, who until just a few years ago was occupied with being a housewife and mother of four, maintaining an apartment in Verona while restoring a farmhouse in the hills above. She had always had a taste for fine wine, so when her husband, Arnaldo, an oenologist at one of the large Veronese wine firms, suggested that the vines at their country house, Le Ragose, ought to be revived and expanded, she decided to take up the challenge. She has since made a career of it. Over the years she planted and pruned, hired a farmer to help with some of the hard work, and "with a little study and a lot of learning by doing" she was soon making wine.

"It started really as a hobby," she said, "but before long it became an obsession, and every year it seems to get more fascinating. Oh, there were problems. You can't imagine the problems unless you're involved

Maria Marta Galli Bortoletto

in winemaking. But my husband helped me when I needed it, and some years the wine has been really quite good, I think."

Signora Galli Bortoletto was showing her modest side. The fourth *Catalogo Bolaffi dei vini d'Italia* gave her Valpolicella Classico the ultimate three-star rating, the only Valpolicella so honored. Other critics have been similarly impressed.

"That is flattering," she said, "though I'm not so sure that others don't deserve the same. Valpolicella is an underestimated wine. Some big companies make it well, too."

She turns out about 30,000 bottles a year, of which some 3,000 are Amarone. Eventually production could reach 100,000 bottles. She also makes for family and friends a lightly sparkling white wine from the same grapes as Soave. Signora Galli Bortoletto's success is not, she insists, the result of any effort to prove a point.

"Anyone who thinks that only men can make fine wine is just sadly naive," she said. "Experience is very important, of course, but once that's acquired, it's not your sex that counts, it's your soul."

Another woman with the soul or whatever it takes to make good Valpolicella is Luisa dall'Ora in Mazzi, who runs the Azienda Agricola Sanperetto at Negrar. Among the men, Giuseppe Quintarelli at Ceré di Negrar makes Valpolicella in the classic style. Mario Soldati, in his first volume of *Vino a Vino*, determined that Quintarelli's must be the Valpolicella closest to that described by Hemingway in *Across the River and Into the Trees*, the frequent mention of which enhanced the wine's legend abroad. The author, like the characters in his book, downed impressive quantities of the wine (along with grappa, which may have originated in the region) while writing at the Gritti in Venice. Quintarelli's Amarone is also noteworthy. Dry, ever so slightly bitter, mouthfilling, a bit woody, and long on the palate, it is the sort of wine to contemplate with patience.

At Masi, a moderately large company with an international reputation, winemaster Nino Franceschetti believes in thinking small, at least in terms of the size of the batches in which he makes his Recioto. Franceschetti, considered one of the foremost winemakers of Italy, specializes in Amarone but makes his sweet Recioto with equal skill and contemplation. The wine comes from the ears of selected grape clusters from vines grown in certain of the company's vineyards. Made in lots of about 2,000 to 5,000 bottles each, though costly, they are in line with the effort and expense involved in their making.

Franceschetti has earned himself a following in the Veronese winemaking community and elsewhere that, it can be hoped, may lead to some beneficial trends. For example, he believes it is a mistake to leave a Recioto very long in wood, or to vinify for a hard wine.

"The beauty of Recioto is its roundness, softness, and harmony," he said. "It should be somewhat fat, but not heavy, and it should not be too tannic. Long barrel aging is not as essential to achieving the desired balance as some people think."

Franceschetti revealed his growing conviction in a theory he calls *vino da luce*, or wine of light. He believes grapes, and the wine they produce, are more dependent on the quality of the sunlight that reaches their leaves than on temperature, precipitation, or even the soil their vines grow in.

"Great wines owe their greatness to the photosynthesis of light," he said. "Bordeaux has the Atlantic; the great German wines have the reflection of sunlight off the Rhine. Here in Verona we have Lake Garda, but we haven't been taking full advantage of it."

Franceschetti wants to see growers return to the more painstaking training of vines onto tilted pole arms, the Trentino method that gives the foliage maximum exposure to the sun's rays.

"Our fathers used the Trentino method and though they didn't have the technology we have now, they sometimes had better grapes to work with. Look at the French: they haven't got our climate, but they have had the good sense to make optimum use of what they have. If we Italians are to prove ourselves, we need to exploit more wisely our superior raw materials. For quality of sunlight no one can match us, but we've got to improve our follow-through."

If everyone had Franceschetti's follow-through, the match would be no contest. His Amarones rank among the nation's most elegant red wines, each remarkable for its individual expression of superior prime materials. That expression is Franceschetti's forte, and it can be sensed in some of the less complex Masi wines as well. For example, Campo Fiorin is a full-fledged Valpolicella until it is pumped into a vat with the lees left over from the fermentation of an Amarone. This induces a refermentation, giving the wine some of the fatness and softness of the Amarone.

"Some people thought that was a stroke of genius," said Franceschetti, "but if you want to know the truth, I started doing it because I didn't want to waste those good Amarone lees. It was an economically motivated experiment that produced a very pleasing result. I understand some other wineries are doing the same now."

Masi also produces a Valpolicella Classico *superiore* from grapes grown in its own vineyards and a crisp, dry, elegant white called Masianco. Its Bianco di Campociesa may be the most admired and costly of all sweet Recioto. The firm's Bardolino and Soave are made chiefly from purchased grapes.

Although my taste is decidedly for the Amarone, some sweet and sparkling Recioto is highly prized in Italy and has found admirers abroad as well. It goes well with fruit, and certain pungent cheeses, but it is probably best on its own before or after dinner. All types of Recioto can be kept for years in the cellar, though it is wise to drink the *spumante* type inside five years.

Amarone has been especially well received in North America recently, one reason a shortage has developed in Italy. Some major houses are trying to increase production, though Amarone is difficult and costly to make. Even with elevated prices, producers make little profit on it. Bertani and Bolla have excellent vintage Amarone available on foreign markets, some of it dating to such fine vintages as 1961, 1964, 1967, and 1969. Though not always easy to find, Amarone has been giving foreigners a taste of how excellent the wines of Verona can be. Unlike many other big red wines of Italy, Amarone is remarkably easy to drink, immediately pleasing to experienced and inexperienced wine drinkers alike. There seems little question that it has a bright future in foreign lands if producers can continue to increase supplies.

Some other firms with good Recioto and Recioto Amarone on the market are Aldegheri, Allegrini, Luigi Righetti, Guerrieri Rizzardi, Santa Sofia, Santi, Fratelli Speri, Fratelli Tedeschi, and Villa Girardi.

As for Valpolicella, most should be drunk within two to four years, though some winemakers insist that their Classico *superiore* from good vintages will benefit from more aging. From exceptional vintages, such wines might even hold up for a dozen years. Still, most Valpolicella sold abroad is not wine to lay down and forget about. Even when a Valpolicella is well made, as it often is, stabilization is a normal process for any wine to be exported. So, once bottled, this wine is not likely to develop much. Secco-Bertani is an extremely reliable and widely available Valpolicella. Among other very good ones are Santi's Castello d'Illasi, which resembles Campo Fiorin, and the Classico of Luigi Righetti, Salvalai, and Fratelli Tedeschi.

Soave, America's Favorite Italian White

Soave has emerged as the most popular of the Verona wines abroad, most notably in the United States, where consumption of white wine has increased dramatically in recent years. Americans drank more Soave in 1977, 1978, and 1979 than they did Chianti, making it the second largest selling Italian wine in the United States after Lambrusco. Soave merits its popularity, for it is refreshing, reliable, and reasonably priced.

Also working in its favor is availability; some 45 million liters of Soave are produced each year, second to Chianti among DOC wines. Thus, when the boom in American consumption of white wine began a few years ago, producers and shippers were able to meet a demand that has continued to grow at a rapid pace. No wonder Soave is considered the most representative Italian wine in the United States today.

Soave's vineyards have been extended well beyond the limits of the picturesque little town dominated by a castle, an inviting tourist stop because of its wine and its position smack beside the Autostrada La Serenissima that runs from Milan to Venice. Soave's DOC zone now extends almost to Verona on the west, to San Giovanni Ilarione on the north, and to Roncá on the east. Most of the better Soave comes from the Classico zone, a rather limited area lying to the north and east of the town.

Its grapes are Garganega at 70 to 90 percent and Trebbiano di Soave from vines of heavy yield. Soave, which must have at least 10.5° alcohol, is light and dry, pale straw with greenish tinges, best to drink within a few months to two years after the harvest. Wines of 11.5° or more of alcohol aged for eight months to develop a fruity mellowness may be called *superiore*. A Soave *spumante* is also produced.

For decades the house wine at the seafood restaurants of Venice, Soave became known elsewhere in Italy soon after the Cantina Sociale di Soave was founded in 1930 by Luigi Zannini, a pioneer of the concept of making premium wines on a large scale. The Cantina Sociale, one of Europe's largest wineries, still dominates production, selling wine not only under its own name but to brand-name bottlers and shippers as well. Some private producers, notably Bolla, have developed their own grape sources in the zone.

Bolla has set the pace in America by making its name almost synonymous with the good quality Soave Classico sold across the United States. Soave Bolla is by now familiar to anyone who knows Italian wine. A family firm headed by Bruno Bolla, it has followed an intelligent strategy to become the Verona area's largest exporter to the United States, supplementing its Soave with Valpolicella, Bardolino, the Reciotos, and Spumante. The 60,000 annual bottles of a special Soave from the family's Castellaro vineyard were distributed initially only in Italy.

From the 3,360 bottles sent to the United States in 1948 to the more than 10 million shipped in 1979, Bolla has maintained a rigorous code of consistent quality, stable prices, and sound promotion. When some other Veronese firms started using the Chianti-style flask a couple decades ago, Bolla refused to follow suit. By now most others are back to normal bottles and still trailing Bolla in sales. (The firm was second to Riunite, the Lambrusco-oriented cooperative complex of Emilia-Romagna, on the U.S. market in 1976, 1977, and 1978.) Like Masi — and one should not neglect Bertani and Lamberti among other big firms — Bolla has proved that the quality and consistency of a wine does not need to decrease as the size of the operation grows.

Bruno Bolla attributes success primarily to the personal way he and his late brother and predecessor Sergio have run the business. A burly, amiable, straight-talking businessman with a doctorate in engineering, Bruno Bolla makes a point of knowing at first hand all of the hundreds of persons who, directly or indirectly, stand behind the company's name.

"We're a big firm, but I can assure you we're not a wine factory," he said. "In a business where quality is everything, you have to know and trust the people who deliver that quality. For instance, we don't just buy grapes on the open market; we buy them from select cultivators only in the Soave Classico zone under a gentlemen's agreement. Our four hundred grape growers belong to what they call the Club Viticultori Soave Bolla, a free association with no legal status whose continuing success is based solely on mutual benefit and respect. We have a system for rating the quality of each grower's grapes, and we reward the best with bonuses and prizes. We provide, free of charge, all sorts of assistance on vine care, fertilization, anything to insure superior quality grapes. As you know, there is no substitute for that."

Bolla is one of the most modern and well-equipped wineries in Italy, with a staff of experienced oenologists to make the wine. More than half the firm's production is sold in the United States.

So much Soave is made in quantity that it is something of a revelation to find a small-scale producer in the zone. Cantina Fratelli Pieropan is a relatively modest enterprise, whose wine from vineyards at Monte Calvarino is often cited among the finest of Soave. The Pieropan Riesling is equally impressive. Santi is another medium-sized winery with a well-earned reputation for quality in Italy, expressed not only in its DOC wines but in a remarkably acidulous white known as Durello.

Recioto di Soave, a dessert wine, sometimes sparkling, is made in somewhat the same way as is Recioto della Valpolicella. It develops a deep golden color, and it can be kept for five or six years. Most of the large firms make this Recioto in limited quantity, as do Pieropan and Santi. Recioto di Soave must have 14° alcohol, a sweeter *liquoroso* version 16°.

Gambellara and Custoza

Gambellara, a white DOC wine made in the zone adjoining Soave on the east in the province of Vicenza, is almost identical to its neighbor, though it is not nearly so well known. The Cantina Sociale di Gambellara produces a white wine comparable to some of the better Soave. Its Gambellara has been selling in Italy at roughly two-thirds the price of Soave, which makes it an excellent value. Enough is produced that more Gambellara will undoubtedly be destined for export.

Gambellara's DOC code provides for a *superiore* of 11.5° alcohol as well as Recioto Bianco, both still and sparkling, and Vin Santo, from the same grapes — Garganega and Trebbiano di Soave — as the dry Gambellara. The Vin Santo of at least 14° alcohol requires two years of aging before it can be sold.

Another DOC wine from Verona province, Bianco di Custoza, seems destined for wider recognition than it enjoys at present. Named for the tiny village of Custoza, a few kilometers southeast of Verona, its vineyards extend into the Bardolino zone along Lake Garda. Bianco di Custoza is made from Trebbiano Toscano, Garganega, and Tocai principally, usually into a still wine, though some *spumante* is produced. Several bottles I have tasted have been equal to good Soave, notably from Cavalchina, Gorgo, San Leone, Santa Sofia, and Villa Medici. More Bianco di Custoza seems to have become available as the demand for white wine increases. It deserves a try as a worthy alternative to Soave. Cavalchina's Pinot Bianco is crisper and more elegant than the Bianca di Custoza.

In the southernmost reaches of Verona province at Bevilacqua in the Po flatlands, Quarto Vecchio makes respectable wines from French varietals: Cabernet, Merlot, and Pinot Grigio. The finest is a *riserva*, from Cabernet and Merlot, aged five years in wood before bottling and capable of improving another five years after that. Much of Quarto Vecchio's production is exported to the United States.

Colli Berici: Mushrooms and Wine

From Vicenza a range of hills known as the Colli Berici protrudes south into the Po Valley. Once noted for underground quarries from which came much of the building stone and statuary used in the Venetian villas designed by Andrea Palladio in the sixteenth century, the hills now serve as a center for various forms of agriculture. Mushrooms and fine wine figure in the range of prestigious products largely through the endeavors of one man: Conte Alvise da Schio, scion of the patrician family of Costozza, a village at the eastern edge of the hills.

Conte da Schio, who describes himself in tones more defiant than boastful as "one of the last true noblemen left in this country," sat at his desk in a small study in his villa one winter morning and related how the American military, through an almost incredible bungle, forced him to abandon his first love (mushrooms) for his second (wine). That course of events, however pathetic, led to the emergence of one of Italy's great Cabernets.

Da Schio's grandfather, also named Alvise, in the 1880s introduced Cabernet, Pinot, and Riesling vines to the Colli Berici in vineyards that had been famous for wine since at least 1330. He and his son Giulio were dedicated winemakers who brought renewed prestige to Berici wines. But when Giulio was killed in battle on the final day of World War I, young Alvise was left with vineyards that did not especially interest him, for he had become infatuated by mushrooms. In addition to the vineyards, the family estate had more than ten acres of caves quarried for stone for Orazio Marinalli, the tireless sculptor who created many of the statues for the region's Palladian villas. Seeing that the caves would make ideal mushroom grounds, Alvise, after taking his degree in mushroom culture at the University of Florence, went to Paris to acquire the spores and other material for his own undertaking.

"I became known as the father of the cultivated mushroom in this country," he said. "I introduced them everywhere, from the Alps to Sicily, all straight from these caves." And, as if to prove his point, he pulled a cloth-bound tome from a bookshelf and plopped it down in front of me. *La coltivazione industriale dei funghi commestibili*, read the title, "Alvise da Schio. 1932."

Alvise da Schio

Between the wars he made a fortune propagating mushrooms, but when the Axis armies started looking for places to hide their materiel, they were naturally attracted to his caves. First the German army moved in, and, as fortunes turned, the Americans arrived to establish an air base in Vicenza.

"After the war I thought I'd be able to return to my mushrooms," he said, "but no, it turned out that the Colli Berici were at dead center of the European military theater, so the American command took advantage of its postwar security rights and sequestered my caves as atomic warhead launching sites.

"It was heartbreaking. In they moved with mines and bulldozers, clearing more space for missiles. I told them, 'Be careful, those caves are centuries old and they need support,' but I guess they thought that was sour grapes. Anyhow, I know some GIs who are thankful that America invented the five-day week, because one Saturday morning when they were on weekend leave the ceiling collapsed, four hectares of caves gone forever.

"Well, I sued for damages and I won eventually, though I still haven't seen any money. There were a few caves left after the collapse, but I rent them out. I was so demoralized I vowed never to return to mushroom cultivation. And from then on I devoted myself to my vines."

The vineyards had been in use right along, but only for wines for the family's consumption and sale in bulk. A perfectionist, Conte da Schio boned up on viticulture and oenology and by 1960 he had brought his Cabernet, Pinot Rosato, and Riesling wines to a level that he saw fit to sell in labeled bottles.

The Cabernet, primarily from Cabernet Franc, is now considered one of the nation's great red wines, even judged by some to be the Italian product closest in nature to the wines of some storied estates of Bordeaux. Though it unquestionably has some of that class, it is unmistakably a product of Costozza, of the volcanic earth and the benign microclimate. Aged in oak in some of the remaining deep, dry caves, it is usually softer and less imposing than the great Cabernet wines of Bordeaux and it takes less time to develop. One cave, the Grotta Orazio Marinalli, contains statues by the old master, providing one of the most artistic settings imaginable for aging wine.

Da Schio's production, which now includes a smooth, fruity Pinot Rosso as well as the Riesling and Pinot Rosato, sells well in Italy. Nonetheless, the Count had consented to ship some abroad, mostly to the United States, though Costozza Cabernet failed to make much of an impression there the first time around. A more recent bid by a U.S. importer fell through after Da Schio went ahead and had labels printed to U.S. specifications and arranged the shipment. "We shook hands on the deal," Da Schio recalled bitterly, "and I never heard from him again."

Da Schio looked out the window onto the statued gardens of his estate and shook his head. "And yet," he said evenly, "I don't hate Americans, though God only knows why." He said he had decided, however, to avoid further foreign dealings. "Much as I'd like to have my wine judged abroad, it just isn't worth the trouble."

Outstanding as Da Schio's wines are, they are rivaled in quality by those of Alfredo Lazzarini on the other side of the Colli Berici at Villa dal Ferro. Lazzarini makes three whites — Bianco del Rocolo (Pinot Bianco), Busa Calcara (Riesling), and Costiera Granda (Tocai) — and three reds — Campo del Lago (Merlot), Le Rive Rosse (Cabernet Franc and Sauvignon), and Rosso del Rocolo (Pinot Nero). All confirm the potential of these hills for outstanding wine.

Lazzarini prices his Pinot Nero slightly higher than the other reds, though I found both the Merlot and Cabernet more to my taste. The Merlot from 1972, an average year, was smooth, round, sturdy enough to last another decade, though by 1977 it was well balanced with the *goudron*, that hint of tar in aroma and flavor, that distinguishes certain Merlots. The Cabernet, also from 1972, was lighter and more refined than the Merlot; though not as big a wine, it was delightful to drink five years later. The Pinot Nero from 1973 was soft, perfumed, apparently approaching a peak after four years.

Other good producers are emerging in the Colli Berici as well. DOC recognition was granted recently for the red Cabernet, Merlot, and Tocai Rosso (a rare vine from Friuli–Venezia Giulia), and the white Garganega, Tocai, Pinot Bianco, and Sauvignon. But Da Schio, a prime mover behind the establishment of DOC, has chosen not to take part.

"At this point, what is DOC going to do for Costozza?" he asked. "Anyhow, I'm too old to worry about all that now."

But age has not dampened his drive to excel. He donned a heavy camel's-hair coat and led me at a rapid gait on a tour of his vines and cantina. After shaking hands and warmly greeting several hired hands, he got into an animated discussion with his cellarmaster about the malfunction of a pump, tapping loudly on barrels and hoses with a walking stick as he made his point about how nobody and nothing worked in Italy anymore.

Colli Euganei: Spas and Vineyards

East of the Colli Berici in the province of Padua lie the Colli Euganei, the sheerness and height of their humped forms dramatized by their abrupt rise from the floor of the Po Valley. In Italy, volcanic hills almost invariably harbor mineral springs and vines. The Colli Euganei have been noted for spas and vineyards since before Roman times. When Petrarch bought a villa there in 1370 he made note of the olive grove and vineyard, apparently one of many that clothed the hills then.

But, as elsewhere, viniculture lapsed for a time; until recently the hills provided wines for consumption in homes, bars, and restaurants, rarely any farther away than Padua, Rovigo, or Venice. A revival that gained impetus after World War II led to DOC for Colli Euganei Rosso, Bianco, and Moscato. The discipline was being expanded to cover Cabernet, Merlot, and Tocai, varietals that should add prestige to the name Colli Euganei.

The Cantina Sociale Cooperativa Colli Euganei at Vó makes all types not only on a large scale but well. The Luxardo de' Franchi firm, which devised the maraschino cherry in Yugoslavia and after the war moved the operation here, is in the wine business as well. Its Monte Venda white and Sant'Elmo red are among the best of their types in the Colli Euganei. The red, made chiefly from Merlot with a measure of Cabernet Franc and a touch of Barbera included, is a warm, dry, generous wine that improves with five years of age. The white, from Garganega, Serprina, and Sauvignon, has a rich golden color and notable strength of character; it is best drunk within one to three years. Both are *superiore*, meaning they contain at least 12° alcohol and have undergone some aging in barrel. Other Colli Euganei wineries make both still and sparkling versions of Rosso, Bianco, Cabernet, Merlot, Moscato, and Tocai, DOC wines that are not well known outside the Venice-Padua area.

Merlot, Cabernet, and Pinot Grigio

Viticulture is so intense throughout the Veneto, a region of small, prosperous cities and luxuriant countryside, that it is sometimes difficult to discern where one wine zone ends and another begins. Even between mountain and valley there is rarely any significant break in the pattern of vineyards, though there are important variations in the sorts of wine they render. Overall, the number of grape varieties, split between foreign and domestic, is astounding.

In the plains, washed by the Piave and other Alpine rivers flowing toward the Adriatic, wine production is variable: industrialized in places, artisanal in others. The subalpine hills extending from north of Vicenza past Treviso to Conegliano and Belluno have a geographical coherence and evident affinity for vines, though the wines made from one zone to the next show distinct variations in character. Merlot has emerged as the predominant grape variety of the central and eastern Veneto, and indeed of all northeastern Italy, due to its prolific nature and the consistent sturdiness of the wines it makes.

Merlot, like Cabernet, the Pinots, Sauvignon, Johannisberg Riesling, and other vines of foreign origin now prominent in Italy, has been around so long it deserves native status. Many French vines were introduced early in the nineteenth century, during the Napoleonic era; by the turn of the century they were cultivated in most regions of Italy. Phylloxera and the subsequent need to graft vines onto American rootstock forced cultivators to be more selective about varieties. In the northeast, where Merlot, Cabernet, and Pinot were well established, they became dominant. But in other parts of Italy, native vines such as Sangiovese, Barbera, Nebbiolo, and Trebbiano were favored.

Merlot, whose vines thrive in the environment of the Tre Venezie, owes its popularity to its soft, tasty, easy drinkability. It can be a rather common wine at times, but when fashioned by skillful winemakers it achieves noteworthy levels as a varietal. Cabernet, widely acclaimed as the noblest of the world's noble vines, often makes more elegant wine, though its vines are slightly less productive and more difficult to cultivate than Merlot.

Both Cabernet and Merlot, which are considered low-altitude vines in northern Italy, do well in flatlands, such as the Veneto's lower Piave and Pramaggiore, Trentino's Adige valley, and Friuli–Venezia Giulia's Grave. The gradual shift of vineyards from the hills toward the plains in northern Italy has been working in favor of Cabernet and Merlot. Mechanized cultivation is more efficient in lowlands, where heartier clones and improved methods of vine treatment have overcome some habitual drawbacks of humid, poorly drained soil.

Cabernet Franc is generally favored over Cabernet Sauvignon in the Tre Venezie, a factor that has aroused the curiosity of some outsiders, who consider the Sauvignon subvariety the worthier of the two. One explanation is that Cabernet Franc is more to traditional local taste, that it makes a rounder, fruitier wine that is ready to drink sooner. Cabernet Sauvignon tends to be somewhat hard and tannic and require aging to reach peak form. Both Merlot and Cabernet (whose subvarieties may often be mixed) are varietal wines in numerous zones of the Tre Venezie.

In Bordeaux, of course, mixing is the rule, though different formulas are followed in the Médoc and Graves (where Cabernet Sauvignon usually dominates Merlot, Malbec, and Petit Verdot) and Pomerol and St. Emilion (where Merlot often dominates Cabernet Franc and the others). However, in many parts of the world, Cabernet Sauvignon stands as a 90 to 100 percent varietal — in California, for example. The trend in Italy seems to be toward Cabernet Sauvignon either alone or as the dominant variety, and the result has been some exquisite wines.

Many winemakers in the Tre Venezie, however, seem to be following the historic Bordeaux patterns of composite wines, even though in some cases it costs them DOC. They have been achieving more complex, more elegant wines than ever before in a remarkable range of styles and flavors. That is why any attempt to "type" Italian Merlot or Cabernet or composites of the Bordeaux genre is no longer valid.

Among the light foreign varietals, Pinot Grigio has emerged in recent times as the favorite in Italy and abroad, so popular that consumers cannot seem to get enough of it. Though it, too, is DOC in many zones, reaching peaks of quality in parts of Friuli–Venezia Giulia and Trentino–Alto Adige, there is decidedly not enough delimited Pinot Grigio to meet the demand. The answer has been a rather ubiquitous product often labeled as Pinot Grigio delle Venezie or Tre Venezie. Enterprising producers have taken advantage of the *vino da tavola* with geographical indication to identify these wines whose authenticity has been the object of considerable skepticism in Italy. It seems likely that Pinot Grigio delle Tre Venezie will become one of the early *vini tipici*, which would at least subject it to some measure of control. Meanwhile, if you want to be sure that you are drinking what the label says it is, it would be wise to limit your choices to DOC Pinot Grigio.

Breganze, Montello, and Venegazzù

The Breganze zone, in Vicenza's province, reaches from Thiene on the west to Bassano del Grappa on the east. Its wines are gaining respect in Italy for their sound quality and reasonable price. More than a thousand growers there in 1950 formed an association to define, improve, and promote their wines. They succeeded in getting DOC status for their Breganze Bianco (at least 85 percent Tocai), Breganze Rosso (at least 85 percent Merlot), Cabernet, Pinot Bianco, Pinot Nero, and Vespaiolo, a white from the native vine of that name, which is also sometimes called Bresparolo.

As a rule, Breganze wines, both red and white, are to drink young when they show a particular delicacy and fragrance. Only the Cabernet *superiore* of 12° alcohol is recommended for aging, and then only for four or five years. The most prized wine of Breganze is Torcolato, a sweet white from Vespaiolo, Garganega, and Tocai grapes, semi-dried and pressed about five months after the harvest. Torcolato is not classified under DOC. Some Breganze wines are now being exported. They are worth watching for: good wines at moderate prices. Maculan is a leading producer of Breganze quality wines. Cantina B. Bartolomeo is also reliable.

Brassano del Grappa is known for its asparagus, its covered wooden bridge over the Brenta that has been destroyed and rebuilt numerous times, and, of course, its grappa, which shares its name with the mountain range north of the town. Good grappa is distilled here from the pressings left over from the countless wines made in the vicinity. Merlot and Cabernet do well in the hills east of Bassano, sometimes reaching heights of great distinction on the soft slopes of the Montello range in the province of Treviso.

The wines of Montello–Colli Asolani, newest of the Veneto's DOC districts, are three: Prosecco (both still and *spumante*), Merlot (whose *superiore* version must have at least 11.5° alcohol and two years' aging), and Cabernet (also with a *superiore* that must have 12° and two years' aging). Merlot dominates production.

At Volpago del Montello, the Conti Loredan fashioned their Venegazzù into one of the most fabled names in Italian wine. Made at the Villa Gasparini Loredan by what is described as a secret method from Cabernet Sauvignon, Cabernet Franc, Malbec, and Merlot, the Venegazzù reserve approaches the pinnacle of stature among Italian wines in the Bordeaux style. It is often found on the wine lists of Italy's most elegant restaurants. A small amount is being exported as well. A Venegazzù Cabernet and Venegazzù Bianco, from Pinot Bianco with a touch of Riesling Italico, are also good wines, though not in the class of the reserve. The Conti Loredan now also make a *méthode champenoise* from Pinot grapes that ranks with Italy's finest.

The Montello hills are known for wild mushrooms and game birds served at the local restaurants in fall and early winter. Some gourmets dispute whether the best restaurant is Da Celeste alla Costa d'Oro at Volpago or Agnoletti at Giavera del Montello. Without deciding that issue, I can confirm that food and wine are splendid at both. The Cabernet made by Leone Agnoletti for his restaurant is an extraordinary house wine, the equal of any varietal Cabernet of the area.

Prosecco: Sparkling and "Simpatico"

North of the Montello hills the Piave valley opens toward Conegliano and Valdobbiadene and another range of Alpine foothills known as the Marca Trevigiana. Vineyards for both red and white wines are among the most carefully cultivated in Italy; the oenological research center and agricultural institute at Conegliano carries out advanced experimentation on vines here, a factor that presents itself in the quality of the wines.

A native variety, Prosecco, gets the greatest share of attention. Its grapes are used for a special white wine whose most popular version is a light *spumante*. Prosecco di Conegliano-Valdobbiadene, which varies in style from delicately sweet to fairly dry, is among the most *simpatico* of Italian sparkling wines. Naturally refermented in either bottle or vat, it becomes a wine of about 10.5° alcohol that may be either a *spumante* or a *frizzante*, the less bubbly version more appreciated locally because it can be drunk with such abandon. There is also a still Prosecco.

The hilly DOC zone in Treviso's province forms a triangle between Conegliano, Valdobbiadene, and Vittorio Veneto. It has what is considered a classic section around the town of Cartizze; wines of 11° alcohol from there may be called Superiore di Cartizze. The various Proseccos and Cartizze show considerable differences in style. The still and *frizzante* versions are allowed to use Pinot Bianco and Grigio grapes with the Prosecco at a maximum of 15 percent. The *spumante* may contain as much as 25 percent Pinot.

Another difference is that winemakers have a choice of how to vinify and, perhaps because this is a center of active ferment in the techniques of production, a dazzling array of styles is evident in the wines. Some use the charmat method; some a rather simple type of refermentation in bottle; others the more complex and time consuming *méthode champenoise*. As a consequence, quality and price cover a rather wide range. But it should be noted that most results are quite pleasing to drink.

Although I have yet to taste a Prosecco or even a Cartizze to equal the finer wines of the Champagne type from Pinot and Chardonnay, most Prosecco costs less than half the price of a Gran Spumante, which makes it an outstanding buy. Not that this section of the Veneto lacks its own contenders in the Champagne field. Carpené-Malvolti at Conegliano makes a vintage Brut from Pinot that has won admirers in Italy and abroad. Antonio Carpené, who heads the firm, is also president of the group of ten producers of the Istituto Spumante Italiano Metodo Champenois discussed in Piedmont.

Prosecco di Conegliano-Valdobbiadene has captured a market in Italy and, very recently, elsewhere. Carpené-Malvolti and De Bernard make all types. The Cantina Sociale at Valdobbiadene makes a fine Cartizze in small batches from select grapes. The Cantina Sociale di Soligo is also admirable. A Prosecco *méthode champenoise* made by still another cooperative — La Monteliana e dei Colli Asolani — recently came on the market after winning raves from local experts. Other wineries with outstanding Prosecco or Cartizze wines are the Cantina Enotecnico Pino Zardetto, which fashions some unique styles; Cantine Nino Franco, whose Rustico is a delightful example of the bottle-fermented *frizzante*; and Mario Rossi, Jr., which sells an interesting *blancs de blancs* of Prosecco and Verdiso grapes under the name FOL; and Canel with both dry and *amabile* Cartizze.

Less emphasis has been placed on still Prosecco, though it is also covered by DOC and can be most attractive. At its best it is dry, light, and fresh with a slight flavor of almonds that can also be scented in its fine bouquet. Like the sparkling versions, it is best to drink within a year or two of harvest. The finest I have tasted came from the Azienda Agricola Dott. A. Cosulich at Collalbrigo outside Conegliano. Other recommended producers are La Quercia, Zardetto, Nino Franco, and the Cantina Sociale di Valdobbiadene.

Prosecco dominates in the Marca Trevigiana, though other wines, including reds, do well there too. Cabernet, Merlot, the Pinots, Malbec, Tocai, and Riesling are cultivated, and the native Raboso (red), Verdiso, and Verduzzo (both white) have survived with a respectable measure of grace. Raboso is especially interesting; tannic and very dry with an acidic vein no longer common in red wines, it is nonetheless tasty in a robust way with an aroma of berries, herbs, and earth that is not to be sensed in more popular wines. Verduzzo is light, dry, and acidic, refreshing when drunk young. Verdiso, a grape now used mostly for mixing, is made into a varietal wine by Pino Zardetto. An astringent but fruity wine, it needs to be drunk within the year.

Descending from the Marca Trevigiana past Conegliano, the Piave valley broadens toward the Adriatic across flat fields interspersed with flat vineyards bordered here and there by towering poplars. The wines of Piave, in which Merlot, Cabernet, Tocai, and Verduzzo are classified as DOC, covers both hill and plain in the provinces of Treviso and Venice. Vines, for the most part planted after phylloxera and World War I, tend to make more distinctive wine in the hills, but some of the plains wine is worthy as well and is now being fairly heavily exported.

Tocai del Piave is light and flowery in the hills where a fine one is made by the Cantina Sociale Colli del Soligo. In the plains it tends to take on more color and body, though it retains a pleasant freshness; Bertoja di Ceneda at Motta di Livenza and Azienda Marcello at Fontanella make it well. Bianchi Kunkler, a large winery at Mogliano Veneto, produces and exports all the Piave DOC wines plus a Pinot Gris.

Cabernet del Piave can be a wine of considerable class and longevity, especially the *riserva,* which is required to have 12.5° alcohol and three years' aging. Merlot del Piave is fresher, rounder, more abundant, with a *vecchio* version that needs 12° alcohol and two years' aging. The Tenuta Giustiniani at Monastier di Treviso makes a good Merlot. At Castello di Roncade, an imposing fortress castle, Barone Giovanni Ciani Bassetti produces both Cabernet and Merlot, as do Azienda Marcello, San Cipriano at Sacile, and the Enoteca I. Cescon at Rai. The latter also makes a good Raboso. Malbec, a grape often mixed with Merlot and Cabernet, is cultivated widely in the eastern Veneto. Several producers make a varietal wine from it that has not been classified.

Clinton, Humble, Beloved American

Another wine that has not been classified is Clinton, or Clinto (or Crinto, or Grinto, sometimes even pronounced Hrinto, as Mario Soldati, one of its advocates, points out). The vine is believed to have found its way from America, probably New York State, in the late eighteenth or early nineteenth century. Just how or why it was imported seems to be a mystery to Venetians, who also seem mystified about the origin of its name. Soldati's informants speculate that it came from an American city, or perhaps a person, but, in fact, there is an American vine of that name of the genus *Clintonia,* whose namesake seems to be the former New York governor, De Witt Clinton. Alexis Lichine's *Encyclopedia of Wines and Spirits* defines Clinton as a "productive American vine giving small, black, spicy grapes yielding wines suitable for blending but little else."

Clinton's Italian admirers would not accept the latter part of that definition, though I suspect most other wine bibbers would. Whatever the case, the wine seems to fall into two categories: rough and rougher. The rough version is called Clinto, according to Soldati, the rougher Clinton, though the etymology like the history remains somewhat obtuse. Riccardo di Corato in 2214 *vini d'Italia* writes that Clinto comes from a vine called Fragola (the term for strawberry) and makes a lighter, more perfumed, and sweeter wine than Clinton. He adds that neither should be called wine in the strict sense of the word because they both derive from vines outside the category of *vitis vinifera*. A term frequently used to describe the wines is *volpino*, which translates as foxy, a characteristic of wines from native North American vines.

But Clinton, or Clinto, had at least one thing going for it. When phylloxera, another import from America, arrived, its vines had a natural immunity. Clinton not only survived, but was planted heavily throughout the Veneto and in neighboring regions. And even after more noble vines were grafted onto American rootstock and returned to production, Clinton lived on, most notably in the hills between Treviso and the mountain city of Feltre.

Soldati, who is known to alternate his sipping with puffs on Toscani cigars (which are to a good Havana what Clinton would be to a Mouton Rothschild), is no wine snob. While others describe Clinton as disgusting, even vulgar, he in a paragraph tells why there are those who love it:

Wine . . . so humble that it is not found in commerce but is bought and sold through direct and private dealings between producer and consumer; wine, in any case, that is so low priced that it surely is not worth adulterating, and, for that reason, the only wine that is *certainly and always genuine;* wine that oenologists scorn for its crudity, for its excess of tannin and color, and for its low grade of alcohol: but, wine that true Venetians, old and young, the farmers of Verona, Vicenza, Padua, Rovigo, Treviso, and Belluno love more than any other as a table wine; and we've even heard that they send it to Belgium when they emigrate to work in the mines.

Well, Clinton, or Clinto, is not about to arrive at your neighborhood wine shop. It is not easy to acquire even where it is grown. An employee of the agricultural institute at Conegliano, who went to some trouble to provide me with a bottle, said that farmers were not only reluctant to sell it but were legally forbidden to make it because when distilled as it often is into grappa it had been found to form excessive methyl alcohol, which attacks the nervous system. Nevertheless, my research continues into the fortunes of this humble, beloved American.

Conegliano: A Wine Called I.M.2,15

Texts at the Conegliano wine school provide little further enlightenment on Clinton, though Professors Giovanni Dalmasso and Italo Cosmo touched on the subject in their classic work *Principali vitigni da vino Coltivati in Italia,* a courageous effort to trace the origins and development of the myriad varieties of vines used for wine in Italy. It took them fifteen years and five volumes to complete the study.

Another project at the school has been the quest for improved vines. The most successful experiment so far resulted in I.M.2,15, a cross of Cabernet Sauvignon and Prosecco that has been found to thrive in the hills around Conegliano, making a red wine of notable class that develops after normal fermentation in two years instead of the three customary here for a Cabernet. The I stands for *incrocio* (hybrid), the M for Manzoni (Professor Luigi Manzoni, who directed the project), the 2 for the vine row, and 15 for the number of the grafted vine. The vine and its wine are now unofficially known as Cabernet Manzoni. The school sells it as I.M.2,15, along with a selection of its other wines.

More recently a hybrid of Pinot Bianco and Prosecco has shown promise. One of the first wines from that vine was a 1976, which, taken straight from the barrel in January, 1977, was full-blossomed and smooth. That wine will be more widely produced in a few more years. Another Manzoni hybrid, I.M.6,0,13 (Riesling and Pinot), has been successfully cultivated in the Veneto and Friuli–Venezia Giulia.

Conegliano is sometimes called the capital of Italian wine, not only for its research and educational facilities, but also because so much equipment used in winemaking is manufactured there. It is a city of 35,000 on the plain where the Marca Trevigiana meets the Piave flatlands, its old quarter skirted by the state road that runs north from Venice to Cortina d'Ampezzo and the Austrian frontier.

The "Rolls-Royce of Barrels"

The Garbellotto barrel factory is one of the many low-slung block and steel structures in Conegliano's *zona industriale*. From the outside Ditta

Garbellotto G.B. & Figlio looks like any other modern Italian plant, making it hard to imagine that behind its rectangular façade the ancient craft of cooperage is performed with a skill that has earned its product the accolade of "the Rolls-Royce of barrels."

Inside, the whine of saws and booming of hammers striking wood can be deafening. So Mario Salvador, an assistant to director Pietro Garbellotto, moved outside to explain the process on a vast asphalt lot where thick slabs of oak were stacked several meters high, the wood darkened by the dampness of a January fog. The oak, brought some 200 kilometers by rail from the forests of Slavonia in Yugoslavia, is selected at the lumber mills for its absence of knots, cracks, and blemishes. After four years of seasoning outside the Garbellotto plant, certain sections of each slab are cut for barrels. The rest is used for furniture.

"As you can imagine," said Salvador, "this wood is rather expensive."

So, of course, are the barrels, but the Rolls-Royce reputation was built on more than price. Inside, only a few machines were visible — saws and various trimming and stamping devices designed by company technicians to do in minutes some incidental work that used to take hours. But that is the lone concession to modernity; the really heavy work is done by hand.

At the center of the plant floor a man with a sledgehammer stood on a scaffold beside a half-completed 500-liter cask inside of which a fire roared. A man standing on the floor splashed water from buckets onto the steaming tapered slabs as the man with the hammer, with sharp, careful blows, drove a heavy iron band down around the barrel's girth, forcing the supple wood together. Joined by wooden pegs, the barrels are thus sealed without glue. The barrel was then inverted and the other end completed the same way, one iron band after another. Then another crew moved in to attach the end pieces, whose wider boards were already joined and pegged, but whose edges had to be trimmed to fit the barrel's circumference, no two of which are ever precisely the same.

Once assembled and dried, the barrels' exteriors are varnished, but the interiors are left raw, washed and soaked with neutralizing agents to diminish the wood's odor. This, of course, never disappears completely but works its way into aging wines to become an integral part of their character. Slavonian oak is valued over all others, even that of the Limousin of France, for the subtle flavor and aroma it lends such fine old wines as Barolo, Amarone, and Brunello di Montalcino. That invaluable interreaction between wood and wine, even young wine, is what Garbellotto barrels are noted for and what, evidently, has made them worth their price to winemakers all over the world.

Back in his office Salvador served wine and talked about the role of barrels in winemaking.

"You hear a lot these days about short fermentation and quick aging in stainless steel and glass-lined vats, young, fresh, uncomplex wines that have no use for wood. Well, despite all that, the demand for our barrels and vats is stronger than ever.

"We're wine lovers here, from Signor Garbellotto down through the ranks. And though it might sound trite to say so, when we know a good wine was made and aged in our barrels, we're proud of it. We feel we're due a share of the credit."

The Rolls-Royce may be going strong, but some barrel makers at the Fiat level are beginning to feel the pinch. More than just a tendency, the movement away from wood aging, even of big red wines, is supported by consumer preference and scientific research, and it is being encouraged by leading scholars of oenology. Some producers of Barolo, Brunello di Montalcino, Gattinara, and Vino Nobile di Montepulciano, to cite a few of many wines required by DOC to undergo extensive barrel aging, are seeking changes in the disciplines. Such modifications take time, but in all probability required maturing in wood eventually will be reduced. Meanwhile, some winemakers are quietly ignoring the rules and holding barrel aging to a minimum.

Even in the field of superior red wine, Italian tastes have been shifting away from hard, robust, well-aged versions to softer, fruitier, younger wines to be served at slightly cooler temperatures than previously. Nowhere is this trend more noticeable than in the Veneto. The transition has gained momentum through the rapid introduction of the new technology that enables producers to make such wines with model efficiency. The current of opinion at the wine schools of Conegliano, San Michele all'Adige, and Alba, which set the pace among Italy's progressive winemakers, is decidedly anti-wood.

Consider the words of one respected academician, Luciano Usseglio-Tomasset: "In my judgment, conservation in wood is without doubt detrimental to the quality of great red wines." He backs that provocative stand with comparative research on a Piedmontese red which after barrel aging demonstrated marked deterioration of basic elements through oxidation and an excessive presence of sulfates (from cleaning operations). If Professor Usseglio-Tomasset is so far one of the few experts who would abolish barrels, an increasing number clearly favors cutting down on their use.

But what about that woody aroma that gives Bordeaux, Cabernet Sauvignon, Barbaresco, and Chianti *riserva* that extra touch of distinction? Usseglio-Tomasset and others argue that in the achievement of that woodiness other desirable elements of the wine are sacrificed and that the overall organoleptic quality of barrel-aged wine is inferior to that of wine aged in oxygen-free containers made of impregnable materials.

As in so many controversies over wine, it all boils down to a matter of taste, and here the Italian antibarrel movement still faces formidable opposition both at home and abroad. In the long run, though, the odds might be in their favor. Not only are barrels costly to build; they are difficult to maintain in hygienic condition. The ideal barrel for giving a woody aroma with a minimal deterioration of other elements, according to Usseglio-Tomasset, is the small 225-liter *barrique* often used in Bordeaux and also employed in the aging of an elite few Italian wines. But it must be of oak and it should be relatively new. Larger barrels not only fail to give much woodiness to the wine; they can encourage excessive oxidation.

As we entered the 1980s, barrels — like petroleum-powered automobiles — were beginning to bear out what the pessimists were saying about approaching obsolescence. With the cost of Slavonian and Limousin oak rising at about the rate that artisan barrel makers were disappearing, it seemed certain that admirers of wood in wine, like drivers, would be forced to pay an ever-increasing price for their indulgence.

The "Ombra" and Artistic "Cucina"

Every province of the Veneto has its own variations on the regional *cucina,* and superb restaurants and *trattorie* to serve them. Venice's choices vary from *tavole calde,* the Italian style snack bar, to the elegant Antico Martini and the always fashionable Harry's Bar, which, despite its name, serves such local specialties as *risi e bisi* (rice with peas), *scampi,* and *fegato alla veneziana* (calves' liver and onions) with a flair that has earned it two stars in the Michelin.

Before their evening meal, Venetians have the pleasant custom of *andare per ombre,* their way of suggesting a visit to a local tavern or two. The *ombra,* a tiny measure of wine, takes its name from shade, specifically that of the bell tower of St. Mark's in whose shadow were the bars that first served it. Today, the custom of *andare per ombre* has spread throughout the region. Though the wine may vary from excellent to rather mediocre, after his customary four or five, the true Venetian seems in no mood to complain.

Good as the city's restaurants are, Venetians themselves will tell you that the places that serve the best food at the most reasonable prices are in the countryside, well beyond the dismal smokestacks of mainland Mestre. More often than not they will steer you toward the hills of Montello and the Marca Trevigiana in the province of Treviso, where, as some gourmets insist with little argument to the contrary, the level of restaurant cooking is rivaled in Italy only by that of Parma. The evidence is entirely convincing: Agnoletti and Da Celeste alla Costa d'Oro in the Montello hills, Villa Cipriani in a magnificent estate at Asolo, Gambrinus in a romantic park with a millstream running through at San Polo di Piave, Da Gigetto, a lively place in an antique setting at Miane, and many more.

At Solighetto, a country town between Conegliano and Valdobbiadene, the Locanda da Lino offers all the elements the Venetians make the trip for: fine food and wine, friendly service, tasteful and comfortable surroundings, and modest prices. It is a happy, warm place that can serve three hundred or so meals in its several dining rooms and terraces and still make the customers feel fussed over. Lino Toffolin, the artist owner, has decorated the walls with paintings, many of them his own. Bearded and wearing a chef's jacket and apron, he cheerfully bustles back and forth between the tables and the *fogher,* the open round fireplace where meats are grilled and roasted on the spit.

Among the openers are *pasta e fagioli* and a type of *lasagne* made with a flattened artichoke, ham, cheese, and béchamel. For the main course, Toffolin brings a grappa of such rare smoothness that he is often asked if anything tastier than *colombini con polenta,* two doves roasted to perfection topped with *salsa peverada,* a sausage and herb sauce, on a bed of polenta. His Prosecco, Cabernet, and Merlot, all from nearby vineyards and recent vintages, complement the food perfectly. And, with the bill, Toffolin brings a grappa of such rare smoothness that he is often asked if some can be bought to take away.

"I don't sell it," he says. "I give it away. But only in small doses."

Pramaggiore and Lison

To the east of the Piave, in the low country against the border of Friuli–Venezia Giulia (and even crossing it in places), three more wines have gained DOC. Merlot di Pramaggiore, Cabernet di Pramaggiore, and Tocai di Lison have been admitted under conditions similar to those of their lower Piave counterparts. Their vines grow in the alluvial soil west of Portogruaro to almost as far north as Pordenone, in Friuli. The zones cover practically the same territory, though the red wines take the name of the town of Pramaggiore and the Tocai that of nearby Lison.

The Cabernet *riserva*, of at least 12° alcohol, is bottled after three years and is capable of a decade more of aging. The Merlot *riserva*, also 12°, is bottled after two years and is shorter-lived. Tocai di Lison, the best of which comes from the Classico zone, is a wine of 11.5° alcohol to drink young when it shows balance between its dry and slightly bitter elements. Tenuta Sant'Anna at Loncon and Tenuta Santa Margherita at Portogruaro have made all three wines known throughout Italy and abroad. The Cantina Sociale di Portogruaro also exports all three. Among small producers the Tenuta La Braghina and the Club Produttori Associati at Pradipozzo are outstanding, but their wines are not easy to come by. A fine Cabernet is made by Dialma at San Stino di Lavenza.

The Vintages

The Verona Wines

	Valpolicella, Recioto, Amarone	Bardolino	Soave
1979	Excellent	Excellent	Excellent
1978	Good, scarce	Good, scarce	Good
1977	Excellent	Excellent	Excellent
1976	Good	Good	Good
1975	Poor	Good	Good
1974	Good	Good	Excellent
1973	Good	Good	Good

	Valpolicella, Recioto, Amarone	Bardolino	Soave
1972	Poor	Poor	Fair
1971	Good	Excellent	Good
1970	Good	Good	(Any previous
1969	Excellent	Great	years probably
1968	Good	(Any previous	too old)
1967	Excellent	years may be	
1966	Good	too old.)	
1965	Fair		
1964	Excellent		

	Colli Berici, Colli Euganei	Piave reds	Piave whites, Prosecco
1979	Excellent	Excellent	Excellent
1978	Fair to good	Good	Good
1977	Fair to good	Good	Fair to good
1976	Very good	Very good	Very good
1975	Good	Good	Fair to good
1974	Good	Good	Good
1973	Good to excellent	Fair	Fair
1972	Good to excellent	Good	Poor
1971	Exceptional	Excellent	Fair
1970	Excellent	Good	Excellent
1969	Good	Good	—

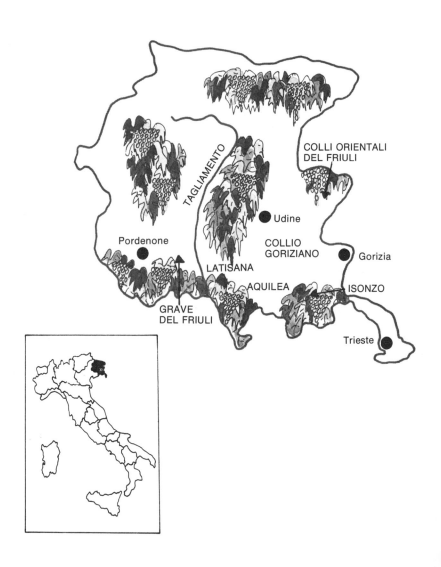

COLLI ORIENTALI
DEL FRIULI

TAGLIAMENTO

Pordenone

● Udine

COLLIO
GORIZIANO

● Gorizia

LATISANA

AQUILEA

ISONZO

GRAVE
DEL FRIULI

Trieste ●

FRIULI·VENEZIA GIULIA

PROVINCES

TRIESTE, Gorizia, Pordenone, Udine

POPULATION

1,235,000

AREA

2,948 square miles

AVERAGE WINE PRODUCTION

130 million liters

DOC WINES

Aquilea (Cabernet, Merlot, Pinot Bianco, Pinot Grigio, Refosco, Riesling Renano, Tocai) · Collio Goriziano (Cabernet Sauvignon and Franc, Collio, Malvasia, Merlot, Pinot Bianco, Pinot Grigio, Riesling Italico, Sauvignon, Tocai, Traminer) · Colli Orientali del Friuli (Cabernet Sauvignon and Franc, Merlot, Picolit, Pinot Bianco, Pinot Grigio, Pinot Nero, Refosco, Ribolla, Riesling Renano, Sauvignon, Tocai, Verduzzo) · Grave del Friuli (Cabernet Sauvignon and Franc, Merlot, Pinot Bianco, Pinot Grigio, Refosco Nostrano and Peduncolo Rosso, Tocai, Verduzzo) · Isonzo (Cabernet, Malvasia Istriana, Merlot, Pinot Bianco, Pinot Grigio, Riesling Renano, Sauvignon, Tocai, Traminer Aromatico, Verduzzo) · Latisana (Cabernet, Merlot, Pinot Bianco, Pinot Grigio, Refosco, Tocai, Verduzzo)

OTHER WINES

Blaufränkisch · Gamay · I.M.6,0,13 · Moscato Rosa · Müller Thurgau · Pinot Spumante · Prosecco · Ramandolo · Riva Rossa · Schioppettino · Sylvaner · Tazzalenga · Terrano del Carso · Torbolino

The Promised Land

F RIULI–VENEZIA Giulia, tucked into Italy's northeastern corner against Austria and Yugoslavia, was the last of the twenty regions to take its present form. It is sometimes equated with another of the Tre Venezie, Trentino–Alto Adige, which indeed shows some similarity in history, geography, and life-style. Friuli–Venezia Giulia, too, has a hyphenated name and cultural divisions of sorts, though members of the Slavic minority of the Friulian hills and the small slice of the Istrian peninsula left to Italy after postwar settlements with Yugoslavia have, for the most part, become thoroughly Italian in spirit, letter, and style.

Witness Sandro Princic, about thirty, blond, blue-eyed, vigorous, self-assured, drawing wine with a bulb-handled "thief" from the top of a vat in the family cellar at Pradis di Cormons, outside Gorizia.

"Taste this," he said, releasing some of the limpid golden liquid into my glass. "To me, our Tocai of Collio is the best wine in the world!"

His father, Isidoro, about sixty, graying, blue-eyed, vigorous, jocular, grinned up the ladder at his son.

"That Sandro," he said in heavily accented Italian, "he's a proud one, isn't he?"

Doro, as everyone calls him, who was born a Slovenian, leaves no doubt about who was the source of Sandro's pride and enthusiasm.

"Till Sandro grew up, I made the wine," he said. "Very good wine, too. Now Sandro, he just wants me to help with the heavy work. All that complicated stuff, he doesn't need the old man around for that."

Then Doro broke into laughter so irresistibly contagious that everybody in the cellar was soon accompanying him: members of the Princic (pronounced *Preen*-sheesh in the Slavic style) family and friends gathered on a Sunday afternoon. As Doro and Sandro bantered about their respective talents as winemakers, we sampled Pinot Bianco, Sauvignon, Cabernet, and Merlot from the vats, and each was eminently praiseworthy. But Sandro had made his point; if there were a candidate for best wine in the world, it had to be the Tocai. But then, with only a few thousand bottles produced a year and only a few hundred of them ever carried out of the province of Gorizia, it may be a while before the world knows about Princic Tocai.

Other winemakers of Collio Goriziano, usually called simply Collio, have their candidates as well, and not only in Tocai. The hills are an elite growing zone, the source of a multiplicity of wines, particularly white, now acknowledged to be among the nation's finest. Sandro Princic is not alone in his conviction that they merit worldwide recognition.

Wines, often good wines, have been made in the hills and plains of Friuli for centuries, as the land passed between Romans, Huns, Byzantines, Venetians, and Austro-Hungarians, among others. But only Picolit, the most cherished of all Italian dessert wines, was ever famous. And, because of floral abortion, a malady that inhibits pollination, its vines have been depleted and it has been exceedingly rare.

Until recently the other wines of Friuli–Venezia Giulia had a hard time establishing their identities. The region, most of which was formerly part of the Veneto, was patched together after World War I and reduced in size after World War II, when portions were returned to Yugoslavia amidst violence, threats, and bitter compromises. The fate of Trieste hung in the balance until 1954, when it returned to Italy. Still the name Friuli–Venezia Giulia remained remote to many other Italians until the earthquakes of 1976 struck, leaving more than a thousand people dead and many towns in ruins. That tragedy probably did more to embed the name Friuli–Venezia Giulia on the Italian conscience than any previous event. Damage to the vineyards was slight, fortunately, and the wines have continued to confirm a conviction that is becoming widespread, that in the modern world of Italian wines, Friuli–Venezia Giulia is the Promised Land.

Promise is a new and refreshing concept to a people who have been historically unlucky and chronically poor. Friulians have shown unparalleled fervor in carrying out a program begun in the early 1960s to assert a natural aptitude for viniculture that had never been fully realized before. With funds provided by the Common Market and local and national institutions, some 5,000 acres of mixed vineyard-farmland was converted to specialized vineyards in less than a decade. The vines were selected from choice Friulian varieties and time-proven imports, most of them planted in hilly areas or select flatlands that have since been classified as DOC zones. The program, which emphasized prestige wines, has already borne fruit, but there is much more to be heard from the winemakers of Friuli–Venezia Giulia.

Orfeo Salvador, head of the region's vinicultural development program, has been a dynamic force behind the regionwide upturn in fortunes. As he put it: "Friuli–Venezia Giulia is one of the great natural wine zones of the world. We have everything here — except enough space."

What space there is, though, is used wisely; the DOC zones were set up with exemplary rationale after years of planning. There are six — Collio, Colli Orientali del Friuli, Grave del Friuli, Isonzo, Aquilea, and Latisana — each defined geographically for its coherence and individuality. Each wine classified in each zone is from a verified grape variety whose name it must bear. (The one exception is Collio, a white from Ribolla Gialla, Malvasia, and Tocai grapes grown in the Collio zone.) No other region has so neat and comprehensible a DOC system.

The New Era: Big Aspirations, Quiet Dedication

Sandro Princic is one of many Friulians, not all so young, who represent the new era in winemaking. Father Doro used to sell wine in demijohns at the going rate per hectoliter. Sandro sells wine by the bottle and already, to some extent, is able to name his price. For the time being he has chosen, wisely, to keep his prices more modest than his aspirations.

So, against even greater temptation, has Mario Schiopetto, Sandro's friend, neighbor, and occasional mentor, as dedicated a winemaker as I have encountered anywhere. Demand for Schiopetto's wines, most of which are bottled in the spring, annually leaves his stock of about 100,000 bottles exhausted — or at least reserved — by summer. Most businessmen in that situation would simply elevate their prices, but Schiopetto, who is as savvy as he is devoted, has other ideas.

"Winemaking is more than a business to me," he explains; "it's my life. My name is only as good as my wine's. I make a comfortable living, but more than that, I'm doing what I want to do. I'm more concerned about integrity than profits."

Like many farm boys during the postwar economic boom, Schiopetto went away, eventually abroad, to work and save money. Years later, he returned to the family property at Spessa di Capriva and found new excitement in working the land.

Mario Schiopetto

"My father made wines, but he called them simply rosso and bianco," Schiopetto recalled. "During my travels I realized there could be more to it than that."

At first he bought grapes from neighbors to supplement his own meager supply. Then when the vineyards known as the Mensa Arcivescovile di Gorizia, which had furnished wine to the archbishopric of Gorizia, became available, Schiopetto acquired the lease and took over some 30 acres of the most privileged vine land in Collio. With a diligence that would drive most men to drink, he made them even better.

"I've learned through making wine that patience is everything," he said. "There's technology, of course, the bag of tricks one can fall back on to correct an error. But errors are made by man, not nature. Man needs to intervene at a certain moment to transmit the essence of the fruit to the wine. And that's the key . . . knowing, feeling intuitively when the moment is right. When you see that the grape is ready, it may already be too late. No, the only way to know the moment is to live with the grapes."

His theory applies to vinification as well, a process he believes should be neither too long nor too short but adjusted to the natural strengths or shortcomings of each batch of grapes.

Schiopetto, hands folded atop the gleaming waxed surface of his dining room table, spoke deliberately, his carefully chosen words and composed manner indicative of a patience that approached the ascetic. He makes twelve, sometimes thirteen different wines in the harvest-vinification epoch that may start as early as mid-August and run through November. That task, so demanding that many nights he sleeps in the cellars next to his fermenting vats so as not to let the moment pass him by, might seem to spread his talents thin. On the contrary, he insists, it keeps him alert, vital.

"I lock the doors, forget about the rest of the world, and give all my attention to my wines," he says. "That's my period of creativity and the end product, the wine, is my medium of expression. Each wine presents a new challenge at its own pace. After all, one can only create one master-piece at a time."

You might expect the source of such eloquence to show a streak of vanity, a touch of the prima donna. Nothing of the sort. Schiopetto, as he moved from barrel to barrel to draw samples of all twelve wines from a recent vintage — examining the color, rotating his glass and sniffing, then sipping a bit and working it around his tongue before spitting it into the cellar drain — received compliments with a skeptical look, occasionally replying with his own coolly balanced evaluation. He performs his work with confidence, even flair, not of the showman, but of the accomplished artist.

They might not all be judged as masterpieces, but I do not recall ever tasting in succession so many wines of such consistent and distinct virtue.

There was not an ordinary wine among them, and one, a Riesling Renano, had a polished, crystalline splendor that brought to mind descriptive terms that could only sound ridiculously excessive. Suffice it to say that I have never before tasted a wine four months old that had so much in its favor.

Schiopetto, to my surprise, accepted my appraisal. "That," he said in a moment of rare self-indulgence, "is one of the most successful wines I've ever made." Upon which he smiled, lifted his glass, sniffed, sipped, and swallowed some.

Riesling Renano is not provided for under Collio DOC, nor is Müller Thurgau, the first of Schiopetto's wines I had tasted. From the 1973 vintage, drunk in May, 1974, I noted at the time that the Müller Thurgau was the ultimate wine in the Rhine-Alsace style I had tasted in Italy. Now, years later, I had found its equal in the Riesling.

"Each year it seems that one wine stands out," he said. "In 1973 and 1978 it was the Müller Thurgau, but other years it's been a Tocai or a Pinot."

Schiopetto allowed that he had so far developed a slightly defter touch with his whites (*le donne*, the ladies, as I believe he called them) than with his reds. The whites are Tocai, Riesling, Müller Thurgau, Pinot Bianco, Pinot Grigio, Sauvignon, Traminer, Malvasia, and Ribolla. The reds are Cabernet and Merlot. He had also made a Moscato Rosa and, for the first time, another rosé, fine and light, from Merlot, that he calls Riva Rossa.

Collio: A Climate for Youth

Schiopetto and his colleagues in Collio are not fanatical about aging wines. Their whites are generally at a prime from five months to two years, and even the reds are designed to hit their stride within one to four years, though from some vintages they may keep well for a decade or more.

Down the winding road toward Capriva is Villa Russiz, where a winery was established in 1868 to support the A. Cerutti orphanage. Its director, Edino Menotti, is a firm believer in youth. He has cut the fermentation on the skins for his red Cabernet Franc, Merlot, and Pinot Nero to three days and swears that they are much the better for it.

"I took a bottle of my Cabernet to a wine conference in Bordeaux a while ago," he said. "I know that sounds terribly disrespectful, but really it was just to drink with friends so we could do some comparing. We never got around to that. I opened it for a French winemaker, who refused to believe it was made eight months earlier. 'Mon Dieu,' he said to me, 'to get a wine that good here you'd have to wait eight years.'"

Well, the reds of Collio may indeed show an unusually supple finesse when young, but they bear only a distant family resemblance to their French cousins. The nature of the grapes in the benign climate of Collio is such that their essence seems to carry over most impressively into young wines with their own measure of breed and nuance. None of the DOC wines of Collio — red or white — have specific aging requirements.

Of all Friuli's wines only the native red Refosco del Peduncolo Rosso improves notably with age. It tends to be very green and tannic until about its third year, when it starts to mellow into a wine of true individuality, somewhat like the Raboso of Piave in the Veneto. A warm, robust, austerely dry wine, Refosco usually does better in other sections of Friuli than Collio.

The same is true of Picolit, a vine from which most growers of Collio seem to keep a respectful distance. But most other Friulian whites — the fresh, dry types — seem to attain their highest levels in Collio, whose hills fold gently against the Yugoslav border for some 35 kilometers from Dolegna to Gorizia. Vineyards there range from 200 to 1,000 feet above the level of the Adriatic, a short way to the south, whose breezes create a year-round climate so comfortable it is sometimes referred to as *aria condizionata.*

Tocai and Other Gems

Tocai stands out among the whites, not because it is invariably the finest but because it is the most widely cultivated and most thoroughly appreciated of Collio's wines. Although Friulians constantly remind outsiders that their Tocai has nothing to do with Hungarian Tokay, the evidence is overwhelming that the vine is of eastern origin. So is the name, from *tukaj,* which means "here" in Slavic, according to local chroniclers. But whatever the origin, by now it must be acknowledged that "here" is Friuli, where Tocai is enamored in a fashion that knows no ethnic barriers.

Collio's winemakers have as diversified a production as can be found anywhere. Everyone makes at least three varieties and some, like Schiopetto, many more. That way they can create their wines one at a time. But whatever else they aspire to, they all make Tocai and regularly serve it at their own tables, because, as some say, "It's a wine so good it goes with anything." In Friuli, where East meets West, "anything" covers an inordinately broad spectrum. Tocai is obviously more suited to grilled fish than to goulash, but it is such a lovely wine, so smoothly balanced between dry, bitter, nutty, alcoholic, and even *abboccato,* between fruity and acidic, between light and firm in body, that it is a pleasure to drink most any time.

Tocai is by no means the only gem of Collio. Edino Menotti at Villa Russiz holds his Pinot Grigio in greater esteem. His is rich and velvety, a pale smoky gold color with copper tinges, the result of leaving the fermenting wine in contact with the skins for a time. Higher in alcohol and somewhat longer-lived than most other Friulian whites, Pinot Grigio varies somewhat in style according to its maker. Marco Felluga, a winemaker at Gradisca d'Isonzo in the plain who has expanded his holdings with some of the most prized land of Collio near Capriva, makes his Pinot Grigio full and opulent. Gradimir Gradnik, on his small estate near Plessiva di Cormons, makes a drier and more delicate Pinot Grigio as do others who vinify their wine off the skins.

The other whites — Pinot Bianco, Malvasia, Sauvignon, the two Rieslings, Müller Thurgau, Traminer, and Ribolla Gialla — can attain notable heights as well, though perhaps not so frequently as do Tocai and Pinot Grigio. Even Collio, sometimes called Bianco del Collio, from the mixture of Ribolla, Malvasia, and Tocai, can rise above the ranks of the ordinary.

Malvasia, a native of the region apparently unrelated to other vines of that name, can develop a pleasant aromatic lushness; it is sometimes aged for three or four years. Ribolla Gialla, another native, is most often light, fresh, and fairly acidic. A version of Ribolla known as Torbolino is made from partially fermented musts. Cloudy, soft, and rather sweet, it is drunk in November and December with roasted chestnuts.

Renato Ferlat, who runs the Azienda Agricola G. Ferlat at Cormons, has been making wine from the hybrid I.M.6,0,13 developed by Professor Manzoni at Conegliano. A cross between Riesling and Pinot, it is apparently unique in the region.

Independents and Cooperatives, Consortiums and Cliques

Wine production in Collio remains prominently in the hands of in-dividual farmers and estate holders with limited output. Doro and Sandro Princic, for example, turn out about 30,000 bottles a year; Mario Schio-petto about 100,000; Villa Russiz about 150,000. Brothers Livio Felluga and Marco Felluga each have winemaking operations in Collio and else-where with outputs that far surpass those numbers, but both are deter-mined to retain the pace and style of the independent grower.

In recent years concepts of small-scale cooperative winemaking new to Italy have been established in Collio, aimed at obtaining superior results at all stages of production from cultivation through vinification and mar-keting. Giovanni Scolaris, an oenologist with a winery at San Lorenzo Isontino, has contracted several growers in the San Floriano district to provide him with grapes for wine made in individual batches. All bottles bear the names of grower and vineyard on their labels. Some of these wines are among the finest of the zone. Gaspare Buscemi, who had been working as a winemaker for such established wineries as Conti Formen-tini, Barone Codelli-Dott. Donda, and Conti di Maniago, also guides a number of small growers through the entire process from planting vines to selling the wine. Buscemi, whose special labels contain detailed data about production, gives the name of grower and vineyard in capital letters and his own in modest italics underneath.

Vittorio Puiatti, partner and chief winemaker at EnoFriulia, buys all grapes and turns them into wines held in awe by Italian cognoscenti. Puiatti, regularly acknowledged by his peers to be one of the nation's most brilliant wine technicians, is awe-inspiring himself, a restless genius whose energy is camouflaged by the appearance of an oversized and some-what disheveled teddy bear. His forte is white wine whose splendor is enhanced by an unerring ability to travel.

Puiatti uses a stabilization process that involves an instantaneous pas-teurization as the wine goes into bottle, a method that does not alter taste to any discernible degree. Steady expansion has made EnoFriulia a rela-tively large winery for Friuli, and perhaps the one that has made the greatest recent impact on the Italian market by providing unrelenting quality in both DOC and non-DOC wines with the volume to have bottles available in all the right places.

Puiatti is one of a number of Friulian oenologists who have contributed to the so-called *metodo friulano,* whose influence on production of white wine in Italy in recent years has been significant. The Friulian method is aimed at achieving the freshest white wines possible by putting only the select free-run must (usually less than 60 percent of the weight of the grapes) through a slow, low-temperature fermentation in an environment that remains as free of oxygen as possible from vinification through bottling. The result is the bright, fruity, acidulous wines that Friuli is now renowned for, wines that often contain ample alcohol ($11.5°$ to $13.5°$) but balance it with a fresh, clean flavor that is best enjoyed within months after the vintage — not because the wines are fragile, but because, in theory, their elements are at a balanced prime when bottled and age can do nothing to improve them.

Collio has an active producers' consortium headed by Conte Douglas Attems, who makes wine at Lucinico outside Gorizia. Its emblem is a man in folk costume trampling a vat full of grapes, a bit of nostalgia that has nothing to do with the way wines are made here today. The consortium takes part in a regionwide campaign of growers' associations to promote all of Friuli–Venezia Giulia's wines. But not all growers belong.

Schiopetto, for one, chose to remain outside, partly because he believes a consortium tends to serve as a common denominator for its members' wines. Instead, he and several other winemakers maintain an informal clique (no symbols, no rules, no dues) that brings them together now and then to help and encourage each other and to criticize each other's wines as frankly as possible between friends.

"We appreciate what writers and critics say about our wines," says Sandro Princic, "but the people we really listen to are our fellow winemakers. We know that they know what they're talking about."

If their objectives sometimes seem loosely defined, members of this clique are as serious as those of the consortium about gaining wider recognition. To date, however, many have shown a certain hesitancy, almost a reluctance, to export their wines. The winemakers of Collio seem to realize that before they conquer the world, they will have to complete their conquest of Italy. For the moment all that seems to be holding them back is their shortage of numbers.

"We're young in this zone," says Schiopetto. "Collectively we lack the experience of growers in some other parts of Italy and France. But we don't lack the natural conditions, the talent, the human spirit to make great wine. We're building a tradition here while we're building our output. Our time is coming. You can count on that."

The following listing of some recommended producers in Collio is determined by the quality of at least one, more often several, of their wines. The practice of making many varieties means that not all wines in all years could be expected to be outstanding. But a basic skill and integrity has been evident in those tasted.

★ Conti Attems, Lucinico
★ Azienda Agricola della Roncada, Cormons
★ Borgo Conventi, Farra d'Isonzo
★ Gaspare Buscemi, San Floriano del Collio (labeled by grower and vineyard)
★ Fratelli Buzzinelli, Cormons
★ Barone Codelli-Dott. Donda, Cormons
★ Ferruccio Castellan, Farra d'Isonzo
★ Carlo Druforka, Oslavia
★ EnoFriulia, Capriva
★ Livio Felluga, Brazzano di Cormons
★ Marco Felluga, Gradisca d'Isonzo
★ G. Ferlat, Cormons
★ Conti Formentini, San Floriano del Collio
★ Gradimir Gradnik, Plessiva di Cormons
★ Wanda e Neda Gradnik, Plessiva di Cormons
★ Marcello Humar, San Floriano del Collio
★ Silvio Jermann, Villanova di Farra
★ Komjanc, San Floriano del Collio
★ Mario Miklus, San Floriano del Collio
★ Fratelli Pighin, Spessa di Capriva
★ Silvestro Primosic, Oslavia
★ Doro Princic, Pradis di Cormons
★ Mario Schiopetto, Spessa di Capriva
★ Giovanni Scolaris, San Lorenzo Isontino (labeled by grower and vineyard)
★ Baronesse Tacco, San Floriano del Collio
★ Villa Russiz, Capriva

A few of their wines have been exported, and more are likely to join them in the near future. Many are available at the handsome Enoteca Regionale Serenissima at Gradisca d'Isonzo, one of the first publicly supported wine-tasting centers in Italy, though there are now many more throughout the nation.

Colli Orientali and Picolit

Collio's low-lying hills around Cormons and Capriva and the somewhat loftier rises near San Floriano and Oslavia, above Gorizia, are among the most privileged viticultural areas of Italy. But the preeminence of Collio, tiniest of Friuli's five DOC zones, gives its wines no exclusive claims to excellence. The adjacent Colli Orientali del Friuli has some exceptional terrain as well. Growers there work with all the varieties found in Collio, sometimes with equally impressive results. And some other varieties, notably the native Refosco, Verduzzo, and the storied Picolit, are indisputably more at home in Colli Orientali than in Collio.

Colli Orientali del Friuli, in the province of Udine, extends some 50 kilometers from San Giovanni al Natisone north across rolling plains past Cividale del Friuli into the foothills of the Julian Alps. Its climate is so consistently favorable that every vintage from 1970 to 1976 was rated excellent. Vine cultivation is somewhat more scattered in Colli Orientali than in Collio, with such exceptions as the Rosazzo hills, where a number of estates turn out wine of true eminence. Foremost among them is Picolit (occasionally spelled Piccolit), a wine that only a few dozen growers in the entire region take the pains to cultivate.

Picolit's vines have been undergoing a revival of sorts after decades of incessant decline. Some growers have found that by interspersing its vines with those of certain other varieties, floral abortion, its pollination deficiency, can to some extent be overcome. Experts have also successfully grafted its vines onto heartier roots. Still, its yield after grapes are picked and partly dried is so low that that factor alone could almost justify its astronomical price.

Talk of a comeback, however, has apparently failed to convince those admirers from the golden years, who are old now and few in number, that Picolit could ever be the same. Maybe not. I have never tasted a Picolit from before the 1964 vintage. And, indeed, any bottles that remain from earlier times are no doubt concealed in the cellars of the privileged. There are certainly none in commerce, and if there were they would be priced beyond what any reasonable person would pay for them.

In the late eighteenth century, Picolit's vines thrived. Fabio Asquini produced the wine at his estate at Fagagna on a scale grand enough to export annually some 100,000 bottles containing about a half-pint each. By the mid-nineteenth century, Picolit was undoubtedly the most prestigious wine of Italy. Its bottles graced the tables of the courts of England, France, Russia, and Austria, where the Hapsburgs had the passing fortune of considering it a domestic wine. Its fame has lived on into this century, so prominently that some now call it Italy's Château d'Yquem. Though such misguided comparisons make me shudder, I can understand what those who utter them are driving at; for Picolit can still be a wine of undeniable greatness.

Italo Cosmo, the scholarly classifier of Italy's wines and vines, asserted that Picolit "can contend with the best dessert wines known today."

Luigi Veronelli, who calls Picolit "very great," once stated that the wine of Rocca Bernarda had no equal. He will get plenty of argument about that, but he did have sentimental reasons for making such a judgment. The late Contessa Giuseppina Perusini Antonini, of the family that owns the Rocca Bernarda estate, was esteemed as the *grande dame* of Italian wine. Before her death at one hundred and one she was still contributing, albeit more morally than physically, to the winemaking operation run by her son, Gaetano, a distinguished scholar, who died in 1977.

Mario Soldati, the irrepressible dilettante, eulogized the Picolit of Fratelli Furlàn tasted on their estate at Abbazia di Rosazzo. He described its color as topaz, its texture as "strangely oily," and detected the scent of, among other things, gardenias and dates and the flavor of pears, peaches, plums, walnuts, almonds, honey, concluding that it was "antique, intense, robust, soft, and delicious . . . and, deep down, bitter, serious, Gothic." In contrast with Château d'Yquem, Soldati pointed out, the Furlàn Picolit was stronger and drier and it was best suited to drinking with piquant blue cheeses, such as Gorgonzola, while Château d'Yquem was strictly for dessert.

The French, it should be noted for the record, also drink Sauternes with foie gras, for which Picolit seems amply suited as well. And some Frenchmen, a fortunate few, like to contemplate Château d'Yquem by itself before or after a meal, just as some Italians do Picolit. But I can only hope that if Picolit is indeed headed into an era of renewed vitality, it will not have to stand constant comparison with the wine of a single great French estate. That is not a kind way to treat a fallen idol trying to get back on its feet.

Most Picolit comes from small and scattered plots in the Colli Orientali or in adjacent zones such as the hills of Buttrio and the western fringes of Grave del Friuli near Udine. In the Colli Orientali, the only zone where it is classified, it must have at least 15° alcohol and be aged two years to qualify as Picolit *riserva* DOC.

Among Picolit producers are Conti di Maniago at Soleschiano, Luigi Valle at Buttrio, Ronchi di Cialla at Cialla di Prepotto, Ronchi di Manzano at Manzano, Fratelli Furlàn at Abbazia di Rosazzo, Volpe Pasini at Togliano di Cividale, Antonio Furchir at Felettis di Bicinicco, Angoris at Cormons, Tavagnacco e Dorigo at Premariacco, Vittorio Nalon at Ara di Tricesimo, Paolo Rodaro at Spessa di Cividale, Livio Felluga at Brazzano di Cormons, and Rocca Bernarda near Ipplis. There will unquestionably be some variation in style and quality among these, and I can by no means vouch for all of them.

Improbable as it might seem to the preceding producers, whose wine comes from hill country, a Picolit from the flatlands of Isonzo has come out on top in recent regional judgings. The 1975 Picolit from the Azienda Agricola Cappelletti at Cave di Selz was awarded by judges a 19.5 rating out of a possible 20, the highest for any wine of that year in the entire region.

Some might question its pedigree, but the Cappelletti Picolit erased any doubt I had that modern-day Picolit was capable of greatness. The wine was pale gold with greenish reflections and had a delicate, flowery bouquet. Its first sensation in the mouth was full, soft, mellifluous, with smooth texture and firm tone. Then the fruit came across crisply and distinctly, always in harmony with its sweetness, which was just right — amabile. And in the end the amarognolo was there, the vaguely bitter taste that gave the wine its unexpected depth. I could understand why the judges found it a half-point short of perfect.

Santo Duca, who runs the Cappelletti winery, cultivates his vines on a plot as flat as a football field, flush against the Venice–Trieste autostrada. He says the Isonzo seaside climate is more beneficial to Picolit than is the hill climate of Colli Orientali, which, if true, might explain why his vines not only look heartier but tend to be more productive. He interspersed his Picolit vines in a total of about an acre with Traminer vines, which favor pollination. Cappelletti's production is only a few hundred bottles a year.

Ranging even farther afield, Mario Pezzi at Bertinoro in the hills of Romagna makes a Picolit called Paradiso, and Giuseppe Molinelli at Ziano in the hills of Emilia makes another. Theirs are solidly in a class with most Picolit of Friuli. Picolit vines have been introduced in other parts of northern Italy, an indication that the wine's revival may be more widespread than the Friulians expected.

Some Old-Timers

Friuli's winemakers seem to thrive on diversity. The region's wine boom was built on the strength of popular grape varieties, not rarities. Still, it is heartening to see that not all the old-timers live on only in memory.

Verduzzo Friulano, whose vines have been cultivated for centuries, rivals Tocai in the hearts of some Friulians, who find its light, even salty, dryness most pleasing when it is drunk very young. Verduzzo is still widely cultivated in the Colli Orientali, where it has DOC status. At Ramandolo in the northernmost part of the zone, some dessert wine is made from Verduzzo grapes semi-dried on mats. Known either as Verduzzo di Ramandolo or Ramandolo Bianco, it was once one of Friuli's most celebrated wines, and is still enjoyed locally. Two superb Ramandolos are made by G. B. Comelli and the Azienda Agricola Dri Giovanni.

Refosco del Peduncolo Rosso was the lone native vine producing red wine that was brought back to prominence after phylloxera. A taste of the Refosco made by Giovanni Monai at Nimis explains why it survived. His is a big, strong wine whose elegance is not lost in its rusticity. Refosco goes nicely with game, particularly venison, though bottles need to be opened well ahead of time to let the air take the edge off its characteristic sharpness.

Tazzalenga, or Tacelenghe (each means *taglialingua* or tongue cutter), resembles Refosco in its rusticity and sharpness and its ability to age. But it is scarcer than Refosco and does not have DOC status. The only producer of Tazzalenga I know of is Cantine Conti Florio at Buttrio.

A few growers in the community of Albana di Prepotto in the Colli Orientali have quietly kept alive a red wine usually called Schioppettino, from the Ribolla Nera vine. Mario Soldati reports that only about 2,000 liters are produced a year, almost none for sale. But if you make a trip to Albana di Prepotto and if you persist, you might be able to taste a glass of what he calls "a great wine, approaching the great ones of Piedmont, but with a grace all its own." The Schioppettino of Giuseppe Toti fits that description.

The popular varieties of Friulian wines are now fairly widely available in Italy. Several wineries also export, notably Angoris, Collavini, Morassuti, and Santa Margherita, all of whom offer a commendable range of wines, whether DOC or not. Angoris, founded more than three hundred years ago, has kept pace with the regionwide surge in development. Under the astute direction of Luciano Locatelli, Angoris production should reach 600,000 cases by 1983 – compared with 350,000 cases in 1977 – of wine from grapes grown in company vineyards. Angoris has played a leading role in introducing the region's wines to Americans. Such other producers as Conte Gianfranco d'Attimis Maniago, Duca Badoglio, EnoFriulia, Livio Felluga, Marco Felluga, Luigi Valle, and Cantina Rubini have also been exporting on a smaller scale. Other wineries are planning to follow suit.

In the Colli Orientali, the following producers, who work on a small scale, are also worthy of mention: Cantarutti Alfieri at Colli di Rosazzo, Domenico Casasola at Ronchi di Rosazzo, Girolamo Dorigo at Buttrio, Carlo Giacomelli at Pradamano, Giuseppe and Enrica Panizzo at Case di Manzano, and Isidoro Tilatti at Corno di Rosazzo.

The Buttrio hills, which lie between the Colli Orientali and Grave del Friuli, produce wine of very good quality that is sometimes labeled as Colli di Buttrio, though not DOC. These wines are especially favored in Udine, a city whose Venetian beauty is dignified by its Gothic character. Udine is the capital of the Friulani, a people whose culture and language, a form of Romansch, has helped give the region a sense of unity and independence.

Grave, Isonzo, Aquilea, and Latisana

The Julian Alps, uniformly peaked and gleaming white in winter, span the region east to west like an elongated lower denture. The plains and rolling hills to their south, washed by the Tagliamento River, are alluvial and rich in places, gravelly and eroded in others, overall appearing better suited to field crops and grazing than winegrowing. Known as Grave del Friuli (the Grave, as in the Graves of Bordeaux, referring to gravelly land), it is the region's largest, most productive, and most geographically variable DOC zone.

Grave covers an area from the Livenza River valley west of Pordenone across the Tagliamento to the hills east and north of Udine, where the earthquakes of 1976 were most devastating. Much of the flatland under vine renders wine for everyday consumption. But in places Grave, too, produces wines worthy of Friuli's newly illustrious reputation.

In the westernmost section of Grave, near Pordenone, the vine nurseries of Rauscedo produce some 30 million cuttings a year. The largest such nursery of Europe, if not the world, Rauscedo has supplied most of the vines planted in Friuli and the eastern Veneto, as well as other regions. The nurseries began their activity about 1920 after phylloxera forced cultivators to seek the most suitable varieties for their terrains and graft them onto American rootstock. Continuing experiments carried out at Rauscedo in cooperation with the research center at nearby Conegliano have realized notable improvements, particularly in vines now widely planted in the plains of Friuli's Grave, Isonzo, Aquilea, and Latisana, and the Veneto's Pramaggiore, Lison, and lower Piave. Careful selection has resulted in heartier clones more resistant to mildew and the other perils of damp soil. The nurseries have also propagated hybrids and strains of traditional vines that are more productive and less disease-prone in all types of climate. The nurseries at Rauscedo are due a major share of the credit when Italians boast, with justification, that the quality of their *prima materia,* the raw materials or the grapes, is overall the best in the world today.

Merlot is the overwhelming favorite of Grave's producers. In 1976 more than half the zone's DOC production was of this fresh, tasty red that is to Friuli and the Veneto what Barbera is to Piedmont and southern Lombardy: a solid wine for regular consumption. In the plains of Grave, Isonzo, Aquilea, and Latisana it only rarely reaches heights of distinction, and even in the hills it is not aimed at the high-price market. But Merlot, as the region's most widely produced and most widely consumed wine, even surpassing Tocai, is the stalwart of the winemaking economy.

Grave del Friuli's DOC wines are seven: Merlot, Cabernet, Refosco (both Peduncolo Rosso and Nostrano), Tocai, Pinot Bianco, Pinot Grigio, and Verduzzo. Among its many wineries, both independents and cooperatives, only a few have gained national attention. Among them are Duca Badoglio at Codroipo, Fratelli Pighin at Risano (who also have holdings in Collio), Conti di Porcia e Brugnera at Pordenone, Villa Sospisio at San Quirino, Cecilia Danieli at Caminetto di Buttrio, Tenuta del Faé at Motta di Livenza (whose winery is actually in the Veneto), Azienda Agricola Kechler at San Martino di Codroipo, Azienda Agricola Plozner at Spilimbergo, and A. Pittau at San Leonardo Valcellina. The Cantina Sociale Cooperativa at Casarsa makes a Refosco and the Cantina Sociale del Friuli Orientali at Bertiolo a Cabernet that rank among the finest of the zone, indicating that cooperative winemaking here is successfully reaching into the quality field.

Isonzo, Aquilea, and Latisana, which gained DOC status only recently, have certain features in common. Their wines come from coastal plains or the gentlest of hills tempered by maritime weather. Growers in each zone, after upgrading the quality of their wines and organizing and defining their production, are now striving to have their wines widely recognized. So far only a few have succeeded.

Isonzo takes its name from the river that enters the Adriatic south of the port city of Monfalcone. The zone begins south of Collio, reaching the island of Grado on the southwest and following the Yugoslav border down the Istrian peninsula past Trieste, the nation's second busiest port (after Genoa). As the only heavily populated and industrialized section of Friuli, it does not look like wine country. But some Isonzo wines, particularly the Picolit of Cappelletti, prove that appearance to be somewhat deceptive.

Cappelletti's Sauvignon, whose vines grow in the Carso hills, is also outstanding. The Tocai, Malvasia, and Traminer are good. Among other reliable producers are Azienda Agricola Bader at Fratta di Romans, Fratelli Brotto at Vermigliano, Eredi Dott. Gino Cosolo at Fogliano Redipuglia (whose Merlot ranks among Italy's finest), and the Cantine di Villanova at Farra d'Isonzo (which makes *spumante* of Prosecco and Moscato grapes in addition to its regular wines).

Isonzo's DOC varieties are Cabernet, Merlot, Malvasia Istriana, Pinot Bianco, Pinot Grigio, Riesling Renano, Sauvignon, Traminer, and Verduzzo. But the truest wine of Trieste, Terrano del Carso, is not classified. Its vines, in the Refosco family, have been largely replaced by more prestigious varieties. A purplish, rather rough-featured, slightly fizzy red that is usually served chilled, Terrano is low in alcohol but high in lactic acid, which supposedly reinforces the blood. Notwithstanding that attribute and its sentimental value, Terrano might offer a clue to why the Slavic people of Trieste, until recently, preferred beer and slivovitz, a plum brandy, to wine.

Aquilea and Latisana once seemed destined to become a unified zone, but their growers elected to seek separate classifications, and in 1976 both were recognized under DOC. Aquilea takes its name from the city settled by the Romans more than two thousand years ago. Its columned ruins are depicted as the emblem on the consortium label. Aquilea's wines are Merlot, Cabernet, Refosco, Pinot Bianco, Pinot Grigio, Riesling Renano, and Tocai. The reds represent about two-thirds of the production with Merlot predominant.

Latisana is named after the town near the mouth of the Tagliamento River bordering on the Veneto. Its wines, the same varieties as in Aquilea except that Verduzzo is classified and Riesling is not, are similar in character to those of the Veneto's Pramaggiore and Lison, though the winemaking tradition is not so well established.

Aquilea and Latisana have benefited from research done principally at Conegliano and Rauscedo to improve grapevines grown in flatlands. If such soil rarely produces great wine, yields are often prolific and quality can be very good indeed.

In Aquilea, the Cantina Sociale Cooperativa del Friuli Orientale at Cervignano, which markets its wines under the trade name Molin di Ponte, makes some wines vineyard by vineyard under the *cru* concept. The cooperative's winemaster is Orfeo Salvador, who also directs regional development. A stickler for quality, Salvador has made Molin di Ponte one of the most prestigious names in northeastern Italian wine. Many grapes come from property owned by Lloyd Adriatico, the Trieste-based insurance firm. A good independent producer in the zone is Azienda Agricola Giacomelli at Ca' Leoni. In the Latisana zone the Isola Augusta winery at Palazzolo della Stella has emerged as a large producer whose emphasis is clearly on quality.

The Cooking: An Intermingling of Imported Flavors

Friuli's array of foods is as awe-inspiring as its profusion of wines. The cooking derives from several corners of central, eastern, and southern Europe and even, in subtle form, from across the Mediterranean. Trieste with its international port, is the melting pot of a *cucina importata,* dishes brought in by Slavic, Germanic, Hungarian, Venetian, and also Jewish and Greek people who have settled there. And though their names and backgrounds often contrast, their tastes and textures intermingle appetizingly on the tables of Friuli's restaurants.

In country homes the fare still tends to follow ethnic lines. As a rough generalization, in the Carnia mountain range north of Udine, home cooking includes pork in its various forms, game, goulash, *Schnitzel, gnocchi* made from either potatoes or soaked bread (and often indistinguishable from the *Knödel* of Austria), thick soups with cabbage as their base, and pastries in the Viennese style. In the lower plains and along the Adriatic, roast meat, poultry, and fish done in many ways prevail, and there are pastas and risottos and plenty of fresh vegetables and fruit.

By now a number of dishes qualify as regional in the sense that they are as universally appreciated as any food could be in Friuli: meat grilled on the *fogolar*, the omnipresent polenta, and *pasta e fagioli*, the humblest and often the tastiest of soups. Foremost among the regional specialties is *prosciutto di San Daniele*. Matured slowly in the soft subalpine air, the hams of San Daniele rival in fame those of Parma. Many gourmets say they are even more *dolce*, which refers as much to their tenderness as their mellow flavor.

Bruno Mantovani, restaurateur and student of regional cooking, notes that you can tell when you have crossed the cultural line from Italian to Slavic when the prevailing tang of the sauces changes from garlic to onions. At his restaurant, Da Bruno in Monfalcone, Mantovani cooks fish with a light touch and selects his wines with the deftness of the master sommelier that he is. He says the problem of knowing which wine to serve with which dish is of recent origin in Friuli.

"In the past the Italians here drank common wine and *grappa* and the Slavs drank beer and Slivovitz," he said. "I still have trouble convincing some people that our white wines, which are among the finest anywhere, are appropriate with fish, and the red wines go better with meats and cheeses."

He pointed out that there are exceptions to the rule. On the island of Grado the sharply seasoned fish soup, or chowder really, called *boreto alla gradese*, goes best with strong red wine.

Many of Friuli's restaurants now offer a full selection of wines. The Conti Formentini serve ten of their own at their restaurant in the fifteenth-century castle at San Floriano del Collio, where the food, the wine, and the medieval setting make for a memorable meal. Parco Formentini and Da Bruno are listed in some guidebooks, but not all the good restaurants of Friuli are.

Al Giardinetto, a cozy place with central European decor in the center of Cormons, is frequented by winemakers and small-town business people. Ezio Zoppolatti, owner, chef, waiter, bartender, is one of those gifted souls who can take any number of orders in succession without writing anything down and come back minutes later with exactly what everybody asked for. His menu is mixed, like the culture of this Collio wine center, and the food is invariably tasty. For pasta he may serve *cannelloni* on the same plate with a *Leberknödel*, which is lighter and more flavorful than any liver dumpling you might find in its native Austria. The venison in wine sauce, when available, is superb, and so is the apple *Strudel*. Zoppolatti's house wines, Tocai and Merlot, are unlabeled, but of the level demanded by customers accustomed to drinking daily some of Italy's finest, freshest wines.

The Vintages

	Collio Goriziano	Colli Orientali del Friuli
1979	Outstanding	Outstanding
1978	Good, scarce	Good, scarce
1977	Fair	Good
1976	Excellent	Excellent
1975	Fair to good	Excellent
1974	Good	Excellent
1973	Excellent	Excellent
1972	Excellent	Excellent
1971	Excellent	Excellent
1970	Excellent	Excellent

	Grave del Friuli	Aquilea, Isonzo, Latisana
1979	Excellent	Outstanding
1978	Good	Fair to good
1977	Fair	Fair
1976	Excellent	Very good
1975	Good	Good
1974	Good	Excellent
1973	Good	Excellent
1972	Excellent	Excellent
1971	Good	Excellent
1970	Fair	Good

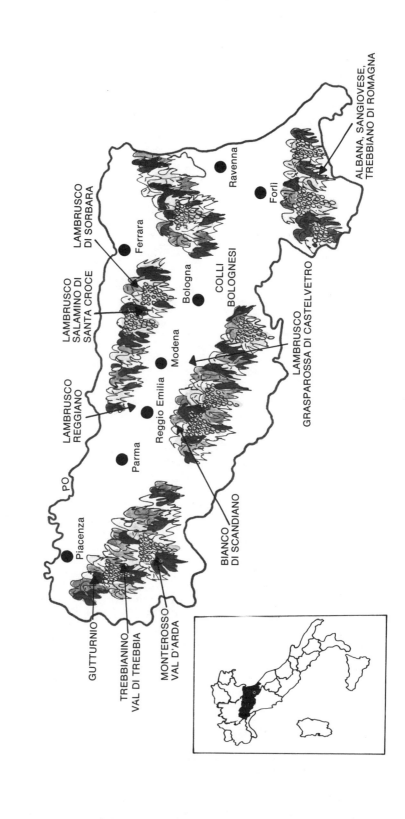

EMILIA-ROMAGNA

PROVINCES

BOLOGNA, Ferrara, Forlì, Modena, Parma, Piacenza, Ravenna,
Reggio Emilia

POPULATION

3,870,000

AREA

8,542 square miles

AVERAGE WINE PRODUCTION

1.05 billion liters

DOC WINES

*Albana di Romagna · Bianco di Scandiano · Colli Bolognesi–Monte
San Pietro–Castelli Medioevale (Barbera, Bianco, Merlot, Pinot Bianco,
Riesling Italico, Sauvignon) · Gutturnio dei Colli Piacentini · Lambrusco Grasparossa di Castelvetro · Lambrusco di Sorbara · Lambrusco
Salamino di Santa Croce · Lambrusco Reggiano · Monterosso Val
d'Arda · Sangiovese di Romagna · Trebbianino Val Trebbia · Trebbiano di Romagna*

OTHER WINES

*Aleatico di Bertinoro · Barbarossa · Barbera dei Colli Piacentini ·
Bianco di Castelfranco · Bianco Val Nure · Bianco Val Tidone · Bo-
narda dei Colli Piacentini · Bosco Eliceo · Cabernet · Cagnina ·
Fogarina · Fortana · Gaibola · Labrusca · Lancellota · Malvasia dei
Colli Piacentini · Molinelli · Moscato · Müller Thurgau · Paga-
debit · Picolit · Pignoletto · Scorzamara · Sparvo · Terra Calda
Scorza Amara*

The Nation's Wine Barrel

APPROACHED from the north, from the Veneto or Lombardy, Emilia-Romagna appears to have but two physical dimensions: length and width. A fertile, often foggy land of vast farms and heavily banked canals, where until the automobile became accessible to the multitudes the bicycle was the chief form of transportation, the northern part of the region looks like the sort of environment that would make a Dutchman feel at home. There the Po, flowing eastward to the Adriatic, supports on its broad shoulders bountiful sources of grain, fruit, vegetables, milk, cheese, and meat.

Sometimes referred to as the breadbasket and the fruit bowl, Emilia-Romagna could just as accurately be described as the nation's wine barrel. The region has solidified its position as the most productive on average in recent years, thanks in great part to the copious vineyards of the Po Valley that provide a decorous touch of vitis vinifera to the otherwise tedious symmetry of field crops. In 1978, Emilia-Romagna produced 1.17 billion liters of wine, one-sixth of the national total of 7 billion liters.

Producers of quality wine in surrounding regions like to remind you condescendingly that Emilia-Romagna is overwhelmingly a source of bulk wines, blending wines, industrial wines to be converted into alcohol and vinegar. But that representation is not terribly accurate. The region makes numerous wines of enviable quality, much of them, but not all, in the DOC zones of the southerly highlands. One lowland wine has escaped the bonds of anonymity to become a runaway international best-seller; it needs no introduction, at least not to Americans.

Whatever else one might be inspired to say about Lambrusco, it could not be described as flat. Its vines, trained onto trellises and trees sometimes higher than basketball hoops, render grapes for a deep purple wine that when poured issues a brilliant pink froth that quickly subsides, the bubbles lingering long enough to give a languid tickle to the tongue.

That sensation pleases not only Italians but millions elsewhere, notably in the United States, where from the mid-1970s on Lambrusco represented more than half the market for Italian wines, prompting the Italian magazine *Civiltà del Bere* to coin the term *Lambruscodotto transatlantico*. In 1979, the "Lambruscoduct" carried more than 10 million cases across the Atlantic and there seemed to be no limit to its supply. Almost singlehandedly Lambrusco had provided the explosive force behind the Italian wine boom in America.

The Lambrusco phenomenon is the stuff fairy tales are made of, but while charming America's young at heart this Cinderella gets kicked around a lot at home. No other Italian wine has been subjected to such scorn and derision, particularly from rival producers and appreciators of "more serious" wines. A Tuscan winemaker offered a typical comment: "Americans gave us Italians Coca-Cola and now we're repaying the debt with Lambrusco." The Coke image is widespread, but that is mild compared with some of the other things Lambrusco's detractors have said about it over the years.

Frank Schoonmaker wasted no words in calling Lambrusco "as nearly undrinkable as a well-known wine could be." Waverly Root, in *The Food of Italy*, wrote: "Every Lambrusco I have ever tasted has been thin and tart, perilously close to vinegar. Since the best Lambrusco comes from Modena, as does the best vinegar, one might wonder whether the Lambrusco grapes which produce wine have not missed their real avocation." (Root's reference was to the rare and expensive Aceto Balsamico di Modena, vinegar aged in kegs of several types of wood to pick up the aroma of each.)

Other critiques have been less acid. Many Italian and English writers accord the wine praise or at least grudging respect for the way the dry version complements Emilian cooking, which is generally conceded to be the richest and most refined of Italy. The fourth *Catalogo Bolaffi dei vini d'Italia* awarded two Lambruscos three stars and several others two, though it did point out that a three-star Lambrusco is one thing and a three-star Barolo quite another.

While I have yet to taste a Lambrusco of such stellar dimensions, I do not count myself among those who universally condemn the wine, either. When well-made and honest (and dry), Lambrusco can be pleasant with a hearty meal.

The most esteemed Lambrusco is made in Emilia's heartland around Modena and Reggio Emilia, where there are now four DOC classifications: Lambrusco di Sorbara (northeast of Modena along the Panaro

River), Lambrusco Grasparossa di Castelvetro (south of Modena), Lambrusco Salamino di Santa Croce (north of Modena around the town of Carpi), and Lambrusco Reggiano (from various communities around Reggio Emilia). Subtle distinctions can be made between the grape types and the wines of each. Debates recur about which is superior, though the Sorbara zone produces what is often recognized as the "classic" Lambrusco.

Among the subvarieties of the Lambrusco grape employed are Lancellota, di Sorbara, Maestri, Marani, Fortana, Salamino, Montericcio, Uva d'Oro, Grasparossa, Viadenese, and Scorza Amara, though it would be needlessly confusing to try to explain the special properties of each. The DOC wines, most often dry but also *amabile*, must have a minimum alcohol content of 10.5° or 11°, and their carbonation must result from natural fermentation. They are wines to be drunk young, with food. Their nuances are not of the sort to ponder.

Perhaps the most convincing argument for Lambrusco's inevitable worth is that it is made and drunk by Emiliani, people whose palates are as discriminating as their appetites are insatiable. Few natives are naive enough to call Lambrusco great, but most will admit that they consume more of it than any other, and not only because they like the bubbles and the modest price.

"Maybe you have to be from here to hold it really in esteem," said Nello Colombi, cellarmaster at the Tommaso Agostinelli winery at Rami di Ravarino, north of Modena. "When you drink a wine every day it has to satisfy you. Some drink it cool, but I open the bottle and let it sit awhile. Then you can taste that it is really a warm wine, frank and harmonious. And, to my taste, it must be very dry, so dry that it cleanses the mouth, with a light sparkle and a hint of bitterness.

"Frankly, I get a little angry when people malign Lambrusco," Colombi continued. "But I suppose it's understandable. There's so much of that fabricated stuff around these days."

The fabricators never look far for grapes; Lambrusco's vines, which thrive on the plain, are among the most prolific of the peninsula. Placed at intervals of about 15 feet in rows 25 feet apart, the vines are trained onto high trellises or, rarely now, the branches of *pioppi* trees, the knotty limbed members of the poplar family that have been dying out lately from a curious malady. The vines spread their foliage across these arbors under which maintenance crews on tractors and carts maneuver through the tunnels. In summer they provide shade from the sun, which beats down here with a relentlessness rarely equaled in the rest of northern Italy. At harvest time, the vine limbs reach eerily through the shifting fog to touch those of the next row over, looking something like giant, shaggy scarecrows holding hands as if to dance a minuet.

International Brotherhood of Wine

Lambrusco production and export are dominated by giants, both privately owned and cooperative. They have succeeded in putting Lambrusco on the world market in ever-increasing quantities. And whether you take their products seriously, as some consumers do, or consider it "pop," as do others, there is no longer any question that in economic terms Lambrusco is a wine to be reckoned with. Much of what is sold as Lambrusco is not DOC, but that does not necessarily mean it is inferior. Use of the name Lambrusco is permitted in *vino da tavola* under specified conditions in a number of areas, notably in the province of Parma, which is expected to gain DOC soon.

Lambrusco sales in the United States have been led by Riunite, Giacobazzi, and Cella. Many other large Italian and foreign-owned firms carry Lambrusco in their lines, but some operate mainly as shippers. Riunite's sales of 6.8 million cases (81.6 million bottles) in the United States in 1979 (most, but not all, Lambrusco) placed it first in volume among imported brands.

Emilia-Romagna's capital, Bologna, is the buckle of the Red Belt, the northern Italian industrial and agricultural complex where Communists dominate not only regional and local politics but control production at many factories and farms as well. It follows that a great deal of Lambrusco is turned out by Marxists, prompting endless jokes in Italy about "red wine" and political taunts about Communist compromises with the capitalist United States.

Riunite, whose full name is Cantine Cooperative Riunite Reggio Emilia, groups some 8,500 growers in a network of cooperative wineries that possess 14 pressing stations and 2 bottling plants under the technical direction of 6 oenologists and 3 chemists. Riunite's administrator, Communist former Senator Walter Sacchetti, is a fiery orator of gravel voice who believes firmly in the benefits of political and economic détente and the international brotherhood of wine. He is a staunch campaigner for the recognition of Italian cooperative wineries as the basic suppliers of wine for the people, maintaining that such large-scale production can be controlled to result in sound wines that sell for a fair price to the consumer and provide a just reward for the cultivator. Obviously a great many wine drinkers, Italian and American alike, confirm that Riunite's formula works.

Much of Riunite's production is imported by the House of Banfi in the United States, an already large firm expanding on both sides of the Atlantic, and one that takes Lambrusco very seriously indeed. Banfi launched Riunite Lambrusco on the U.S. market in 1969 after carefully studying American tastes in beverages and finding that they ran to the sweet, fruity, and bubbly. At that time most Lambrusco was dry, but Riunite agreed to put its emphasis on the *amabile* and was soon rewarded with sales that bore out what Banfi's studies anticipated and more.

Although a share of Riunite's exports to the United States consists of Lambrusco Reggiano (including a small amount of *secco*), most is not of controlled name and origin. But, as Sacchetti insists, "All our wine is of DOC standard. And despite what some people say, Lambrusco *amabile* is as valid under organoleptic analysis as is Lambrusco *secco*. In fact, the only difference between them is that one contains residual sugars and one doesn't. It's merely a variation in the alcoholic fermentation."

Sacchetti explained that the main reason most Riunite Lambrusco is not labeled DOC is a cost consideration. For instance, by using a screw-on metal cap instead of the cork required for DOC Lambrusco, the cooperative cuts costs by millions of lire a year. The former senator bristles at the suggestion of artificial carbonation. "Absolutely not," he said. "All Riunite Lambrusco is naturally refermented. It is all quality wine."

As in all Lambrusco exported to the United States, the degree of pressure from this natural carbonation is held under U.S. definitions for sparkling wines, which are heavily taxed. So Lambrusco is properly defined as *frizzante* rather than *spumante*.

Wine critics and connoisseurs in the United States have had a field day scoffing at this "pop" wine *all'Italiana*, but contrary to their expectations, Lambrusco's bubble has not burst. As one U.S. importer of what he called the "magic liquid" put it: "For years the detractors said that those young Americans who stepped up from Coke to Cold Duck to Lambrusco would abandon it when they graduated to the serious wine level. What they failed to realize is that for every graduate of the Lambrusco school, two graduates from the Coke school are waiting to enroll. And they're not all kids either."

Lambrusco's enduring success in America has also forced Italian doubters to swallow their words. And to the amazement of the nation's *buongustai*, Lambrusco *amabile* has recently taken off in Italy. Riunite, which sells most of its Lambrusco and white and rosé wines in the United States, now sells some 35 percent of its total production in Italy, and about half of that is *amabile*. Other Lambrusco producers have noted the trend as well and are vinifying to meet it.

Not "Pop" to the Natives

At home, in Emilia, where it is not a "pop" wine and the *secco* is still favored, Lambrusco sales have shown no sign of ebbing either. That explains why a prestige winery like Tommaso Agostinelli continues to function the way it does. Its production of about 150,000 bottles a year is modest for Lambrusco. But the winery, whose owner is a Bolognese businessman, has an unsurpassed reputation for integrity and quality, neither of which is easy to come by in Lambrusco country these days.

Agostinelli Lambrusco is made by a traditional, rather intricate method. From 60 percent Lambrusco di Sorbara and 40 percent Lambrusco Salamino, the grapes are picked on the late side, after mid-October usually, and fermented four or five days on the lees. Then one-tenth of the wine is drawn off and filtered. This *filtrato*, low in alcohol and sweet, is set aside while the rest of the wine is put through a normal fermentation, then racked by transferring it from one oak barrel to another until late February or early March. Then the *filtrato* is added to induce a refermentation when the wine is bottled. The corks are tied down with string and the bottles are stored horizontally until July, then vertically until they go on sale at summer's end. Agostinelli is one of a few wineries that sell all their wine by vintage.

Nello Colombi, a wiry man wearing baggy blue coveralls, walked from barrel to barrel, checking the coded numbers chalked on like the markings on railroad boxcars, telling when each batch of wine had moved and from which barrel it came.

"Because it's inexpensive, people think Lambrusco is easy to make," said the cellarmaster. "I guess they think we put a pill in the bottle to make the bubbles and that's all there is to it. Well, it isn't Champagne, but I can tell you there's plenty of work involved in Lambrusco too."

Agostinelli Lambrusco, which costs a bit more than some others, is markedly better than most. Its market has remained principally in Italy, with some exports to Switzerland and Germany. The quantity apparently has not been sufficient to interest buyers for the U.S. market. Nor is the production of Casimiro Barbieri, who makes Lambrusco in the basement of his home at Magazzeno in the Castelvetro zone. Barbieri, whose wine shares with Agostinelli the distinction of being the Bolaffi three-star Lambruscos, sells about 500 bottles a year after meeting the demands of family and friends.

Two independent Lambrusco producers who work on a larger scale but well are Contessa Matilde and Chiarli. Good bottles are also available from Cancarini-Ghisetti at Villanova di Là, Nedo Masetti at Carpi, Cantina Simoni at Modena, and Severi Vini at Barriovara. Cantine Cavicchioli at San Prospero in the Sorbara zone makes two red Lambruscos that are among the best available and a white, vinified from Lambrusco grapes, that is not only out of the ordinary but excellent.

Other cooperatives besides Riunite prominent on the market are the Cantina Sociale di Santa Croce, UCS (Unione Cantina Sociale), and CIV (Consorzio Interprovinciale Vini). The latter is an association of 4,300 producers who make and bottle wine from their vineyards exclusively.

There is, as well, Lambrusco that is not called Lambrusco. One that stands out is Labrusca, made using the charmat method by Lando Lini, an engineer at Canolo di Correggio. A brilliant cherry pink, joyously explosive *spumante,* Labrusca was originally made by Lini exclusively for a group of friends, most of whom showed up for an annual party at his home. But word got around and now Lini makes enough to sell some on the side.

Other red, usually bubbly wines made in the Modena and Reggio-Emilia zones include Lancellota, Fortana, and Fogarina, which are largely of local interest, and Terra Calda Scorza Amara, a special type of Lambrusco not widely distributed but highly regarded in the area where it is grown near Reggio. Dark and tannic with a bitter vein, good Terra Calda Scorza Amara is available from Remigio Medici & Fratelli and Ina Maria Pellerano.

Some white wines of more than routine interest are produced in the

Emilian low country. Bianco di Scandiano, in dry, sweet, and *spumante* versions, recently gained DOC. Bianco di Castelfranco, a dry wine from around the town of that name near Modena, is expected to be recognized soon.

A Zest for Good Eating

Emilia-Romagna's Communists may not always be the world's most militant, but they are probably its best fed. Bologna is also the capital of that rather bourgeois national pastime known as *la gastronomia,* the practice of which transcends all political lines. Bologna *la grassa,* Bologna the fat, is one of Italy's most handsome and livable cities, the hub of a region whose cooking varies considerably in style and content. But from Piacenza on the west to Rimini on the east, the zest for good eating rarely fluctuates in intensity. Restaurants, especially in Emilia, can usually be relied upon to serve good Lambrusco, though with such superb food one can be excused for succumbing to the temptation to drink one of the region's other fine wines. Enough are available so that even if one's taste does not run to Lambrusco there is never any need to follow the example of the proprietor of one of Emilia's noted restaurants, who, through a meal and afterward, sat sipping Coca-Cola. That eccentricity might be taken as the ultimate putdown of Lambrusco were it not for the likelihood that the man's doctor had issued that most familiar of orders in Italy: to give his liver a rest.

Bologna, with such celebrated restaurants as Bacco, Diana, Dante, Notai, Palmirani, Al Pappagallo, Rosteria Luciano, Al Cantunzein, and Don Chisciotte, has no exclusive claim to excellence in regional cooking. Temples of gastronomy can be found in all the region's cities and in towns and villages across the countryside. The cooking is rich and generous, sometimes rustic, sometimes refined, turned out with the incomparable relish of a people who really love to eat. In that sense and others it resembles the cuisine of Lyons and its surroundings in France. Like the Lyonnais, the chefs of Emilia-Romagna have a wealth of produce grown or raised locally as a base for composing endless variations on familiar themes.

The variations composed by Giuseppe Cantarelli and his wife Mirella are so delectable that their homey *trattoria* in the tiny farming community of Samboseto is invariably listed among the great restaurants of Italy. Yet it is so inconspicuous that I drove past it twice on the misty

day when I found it, years ago, behind the family food store with only
a faded sign (since repainted) on a plastered wall to indicate its presence. Though its two Michelin stars supposedly make it worthy only of a
detour, Cantarelli's devotees regard the place as a mecca worth long
journeys to Samboseto in the otherwise unspectacular hinterlands of the
Po north of Parma.

Cantarelli, Peppino to his friends, is a temperamental perfectionist
with a genius for coordinating meals that sometimes range, in the Italian
context, rather far afield. His menu and wine list reveal an unabashed
emulation of things French, though he has in no way let the Gallic
influence overwhelm him. Despite the presence of duck in Cognac and
a soufflé of tongue on the menu, most specialties are of local origin and
bear the unmistakable stamp of Cantarelli's inventive individualism.
His flair is tempered by the composure of his wife Mirella, who guides
with a sure and graceful hand a kitchen crew of local women, most
on the hefty side, who also double as waitresses when the *trattoria*
reaches its capacity of about sixty guests.

The wine list includes numerous great bottles from Italy, France,
and Germany, but Cantarelli wisely suggests wines of his own production. They include a *frizzante* white called simply Vino Bianco, from
Riesling, Malvasia, and Trebbiano grapes that with a Cantarelli meal
can seem to rival Champagne; an excellent still, dry Riesling; an exemplary Lambrusco; and a still, red Scorzanera (from the Scorza Amara
grape also used for Lambrusco), whose depth and class are well beyond
the scope of most other wines hereabouts. All three come from vines in
the nearby plains and hills.

The *prosciutto* of Parma is never pinker and more succulent than here,
but *culatello,* from the softest part of the pig's posterior, is even more
flavorful, so much so that the people of the Parma area usually keep
that part to eat themselves. The *tortelli di erbetta,* squares of golden
handmade pasta as light as any I have ever tasted, are filled with a
ricotta and herb mixture and served with drawn butter and grated
Parmesan from the cheesemaker just down the road. Main-course dishes
include duck, game hen, and pheasant cooked in a number of imaginative ways. But the tastiest of all might be the humblest. *Padellete,* pork
ribs with white beans baked in a casserole somewhat on the order of a
cassoulet, was a meal popular with peasants who often ate even better
than the aristocrats.

A Cantarelli meal is best concluded with the house nocino, a liqueur made from green walnuts steeped in eau-de-vie. A specialty of the area often made in homes, its bitter, tonic qualities are reputed to aid digestion.

Cantarelli's brilliance is no isolated phenomenon. The province of Parma probably has more outstanding restaurants per square kilometer than any other of Italy. Parma itself boasts Aurora, Angiol d'Or, Al Dsevod, and La Filoma. But the community of Busseto, which includes Samboseto, is the most frequent target of Italian gastronomes. Busseto is also noted as the home of Giuseppe Verdi, whose stature seems far greater to the people of Italy than most of the statesmen and militarists numbered among its favorite sons. Why else would the composer's portrait grace the 1,000-lire note, the Italian equivalent of the dollar bill?

Verdi, so they say, was an indefatigable gourmand. If he were alive today, he would not have to travel far from home to satisfy his appetite. Right next to his birthplace at Roncole Verdi is the restaurant Guareschi, founded by the author and caricaturist Giovannino Guareschi, creator of the fictional priest Don Camillo, a favorite character in popular Italian literature. Guareschi's son Alberto is the chef and host, whose approach to his calling is lower key than Cantarelli's but whose cooking is no less appealing. In Busseto itself there are Il Sole, whose setting is as unpretentious as the food is sumptuous, and I Due Foscari, owned by the celebrated tenor Carlo Bergonzi, whose dining room has the fanciful trappings of an opera set, with dishes to match the surroundings.

Emilia's range of typical food is too vast to ponder at length, but one should never leave the region without trying *zampone*, the stuffed pig's-foot sausage traditionally made in Modena province and now available nearly everywhere in Italy. *Zampone* and the less revered *cotechino*, which is similar, are the highlights of *bollito misto*, though they are often served on their own either with white beans or with mashed potatoes and lentils, which reputedly bring prosperity when eaten at the New Year. With *zampone* the recommended wine is Lambrusco, whose sparkling astringency cuts through the richness of the meat and even, it is said, inhibits more than other wines do the formation of cholesterol in the blood.

Hill Wines: The Pleasure of the Unexpected

Emilia-Romagna's wines might be split into two general categories, those from the plains and those from the hills, though visitors sometimes remain unaware of the latter's existence. That is understandable, for the hills are often hard to spot from the main arteries, from the Bologna–Milan and Bologna–Venice highways or the Via Emilia, the Roman road that gave its name to half the region. But, in fact, there are hills aplenty. The region's southern border (with Liguria, Tuscany, the Marches, and the Republic of San Marino) is defined by the Apennines, which rise in places to heights suitable for skiing.

Emilia-Romagna's finest wines come from hill country, most notably from Romagna, whose DOC zones are now quite well known, but also from Emilia, where many remain to be discovered. The hill wines consist of many types and styles, some fascinating natives and some promising new varieties.

The westernmost part of the region, the hills southwest of Piacenza congruent with Lombardy's Oltrepò Pavese, is the home of Gutturnio dei Colli Piacentini, a red DOC wine of about 12° alcohol made from Barbera and Bonarda grapes. Usually fresh and smooth after light aging, Gutturnio can equal some Oltrepò reds, though overall it seems less distinctive. A conspicuous exception is the Gutturnio of Valentino Migliorini, a restaurateur at Caorso near Piacenza who doubles as a winemaker at his cantina in Piedmont's Monforte d'Alba. Migliorini's Gutturnio is smooth, soft, and stylish, thus bearing only a vague resemblance to other red wines of the Colli Piacentini, which for the most part show some roughness on the edges. Migliorini also makes two fine light sparkling wines — a dry Trabense (from Trebbiano, Ortrugo and Malvasia) and a demi-sec Malvasia — from grapes grown in the Piacenza hills. Working with his oenologist adviser Sergio Galletti, whose specialty is *méthode champenoise*, Migliorini came up with a Pinot *spumante* called Valentino Brut from the 1978 vintage that rivaled the finest Champagne-style wines. That completed his line of house wines that is indisputably the most distinctive of any restaurant in Italy.

The Gutturnio zone is split into three parts. The better-known vineyards lie around the town of Ziano Piacentini, just a few kilometers from the Lombardian wine center of Santa Maria della Versa. Winemakers here are naturally more oriented toward the Oltrepò styles than toward those of other parts of Emilia. Reliable producers at Ziano are Pietro Calabresi, with the vineyard La Solitaria, Cavaliere Armando Clementoni, Remo Crosignani, and Giuseppe Molinelli & Figli.

Molinelli makes a number of non-DOC wines: Barbera, Bonarda,

Malvasia, Müller Thurgau, and two rare and excellent white dessert wines. His Picolit is one of the few made outside Friuli; his namesake, Molinelli, is made from a unique grape of his own discovery. Aged in wood, Molinelli has 15° to 16° alcohol and can be kept for about a decade after bottling.

Malvasia di Ziano is also expected to gain DOC status. Barbera and Bonarda of the Colli Piacentini are sold as varietals that may someday rival those of the Oltrepò.

The nearby valley of the Trebbia River has a white DOC wine called Trebbianino Val Trebbia, which as yet has not created much of a stir outside the Piacenza area. To be drunk young, it is dry and light with a bit of prickle on the tongue.

The Trebbia Valley, according to some chroniclers, is the home of the Trebbiano grape. If so, it has made an important contribution to the world of wine, not only in Italy, where Trebbiano is the chief component of white wines in Romagna, Tuscany, Umbria, and many other regions, but in France as well. There it is known in the Midi, where it is widely employed, as Ugni Blanc, and in the Charentes as St. Emilion, source of the wines that are distilled into Cognac. But the Trebbiano grape makes up only a small part (from 15 to 30 percent) of the mixture for Trebbianino Val Trebbia, which is dominated by Ortrugo and Malvasia Candia with some Moscato and Sauvignon included.

To the east, the Arda River valley, also in the province of Piacenza, has a white DOC wine with the somewhat confusing name of Monterosso Val d'Arda. Made from the same varieties as is Trebbianino, but with Malvasia Candia and Moscato dominating, Monterosso becomes a delicate wine with good fruit and a pleasant measure of sweetness. A sweet Monterosso *spumante* is similar to some of the Asti wines. There is also a Monterosso *amabile*.

The Azienda Agricola Pusterla at Vigolo Marchese produces a very good version of the dry Monterosso Val d'Arda, along with a fine, light Gutturnio. If other producers can equal the Pusterla Monterosso, the wine has a promising future. Two other similar white wines made in Piacenza province are DOC candidates: Bianco Val Nure and Bianco Val Tidone.

The Apennine foothills south of Piacenza, Parma, Reggio Emilia, and Modena have in recent years undergone rather extensive new plantings in vines, such as Riesling, Sauvignon, Barbera, the various Pinots, Malvasia, Cabernet, Merlot, and Moscato. With time, wines there might be expected to approach the quality of those now being produced in the Colli Bolognesi, southwest of Bologna, a zone emerging rapidly as one of the region's elite.

Active Ferment in the Colli Bolognesi

Steeply sloped and rounded on top, the Colli Bolognesi have a cool, inviting look when approached in summer from the hot Po Valley. Narrow roads traverse them roller coaster fashion, plunging down the side of one camel-hump rise to bridge a stream and wind back up another. The zone, recently included in DOC, is centered around the remote hill town of Monte San Pietro between Bazzano and Sasso Marconi. The hills have the unmistakable look and feel of fine wine country, yet the name Colli Bolognesi is still scarcely recognizable outside the Bologna-Modena area.

Colli Bolognesi, whose appellation should include either the appendage Monte San Pietro or Castelli Medioevali or both, has six DOC wines: Barbera, Merlot, Sauvignon, Pinot Bianco, Bianco (from Albana and Trebbiano), and what is now called Riesling Italico. Technically, however, the latter is not Riesling but rather Pignoletto, from a vine that may have been brought south from the Rhine centuries ago but has since come to be considered indigenous to Bologna's hills. In fact, studies at Conegliano have confirmed its individuality, and the name was in the process of being officially amended from Riesling Italico to Pignoletto. Cabernet Sauvignon has been scheduled to become the seventh DOC wine. Colli Bolognesi's wines, generally dry, are often lightly *frizzante* and sometimes *spumante*. They are most pleasant to drink young when, whether red or white, they can have remarkable vivacity and strength of character. Only Barbera undergoes aging; after three years in wood it can be labeled *riserva*.

The appendages to the appellation are the result of a division between the two producers' consortiums, one called Monte San Pietro, the other Castelli Medioevali, though both include members throughout the DOC zone. Some say the split is political, others that it resulted from "differences in agricultural concepts," but whatever the interpretation, feelings on both sides are rather bitter. Castelli Medioevali has more members, many of them small-scale growers who were expected soon to concentrate their production in cooperatives, which should result in more uniform quality than at present. The Monte San Pietro consortium has a cooperative of its own, the Cantina Sociale Consorziale Monte San Pietro. For the moment, though, the area's best wine is made by independents.

Aldo Conti is one. A founder of the Monte San Pietro group, he was in a sense a pioneer as one of the area's first winemakers to sell his products by the bottle. On his Tenuta di Monte Maggiore, Conti produces not only the DOC wines but some special creations that also show his unique touch. There is Mezzariva Bianco dell'Abbazia, made chiefly of Albana, and Bianco del Monte Avezzano, from Trebbiano, but his proudest wine is Bianco Roncandrea, a perfumed dry white from a hybrid of Riesling and Pinot Bianco, the result of Conti's own patient grafting and induced pollination.

As Conti explained it, "I made my money in business and amuse myself by losing it in wine," though he confessed that whatever the financial consequences, winemaking was his most satisfying venture. "Absolutely," he said, grinning sardonically as he patted his shock of gray hair, "but it helps to be a thoroughbred nut case like myself or you might let it get you down." To keep his late middle-aged spirit lively, he opened the Ustari da Matusel in the center of Bologna, a restaurant where he chats informally with guests (who are mainly under thirty) and provides imaginative dishes to go with his wines. His Merlot has won top honors in serious competition and his Barbera is among the smoothest of the breed made anywhere. But his favorite seems to be the Roncandrea, which he also calls Laudetur Vinum. "*Che vino!*" he announced, inhaling its flowery aroma. "Perfume, that's what it is. And to think I had to open a restaurant to sell it."

There was only a grain of truth in that statement, though Conti's, like the other good wines of the zone, are not as widely recognized as they deserve to be. Typical of his iconoclastic approach to winemaking, Conti does not state the vintage on the label. ("It only confuses people," he explained. "When I bottle it, it's ready.") And he gives the alcohol content at no more than 12° or 12.5°. ("Actually it's higher," he admitted, "but if you put 13.5 on the label it scares people, at least in Bologna.")

The outstanding varietal wines of the Bologna area are made by Enrico Vallania on his Terre Rosse estate above Zola Predosa. Not all are DOC, but as Vallania, a philosophical physician and oenologist, looks at it, Colli Bolognesi is not worth much on a label anyway. The names of his wines are worth something, though perhaps less in Bologna than other places. They read like an honor roll of the vines of France: Cabernet Sauvignon, Merlot, Chardonnay, Pinot Grigio, Pinot Bianco, Sauvignon, Riesling. Only in Friuli do individual producers work with such a noble array, and only rarely anywhere do they equal Vallania's results.

It would be difficult to pick a best wine out of the Terre Rosse battery, but the predominant product is Cabernet Sauvignon, whose nature seems best to meet the objectives of Vallania's inspired artistry. He has proved the potential for the low-lying sections of the Colli Bolognesi, where even from substandard vintages, such as 1976, his Cabernet is impressive.

"The climate and geography of many sections of Italy are better suited to Cabernet Sauvignon production than is most of Bordeaux," said Vallania, who has made a long and careful comparison of conditions. "The same could no doubt be said for parts of California and for other nations. The order is changing in quality wine production throughout the world, and those of us who have the privilege of working with Cabernet Sauvignon are aware of its outstanding capabilities. To me, there's no question that Cabernet is the red wine of the future in Italy."

Vallania is nearly as enthusiastic about Merlot, though he readily admits that Italians, himself included, have not done enough to bring vine cultivation to the level realized at those few French estates where time and economic privileges have favored the quest for perfection.

"The superiority of those estates that stand above all others is not just some quirk of nature," he said, "and it's not really much of a mystery. In Italy, because wine prices have remained relatively low and now today because labor costs are so high, we have not been able to practice certain procedures that would clearly result in superior quality, the personal touches that one can afford when one's wine sells for elevated prices but can't even consider when one is in a low-profit or break-even situation, as so many small estates in Italy are. Consider training methods. The French use head-trained vines with more plants per hectare and fewer clusters per vine, which would be preferable here for Cabernet, Merlot, and Pinot, though by now it's economically prohibitive. Even more important, though, are those intricate maneuvers that must be carried out to improve a vineyard, though they involve sacrifices that few growers can deal with. I'm talking about the thinning of the vines after budding to cut back yield and improve the quality of grapes, the seasonal improvements that require daily attention, but that's not all. The real

Enrico Vallania

key is selection. Once your vines are fully grown, you should go through the vineyard and pick out the weaker ones, cut them off and graft shoots from the stronger ones onto the stumps. Year after year, until every vine is strong. These are the things they've done at Pétrus and Lafite and Romanée-Conti, and they are the indispensables that superiority is based on. How many growers in Italy do it? I don't know. Certainly very few and on a very limited scale. My age prevents me from doing it to the extent I'd like to. How I wish I were young enough to start over!"

Well, youth has not eluded Enrico Vallania's wines, which reflect not only patience and skill but the personal exuberance of the winemaker. "I like wines to be vigorous and refreshing, full of fruit and flavor. And I also like to drink them a few degrees cooler than most people do," said Vallania. "The big, heavy, aged wines like Barolo are fine once in a while, but you can't make drinking them a habit. My Cabernet? I could drink it every day."

The 1971 vintage produced Cabernet of immense dimensions, too big for Vallania, who has been progressively lightening his wine through vinification techniques that bring it to a peak at from two to five years after the harvest. He has done away with barrels, whose use he considers more harmful than beneficial to Cabernet, meaning that his wine lacks the wood that international connoisseurs value so highly. But under taste analysis — in terms of fruit, body, balance, color, flavor, and aroma — Vallania's Cabernet Sauvignon can approach perfection.

The whites, particularly the Chardonnay and Sauvignon, are the most convincing arguments against the widely held belief that those French varietals thrive only in the Tre Venezie. Word has got around slowly, and Vallania's wines have been showing up in wine shops and restaurants through the Po Valley, startling those consumers who notice that they come from Bologna. One fine place that has known about the wines of Terre Rosse for a while is the Rocca restaurant at Bazzano, just down the road from Zola Predosa, with its *tagliatelle duchessa* and a tempting assortment of *fritto misto all'Italiana*.

Another good winery in the Colli Bolognesi is the Tenuta Bissera of Bruno Negroni, whose wines occasionally rival Vallania's and Conti's. Many growers in the zone are experimenting with varieties outside the norm — Montepulciano and Tocai Friulano, for two — with encouraging results. The atmosphere of active ferment in Colli Bolognesi winemaking seems destined to be much more widely felt someday.

On the fringes of Bologna are other good wineries, not all of which produce DOC wines. Perhaps the most fascinating vinicultural venture in the area is taking place at Gaibola, just outside the city limits, where a young winemaker named Marzio Piccinini grows vines in an ancient chalk quarry rich in active, or what Italians refer to as a "living," limestone. Piccinini's wines, all white and all called Gaibola followed by the varietal name, are Sauvignon, Moscato Giallo (which Luigi Veronelli describes as a *"vino erotico"*), Albana, Garganega, Bura (apparently originally Tocai Friulano), and Pignulein (or Pignolino, which might be Pignoletto). Piccinini, at his Podere I Tre Lucchetti, prunes his Pignulein vines so severely that each yields only about a liter of wine. *Amabile*, though not terribly rich, Pignulein sells for much more than the others. Veronelli recommends it with codfish or hare, strange-sounding combinations, but having tried neither, I am in no position to judge.

Romagna, Where Water Turns to Wine

Emilia and Romagna, by general agreement, coincide at Bologna, though elsewhere the line between them has not always been explicitly defined. It has been said that the reason the two were joined in a single region was to avoid the inevitable conflict that drawing a line between them would have provoked. That seems no more unlikely than the definition offered by the writer Antonio Baldini: "Descending from Bologna toward Imola and asking for a drink at any house, as long as they give you water you are in Emilia, but where they start to give you wine is the beginning of Romagna."

Indeed, wherever you travel in Romagna, high or low, you will never be far from a source of wine. Romagna's concentration of vines is the heaviest of the peninsula, particularly in the province of Ravenna, which most years produces more wine grapes than any other of Italy.

Romagna has all the region's seacoast, extending from the mouth of the Po on the north to Cattolica on the south. It also has an ample share of superabundant flatland and a smattering of hills, where some of the region's most distinctive wines are made. The hill wines can be excellent, but much of the valley grape production goes into cheap wines, brandy, wine concentrates, wine-based drinks, and even vinegar. Many farmers consider grapes just another fruit crop that thrives in this warm, misty land of plenty.

Bosco Eliceo is the only plains wine that has gained much notice, and that because its character is well beyond the ordinary. Made from Uva d'Oro, whose vines, some say, have been traced to Burgundy, Bosco Eliceo is grown around the Comacchio, the Adriatic lagoon north of Ravenna famous for its eels. Deep purple, warm, generous, dry, acidic, it has some of the mellowness of, say, a Merlot with some of the rusticity of, say, a Clinton. But in the end it is not much like either. It is good with sausages and grilled eels. It should also be ideally suited to having eels cooked in it the way chefs of Bordeaux do their exquisite *lamprois à la Bordelaise,* lampreys stewed in red Bordeaux.

The hills along Romagna's southern flank have three DOC wines: the white Albana di Romagna and Trebbiano di Romagna and the red Sangiovese di Romagna. Their DOC zones correspond more or less within a vast area stretching from just southeast of Bologna to just west of Rimini. Most vineyards lie south of the Via Emilia as it passes the cities of Imola, Forlì, and Cesena, and north of the mountain frontiers with Tuscany and San Marino.

Albana di Romagna is the region's most popular and versatile white wine. It comes in dry and sweet versions, still and sparkling. When dry it tends to be fairly delicate, with a lightly bitter vein and marked acidity. It goes well with highly seasoned fish dishes. When sweet, or rather *amabile*, for it is never lush, it goes well with fruit tarts or as a light *aperitivo*.

Albana is being made admirably well by a growing number of producers, which accounts for its ever more illustrious reputation nationally. It is even under consideration for DOCG, though it hardly seems to have arrived at that elite level yet. Still, as a white of more than routine appeal in an era when wines of its genre are in great demand, Albana has enough economic — and political — interest behind it to soon realize its potential. By 1980, talk of "launching" it in the United States and other nations was no longer idle. Albana may soon be competing strongly in those markets now dominated by Soave, Verdicchio, and Frascati.

The finest traditional-style Albana I have come across was a *secco* from Cavaliere Mario Pezzi, made at his Fattoria Paradiso outside Bertinoro. That was golden, smooth, elegantly balanced, an example of how good the wine can be. The Fratelli Vallunga at Marzeno di Brisighella, the pacesetter among Romagna's wineries today, makes an Albana *secco* that is outstandingly fruity and fresh, its style remindful of some of the fine whites of Friuli. The Vallunga Albana, especially from the exceptional 1977 vintage, stands as an ideal that other wineries would be well advised to try to equal. Vallunga's Albana is best within a year or two; Pezzi's might hold up well for up to four years because it is made in a more artisanal style. The *amabile* version tends to last longer because it is slightly stronger. Regular Albana, either still or *spumante*, must have 12° alcohol, the *amabile* 12.5°.

Trebbiano di Romagna, lighter, fresher, and often more acidic than Albana, is generally to be consumed within a year or two at the most after production. Until recently, it was considered little more than a local carafe wine that did not travel well. But the new technology is promising to change that image. Fratelli Vallunga, Francesco Ferrucci at Castelbolognese, and other progressive winemakers in the zone are now making fine Trebbiano capable of withstanding shipping. The increasing use of white wine in Italy and abroad will undoubtedly boost Trebbiano, too.

On its own, the Trebbiano grape traditionally made a rather thin wine, frequently flawed by sourness and excessive oxidation. But these days, thanks to new techniques, Trebbiano di Romagna often turns out bright, crisp, clean, even fruity. DOC also provides for a *spumante*. Both still and sparkling Trebbiano must have at least 11.5° alcohol.

Though the red Sangiovese di Romagna has been growing in stature, its importance still lags behind its availability. With 40 million liters a year — far more than DOC Lambrusco — it dominates premium wine production in Emilia-Romagna and ranks third in volume behind Chianti and Soave among Italy's DOC wines. And yet, until recently, it was scarcely known outside the region. Why? Same old story: the natives drank it up, never dreaming that its homespun goodness would be appreciated elsewhere. By now it has been recognized that Sangiovese di Romagna has an international future as it enters the world trade channels opened up by Lambrusco.

Sangiovese, with minimum alcohol of 11.5°, is neither very complex nor adapted to much aging, though the *riserva superiore* requires 12° alcohol and two years in barrel. From certain producers and certain vintages it has an aptitude for developing style and tone generally associated with red wines of greater standing and higher price. Three Sangioveses that warrant most serious consideration are made by Otello Burioli & Figli at Longiano, by Conte G. Battista Spalletti at Savignano sul Rubicone, and by Fratelli Vallunga at Marzeno di Brisighella.

Burioli's wine has such forthright goodness that its depth may take a while to become apparent. Full-bodied and smooth, with cheese it shows all the elegance of a superior aged Chianti. That is no coincidence, for Sangiovese is made from a Romagnan strain of the grape that is the mainstay of Chianti. Tuscan winemakers usually mix their Sangiovese with other grapes, but Sangiovese di Romagna is a 100 percent varietal. Spalletti's Rocca di Ribano is more tannic and austere than the Burioli wine, more delicately balanced. It probably could age well for five to eight years, but after two it can be delightfully drinkable.

The Fratelli Vallunga make Sangiovese at their winery in the hills south of Faenza. Tommaso Vallunga, a modern master, has also created a special Sangiovese called Brisiglé, from grapes grown by Bruno Benini, expressly for the Gigiolé restaurant at nearby Brisighella. The food of Gigiolé is worth the half-hour drive from the *autostrada,* and if you ever make it, do not miss the best Vallunga wine of all, Rosso del Armentano. In it, Sangiovese has been mixed with about 30 percent Cabernet and 10 percent Pinot Nero in one of the most successful formulas for red wine of the region. Rosso del Armentano is not especially big, but it is immensely pleasing, perfectly rounded with some of the flowery softness sometimes sensed in the finest *crus* of Pommard and Volnay in the Côtes de Beaune. Vallunga makes only about 25,000 bottles of this lovely wine a year.

A number of other producers make good Sangiovese, a popular, modestly priced wine good to drink, as a rule, within three or four years. Most Sangiovese is still consumed in the region, though it unquestionably has the potential for wide distribution and export. Good bottles are available from Cantina Baldini, Cantina PEMPA, Cantina Sociale Riminese, La Casetta, Pasolini Dall'Onda, Fattoria Paradiso, Conti Guarini Matteucci di Castelfranco, Giuseppe Marabini, Tenuta del Monsignore, and Arturo Tesini.

Corovin, the largest cooperative winery in Europe, with annual production of 180 million liters, groups 10,000 cultivators in a chain of 14 cooperatives. With headquarters in Forlì, Corovin sells some 40 million liters of wine a year in bottle, including the DOC wines of Romagna and Lambrusco. Another Corovin product was a white wine launched in the United States under the name Crista Bella. The subject of an expensive advertising campaign, Crista Bella was distributed by Tribuno, an autonomous division of Coca-Cola. Although its quality was acceptable for a white table wine, some elements of the Italian wine industry viewed Crista Bella, like Sotto Voce, Bell'Agio, and other so-called fantasy wines, as a potential threat to the improved image of control projected by DOC wines in the United States because these products ("born yesterday," as the magazine *Civiltà del Bere* put it) give no indication of origin, authenticity, or tradition behind their names. By 1980, Crista Bella and Sotto Voce had been canceled in the United States, though Banfi's Bell'Agio was still selling.

The Wines of Paradise

Good as many wines are now, the consensus is that the hills of Romagna have the capacity for greater things. Some growers are striving to reach new heights with old vines and new. One who has already succeeded most admirably is Mario Pezzi at Bertinoro.

Pezzi, in his meticulous manner, has converted sections of his family's cattle ranch into a haven for vines that he calls Fattoria Paradiso. His sprawling white villa, which also houses his cantina and a wine mu-

Mario Pezzi and daughter Graziella

seum, is encircled by vineyards in which he grows three popular varieties and four other extraordinary types, two of his own realization. They are Barbarossa, whose vines he discovered by accident and which he named after Frederick I, the red-bearded Holy Roman emperor who once resided in the castle at Bertinoro, and Pagadebit, white and lightly sweet, whose name means "pay debt." These two rarities are probably his finest wines, though his Picolit and Cagnina are exceptionally good sweet wines, and there is nothing common about his Albana or Sangiovese either.

As wine estates go, Fattoria Paradiso is neither too large nor too small but of a size that Cavaliere Pezzi has determined is workable and profitable while allowing the boss to run the entire show. He has been getting plenty of help lately from his daughter Graziella, a college graduate who seems determined to follow in her father's footsteps. Fattoria Paradiso is as neatly laid out and tidily maintained as a farm can be, no waste, no shortage, nothing left to chance except the whims of nature. Pezzi is an innovator, but of the sort who plots his every move.

His Pagadebit, from the almost obsolete Pagadebit Gentile vine, is perhaps his proudest achievement. That wine is so charmingly delicate in color, scent, and flavor, so precisely *amabile,* so clean and fresh that it is difficult to name a food to go with it. Some recommend it with cream soups, fruit, or dessert, but Pezzi himself prefers to drink it in tiny, contemplated sips. Italo Cosmo tasted Pagadebit on a visit to Bertinoro and told Pezzi that it should be valued among the great dessert wines of Italy. From some vintages it comes out almost dry, though no less distinctive.

Barbarossa is equally unique. Pezzi, who described its discovery as a miracle, took its few vines and carefully propagated them until he could grow enough grapes to make wine. He has been rewarded with a strong, dry red of outstanding depth and nuance. It is a big wine that goes with game, but Pezzi also recommends serving it with roasts and truffles. He suggests opening the bottle hours before serving and then only when the wine is five years old. Barbarossa's limited production is all that has prevented it from becoming known as one of Emilia-Romagna's outstanding red wines.

Pezzi has been able to achieve a greater yield from his Picolit vines than most growers do in Friuli. But its production still is difficult, which explains why this rich and luscious wine is his most expensive. Cagnina is a red dessert wine made from select clusters of Canaiolo Nero grapes known locally as Cagnina. Only a few growers around Bertinoro and Cesena make it. The most remarkable thing about Pezzi's Cagnina is its brilliant ruby-violet color. Grapy and fresh, it should be drunk young, when its bold sweetness goes well with rich desserts such as fruit and nut cakes. The vineyards of Bertinoro are also known for Aleatico, another sweet red wine used for dessert or *aperitivo.*

Pezzi's wines are a feature at La Frasca, in Castrocaro Terme, which has one of the outstanding wine lists of Italian restaurants. Gianfranco Bolognesi, owner and sommelier, has adopted a system of offering menus at various price levels with wines included. The food is predominately Romagnan, which is perhaps not as rich as Emilian but concedes nothing in quality. The wines, too, are often Romagnan, though only the finest. Bolognesi's impeccable palate has led him to stock bottles from many regions, a veritable honor roll of the great wines of each.

The Vintages

	Lambrusco	*Gutturnio dei Colli Piacentini*
1979	Good, scarce	Excellent
1978	Excellent	Excellent, scarce
1977	Uneven, some good	Fair
1976	Good	Very good
1975	Excellent	Fair
1974	Good to excellent	Good to excellent
1973	Good	Fair
1972	(Not a wine to age)	Poor
1971	—	Excellent
1970	—	Excellent

	Albana, Trebbiano di Romagna	*Sangiovese di Romagna*
1979	Excellent	Excellent
1978	Good	Good
1977	Exceptional	Exceptional
1976	Fair to good	Fair to good
1975	Excellent	Excellent
1974	Good	Good
1973	Excellent	Good
1972	—	Good
1971	—	Excellent
1970	—	Excellent

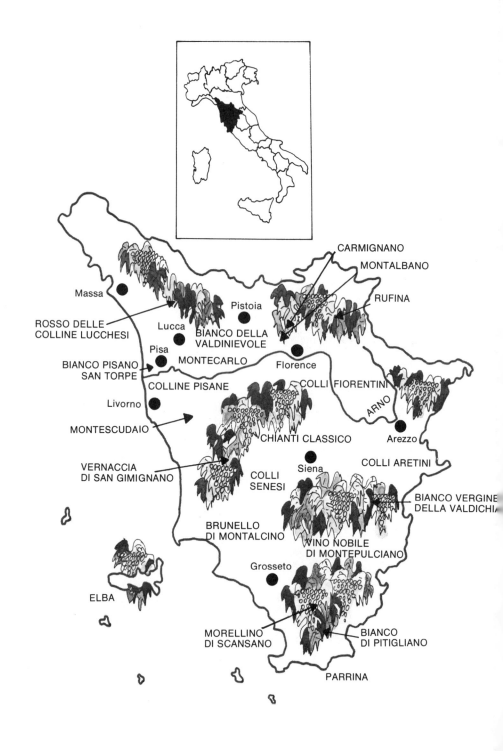

CARMIGNANO

MONTALBANO

RUFINA

Massa

Pistoia

ROSSO DELLE
COLLINE LUCCHESI

Lucca

BIANCO DELLA
VALDINIEVOLE

Pisa

BIANCO PISANO
SAN TORPE

MONTECARLO

Florence

COLLI FIORENTINI

COLLINE PISANE

ARNO

Livorno

MONTESCUDAIO

CHIANTI CLASSICO

Arezzo

VERNACCIA
DI SAN GIMIGNANO

COLLI
SENESI

Siena

COLLI ARETINI

BIANCO VERGINE
DELLA VALDICHIA

BRUNELLO
DI MONTALCINO

WINO NOBILE
DI MONTEPULCIANO

ELBA

Grosseto

MORELLINO
DI SCANSANO

BIANCO
DI PITIGLIANO

PARRINA

TUSCANY

PROVINCES

FLORENCE, Arezzo, Grosseto, Livorno, Lucca, Massa Carrara, Pisa, Pistoia, Siena

POPULATION

3,500,000

AREA

8,876 square miles

AVERAGE WINE PRODUCTION

470 million liters

DOC WINES

Bianco della Valdinievole · *Bianco di Pitigliano* · *Bianco Pisano San Torpé* · *Bianco Vergine della Valdichiana* · *Brunello di Montalcino* · *Carmignano* · *Chianti (Classico, Colli Aretini, Colli Fiorentini, Colline Pisane, Colli Senesi, Montalbano, Rufina)* · *Elba (Bianco, Rosso)* · *Montecarlo Bianco* · *Montescudaio (Bianco, Rosso, Vin Santo)* · *Morellino di Scansano* · *Parrina (Bianco, Rosso)* · *Rosso delle Colline Lucchesi* · *Vernaccia di San Gimignano* · *Vino Nobile di Montepulciano*

OTHER WINES

Aleatico · *Ansonico di Giglio* · *Bianco di Candia* · *Bianco di Chianti* · *Bianco Val d'Arbia* · *Brusco dei Barbi* · *Castello di Monte Antico* · *Galestro* · *Grana* · *Gran Spumante* · *Montecarlo Rosso* · *Montepescali* · *Moscato d'Elba* · *Moscadello or Moscadelleto di Montalcino* · *Nuovo Fiore* · *Procanico* · *Riesling* · *Rosato di Bolgheri* · *Rosato di Rigutino* · *Rosso di Cercatoia* · *Rosso Toscano* · *Rosso dei Vigneti di Brunello* · *San Giocondo* · *Sassicaia* · *Solera Dry* · *Tegolato* · *Testucchio* · *Tignanello* · *Tocai* · *Vin Santo Toscano*

Chianti: The Quintessential Wine

THE Apennines that separate Emilia-Romagna from Tuscany, though no longer difficult to cross, remain, as ever, precipitants of change. The trip across the mountains, whether on the Autostrada del Sole or one of the slower, winding roads across the nation's spine, dramatizes the contrasts between one region and the other, and even between one town and the next. It can provide the observant traveler with insights into why the Italian people have retained so much of their localized individuality — the vitality, the pride, and the pathos involved in living in their own special place.

Entering Tuscany, near the crest of the range, one is hardly struck by the differences. But as you bear south toward Florence, as forests of pine yield to chestnut and oak, then open into pastures and terraced fields interspersed with olive trees and vines, the sense of change is palpable and mounting, registered not only in the passing kilometers but in a sensation of rolling back through time. The images are masterful and pure. A stone farmhouse, roof sagging above a graceful arch, geraniums planted in discarded seed oil cans, the scene animated by chickens pecking for grain strewn about the yard. A castle's tower, Ghibelline (you can tell by the fishtail shape of the bastions jutting from the parapets), looms beyond a row of cypresses, the sky of a hue so delicate it might have been done by Botticelli.

By the time Florence comes into view, Brunelleschi's Duomo, the Palazzo Vecchio, and Forte Belvedere rising over the medley of terracotta roofs, you have reached the heartland, the wellspring of Renaissance Italy's artistry, intellect, and soul. And yet, after descending the hills to mingle in the narrow streets with the Florentines and their ever-present visitors, you find no evidence of the throb and glitter of a metropolis, but rather the deliberate, dignified pace of a big country town. Venerable Florence, fortified in stone, endures its throngs of tourists as it withstood invasions by outsiders in the past, maintaining, almost stoically, its sense of balance, civility, and good taste.

With such strength of character and an inborn eye for beauty, Tuscans built their cities and towns and shaped their countryside into an archetypal setting, the most Italian of places. Their land could not be called abundant, but in a sense it is rich: in its rewards to those who work it wisely, and as a source of inspiration to generations of a people who, perhaps more than any other, have shown the world what genius is.

It seems only natural that Italy's quintessential region should make its quintessential wine. Chianti has long been the most widely known and representative name in Italian wine, the one whose fortunes for decades reflected those of production nationwide and whose traditional container, the straw-covered flask, symbolized the trade. Today, the *fiasco* is approaching obsolescence, in part because of the excessive cost of making its hand-woven straw base and in part to the advantages producers have found in selling their wine in regular bottles. But Chianti, significantly, is as vital as ever before.

Though Chianti does not seem destined ever to be considered the greatest wine of Italy, or even of Tuscany, it is both historically and currently the most eminently intriguing. For even with centuries of tradition behind it, Chianti must be considered a contemporary wine in a state of flux. There are so many new vineyards, inspired producers, and fresh ideas around nowadays that it might take another decade or more for Chianti to establish its ultimate status in the hierarchy of Italian wines.

Chianti, in its seven units and their fringes, is the largest DOC district of Italy, both in territory and volume of production. Its more than 1 million acres stretch halfway across the peninsula from Pisa to Arezzo and from north of Florence half the distance south to Rome. From some 150,000 acres of vineyards, nearly 7,000 registered growers produce grapes for more than 100 million liters of DOC Chianti annually. And production has been increasing. Yet there are few places in Chianti's vast area where viticulture appears to be intense.

Hillside vineyards, which are still not all specialized, share estate land with olive groves, grain fields, and woods, a reason why the Tuscan landscape has retained a rustic elegance, a beauty at once wild and tamed that has captured the imagination of artists, poets, and travelers for centuries. Fortress castles, patrician villas, lonely farmhouses, winding graveled lanes flanked by cypresses and umbrella pines, hillsides splashed with yellow-flowered broom in late spring, woods of scrub oak, chestnut, and juniper: in Chianti's hills man and nature have found compatibility by never demanding too much from one another.

In such a setting it is not heartening to see a slope stripped of its habitual vegetation and put solidly to vine, for straight lines never figured prominently in the symmetry here. But economics is economics, and the demand for Chianti, after leveling off in the mid-1970s, is growing once again.

Despite its popularity, Chianti remains an enigma, as much in its homeland as abroad. It has gradually shifted its role from that of a wine to drink young to one that can age nicely, even magnificently from certain vintages and certain producers. And in that sense it has been undergoing a crisis of identity. While seeking amnesty for some unfortunate episodes in its otherwise proud past, Chianti faces a promising future not devoid of uncertainties.

If Chianti's new style of success is to continue, problems of costs, chiefly for labor, must be overcome. Most vineyards are in rather rough country, so cultivation has not been highly mechanized. Those gritty men who have been tending the vines by hand are growing old and their sons have shown little willingness to work the vines for wages below what factory hands are paid. The disconcerting choice left to landowners is to pay wages competitive with industry or to mechanize production, either of which means that costs must go up. So producers of Chianti, like those of almost all Italian premium wines, face the inevitability of raising prices while striving to keep their products in the extraordinarily competitive position they have been in. Some are bracing for a crunch.

But the makers of Chianti have weathered crises before, some so severe that it is a tribute to their resilience that the name survived with a measure of dignity, for few wines on earth have had such a turbulent history. Some producers have opted out, preferring to let wines that could be called Chianti carry other names. Still others have branched out, using their experience to make special wines — some from old vines, some from new, some carrying a special mark of distinction. But most have stuck with the name Chianti, confident that it will prove in the long run to be more of a boon than a burden.

How and when Chianti got its name is a matter of some conjecture; how far the wine has come since its early days is a matter of continuing controversy. Tuscans are skeptical folk, wary (though often envious as well) of him who is *furbo,* a term that means shrewd or cunning or even dishonest — as long as one gets away with it. But still it seems naïve, if not malicious, of them to persist in the often-expressed notion that much of what is sold as Chianti is hauled in by tanker trucks from wine factories to the south, even though it is true that Chianti is allowed a "correction" of up to 15 percent with wines or musts that may originate in other places.

Tuscans, who are thrifty to the point of parsimony, still have access to bulk wines straight from the farm, sometimes very good, sometimes not, but always, they insist, *genuino* and always moderately priced. So it is probably no wonder that they consider the cost of DOC Chianti, which often sells for more than $2.50 a bottle in Florence, as being terribly inflated. Even at home, Chianti has a long way to go.

Good Times and Bad

The Etruscans, the mysterious people whose language has only recently been deciphered, cultivated vines and made wine in Tuscany more than three thousand years ago. As evidence they left behind in their tombs vases, amphorae, and murals depicting happy wine drinkers. Their Roman conquerors were proficient winemakers as well, but when the empire declined, so did the vineyards. The clergy and the nobility revived them in the Middle Ages.

Lamberto Paronetto, in his book *Il Magnifico Chianti,* wrote that part of the continually disputed terrain between Florence and Siena might have been called *Clanti* as early as the eighth century. He notes, however, that the popular version of the derivation of the name Chianti is from *clangor,* a Latin term for a trumpet's blare as in a baronial hunt. Whatever its origin, the name had been cited in literature by 1260. In the thirteenth and fourteenth centuries, the area's feudal barons took part in the Lega del Chianti, a league to protect their various interests, one of which was wine. The League's territory ranged over an area now in Siena's province around the towns of Radda, Gaiole, and Castellina, covering about 40 percent of what is now the Chianti Classico zone.

Early references to Chianti as a wine were more often to white than red, though today white wines made in the zone cannot be called Chianti, at least not for the time being. The red wine of Florence's domain was known as Vermiglio in the late Middle Ages or as Florence Red when it was shipped to London as early as the thirteenth century. The Renaissance brought the art of winemaking to unprecedented heights in Tuscany, in the quality of the wine and in the techniques and rituals that grew around its production, bottling, and service. Chianti, or Vermiglio, was certainly one of the world's first dry red wines, coveted by the elite and quaffed by the masses in the heady atmosphere of Renaissance Florence.

The flask had been in use for at least six centuries before it made an impact on the world's wine markets, about 1860, after glass containers were perfected to permit cork sealing. Somewhat earlier, Bettino Ricasoli, the "Iron Baron," who became the second prime minister of a newly united Italy, made wine at his castle at Brolio, where he devised a formula for making Chianti from a composite of grapes by a method that is still in use to a large extent today.

Chianti's success encouraged imitation by neighborhood growers who liked the name and saw no harm in putting their own wine in flasks and calling it Chianti. But as transportation improved and "Chianti" production spread up and down the peninsula, growers in the authentic zones tried to check the impostors. Consortiums were formed, first by Chianti Classico in 1924, then by Chianti Putto in 1927, to organize producers and protect their wine's name. They managed to have the growing zones defined by law in 1932, but in the troubled period between two wars and the advent of Fascism, the Italian legal system was often encumbered by matters of greater gravity than wine fraud. Chianti's reputation hit appalling lows in the years following World War II. Only since DOC came into being could producers report real progress in restoring dignity to Chianti's besmirched name.

"Historic Compromise"

Chianti's recovery gave impetus to the general resurgence of Italian wines. The self-discipline shown by Tuscans in formulating a comprehensive code to control winemaking became the model for creating throughout Italy consortiums around which the DOC legislation of 1963 has been put into effect. The Chianti Classico consortium led the way. Since its foundation it has more than doubled the size of the original Classico zone, and it has remained a pacesetter in upgrading standards and in promoting its wines. It now has more than 700 members, nearly 300 of whom sell their own wine in labeled bottles. The consortium's emblem, the *gallo nero* (black rooster), is undoubtedly the most widely recognized symbol of quality wine in Italy today.

But the *gallo nero* is not the only badge of integrity in Chianti. The rivalry with the Putto consortium, whose name comes from its emblematic baby Bacchus entwined in a vine, is outwardly correct, but bitter behind the scenes. Nonetheless, not long ago the consortiums reached a difficult agreement that committed them to working for DOCG in full cooperation. This *"compromesso storico,"* as it has been called in light-hearted reference to a "historic compromise" reached between Italy's Christian Democrat and Communist political factions at about the same time, is believed to have cleared the way for Chianti's eventual elevation as a unit to the higher level. But, as Paolo Desana's national DOC committee has reminded the Tuscans, the details involved in guaranteeing the production of such a vast area will take a while to work out.

The recently expanded Putto confederation, the largest producers' association in Italy, has many more members than does the Classico consortium and a correspondingly greater volume of production. Its members' nearly 1,900 properties are scattered through the other six recognized DOC zones: Montalbano, Colli Fiorentini, Rufina, Colli Aretini, Colli Senesi, and Colline Pisane. Between them, if for no other reason than their sheer strength of numbers, they turn out more good Chianti than do Classico's adherents. Putto has been proclaiming this for years, but as far as the world's consumers, dealers, critics, and writers are concerned, the fact has been falling on deaf ears.

In defense of the Chianti Classico consortium, it seems fair to say that a greater percentage of wine sold under its *gallo nero* emblem is first-rate. But the widespread and persistent notion that the term "Classico" denotes intrinsic superiority is harmful to the general health of Chianti and should have been discarded long ago. It should further be noted that producers of Chianti in the delimited zones are not required to belong to any consortium, but they are required to meet legal standards to carry the DOC on their labels. Not all good Chianti can be identified by a black rooster or a Bacchus on the neck label. There are, in addition, several other active consortiums, mainly on the periphery of the delimited zones, seeking DOC for their areas' Chianti.

DOC disciplines have set slight differences in the standards for Chianti Classico and the Chianti of the other six zones and those fringes entitled to the name. Classico has a lower maximum yield of grapes per hectare and a 12° minimum alcohol content against 11.5° for other Chianti. All Chianti must be kept until the March 1 after the harvest before being sold; to be called *vecchio* it needs more than two years' aging, to be called *riserva* more than three years. Classico *riserva* must have at least 12.5° alcohol, Chianti *riserva* at least 12°. The Putto consortium, however, has voluntarily and wisely set its standards equal to Chianti Classico's.

The grape formula for all Chianti is flexible enough to allow for variations in style and type, ranging from deep violet to light ruby in color, and in taste from rather full, complex, aged versions to sprightly young wines to be drunk within a year or two. The mixture is of red Sangiovese at 50 to 80 percent, red Canaiolo at 10 to 30 percent, and two light grapes — Trebbiano and Malvasia — at 10 to 30 percent. The heavily pigmented Colorino grape is often used in the *governo all'uso toscano.*

Though some producers avoid on principle the permitted 15 percent correction, others take advantage of it to tone up their Chianti, particularly from weak vintages. Traditionally, much of the musts or wines used came from the deep south, notably Apulia, but a recent trend has been toward use of Cabernet and Merlot, sometimes grown locally. Also Montepulciano d'Abruzzo, which is similar in character to Sangiovese, though more robust, has been growing in favor.

Chianti, Old and New

Governo, like the flask, has been losing ground in Chianti's recent evolution. For flask wines most makers used *governo* to give to Chianti a certain youthful zest and roundness that suited not only the typically rustic Tuscan cooking but concepts of eating *all'Italiana* in many other places. The *governo all'uso toscano* consisted of adding the musts of from 5 to 10 percent of the grapes, which had been set aside and semidried on mats, to vats of normally fermented wine. That practice, which induced a refermentation while increasing color, alcohol, and the glycerol level, is now in decline. One reason why is that it can leave the wine more vulnerable to deterioration, which may be marked by volatile acidity that results in "off" odors, while oxidation causes the flavor to fade or grow flabby. Also, producers now have at their disposal techniques to realize effects similar to *governo* with less risk and bother. Increased emphasis has been placed on controlling the malolactic fermentation to reduce volatile acidity and increase stability, a step that was all too often neglected by Tuscans in the past.

The flask, meanwhile, has become a victim of technology as well (or, should we say, rather, of modern concepts of design and marketing). Those wizened country women who used to scratch out a living weaving the bases priced the flask out of the market. Anyway, that is the excuse wine producers usually give for the flask's demise, though some bottle makers in the region insist that they can manufacture an authentic 1.5-liter flask that, once labeled and corked, would cost no more than bottles and could be packed and shipped just as economically. As Giovanni Bartolozzi of Vetreria Etrusca put it: "Cost isn't the decisive factor working against the flask. It's image. Chianti makers don't want to be saddled with an old-fashioned container. They want consumers to associate Chianti with Bordeaux, so they've adopted the Bordeaux type of bottle."

A great deal of Chianti is still sold in oversized containers in Italy, but the flask is less and less apparent. Its successors lack that flare for ready identity that was perhaps the key factor in Chianti's rise to fame. Classico's producers have selected a nondescript 1.5-liter magnum. Putto's came up with the squat, slope-shouldered *toscanello* of the same size, whose proportions are as gawky as the flask's were graceful. And there is also something called the *chiantigiana* in circulation, still another inducement to producers to sell their wines in Bordeaux-style bottles. Neither the *fiasco* nor the *governo* is dead yet, but their days, and thus those of the old Chianti, seem numbered.

The new Chianti has not asserted its total personality yet. It is no longer a secret that use of the light Trebbiano and Malvasia grapes in Chianti has been reduced to below the prescribed DOC minimum and in many cases to nothing, all with the tacit approval of the consortiums. In theory, the result should be wine of deeper color, bigger body, and greater aging potential than before. And yet much Chianti on the market today is rather light, fruity, fresh, not the sort of wine that needs to be laid away for years.

The reason for this apparent contradiction is that the new oenology has given the winemaker a greater number of variables to choose from. You will hear sharply diverse points of view in the Tuscan hills these days about what Chianti's character should be, and you will taste the differences in the wine. For every producer who aims for a deep, robust, aristocratic wine to be aged in barrel into *vecchio* or *riserva* there seems to be another who favors vinifying toward the light and bright in wine to be drunk within a year or two, a style that has more to do with stainless steel than Slavonian oak. Not that the choices are strictly black and white; some producers make a little of each.

With all those excess light grapes around, producers in Chianti have been pushing for the launching — or, historically speaking, the redis- covery — of white Chianti, though already use of the name Chianti with Bianco has been excluded by authorities. Another welcome result has been a noticeable increase in the production of Vin Santo.

The prime emphasis remains on red wine, Chianti of more consistent quality and greater prestige, whether or not it is labeled *riserva*. With each vintage more good wines appear, making this an era of unprece- dented excitement and confusion for Chianti admirers. The candidates for the top category are emerging at an ever-increasing tempo, at a rate that makes them difficult to keep track of.

The practice of letting Chianti age before selling it is by no means novel, for many winemakers have traditionally turned over at least part of their crop to barrel aging. But few of their number, perhaps two dozen, could state that their *riserva* or *vecchio* Chiantis were well known outside Tuscany before 1970. By 1980 the number of producers selling aged Chianti in bottles must have been at least 1,000. Their wines, often estate-bottled and often of limited supply, have been making slow but steady progress in the quality markets, both in Italy and abroad. Some large wineries and shipper-bottlers have well-established reputations for their bottled and aged wines of sound quality with the all-important ca- pacity of meeting consumer demand.

But the very finest Chiantis are rarely produced in great quantity. It is difficult to pinpoint where they come from, though one can single out certain terrains throughout the seven zones that have superior condi- tions of soil or beneficial microclimates or better-established vines or, perhaps most importantly, a winemaker of exceptional skill. Luck and the weather play their roles as well.

Chianti Classico has been getting an inordinate share of the attention, not only because of the myth of its inherent superiority (which its makers, naturally, believe themselves), but also because its wines have been proving increasingly to be worthy of the *gallo nero* reputation for quality. Occasional duds appear bearing the emblem, but the consortium, which controls more than 90 percent of Classico production, has been diligently trying to shape them up as well. Some years, more than half the wine tested has been rejected by the consortium as substandard, as in 1976 when poor weather took its toll. The Classico zone enjoys the advantages of a close-knit organization and a certain geographic coherence. It covers some 200,000 acres in a rough ellipse that reaches from just south of Florence to just north of Siena, centered in Greve, a market center in one of its few flat-bottomed valleys.

The other six DOC Chianti zones are dispersed through the provinces of Pisa, Pistoia, Florence, Arezzo, and Siena, completely encircling Chianti Classico in an area of about 750,000 acres. Chianti dominated by the Putto confederation has a greater variation of terrain and climatic conditions, a greater range of styles and of quality. Still, anyone who attempts to compare generically and qualitatively the character of Chianti Classico as opposed to Chianti is on shaky ground indeed. When it comes to class, each Chianti should be judged by its individual attributes, not by the group its producer belongs to.

Florence's Domain

The bottle of Chianti I recall enjoying most, and indeed one of the finest red wines I have ever tasted, would seem to have lacked the necessary credentials. It was not very old, not a *riserva,* not a Classico, and it was made using the *governo.* La Querce 1970, a Putto, it came from the Colli Fiorentini at Impruneta, about 10 kilometers south of Florence. When I bought it and drank it in 1974 it cost 3,500 lire, an astronomical price for a relatively young Chianti. It was worth it and more. Balanced, luxuriant, with unusual depth and strength (14.5 percent alcohol), it showed nuances in its bouquet and flavor that no wine that young should have been expected to have. Evidently those features, both tangible and nebulous, that made the wine great had melded at that propitious moment. I have since tried the 1970 *riserva* and other vintages from La Querce, all made by *governo,* and none has equaled that first bottle.

Attilio Pieri, manager and winemaker at the estate owned by Gino Marchi and Grazia Montorselli, listened intently as I told him of my experience. Yes, he said, it was true that 1970 was a great year for La Querce (though not generally for Chianti), undoubtedly the finest since he became *fattore* in 1968. Yes, the wine fetched an extraordinarily high early price, apparently the highest for any Chianti anywhere. Why? Because it was exceptional and there had been a demand. No, he did not agree that it reached its peak in 1974, but everyone is entitled to his opinion. The 1970 *riserva,* he believed, had many good years left in it.

Attilio Pieri

Pieri, calm, slim, craggy-featured, seemed surprised and amused by the course of our conversation. He explained that all his 1970 Chianti — some 30,000 liters from 16 acres of vines — had been vinified together and then, after the *governo,* separated into smaller barrels as either regular Chianti or *riserva,* which stayed in the wood three years. He practices *governo* for the reserve wine, he said with a shrug, because that is the way he makes Chianti. Period.

That explanation seemed good enough for me, but I remain, nonetheless, puzzled. Perhaps when the 1970 *riserva* rounds into full form, if it has not already, some of my doubts will be resolved. Still, there is no question that La Querce can be a very special wine. Pieri, who worked his way through first agricultural, then accounting schools in the prewar days by making and selling contraband grappa near his native Lucca, vows he has no secrets and uses no tricks in making either Chianti or La Querce's equally fine olive oil.

"I prune carefully, I use manure, no chemical fertilizers ever, and I employ every honest means I can to make a good wine. But if it isn't up to La Querce standards, it's sold at the bulk rate, not bottled. I try to keep the process natural from beginning to end. Come to think of it, these days maybe that is a secret."

As traditional suppliers of wine to Florence, the vineyards of Colli Fiorentini and the adjacent Montalbano and Rufina have long-established rights to the name Chianti. The zones stretch from near Pistoia on the northwest (Montalbano) around the southern and eastern limits of Florence (Colli Fiorentini) to the town of Dicomano on the northeast (Rufina). *Governo* is probably still practiced here more than elsewhere because of the demand for fresh flask wines on the tables of Florence. But the trend toward bottled and aged wine is prominent as well.

Each of the three zones has vineyards and vine-growing areas capable of producing wines that can stand with La Querce in the front ranks of all Chianti. In Montalbano, which encompasses the DOC zone of a special red wine known as Carmignano, excellent Chianti is made by, among others, Nobil Casa Contini Bonacossi at Capezzana, Fattoria di Artimino at Artimino, and Bibbiani at Capraia e Limite. In the Colli Fiorentini, Montespertoli is the center of an exceptional area where the names of Ottorino Buti and Novello Parri are among the noteworthy. Parri and his son Luigi make Chianti from three estates: Tenuta Corfecciano, Tenuta Il Monte, and Tenuta Ribaldaccio. Pasolini Dall'Onda Borghese at Barberino Val d'Elsa makes a Chianti in the best of traditional styles.

Still more producers in Colli Fiorentini and Montalbano rate special mention, among them:

★ Collazzi at Colleramole Impruneta
★ Colonia at Cerreto Guidi
★ Dianella Fucini at Vinci
★ Fattoria Lilliano at Antella
★ Fattoria La Pagnana at Rignano sull'Arno
★ Fattoria Il Palagio at Figline Valdarno
★ Fattoria di Sammontana at Montelupo Fiorentino (from the properties of Andrea & Ezio Gigli, Peruzzi, and Conte Dzieduszycki)
★ Fattoria Giannozzi at Certaldo Alto-Marcialla (the estate of Luciano Giannozzi, president of the Chianti Putto consortium)
★ Fattoria Terranova at Reggello
★ I Golli at Romola
★ Passaponti at Marcialla
★ Pillo at Gambassi (the winemaker is Bianchina Alberici, who also makes Buttafuoco in Lombardy's Oltrepò Pavese)
★ Ugolino at Mortinette Ugolino

Rufina: "Poco ma Buono"

Rufina, smallest of the seven Chianti zones, makes some of its grandest wines. The popular expression *poco ma buono* applies here — another way of saying good things come in small packages. Marchesi de' Frescobaldi and Spalletti are the biggest names. The list of smaller estates adds to the honor roll of Chianti that in terms of the concentration of quality wines may be matched only in certain parts of Chianti Classico, notably the area around Castellina, Radda, and Gaiole that comprised the original Chianti League.

Spalletti, controlled by the Cinzano Vermouth firm of Piedmont, has cellars in the town of Rufina. Spalletti makes its respected Poggio Reale Riserva from the estate of that name, along with other Chianti, Orvieto, and other types of wine. Smaller Rufina estates of note are Busini, Camperiti, Fattoria Altomena, Fattoria di Bossi, Fattoria di Selvapiana, Fattoria di Vetrici, Grignano, Petrognano, and Tenuta di Poggio.

Marchesi de' Frescobaldi, who trace the winemaking members of their famous family back to the fourteenth century, are unique among the large-scale wine firms of the area in that they make all their wine exclusively from grapes grown on their eight estates. In fact, each property is a complete winemaking unit run independently, except that bottling is done at the Pontassieve plant that also serves as a point of coordination.

Marchesi de' Frescobaldi is a family enterprise controlled by three brothers who above all else consider themselves cultivators. The brothers — Vittorio, Leonardo, and Ferdinando — manage to look more like *marchesi* than men of the soil but they run their extensive operation with a precision that can come only from knowing every row of vines, every cask, every hired hand on each of the properties. They also divide duties in a business of international scope with Vittorio as president, Ferdinando as commercial manager for Italy, and Leonardo as manager of foreign sales.

Taken together, the Frescobaldi vineyards represent one of the largest, if not the largest, family-owned wine holdings in Europe with a total of more than 500 hectares (1,335 acres) of vines in both Rufina and Colli Fiorentini. Besides Chianti they produce Vin Santo, white and rosé wines, a *vino novello* called Nuovo Fiore, and a Champagne-type *spumante*. Although the brothers prefer not to make judgments on the quality of wine from each estate, there is no denying that Nipozzano excels for Chianti of the *riserva* class and Pomino stands out for its white and Chianti of youthful tone.

The Castello di Nipozzano passed into the family in the last century, when the daughter of Marchese Vittorio degli Albizi, an innovative winemaker who won numerous awards for his skills, married a Frescobaldi. Nipozzano has since been expanded into a major property whose wine illustrates how good the Chianti of Rufina can be. Bottles dating to 1864 are kept in the cantina. The 1974 vintage, which was rounding into form by 1980, showed the color, body, balance, and aging potential that if realized more consistently throughout the seven zones would earn Chianti the reputation of one of the world's truly great wines, as some of its boosters now claim it to be. I strongly suspect that the 1974 Nipozzano contained no white grapes.

One Nipozzano plot produced such a grand wine in 1974 that the Frescobaldis decided to bottle it separately under the name Montesodi. The 4,850 bottles were selling for about 15,000 lire apiece in 1980, which made Montesodi one of the most expensive recent red wines in Italy. Marchese de' Frescobaldi planned to bottle it only in exceptional years.

Nipozzano reflects the master touch of Luciano Boarino, the Piedmontese technical director whose experimentation with the vines and wines of Frescobaldi has further enhanced the firm's reputation. The Chianti of Pomino is distinguished by its aroma, which Boarino credits in part to the 10 percent Cabernet Sauvignon and in part to the uncommon height of the estate's vineyards. "What high altitude costs in body, it often makes up for in fragrance," Boarino explained. The Cabernet is permitted, as it is in Chianti of a few other estates, because it was traditionally cultivated at Pomino.

The upper vineyards of Pomino, which lie between 2,000 and 2,300 feet above sea level, are planted in Pinot Bianco and Grigio, Sauvignon, and, more recently, Chardonnay. These vines, foreign to Tuscany, have given Boarino his greatest challenge and his greatest satisfaction. Pomino Bianco is singular among Tuscan whites, crisp, clean, fragrant, fruity, with class remindful of some Pinots of Friuli but with character exquisitely its own.

Two other large Chianti firms have headquarters at Pontassieve on the edge of the Rufina zone. Ruffino and Melini are known throughout the world for the wines they market in both standard bottles and larger containers. Though they purchase grapes for some of their wines, each makes special wines from its own vineyards in Chianti Classico and elsewhere.

I. L. Ruffino, whose winery spans the main Florence–Pontassieve road, is a dependable giant with a sound line of wines from Tuscany and other regions. But its main focus has always been on Chianti, and through the years its name has probably been the most recognizable in Italy and abroad among all producers of the wine. The firm, owned by the Folonari family, bottles both DOC Chianti Classico and Chianti, some of the Classico under the names Riserva Ducale and Gold Label. Those prestigious wines from the best vintage years are made with the selectivity and care usually associated with small estates.

Melini, which is part of the Winefood group, produces both Chianti and Chianti Classico, where it has extensive holdings. It also makes Orvieto and other wines, which are bottled at Pontassieve. The firm was founded by the Melini family in 1705. In the last century, Adolfo Laborel Melini devised the so-called *strapeso* flask of glass strong enough to permit bottling with corks. That enabled Melini and other producers to ship their Chianti throughout the world and build the image of the flask.

Big Business in Classico

Three other big names in Chianti — Barone Ricasoli, Marchesi Antinori, and Conti Serristori — were winemaking operations based on properties of those noble families in Chianti Classico. Steady expansion has diversified their product lines.

The Società Vinicola Conti Serristori, now controlled by Winefood, still bases its solid reputation on its Chianti Classico Machiavelli. That wine comes from vineyards at Sant'Andrea in Percussina once owned by the Serristoris' ancestor Niccolò Machiavelli, who did much of his important writing there while in exile from Florence. Serristori produced a special Chianti Classico *riserva* from the 1975 vintage, 10,470 bottles labeled Ser Niccolò Machiavelli. It makes other wines as well, including an Orvieto, a rosé, a Vin Santo, and a Brut Spumante.

Marchesi Lodovico and Piero Antinori were once noted primarily for their Villa Antinori Chianti Classico, but the firm has moved smartly to develop an imaginative and imposing array of quality wines. The Antinori assortment includes Chianti Classico and Chianti and Orvieto Classico from the family estate of Castello della Sala. Others are Villa Antinori Bianco, Rosato di Bolgheri, a Sherry-style Solera Dry, Aleatico, Vin Santo (both white and a rare red), a Brut Spumante made by the *méthode champenoise* from grapes purchased in the Oltrepò Pavese, and a *vino novello* called San Giocondo from grapes grown in the Tuscan hills, one of the first and most successful new wines around. Antinori also makes Tignanello and distributes Sassicaia, two extraordinary red wines that will be discussed later.

Piero Antinori is without doubt one of the most brilliant activators in the art of making wine and the techniques of selling it at work in Italy today. At once progressively innovative and respectful of useful tradition, Antinori is young, intelligent, shrewd, and eloquent, with the energy to make things happen in a way that would quickly exhaust more common men. The Antinoris can trace their family heritage in wine back to the fourteenth century, when one Giovanni di Piero Antinori was enrolled in the guild of *vinattieri*. But Piero Antinori, though a nobleman with his feet firmly planted on the stones of Florence, is not one to dwell on the past.

"Sometimes when I look around Italy I try to imagine what the wines would be like if other grape varieties were planted in certain places," he said. "Here in Tuscany we have Sangiovese and Trebbiano, fine, hearty varieties. But if we had Cabernet Sauvignon or Nebbiolo for the reds and, say, Chardonnay or Pinot or Riesling for the whites, we might have even greater wines."

Antinori's is not idle dreaming. The firm has planted Cabernet in certain of its Tuscan vineyards and Pinot and Chardonnay at Orvieto. If Antinori had his way he would eliminate the light grapes altogether in Chianti and put Cabernet in their place. The problem, of course, is the DOC discipline.

"I know things are slow to change," he said. "This is Italy, after all. But I'm an optimist. I think there's a good chance that we can change the discipline for the better. And sooner than you might think."

Cantine Antinori at San Casciano Val di Pesa contains the ultimate in equipment for production of white wine and a Bordeaux-style setup for some of the reds, all under the direction of oenologist Giacomo Tachis. Antinori's aim is to perfect the system to process each wine in the most suitable manner, which means there is plenty of experimentation under way.

"Frankly, we Tuscans have been rather backward when it comes to techniques," said Antinori. "We're just learning to work well with whites and we're not exactly in the avant-garde with reds either. I repeat, I'm an optimist. Our traditional wines are already very good, but wait until you taste the Tuscan wines of the future."

Piero Antinori

For the present, all the wines of Antinori can be appraised in Florence at the Cantinetta Antinori, a bar-restaurant on the ground floor of the Palazzo Antinori on, naturally enough, the Piazza Antinori.

Barone Ricasoli's Castello di Brolio was for decades the most vaunted name in Chianti with a reputation passed down from the Iron Baron through the generations. From its formidable base in the southerly hills of Classico, the family built a wine empire headed by Barone Bettino Ricasoli, who remained for years a force behind the Chianti Classico consortium and possibly the most respected figure in Tuscan wine. Then, in the mid-1970s, Ricasoli made two moves that sent shock waves through the Italian wine industry. He sold controlling interest in the firm to Seagram's, the American conglomerate, and not long afterward he (along with Antinori) quit the Classico consortium.

Both steps made perfect sense if analyzed in strictly business terms; Seagram's provided the capital for growth and development, and with a name of his stature Barone Ricasoli did not need the consortium behind him. But not all Ricasoli's peers, or other Tuscans, tend to think in strictly business terms. There was talk of a *tradimento* — whose mildest interpretation is "sellout" — to the Americans, along with grumbling about the irreparable harm done to the *gallo nero*. Even before that, an undercurrent of opinion had it that Brolio was not what it used to be; now such talk broke into the open. Indeed, there were signs that Brolio, like a few other Classicos from long-established estates, was not keeping pace with the emerging competition. Although the price of Brolio *riserva* remained at the top of its category, its quality, perhaps, had not. The *Catalogo Bolaffi*, for example, had been giving Brolio *riserva* one star for quality while handing out two or three to other Chiantis, some mere upstarts. But one should not judge Brolio or Ricasoli too harshly, remembering that overworked phrase from the sports world, "Wait'll next year!" can apply in winemaking as well.

Barone Ricasoli would never need an alibi for its Torricella, one of those uncommon dry white wines that benefit not only from barrel age but from a decade, sometimes more, in bottle. Made from Malvasia grapes gathered in the Brolio vineyards once owned by Galileo, it can serve as a table wine with fish, but its opulence probably comes across best as a well-chilled *aperitivo*. Ricasoli may still have bottles of the 1955 and 1957 Torricella to sell. Ricasoli Vin Santo is also noteworthy.

Castello di Meleto and Bertolli are two other large firms whose Chianti Classico is well known abroad. Bertolli also makes regular Chianti and other wines.

Two cooperatives have brought their production to the level that places them among the major Chianti Classico producers in terms of volume. Castelli del Grevepesa gets its grapes from 183 estates, large and small, and vinifies them at its winery at Ponte di Gabbiano. Its production reaches some 6 million liters a year, about a quarter of it marketed directly in bottles, flasks, and magnums. The Agricoltori del Chianti Geografico near Gaiole produces about 3 million liters of Chianti Classico a year, but markets only about 350,000 liters under its own Chianti Geografico label.

The Old Guard: Keeping Step with the New

Behind the giants is a nucleus of medium to large estates, often the properties of aristocratic families, whose Chianti Classico in bottles has been on the market for years in great enough quantity to have established solid reputations. Their names, familiar in Italy and often abroad, are the foundation upon which Chianti's renewed prestige has been built. Prominent estates in this group and their owners:

★ Badia a Coltibuono, Piero Stucchi-Prinetti
★ Calcinaia, Conte Neri Capponi
★ Casenuove, Pietro Pandolfini
★ Castello di Cerreto, Marchese Emilio Pucci (the peripatetic fashion designer)
★ Castello di Uzzano, Conti Castelbarco Albani Masetti
★ Castello di Verrazzano, Cavaliere Luigi Cappellini
★ La Pesanella, Grande Ufficiale Remo Ciampi
★ Lilliano Rosso, Principessa Eleonora Ruspoli Berlingieri
★ Mocenni, Nicolò Casini
★ Monsanto, Fabrizio Bianchi
★ Montagliari, Lorenzo and Giovanni Cappelli
★ Montepaldi, Marchesi Corsini
★ Nozzole, Letizia Rimediotti Mattioli
★ Palazzo al Bosco, Renzo Olivieri Eredi
★ Pian d'Albola, Principe Ginori Conti
★ Straccali, Tina and Franca Straccali
★ Tizzano, Conte Filippo Pandolfini
★ Vicchiomaggio, a corporation
★ Vignamaggio, Contessa Elena Sanminiatelli Castelbarco
★ Vignavecchia, Franco Beccari
★ Villa Cafaggio, Stefano Farkas

These wines represent the established elite of Chianti Classico, widely appreciated for their integrity and reliability. They include several wines consistently ranked among the finest Chianti of all, perhaps most consistently the Vignavecchia *riserva*.

In the quality markets these stalwarts set the pace, but the ranks of the old guard sometimes find themselves looking sideways to be sure they are keeping step with the new. Names that were scarcely known just a few years ago keep popping up when Chianti Classico is judged on absolute quality and not on established reputations.

Thus Poggio al Sole, from a tiny estate turning out some 15,000 to 20,000 bottles annually, was unofficially dubbed "wine of the year" after its 1975 vintage went on sale in 1977. Made using the *governo* by estate manager Aldo Torrini, Poggio al Sole was judged by the Lega del Chianti, a wine society remindful of the Chevaliers du Tastevin of Burgundy, as best wine in a tasting at Gaiole. Other critics tended to support that decision. A harmonious, full-bodied wine, it seemed best suited to drinking within two to four years. Poggio al Sole also is made into *riserva* from good vintages.

Among the emerging Classico, the sentimental favorite is Savignola Paolina, made by an energetic octogenarian on her diminutive plot of land adjacent to Vignamaggio. The wine is named for the estate, Savignola, and its plucky creator, Paolina Fabbri, who personally directs all the work. Signorina Fabbri, a relative newcomer to winemaking, says she developed her style in her seventies and is now enjoying the fruits of her labor in her eighties. And, indeed, her Classico is among the most respected and expensive on the market. A traditionalist, Paolina Fabbri believes, as did many of her no longer active contemporaries, in following the phases of the moon in all stages of winemaking and in the benefits of thorough wood aging.

Coralia Pignatelli della Leonessa, proprietess of Castell'in Villa near Castelnuovo Berardenga, provides indisputable evidence that women — princesses at that — can make wine as well as men. "As well? I think better," she said. "Women are more sensitive to subtleties, more refined in their tastes. If more women were involved, we'd have finer wine." Princess Pignatelli backs her spirited position with a Classico that should be the envy of most of her male competitors in Chianti. One might be tempted to describe Castell'in Villa as soft, smooth, seductive, etcetera, terms the princess would certainly not dispute, but her style also allows for a measure of tannin and wood. She applies her special touch to a production of nearly 400,000 bottles a year of a wine worthy of a princess — or even a prince.

Next door to Castell'in Villa is Pagliarese, another property owned by a woman, Alma Biasotto Sanguinetti, but in this case she leaves the winemaking to the men. She attributes the superb balance and breed of her estate's wine, even in such mediocre years as 1972 and 1976, to the prominence of beneficial minerals in Pagliarese's soil, elements she says are not so prevalent elsewhere. Pagliarese *riserva* is often listed among the finest Chianti made.

Other estates in Chianti Classico, some small, some rather large, some old, some new, have been making wine of real validity, though not all is exported. Here are some Chianti Classico estates whose wines from the vintages between 1969 and 1978 have proved to be excellent:

★ Berardenga at Castelnuovo Berardenga
★ Bozzagone at Castellina in Chianti
★ Caggiolo at Castellina in Chianti
★ Capannelle at Gaiole
★ Carobbio at Greve
★ Castello di Cacchiano at Gaiole
★ Castello di Monteriggioni at Monteriggioni
★ Castello di Mugnana at Greve
★ Castello di Rencine at Castellina in Chianti
★ Castello di Volpaia at Radda
★ Castelruggero (Le Macchie) at Strada in Chianti
★ Castelvecchi at Radda
★ Cerasi at Castellina in Chianti
★ Fattoria Aiola at Vagliagli
★ Fattoria della Barone at Panzano
★ Fattoria della Lodoline at Vagliagli
★ Fattoria di Castagnoli at Gaiole
★ Fattoria Le Pici at San Gusmé
★ Fattoria Montecchio at San Donato in Poggio
★ Fattoria Poggiarello at Castellina in Chianti
★ Fattoria di Selvole at Vagliagli
★ Filetta at Lamole
★ Fonterutoli at Castellina in Chianti (from the estate of Lapo Mazzei, president of the Classico consortium)

★ Fortilizio Il Colombaio at Querciagrossa
★ Godenano Secondo at Castellina in Chianti
★ Grignanello at Castellina in Chianti
★ Il Campino at Barberino Val d'Elsa (which claims to be Classico's smallest producer with 1,250 bottles a year)
★ Isole e Olena at Barberino Val d'Elsa
★ La Bricola at Sambuca Val di Pesa
★ La Mandria at Gaiole
★ Le Bocce at Panzano
★ Monte Vertine at Radda
★ Nittardi at Castellina in Chianti
★ Petroio at Quercegrossa
★ Petroio Via della Malpensata at Radda in Chianti
★ Podere Spadaio at San Donato in Poggio
★ Rignana at Greve
★ Tenuta La Novella at San Polo in Chianti
★ Salcetino at Lucarelli
★ San Leonino at Castellina in Chianti
★ Valiano at Vagliali
★ Villa Cerna at Cerna

The list could probably be doubled in number, for there are so many fine bottles of Classico available. Most can be found for sale at the Enoteca di Chianti Classico in Greve.

A Foreign Touch

Foreigners, who have long been attracted to these enchanting hills, have settled in the Classico zone by the hundreds, buying up farmhouses, villas, and even castles, sometimes with enough land to make wine of their own. The roster of Chianti Classico producers includes such names as Hargittai, Lüneburg, François, Gutierrez de la Solana, Van Straten, and Hamilton.

Prominent among these *stranieri* is John Dunkley, an Englishman, who arrived on the scene in 1971. After weighing his assets, he decided he could afford to leave his advertising career in London and live comfortably if modestly at Riecine, his restored farmhouse with five acres of vines and a swimming pool overlooking the quiet town of Gaiole. With his Italian-born wife, Palmina, as full-time partner, he went to work on the vines, keeping what he could of the old ones and coaxing along the new with a copy of *General Viticulture,* the vineyard keepers' bible from California, always close at hand.

"There was a bit of bumbling about at first," Dunkley recalled, "but everyone was so warm and helpful. Our main source of information was neighboring farmers, but people from big firms and the *consorzio* helped as well. When they gave advice, it was good advice."

It must have been. By 1973 the Dunkleys not only had their wine accepted as Chianti Classico, but to the surprise of everybody, including themselves, when it went on sale in 1975 it was immediately judged to be exceptional. Riecine's praises were soon being sung not only in Italy, but in faraway England, and even in the wine column of the *Chappaqua Patent Trader* in New York State. Later vintages have often been as good or better. Dunkley, who still seems a bit stunned by his wine's acceptance, has consented to export some to Britain, the United States, and Hong Kong. But with a production of only about 12,000 to 15,000 bottles a year, he has had to limit sales. Although he says that the label, which depicts their home, was meant to be a spoof of the grand castles and villas that appear on others, it turned out to be one of the more artistically conceived of the zone.

"I'm immensely pleased," said Dunkley, whose trim bearing, sharp features, and graying blond hair give him the appearance of the movie version of an aging British army officer. He sat under the pergola in front of his house, sipping the excellent white wine he has been making and selling in minuscule amounts as well, and talked about winemaking.

"This is not an easy business," he said. "By doing 50 to 60 percent of the labor ourselves, with the olives, we break even. That's all we ever planned to do. We're in a position where we can't make any money, but we can't literally lose any either. And our reward is all this wonderful wine to drink."

Dunkley said that neither he nor any other small-scale producer he knew of was getting anywhere near the maximum yield of grapes per hectare allowed by Chianti Classico (11,000 kilograms, or 7,700 liters of wine, which translates into about 3,000 bottles from an acre). "We're lucky if we get half that," he said.

The Dunkleys had hired two farmhands, both close to seventy, to help tend the vines, but he said they had no idea how they would replace them if they were no longer available.

"That's something we could deal with, I suppose, but some producers

John Dunkley

couldn't. I believe that if Chianti, and good Italian wine in general, is to survive, that quality might have to be raised a bit, yes, but the price will have to be tripled. I don't see any other way to pay the costs of maintaining high standards."

Colli Aretini, Colline Pisane, and Colli Senesi

Colli Aretini, though it produces a significant quantity of wine, so far has not oriented much production toward estate bottling. Much of its Chianti is sold to bottling firms or simply sold in bulk directly to consumers. Indications are, though, that this situation is changing and that more producers are now bottling and selling their wines. Among those who now do so with impressive results:

★ Castello di Montegonzi at Cavriglia
★ Fattoria di Chiaravalle at Giovi
★ Fattoria di Marcena near Subbiano
★ Fattoria di San Fabiano at San Fabiano
★ Fattoria di San Vittorio at Foiano
★ Fattoria La Trove near Arezzo
★ Marengo at Palazzuolo Alto
★ Monte Petrognano at Quarata
★ Podere di Cignano at Bagnoro Montoncello
★ Savoia Aosta at San Giustino Valdarno
★ Villa La Selva at Monte Benichi Bucine

Colline Pisane, the hills southeast of Pisa, has the gentlest climate of the seven Chianti zones because of the proximity of the Mediterranean. Its Chianti is not widely known, though some good wine is made there, often on the soft, light, fresh side. Good estate-bottled wines include:

★ Bellagotti at Terricciola
★ Fattoria Cempini Meazzuoli at Terricciola
★ Fattoria Gaslini at Badia di Morrona
★ Fattoria di Piedivilla at San Pietro Belvedere
★ Vino del Caratello at Soiano

These and other Chiantis of the Colline Pisane, as well as the wine of the newly designated DOC zone Bianco Pisano di San Torpé, can be tasted at the attractive *enoteca* in the center of Terricciola.

Colli Senesi, the largest Chianti zone, has three separate sections: one wrapping around the southern half of the Chianti Classico zone from Certaldo to Siena and on past Castelnuovo Berardenga; one surrounding Montepulciano; one surrounding Montalcino. The province of Siena stands alongside Cuneo in Piedmont (with its Barolo, Barbaresco, Nebbiolo, Barbera, and Dolcetto) as the most important provider of prestigious wine in Italy. In addition to its fine Chianti (from both Colli Senesi and the original section of Chianti Classico), Siena's DOC wines include Vernaccia di San Gimignano, Vino Nobile di Montepulciano, and the by now legendary Brunello di Montalcino. Siena also boasts some unclassified wines of distinction. The beautiful medieval city is also the home of the Enoteca Permanente Nazionale, the national wine museum, in the Fortezza Medicea, a recommended stop for any traveling oenophile.

In some seasons, particularly winter, Siena's countryside looks so starkly barren that one might wonder if anything could grow in its bleached and cracked clay soil. But the earth has an affinity for grapevines and olives, a fertility that expresses itself in the soft silver-green tones of spring and early summer. It is sometimes said that the gentleness of the land carries over into the character of the people. The most obvious manifestation of this, if it is so, is in their speech. Where the Florentine dialect has its peculiar transformation of the hard *c* to a guttural *h*, the Sienese dialect is purer, softer, the model for the modern Italian tongue.

The quality of wine produced in these hills ranges from the commonplace to the divine. The commonplace often ends up in flasks or the newer large containers that are shipped from bottling plants at such wine centers as Certaldo and Poggibonsi to many parts of the world. They are not always a credit to the Chianti family, but they do contribute strongly to the home economy.

The divine include not only Brunello, Vino Nobile, and Vernaccia, but numerous Chiantis. From the hills just east of Siena comes one, Castelpugna, made by Conte Carlo Alberto Fumi Cambi Gado. Another comes from the Chigi Saracini estate called the Azienda Agricola Madonna near Castelnuovo Berardenga, the property of the Accademia Musicale Chigiana, which is financially controlled by the Monte dei Paschi di Siena bank. (Monte dei Paschi di Siena also controls Fontanafredda of Piedmont.) Near Montalcino, Emilio Costanti, whose Brunello is deservedly among the most renowned, also makes a Chianti that ranks with the absolute best.

Country and small-town restaurants in the area frequently serve good Chianti of local production. Notable among them are Pulcino at Montepulciano, Le Grotte in Sinalunga, the Fattoria l'Amorosa south of Sinalunga, the Trattoria La Torre beside the monastery of Monte Oliveto Maggiore, and La Chiusa at Montefollonico, the next hill town north of Montepulciano. At La Chiusa, Umberto Lucherini and his wife, Dania, with a battery of cheerful country women, provide specialties often based on recipes from the area's bucolic past and nearly all made from produce of their own farm. Even in Tuscany, where the traditions of food and wine seem to be adhered to more faithfully than in other regions, the Lucherini menu is extraordinary: a full range of *antipasti*, thick country soups, homemade pasta and whole wheat bread, meat and aged *pecorino* cheese from field-grazed animals served with some of the best wine of Siena and other choice parts of Italy.

Among many fine Chiantis of the Colli Senesi are these:

★ Cantine Baroncini at San Gimignano
★ Casale del Bosco at Montalcino
★ Cercignano at Colli Val d'Elsa
★ Cusona at San Gimignano
★ Fassati at Pieve di Sinalunga
★ Majnoni Guicciardini at Vico d'Elsa
★ Montemorli at Poggibonsi
★ Montenidoli at San Gimignano
★ Rosso di Casavecchia at Monteriggioni
★ Tenuta La Lellera at Montalbuccio
★ Vecchia Cantina at Montepulciano

The recent expansion of the Putto confederation has put many Colli Senesi wineries under its aegis, but the old emblem of the local consortium, a she-wolf nursing two infants over a black and white triangular shield, is still often seen on bottles.

The Galaxy of Tuscan Reds

With Chianti in the galaxy of Tuscan red wines that derive primarily from Sangiovese are some with even more luster and some with less, but all seem to revolve inevitably around Chianti. There appears to be no limit to the variations and combinations winemakers have come up with in working with this noble grape.

In the Chianti zones dozens of wines could qualify, the most obvious being Vino Nobile di Montepulciano and Carmignano. Vino Nobile, in fact, is considered technically a Chianti by Professor Pier Giovanni Garoglio, one of the most distinguished authorities on Italian wines. Carmignano was a Chianti until its growers were permitted just recently to return to the historic appellation with a slight modification of grape types. Brunello di Montalcino could not be a Chianti because it is made exclusively from the Brunello grape, a strain of Sangiovese Grosso, which can, however, be used in the Chianti composite. Some isolated exceptions to Chianti are also worthy of note.

One is Testucchio, made by a young oenologist named Massimo Schiavi near Montespertoli. He uses only red-wine grapes, including Sangiovese and the rarer Occhio di Pernice, Mammolo, Ciliegiolo, and Prugnolo, all from old vines, some trained onto the traditional support, the runty, gnarled *testucchio* tree. Schiavi came up with a wine of impressive tone with his first vintage of 1973. Very deeply colored, full-bodied and solid, even hard, it has evident aging potential and goes well with Tuscan country dishes.

Another is Tegolato, made at the Antico Castello di Poppiano at Barberino Val d'Elsa from select grapes that could go into Chianti. It is aged in small barrels under the *tegole*, the roof tiles from which it takes its name. Changes in temperature cause the wine to work and rest with the changing seasons and thus develop in a few years the qualities of an older wine. A bottle of 1964 vintage drunk in 1974 tasted like a fifteen-year-old (and superb) Chianti. Tegolato, from the estate of Principi Kunz Piast d'Asburgo Lorena, who trace their lineage to the Hapsburgs, carries a princely price.

The most important innovation in the Sangiovese family is the Tignanello of Marchesi Antinori, which has quickly acquired the status of aristocrat among Tuscan red wines. Made from Sangiovese, Canaiolo, and Cabernet Sauvignon, the grapes are selected from the Tignanello plot of the Antinoris' Santa Cristina vineyards in Chianti Classico. Tignanello's masterfully designed label spells out details of production of a wine that has been widely proclaimed as great.

The label for the first Tignanello from the 1971 vintage stated that 95,443 liters were made from 76,682 vines and that the wine was aged in small oak barrels and bottled on February 12, 1974. That vintage made a big, complex, tannic wine that contained a bit of light Malvasia. In the ensuing vintages (Tignanello is made only in excellent years) of 1975, 1977, 1978, and 1979, Cabernet Sauvignon was included at about 10 percent, making the wine even more elegant in body and aroma.

"There was a marked improvement," said Antinori. "The Malvasia lent some bouquet but, unfortunately, it shortened the wine's life because Malvasia has a tendency to oxidize. Cabernet seems to have everything that Sangiovese lacks — the body, color, and aroma plus the longevity. Now we have a wine of even greater depth and life span. The '78 is the best so far."

Antinori considers Tignanello a model for what Chianti *riserva* could be, though he has no intention for the present of calling it Chianti. Some experts have ranked Tignanello with the absolute greatest red wines of Italy. Its price will undoubtedly climb beyond the level of about $7 to $10 it had been selling for in Florence. But one can hope that Marchesi Antinori with their business acumen will let Tignanello establish its justified price on international markets, something Brunello di Montalcino never had the chance to do.

Brunello di Montalcino: Price and Perseverance

Scarcely even known in Tuscany a decade ago, Brunello di Montalcino is now the most fabled wine of Italy. Its fame has been carried abroad with the wondrous note that it can outlast some of the longest-lived Bordeaux and may, in some cases, cost more. Such fanfare would seem to be a marvelous boost for the prestige of Italian wines, proof that they, too, have taken their place among the world's *crème de la crème*. But behind Brunello's image of serene supremacy lie some vexing problems of the sort that cannot be wished away.

Brunello's image was built from the beginning by the Biondi-Santi family, whose ancestor, Clemente Santi, won a citation for a wine of that name in 1865. Clemente's son Ferruccio Biondi-Santi, who isolated and propagated the Sangiovese Grosso vine in his vineyards at Il Greppo, is often recognized as the founder of Brunello di Montalcino. He, his son Tancredi, who died in 1970, and his grandson Franco, who now runs the estate, have all made reserve wines of unquestioned greatness, using Ferruccio's formula of taking only the choicest grapes in fine years, vinifying them naturally, and letting the wine age long in Slavonian oak and much longer in bottles. Ferruccio's legacy included a wine from 1888 that has been sold for astronomical prices. Many more old vintages remain in the cellars at Il Greppo or in wine shops and restaurants in Italy, waiting for those buyers willing to spend 30,000 lire or, often, much more for a bottle. Even the latest vintage in bottle, the 1974 non-*riserva* was listed at 11,000 lire ($13.70) in 1979. The 1970 *riserva* cost 24,000 lire, the 1964 79,000 lire, the 1945 293,000 lire, the 1925 1,130,000 lire, and the 1891 4,000,000 lire ($5,000). The 1888 was no longer listed; presumably the few remaining bottles were available only to bidders.

Over the decades neighboring landowners joined the Biondi-Santis in making Brunello, but not without protests from the family that originated the name. By 1966 enough were making good Brunello to earn its recognition as one of the earliest DOC wines of Italy. Though choice Brunello had a special reputation among Tuscans able to afford it, it was not really "discovered" by other Italian connoisseurs until about 1970. The distinguished black label of Biondi-Santi soon became the nation's most esteemed, the glory of the well-heeled collector's cantina and a badge of arrival for the *nouveau riche*.

Several other Brunello producers followed the lead, some boldly putting their prices up close to Biondi-Santi's, making Brunello generally the most expensive wine of Italy. But others balked, realizing that the trend threatened to price their wines out of reach of all but the very rich. When the producers' consortium was formed in 1967, the Biondi-Santis remained outside. Some say that the reason was their refusal to accept use of the name Rosso dei Vigneti di Brunello for a younger wine from Brunello vines, others that they came up against charges of "money madness" by producers who wanted to arrive at a uniform price structure that would favor their wines as a unit. Whatever the reason, the bitterness has remained on both sides.

Franco Biondi-Santi, who was accused of arrogance and worse, was shaken by the depth of feeling against him. He seemed shocked and hurt that his right, as head of the estate that created Brunello, to practice laissez-faire economics should be brought into question. He has always known he could get his price, sooner or later, and the way he sees it, the others are free to get their prices too.

Soft-spoken and aristocratic, Franco Biondi-Santi is a patient man of handsome appearance and impeccable manners and taste. He has a college degree in oenology and, even more important, he is totally dedicated to his profession. And yet, when it comes to prices, there might be something to not only what his rival winemakers say but what other people elsewhere have expressed.

A distributor in San Francisco who was among the first importers of Biondi-Santi Brunello in America admitted he was having trouble selling the wine at those prices. The New York and London markets seemed just as reluctant. Even in northern Italy enthusiasm seemed to be on the wane. A prominent restaurateur in Emilia-Romagna complained that when customers asked for Biondi-Santi Brunello and then asked the price, they changed their minds and ordered an older *grand cru* from Bordeaux for less money. The feeling in many quarters is that Biondi-Santi's Brunello is no longer a drink but a collector's item. People in the wine trade speculated that Biondi-Santi and such other highly regarded producers as Emilio Costanti and Fattoria dei Barbi had already priced themselves out of the international market before they ever really got onto it.

Less sensitive winemakers might not care, but Franco Biondi-Santi does. At first he seemed puzzled that foreigners, particularly Americans,

Franco Biondi-Santi

seemed reluctant to pay the prices Italians were paying. But recently he decided to follow a strategy of placing his wines discreetly on the U.S. and British market at select shops and restaurants. After a visit to the United States, he expressed confidence that his wines were beginning to make an impact there, though not a widespread one.

Biondi-Santi, aided by his son Jacopo, has limited Il Greppo's vineyards to some 45 acres, as much as he can supervise personally. Only vines of ten years or older are used for Brunello, the best grapes for *riserva* in fine years, and the second choice for what he calls *annata* (or vintage). With grapes from the younger vines he makes a red *vino da tavola* called simply Greppo. In poor years, such as 1972 and 1976,

Biondi-Santi sells all his wine in bulk rather than make Brunello. Even in good years he is lucky to produce 50,000 bottles of Brunello; the *riserva* is never sold until six years after the harvest.

Biondi-Santi, whose country home, the elegantly renovated ancestral estate, Il Greppo, adjoins the cantina, discusses wine as a technician, a craftsman who pretends no extensive knowledge of what his worldwide competition is. He is a model Tuscan, but in the Sienese sense, which signifies a gentler approach to life and perhaps a less cosmopolitan outlook than the Florentine counterpart might show. Though he has certainly used his training and experience to make some adjustments in the winemaking processes and allowances for each crop's exigencies, he insists that basically nothing has changed. He aims for a Brunello in the tradition of his father's and grandfather's — that is, tannic and high in alcohol, extract, and acids, austere, warm, rich in body and color and infinitely complex. If other such wines could be described as big, Biondi-Santi's might be considered enormous.

As a consequence, his Brunello is for people who have not only the money but the perseverance to let it sit for years, even decades, for the reserves do not even begin to open up until they are ten years old, and then they may go on for longer than the average person's lifetime. All this is admirable, though it makes Biondi-Santi's wines not only among the world's most expensive but the hardest to get to know. In 1978, I was able to taste his best *riserva* bottlings from 1945 to 1971. The 1971 and 1970 were still hard, years from their optimum, but extraordinarily rich and promising. The 1969 and 1964 had arrived, especially the latter, which at that point may have been as excellent as it will ever be, though it was still robust and obviously had good years remaining. The 1961 and 1955 showed the qualities of graceful age that make Brunello so exceptional among the world's old red wines. The 1945 showed its years even less than the previous two. It was still round, complex, though its deep ruby color showed *pelure d'oignon* on the edges and the intensity of tannin and acids that persist so long had decidedly lessened. Still, had it been a wine other than Brunello, it might have been taken for ten or fifteen years old, rather than thirty-three.

Legendary Status, Mixed Reviews

Brunello production, though restricted to approved sections of the community of Montalcino, has been increasing at an astounding rate.

Much of the available vineyard space has been bought up in recent years by both local cultivators and outside interests with Italian as well as foreign money behind them. Between 1967 and 1978 the number of registered Brunello properties increased from 37 to 80 with an eightfold increase in land under vine and a tenfold increase in wine produced — from 207,714 liters to 2,146,760. And production will rise considerably when recently planted vineyards reach full bearing in the early 1980s.

The newcomers include some prominent investors. The Cinzano vermouth firm, with Coca-Cola money behind it, headed a group that purchased Col d'Orcia, an estate that has produced wine for years. Marchesi de' Frescobaldi is involved with a group known as Enoviticola Senese, which had French, German, and Spanish investors as well. Their estate, Castelgiocondo, brought out its first bottles in 1980, not all Brunello. The most talked about outsider was House of Banfi, the largest U.S. importer of Italian wines, which had prepared some 1,000 acres of vines (though only 125 in Brunello) at a place called Poggio d'Oro, or Golden Hill. Given Banfi's Midas touch, the new estate will probably live up to its name someday.

With all this new activity, the legendary estates of Brunello are being pushed to uphold their preeminence. The most legendary Brunello is produced by Biondi-Santi, Fattoria dei Barbi, and Emilio Costanti, who in some years charges about as much for his *riserva* as does Biondi-Santi. By 1979, only twenty-five estates sold Brunello under their own labels; some were very good, only a few exceptional. Each year, more Brunello from these less proclaimed producers has been finding its way abroad, providing the legends with their first real taste of international competition.

Only recently have non-Italian wine critics begun to venture opinions about Brunello. The reviews have been mixed, reflecting as much perplexity as admiration. That is understandable, for some wine that has arrived in foreign lands in recent years has not shown Brunello at its best and has not always been equal to its price. In some cases, it might have been too young; the fine 1970 and 1971 vintages were ready from some producers but not from others. The subpar 1973 vintage, which was widely distributed, represented wines that simply could not stand up to the four or five years (for *riserva*) in barrel required by DOC. The 1973s were not very good to begin with, and by 1980 most bottles had dried up.

Many wine lovers willing to pay the price have expressed disappointment in their early experiences with Brunello, and some consumers, experts and nonexperts alike, have found the cost little short of scandalous. Too bad, for Brunello at its best could take its place in the front ranks of the world's aged red wines. But so far authorities and critics with the power to put it there are not universally convinced of Brunello's class. I suspect that the main reason for this is that they have not always been exposed to the best vintages at their prime. Unfortunately, price makes such exposure difficult to come by.

The Other Side of the Coin

The rivalry that has upset the normal equilibrium of the quiet fortress town of Montalcino may still work itself out by one or another of the laws of economics, because some opponents of astronomical prices now make wines of very high quality and reasonable value. A leader in this trend is the Tenuta Il Poggione, owned by Leopoldo Franceschi and run by Piero Talenti, one of the sharpest of that breed of unsung heroes the Tuscans call *fattori*.

Talenti, a Romagnan by birth, has a degree in oenology and, like Franco Biondi-Santi, assumes the title Dottore. But there the similarities seem to end. A fiery, frank man whose light complexion makes him look more like what most people might consider an Austrian than an Italian, Talenti has definite views about what Brunello di Montalcino's image ought to be, which is quite a distance from what it is.

"Brunello should be accessible to people at a justified high price, because it is truly a great wine," he said. "But great wine does not have to be reserved for millionaires."

Talenti was seated at a plain wooden desk in his office in an isolated corner of the unmarked stone building that houses the Poggione winery next to the post office in Sant'Angelo in Colle, a village of maybe eighty inhabitants that enjoys a bit of renown in these parts as the home of Radio Toscana Sud (run by two young men who were wearing jeans and t-shirts while conducting the morning's broadcast).

The Poggione holdings render enough grapes to make about 80,000 bottles of Brunello a year, plus such other fine wines as a white Vin Biondo, a lightly sweet *spumante* from Moscadelleto grapes, Rosso dei Vigneti di Brunello, and a superbly dry Vin Santo. As such it is among the largest wineries in the Montalcino area at present and its wines are unquestionably among the best values.

Talenti defies some of the traditional rules for making Brunello and gets away with it admirably. His wines from 1971, 1972 (a year in which many could not meet Brunello DOC standards), 1973, 1974, and 1975 were excellent. The 1975 was the most drinkable Brunello made in the decade of those I had tasted by 1980.

"You know what the traditionalists will tell you about our Brunello: that it won't last," he said with indignation. "Well, don't you believe it. I wish I could be around to taste my wine against theirs in fifty years, because whoever is will be in for some surprises."

Talenti puts the wine through what he calls a "normal" fermentation as opposed to the "prolonged" practice of others, and he keeps barrel aging to the required minimum for both the regular Brunello and the *riserva*.

Piero Talenti

"You can drink the wine within months, and it's good, which disproves all the bunk that's been said and written about Brunello being by nature forbiddingly hard," he said. The regular Rosso dei Vigneti, from younger vines, is made to drink starting in the year after the vintage, when it is among the most satisfying young red wines of Italy. Talenti is convinced that from such substandard vintages as 1972, 1973, and 1976, Rosso dei Vigneti at about a third the price is a better wine than Brunello.

"Four years in barrel is too long for any wine," he asserted, "and the five years in barrel for *riserva* is ridiculous. I favor a year in barrel for vintages on the light side and two years maximum for the great vintages. After that the wine develops its aroma and flavor better in bottle. And that's a quality factor known in most of the world's great red wine areas by now, but you can't convince the traditionalists of it here. Some of us want to change the DOC rules to cut back barrel aging, but so far we're not getting very far. They accuse us of looking for economic shortcuts. Nonsense. My position is that they can keep their wine in wood as long as they like. Fine. But those of us with other ideas — legitimate ideas backed by ample research — should have some options too."

Il Poggione, which has increased exports to the United States, has been greeted with more satisfaction generally than have bottles from the traditionalists. Not only does Poggione cost much less, it is ready to drink soon after bottling, and yet it has breed and aging potential to carry the Brunello name at its proudest.

Talenti's position is generally supported by Ezio Rivella, the dynamic general manager of House of Banfi's Italian division. Though Banfi's reputation has been built on the strength of Lambrusco and other popular wines, chiefly the so-called soft or mellow types, it has been moving into the prestige field in a manner that should soon start to attract attention. But for the time being, Banfi and Rivella have been treading lightly in Montalcino while preparing the base for a wine intended to respond to both ancient tradition and recent consumer trends. For this they are spending some $36 million to prepare one of the world's largest wine estates.

Of the nearly 1,000 acres planted by 1980 at their new property near Sant'Angelo in Colle, only 125 acres were in Brunello, an object of curiosity locally. Most remaining acreage has been planted in Moscadello, the local version of the Moscato Bianco grape, whose history here surpasses Brunello by hundreds of years. Moscadello was among the most treasured wines of Tuscany when tastes ran to aromatic dessert wines. Banfi and Rivella are convinced that those tastes are coming back (consider the recent success of Asti, not to mention Lambrusco). The investment is significant in the way it combines business with a respect for tradition that should hasten the revival of Moscadello and aid its elevation to DOC. Rivella plans to make a lightly sweet sparkling wine that should be somewhat remindful of Asti but very much its own thing. Eventually nearly 2,000 acres may be planted, under a scientific system aimed at mechanical harvesting.

Rivella denies that the Banfi move in Montalcino downplays the importance of Brunello, though he agrees the red wine's future is not entirely secure at this point. With 125 acres in Brunello vines, Banfi has the potential to become one of the largest producers of that wine, though what percentage of grapes eventually will go into Brunello will depend on both the quality of each vintage and the future success of the wine in general.

"As an outsider, I'm compelled to speak softly," said Rivella, a native of Piedmont, whose expertise has earned him a reputation as the "wizard of white wine" in Italy. But Rivella's presence has already been felt in the inner circles of Montalcino wine production and his words and actions are not being ignored. He, too, believes that two years should be the maximum barrel age for any red wine, no matter how big, and from weaker vintages one year is sufficient. He says that small, new barrels are not a practical consideration, and that the larger casks of Tuscan custom are satisfactory.

"I'd be tempted to make a red wine from Brunello grapes and sell it at a higher price than Brunello, to make a point, because it would be a better wine," he said, echoing Talenti's thinking. Well, Rivella will have plenty of time to ponder that, though the first Banfi Brunello from the few old vines on the property was already in circulation and the new vines will not be used until the mid-1980s. The Moscadello should début about 1982.

Rivella described Montalcino as a truly elect wine zone, "but not only for Sangiovese." Banfi has planted several hectares in Cabernet Sauvignon. "Purely experimental," says Rivella with a trace of irony in his tone. Technically, only approved varieties can be planted in Montalcino and Cabernet is not one of them. That move, too, was based on careful analysis of soil, climate, and other conditions that proved to be just about ideal.

Ezio Rivella

The Drawbacks of Starting at the Top

Brunello production will probably begin to approach its limits in the late 1980s because the approved area (in which olive trees may not be removed for vines) is only about 2,500 acres. Maximum yield of 7,000 liters of wine from a hectare (or about 3,750 bottles from an acre) is never achieved because select grapes are used. The wine must have 12.5° alcohol and be aged four years in wood to be called Brunello di Montalcino, five years in barrel to be labeled *riserva*. When it goes into bottle, Brunello has a deep ruby color that gradually takes on garnet and orange tones with age. It can be sold only in Bordeaux-style bottles not exceeding 75 centiliters.

Brunello di Montalcino has benefited from four magnificent recent vintages — 1970, 1975, and 1979, which were all abundant, and 1977, which produced average quantity. Some estates had a great year in 1978, while others had only a fair harvest, often reduced by humidity or hail. The Montalcino zone, whose westernmost point is about 45 kilometers from the sea, benefits from micro-climates especially conducive to the cultivation of grapes, as well as olives and fruit.

None of the estates registered at present is equipped to make Brunello on a large scale. Quality standards are high here and when DOCG arrives they should be even higher. The consortium, despite the absence of Biondi-Santi and Fattoria dei Barbi, still supervises 92 percent of production. In addition to those already cited, the following estates and their owners are noteworthy:

★ Altesino, Giulio Consonno
★ Argiano, Loffredo Gaetano Lovatelli
★ Camigliano, a corporation
★ Campogiovanni, a corporation
★ Canalicchio, Silvano Lambardi
★ Canalicchio di Sopra, Fratelli Pacenti
★ Capanna, Cesare Cencioni
★ Caparzo, a corporation
★ Casale del Bosco, Silvio Nardi
★ Castiglione del Bosco, a corporation
★ Chiesa di Santa Restuita, a corporation
★ Colombaio di Montosoli, Nello Baricci
★ Lisini, Elina Lisini
★ Pertimali, Livio Sassetti
★ Poggio alle Mura, a corporation
★ Tenuta di Sesta, Giuseppe Ciacci
★ Valdicava, Bramante Martini
★ Val di Suga, Sereno Freato

Among the special wines of Montalcino, Moscadello and Vin Santo have historical standing. A curious red wine is Brusco dei Barbi, made at the Fattoria dei Barbi from Brunello grapes but using the *governo*. Francesca Colombini-Cinelli, who owns the estate, serves it with country food at the tavern on the grounds. Big and bold, Brusco dei Barbi has a sort of rustic elegance that goes well with salami and good aged *pecorino* and *cacciotta* cheeses.

Use of the name Rosso dei Vigneti di Brunello has been the source of a continuing controversy among producers here, though nearly all make a wine from Brunello grapes to be sold within two or three years after the vintage. Common Market norms forbid use of the term Brunello in the name, because it supposedly could cause consumers to confuse it with the DOC product. In 1978, Italian authorities told producers to stop using the name. Most have persisted, however, arguing that the appellation is perfectly accurate because the grape is called Brunello. The latest word was that authorities were reviewing the situation after conceding that producers might have a legitimate point. Meanwhile, Rosso dei Vigneti di Brunello remained on the market under that name.

Brunello producers protested when Barolo and Barbaresco were selected earlier for DOCG, believing, as any winemaker would, that theirs was more deserving. Some grumbled that the selection was a political fix. But, on examination, Barolo and Barbaresco had not only more impressive historical credentials behind their names but a more uniform current structure of production and more evidence of unity, self-discipline, and control shown by the consortium and individual wineries. Brunello producers, understandably, regard DOCG as a badge of achievement rather than what it is designed to be: the ultimate imposition of quality control. At any rate, by mid-1980, no wine was yet officially DOCG.

Within its limited production zone, Brunello di Montalcino has natural conditions for greatness rarely equaled in the world's wine zones. Some of this greatness has been realized, but it will take many more years, maybe even decades, for Brunello di Montalcino to establish its unique value in the way that other pockets of greatness such as Barbaresco or the Côte de Nuits have by standing up to the extended trials of selling on a wide and discriminating market. Starting at the top (in terms of price) may prove to have more drawbacks than advantages, for Brunello di Montalcino will be constantly called on to prove its greatness. So far this proof has been rather nebulous.

Vino Nobile di Montepulciano: Still King?

Vino Nobile di Montepulciano is often twinned with its Sienese neighbor Brunello as Tuscany's other "great" wine. It was the third Italian wine tapped for DOCG status, though almost simultaneously with Brunello. It has been recognized for centuries as a special wine that has inspired its admirers to wax lyrical about it. The most quoted enthusiast was Francesco Redi, the poet-physician who in his *Bacco in Toscana,* written in the seventeenth century, exclaimed: *"Montepulciano d'ogni vino é re."* Producers since have been unable to resist citing Vino Nobile as king of all wines, but I sometimes wonder if it is now as regal, relative to others available, as it was when Redi was composing his dithyramb to Bacchus.

Vino Nobile, whose vineyards surround the gorgeous hill town of Montepulciano, can be an elegant wine, at its best equal to the finest Chianti, which is commendable indeed. And yet, though I do not wish to malign it, I am not convinced that it has shown the general class or consistency of production to be placed alongside Barolo, Barbaresco, and Brunello in the elite category of DOCG wines. Vino Nobile, as Professor Garoglio asserted, is essentially a Chianti; its grape composition can result in a wine that could be sold under the name Chianti, though its makers can point out technical differences between the two. The principal grape is here called Prugnolo, which is just another name for Sangiovese Grosso. The *nobile* supposedly refers to the tradition of selecting only "noble" grapes for the wine.

Certain production regulations differentiate Vino Nobile from Chianti: *governo* may not be used; Vino Nobile must be aged a minimum of two years (to Chianti's five months), three years to become *riserva* (like Chianti), and four years to attain the special status of *riserva speciale*. Vino Nobile, which must have at least 12° alcohol, may be sold only in Bordeaux-type bottles of three-quarter liter or less; Chianti can be sold in larger containers. But the real difference is in a name, and Vino Nobile's high-sounding appellation can be worth more on the market.

The formula for Vino Nobile is Prugnolo at 50 to 70 percent, Canaiolo Nero at 10 to 20 percent, Malvasia del Chianti and Trebbiano Toscano at 10 to 20 percent (so far all Chianti grapes), plus Pulcinculo (another name for Grechetto Bianco) and Mammolo, which between them may be included at up to 8 percent. Some admirers, perhaps striving to set Vino Nobile apart from Chianti, note the special bouquet of Mammolo, but that grape is used only minimally and anyway is optional. Many producers of Vino Nobile also make Chianti Colli Senesi, which is invariably a lesser wine, precisely because the select grapes go into the more expensive Vino Nobile.

Lest anyone suspect that there is no such thing as a noble Vino Nobile, let me assure you that there is. The noblest, time and again, has come from Poderi Boscarelli, a small estate near the village of Cervognano. Produced by Ippolito and Paola De Ferrari Corradi, a handsome couple from Genoa, the Boscarelli Vino Nobile is distinguished by its robustness, color, fruit, and rotundity. Other good Vino Nobile, invariably leaner in body and more austere in constitution, seems to whisper its message, but this one stands up and talks to you. Its monarchical bearing is undeniable even though its creators have been trying to give it a low profile.

As we compared the 1973, 1974, and 1975 vintages in the dining room of their comfortably rustic villa surrounded by some 22 acres of vines in the low hills of the Valdichiana below Montepulciano, the De Ferraris reminisced about how their wine, almost despite itself, became the envy of Montepulciano.

"We could have bought a yacht for the same price," said Ippolito De Ferrari, who owns a textile firm in Genoa and escapes to Tuscany only on weekends and for a few weeks every summer. "That would have been a lot less work." But instead they bought Poderi Boscarelli, which they learned about through Paola's father, who came from Cervognano, and in the early 1960s they started restoring the old farmhouse and putting in a few new vines.

"It started out innocently enough," she recalled. "We didn't know the first thing about winemaking but we did know that Cervognano was famous locally, because even the wine made there using the crudest methods was superior." The first few hectares were put in under the supervision of a caretaker (who still tends the vines), and in 1968 they made their first wine.

"Our intention was to make enough for home use and sell the grapes we didn't use," Ippolito recalled. "We bought a new barrel and then another, and after that it just kept growing." The vineyards were expanded annually through the 1960s to 11 acres for Vino Nobile and 11 for Chianti. The De Ferraris have concentrated on the Nobile, selling either the grapes for Chianti or the wine in bulk, except for one year when they sold a barrel to be bottled and exported to the United States. That Chianti was a superior example of its type.

"One year," Paola said, "we made the mistake of enrolling in the cooperative, not realizing that by doing so we had to consign *all* our grapes to it or pay a fine. After paying the fine, we dropped out, because by then we realized that the wine was just too good to compromise, and we started bottling it and selling it."

That involved expanding the cantina. "We thought we'd reached our limits and then we realized we needed more space, so we'd knock out a wall, then another, and put in vats and barrels," Ippolito recalled. "Some people have beautiful old cellars with vaulted ceilings and all the trappings, but ours is such a mess we won't even let you see it."

Although their aspirations have remained, all things considered, modest, the De Ferraris, as outsiders, have felt the pressures inevitably brought to bear by the in-group of winemakers in the Montepulciano area, some of whom own estates that have been producing respected wine for decades, even centuries. Any hopes of rapport were dashed when the De Ferraris were invited to join the consortium and politely declined.

"We simply couldn't see the advantages it offered a small operation like ours," Ippolito said. "We make sure our wine meets all the technical regulations and quality standards of DOC and then we go beyond that by having it meet our own standards. If we don't think it's good enough, we don't sell it." That happened in 1972 and 1976. "Anyhow," he continued, "we can handle our own promotion and sales. It seemed to me the consortium involved paying dues for nothing."

To make matters worse, their Vino Nobile started drawing raves in the mid-1970s from writers and critics, who by now rank it by consensus as the finest Vino Nobile. While not denying the obvious, the De Ferraris admit to a measure of discomfiture over their unintended achievement of showing up the local producers. "It's led to hard feelings and ostracism that can be really unpleasant," Paola said. "And one result is that we don't sell the wine through local retailers because we don't want to invite comparisons that might aggravate feelings."

The only exceptions are a couple of restaurants in the neighborhood run by friends and the Enoteca Regionale of Sandro Morriconi at nearby Pienza. Morriconi, one of the most astute wine dealers around, sells the wine nationally by mail order through his Club delle Fattorie. Otherwise, the De Ferraris sell their Vino Nobile to restaurants and shops in other parts of Italy north and south, and in the United States and Germany.

Neil Empson, who exports the wine to the United States, proposed to take their whole production of about 10,000 bottles one year. "I told Neil I was flattered by the American response," said De Ferrari, "but I refused. After all, winemaking is still a hobby to us and much of the satisfaction is getting reaction in Italy, the comments you hear when you stop in a restaurant or a wine shop and people say nice things about your wine."

"Especially from people who know wine," Paola added. "That provides real motivation. All the time and work involved, not only in the vineyards and in making the wine but the bottling, corking, labeling, which are all done by hand, and the bookkeeping. It all seems worthwhile when you know people appreciate what you're doing."

The De Ferraris let their wine express itself naturally. Not only do they refuse ever to use the 10 percent correction with other wines or musts permitted under DOC, they also avoid filtration or any form of stabilization. They are not keen on much wood aging either, though they consent to three years in barrel for *riserva* to satisfy certain tastes. But they draw the line at *riserva speciale*. "Four years in barrel is too much," Ippolito said. "My own preference is for wine aged the normal two years in barrel and then in bottle."

Paola De Ferrari, who spent some of her early years near Montepulciano and who stays alone on the farm at crucial times when her husband and two school-age sons are in Genoa, seemed willing to make a career out of Vino Nobile. But her husband was reluctant to leave a successful business for the risks of winemaking. "Maybe someday," he said wistfully. "It's something to think about."

The De Ferraris have decided, come what may, to limit their production of Vino Nobile to 20,000 bottles from select grapes in good years. "We have the vineyards to expand production well beyond that," Paola said, "but we won't. We couldn't give it the attention we do now. Not only that, if it got too big, making wine wouldn't be fun anymore."

The only other Vino Nobile I know of that approaches the Poderi Boscarelli in its robust character is served at the Pulcino restaurant near Montepulciano. It comes from the property of Gabriella Matassini Ercolani. The other good ones tend to be more austere in the local tradition of aged red wines. Commendatore Adamo Fanetti and his son Giorgio have been leaders in the drive to establish the wine's widespread reputation and its acceptance as DOCG. The subtle grace of the Fanetti Vino Nobile needs plenty of breathing time at room temperature to be appreciated. Other respected names in Montepulciano are Fattoria di Gracciano, owned by Franco Mazzucchelli, whose Vino Nobile is exported to the United States and Britain; Fratelli Bologna Buonsignori; Cantine Riunite di Cavaliere Mario Contucci; and Fassati, which was among the first to be exported, primarily to the United States. The Vecchia Cantina di Montepulciano, a cooperative founded in 1937, seems to be the largest winery of the zone and, despite its name, the most modern — at least in appearance.

Carmignano: A Touch of Finesse

Carmignano, an enclave in the Montalbano Chianti zone west of Florence, was granted DOC status in 1975. Its growers still have the right to make Chianti, and most do, but some are putting prime emphasis on building the prestige of Carmignano, which varies ever so slightly from Chianti. The notable difference is the inclusion of Cabernet grapes at 6 to 10 percent, a dose that — when detectable — can give a touch of finesse to what would otherwise be a privileged Chianti.

The privilege is not only in the exceptional terrain, exposure, and microclimates of so many vineyards in the balcony of hills around Carmignano and Artimino, but also in a winemaking tradition that goes back to ancient times. The quest for quality has been led by the Nobil Casa Contini Bonacossi and its Villa di Capezzana, more names to list among the great in Tuscan wines. Ugo Contini Bonacossi was a prime mover in having Carmignano recognized as an independent wine zone, a maneuver that some Chianti people considered superfluous for a mere 6 to 10 percent difference in grape content. But the claims had some historical validity; documents approved by the Grand Duke of Tuscany in 1716 geographically defined Carmignano as a wine entitled to a name protected against fraudulent imitation. (At that time, however, Cabernet grapes could not have been used in the composition because they had not been introduced in Tuscany.)

Whether the move merited the effort remains to be seen. Carmignano is not yet a household word in the world of Italian wine, though with Capezzana and several other estates producing wines of consistent excellence under the name, it already carries considerable prestige and seems a natural for DOCG before long. Carmignano must have 12.5° alcohol and be aged eight months before being sold, three years for *riserva*.

Carmignano *riserva*, particularly from the Contini Bonacossi, is notable for its elegance and complexity. It is not an exceptionally robust wine, in the sense of Brunello or Barolo, though it has the capacity to age well — for a decade or more from such fine vintages as 1971 and 1975. Its bright ruby color takes on garnet tones with age and its dry flavor tends to gain harmony while becoming soft and velvety after about six years. Carmignano goes beautifully with fowl, especially the game birds such as thrush and quail that Tuscans roast on the spit in autumn and winter.

Capezzana also turns out good Chianti in both bottle and flask. Following the pattern of using grapes from young (or old) vines not up to Carmignano or Chianti DOC standards, the estate also has a good "jug" wine called Poggetto, Vino Toscano. A limited amount of Capezzana Bianco is also sold, outstanding among the white wines of the Chianti zones.

Capezzana and such other producers of fine Carmignano as Fattoria Il Poggiolo, Fattoria di Bacchereto, and the ancient and renowned Fattoria Artimino, also make Vin Ruspo, a most pleasing rosé with an intriguing little *storiella* behind it.

Each harvest, as they tell it now, those wily Tuscan peasants who did the picking would spill enough must from the tubs they hauled the grapes in to fill a couple of demijohns of their own. These they spirited home after dark. From the must of both red and white grapes they made a light wine that fermented in the demijohns. It was good to drink young, though they tried to save enough to refresh themselves during the hot days of the summer grain harvest. Today most Vin Ruspo in commerce is made in glass-lined vats, though some producers say they still make it in demijohns. A hearty rusticity distinguishes Vin Ruspo as one of the better rosés I have come across in Italy, with the guts to accompany not only a wide range of antipasto and pasta but most meats as well. Producers have requested DOC for Carmignano's Vin Ruspo.

The Resurgence of Tuscan Whites

Although Tuscans, like Piedmontese, consider white wine to be of secondary interest, present-day consumer tastes have helped generate a trend in favor of *bianco*. In the Chianti zones, a push was underway for a DOC white, though the wine almost certainly will not be able to use the name Chianti in its appellation, because Chianti now legally refers to a wine rather than a geographical entity. Whatever it is called, it will take several years to accomplish recognition. Not only were the Chianti consortiums at odds over the composition of this so-called Chianti Bianco, but many producers obviously needed to brush up on the techniques of white wine production.

A new white wine called Galestro was introduced by Antinori, Frescobaldi, Ricasoli, and Ruffino in mid-1980 in cooperation with the Chianti Putto consortium. Unique among Italian wines in that it had a maximum permitted alcohol grade (10.5°), it was made from Trebbiano with other light varieties such as Sauvignon, Chardonnay, and Pinot Bianco included. Light, fresh, and fruity, it appeared to be a prototype for the new Tuscan white; its producers have already begun a campaign for DOC. Meanwhile, the Chianti Classico consortium was developing a white wine called Bianco della Lega, which was expected to be launched next year with the wine of the 1980 vintage.

Five white wines from within or near the various Chianti zones already have DOC status. They have been increasing their followings in Italy, and to some extent abroad. They are Montecarlo Bianco, Bianco Vergine della Valdichiana, Bianco della Valdinievole, Bianco Pisano San Torpé, and Vernaccia di San Gimignano. The latter is the most firmly established, in part because it comes from around the towered town of San Gimignano (someone who must never have ventured within its walls once labeled it "the Manhattan of Tuscany"), a lovely medieval place that figures prominently on the itinerary of regional tours.

Vernaccia, made chiefly of the grape of that name (apparently unrelated to the Vernaccia of Sardinia and other places), is unique among Tuscan white wines in that it theoretically contains no Trebbiano or Malvasia. Vernaccia di San Gimignano has been around a long time — it was praised by Michelangelo Buonarotti junior in 1643 — and until fairly recently it probably had not changed all that much from the old days. Traditionally it was a wine to age, whose bronze tones were largely the result of contact with air during the vinification and with wood afterward. Vernaccia was noted for its somewhat woody flavor with a lightly bitter vein, pleasant to sip like sherry.

That image has been changing lately. Though Vernaccia still keeps rather well for a white wine, it is now more often than not of a pale golden color, fresh, smooth, dry, and agreeably rounded — a fine, even elegant table wine that is perhaps at its optimum in its first two years. This evolution has been brought about by introduction of techniques that — to my taste, at least — have made Vernaccia more attractive without compromising its fundamental virtues. It is good with fish, and it has enough to it, including that lightly bitter vein, to make it still worthy of sipping alone.

Fattoria di Pietrafitta and Cusona of Guicciardini Strozzi are the most respected names in Vernaccia di San Gimignano, with good reason, for they have made very good wines for years. Lately other producers have begun to rival them; the list includes Castello di Pescile, Fattoria della Quercia, Cantine Baroncini, Fattoria di Monte Oliveto, Il Raccianello, Conca d'Oro, Casale, Fattoria Tollena, Ponte a Rondolino, and Vagnoni.

The Valdichiana, the valley that runs south from Arezzo past Montepulciano, has been more celebrated for its beef than its wine, though these days the huge white steers that were used for *bistecca alla fiorentina* are seen less and less on its gently rolling surface as vineyards become ever more apparent. Bianco Vergine is not famous yet, but there are indications that one of these days it may be. Made from 70 to 85 percent Trebbiano with a measure of Malvasia and other varieties, Bianco Vergine at its finest can stand among the best dry whites of Tuscany. One of its finest comes from the Fattoria di Manzano, on the plain below Cortona, a medium-sized winery with the potential capacity to establish a reputation well beyond the province of Arezzo. The wine is light golden, dry and delicate in flavor, richly textured with a bitter almond undertone. From good vintages it reaches a peak after a year, though it is also good younger.

Rosso di Manzano, from the same *fattoria,* is fundamentally a Chianti without the right to the name. It, too, is an outstanding wine of the type, rich, deep, and smooth, though the winery does not age it in wood. If it did, it might have a red wine of major importance, for the elements of greatness seem to be there.

Another excellent Bianco Vergine della Valdichiana is made by Aldo Casagni at Rigutino near Arezzo. He also makes a good rosé called Rosato di Rigutino and Vin Santo, both *secco* and *amabile,* of unsurpassed quality. Other Bianco Vergine producers of note are M. Baldetti at Pietraia-Bassebozze; Molino della Vecchia, Bruni Gazzini, and Bertini, all near Cortona; and the Vecchia Cantina at Montepulciano. Spalletti of Rufina also produces and exports Bianco Vergine.

Trebbiano's monopoly on the white wines of eastern Tuscany is not under serious challenge, for its prolific yields have made it an irreplaceable variety to many producers. But some have ventured into the unknown and come up with rewarding results. Of special note are the Tocai of the Fattoria di Marcena, pale, crisp, and dry, a rival to many

Tocais of Friuli and the Veneto, and a Riesling made by Primo Barelli at the Castello di Sorci, near Anghiari, a wine to compare with some Rieslings of Alto Adige and the Oltrepò Pavese. That Riesling is sometimes available along with a hearty red at Barelli's rustic restaurant beside the castle, where country women prepare traditional dishes of the upper Tiber valley with all the good tastes of the earth. The experiments with low-yield, high-quality vines from other places may well lead to more plantings that could give Tuscany some of the variety in white wines that more northerly regions have.

Montecarlo, which some consider the region's reigning white wine, is dominated by Trebbiano (at 60 to 70 percent), though the inclusion of such strangers as Pinot Grigio, Roussane, Sauvignon, and Sémillon give it a mark of distinction. The vineyards surround the town of Montecarlo in the province of Lucca. Production is slight and much Montecarlo is consumed in nearby tourist centers such as Pisa, Viareggio, and Forte dei Marmi where seafood dominates the menus. Montecarlo is delicate, pale yellow, and smooth, with an appealing balance between fruity and flinty dry. As a rule, it should be drunk from six months to two years after the vintage, though Tuscans often keep it longer.

The Fattoria del Buonamico and the Fattoria di Montecarlo make wine of superb tone, certainly among the finest whites of the region. The Fattoria del Buonamico was founded by the Vanelli family as a supply base for wine and other farm products served in its Gatto Nero restaurant in Turin, which some Italians consider the finest Tuscan restaurant anywhere. The vineyards have been expanded somewhat, and now the wine is sold commercially and even exported. The Fattoria del Buonamico also makes an unclassified red that can be even better than the white. In 1975, for example, it was magnificent, so impressive that it was given a special name — Rosso di Cercatoia — and sold at double the price of the white. That 1975 ranks as one of the finest Tuscan reds of that vintage. It is dominated by Sangiovese with some not-so-common varieties included. Soft, round, mouth-filling, it was perhaps closest in type to a Carmignano, though its richness and bouquet were reminiscent of fine Burgundy.

The Fattoria di Montecarlo rivals Buonamico in quality. Other recommended producers are Attilio Tori, whose wine is called Cerruglio; M. Passaglia; Fattoria del Teso; and Fattoria La Torre, which also makes a good red.

Bianco della Valdinievole, from the province of Pistoia near the spa of Montecatini Terme, gained DOC status so recently that it has not had time to establish its name in Italy. But wines from the zone, both white and red, have been noted for centuries for their character. Bianco della Valdinievole is made from Trebbiano into a pleasantly light wine, sometimes with a hint of fizz, that goes well with fish. The discipline also includes a Vin Santo from the same grapes as the Bianco, but semi-dried and pressed into a wine to be aged at least three years.

Bianco Pisano San Torpé was named DOC in 1980 on the strength of a campaign by its active consortium. The zone covers a large area south-east of Pisa in much the same location as Chianti Colline Pisane. The grapes are again Trebbiano, with some Malvasia and Canaiolo Bianco included. Its most prominent wine to date is called Gello, from the Fattoria di Gello near Lavaiano on the Arno's alluvial plain. A flinty dry, pale, crisp wine, Gello won an "Oscar" in 1970 as the best white in one of Italy's numerous wine competitions. Other reliable producers include Fattoria Gaslini, Fattoria di Piedivilla, and Fratelli Salvadori.

Tuscan Cooking: Sublime Simplicity

Ranging into the mountains north of Lucca toward the borders of Emilia-Romagna and Liguria, the wines and the food, like the scenery, become more rustic, sometimes in the most appealing ways. I remember a red called Grana served at La Greppia, which has to be the most ramshackle setting yet for *la grande cucina Italiana* — a mountain hut with corrugated roof on a windblown, treeless, boulder-strewn plateau high in that part of the Apennines known as the Garfagnana. The interior was warm and cheery in a homey way, and the food cooked and served by Signora Vincenzi was more than enough reward for the ascent through countless curves in a somber, late-fall landscape. There was antipasto of mountain *prosciutto* and salami, freshly baked whole wheat bread sliced thick from basket-sized loaves, two types of *cannelloni* — one with béchamel and cheese, the other with ragout — followed by spit-roasted wood pigeons and field greens, fresh *pecorino*, and through it all that robust Grana made by the Signora's father down the mountain at San Romano.

That sort of eating is, admittedly, on the excessive side these days, but there is something about medieval Lucca and its unspoiled hill country that make a modern light diet seem needlessly restrictive. And, after all, Italians will tell you that Tuscan cooking is the most healthful because it is the most natural, the most simplistic. But that term *simplistic* can be deceptive; it should not be taken to mean that Tuscan cooks, because they perhaps fuss less with their preparations than do Emilia-Romagnans, for example, care less about the food they eat. Tuscans have a knack for elevating the humblest country dish to tasty respectability and even, on occasion, to the sublime.

What could be simpler than what is known variously as *fettunta, panunto,* or *bruschetta,* depending on the locale, a slice of bread grilled on the coals, then rubbed with raw garlic, sprinkled with salt and flooded with olive oil, preferably *extra vergine* while it is still slightly sharp after being cold-pressed? Or *crostini,* toast spread with warm chicken-liver paté flavored with sage, onions, *prosciutto,* capers, and anchovies? Or *minestrone* done in a hundred different ways, depending on vegetables in season, thickened on succeeding days with stale bread and fresh flavorings to become a *ribollita,* the heartiest and most flavorful of soups? Or *bistecca alla fiorentina* grilled artfully over coals so the outside is crusted and the inside is still a succulent pink? Or *fagioli,* lowly white beans, simmered to tenderness and served with olive oil and a few twists of fresh pepper, a side dish that can send its admirers into states of ecstasy?

Tuscans are country-oriented people who know too well the essentials of taste to be fooled by frills in either food or drink. That probably explains why the region's "fancy" restaurants (and there are indeed not many) are the lone outposts of that genre of cuisine sometimes called international, which often turns out to be imitation French with a few choices like *spaghetti alla carbonara* or grilled *scampi* thrown in for a native touch. Most restaurateurs stick to the basics: unadorned surroundings with menu recitable in a matter of moments and wine choices restricted to *"rosso o bianco?"* Here at least that slim selection is usually eminently satisfactory. In any case, it will have to do.

The inspiration for Tuscan cooking can be traced directly to the country kitchen, to the hands of farm wives who, after working in fields, olive groves, and vineyards beside the men, tend livestock, clean house, keep a vegetable garden, wash and sew, and still cheerfully twice a day turn out meals that would make the finest chefs of Florence proud. How many great Italian cooks drew their inspiration from these Italian mammas everywhere who, toiling away in their one domain, the kitchen, run not only their households but, in a not altogether oblique sense, the country? Though political analysts do not often dwell on motherhood and cooking, a case could be made for these institutions as the bonds that hold this schismatic nation together.

Coastal Wines: Emerging from Obscurity

Wines are made all along the Tuscan coastal plains and hills from Massa and Carrara south to the Argentario peninsula and on the islands as well. Though the northwestern corner of Tuscany has no DOC zones, wines of character are produced in the marble-rich hills facing the sea above Massa and Carrara. Near Aulla in the Lunigiana hills and the Magra River valley, both reds and whites served by the flask in *trattorie* seem too good to remain anonymous for long. Their vines, from a dozen varieties and more, have such names as Durella, Morone, Rosaria, Bracciola, Foscara, in addition to the more familiar. Until recently they had been propagated casually, interspersed and mixed, the resulting wines identifiable only by those who knew their makers. All that is beginning to change, but the discipline required for recognition is still not very evident here, though Bianco di Candia has become a candidate for DOC and others will undoubtedly follow. In the meantime, the wines of Tuscany's northernmost coastal area remain treasures for the adventurous to seek out.

The hills of Lucca have a DOC red wine called Rosso delle Colline Lucchesi, still another variation on Chianti. It includes a bit of Ciliegiolo and Vermentino grapes as well as the Chianti varieties. Though it was recognized early — in 1967 — as a DOC wine, it has not received much notice outside the Lucca-Pisa-Montecatini area, where it is generally drunk young and cool.

The obscurity is easily explained, according to Bruno Nannini, head of the Rosso delle Colline Lucchesi consortium and creator of San Gennaro–Leoni, the zone's only wine of more than local renown. "I've tried to interest the others in some promotion," he said, "even the most elemental propaganda to let the rest of the world know we make good wine here. But every time I start something, it turns out I'm the only one who goes through with it. And you can't have a one-man consortium."

No, but Nannini, who voices his determination in soft tones, will go on trying and will possibly succeed almost singlehandedly in making Rosso delle Colline Lucchesi better known. His San Gennaro expresses *governo* at its classic best — lively, fruity, yet smooth and refined in wine capable of long aging. "Here's the difference," said Nannini, pointing to grapes drying on cane mats six weeks after the 1978 harvest. "Concentrated musts are no substitute for these. You wonder why they don't bother with *governo* in Chianti nowadays. There's a simple explanation. It's too much trouble. Yes, I know, they say *governo* wine won't age. What they're really saying is that they don't comprehend the process or the purpose. *Governo* should enrich and stabilize the wine in a natural way. Here, taste this."

Nannini drew some 1971 *riserva* from a barrel in his cantina near the crest of San Gennaro, a hill community like many of Lucca more noted for olive oil than wine. This Rosso delle Colline Lucchesi was extraordinary, the equal of many fine Chiantis of that year with an aroma more pronounced than in most reserve wines from Sangiovese. "See, that was made using *governo*," said Nannini, "and it hasn't reached its prime yet. Taste it again in a year or two and tell me if *governo* is only for young wine."

Young or aged, most wine of Lucca never travels far from home, so there is plenty around to enhance the rustic local cooking. At Ponte a Moriano, 9 kilometers north of Lucca, the Trattoria La Mora offers traditional dishes — bean soups, homemade pasta and pastries, game, fowl, polenta — with the finest wines of the zone. Sauro Brunicardi, who runs the family restaurant beside the fast-flowing Serchio River, has collected Lucca's wines along with other fine bottles from Tuscany and other regions in his *enoteca* across the lane.

Down along the coast past Pisa toward Livorno, some wines are emerging from obscurity as their producer consortiums succeed in having them officially recognized. Montescudaio, a hilly zone southeast of Livorno, gained DOC in 1977 for its Bianco, Rosso, and Vin Santo. The Bianco, from Trebbiano at 70 to 85 percent plus Malvasia and Vermentino, is dry and refreshingly light, ideal with fish. *Cacciucco,* the piquant fish stew of Livorno, is such a hearty concoction, however, that a rosé or even a red might be better suited to it. Montescudaio Rosso, from Sangiovese at 65 to 85 percent with Trebbiano and Malvasia making up the difference, resembles the lightest styles of Chianti with its bright cherry hue and unimposing drinkability. Montescudaio Vin Santo is made from the same grapes as the white but semi-dried; it must have at least 14° alcohol and be aged three years. Good rosé is also made in the hills. Like much of maritime Tuscany, Livorno province shows outstanding potential for viticulture with some already conspicuous successes among the scattered styles of winemaking.

Sassicaia, Thoroughbred Cabernet

That Sangiovese is the base of all Tuscan red wines, great and small, is gospel. Well, anyhow, it was gospel and might still be had it not been for Marchese Mario Incisa della Rocchetta and Sassicaia. But what, as any self-respecting Tuscan might ask, is a marquis from Piedmont, home of Nebbiolo and other noble vines, doing growing the noblest of French vines in Tuscany, which has a noble vine or two of its own? And why, of all places, at Bolgheri, where the wines were always rather common and, to make matters worse, reputedly had sea salt in their flavors?

Marchese Mario Incisa della Rocchetta might have asked himself questions of the sort often in the years before Sassicaia came out of its shell, emerging with more than just the usual modest aspirations expected of Italian Cabernet. Some Tuscans still shake their heads in disbelief, but none would any longer dare question Sassicaia's credentials, especially after the astounding triumph in London. There, in a showdown of world Cabernets sponsored by *Decanter* magazine in 1978, Sassicaia swept the field of 34 wines from 11 nations, winning unprecedented perfect scores of 20 from 2 of 5 panelists and the unanimous accolade of "the best wine in the entire tasting."

"I wasn't surprised," Incisa recounted later, "but at one point in my life I would have been."

That point was in the 1940s after Incisa's family acquired the Tenuta San Guido, a huge tract of land south of Livorno along the Aurelian Way, which followed the Mediterranean from Rome to Gaul. This part of the Maremma, the Tuscan coastal section noted for its reminders of the Etruscans and for such natural provisions as borax and wild boar, had never been distinguished by its wines. But Incisa stubbornly went ahead with a project he had had in mind since student days, and in 1942 planted a hectare of Cabernet Sauvignon on a hill called Castiglioncello. He selected that site at more than 1,000 feet above sea level because it was ideally exposed and high enough, he reasoned, to escape salty breezes.

He made his first wine a few years later, using methods that were part Tuscan (the *governo*, of course), part French (*barriques* of the Bordeaux type were found for aging, though they leaked), and part Piedmontese (such a heritage was not to be neglected). The result was disastrous. He and his Tuscan counsels, who suffered through a tasting, were unanimous in pronouncing it swill, but nobody was quite sure why. Incisa turned his attention to other agricultural pursuits.

Then, years later, purely out of curiosity, Incisa decided to sample some bottles that had been put away at the rate of about 200 liters a year. Having been made in true country style, the wine was rustic and dense and heavy with sediment. It often showed an excess of volatile acidity, but wine from every vintage, even the medium years, was drinkable, and some vintages gave hints of greatness. Scarcely able to believe it himself, Incisa offered it to friends worldly enough to appreciate something besides Chianti. They too found positive points. Incisa renewed his interest in winemaking, eventually even dropping the *governo* and buying some barrels that did not leak.

The earlier problem, which everyone had overlooked at the time, was that Cabernet Sauvignon was not ready to drink in the spring following the harvest, as the light-hearted local wines were. The tar and herbs and tannin that the local experts found so disgusting were positive factors that needed time to express themselves in harmony.

Still Incisa, a dapper nobleman of the country-gentleman mold, saw no reason to make wine for profit, because his estate was already thriving on such products as flowers and thoroughbred racehorses. Though he gradually increased production of Cabernet, planting an additional small vineyard at lower altitudes in a place called Sassicaia (where sea salt has never presented a problem), he made just enough wine to keep family and friends happy.

Then in the mid-1960s, young Piero Antinori, Incisa's nephew, suggested that Sassicaia had too much class to be considered just a hobby wine, and he managed to persuade his uncle to make some available for sale in bottle. Wine from the 1968 vintage was labeled and sold through Marchesi Antinori's commercial channels and Incisa's son Niccolò was recruited as commercial manager. The 7,300 bottles sold quickly and generated a triumphant response from Italian experts.

Emile Peynaud, a leading oenologist from Bordeaux and friend of the family, offered practical advice, although his assistance has remained informal and infrequent. Incisa is still in charge of Sassicaia, relying on occasional suggestions (if he agrees with them) from Antinori's chief oenologist, Giacomo Tachis. The wine is fermented in open wooden vats and, after racking, aged in *barriques* for about two years. Because the storage rooms are situated in a converted flower hothouse above ground level, they are kept at an air-conditioned low temperature. Then the wine is taken to Antinori's cantina near Florence for bottling and two more years of aging before being sold.

Incisa recently expanded vineyards to a total of 4.5 hectares (slightly more than 11 acres) and added a few Cabernet Franc vines to the predominant Cabernet Sauvignon. The capacity of 20,000 bottles from the 1978 vintage was to be increased eventually to 30,000 bottles, but no more. Sassicaia will be kept at the dimensions of a small family estate.

Sassicaia has a Bordeaux style, as many admirers have noted, arrived at through conscious emulation. But there are notable differences. For one, the wine consists almost entirely of Cabernet Sauvignon; the great Bordeaux are invariably composites. Also cultivation methods differ; Sassicaia has fewer vines per hectare than do the great French estates and the vines are pruned longer in the cordon style and yield more grapes per plant than do the head-trained Bordeaux vines. Another contrast is in size; Sassicaia is much smaller than Margaux, Lafite, Cheval Blanc, and most top Bordeaux properties and produces much less wine.

Sassicaia does seem to have a clear advantage over Bordeaux in climate. Its vintages have been remarkably consistent. For instance, the 1972 harvest, a disaster for most areas of Tuscany, produced the Sassicaia that swept the London tasting. Like a number of Italy's great wines, Sassicaia is not DOC and therefore carries the humble designation *vino da tavola*. Though he disapproves of the term and the concept behind it, Incisa is not worried. Sassicaia's reputation is now beyond the scope of such petty distractions. It took time, but somehow the marquis from Piedmont put it all together and came up with a thoroughbred, an Italian Cabernet that ranks as a serious contender in the world's most elite field of wine.

Elba: A Place in the Sun

From Bolgheri the mass of Elba can be seen across the water to the south, its rocky, sun-scorched mountains from afar looking as formidable as they must have in Napoleon's time. But as the ferry from Piombino approaches the island's capital, Portoferraio, the outlines of new villas and hotels and the animation provided by cars plying the curvy roads reveal that this is no longer the mecca for escapists it once was. But Elba remains a pleasant place to bask on a beach, swim in clear water, eat seafood fresh from the trawler, and drink wines as individualistic as any in Tuscany.

The dominant grapes, Sangioveto (a variation of Sangiovese) and Procanico (the Elba version of Trebbiano), are familiar, but the wines decidedly are not. Some say the island climate, particularly in the valleys south and east of Portoferraio toward Porto Azzurro, gives the whites their attractive sunny taste and the reds their sound body and depth, but the real difference probably is emitted by the ferrous earth of an island that has long been Italy's major source of iron. The old-style vineyards are the prettiest; the vines emerging from the rust-hewn soil are trained onto bamboo poles set teepee style. Inevitably, this touch of local color is being erased by the advent of mechanization.

Though Napoleon admired the island's wines during his brief exile, the Elbans themselves traditionally cut them with water to diminish the natural tendency to high alcohol and heavy bodies. One wine, though I am not sure why, is still called Acqua Matta — or "Crazy Water." Until recent decades the island's chief grapes were the white Biancone and Moscato and the red Aleatico, which is still used for a rich dessert wine. The relatively recent domination of Sangioveto and Procanico has heralded a trend toward lighter, drier wines. Under DOC rules Elba Rosso and Elba Bianco vines must be controlled for low yields. The wines are fruitier and less alcoholic than before — the white 11° minimum, the red 12° — and nowadays even the islanders usually drink their wines neat.

One of the oldest winemaking families of Elba, Gasparri, is still prominent. The M. Gasparri & Co. winery is now run by Aulo Gasparri, who turns out fine Procanico and Sangioveto, Aleatico di Portoferraio, Moscato, and a dry Gran Spumante, also from the Procanico grape. Other producers of note include Tenuta Acquabona, Podere La Pianella, Azienda Agricola di Mola, Lupi Rocchi, Vinicola Elbana, the cooperative Enopolio di Portoferraio, and La Chiusa di Magazzini, run by a dedicated woman who in a few years has personally made her wines Elba's foremost in quality.

Giuliana Foresi is one of a growing number of Italians who have given up city life to return to the land. Not many had such a lovely place to come back to as La Chiusa di Magazzini, her family's summer estate overlooking the bay of Portoferraio. Yet, with all the trappings of Old World gentility around her, Giuliana Foresi did something none of her

Giuliana Foresi

male predecessors who possessed the estate ever dreamed of doing in the four centuries since the family settled there after Cosimo I de' Medici founded Portoferraio: she put on work clothes and learned to hoe, spray, drive a tractor, prune, and pitch manure, to pick grapes and press them, operate a derasper, to rack, fine, age, bottle, label, and sell wine.

And though she does not always perform all these tasks alone, no wine-maker anywhere can say he (or she) has put more into the final product than Giuliana Foresi has.

Still, save for a healthy tan and some calluses on her hands, Signorina Foresi does not show signs of being overworked. A petite, middle-aged blonde, in conventional feminine attire she could still pass for the Milan advertising executive she was until 1972. Her passion for winemaking was a late-blossoming phenomenon that does not date to her childhood when the local *contadini* did the rough work and her father, a Livorno physician, supervised the vinification. His last vintage was 1972, and Signorina Foresi, who by then was an active if not-too-well-informed participant, was left with some 11 acres of the island's finest vineyards. By then the labor situation had made the absentee-landlord type of winemaking on small plots a financial liability, so she was confronted with a decision that "might have been tough, but wasn't."

"Though I had lived more on the mainland, I always was an Elban at heart," she said, "so nothing seemed more natural to me than leaving my job and coming home to run the vineyards. As it turned out, winemaking is more difficult than I'd figured, but I've never regretted my decision."

Working days, with a little help from neighborhood farm laborers, and studying nights, she not only continued La Chiusa's winemaking operation but improved it. She mechanized where she had to and bought some new equipment.

"You know, the hardest thing I've faced, and I still haven't made up my mind, is replacing those lovely old wooden fermenting vats with stainless steel ones," she said. "Oh, I know it will have to be done eventually, but it's going to ruin the aesthetics of my cantina. To me, aesthetics are an important part of winemaking."

Like everything else about La Chiusa, the cantina was designed with an abundance of good taste. The estate, with its towered main house, tiny chapel, and farm buildings, is flanked by palms and cypresses and surrounded by an eighteenth-century wall that gives it the appearance of a French *clos*. Giuliana Foresi's vines, which are purposely held to half the permitted yield, annually produce some 12,000 bottles of wine with all the grace and charm of its home and its maker. The white, aged briefly in oak barrels, is straw-colored, very dry and smooth, nicely balanced between fruit and acid with a hint of the nearness of the sea about it. The red shows even greater class. Deep ruby, full-bodied, lightly tannic, it can be vigorously pleasing to drink after two years of wood aging, but kept longer it tends to round into a wine of depth and elegance. From some vintages it can age for a decade or more.

Elba is the largest island in the Tuscan archipelago, which also includes Giglio, Giannutri, Capraia, Gorgona, and the remote Monte Cristo. Each, of course, has wines, but only those of Giglio enjoy any more than a local reputation. Ansonica di Giglio, from the grape of that name, is about as colored as a white wine can be. But if you are not put off by the rich amber hue, as deep as that of a well-aged Cognac, the Ansonica from Le Cannelle is a dry, vigorous, amply scented wine that can go very nicely with a plate of grilled fish. There is also a dessert version made.

On the mainland, in the province of Grosseto, many very good table wines are now produced, the most noted being the red and white of La Parrina, near Orbetello, which are DOC. Attractive wines from the estate of the Marchese Spinola Giuntini, the white is from Procanico (Trebbiano) at 80 percent with the rest Ansonica and Malvasia, and the red from Sangiovese at 80 percent with the rest Canaiolo, Morellone, and Colorino. Known as Vino Etrusco, an allusion to the Etruscan civilization that thrived in this southernmost section of Tuscany, the labels were inspired by designs found in ancient tombs. The Parrina wines are favorites in the resorts of Porto Ercole and Porto Santo Stefano on the Argentario peninsula. Well made and moderately priced, they are among the most satisfying of those wines that Italians call *scorrevole* — fluent or flowing, delightfully easy to drink.

The nearby Cantina Sociale di Montepescali also produces good red and white wines on the lonely hillsides of the Maremma, an area, long abandoned because of malaria, that has only recently begun to realize its capacity for fine wines.

To the east, around Pitigliano and Manciano, are the vineyards of Bianco di Pitigliano, a delicate wine from Trebbiano, Greco or Grechetto, Malvasia, and Verdello grapes. The most heavily produced DOC white wine of Tuscany, it has been gaining popularity in central Italy. Bianco di Pitigliano is made and bottled most prominently by the Cantina Cooperativa di Pitigliano, which exports some of its growing production.

A recent Tuscan DOC wine, Morellino di Scansano, was officially recognized in November, 1978. A red from Sangiovese with a 15 percent addition of local varieties permitted, Morellino is warm, dry, and lightly tannic with at least 11.5° alcohol. A *riserva* version must have

12° alcohol and be aged at least two years, one in barrel. Part of the DOC zone, around Manciano, Magliano in Toscana, and Roccalbegna, overlaps that of Bianco di Pitigliano. The two Morellino di Scansano wines I have tried were distinctly promising, one from the Fattoria Palazzaccio, the other from Libero Sellari-Franceschini.

An excellent unclassified red wine from the neighborhood is Castello di Monte Antico, made by Giorgio Cabella at his Fattoria di Monte Antico e dell'Abbadia Ardenghesca near Civitella Paganico, just outside the Brunello di Montalcino zone in the province of Grosseto. Big and robust, because of its base of Sangiovese Grosso (with some Canaiolo, Colorino, and Trebbiano included), with age it can rival its more vaunted neighbors in the province of Siena. Cabella also makes from Trebbiano and Malvasia a fine white wine called Ardenghesca. Suave and sumptuous, it is best to drink young.

Vin Santo, the People's Choice

Chianti's legendary popularity notwithstanding, the wine most beloved by Tuscans is Vin Santo, whose soft, often sweet, vinous qualities please almost everybody from grandmas to teething infants. It comes in many forms from many sources, the best appreciated generally being from the barrel put away in the attic of nearly every farm home. It is usually sweet, or at least *abboccato*, though a respected school of thought insists that real Vin Santo must be dry.

I go along with Aldo Casagni of Rigutino, who makes both dry and lightly sweet Vin Santo at his farm outside Arezzo, each as fine in its way as any I have tasted. He says the relative sweetness depends primarily on the sugar content of each batch of grapes, a factor that varies from year to year and from one plot or grape variety to another. "The one rule of good Vin Santo is that its sugar must be completely natural," said Casagni. "Of course, in many cases it isn't."

Traditionally, Vin Santo was made from grapes semi-dried by hanging from the beams of farm kitchens, where they picked up a smoky aroma, then pressed and fermented into wine sometime between Christmas and Easter. But today other less quaint methods are often used to dry the grapes. Still, the real Vin Santo — which must be sealed in small barrels and kept in an environment where it feels the cold of winter and the heat of summer for three to five years — is treasured. Bottles from prestige wineries sell for double the price of the best *riserva* Chianti of the same year.

Vin Santo Toscano seems destined to become DOC one of these days in what would be Tuscany's first regionwide classification. However, its grapes would come only from designated areas, and the wine naturally will have to meet a set of standards of production and quality, including a minimum alcohol content of 14°. Vin Santo is made from such traditional Tuscan grapes as Malvasia and Trebbiano primarily, though other types may also be included.

Numerous legends exist about the origin of the name, though the most probable reason it came to be known as "holy wine" was through its use in religious rites and ceremonies. Sweet Vin Santo is a unique dessert wine, well suited to cakes and pastries, particularly the hard almond biscuits known variously as *ricciarelli, croccanti, ghiottini, spaccadenti,* and *cantucci di Prato,* which are softened by soaking in the wine. Sweet Vin Santo can also be used like Porto as a sipping wine before or after a meal. Dry, it makes an excellent *aperitivo.* Vin Santo's colors range from light golden to deep bronze. There is also a red Vin Santo, though the only one I know of in commerce is sold by Antinori.

Good Vin Santo is produced by thousands of Tuscans, though usually in such preciously limited quantities that they do not sell it. Rather it is kept aside as a symbol of hospitality, to be served with the spontaneous generosity that lives on in country homes. Even the everyday table wines produced on Tuscan farms, though sometimes made under rather primitive conditions, usually turn out to be hearty and frank with the rough-hewn but natural grace of the good people who make them.

The Vintages

	Chianti	Brunello di Montalcino	Vino Nobile di Montepulciano
1979	Exceptional	Exceptional	Exceptional
1978	Scarce, some excellent	Uneven, some exceptional	Scarce, some excellent

	Chianti	Brunello di Montalcino	Vino Nobile di Montepulciano
1977	Scarce, some great	Exceptional, not abundant	Scarce, some exceptional
1976	Poor to fair	Poor to fair	Poor
1975	Excellent	Excellent, some great	Excellent, some great
1974	Good	Fair	Good
1973	Fair to good	Fair to good	Excellent
1972	Poor, little wine made	Poor, some acceptable	Poor
1971	Excellent, some great	Excellent	Poor to fair
1970	Excellent	Great	Exceptional
1969	Good to excellent	Fair	Good
1968	Very good	Good	Excellent
1967	Good to excellent	Good to excellent	Exceptional
1966	Fair to good	Good to excellent	Excellent
1965	Fair to good	Poor	Poor
1964	Good to excellent	Excellent, some great	Excellent
1963	—	Poor	—
1962	Excellent	Poor	Outstanding
1961	Good	Excellent	Good
1960	—	Poor	—
1959	—	Poor	—
1958	Excellent	Excellent	Excellent
1957	Excellent	Excellent	Very good
1956	—	Poor	—
1955	Excellent	Exceptional	Very good
	Vernaccia di San Gimignano	Montecarlo Bianco	Elba Bianco and Rosso
1979	Excellent	Excellent	Excellent

	Vernaccia di San Gimignano	*Montecarlo Bianco*	*Elba Bianco and Rosso*
1978	Scarce, some excellent	Uneven, some good	Good
1977	Scarce, excellent	Scarce, some excellent	Excellent
1976	Poor	Poor	Good
1975	Excellent	Excellent	Fair
1974	Excellent	Good	Fair
1973	Excellent	Good	Excellent
1972	Fair to good	Poor	Fair
1971	Excellent	Good	Excellent
1970	Exceptional	Excellent	Exceptional

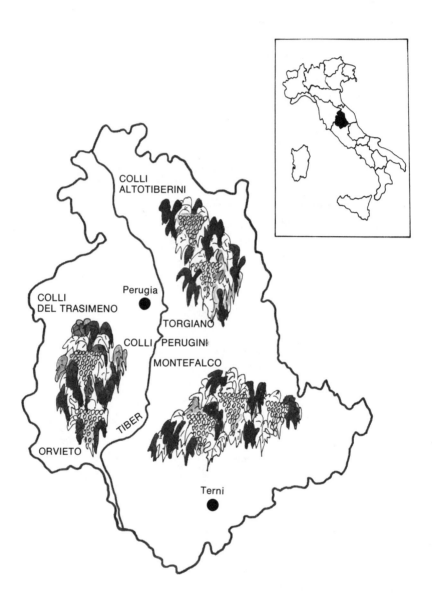

COLLI
ALTOTIBERINI

COLLI
DEL TRASIMENO

Perugia ●

TORGIANO

COLLI PERUGINI

MONTEFALCO

TIBER

ORVIETO

Terni ●

UMBRIA

PROVINCES

PERUGIA, Terni

POPULATION

795,000

AREA

3,270 square miles

AVERAGE WINE PRODUCTION

70 million liters

DOC WINES

Colli Altotiberini (Bianco, Rosso, Rosato) · Colli del Trasimeno (Bianco, Rosso) · Montefalco (Rosso, Sagrantino) · Orvieto · Torgiano (Bianco, Rosso)

OTHER WINES

Almonte · Amelia · Cabernet Sauvignon · Castel Grifone · Collazzone · Collepepe · Colli Perugini · Lago di Corbara · Marsciano · Merlot · Monteforcone · Montegabbione · Montegiove · Musignano · Nebbiolo di Gubbio · Orvieto Rosso · Pinot Bianco · Riesling · Santa Giulia del Poderaccio · Scacciadiavoli · Solleone · Tocai · Todi · Tudernum · Vernaccia di Cannara · Vin Santo

Visions across the Vineyards

I N Umbria, time stood still so long that even the countervailing influences of the space age have not forced it to drop its Old World pose. They call it the green heart of Italy, because it lies at the center of the peninsula and is still verdant with woods and pastures, and also because it typifies the rustic, nostalgic, unadorned goodness of the earth and the mystic spirituality of the Italian people as expressed through the nation's patron saint, Francis of Assisi.

It is a land of resolute contrasts, improbable juxtapositions, unexpected experiences that derive from the existing realities of different eras being played off against each other. The ancient towns, stark and stoic atop their hills, stand out against the soft green-amber-golden hues of farmland rolling off lazily toward distant mountains. Along the highways you may still spot a team of oxen pulling a painted wooden cart, the great white animals nodding languidly at tandem trucks thundering past toward distant cities.

The people in a country village, their features so curiously mixed between ancient Umbrian, Etruscan, and Latin, Goth, Hun, and Gaul, regard you with cool suspicion when you approach: another invader threatening to upset the tranquility of a summer afternoon? No, merely a pilgrim come to try the wine. Your impromptu host becomes your instant friend, who will not let you go until you have drunk your fill in a cool cantina and sampled homemade *prosciutto*, salami, *pecorino*, and cakes, and vowed repeatedly to return some Sunday with your family for a real feast.

Few Umbrians will thank you if you point out similarities in their way of life and the Tuscan, apparent as they may seem on the surface. They are used to it, but they resent it, and they may tell you politely but firmly that you do not understand much about Umbria if you regard it as an adjunct of Tuscany or Latium or any other region.

Consider the wine. True, Umbria's major grape for red wine is the Tuscan Sangiovese, and the chief grapes for white wine are the Tuscan

Trebbiano and Malvasia. And yet, maybe it is the soil, the warmer, land-locked climate, the subtle variations in methods followed by winemakers from one region to the next, but any resemblance between Umbrian wine and Tuscan is purely coincidental. And whatever you do, never let an Umbrian hear you say that Tuscans invented Vin Santo, tanta-mount to implying that St. Francis was born in Arezzo.

As the only Italian region that does not figure in the national outline, Umbria can be approached by land from every angle, from the Marches, Latium, or Tuscany, over mountains or across plains, via the Auto-strada del Sole or along winding country lanes. I prefer to travel on the latter, because they seem more in keeping with Umbrian character and because the wines you find along rural roads, if sometimes humble, are never served in disposable plastic cups. There is no more dramatic ap-proach to Umbria than along the road that runs from the Via Cassia, the ancient Cassian Way that linked Rome and Florence, to Orvieto, de-scending on the town in hawklike swoops that afford visions across the vineyards of the Gothic Duomo, its splendid façade rising majestically above the medieval rooftops.

The Golden Days of Orvieto

Orvieto, planted since Etruscan times on a bed of volcanic rock, is one of Italy's loveliest wine towns, offering visitors through the centuries such a seductive lieu for sipping that they might be excused for being taken in by all the poetic pandering behind the wine's worldwide fame. Still, Orvieto was no doubt a great wine once upon a time, relatively speaking, when standards were different, when lightly sweet, golden wines kept cool in deep cellars and wells were coveted by popes and Renaissance painters (and possibly even common souls, though nobody ever bothered to interview the man in the street in those days).

The historical importance of Orvieto's wines is thoroughly docu-mented. The gradual, well-exposed slopes in the Classico zone surround-ing the town and overlooking the Paglia River consist of clay and vol-canic substances known since ancient times to be auspiciously suited to vine cultivation. Local taste, probably since the Etruscans settled here, have favored white wine, though some red wine made in the area is of excellent quality.

There is no way of knowing how good the wine of Orvieto was in Etruscan days because those people were not inclined to record their pleasures in writing, but, judging by their art and the evidence of the efforts they put into its making, it must have been most rewarding. The Etruscans dug deep into the town's stone base for the dual purpose of excavating tufa for building and of constructing sophisticated, multi-level cellars for making wine. Their system was based on the force of gravity: crushing was carried out at ground level, fermentation at the next level down, aging in the lower grottos, where temperature was cool and constant. Have later systems ever been so ingeniously functional?

Over the years Orvieto maintained its standing as one of the peninsula's most esteemed wines. Luca Signorelli demanded part of his payment in wine for decorating the Cappella Nuova in the Duomo. Pinturicchio, another celebrated contributor, requested a steady supply of wine, which he got. In fact, he got so much that his contract was rescinded after a year "for having consumed too much azure, too much gold, and too much wine."

As an *abboccato* wine, Orvieto's fame endured well into this century, aided no doubt by the *pulcianella*, the squat straw-based flask it was most often sold in until recent times. Not long after World War II, however, as tastes gradually shifted toward dry white wines, Orvieto producers failed for a time to match the emerging national competition. The Tuscan Chianti firms that controlled a large share of Orvieto production shifted quickly to the dry, but still the image and sales slumped. The *pulcianella*, expensive and clumsy to ship, was a factor in the decline.

Producers soon realized that Orvieto, in addition to a face-lift, needed a thorough revision of its age-old personality. The initial cosmetics had not been enough. The larger wineries raised the money to invest in the new technology that in just a few years transformed Orvieto from a soft, lightly sweet, golden country wine to a crisp, rather dry, pale straw-colored cosmopolitan beverage. Most firms are still paying off debts on their new plants and equipment but, riding the crest of the worldwide white wine wave, they have found Orvieto in the last few years to be a better investment than Chianti.

A key figure in the comeback has been Piero Antinori, who heads the largest winery and presides over the newly unified consortium of Orvieto and Orvieto Classico. Antinori, whose Umbrian base is the centuries-old family estate of Castello della Sala, credits the positive economic situation to sound fundamentals: gradual, quality-controlled expansion of production of a good basic wine made using advanced techniques and sold at a reasonable price.

"Orvieto has always been an excellent zone for white wine," says Antinori, "though as in other areas where a thorough transition has taken place, there is a constant need to review developments. We've been striving to elevate overall quality and I think we've been successful in surpassing the general level of DOC white wine from other parts of Italy. But that isn't enough. We're experimenting intensely with cultivation and vinification techniques. I'm personally not convinced that the present grape formula for Orvieto need be the ultimate. We're doing some tests with Pinot and Chardonnay grapes that aren't conclusive yet, but it could be that use of those varieties in the formula could be a positive quality factor."

What if it turned out that Pinot and Chardonnay on their own made superior wine? "I don't exclude any eventuality," said Antinori, his tone, like his smile, revealing that he had contemplated the idea. "Winemakers everywhere should explore all possibilities, cautiously, rationally, of course, with an eye to making the best wine conditions can afford. We should not let our notions of tradition or our wine laws inhibit the pursuit of excellence."

The formula for Orvieto prescribed by the DOC discipline of 1971 calls for Trebbiano Toscano at 50 to 65 percent, Verdello at 15 to 25 percent, and Grechetto, Drupeggio, and Malvasia Toscana at 20 to 30 percent between them. Orvieto has a large production zone, extending into Latium, though much of the better-quality wine is made in the Classico zone in the environs of the town. Vineyard expansion has been steady in recent years, and more land is available, indicating that production will increase from the approximately 8 million liters a year level of the late 1970s. About 3 million liters of that were Orvieto Classico.

A Question of Character

Antinori's assessment of Orvieto's status seems accurate, though some long-standing admirers of the wine might argue that the recent evolution in techniques instead of changing the wine's personality buried it. Orvieto's growing success on national and international markets indicates that the emphasis on the dry version is economically sound and that the wine has emerged as a worthy representative of the new breed of Italian white. But, as the respected English wine authority Michael Broadbent commented after tasting a well-known Orvieto in London not long ago: "This is certainly a good, clean, well-made wine, but it has nothing whatever to do with my conception of Orvieto. Is it possible that technology has carried things too far in this case and compromised traditional character?"

That crucial question could be posed about dozens of other white wines, not only Italian ones; the answer, obviously, lies on the palate and in the mind of the perceiver. Exponents of the new breed, most prominently Ezio Rivella, assert that the current techniques result in the purest possible white wines, and that rather than compromising character, more than ever before they truly express the nature of the grapes. "What some people described as character," Rivella once said, "was chiefly flavors and aromas that did not derive directly from the grape." Rivella and others maintain that oxygen, wood, and aging are to be avoided at all costs because they detract from the all-important quality of freshness.

As a weathered witness of both styles — the oxidized, woody, heavily flavored, often flat Orvieto, Frascati, Vernaccia, etcetera, of yore and the super-clean, pasteurized, young, flawless, but often rather neutral whites of recent years — I lean toward the new, but not without reservation. A breath of air, a hint of wood, a little bottle age lend to certain white wines something that when skillfully controlled can be beneficial.

DOC regulations for Orvieto, both *secco* and *abboccato,* specify that no more than 65 percent of the weight in grapes be transformed into wine, meaning that only the free-run must is used. Orvieto should have a pale color and delicate aroma and flavor with at least 12° alcohol. Both versions are best to drink young.

Production has become ever more concentrated in the hands of the larger wineries able to afford the necessary equipment. The biggest and just possibly the best is Antinori's Castello della Sala. Other Orvieto producers working on a relatively large scale are Bigi (controlled by Winefood), Bertolli, Luigi Cecchi, Ricasoli, Ruffino, Serristori, Spalletti, and the Centrale Cantine Cooperative. Smaller-scale producers of Orvieto Classico with good reputations are Barberani, Cellini, Achille Lemmi, Papini, Petrurbani, Conte Vaselli, Vincenzo Cotti, and Tenuta Le Velette.

Interestingly, after the historic change of course of recent years, the *abboccato* is showing signs of a revival. Some producers are speculating that its semi-sweet flavor will appeal to the emerging youth market in Italy and abroad. So, ironic as it may seem, the proportion of *abboccato* is now expected to increase. But it will probably never again be quite like those wines that appealed to Etruscans, Renaissance painters, popes, or even Michael Broadbent, because Orvieto's producers, with all that money tied up in new equipment and renewed hope, are not inclined to look backward.

Orvieto Rosso, Nonexistent but Good

I remember those days, more than a decade ago now, when I lived in Rome and escaped frequently to Umbria, where the wine and food were always appetizing, even in the simplest country places. Each *trattoria* and *osteria* around Orvieto then, and there were many, boasted that its wine was either its own production or made expressly for it by a *contadino* whose name and address would be given out only if the proprietor were sure he had enough wine available so his own supply would not be interrupted. The open white wines of Orvieto were still often *abboccato* then, though only lightly so and always with a pleasantly bitter tang, never so sweet that they were not refreshing. Frequently, though, the white wines lost their liveliness and started to darken through the summer, so that by autumn you were better off drinking red wine.

Come to think of it, the red wines of the Orvieto area (which were customarily referred to as *nero* — black — rather than *rosso*) often were more impressive than the whites. They were sturdier, naturally enough, with full body and deep color. Though they were not always perfectly balanced, by the fall after the harvest and on into the next year, some took on tones of elegance that made them a robust match for a meal built around roast meat and game. These *vini neri* were usually placed down on the table, which was as likely to be covered with paper as cloth, with no pretention whatever, in a worn flask or a painted pitcher. The names of their producers, which I often jotted down, have faded from memory now.

Orvieto Rosso, like Chianti Bianco, does not exist on paper, so you will not find it on a label, though you might still come across it in a country inn. Good red wines made in the area and sold in labeled bottles include Rosso di Spicca from Tenuta Le Velette of Orvieto, Montegiove from Achille Lemmi of Monteggabione, and Santa Giulia del Poderaccio from Conte Vaselli at Castiglione in Teverina. That last wine, whose vineyards are actually in Latium, is renowned for its longevity.

Umbria has only two provinces, Perugia and Terni. The second, whose seat is a steelmaking center on the Nera River, comprises an underprivileged share of the territory, but it does include Orvieto. The remainder of Terni's province, in the southern part of the region, has no wines of more than local repute. Good country wines, red and white, can be found through the hills east of the Tiber from Lake Corbara to Baschi, Guardea, Lugnano in Teverina, Amelia, Giove, and Penna in Teverina. Castello di Montoro, made by the Marchesi Patrizi Montoro near Narni, is a robust red wine.

Perugia, the regional capital, counts most of Umbria within its province, most of the monuments, most of the scenery, most of the wines. A thriving city of 150,000, it was founded by the Etruscans on a lofty hill. In recent times it has expanded downward and outward, scattering apartment blocks and factories through the surrounding valleys. Its center has a splendid collection of galleries, museums, and historic sites, well worth visiting, though Perugia's pace sometimes seems almost too rapid for Umbria. The cadence is more leisurely in outlying places — Assisi, Spoleto, Gubbio, Norcia, Spello, Trevi, Todi, Montefalco, Città di Castello, Città della Pieve — where history does not always appear to be a thing of the past.

The province of Perugia, with four DOC zones and promise of another — has the makings of real oenological significance, though much of the potential has yet to be developed. Torgiano has wines of international stature, and Colli del Trasimeno is beginning to attract attention beyond the region. But Colli Altotiberini and Montefalco with its Sagrantino are scarcely recognizable beyond Perugia. Alongside the DOC wines, which will soon include Colli Perugini, the province of Perugia possesses an extraordinary wealth of wines to discover.

Torgiano: One-Man Show

In theory the name may apply to qualified red and white wines made by any producer in the zone just south of Perugia, but in practice Torgiano is a one-man show. Giorgio Lungarotti, at an age when most men of his means would be comfortably retired, commands his benevolent monopoly with the inspired dynamism of a newcomer, expanding, revising, perfecting a winemaking operation that has been considered a model of its genre for years.

A trim, towering figure, Lungarotti strides through his recently en-

Giorgio Lungarotti

larged and renovated cellars with the air of a fleet admiral inspecting his flagship, scanning the works with an eye attuned to catching any detail that might be out of place. From the edge of Torgiano, with the tower of the Roman god Janus (Giano) which gave it its name, Lungarotti can point to the village of Brufa across 7 kilometers of sunwashed low hills over a landscape of vineyards that, if not all his own, nonetheless contribute to his enterprise.

Torgiano is not a Lungarotti trademark, though it might as well be because he is the only commercial winemaker in a DOC zone whose name has come to be synonymous with his own. Other growers have every right to make and bottle Torgiano Rosso and Bianco too, but so far none has risen to the challenge, apparently because Lungarotti's system of buying grapes and making wine has worked to their mutual benefit and satisfaction. Anyhow it would be extremely difficult to match Cantine Giorgio Lungarotti for quality, price, or consistency of products. With a long-standing market at home and a growing following of admirers abroad, Lungarotti is Umbria's central figure in the quality field and, indeed, one of the most respected names in Italian wine today.

Lungarotti, who holds a doctorate in oenology, has put his learning to extended good use, building a modest family business into a wine empire in the heart of Umbria that turns out nearly 2.5 million bottles of DOC wine a year. The red Rubesco and white Torre di Giano, both trade names for his DOC Torgiano wines, are the bases of his reputation, though the line also includes a Vin Santo, a rosé called Castel Grifone, a Sherry-style Solleone, and, just recently, Traminer and Cabernet Sauvignon. That range reflects his tireless approach to his calling. His skills have been supplemented recently by the counsel of Corrado Cantarelli, one of Italy's leading scholars in the field of oenology, and now by his daughter Teresa, a recent graduate who has joined the operation.

Torre di Giano is dry, fresh, lightly perfumed, distinct from both Orvieto or Tuscan whites. One difference might be that the acidic bite of the dominant Trebbiano is softened by the soft fruitiness of Grechetto at 15 to 35 percent. A very limited amount of Torre di Giano is put aside in great vintages as special reserve, though bottles are rarely seen in commerce.

When Rubesco first gained national prominence, which was not so long ago, it was often associated and compared with Chianti because the composition is almost identical: Sangiovese at 50 to 70 percent, Canaiolo at 15 to 30 percent, Trebbiano at 10 percent maximum and other dark varieties at 10 percent maximum. But by now Rubesco is recognized for its unique tone, thanks in part to the inclusion of Ciliegiolo and Montepulciano grapes, but perhaps more essentially to the climate and soil of Torgiano. Although there is no specified aging requirement for Torgiano under DOC, Rubesco is well aged in both large oak casks and bottle before going on sale; the *riserva* may spend as long as four or five years in barrel. The reserve wine from the great years, again produced in small quantities and sold in numbered bottles, is robust, austere, long-lived, convincing evidence that red wine has a prominent place in a region historically dominated by white.

Just in case any doubters remain, Lungarotti recently started making a Cabernet Sauvignon that should apply the coup de grâce. His first Cabernet from the 1974 vintage from vines planted in low-lying fields a few years earlier was powerful, rich, perfumed. It needed age to tone down a certain aggressiveness, but indications were that it will achieve a level of greatness all its own. The outlets for these special Lungarotti wines are so limited that the only sure way to obtain them is to visit Torgiano.

Other places can offer more in the way of culture, drama, and day and night activities, but for a taste of gentle Umbria in all its rural dignity, Torgiano is hard to beat. Equidistant from Rome and Florence and just a few minutes' drive from Perugia and Assisi, it is an ideal spot for the travel-weary wine lover to pull himself together. The recommended resting place is (what would you expect?) Lungarotti's Le Tre Vaselle, a rustically elegant new hotel-restaurant in the center of town. There the food is Umbrian with some deft touches from outside. The wines also include a few selections from elsewhere, notably in the Champagne field, though few guests ever venture beyond Lungarotti's own products.

The *antipasti* include local *prosciutto* and salami and vegetables prepared in various ways, accompanied by *pizzetti*, crisp, thin little pizzas flavored with fresh herbs. *L'imbrecciata* is a hearty peasant soup of chick peas, haricot beans, and lentils. As elsewhere in Umbria, flavorful pork, veal, chicken, and lamb are the bases of main courses, but an irresistible choice when available is *piccione alla spoletina*, pigeon or dove cooked with black olives, a special dish from nearby Spoleto. Umbria is reputed to be the nation's leading source of truffles, both black and white, which during the autumn figure exquisitely in the sauces. The most famous of the region's pastries is *torcolo*, an egg cake to be dipped into sweet (and only sweet) Vin Santo.

Writing about wine, for all its pleasures, like any job has its dull moments. The tour of the new winery is perhaps the dullest, downright excruciating after you have seen your first hundred or so continuous presses, stainless steel vats, automated bottling operations, etcetera. Next in order of boredom is the wine museum, but I can no longer state that once you've seen one you've seen them all.

Credit for that revelation is due largely to Lungarotti's gracious wife, Maria Grazia, whose Museo del Vino around the corner from Le Tre Vaselle is the most stimulating display of the glories of wine's past that I have witnessed. Though not large, it is packed with relics, both humble and grand, all so tastefully selected and cleverly arranged that no matter how many collections of wooden presses, hand-blown bottles, chipped and dented drinking vessels, and other clichés I had seen in the past, I came away feeling enlightened. Signora Lungarotti has illustrated the displays with her own brilliant photographs. The collection of pottery and ceramics, mostly from Umbria, is the highlight of this most attractive museum.

Perugia's Hills: Naturally Endowed

The central Umbrian hill country fanning out south of Perugia toward Spoleto, Todi, and Città della Pieve includes some of central Italy's most naturally endowed territory for quality wine, though only in

Torgiano has that potential been realized in recent times. Moves are afoot to upgrade the consistency and prestige of wines from other zones. For example, at Montefalco an historically significant wine known as Sagrantino has been resuscitated by DOC, which has also modernized its character. In the old days, Sagrantino, also known as Sacrantino or Sacramentino, apparently in reference to the Sacrament or the Sacramentine religious order, was a smooth, sweet red wine made from semi-dried *passito* grapes. Although a few producers still make it that way, often a touch *frizzante,* the current practice is to carry out a complete alcoholic fermentation that results in a strong, dry, rich, deep purple wine with an attractively bitter finish, somewhat reminiscent of Recioto Amarone. Sagrantino vines, indigenous to the area, can be grown in the community of Montefalco and parts of Giano and Bevagna for the DOC wine. Though hard to find, Sagrantino is available with appropriate roast meats and other generous Umbrian dishes at the restaurant Il Molino in Spello, the ancient town propped so strikingly on its steep hillside. Domenico Benincasa and Adelio Tardioli make good Sagrantino. There is also a Montefalco Rosso DOC, invariably dry and lighter than the Sagrantino. It is made primarily from Sangiovese with Trebbiano and Sagrantino.

A large zone known as Colli Perugini has been nominated for DOC with a Rosso from Sangiovese with a bit of Merlot and Barbera and a Bianco from Grechetto, Malvasia, and Trebbiano. Colli Perugini will take in the hilly area south of Perugia along the valleys of the Topino as far as Foligno and the Tiber as far as Todi. Already a number of good wines are being made in the zone, some along the lines proposed for DOC and some along purely individual lines.

One that falls into the individualistic category is Scacciadiavoli, or "chase away devils." Made from Barbera and Sangiovese grapes, it is a rustic, dense, tasty country wine from an area between Todi and Foligno. Another is the Vernaccia of Cannara and Bevagna, but here Vernaccia is a sweet red wine made from Cometta and Corvetta grapes. (It has nothing to do with the various vines known as Vernaccia used for the wines in San Gimignano, Sardinia, and the Marches, which are each distinct varieties unrelated to the others.) The red Vernaccia of Cannara and Bevagna is produced from semi-dried grapes into a thick, fragrant wine that is drunk up in the late winter and early spring after the harvest. Occasionally *frizzante,* it is used in a local religious ceremony at Easter and served generously during and after the holiday feast.

Many more unusual and good wines are made in the hills of Umbria, some from uncommon grape varieties. The white wine of Marsciano is based on Garganega, the chief grape of Soave, which is rarely found outside the Veneto. (Marsciano's red wine is made from conventional varieties, including Sangiovese, and can be excellent.) The Nebbiolo grape of Piedmontese origin is found in some red wines around Spoleto, though oddly enough a wine called Nebbiolo di Gubbio, from the environs of that well-preserved medieval town, is actually made from Dolcetto, another Piedmontese variety. White wines at Collepepe and Collazzone often contain Sauvignon. Other varieties used in Umbrian wines include Tocai Friulano, Riesling, and Traminer. Merlot has been cultivated here for more than a century. Though usually mixed with Sangiovese, Merlot can make a splendid wine on its own, as Ruggero Veneri at Spello has proved.

The wines of Todi, the Roman Tudernum, which guards the Tiber from a lofty position, has very good red and white wines, some marketed under the name Tudernum. They can be enjoyed at the Ristorante Umbria just off the town's central piazza, where the setting, the view, and the food are Umbrian classics. Almonte, made by Ugo Vagniluca at Frontignano di Todi, may be the best red wine of the area. Among other quality wines of Umbria that are not DOC, the red and white Musignano of G. Andreoli at Città della Pieve and the red and white Monteforcone from the village of that name northwest of Perugia stand out.

Vin Santo is made everywhere in Umbria, too often industrially, but still lovingly by some. The process is more or less equivalent to the Tuscan; the chief differences are over which region originated it and how it should taste. Umbrians, who can rattle off historical references as nimbly as can Tuscans, claim it as their own and pooh-pooh the notion that dry Vin Santo has any validity in tradition. No, they insist, Vin Santo should be rather sweet, warmly alcoholic, soft, smooth, and smoky in flavor from hanging the grapes near the hearth to wither. In Umbria Vin Santo is often made from Grechetto grapes; in Tuscany Malvasia dominates. Vin Santo is not DOC in any part of Umbria, though if the Tuscans achieve a regionwide classification as expected, the Umbrians can hardly be denied the same.

Colli del Trasimeno: A Fait Accompli

Due west of Perugia lies Lake Trasimeno, Italy's next largest body of inland water after the Alpine lakes. Nearly round, with three islands protruding from its shallow waters, it has a vast basin ringed by hills and mountains so distant that even on clear days their vegetation appears as a uniform smoky green. Despite its placid beauty, Trasimeno has a melancholy nature, noted since the days when Hannibal routed the Romans near its shores. Malaria kept people away until recent eras, which explains why there are only a handful of small towns around it and precious few remnants of history.

The gradually sloped, well-exposed land in the vicinity basks in sunlight reflecting off the lake, providing a luminous environment for vines. Although Colli del Trasimeno covers a large area with significant production of DOC red and white wine, so far the name is not as widely known or appreciated as it might be. Forces are at work to change all that.

The most irresistible force is being provided by Ferruccio Lamborghini, whose famous name has been linked to, among other products, tractors, furnaces, and a sleek sports car called the Miura. After pedaling away from his family's Po Valley farm on a bicycle when he was sixteen, Lamborghini combined his mechanical genius with charismatic energy to propel himself to the top of Italy's industrial heap. But by 1969 he decided that what he needed most was some fresh air, so he sold his various manufacturing enterprises and bought a large tract of woodland near Lake Trasimeno for a totally new venture. Naturally, Lamborghini did not tread lightly in entering his new career. Before anyone had a chance to check on what he planned to do with the land, he took some American-built Caterpillars and leveled more than three-quarters of the property's nearly 450 acres of trees.

"I presented them with what you might call a *fait accompli,*" he recalled, grinning at the memory of his own incredible brashness. "When the authorities did show up, I told them: 'You've got two choices, put the handcuffs on me or let me go ahead and make wine.' They weren't too happy about that but I went ahead and made wine."

He planted 160 acres of vines on the estate named La Fiorita and installed an up-to-the-minute winery under the supervision of his eminent oenologist friend Giorgio Gray. The first crop of suitable grapes came in in 1972 and before long the wine was bottled with the fighting bull that

Ferruccio Lamborghini

had emblemized his cars and tractors emblazoned in black on the label. At that point the only challenge left was to sell it, something at which neighboring winemakers had not shown much success. But Lamborghini charged ahead with advertising, including billboards through the Umbrian countryside, a vigorous campaign capitalizing on his name. By the late 1970s he had almost singlehandedly put Colli del Trasimeno on the wine map and was shipping cases to at least half a dozen foreign nations, including the United States.

"I get to all the wine fairs," he said at a recent Vinitaly in Verona, "and I get a real kick out of them. I like being with all those people. You realize, of course, that I'm not in this for the money. I'll never make back my investment, but I don't care. I made all I need out of this." He patted the hood of a red Miura that was part of his display. "No, mostly I'm just looking after my health."

Lamborghini expects production to reach 800,000 bottles a year eventually, split between white — from Malvasia, Trebbiano Toscano, Verdello, and Grechetto grapes — and red — from Sangiovese, Ciliegiolo, Montepulciano, and Gamay. He also plans to introduce a rosé. Although other winemakers in the Colli del Trasimeno zone still seem a bit awed by his dynamic personality, there is no question that Lamborghini has helped them all by promoting the Trasimeno name nationally and internationally and backing it with wines of sound quality.

"I think some local people are even learning a few things about winemaking from us," said Lamborghini with mock secretiveness, "but don't tell them I told you so."

Lamborghini is more administrator and strategist than winemaker, though he has been learning the secrets of the trade while keeping a scrupulous watch on the operation. An innovator, he was preparing a second 160-acre segment of vines under a system of such expensive and unprecedented scope that to hear other cultivators in tradition-minded Umbria talk, it could not have aroused greater curiosity if a UFO had landed at La Fiorita.

Lamborghini has been treating the excavated land with a natural fertilizer based on hog manure, liquefied and applied through an elaborate complex of dikes, pools, spillways, tubes, and spraying apparatuses. By his estimation, this will leave the land so fertile that the new vines will come into full production a year or possibly two earlier than normal. If so, the early profits might even cover the cost of the fertilization system, which was to be removed when the vines were planted.

"It's a new idea," said Lamborghini, piloting a worn Peugeot diesel car along the tractor tracks of La Fiorita. "And new ideas are what I built my career on in every field. I didn't come here to do things like everybody else."

His only fear, so it seems, is boredom. "If I don't have anything else to do," he said, "I'll get on one of my bulldozers and spend the day digging a hole. Then the next day, if I still don't have anything to do, I'll go fill it in."

The Cantina Sociale del Trasimeno at Castiglione del Lago is the largest producer of Colli del Trasimeno DOC wines; the cooperative also makes a non-DOC rosé called Duca della Corgna which can match the DOC wines for quality. Angelo Illuminati makes an excellent red wine at his Belvedere estate near Villastrada. The Sovrano Militare Or-dine di Malta (Knights of Malta) have an imposing castle at Magione where they make DOC wines. The red is particularly recommended.

Colli Altotiberini: Court Jester to Crown Prince

North from Perugia along the E7 highway lies Umbria's newest DOC zone, the Colli Altotiberini, stretching through the peaceful hills along the Tiber to the border of Tuscany. The aptitude for vines had been known here since Città di Castello was the Roman colony of Tifernum and Pliny the Younger had a villa in a place now known as Colli Plinio and praised the goodness of the wine. But over the centuries poverty, neglect, antiquated techniques, and lack of local demand for serious quality had reduced production to rudimentary levels. With perhaps a dozen exceptions — mainly well-to-do landowners who made a bit more good wine than they consumed and sold the excess in labeled bottles — the wines of the upper Tiber valley were rustic and anonymous and invariably sold in bulk. Tobacco was king and wine was little more than court jester: spontaneous, amusing, sometimes full of charm, but often rather ill-bred and coarse.

Farmers devoted most of their capital and time to more rewarding crops, so the impetus for change had to come from other quarters. It was unexpectedly provided by a group of young businessmen and professionals who formed a society known as the Accademia Enoculturale Altotiberina with the stated purpose of developing, promoting, and defending the quality of local wines. With a boldness that left old-timers shaking their heads in amusement, Gilberto Nardi, insurance salesman and mathematics professor, and Bruno Mangoni, who sells products for infants, launched a campaign for DOC, a long shot that overcame the doubts of nearly everyone, most conspicuously the hard core of local wine producers.

"Ten years ago when you'd mention DOC to some of them, they'd just laugh," Nardi recalled. "To them it was an impossible dream and they weren't so sure they wanted it anyhow." Gradually, though, as the international boom in Italian wine developed and the Common Market clamped down on vine cultivation in all but officially designated areas, winemakers began to see the light. Almost overnight some came up with wines worthy of labeled bottles to be presented at tastings, dinners, fairs, and other promotional events sponsored by the Oenocultural Academy.

"We had to be somewhat selective," said Nardi, "but basically the quality factor had been there right along. We encouraged producers to brush up on techniques, to get serious. They finally responded, and that was the key. This isn't Barolo or Brunello country, but our wines have that authenticity, that intrinsic goodness that is not so easy to find anymore."

The uphill battle culminated in December, 1978, when the national DOC committee cleared Colli Altotiberini for recognition of its Rosso, Bianco, and Rosato. Some eighty producers had joined the new consortium with the Academy's smiling bronze Bacchus as its emblem. As producers prepared for their first vintage of DOC wines, new optimism could be sensed in the upper Tiber valley. If tobacco was still king, wine was by then crown prince. As one producer of both put it: "Land grows tired of tobacco, but not vines. I now see my future in wine."

Colli Altotiberini Rosso and Rosato are made from Sangiovese at 50 to 70 percent, Merlot at 10 to 20 percent, with the possible use of other dark and light varieties. The Merlot, planted hereabouts for a century, lends aroma and softness that distinguishes them among Sangiovese wines. The Bianco is made from Trebbiano Toscano at 70 to 90 percent, Malvasia Bianca, and other light varieties, which here often include Tocai, Riesling, and Pinot for a different touch.

Some producers in the Colli Altotiberini have been making a name for themselves beyond the region. Castello di Ascagnano, guided by Angelo Valentini, who also manages the Fattoria di Artimino in Tuscany's Carmignano zone, has two wines of unusual interest. Fior di Mosto is a first-rate rosé designed to drink young, though its naïve labels, each an original artistic work, have made the wine a collector's item that sells for an unusually high price and often ends up sitting on shelves as decoration. Riserva del Re is the prestige red, austere and well aged and romanticized by the legend of King Ludwig I of Bavaria, who bought the castle for his beloved Marchesa Marianna Florenzi in 1832 and spent summers there with her. The growing reputations of these wines are a credit to Valentini, who combines his love of the arts, fine wine, and fine (organically raised) food in his management philosophy, which is reflected in the quality of Castello di Ascagnano's products.

Castello di Ascagnano, south of Umbertide, is the most grandiose estate in these hills, a fortress overlooking the Tiber surrounded by an immense tract of land used for raising thoroughbred racehorses, dairy cows, honey bees, and fruit and vegetables.

Across the river lies the Colle del Sole, 100 acres of model vineyards created by Carlo Polidori, a builder who turned to winemaking in the late 1960s. His Rubino, considered the zone's "classic" red, and white Verdello have won national awards for excellence. And yet Polidori has had trouble selling the approximately 300,000 liters of wine he produces annually.

"I sell 90 percent of my wine in bulk and 10 percent in bottles," said Polidori. "Unless I can reverse that situation I might not be able to afford to stay in this business. I'm hoping DOC will make the difference by opening up new markets."

Polidori, plump and bespectacled, might look more like a banker than an agriculturist were it not for the floppy beret he often sports. He is modest about his winemaking skills, giving much credit for quality to the "ideal environment" of Colle del Sole. "This is one of those privileged places that produce perfect grapes for wine, thanks to the climate, soil,

Carlo Polidori

and altitude. Our wines arrive naturally at 11.5 to 13 degrees alcohol and balance out in terms of acids and other components. We don't need sugar, concentrates, unhealthful additives that wines from cooler climates often do, and we don't need to worry about the excessive strength of hotter climates. So winemaking here is easy, but wine doesn't just make itself. Let's be frank. My wines are very good and honest and so are some others in the zone. But we could all use some expert help in making them even better."

Polidori's point is well taken. Nobody in the Colli Altotiberini should yet feel that his wine is at the ultimate level, though Polidori perhaps comes closer than any. Neighboring producers Tenuta di Montecorona Antognolla, which is owned by an insurance company and works on a relatively large scale, and Pie' di Murlo, run by Alfio Tondini and son Claudio on a minuscule scale, have also produced admirable wines. The Tondinis' red Brunesco and white Chiaro di Bruna are tributes to studied techniques applied at the artisanal level.

North of Umbertide at Montone, Giuseppe Rossi has renovated his small winery with the financial backing of some Milanese friends, and is making a superb Tocai as well as the Colli Altotiberini DOC wines. Giulio Foggi, a Tuscan brought in by Enrico Vivarelli Colonna to make mostly red wine at Roscetti, also produces a fine, lightly *abboccato* Tocai that holds up for years as an *aperitivo*.

Other producers of note in the Colli Altotiberini are Antonio Gasperini with San Rocco, Dante Brighigna, Carlo Ferri, and Fratelli Renzacci with Citernino, Principe Baldassarre Boncompagni Ludovisi Rondinelli Vitelli with Panicale, Azienda Agraria Bizzi with Rosso and Bianco dei Bizzi, Silvio Nardi (who also produces a Brunello di Montalcino) with Montione, and Dr. A. Cristini with Collecchio.

The Vintages

	Orvieto	Perugia Area Rosso, Bianco
1979	Excellent	Excellent
1978	Excellent	Excellent
1977	Excellent	Excellent
1976	Excellent	Fair to good
1975	Good	Exceptional
1974	Excellent	Very good
1973	Excellent	Good
1972	Fair	Fair
1971	Excellent	Excellent
1970	Good	Great

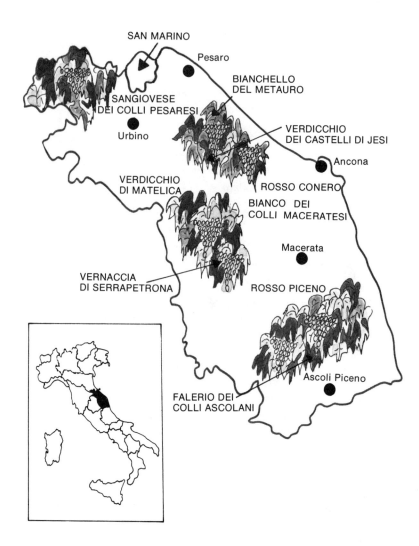

SAN MARINO

Pesaro

BIANCHELLO
DEL METAURO

SANGIOVESE
DEI COLLI PESARESI

Urbino

VERDICCHIO
DEI CASTELLI DI JESI

Ancona

VERDICCHIO
DI MATELICA

ROSSO CONERO

BIANCO DEI
COLLI MACERATESI

Macerata

VERNACCIA
DI SERRAPETRONA

ROSSO PICENO

Ascoli Piceno

FALERIO DEI
COLLI ASCOLANI

THE MARCHES

PROVINCES

ANCONA, Ascoli Piceno, Macerata, Pesaro-Urbino

POPULATION

1,370,000

AREA

3,744 square miles

AVERAGE WINE PRODUCTION

220 million liters

DOC WINES

Bianchello del Metauro · Bianco dei Colli Maceratesi · Rosso Cònero · Rosso Piceno · Sangiovese dei Colli Pesaresi · Verdicchio dei Castelli di Jesi · Verdicchio di Matelica · Vernaccia di Serrapetrona

OTHER WINES

Bianco Piceno · Montepulciano · Moscato del Cònero · Rosato di Collameno · Rosato di Montanello · Rosso Rubino di Matelica · Rutilus · Sangiovese · Trebbiano · Tristo di Montesecco · Verdicchio di Montanello · Verdicchio di Serrapetrona (Spumante) · Vin Santo Marchigiano

The Land of Verdicchio

THE Marches in its unassuming way is one of the most agreeable Italian regions to be in. Maybe that is why they say that those natives who leave never stay away long. Though the region has the elements that appeal to tourists — natural beauty, art, historical monuments, sea and sun, mountains, religious shrines, picturesque towns, fine food and wine — perhaps a lack of the spectacular has kept the Marches off the beaten paths of international travel. An annual exception must be made for July and August, when outsiders, mostly from northern cities and German-speaking countries, swarm the Adriatic beaches in pursuit of their annual suntans. Otherwise, for ten months a year, the Marches is there to be quietly enjoyed by visitors who will soon realize why its people always come home again.

Rippled by hills that taper toward the east along rivers flowing from the Apennines to the Adriatic, the Marches region has well-exposed contours and a gentle climate to support its age-old cultivation of vines and olives in land that is only moderately fertile. Vineyards and olive groves are interspersed with field crops around the hill towns, whose earthen pastels become confused with the colors of the surrounding parched clay fields in late summer, so that sometimes all that is discernible about them from a distance is a silhouette of steeples, domes, and rooftops against a hazy sky.

This is the land of Verdicchio, an indigenous vine that, according to legend, was producing wine when Alaric, king of the Visigoths, passed through in A.D. 410 and took along some barrels to encourage his troops as they sacked Rome. But only in recent times has Verdicchio gained an international reputation linked to the worldwide thirst for dry white wine, a peculiar amphora-shaped bottle, and a nice-sounding name that alludes to the pale green of the grapes and the wine. The heartland of Verdicchio is the hills along the Esino River in the center of the region between the port of Ancona and the paper manufacturing center of Fabriano just across the border from Umbria.

Though planted rather widely in the Marches, even beyond the two DOC zones of Castelli di Jesi and Matelica, Verdicchio vines are rarely seen in heavy concentration. One reason is that the vine is somewhat delicate and difficult to work with, another that the land here is rather steep and has long been fragmented into small plots with different owners. Also, the boom in Verdicchio is a relatively recent phenomenon and cultivators have not yet been able to prepare vineyards to meet growing demand for the wine at home and abroad. By the late 1970s, production of DOC Verdicchio dei Castelli di Jesi had surpassed 11 million liters a year; in the smaller zone of Matelica only about 600,000 liters were produced. Still, that was enough to maintain Verdicchio's standing internationally as second in popularity to Soave among Italy's DOC white wines.

The harbinger of this fame has been the amphora bottle that came to represent Verdicchio much as the flask came to symbolize Chianti. But while the flask has been disappearing, the amphora seems to be here to stay. Though expensive to manufacture, fill, and transport, the amphora, in forms that vary somewhat from producer to producer, seems too valuable a symbol to discard. Some serious wine drinkers object to this odd container as a gimmick, but others have obviously taken to it as an amusing bottle that is instantly recognizable and contains a sound and unimposing wine that goes very well indeed with fish, as well as chicken and other light meats.

Verdicchio dei Castelli di Jesi is named for the fortress towns that top the hills around Jesi, an ancient city noted historically as the birthplace of Friedrich II of Hohenstaufen, the brilliant Holy Roman emperor. The zone covers a large territory in the provinces of Ancona and Macerata but curiously enough Jesi itself is just outside the DOC zone. The wine is made from Verdicchio grapes with Trebbiano Toscano and Malvasia Toscana permitted at up to 20 percent. Wines from most of the zone, excluding only a small section of recent exploitation, may be called Classico. Light and delicate but distinctive in aroma and flavor with a slightly bitter aftertaste, Verdicchio is generally a still wine of about 12° alcohol. It is best to drink within a year or two, the reason why few producers state the vintage on the label. The wine may also be made into a *spumante,* its traditional form, one that it adapts to extremely well.

Fazi-Battaglia was the promoter of both the amphora and the widespread commercialization of Verdicchio. The firm, owned by the Angelini family of Ancona, was originally established in the hills at Cupra-montana where it made the sparkling and *frizzante* Verdicchio popular locally. In 1952, the owners decided to build a new Fazi-Battaglia winery next to the railway station at Castelplanio in the valley and to make a still Verdicchio to be promoted nationally. To emphasize the association of Verdicchio and fish, they devised the amphora, reasoning that Ancona was founded by the Greeks, who used earthenware amphorae for ship-ping wine. To relate its story, Fazi-Battaglia added the *cartoglio,* the little scroll tied with straw to the neck of the bottle, another trademark the firm maintains despite the extra expense.

The amphora and the wine were such a success in Italy that they were soon sent abroad. In recent years more than half of Fazi-Battaglia's sales have been in foreign lands, most notably the United States. The firm has been incorporated as Titulus S.p.A. and has expanded production to some 4 million to 5 million bottles a year. Most of this is Verdicchio, but the line also includes Rosso Piceno and Rosso Cònero, both DOC, as well as some red Rutilus and Rosato di Collameno table wines.

By local standards, Fazi-Battaglia, the region's largest winery, seems gigantic, but on an international scale it is only of medium-large di-mensions. Fazi-Battaglia has held the line on expansion while buying and developing vineyards to bring its total holdings to some 500 acres, enough to produce about 80 percent of the grapes it converts into wine. This more costly practice is designed to gain greater control over quality in a zone where small-scale cultivation is becoming increasingly impractical and unprofitable. Verdicchio vines require ample space because they form clusters only at their growing points, which necessitates pruning for long shoots. Though vigorous when conditions are right, the vine is susceptible to peronospora and oïdium, requiring frequent treatments in damp seasons.

The trend in the Castelli di Jesi is away from the family farm and toward a concentration of production in larger wineries. Other firms have been following Fazi-Battaglia's lead in installing the modern range of equipment needed for white wine, an expense not fully evident at the retail level because producers have chosen to spread the investment over a long term and keep their prices competitive.

Everyone for Himself

Even if Verdicchio is not often eulogized by experts, the standard here may be as high as for any popular white wine of Italy at the moment. It seems to me that variation in quality from the best to the worst in Verdicchio is less dramatic than in other well-publicized DOC wines such as Soave, Orvieto, and the whites of the Castelli Romani. If so, credit may be due to the intrinsic virtuosity of the grape and, just possibly, to the competitive spirit shown by the major wineries. The Classico consortium is weakened by the absence of Fazi-Battaglia in a zone where the motto seems to be everyone for himself, but always with an eye on Fazi-Battaglia, which remains the pacesetter and, naturally enough, the target of a disproportionate share of intramural sniping.

Michele Miglietta, lawyer and able front man for Fazi-Battaglia director Bruno Petracci, is not worried about the competition. He points out that the firm cannot meet all orders either in Italy or abroad and that all signs point to Verdicchio's increasing popularity. The firm's success on foreign markets has enhanced its standing nationally. "It makes an impression on Italians when they go to New York or London and see how prominent our wines are there," said Miglietta. "When they come home, they look for Fazi-Battaglia. We actually make slightly less profit on the wine we send overseas, but we wouldn't sacrifice the prestige involved with foreign sales for anything."

Several other Verdicchio firms have been building international reputations, among them Cantina Sociale di Cupramontana, Cantina Sociale Val di Nevola, Castelfiora, Fratelli Torelli, Garofoli, Tombolini, and Umani Ronchi. Several important shippers also include Verdicchio in their export lines.

Armando and Corrado Castellucci are often singled out among producers in the Castelli di Jesi who work on a rather small scale (300,000 bottles of Verdicchio a year). They, too, have exported some wine from their plots of land at Serra de' Conti and Montecarotto.

Among the producers who work at the industrial level, Gioacchino Garofoli at Loreto makes wines unsurpassed for quality. A family firm, it was founded in 1871, when Loreto (a shrine since the house of the Virgin Mary was transported there by angels) was still an enclave independent from Italy. The firm is now run by two generations of Garofoli: Dante and Franco and Carlo and Gianfranco. Most of their Verdicchio, from vineyards at Serra de' Conti and Montecarotto, is still wine, but the winery has been moving adroitly into the Champagne field at two levels. One *spumante* is made by the charmat method, which develops its distinctive bouquet; the other is a *méthode champenoise* with finesse, proof of Verdicchio's natural aptitude as a sparkling wine. The Champagne type, known as Gran Spumante Nature, is put through the full process that takes two years, much of it upside down in the *pupitres* for which the Garofoli have been clearing space in their cellars beneath the modern plant. Production has grown beyond 50,000 bottles a year.

The Garofoli Gran Spumante demonstrates the expertise of winemaster Gaetano De Fusco, who left his southern home, Taranto in Apulia, to study at Conegliano in the Veneto and then settled in the Marches, halfway between. That sort of mobility has opened up new vistas in Italian winemaking by giving enterprising producers like the Garofoli the chance to select from a nationwide pool of talented oenologists rather than being limited to hiring locally (or doing everything themselves), as was the case less than a generation ago.

Verdicchio di Matelica: Hard to Get

Verdicchio dei Castelli di Jesi dominates the market, but insiders who have made comparisons of the two over time seem to lean to Verdicchio di Matelica. It could just be that the people of the Marches still hold ample reserves of sympathy for country wine, which corresponds to the image cast by Matelica as against the industrialized reputation of Jesi. And it almost certainly has something to do with being hard to get; you can find a bottle from Jesi on almost any supermarket shelf, but you have to search for Verdicchio di Matelica.

Among the few active producers of the Matelica zone, the name Mattei stands out, not only because of its good wines but also because of its connections with a giant figure in recent Italian history. Enrico Mattei, though a public servant as head of ENI, the national fuel concern, was one of the most influential and respected men in Italy and a decisive force in the politics of oil in the Middle East before his death in 1962 in an airplane crash the circumstances of which are still a subject of active controversy. Enrico Mattei and his brother Italo started a winery in Matelica, and Italo stayed home to run it and raise his seven children. Italo Mattei established a reputation for his Verdicchio that led to numerous citations before his death in 1974. His widow, Leonella, and those of their seven children not engaged in other pursuits (such as oil) have kept the winery going in the cellars of their old-fashioned home with an interior courtyard just off the Piazza Enrico Mattei.

"We've maintained the standards," said Leonella Mattei, "which means we produce Verdicchio of only a certain quality. My husband wanted it to remain a family operation and that's what it is." Nearly every other winery made Verdicchio in 1978, but not the Mattei family, who chose to sell their wine in bulk instead. "It didn't have the thirteen degrees of alcohol we require," explained Alessandro Curzi, a son-in-law, who, like other members of the close-knit family, seemed to contribute on a sort of share-the-work basis that left unclear just who was in charge. Curzi, a surgeon at the local hospital, likes to work in the vineyards. His wife, Rosangela, is also active, not only with the vines but the books. Curzi, who came to Matelica from Jesi, is convinced that his adopted home produces superior wine. "I might sound like a traitor, but there's no question about it," said the young physician; "when the Verdicchio of Matelica is made in an artisanal way, it's the best."

The Azienda Agricola Italo Mattei uses Verdicchio grapes exclusively, even though the Matelica DOC allows for 20 percent Trebbiano Toscano and Malvasia Toscana. In good years Mattei produces about 40,000 liters of wine — Verdicchio and a Rosso Rubino di Matelica that is of similar class, though it is not DOC. Very dry and strong with a nice bitter finish, the Mattei Verdicchio may be even more of a fish wine than the somewhat fruitier Verdicchio of Jesi. Despite its strength, it slips down with the greatest of ease.

Another good Verdicchio di Matelica, whose production zone includes several neighboring communities in the provinces of Macerata and Ancona southeast of Fabriano, is La Monacesca, made by Casimiro Cifola, whose wine seems to be more widely available than Mattei's. The only other producer of notable size is the cooperative Enopolio di Matelica, though some independent producers have bottles for sale if you happen to reach them at the right moments.

Good Verdicchio is made outside the DOC zones in several places in the Marches, and its grapes are included to some degree in many of the region's white wines. The vine has been planted elsewhere, mostly in Umbria, but it rarely results in wines to compare with the home versions.

From the Scattered to the Specific

In the Marches, as in other rural environments of central Italy that until almost yesterday were considered remote, the pattern of viniculture has quickly shifted from the scattered to the specific. Those unpredictable country wines with special names and personalities can still be found in the hamlets that dot these green hills, but everywhere the emphasis is being placed on vines and wines whose promise is strictly modern. Verdicchio is the prime example, though two DOC red wines, Rosso Piceno and Rosso Cònero, are gaining prominence nationally and just lately internationally for their sound qualities. The climate is conducive to wines with the strength and body to make them ideal blenders, but the days of anonymous bulk wine production here are rapidly drawing to a close.

Bianchello del Metauro, from the hills around the Metauro River in the northernmost province of Pesaro-Urbino, has established a clique of admirers of what is sometimes called *vinello*, the light, fresh sort of wine you can drink with abandon. Bianchello, literally "little white," is made from the Bianchello or Biancame grape, with Malvasia Toscana permitted at a maximum of 5 percent (for fragrance). Pale straw in color, flinty dry and delicate with the subtlest of fruity bouquets and a palate-cleansing acidity, Bianchello is best to drink in its infancy. Much of the less than a million liters produced annually is drunk up by the end of the summer vacation period in the seafood restaurants from Rimini to Senigallia. Anzilotti Solazzi of Fano is the only producer of this pleasant wine with a nationwide reputation, though other good Bianchello is available on the spot.

An interesting white wine from the hills just south of the Bianchello del Metauro zone is Tristo di Montesecco, whose producer is Massimo Schiavi, the oenologist behind the red Testucchio discussed in Tuscany. Made from Trebbiano Toscano with some Riesling Italico, Pinot Grigio, and Malvasia di Candia included, Tristo di Montesecco is very dry with exceptional aroma, a wine to drink fairly young with fish or poultry. Why it is called Tristo, whose meanings range from *gloomy* to *wretched*, is not clear: possibly somebody's idea of a joke.

The province of Macerata has a wine, recently DOC, known as Bianco dei Colli Maceratesi, which when well made can rival the finest white wines of the region. From Trebbiano Toscano at 50 percent with Maceratino at 30 to 50 percent and Malvasia Toscana and/or

Verdicchio at 15 percent maximum, it is a versatile white that goes as well with antipasto, soups, or light meat as with fish. Pale straw yellow, it has a distinctive aroma and fresh, dry flavor. Recommended producers are Villamagna at Macerata and Attilio Fabrini at Serrapetrona.

Falerio dei Colli Ascolani, whose DOC zone is in the hills around Ascoli Piceno, is made from Trebbiano Toscano at 80 percent with some Passerina, Verdicchio, Malvasia Toscana, and Pecorino grapes. Its light perfume and acidic freshness go best with fish. Most Falerio, like the non-DOC white wine known generically as Bianco Piceno, is drunk up locally. Neither is often seen outside the southern part of the Marches.

Rosso Cònero: After the Beach Crowd Goes Home

That the Marches produces more red wine than white, at least in the quality field, is a secret its people have kept to themselves. They bring the *rosso* out of their cellars after the beach crowd goes home and they drink it with the grilled meat and game they seem to savor as much as seafood.

Lamberto Fiorini, burly host at the Emilia restaurant on the cliffs of the Monte Cònero promontory above Portonovo, was noncommittal when I asked which Verdicchio he favored. "They're all good," he said diplomatically but without much enthusiasm. "I serve three brands at the restaurant, but I'd have more, certainly some from Matelica, if they weren't so difficult to acquire. The tourists demand Verdicchio with seafood, naturally, so that's what we serve most of."

Emilia is one of the finest seafood restaurants of Italy's Adriatic coast, famous for its *brodetto*, a soup that may contain a dozen types of fish (and of which every chef and housewife in the Ancona area has a personal version), as well as its mollusks, crustaceans, and deep-sea fish, all fresh and all imaginatively prepared. But Lamberto Fiorini and his wife, Elia, whose mother, Emilia, founded the place, are equally proud of their meat, poultry, and game specialties.

"You know what I drink with my meals?" said Fiorini, beaming like a schoolboy about to reveal a secret. "A Rosso Cònero made by a farmer near here. I bottle it myself and serve it when people ask for something besides fish. You stay and have lunch tomorrow and I'll have Elia cook some *faraona* [guinea hen] to go with it."

I stayed for lunch and had Elia Fiorini's *faraona in potacchio* (with a sauce of olive oil, wine, garlic, rosemary, and tomato) with the Rosso

Cònero, a well-rounded country wine of deep ruby color, loaded with the rich flavor of the Montepulciano grape. Lamberto Fiorini's point was well taken; in the Marches, where fish is as fresh as you will find anywhere, the diet is not confined to seafood and the wines are not confined to white.

The everyday fare of the Marches is based on pasta followed by either fish or meat, often simply grilled. Some regional dishes are worthy of special note. The most famous pasta is *vincisgrassi*, which originated in Macerata, reportedly as a chef's attempt to honor an Austrian prince by the name of Windischgrätz, a general in the forces occupying the Marches in the early nineteenth century. A type of *lasagne*, its ingredients include butter, cream, *prosciutto*, and black truffles. *Porchetta* can be outstanding here, distinguished by the special herbs the roasting pig is stuffed with. Other meats, such as duck and rabbit, are often prepared *alla porchetta*, which means they have the same basic flavorings, dominated by wild fennel and garlic. Ascoli, founded by the Picenians, is a handsome inland city linked to Rome and the Roman way of life by the Via Salaria. Among its other specialties are *olive all'ascolana*, plump olives stuffed and deep-fried, which are renowned and often imitated in other parts of Italy.

Rosso Cònero is the most robust of the Marches' red wines, its depth and sturdiness attributable to Montepulciano, which may be mixed with up to 15 percent of Sangiovese, though some producers prefer to keep it a thoroughbred. Rosso Cònero is not noted for longevity, but from superior vintages it can round into a wine of real grace after four years or so. The slopes of Monte Cònero, though noted for their wines since the Greeks settled there, have only recently been planted heavily in specialized vineyards that have put a modern face on the ancient landscape. The DOC zone ranges beyond the massif to Castelfidardo near Loreto and inland as far as Osimo and Offana. Production has been increasing; in good years more than 2.5 million liters have been recorded.

Garofoli produces an outstanding Rosso Cònero of 100 percent Montepulciano grapes grown in vineyards at Massignana and Paterno. Well aged in oak casks and bottles, it is a red of firm body and smooth texture. The 1974, drunk in 1979, was in prime form, austerely dry and harmonious with a pleasant bitter undertone and a hint of tannin that indicated it had plenty of life remaining. Castelfiora is another good producer working on a moderately large scale. Fazi-Battaglia, Umani Ronchi,

Fratelli Torelli, Fattoria Le Terrazze, and Cesare Serenelli are other producers of note.

An excellent but scarce Rosso Cònero is made by Don Antonio Marinoni at his minuscule Vigna del Curato in Sappanico, a village on the edge of Ancona. Don Antonio, a native of Lombardy, spent many years as priest at Ancona's Chiesa delle Grazie before requesting a transfer to the small parish at Sappanico to be nearer his vines. He has since become a local personage, a devoted cultivator and winemaker whose Verdicchio dei Castelli di Jesi and sweet Moscato Nobile del Cònero are also wines of distinction. His sales are mainly to visitors, who come from near and far to taste his wines.

Rosso Piceno: A Propitious Combination

Rosso Piceno surpasses even Verdicchio as the Marches' leading DOC wine in terms of quantity, though it has a long way to go to make its name as well known. But Rosso Piceno does seem to have some factors working in favor of future prominence: a large DOC zone with room for development, fine climate with some points of extremely favorable terrain, and, perhaps best of all, a propitious combination of grape varieties. Sangiovese on its own is not always adequate in terms of body, color, and strength, but its more robust cousin, Montepulciano, can give it some of what it lacks without changing its character significantly. Some winemakers submit that Montepulciano, which prevails in the Abruzzi, is nobler than Sangiovese even if its wines are not quite as long-lived in general. Montepulciano closely resembles Sangiovese Grosso in character and the success of both varieties seems to depend heavily on their adjustment to habitat.

The DOC formula for Rosso Piceno is Sangiovese at 60 percent or more and Montepulciano at 40 percent maximum. Trebbiano and/or Passerina may be included at 15 percent, but the tendency here is to minimize or exclude the light grapes, especially in wine for aging. Minimum alcohol is 11.5°. A *superiore* version can be made in a restricted zone in the province of Ascoli Piceno, between the city and the coast in the southernmost hills of the region above the Tronto River. The *superiore* must have 12° and be aged a year.

In the vast territory of Rosso Piceno, which spans much of the hilly eastern portions of the provinces of Ascoli Piceno, Macerata, and Ancona, vine cultivation is intense in places, lackadaisical in others. Some 12 million liters of Rosso Piceno are made in good years though the quality varies markedly from one producer to another. Only recently have wine-makers begun to concentrate on high-quality bottled wine from a zone that previously sold much of its production anonymously to outsiders. Large producers — Fazi-Battaglia, Umani Ronchi, and the cooperatives of Cupramontana and Val di Nevola — have been distributing their Rosso Piceno throughout Italy. Some shippers of Verdicchio now in-clude Rosso Piceno in their export lines.

Some of the best Rosso Piceno is made on a relatively small scale. Names to note are:

★ Antica Cantina Sant'Amico at Lido Saltamartini
★ Boccabianca of Conte Giovanni Vinci Gigliucci at Cupra Marit-tima
★ Giuseppe Pennesi at Sant'Elpidio a Mare
★ La Torraccia of Piero Costantini at Passo Sant'Angelo
★ Michetti & Erbagi at Faiano di Ascoli
★ Picenum of the Consorzio Agrario Provinciale at Ascoli Piceno
★ Tattà of V. & R. Ciarrocchi at Porto San Giorgio
★ Vallone at Sampolo
★ Vigneti Emidi of Stanislao Emidi at Montalto Marche
★ Villamagna of Conti Compagnucci-Compagnoni at Montanello
★ Villa Pigna at Marina del Tronto

Villamagna is the result of another happy combination, a husband and wife who keep their duties clearly divided. Conte Alberto Compagnucci-Compagnoni, a descendant of the family that possessed the Villamagna estate in 1550, runs the business, and his wife, Valeria, a native of Friuli–Venezia Giulia, is the winemaker. From 37 acres of vines on the edge of Macerata, they produce not only Rosso Piceno but a Rosato di Montanello from Sangiovese grapes, a Bianco dei Colli Maceratesi DOC, and a non-DOC Verdicchio di Montanello. From the 1977 bottling, that Verdicchio might have been the best still wine from that grape I had tasted. It had the perfume, fruit, texture, and lingering flavor of some of the classiest white wines of the north with the unmistakable bite and bitter undertone of Verdicchio.

Valeria Giacomini Compagnucci-Compagnoni developed her passion for winemaking by osmosis, or so it would seem. She grew up in Friuli and Bordeaux, where wine is a subject of special interest, and though she never formally studied the craft, she took to it naturally, developing her skills in Argentina, where she and her husband lived for a time, and in the last fifteen years in the vineyards of Villamagna. Though she holds reserves of respect for the privileged vineland of Friuli and Bordeaux, she does not consider herself deprived working in the Marches, some 20 kilometers from the Adriatic, in the gentle hills of Macerata. At the new winery she makes some 200,000 bottles of wine a year, of which the Rosso Piceno has the most illustrious reputation. With its deep ruby color and soft, rotund qualities, the Villamagna Rosso Piceno is a wine for moderate aging that can be excellent after a couple of years. The balance between Sangiovese and Montepulciano results in a red wine of outstanding smoothness with depth and staying power.

Valeria Compagnucci-Compagnoni, a blonde whose complexion turns rosy in the summer sun, likes to work in the vineyards though she now leaves the heavy labor there to a field crew and follows the advice of a viticultural expert. After a fine year in 1977 and exceptional vintages in 1978 and 1979, she seemed to feel that her wines had arrived. "We've won awards," she said, "but the name Rosso Piceno is still not as well known or respected as it ought to be. We're counting on an individual reputation."

Alberto Compagnucci-Compagnoni, who has seen the pattern of agriculture in the Marches evolve for more than half a century, is not convinced that the current movement toward restricted cultivation and production by cooperatives is any improvement over the old free market practice of selling wine in bulk to private producers in other regions.

"Granted, some cooperatives in Italy make respectable wine," he said. "But the concept is all wrong. How can you have any self-respect as a grower and sell your grapes to a cooperative where you have no control over the final product? I'll tell you a little secret. Too often cultivators sell their best grapes privately and unload the rest on the cooperative, to be made into standardized wine sold in bulk. The tricks in this business are endless."

Compagnucci-Compagnoni, whose gentlemanly manner and attire and faith in free enterprise seem almost anomalous in modern-day Italy, can credit Villamagna's success to a resourceful quest for quality. "What are all these wine development programs you hear about in Italy and the European Community doing for the private producer of quality wine? Exactly nothing," he said. "I'm not complaining about the lack of funds.

No, what I object to is this attitude of negating the work of serious producers, of virtually ignoring the existence of the finest, most honest wines of this nation while the powers that be seem to be pointing toward a mass standard of mediocrity. Making fine wine is a labor of love that only special people like my wife are willing to make the sacrifices for. As a business investment, it's pure folly."

Despite the complaints, Valeria and Alberto Compagnucci-Compagnoni obviously enjoy their work and the challenge involved in making their wines better known. Today the name Rosso Piceno is worth but a fraction that of Barolo or Brunello, but with wines available of the class of Villamagna and a few others, the gap should soon begin to close.

Vernaccia di Serrapetrona, a Sparkling Anachronism

The other DOC wine of the Marches is an anachronism, a sparkling red, often sweet, made from still another grape called Vernaccia grown around the remote mountain village of Serrapetrona. Each of the few producers of Vernaccia di Serrapetrona lays claim to authenticity to the product of an ancient tradition whose origin is vague enough to allow for varying interpretations. The producers I know of are Franco Tallei, Antonio Claudi, Umberto Francioni, Raffaele Quacquarini, and Attilio Fabrini. Only Fabrini has a nationwide reputation, not only for his extraordinary Vernaccia but for his other wines as well, all made with a determination that seems to heighten with each vintage.

"I'm an old man," said Fabrini with a genial lack of conviction as he led me through the complex of old and new buildings that include his home, office, and multileveled cantina, all enclosed by a sharp curve in the Via Leopardi, the steep main street of Serrapetrona. True, Attilio Fabrini is not as young as he would like to be, but there is nothing antiquated about his style of winemaking. In fact, his innovation of *méthode champenoise* has prompted his competitors to accuse him of breaking with tradition. Fabrini laughs that off, submitting that the Champagne method is more closely related to the type of bottle refermentation that had been the practice here until recently — though in a rudimentary form — than is the charmat method used by the others. Tradition aside, Fabrini's elaborate pioneering has been amply rewarded. His Vernaccia di Serrapetrona, both *secco* and *amabile,* have singular status among Italy's sparkling red wines and his Verdicchio *nature* is often ranked with the nation's outstanding Champagne-style wines.

Attilio Fabrini and nephew

Vernaccia production is intricate. Fabrini uses 80 percent of the so-called Vernaccia Nera grape and 20 percent Sangiovese. At harvest time the Sangiovese and half the Vernaccia grapes are each fermented separately. The remaining half of the Vernaccia grapes are placed on trays to dry until late December or early January, when they are pressed into a heavy, sweet must to be added to the other wines, which are then combined. This *governo* induces a refermentation that lasts two months. Then the wine is put through a bottle fermentation that lasts at least two years with all the steps involved in Champagne, including the addition of sugar and select fermenting yeasts and phosphates from Champagne.

"The basic process follows a custom that dates back to at least 1442, according to documents of the community of Serrapetrona," Fabrini explained. "Of course, the *méthode champenoise* is an added extravagance that I started using in 1971. So it takes me two years to accomplish what the other producers can do with charmat in twelve days."

As we toured the cantina, Fabrini told about his late developing realization that only the Champagne method could lead to the quality he sought in Vernaccia and Verdicchio. "There's no substitute for it," he said. "The bouquet, the finesse, the *perlage* can't be achieved in any other way. Of course, the results are different between the Vernaccia and the Verdicchio, but the quality is about equal."

With the Verdicchio he makes both a *secco* and a *nature,* which does not include the *liqueur d'expédition,* the dose of sugar and brandy. "The *nature* is finer," he said, "so I'm aiming most of my Verdicchio production at that now, in the good years, of course." The Verdicchio was ranked among the ten best Champagne-type wines of the nation by Adriano Ravegnani in his book *I cento vini d'Italia.*

Fabrini also makes a fine still Verdicchio that is not DOC, a Bianco delle Colli Maceratesi DOC, and a non-DOC Sangiovese. He recently planted some Montepulciano vines in his Pian delle Mura vineyard, hoping that the DOC zone for Rosso Piceno would be enlarged by a few kilometers to take in his vineyards. "Rosso Piceno can be a superb wine," said Fabrini, "because Montepulciano adds character to Sangiovese."

We drove over to Pian delle Mura, several kilometers from Serrapetrona in the community of San Severino Marche, where some 30 acres of vines below the crest of the hill catch the sun from dawn to dusk. The Vernaccia vines, old and thick in the trunk, are apparently unique and indigenous to the hills around Serrapetrona, one of those peaceful backwaters that no outsider would consider visiting were it not for its special wine.

The Vernaccia di Serrapetrona DOC zone includes the communities of San Severino and Belforte, east of Tolentino in the province of Macerata. Pian delle Mura overlooks Serrapetrona, whose pastel buildings are stacked on a hillside topped by a small stone castle with a turret. The architecture and lay of the land somehow seem more reminiscent of France's Languedoc than of neighboring sections of Italy. But then, the Marches has a quality of its own that relates only vaguely to adjacent regions: Romagna, Tuscany, Umbria, Latium, and the Abruzzi. It is difficult to be precise about a particular Marches style because from Ancona to Macerata to Ascoli Piceno there are already worlds of difference.

The Vernaccia of Attilio Fabrini is a ruby-purple color with a pleasing fragrance, persistent bubbles, and light red foam. Whether dry or sweet, the Vernaccia flavor is unmistakable, grapy with a bitter undertone. Minimum alcohol is 11.5° under DOC, though the sweet version leaves a portion of that undeveloped as residual sugar. The *secco* is a fine *aperitivo*, though it also goes well through a meal, and the *amabile* is best with desserts, especially fruit tarts. Both are also suitable for meditation. Fabrini suggests serving them in the old-style Champagne cup rather than the flute, and at cellar temperature rather than ice-cold.

Verdicchio *nature* might be Fabrini's finest wine. The old-timers around Cupramontana who used to make *frizzante* Verdicchio rather than still might have been aware of something many modern winemakers have missed: that the grape converts beautifully into dry *spumante*. In that regard, it may have more natural aptitude than any other native Italian variety. Verdicchio *spumante* is different from the Pinots and Chardonnays, but not so different that it does not merit comparison. Adriano Ravegnani's estimation is not exaggerated; Fabrini's *nature* has the class to rank with Italy's greatest sparkling wines and the personality to stand by itself. These special *spumanti* sell for relatively reasonable prices in Italy, a fraction of Champagne. But excessive taxes on sparkling wines in the United States and Britain have prevented their widespread distribution there. Too bad, for some of them are among the liveliest examples of Italian oenology.

Among the many less acclaimed wines of the Marches are numerous versions of Verdicchio, Trebbiano, Malvasia, Montepulciano, and Sangiovese, including some fine examples of their type. Vin Santo Marchigiano, which may at times equal the best of Umbria and Tuscany, is distinguished by the use of Drupello and Verdello grapes as well as Malvasia and Greco.

The potential for excellence in the wines of the Marches has only begun to be realized. The region's red wines have an intrinsic goodness that demands wider appreciation. And even Verdicchio seems capable of greater things, possibly in the Champagne field. Winemaking in the Marches has long been considered an easy, natural endeavor that in the past was perhaps taken a bit too casually. DOC and the international success of Verdicchio have alerted some producers to the reality that when made with skill and passion, their wines, both red and white, can stand with Italy's elite. For examples of how to succeed in the quality field, the aspirants need look no farther than to the achievers in their midst.

The Vintages

	Rosso Cònero	Rosso Piceno
1979	Exceptional	Exceptional
1978	Excellent	Good to excellent
1977	Excellent	Excellent
1976	Poor	Poor
1975	Excellent	Excellent
1974	Excellent	Good, some great
1973	Very good	Excellent
1972	Fair	Fair
1971	Excellent	Good
1970	Fair	Fair to good

	Verdicchio
1979	Excellent
1978	Fair to good
1977	Exceptional
1976	Poor
1975	Excellent
1974	Fair
1973	Good

ALEATICO DI GRADOLI

EST! EST!! EST!!!

Viterbo

Rieti

CAPENA BIANCO

CERVETERI

TIBER

MONTECOMPATRI COLONNA

ZAGAROLO

CESANESE DI OLEVANO

CESANES DI AFFILE

Rome

MARINO

FRASCATI   COLLI ALBANI

COLLI LANUVINI

VELLETRI   CORI

CESANESE DEL PIGLIO

Frosinone

MERLOT, SANGIOVESE TREBBIANO DI APRILIA

Latina

LÁTIUM

PROVINCES

ROME, Frosinone, Latina, Rieti, Viterbo

POPULATION

5,000,000

AREA

6,480 square miles

AVERAGE WINE PRODUCTION

510 million liters

DOC WINES

Aleatico di Gradoli · Capena Bianco · Cerveteri (Bianco, Rosso) · Cesanese di Affile · Cesanese di Olevano Romano · Cesanese del Piglio · Colli Albani · Colli Lanuvini · Cori (Bianco, Rosso) · Est!Est!!Est!!! di Montefiascone · Frascati · Marino · Merlot di Aprilia · Montecompatri Colonna · Sangiovese di Aprilia · Trebbiano di Aprilia · Velletri (Bianco, Rosso) · Zagarolo

OTHER WINES

Aleatico di Terracina · Baccanale · Castel San Giorgio · Cecubo · Colle Picchioni · Colli Cimini · Colli Etruschi · Colli Rufeno · Colli Sabini · Falerno · Falernum · Fiorano · Grechetto di Gradoli · La Selva · Maccarese · Marmorelle · Mentana-Monterotondo · Monte Giove · Moscato di Terracina · Quintaluna · Romagnano · San Clemente · San Michele · San Vittore degli Uccellatori · Torre Ercolana · Torre in Pietra

Rendering All Things Roman

R OME no longer dominates Italy as it has at times in the past, but it does maintain its eternal hegemony over Latium, claiming the best — and the worst — from all corners of the region and rendering all things Roman. Thus the city may seem satiated, teeming with excess, while outlying parts of Latium often appear drained, forlorn, even scruffy, the holdout population watching its sons and daughters, its produce, its ideas, its spirit drawn relentlessly down the roads to Rome.

Although it may look that way in places, Latium's rural folk have not relinquished agriculture. There is Rome to feed, after all, and millions of consumers thirsting for those white wines whose magic links to Rome have carried them to worldwide fame and fortune. All the renowned wines of Latium are white — Frascati, Marino, Colli Albani, Est!Est!! Est!!! and the region's small share of Orvieto. Historically *abboccato*, now many are dry. Overall, they are probably better than ever: cleaner, fresher, better suited to travel, though none of the popular whites can lay claim to greatness.

Latium is the most productive wine region of central Italy, surpassing Tuscany and usually ranking fifth nationally in volume (behind Emilia-Romagna, the Veneto, Apulia, and Sicily). Latium ranks second nationally in the number of DOC zones — eighteen — behind Piedmont and in a dead heat with Apulia. Some outsiders criticize this wealth of DOCs as not fully merited, the result, they imply, of being close to the Powers That Be in Rome. Well, if it never hurts to be within whispering distance of Rome's inner circles, it must be acknowledged that Latium has been one of the nation's most actively motivated regions in improving and promoting the quality of its wines, notably through the development of cooperatives.

Curiously, in a region where more than 90 percent of DOC production is currently in white wine and the share seems to be increasing, the consensus among qualified observers is that Latium's highest-quality wines are red. Some can be found among the DOCs. But several of the grandest red wines are unclassified, rare, the products of dedicated wine-makers working on a limited scale.

Here and there as you roll south toward the capital, Latium's ancient beauty reigns: across the Sabine Hills where the towns seem intact even if increasingly abandoned; down the Tiber, winding like a green serpent through a path of lush foliage; over Lake Bolsena, whose serenity has survived at least three millennia of human habitation.

Several options apart from the Autostrada del Sole are open to travelers approaching Rome from the north, among them roads that bear Italian-ized Roman names: the Via Aurelia, which follows the coast to France; the Via Cassia, which leads to Siena and Florence; the Via Flaminia, which traverses Umbria toward the Adriatic; and the Via Salaria, that leads to Ascoli Piceno in the Marches. The closest thing to a wine route is probably the Via Cassia.

After entering Latium at Acquapendente, which has a white wine called Quintaluna and red and white wines from the Colli Rufeno, the Cassia veers east around Lake Bolsena. Around its ample, craterlike basin grow vines for two DOC wines that provide a study in oenological contrasts. One is red, sweet, scarcely known; the other is white, now usually dry, its legendary status so pathetically overstated that its name, though in triplicate, is almost lost in a crescendo of exclamation points. Aleatico di Gradoli and Est!Est!!Est!!! di Montefiascone do have one thing in common, though: they have both been around a long time.

Aleatico, apparently the Lugliatico vine of antiquity, is cultivated in many parts of Italy, from Romagna and Tuscany to southern points. But only in Gradoli and Apulia does it make DOC wines. Aleatico di Gradoli is appreciated for its bouquet, in which some detect roses, and for its unaggressive sweetness, which some compare to that of certain ports, though its character is singular: smooth, soft, fruity, whether in the *naturale* version of about 12° alcohol or the stronger *liquoroso* of at least 16°. It is used both as *aperitivo* and after dinner, as well as for casual sipping. It might be best of all with fruit, delicious when spooned from the center of a slightly chilled cantaloupe. The Aleatico Nero vines grow in loose volcanic soil around Gradoli and Grotte di Castro. The only producer I know of is the Cantina Oleificio Sociale di Gradoli, whose wine is difficult to find outside the area but worth searching for.

Other red and white wines of the Bolsena area are known as Colli Etruschi, and another dry red wine of some class is Grechetto, or Greghetto di Gradoli, from the dark grape of that name with some Sangiovese. (There is also a light Grechetto grape prominent in central Italy.)

Est!Est!!Est!!! Another Man's Yquem

If through some twist of fortune you have not heard the story of how Est!Est!!Est!!! got its name, you have been spared one of the most overworked publicity ploys in the history of wine. But there is no denying that the legend of Bishop Johannes Fugger of Augsburg and his trusted servant Martin, who traveled ahead to scout out the inns with good wine and mark them with an *"Est!"* has realized miraculous results. Had it not been for the tale of Martin's ecstatic triple endorsement of the wine at one town inn, the eminently unremarkable wine of Montefiascone might have seen the handwriting on the wall long ago.

But perhaps I am being too harsh. One man's Est!Est!!Est!!! might be another man's Yquem, after all, and Bishop Fugger's folly, fatal at that, might have had something behind it in 1111, when the wine-loving prelate lingered in Montefiascone and never reached his destination, the coronation of Emperor Henry V in Rome. The wine apparently was referred to as Moscatello then, meaning it might have been made from grapes in the Muscat family and not from the Trebbiano, Malvasia, and Rossetto (Trebbiano Giallo) grapes of today. Whatever the case, Bishop Fugger was so fond of it that his epitaph (written by Martin) in the church of San Flavio attributes his death to too much Est!Est!!Est!!!

Bolsena has another tragicomic reference to a religious figure. Dante condemned Pope Martin IV to purgatory in the *Divine Comedy* for drowning the luscious eels of the lake in wine (Vernaccia, however) before eating them. The plump and tasty eels are still considered the leading delicacy of the clear waters of this deep lake.

Like its even more illustrious neighbor, Orvieto, Est!Est!!Est!!! was historically rather lush in flavor and deep golden in color. In recent decades it, too, has been sold in *pulcianella* flasks. It has undergone a similar change in personality to become generally dry (though an *abboccato* version is permitted under DOC) and lighter in color. So far, the conversion has not been as successful qualitatively as Orvieto's. Although the wine has a definite attraction to tourists, romantics, and other susceptible types, it has rarely enjoyed much favor among discriminating wine drinkers. Indeed, some points various critics have raised about it are enough to cause Bishop Fugger to roll over in his grave.

Were the Bishop and Martin alive today, they might not have got as far along the Cassia as Montefiascone, but rather have ended their journey in the town of Bolsena on the northeast corner of the lake, where Italo Mazziotti makes what is generally conceded to be the finest white wine of the zone.

Mazziotti, whose thoroughly professional approach to winemaking contrasts with the flamboyant image of the wine he makes, admits somewhat modestly that, yes, his is the most qualified wine of the name. It should be pointed out that he does not use any exclamation points whatever on his labels, preferring simply "Est Est Est" in gold lettering with a couple of coats of arms and some medals. All in all, rather dignified and sober, fitting for a good, clean, fresh white of balanced aroma and flavor and medium straw-golden color.

Its class surprised me. I had been to Bolsena's shores several times before I met Italo Mazziotti, but the wines there had been disappointing, almost universally *fiacco* — flat, tired, uninspiring — and whether *secco* or *abboccato* had never lived up to the legend. Mazziotti nodded understandingly when I described my previous experiences. Actually, he said, the white wine of Montefiascone was often decent fresh from the barrel during the months after the vintage, but until recently, once bottled and shipped, it faded fast.

Mazziotti pointed out the numerous awards and citations for his family's wines in the office of his cantina, a plain yellow plaster building on a quiet road running off the Cassia. "My father, his name was Gerardo, was the only exporter of Est Est Est to the United States in the days before World War II and immediately after," he said. "He was a conscientious winemaker, but in those days shipping involved a considerable element of risk and the wine didn't always arrive overseas in acceptable condition. Cultivation, vinification, and stabilization were not so scientific then."

After his father and brother died, Italo Mazziotti, a graduate oenologist, decided to do more than merely continue the successful family tradition of buying grapes and making wine. A decade ago, he bought a tract of land called Colle Bonvino, appropriately enough, above the eastern shore of Bolsena and planted more than 60 acres of vines on hillsides sloping toward the afternoon sun off the lake. "Look at this layout," he enthused. "You couldn't ask for a better location for a vineyard." The property even includes an Etruscan tomb, no rarity in this area.

Italo Mazziotti

Mazziotti admits that his Est Est Est has improved markedly since he began growing his own grapes, but he also gives some credit to new techniques and equipment. The grapes are crushed with a Vaslin horizontal continuous press, for example, and only free-run must is used in a low-temperature fermentation. One result is a cleaner, crisper wine that travels well, thanks in part to a postbottling "hot shower" pasteurization process.

Another result has been increasing demand for the wine in Italy. "We used to send about half our Est Est Est out of the country, but lately our sales have been growing internally, especially in Milan, Turin, and other northern cities. However, Romans don't seem so fond of the wine," said Mazziotti, who did not appear at all worried. "I guess it's because it's not soft like their Frascati and Marino."

Mazziotti, who also produces an *abboccato* Est Est Est as well as a good red table wine, confirms the promise of Bolsena's splendid hillsides for quality wine. Indeed, if other producers begin to follow his lead, as seems inevitable with the new technology becoming available, even the experts might be compelled to retract some of their disclaimers about the DOC wine of Montefiascone. Heaven knows, Est Est Est, or Est! Est! Est! or Est! Est!! Est!!! if you insist, could use some authoritative acclaim.

Signs of Change

Italy has no Mason-Dixon Line defining where the north ends and the south begins. The so-called Mezzogiorno is generally considered to be below Rome, but even in the southern reaches of Tuscany and Umbria and now here in northern Latium, signs of change can be noted in the landscape and vegetation, the style of building, human attitudes and activities, the taste of food and wine.

The terrain has begun to look arid, sparse, scorched in places, especially near the sea. Here and there in the towns there is an air of indolence and a touch of squalor. From one to four in the afternoon, and often later in the heat of summer, they are ghost towns with shutters closed, blinds drawn, and doors barred until the end of the siesta. Then, as the welcome cool of evening settles in, the piazzas come alive, the bars fill up with old men playing cards and drinking white wine, and young men gather on the street corners, taking respites from piloting their unmuffled cars and motorscooters to and fro with enviable bravado and a racket that drowns out all conversation in their path.

Perhaps the surest indicator of change is in the speech. Whether the cadence is slower or faster (depending on the emotion content of the situation), the words are less clearly enunciated than they were back in Siena and Perugia. The consonants soften, so that *c* begins to sound like *g*, *t* like *d*, *p* like *b*, and the pitch heightens. Even in the countryside you begin to hear the street language of Rome, *romanaccio,* a boisterous, blasphemous, ungrammatical vernacular of joy, sorrow, poetry, ridicule, complaint, filled with puns, slurs, curses, shouts, wails, and double-entendre. For feeling, color, and volume it is matched only by the dialect of Naples.

South along the Cassia from Montefiascone, the first city is Viterbo, whose high stone walls and active ancient quarter give it an invitingly medieval air. Here you can either continue to follow the Cassia through Vetralla and Sutri, past grottos that may have been carved out of the soft volcanic stone by Etruscans, or branch off on the Via Cimina past Lago di Vico to Ronciglione. All through these hills that run from the Mediterranean to the Apennines good table wines are made, the reds from Sangiovese, Canaiolo, and Montepulciano, as a rule, and the whites from Malvasia and Trebbiano. If only a few are recognized outside their locales, it is not because they lack admirers, who tote them home in demi-johns or drink them from carafes in their local *osteria.* Many wines here, both red and white, have a vein of *abboccato* set off against a hint of bitter almond, soft, pleasant wines that go well with the grilled lamb and pork and *porchetta* and the substantial pastas that are sharper in flavor here because they are topped with *pecorino romano* rather than the milder Parmesan.

To date, there are only two DOC zones in Rome's northern environs: Cerveteri, with both Rosso and Bianco, and Capena with Bianco. More are expected, such as Mentana-Monterotondo from the Sabine Hills, and many others are worth at least passing notice. Along the Cassia between Lake Bracciano and the town of Campagnano di Roma lie the vineyards of Baccanale, a red wine from a unique combination of Latium's native Cesanese with Cabernet Franc and Carignano. Either dry or *pastoso* (another term for the lightly sweet mellowness so typical here), it is best when young. The Colli Cimini near Lago di Vico have red and white wines with enough uniformity in quality to aspire to official status some-day. Numerous good, unpretentious wines are made to the east, across the Tiber around Rieti, Rocca Sinibalda, Subiaco, and Tivoli.

Cooperatives throughout the zone have helped not only to improve standards but to identify and develop various wines. The Cantina Sociale Feronia provided the impetus for Capena Bianco becoming DOC. The wine, from vineyards around Capena, Morlupo, and Fiano Romano, is made from Malvasia at 55 percent maximum, Trebbiano at 25 percent minimum, and Bellone and/or Bonvino at 20 percent maximum, making it similar in structure to the more famous wines of the Castelli Romani. The *superiore* version of Capena Bianco, with at least 12° alcohol, surpasses many Castelli wines in class. Another good cooperative, the Cantina Sociale Colli Sabini near Magliano Sabina, produces white and red wines that until recently were sold almost entirely in bulk, though their quality merits bottling.

Cerveteri is well noted for its Etruscan tombs; as the center of a large and rather promising vineyard area it is also attaching its name to red and white wines. The Cerveteri DOC zone extends north into the communities of Civitavecchia and Tarquinia, near the coast, and inland to Allumiere and Tolfa through mineral-rich hills that were once a center of the Etruscan civilization. Cerveteri Rosso, from Sangiovese and Montepulciano with a bit of Cesanese, is dry, balanced, and fairly robust with at least 12° alcohol. Cerveteri Bianco, from Trebbiano at a minimum of 50 percent, Malvasia at 35 percent, and other varieties (including Tocai and Verdicchio) at 15 percent maximum between them, may be either dry or *abboccato*. Delicate and fresh with at least 11.5° alcohol, it is best young. The Cantina Sociale Cooperativa di Cerveteri, largest producer of both types, maintains a commendable level of quality.

In Cerveteri, as elsewhere in this territory of both natural and hand-carved caves, wine was traditionally made and stored underground in barrels of chestnut. These caves and other simple locales where wine was served straight from the barrel along with cold cuts, cheese, bread, and olives, came to be known as *frasche* or *fraschette* after the laurel branches hung outside the door when the new wine was ready to drink and left there until the last barrel was drained. That happy custom lives on in Cerveteri and throughout much of the hill country of Latium.

Closer to Rome, near the Via Aurelia at Torre in Pietra, red and white wines of special attractiveness are made. The red Castello di Torre in Pietra is dry and robust with a touch of its own sort of elegance. Across the Via Aurelia lies the spacious agricultural enterprise of Maccarese on the flats adjacent to the beach resort of Fregene. Wines there are produced by a corporate winery, Maccarese S.p.A., which reportedly is part of the extensive holdings of IRI, the semi-official conglomerate that controls a major share of the nation's industry. The Maccarese white wines, from Malvasia, Trebbiano, and sometimes Sauvignon and Sémillon, are best when young. The red, from Cesanese with Merlot and Montepulciano, can be special from those vintages that support aging. The Castel San Giorgio *riserva* is strong, smooth, opulent. Aged five years in oak casks, it excels with game and roast beef. It is one of the unexpected delights of the Roman countryside, which is better noted for tender artichokes, sweet peas, and short-lived white wines than for superior aged reds.

Rome: The Show Is The Thing

Rome, with all its impossible contradictions, is still the most entertaining city of Europe. You may love it or hate it (or both, as is the case with me), but if you ever get to know it well, you will never lose your compulsion to return, to walk its streets and witness once again the endless drama of *la vita romana*.

The show, like the setting, has a bit of everything, possibly too much of everything, especially decibels. Between crescendos of joy, laughter, song, amidst choruses of bells, magnified street sounds, blaring car horns, there are occasional peaceful moments, awkward, eerie, the silence of the ages. As a backdrop there is the Rome of the caesars and the popes, the princes and the paupers, the artists of the Renaissance and the architects of a form sometimes known as "Mussolini modern," devoid of both function and taste. The mood shifts from pompous to sacrosanct, from serious to absurd, from good clean fun to so hopelessly degenerate that you might be tempted to get up and walk out. Well, if you do, do not expect your money back.

Naturally, you will want to eat and drink while taking in the performance. True, you do not always eat and drink as well in Rome as you do in some other Italian cities, but you must consider that the joys of table here go beyond mere appreciation of what you consume. If your waiter sets down only one tumbler for white wine, red wine, and *acqua minerale,* and takes an hour and twenty minutes between serving the pasta and the next course, do not feel slighted and do not get angry. Best to take it in stride, adopt the Roman philosophy of *chi se ne frega?* and join the act. If they don't care, why should you?

In the restaurants, the show is the thing. Why else would Alfredo alla Scrofa, where the self-dubbed "King of Fettuccine" Alfredo himself assembled his masterpiece before the customer's eyes, be the most famous place in town? Over the years, I have had my favorite Roman restaurants and *trattorie,* but I do not dare name any for fear that in the ephemeral pattern of Roman eateries they will presently change owners or cooks or deteriorate in some other way or even disappear. You could follow the

Michelin, if you are cautious, or the more recent *Guida dell'Espresso,* if you are bold. But as mealtime approaches, perhaps the surest way to find a decent Roman *trattoria* (though it requires a few words of Italian) is to carefully size up passersby until you spot a well-fed type with a contented expression (important because it indicates that he does not suffer from indigestion). Step up to him and say: *"Scusi, ma dove si mangia bene?"* Chances are he will be heading there himself.

Surely there is no excuse for ever feeling bored or lonely while dining out in Rome. If you are in a touristy part of town, between Trastevere and Piazza Navona, for instance, you will be serenaded by the most motley succession of musicians you have ever laid eyes on, enterprising dabblers in the art of eliciting sounds from the violin, accordion, guitar, clarinet, Jew's harp, kazoo, harmonica, and vocal cords. My favorite, because his dignity never falters no matter how abusive the audience reaction, is a veteran called Garibaldi who tootles on the cornet and is rumored to be among the wealthiest men in town.

La cucina romana, for all its historical references to the lavish feasting of the titled and well-to-do, is predominantly a heritage of the popular and the poor. Many of the city's food specialties are based on simple things: pasta, oxtail, kid, salt pork, calves' innards, sheep cheese, bacon, pungent herbs, and exquisitely flavored fresh vegetables and fruit. When you think about it, it really does not seem so strange that the cooking of the poor survived while many of those elaborate and exotic dishes fashioned so grandly for the banquets of Imperial Rome and, later, for the papal court and the aristocracy, are now all but forgotten. Those concoctions were probably too much work to prepare anyway.

Remember that even the poor people of Rome have never been content just to fill their bellies; eating is a sensual experience and Romans, as much as any Italians, perhaps more, seem to like to have their senses stimulated to the hilt. That may explain why their food is so laden with flavor — so piquant, aromatic, strong. A truly elemental Roman pasta is *spaghetti all'aio, oio, peperoncini,* which is simply a sauce of bubbling hot olive oil into which heavy doses of chopped garlic and chili peppers and a smattering of parsley are sizzled for a few seconds before being dumped over a heap of thin spaghetti cooked *al dente.* Other popular pasta sauces — *alla carbonara* and *alla matriciana,* one with eggs and one with tomato sauce and both with *guanciale,* bacon from the pig's jowl — were stolen from other places, as were many of the special Roman dishes.

Lamb, the real milk-fed baby lamb called *abbacchio,* is the favored meat, though the Romans often choose to smother its subtle flavor by braising it *alla cacciatora* (hunter's style) with oil, vinegar, garlic, anchovies, and rosemary. *Coda alla vaccinara*, oxtail stewed in a sauce rife with onion, tomato, and especially celery, is another tasty dish of the poor. Both meat and fish are often cooked in *agrodolce* (sweet and sour sauce), a concept that dates to ancient Rome.

Rome is surrounded by gardens that keep the city supplied with a sumptuous array of fresh produce. Peas are rarely so sweet as here, though artichokes are the glory of the Roman countryside. Why they are more tender and tasty than those of anywhere else is for botanists to ponder, but there is no question that they are. These *carciofi* are most often prepared *alla romana* (cooked in a casserole with oil, mint, and garlic) or *alla giudia* (flattened and deep-fried in olive oil), a dish of the city's ancient Jewish quarter.

Note that few Roman foods go well with wine. Their flavors are clearly too aggressive. Even the sheep cheese, *pecorino romano*, is usually so sharp and salty that it is used for grating and not nibbling as the milder Parmesan often is. Maybe that is why Romans have been so exasperatingly undiscriminating about wine over the years, and why it never seemed to occur to them — until recently — that there might be some more worthy nectar of the grape than the whites of the Castelli Romani.

Some Romans will tell you that the Castelli wines go with anything, even meat. Granted, as whites go, they might be described as "all-purpose," partly because they lack the crispness, the bite that makes some other whites so refreshing but so limited in usefulness with food. So maybe the Romans have a point; with the barrage of flavors of a typical Roman meal, you want a wine that slips down easily and does not require much attention. That, in the final analysis, is probably the outstanding quality of the whites of the Castelli Romani.

Wine, Water, and Song

Though I try to respect proverbs, when it comes to drinking wine I really cannot advise always doing as the Romans do. One of the city's favorite drinking songs begins:

> *Ma che ti frega,*
> *Ma che t'importa,*
> *In nostro vino ci mette l'acqua.*

The gist is that you should not worry that they water down the wine. Indeed, I have found that many open wines sold in *trattorie* and *osterie* of the city can be made somewhat palatable by being blended with mineral water, but the line must be drawn at Coke, other soft drinks, and beer. And yet, through years of cringing as Romans blended these and other beverages into cocktails based on the rust-colored *bianco* of the Castelli, I must concede a certain degree of empathy. All too often the wine was really that bad. But why?

The root of the problem is the Malvasia grape in its various subvarieties, the main component of Frascati, Marino, and other Castelli whites. Malvasia has a greater tendency than do other light grapes to oxidize in wine. The old techniques of fermentation on the skins in open vats and aging in barrels involved exposure to the air. Often a wine that was very good to drink in a cellar in the towns of Frascati or Marino in the early spring, with all the bouquet, softness, and freshness that typified its youth, would begin to fade after being pumped into tanks or demijohns, trucked the 20 kilometers into central Rome, and pumped or siphoned again into the refrigerated glass tanks that *trattorie* stored it in. By the time the last liters were drawn off into carafes, the wine was often flat, sour, clearly off.

Some winemakers and innkeepers improvised methods of keeping the wine stable a bit longer, such as excessive sulfur dioxide or other chemicals, but the result was often a headache or an attack of *mal di fegato,* as Romans call any affliction of the digestive tract. No wonder Romans packed into cars, buses, and trolleys on Sunday and headed out to the hills to drink the authentic Castelli wines on the spot.

The situation has improved of late. Horizontal presses, stainless steel vats, refrigerated fermentation, pasteurization, oxygen-free bottling in wineries that can afford the equipment have effectively combatted the oxidation problem. Thus the bottled wine is purer than ever before and it can travel. But it is not the same; many Romans seem to resent that.

Marco Trimani, journalist, scholar, and the city's foremost retailer of quality wine, described the trend. Frascati and Marino are selling better than ever in other parts of Italy and abroad, he said, but sales have been decreasing steadily in Rome. Meanwhile, Romans are buying more Piedmontese reds, Friulian whites, certain other prestige wines from the north. Open wines from the Castelli are still sold in restaurants, *osterie,* and shops (Trimani himself carries a couple that are drawn through brass taps into the customer's empty containers), but the tradition seems to be dying, another Roman victim of modernism.

Trimani, whose philosophy is more that of a missionary than a merchant, submits that Rome should be the capital, the showcase of Italian wine. "Wine is one of the most attractive, positive features of Italian life today, a national treasure," he says. "More foreigners visit Rome than any other Italian city, but in nine places out of ten where wine is sold visitors are bound to be disappointed, because there is so little choice. Naturally, there are some exceptions, but not nearly enough."

The leading exception is his own Enoteca Trimani on the Via Goito, which carries possibly the most complete selection of quality wine in Italy. All regions are represented, except Molise, and all wines are selected for their authenticity and validity. The shop has served as an information center and supply base for some of the research on this book.

Trimani's enthusiasm is most pronounced when he discusses the wines of his home region. He is not alone among experts in the conviction that, fine as many whites are, much of Latium's territory is best suited to vines for red wine. He has numerous bottles on his shelves to back the point, including one of his own creation from his family estate near Rieti, known as San Vittore degli Uccellatori.

Fiorano: A Secret Shared by a Few

The noblest Romans of them all are called Fiorano, three non-DOC wines produced on the outskirts of the city by a prince whose success refutes the widely held notion that Rome is not a wine town. Alberigo Boncompagni Ludovisi, Principe di Venosa, established his few acres of vines along the ancient Appian Way 15 kilometers from the center of Rome and a few hundred meters across the meadows of the Campagna Romana from Ciampino, Rome's second airport.

It is hard to say which of the three Fiorano wines is most remarkable because all stand out from the other wines of Rome. The red comes from equal parts of Merlot and Cabernet Sauvignon and the whites are the results of single varieties, one from Malvasia di Candia and one from Sémillon, the major light grape of Sauternes and Graves. Certainly Fiorano Rosso has made the most profound impression upon cognoscenti. Though it shares the breed and structure of some fine Bordeaux, the Roman climate tends to bring it to more consistent peaks; there are none of those lapses into the thinness that the French refer to as subtle.

Fiorano Rosso, with its richness of extract, needs plenty of bottle age to develop finesse after two to three years in barrel.

Fiorano Bianco from Malvasia di Candia may be the finest dry white of Latium, a wine whose quality varies of necessity from vintage to vintage but from the best of them shows an elegance that few if any of the region's many DOC whites ever achieve. This white is aged in barrel for up to two years and can maintain its quality for several years more even though it is not subjected to the sort of treatment that white wines made on a larger scale are now routinely put through. Fiorano Bianco is proof that even Malvasia grapes, when picked at the right moment and processed in small quantities under immaculate conditions, can avoid undesirable effects of oxidation and instead develop into wine of attractively smooth texture, complex flavor, and golden hue. Unfortunately, few winemakers can afford to risk this artisanal type of vinification, but Principe Boncompagni Ludovisi obviously would not have it any other way.

The Fiorano Sémillon bears little resemblance to Sauternes. Among other things the *pourriture noble*, the rot that ennobles the great dessert wines of Bordeaux, simply does not occur in the Campagna Romana. Still, this Fiorano, though only vaguely sweet, is a most refined wine of its type and a rarity in Italy, where Sémillon has never caught on the way some other French varieties have. It is light and delicate, probably best as a predinner drink.

The greatness of Fiorano is a secret shared by a few, for the several thousand bottles (all numbered) are annually parceled out to loyal wine dealers and restaurateurs, who in turn reserve it for special customers. Only occasionally do bottles show up in a restaurant or *enoteca* elsewhere in Italy and there is simply not enough for export.

Frascati: Focusing on the Dry

From the plains of Fiorano it is just a short hop into the hills known variously as the Colli Albani, Castelli Romani, or Colli Romani, a circle of volcanic rises overlooking Rome from the southeast. The Alban Hills, flanked by the Autostrada del Sole and the Appian Way, predate Rome as a center of civilization; the town of Albano is believed to have been founded by Ascanius, son of the Trojan hero Aeneas, about 1150 B.C. Even today there is an air of antique remoteness about them, bizarre and inscrutable, especially in their upper reaches, as though amidst their crater lakes and chestnut woods, their cool glens and forbidding gorges, they were still harboring pagan gods.

Quantitatively (and in a sense qualitatively) speaking, the Castelli Romani are among the most important wine areas of Italy. On the lower slopes, around villas, castles, half-rural and half-suburban towns lie the vineyards of six distinct DOC zones: Colli Albani, Colli Lanuvini, Frascati, Marino, Montecompatri Colonna, and Velletri. Most current production is in dry white wine, though sweet, semi-sweet, and *spumante* versions are permitted in places, and Velletri has both red and white wines under its name.

Frascati ranks as the premier Castelli wine, both in volume of production and prestige. Its reputation has survived more than a fair share of abuse and scandal, perhaps the most damaging being that Roman hosts perennially passed off their questionable-at-best house wine as "Frascati," knowing that most tourists would recognize the name and not the taste. Today, DOC provides a measure of protection, though waiters are still not above replying "Frascati" when asked the origin of almost any open wine.

The vineyards of Frascati gravitate rather extensively around the town of that name, distinguished by its patrician villas, such as the elegant Villa Aldobrandini. The DOC zone also includes sections of Monteporzio Catone, Colonna, Grottaferrata, Montecompatri, and even the southeasternmost part of the community of Rome. Although Frascati is now most often a dry wine, it can be sold in several versions, all variations on a central theme. Its composition, at least on paper, is devilishly complex; the prescribed grapes are Malvasia Bianca di Candia (also known locally as Malvasia Rossa), Malvasia del Lazio (also known as Puntinata), Greco (also known as Trebbiano Giallo), and Trebbiano Toscano, present in varying degrees, with the possible addition (at 10 percent maximum between them) of Bellone and Bonvino (the latter also known as Bombino Bianco). These grapes recur in varying measure through the formulas of all the Castelli DOC white wines.

Basically, Frascati is either dry or sweet, though there are shadings even within those general categories. Dry Frascati may be known as either *asciutto* or *secco*, the latter supposedly a smidgen drier than the former, though neither can have more than 1 percent residual sugar. Then there are the sweet versions, one called *cannellino* (yet another variation on *dolce*), which has 3 to 6 percent residual sugar, and the other *amabile*, with 1 to 3 percent residual sugar. Minimum alcohol for all these types is 11.5°, though when the wine has 12° or more of natural alcohol it may be labeled *superiore*. Frascati may also be made into a *spumante*, though little of that is on the market.

Cannellino was once the preferred style. Some Romans still insist that given the grapes and the natural conditions of the zone, Frascati is best as a sweet wine with the special aroma, softness, and velvety rotundity that set Malvasia apart. Also, the sugar helps it to survive and the inevitable maderization over time is more attractive in a sweet or strong Malvasia than in a dry or light one. Both scientifically and aesthetically, backers of *cannellino* are justified. But for the time being, the attention of all the large wineries and most of the small is focused on the dry.

The general quality of Frascati has now reached an unprecedented level of consistency, thanks not only to DOC but to extensive investment in new vines and equipment. Though in theory you should never find a bottle of bad wine on the market, remember that Frascati, like other Castelli whites, is designed to be drunk young, so it is wise to consume it within a year of the vintage, never more than two.

Although no Frascati stands out clearly above the crowd, I have long been impressed by San Matteo, in both *secco* and *cannellino*, and more recently by the wine of Fratelli Mennuni. The Mennuni Frascati has the lightness in color and flavor that now typifies the wine, but it also seems to have a touch of something extra, an elusive quality, not fully definable, that from the 1978 vintage, anyway, would have earned it a point over most others in a comparative tasting. The brothers Mennuni, Michele and Giorgio, recently completed a new medium-large winery below the town of Frascati, a clean, well-lighted place with all the charm of an airplane hangar. But one should not always judge a wine by its home base nowadays. As Michele Mennuni explains it, the key to quality for a winery that buys grapes, as most do in Frascati, is to develop a network of conscientious growers in the right locations. "We only buy grapes from hillside vineyards," said Mennuni, pointing out his office window to the nearby inclines where most come from. "And you have to be choosy. We're a growing company trying to establish an international reputation, so we have to be sticklers about the quality of our grapes and our wine."

Fratelli Mennuni have produced about 1 million liters of Frascati a year, though they plan to increase that gradually while reducing production of the various non-DOC wines — red and rosé — made at present. They are banking on continued expansion of the world market for white wine. They also seem to be banking on youth. Most of the cellar team, including Michele Mennuni's sons, Alessandro and Gianbruno, appeared to be under thirty.

The largest Frascati producer is Fontana Candida, part of the Winefood group, whose recent acquisition of most of the operation of Valle Vermiglia increased its plant capacity to more than 5 million liters. Fontana Candida's sales are almost exclusively of Frascati and Frascati *superiore*, some sold in the slope-shouldered bottle with the familiar red, white, and gold label under a netting of gold wire. Other reliable producers of Frascati include Conte Zandotti, A. De Sanctis & Figli, Castel De' Paolis-Lepanto, the Colli del Tuscolo cooperative, and Gotto d'Oro, the trade name of the Cantina Sociale Cooperativa di Marino.

Marino: First in Some Roman Hearts

Marino may be the perennial second in prestige among the Castelli wines, but in the hearts of some Romans it has always been first. Lying 10 kilometers southwest of Frascati along the road to Castelgandolfo, the town of Marino is known for its annual festival with a fountain spouting wine and for the appealingly simple *osterie* where wine flows almost as freely year around. Subtle variations in the proportions of Malvasia, Trebbiano, and other grapes make for minute distinctions in aroma and flavor, but in terms of quality there is little to choose between Marino and the wine of its more ballyhooed neighbor.

Marino, whose DOC zone includes parts of the communities of Castelgandolfo and Rome, is most often *secco,* though *amabile* and *spumante* versions exist; its *superiore* must have at least 12.5° alcohol, half a degree more than Frascati's. Marino has undergone a remarkable transition in less than a decade, largely through the expansion of a giant cooperative. But some traditionalists persist in working on an artisan scale. One is Paola Di Mauro, who among winemakers of whatever age, sex, background, or motivation is truly one of a kind.

"I'm a little strange," she reminded me two or three times as she talked about her winemaking activities. Well, admittedly her attitudes about wine and life in general differ considerably from the norm, which may be why she seemed so content. A bright, articulate, thoughtful woman, she seemed about as sane, as free of complexes as a person in this business could be. Paola Di Mauro said she had no worries, not even about the millions of lire she loses each year making wine.

"The only way you can make a profit on wine is to sell it at a high price," she said. "I'd rather give it away to my friends and laugh at the loss, the same way you'd throw away money on any other expensive hobby." Fortunately, she had the money, from the family iron business.

The truth is, though, that she does not give it all away. The clients for her Marino and red Colle Picchioni include some of the most important shops and restaurants of Rome, among them the Grand Hotel. Her Marino is considered by some to be the finest traditional-style white of the Castelli. To my taste, the Colle Picchioni is even better, certainly among the region's outstanding red wines. Not a bad showing for a teetotaler.

"That's right," she repeated when I thought I had misunderstood, "I'm a teetotaler. Wine makes me dizzy. Oh, I'll taste a mouthful now and then. You might not believe this, but not drinking sharpens my palate. I can pick out nuances in wine that others can't."

Signora Di Mauro bought the property a number of years ago because she liked the lay of the land, overlooking Rome with a view of the sea to the west and with the Pope's summer palace at Castelgandolfo dominating the hill behind. Her architect son designed the villa with plenty of wrought iron, tile, wooden beams, and antique furniture, all surrounded by vines like a French château, but with olive trees hundreds of years old as an Italian touch. The previous owner was a Frenchwoman, who had some vines planted, though when Signora Di Mauro moved in, the neighbors warned her that the wine was no good. "They were right," she recalled. "It was close to vinegar."

"I decided something ought to be done about it," she said. "After all, this is a DOC area, the vines were healthy. Some were about thirty years old and some others about fifty. And look at this soil: volcanic, friable, perfect for vines." She scooped up a handful and let it sift back evenly to earth. "So I went to the research institute at Velletri for advice. They were very encouraging. I got literature on viticulture and oenology and started to read. Everybody, including my husband, insisted I was crazy, especially since I don't drink wine. But I'm that way. When I start something, I have to see it through."

She planted more vines and, with the aid of her one helper, a farmer who lives in another new house on the land, has built production to about 30,000 bottles a year from 9 acres of vines. For Marino she planted new Malvasia and Trebbiano vines. Her Marino is rather unique these days because she does the fermentation partly on the skins and ages it in wooden barrels and bottles before selling it. Hence it has a deep amber color and a rich, vaguely caramelized flavor, smooth texture, and a hint of *amabile,* but just a hint.

"I can afford to make it that way because I'm a small, personally involved producer," she said. "I think that's why my Marino has personality and why the mass-produced wine is rather characterless. Now, I don't mean to be snobby about this. You can buy an outfit at Valentino [the Rome designer] or at Standa [a department-store chain] and be perfectly satisfied with each. They're both valid. It depends on what you're looking for."

For the red Colle Picchioni, Signora Di Mauro took advantage of the Merlot, Cabernet, and Sangiovese vines already there, added more of the same, and again followed traditional lines to achieve a wine of rare finesse, worthy of a château. It bears a resemblance to Fiorano, but only a vague one. Both are examples of what can be achieved in the Campagna di Roma with inspiration and a bit of courage.

Courage because the planting of atypical vines is now officially frowned on in Common Market countries. In the Castelli Romani, as in all other classified wine zones, only recognized and approved vines may be planted. Growers nonetheless sometimes put in vines of their own choosing at their own expense, though the practice is forbidden under current EEC policy. So those who want to try something new and different, such as Cabernet Sauvignon or Tocai Friulano in the Alban Hills, are not only denied the financial support that other growers are entitled to but are technically considered to be violating norms, an act for which they could be penalized.

As Paola Di Mauro put it in an uncharacteristic moment of displeasure: "The current policy seems to be aimed at inhibiting the individual with the ambition to try to achieve something special, something extraordinary, perhaps something great. I'm sorry, but I don't think that's any way to maintain a national heritage."

At the Cantina Sociale Cooperativa di Marino, concepts of heritage are of necessity quite different from Paola Di Mauro's. The Marino, Frascati, and non-DOC red and rosé wines sold under the name Gotto d'Oro are standardized, no question about that, but as the cooperative's directors would argue, it is an admirable standard that took a tremendous combined effort to achieve. As a result, some 450 cultivators in the Marino zone now work with a new sense of security and responsibility and perhaps even renewed pride. Theirs is one of the largest and most successful cooperatives of Italy, with three plants and a total capacity of 24 million liters.

Giuseppe De Sanctis, commercial director, explained that in the years before and since the first fully modernized Gotto d'Oro winery went into production in 1973, the program has been directed at achieving and maintaining quality on a mass scale. "We have always aimed at a world market, not just a local or national market, but before we could begin exporting we were compelled to have a product of unquestioned quality," he said. "Exportation has been beneficial because it has kept us constantly alert." De Sanctis noted that some 30 percent of production is exported and the rate is increasing. "I think that's confirmation of success," he said. "But it took time and work. Only lately have we begun to realize the fruits of our labor."

The modern winery system was set up by Ezio Rivella, who still serves as an adviser. Rivella is the leading Italian advocate of the pure and fresh young wines that were a special challenge here because of the oxidation problem. He, perhaps more than any other person, is responsible for the new looks and flavors in the white wines of the Castelli Romani, for the concepts, techniques, and stable results he pioneered at Gotto d'Oro are now emulated by the several cooperatives and numerous private wineries of the six DOC zones.

More Whites and the Lone Castelli Red

Velletri enjoys a measure of renown in Latium for both its white and red wines, but the other DOC white wines of the Castelli, though appreciated locally, have yet to make a widespread impression. There is little to differentiate them from the more popular Frascati and Marino; it seems doubtful that even experienced tasters could always pick them out.

Colli Albani, an extensive zone, includes parts of the communities of Albano, Ariccia, Rome, Pomezia, Ardea, Castelgandolfo, and Lanuvio. Much of its DOC wine, which may be *secco, amabile,* or *spumante,* with a *superiore* of 12.5°, is turned out by the large Cantina Sociale Colli Albani at Cecchina.

Colli Lanuvini, from the southwestern part of the hills around Genzano and Lanuvio, is made only in *secco* and *amabile* with no *superiore.* Giorgio Tupini at Genzano makes a white wine that carries the additional name of Colle San Gennaro. Some Colli Lanuvini wine can be found under the Valle Vermiglia label.

Montecompatri Colonna takes the name of two towns in the northern-most section of the Alban Hills on either side of the Autostrada del Sole. The wine, which may also take the name of either town alone, is made in *secco* and *dolce* versions with a *superiore* of 12.5°. Bottles are not often seen in commerce, even in Rome.

Velletri, at the southern extreme of the hills, seems to enjoy certain advantages that distinguish its wines, particularly the Rosso, the lone DOC red wine of the Alban Hills. The Bianco is sometimes more deli-cate than the others, though some detect a special aroma in both the *secco* and *amabile* versions and a bitter undertone in the flavor. Velletri Rosso is made from almost equal measures of Sangiovese, Montepulciano, and either Cesanese Comune or Cesanese di Affile (or both). Bombino Nero, Merlot, and Ciliegiolo are also permitted at a maximum of 10 per-cent. The result is a dry, well-balanced wine of fairly deep ruby color, smooth and a touch tannic, though it does not age all that well. The Produttori Vini Velletri Consorzio makes very good wines of both colors, as does the Casa Vinicola Pavan at Lariano.

One enthusiastic winemaker of the Alban Hills is Anthony Quinn, the American actor, who has a house near Velletri surrounded by vines. People who have tasted them say the wines are excellent, especially a red he calls Rosso dei Figli. He reportedly does much of the work himself. As far as I know, though, Quinn does not sell the wines commercially. Another producer in the area is Marino Camponeschi, who owns Rome's Piccolo Mondo restaurant and serves his white and exceptionally good red wines from his Vigna Camponeschi there. Principe Pallavicini at Colonna makes good white and red wines sold under the name Mar-morelle.

Cesanese: A Change of Complexion

Zagarolo could almost be considered a Castelli wine because its vine-yards are adjacent and the grapes for the DOC wine are virtually the same as its neighbors'. But the little town with the strange-sounding name lies at the foot of the Prenestina Hills that range off to the south and east toward the borders of the Abruzzi and Campania. Zagarolo Bianco, whether *secco* or *dolce,* is hard to find, except in the town's *trattorie* or *frasche* with their laurel branches above the door advertising its availability. There, if you are adventurous and have a strong stomach, you might even want to try it with *coppiette,* strips of horse or donkey meat dried in the sun and flavored with red peppers.

At Zagarolo the landscape changes abruptly, signaling that the sprawl of latter-day Urbe lies behind and the rugged uplands of southern Latium lie ahead. As you point southeastward toward Frosinone and Monte Cassino, you enter the Ciociaria, a land of oak woods and steep pastures, mixed crop farms, and country towns whose more recent structures are often quaintly superimposed on the building of earlier ages. The wine suddenly changes complexion, too, from white to red. Soon after Palestrina you arrive in the homeland of Cesanese, Latium's lone contribution to the hierarchy of Italian red wines. Not that Cesanese could be considered noble — yet — but it does have the sort of breed to aspire to greater standing.

Three small Cesanese zones have been delimited, all snuggled within a triangle formed by drawing lines between the towns of Palestrina, Subiaco, and Anagni. Why it took three zones to represent what is essentially one wine (with a perplexing range of variations) is hard to determine, though the reason can no doubt be traced to that touchy area of local pride and tradition. All Cesanese, whether of Affile, Piglio, or Olevano Romano, is made from at least 90 percent Cesanese di Affile or Cesanese Comune grapes, usually combined. The remaining 10 percent may consist of Ottonese (also known as Bombino Bianco), Barbera, Montepulciano, Passerana or Passerina (as Trebbiano Toscano is called locally), and Sangiovese.

Cesanese di Affile and Cesanese di Olevano Romano each comprise six styles: *secco, asciutto, amabile, dolce, frizzante,* and *spumante* (the bubbly types are both sweet and refermented naturally). Cesanese del Piglio does not include the *frizzante* and *spumante,* but it does take in the two dry and two sweet versions. All have minimum alcohol of 12°, of which at least 10° must be developed in the sweet wines.

The few experts I know of who have tasted their way through the gamut of Cesanese DOC wines have reacted positively, even enthusiastically, to their quality. Roberto Cuccodoro, assistant director of the Enoteca Trimani in Rome, for one, said he considered certain both dry and sweet versions of Cesanese di Affile outstanding, even if they are nearly impossible to find outside the town.

The Cantina Sociale Cesanese del Piglio makes a dry wine that with moderate aging takes on bright ruby-garnet tones and shows excellent balance between its soft, fruity qualities and a lightly bitter, tannic vein. Equally classy is the dry wine from the Cantina Sociale Vini Tipici Cesanese at Olevano Romano. Cuccodoro also recommends the *dolce* from that cooperative. Cesanese in the dry range is usually served cool and the sweet and bubbly versions are served well chilled.

Production of Cesanese has been increasing, especially in the cooperatives, reason to anticipate seeing more of this promising red wine on the market soon. As a varietal, which it is in all three DOC zones, Cesanese seems to be as well adapted to sweet as dry. That quality is not being ignored by producers here who have watched sweet Lambrusco catch on throughout Italy lately.

Cesanese grapes figure in the composites of several of Latium's finer red wines: Velletri, Castel San Giorgio, and Cerveteri Rosso among them. In a supporting role, Cesanese has made its most convincing showing close to home, in wines from hillsides around Paliano and Anagni. One fine example is La Selva, made from Barbera and Cesanese grapes by Principe Ruffo di Calabria on his vast wooded estate, much of which has been turned into a wildlife preserve open to the public. Together Cesanese and Barbera make a strong, big-bodied wine that, after aging in small barrels of local chestnut wood, develops an inimitable bouquet and a smooth, refined flavor. However, like its name, La Selva retains a hint of its wild surroundings, a trait that makes it all the more attractive with hearty meat dishes and game.

Torre Ercolana: The Melody Lingers On

Anagni, a small but historically propitious town poised on a lofty hilltop like a herald angel, is renowned for its four popes and its Romanesque-Gothic cathedral, setting of the excommunications of Barbarossa and Philip the Fair. However, its attractions are not exclusively of an ecclesiastical nature; Anagni is also noted for its wines, foremost among them a contemporary legend known as Torre Ercolana.

The legend arose in the 1960s after word got around that Luigi Colacicchi, maestro of the Rome Philharmonic Orchestra and a native of Anagni, had a little vineyard back home where he nurtured a red wine so grand that it had to be tasted to be believed. The catch was that

Colacicchi, an artist in more fields than one, was willing to sell only between 800 and 1,500 bottles of Torre Ercolana a year, providing the vintage was up to par.

From the superb 1968 vintage, he drew up two series of labels. On the first he wrote by hand that the reserve consisted of 1,480 bottles; on the second he had printed in red ink that the reserve consisted of 1,396 bottles — a mysterious loss of 84. Marco Trimani, his exclusive retailer, explained the diminution: "The Maestro always set some wine aside to remember his friends with and between the hand-lettered and the printed labels he remembered a few more."

My introduction to Torre Ercolana was with that 1968. I had heard wine described in musical terms before — those allusions to instruments, tempos, sounds that wine writers sometimes resort to when they tire of citing fruit and flowers. But this went beyond mere violins or trumpets, andantes or allegrettos. My first mouthful of Torre Ercolana was like my first earful of Beethoven's Fifth: so overpowering it left me grasping for adjectives to describe it. But, come to think of it, most adjectives would not do anyway. How can you put a symphony into words?

The Maestro is gone now, but the melody lingers on. Upon Luigi Colacicchi's death a few years ago, the legacy of Torre Ercolana passed to his nephew and unsung partner, Bruno Colacicchi, who may try to tell you that all he is doing is trying to follow his uncle's score. Bruno Colacicchi, who tempers his devotion with an easygoing, rather dapper air, his erudition with an engaging dose of small-town humor, nonetheless seems to lack none of his uncle's skill in directing a minuscule but magnificent winemaking operation. There has been no letdown in the quality of Torre Ercolana.

Colacicchi, administrator of the Principe del Piemonte religious society in Anagni, maintains the vaulted subterranean cantina in the heart of the town's medieval quarter where the Colacicchi family has made wine for generations from grapes grown in vineyards outside the town walls. "As you can see, nothing has changed," said Colacicchi, pointing to cobwebs on the ceiling and offering a thick sandwich crammed with slices of local cheese to go with the wine. With a dipper he scooped some deep purple liquid of the 1978 from an open aeration vat into a tumbler, the first of three vintages he offered as a demonstration of how the wine developed.

Colacicchi rated the 1978 vintage the best since 1970, though the wine was still rather coarse with exaggerated fruit, tannin, and color six months after the harvest. The 1977 was almost as good a year, and it was rounding into form. The 1976, a medium year, was nearly ready for bottling. Of the wines in bottle, the 1975 vintage was superb and the 1970, of which only a few bottles remained, was the greatest of all.

"That was one of those years when the Cabernet, Merlot, and Cesanese grapes all matured perfectly," Colacicchi explained. "The secret, the genius of Torre Ercolana is in fact the balance of the local Cesanese against the more precocious French varieties. In hot, dry years the Cesanese develops magnificently and the Cabernet and Merlot less well, but the Cesanese can carry them. Just the opposite occurs in cooler, damper years, when the Cabernet and Merlot carry the Cesanese. That's why you'll taste a marked difference in character in different years but also why we almost never come up with an unacceptable wine."

Success is also due to meticulous care of the tiny vineyard of about 2 acres that produces enough grapes for about 2,000 bottles (a quarter of them a white called Romagnano). Colacicchi is doubling the area in vines for the dark grapes, about one third in each variety, but they will not make acceptable wine until the mid-1980s.

As we tasted the different vintages, one of Colacicchi's two helpers worked a hand pump that moved the 1978 wine first out of the aging cask while the dregs were drawn off and the wine aerated and then back in to spend three months before the next racking. "No new technology here," said Colacicchi. "Even for the white wine (from Malvasia), we do a standard, natural fermentation followed by aging in barrel with four rackings a year. No filtration, sterilization, pasteurization. You won't find wine anywhere that is more natural or made with such loving care. And what do we get for it? The right to call it *vino da tavola*.

"I could, of course, use mostly Cesanese grapes and make a Cesanese del Piglio DOC," he said. "That's what the Ministry of Agriculture advised when I raised the problem with them. But who wants DOC when they can have Torre Ercolana? I tell you, it's insane and getting worse. Lots of winemakers like me in Italy are facing the same obstacles, which seem to have been created to protect the cooperative and big-money interests. Our problem is that we're mostly small and scattered and can't get organized long enough to make our voices heard."

The latest insult was a ruling that non-DOC wine could not be sold with labels indicating the number of bottles made in a given year and could not be called *riserva* or anything similar, he complained. "Besides that, they tell me I can't call the white wine Romagnano anymore, even though that's what the plot of land has been called since time immemorial and is a trademark. You know why? Because there's a wine from around the town of Romagnano Sesia in Piedmont which has been granted exclusive rights to the name, even if it's not DOC."

Colacicchi, who had been alternately puffing and chewing on a long thin cigar as he vented his indignation, suddenly brightened. "Oh, I suppose I shouldn't let it get me down. At least they haven't told me I can't make wine or sell it — yet."

Selling Torre Ercolana is the least of Colacicchi's problems. After his annual allotment to Trimani and his growing list of regular clients, there is scarcely enough left over for his friends, let alone any potential buyers from abroad.

"This American dealer showed up here," said Colacicchi. "What was his name? Nice man. I think he said his family came from Caserta. Anyway, he asked me . . . no, insisted I supply him with three thousand bottles annually. I said, sir, what you're asking for is three years' supply a year. That didn't seem to faze him. Oh well, it's nice to know that even in America they believe in miracles."

Southern Latium: The New vs. the Historic

Bruno Colacicchi is not alone in working with French grapes in the area around Frosinone. The agricultural experimentation center at Sanmichele, near the abbey of Monte Cassino, has been successfully cultivating Cabernet, Pinot, Petite-Sirah, and Sémillon vines whose grapes show up in the wines made at the station and in those of a few other producers. So far, no wines of the southern Ciociaria have been delimited.

Heading southwestward toward the sea from Anagni, after crossing the range of hills known as the Monti Lepini, the road descends into what was once the Pontine Marshes and now is flat and fertile farmland known as the Agro Pontino. On the northern edge of the plain and extending into the hills is the DOC zone of Cori, which covers an area above the town of that name and below it as far as Cisterna on the Appian Way. Cori Bianco is made from the same grape varieties as the Castelli whites and in similar proportions into *secco*, *amabile*, and *dolce* versions of at least 11° alcohol. The Rosso, from Montepulciano at 40 to 60 percent, Nero Buono di Cori at 20 to 40 percent, and Cesanese at 10 to 30 percent, is dry, soft, pleasant enough when drunk fairly fresh.

Aprilia, a homely farm town at the junction of the Via Pontina and the Via Nettunese, gives its name to three DOC wines from the Pontine flatlands between the Castelli Romani, Pomezia, Anzio, and Latina. Merlot d'Aprilia, Sangiovese d'Aprilia, and Trebbiano d'Aprilia are all made from grape types imported from regions to the north. Farmers from the Veneto and Romagna were rewarded for settling here when the marshes were drained in the 1930s because of their experience in working reclaimed land back home. Some have done an admirable job of cultivating vines, though few would pretend this is a prime area for viticulture and some ponder whether Merlot, Sangiovese, and Trebbiano were the best choices of vines. Cabernet vines do extremely well, but the wines often turn out too strong. DOC sets strict standards of production, holding the maximum yields of all three types to 8,000 kilograms per hectare and limiting the transformation of grapes to wine to 60 percent of the weight for Sangiovese and Trebbiano and 65 percent for Merlot. All wines must have 12° or more alcohol and consist of at least 95 percent of the varietal grape.

Most production of both DOC and non-DOC wines of Aprilia is carried out by the immense Cantina Sociale Enotria, whose capacity of some 26.5 million liters surpasses even that of Gotto d'Oro. The wines of Enotria are always acceptable and moderately priced, but they do not rise above the everyday category. Of the three, Merlot tends to be the most impressive after two to three years of aging. Sangiovese is considered a red wine, though it is often closer to rosé in color and body and is best when fairly young and cool. The Trebbiano is usually smooth, balanced, light in body, and is best very young.

The old road through the Pontine Marshes was the Appian Way, but the scenic route south follows the coast, skirting the flatlands that, however productive, are somewhat dreary and out of character in Latium. From Anzio and Nettuno the sand beaches stretch to Sabaudia at the foot of the Circeo peninsula, where the enchantress Circe retained Odysseus and turned his men into swine. On the hills behind the ancient ports of Terracina, Gaeta, and Formia — and south into Campania — grew the vines for the most vaunted wines of ancient Rome, Cecubo and Falernum. Wines of those names are still made hereabouts today, though they are not true to type, for the Romans had a liking for

the sweet and syrupy, sometimes with the added flavors of such pre-
servatives as resin, pitch, salt water, and honey. It would be fascinating
to hear what Cicero, Pliny, Horace, and Virgil would have to say about
the current products, which, in any case, certainly show more intrinsic
virtue than the wines of the Pontine flatlands. Despite their present
quality and historic status, none has gained the protection of DOC.

Two dessert wines of Terracina, the golden Moscato and the deep
red Aleatico, both strong and luxuriant, would seem to fit the Roman
mold better than do the modern Cecubo and Falernum. The Cantina
Cenatiempo at Formia makes a dry but rich and full-bodied Cecubo
from Abbuoto, Negroamaro, and San Giuseppe Nero that ranks among
the finer reds of Latium. The dry, red Monte Giove of Sangiovese and
Cesanese grapes can show special character from some vintages.

The precise home of Falernum is disputed by Latium and Campania;
it seems that the wines of that name in antiquity were produced in both
regions, though the center probably lay in what is now Campania.
Cenatiempo makes a dry, light amber wine called Falernum from Falanghina, Negroamaro, and Cicienello grapes grown in both regions.
That should not be confused with the dry, red Falerno also made by
Cenatiempo and others from Aglianico (the outstanding dark grape of
Campania) along with Negroamaro, San Giuseppe Rosso, Falanghina, and others. Falerno (Italian for the Latin Falernum) is a big,
bold wine of true character, noted for its full aroma that becomes with
age a refined bouquet. Producers of Cecubo, Falernum, and Falerno
have reason to aspire to greater renown for their modern wines that, although they may not share the taste of the old, are certainly due a share
of the antique luster.

The Vintages

	Castelli Romani	Cesanese
1979	Excellent	Excellent
1978	Good	Excellent
1977	Very good	Very good

	Castelli Romani	*Cesanese*
1976	Fair	Poor
1975	Good to excellent	Excellent
1974	Fair to good	Good
1973	Good to excellent	Very good
1972	—	Fair
1971	—	Excellent
1970	—	Excellent

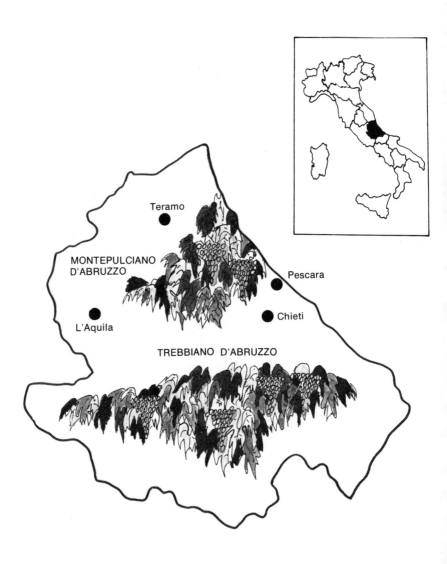

Teramo

MONTEPULCIANO
D'ABRUZZO

Pescara

L'Aquila

Chieti

TREBBIANO D'ABRUZZO

THE ABRUZZI

PROVINCES
L'AQUILA, Chieti, Pescara, Teramo

POPULATION
1,200,000

AREA
4,550 square miles

AVERAGE WINE PRODUCTION
250 million liters

DOC WINES
Montepulciano d'Abruzzo (Cerasuolo) · *Trebbiano d'Abruzzo*

OTHER WINES
*Moscato · Pinot Grigio · Riesling Renano · Sejve Villard 12.375 ·
Spumante · Traminer · Veltliner · Vin Cotto*

Wolves, Bears, and Strong Black Wine

MENTION the Abruzzi to an Italian from somewhere else and you may be told of a lofty wilderness where fiercely proud mountain people share their habitat with wolves, bears, and deer, where crafts such as weaving and pottery making are still going industries, where woodsmen and shepherds keep the womenfolk near the stove as they devour hearty food and drink amply of strong black wine, where quaint customs and costumes remain realities. Most myths contain some truth, perhaps in greater measure when they concern the Abruzzi than some other regions.

Certainly, if you enter the Abruzzi from Latium, between the Gran Sasso and the Maiella ranges with the highest peaks in the Apennines, you may gain the impression of having arrived back at a much earlier point in time. Even from the *autostrade* that link Rome and L'Aquila in an hour and Rome and Pescara in two, you will spot walled and fortified towns, clinging with dramatic severity to rocky spurs above every strategic point of passage, impenetrable, stoic places where today people grow old poking at the coals of wood fires. But even there amid the stones, signs of encroaching modernism strike you: the TV antenna on every still-inhabited dwelling, the general store with packaged pasta in a place where a decade ago no self-respecting housewife would have dreamed of not rolling her own, the Bar Centrale with a shiny new espresso machine hissing steam and with shelves of wine in labeled bottles from the *cantina sociale* down the valley.

As for the wolves, bears, and deer, most of the few that remain roam in the Abruzzi National Park. The woodsmen and shepherds are still around too, but like weavers and pottery makers, they are fewer in number with the passing years. Even the hearty food and strong black wine can still be found, though neither seems as potent as it used to be.

"I agree that it's sad to see the old things go," said Rino Moretti, who may be the region's most respected innovator in the field of oenology, "but let's face it, if new techniques and ideas hadn't been introduced

Rino Moretti (left) with Casal Thaulero cellar worker

here, the wine of the Abruzzi would still be unknown outside the region, as it was in the 1960s. You can get as nostalgic as you want about country wine and all its alleged virtues, but the fact is that most country people are incapable of making wine of consistent quality. And I don't mean from one year to the next — after all, we all have to deal with good and bad vintages — but from one barrel to the next or one bottle to the next. I'm all in favor of the little guy who makes wine, but if he wants to compete on the market, he can't ignore rational techniques any more than a large operation can."

Moretti, who designed the winemaking facilities of the Casal Thaulero cooperative at Roseto degli Abruzzi and guided the winery through the formative years as it quickly became the region's model for quality on a significant scale, has recently gone into partnership in an independent firm called Meridiana. Like most winemakers I encountered in the region, Moretti expressed undivided optimism about the future of

Abruzzi wine, which in less than a decade has emerged on national and international markets and gained a reputation for quality and value. The consensus is that the Abruzzi has only begun to exploit its potential for quality wine.

Though the region is not especially large and its prime agricultural land is limited to the hills along the Adriatic and valleys along the rivers that drain its high mountains, the Abruzzi has increased production of DOC wine beyond the approximate tenth that corresponds to the national average. Its two lone DOC categories, Montepulciano d'Abruzzo and Trebbiano d'Abruzzo, are regionwide, a situation that many producers now view as inopportune but that does allow for handy consumer identification.

Montepulciano d'Abruzzo actually comprises two types of wine, a red and a rosé known as Cerasuolo for its cherry hue. The two Montepulciano types, whose basic alcohol must be 12°, may include up to 15 percent Sangiovese. Trebbiano, whose base grape may be either Trebbiano d'Abruzzo or Trebbiano Toscano or a combination of the two, may also include up to 15 percent Malvasia Toscana, Cococciola, and Passerina grapes. Its minimum alcohol is 11.5°. The red Montepulciano may be called *vecchio* when aged two years.

Some winemakers of the Abruzzi complain that the regionwide classifications do not take into account special zones of viticultural excellence. Although most producers have been too busy building and improving wineries and vineyards since Montepulciano was recognized in 1967 and Trebbiano was tapped in 1972, indications are that requests may eventually be made to the national committee for individual recognition of certain zones, or at least for the right to cite their names as subdenominations on the label.

The Mystery of Montepulciano

The Montepulciano vine reigns supreme in the Abruzzi. Appreciated for its heartiness and the robust generosity of its grapes, it accounts for some three-quarters of the region's DOC production. Montepulciano d'Abruzzo ranks among the ten most prominent DOC wines of Italy, with a volume of some 15 million to 18 million liters a year. The name Montepulciano comes from the Tuscan town where Vino Nobile is made, no question about that, but it is by no means certain that the vine originated there.

Two theories exist about how the vine, which is now more heavily diffused in the Abruzzi than anywhere else and the cultivation of which has spread into all neighboring regions, came to be called Montepulciano. One is that centuries ago, when the wool merchants of the Florentine Republic opened trade routes into the grazing land of the Abruzzi, Tuscan traders introduced a vine from their home to the Abruzzesi, who adopted it and gradually made it their preferred source of wine.

The second supposition, the more plausible to the Abruzzesi, is that the Tuscan wool traders noted the similarity in a native vine of the Abruzzi and the Sangiovese Grosso of Montepulciano and the native vine came to be called *tipo Montepulciano*. Over the years, the *tipo* was dropped and the name Montepulciano stuck. Backing the second thesis is the evidence that Montepulciano vines are to be found in the Marches, Umbria, Latium, Campania, Molise, and Apulia, within a radius whose axis is the Abruzzi. Curiously, the vine is not often cultivated today around Montepulciano or in most other parts of Tuscany, and evidence indicates that it may never have been. The Abruzzesi reason that if the Montepulciano vine had been in Tuscany all along, it probably would have superseded the Sangiovese vine because in many ways it seems superior. However, it matures later and Tuscany is somewhat cooler than the Abruzzi.

Leaving such regional differences aside, it seems clear that Montepulciano does extremely well in much of the Abruzzi whose growing conditions in certain sections can rival nearly any of the peninsula. As one producer put it, "We've got the southern sun and Adriatic influence combined with a somewhat northerly climate and terrain. If you pick the spot carefully, you can virtually duplicate any of the prime wine zones of the north — Piedmont, Tuscany, Friuli, even Alto Adige."

As for Trebbiano, the theory is that the vine called Trebbiano d'Abruzzo or Trebbiano Nostrano derived from the Bombino Bianco of Apulia. But Trebbiano Toscano did indeed come from Tuscany. Different winemakers favor one or the other, sometimes depending on climate. In cooler places, the Tuscan variety seems to thrive and under warmer conditions the Abruzzi version does better. Overall, Trebbiano Toscano appears to be gaining the upper hand for its resistance and for its adaptability to modern vinification methods. Its grapes are supposedly less subject to oxidation than are those of Trebbiano d'Abruzzo.

The Cassa per i Mezzogiorno, the fund for development of the south, has pumped money into the Abruzzi's winemaking facilities with results particularly noticeable in the cooperatives. Casal Thaulero stands out as the first Abruzzi winery to establish itself internationally. The cooperative, which draws its grapes from vineyards in the hills above the Adriatic resort of Roseto degli Abruzzi, has a capacity of some 16 million liters, much of it DOC or at least with the potential to be DOC. Casal Thaulero produces much more Montepulciano, both red and Cerasuolo, than Trebbiano. From each good vintage a select 300,000 to 350,000 liters of red are aged for two years in oak barrels and sold as the winery's prestige product, one of the better cooperative wines of central Italy. The new chief oenologist at Casal Thaulero is Giulio Silvestri.

Rino Moretti, who still speaks proudly of the winery where he spent ten years, credits Casal Thaulero's success to the vinification system, which he designed himself, and to the innate quality of the area's grapes, especially Montepulciano. Moretti, a native of Umbria and a graduate of Conegliano in the Veneto, is convinced that Montepulciano is one of Italy's great red wine grapes, more important than Sangiovese.

"Sangiovese does well in some places, such as Montalcino, but not so well in others," said Moretti, "and where it doesn't do so well you get wines weak in color and body. Let me tell you a secret. If you take a lightweight Chianti and blend it with a little Montepulciano d'Abruzzo, you'll notice a marked improvement in tone. People in the Abruzzi have known that for ages, which explains why Sangiovese never caught on here the way it did in other regions. Here we sometimes use Sangiovese to tone down the Montepulciano when it gets too big and strong. But basically, when Montepulciano is carefully made, Sangiovese isn't needed."

Several producers in the Abruzzi noted that Montepulciano's role as a blending wine is not a thing of the past. It not only gives a boost to Chianti but reportedly does wonders for Barbera and Valpolicella, even today. "Not so much goes north now, because we keep more at home to bottle and sell," said Moretti, "but the demand is still there."

"Enormous Possibilities"

Giovanni Alberton, a specialist in viticulture and oenology from the Veneto, who makes wines called Duchi di Castelluccio, backs Moretti's enthusiasm for Montepulciano and even carries the case a step beyond. "I think Montepulciano is in a class with Nebbiolo," said Alberton, who worked with the Nebbiolo grape in the excellent Antica Casa Vinicola

Scarpa at Nizza Monferrato in Piedmont before he came to the Abruzzi. "Look at that texture," he said, swirling some wine from the 1975 vintage around in a glass and observing its legs. "It has everything a modern red wine needs . . . body, color, strength, aroma, depth of flavor. It was once believed that Montepulciano was naturally rougher than most other red wines, but I'm convinced that was a consequence of old vinification methods used here. Today, with a controlled fermentation, Montepulciano can be turned into a wine of unquestioned greatness."

Like many progressive winemakers in Italy, Alberton does not feel harnessed by traditional practices such as long fermentation and excessive barrel age. In fact, for Duchi di Castelluccio, barrels have been rejected as detrimental to the development of Montepulciano's complete attributes. "Bottle age, not barrel age, is the essential factor in developing Montepulciano's bouquet," said Alberton. "The wine has so much to it already that it doesn't need the woodiness and tannin that a barrel would give it. We feel the balance is better arrived at by letting the wine express itself."

Duchi di Castelluccio is the trade name of Scali-Caracciolo, a private winery whose first vines were planted in 1971 and which has already created a flurry whose impact is being felt beyond the region. The property of Francesco Scali, whose mother was a descendant of the Caracciolo family that owned the castle of the Duchi di Castelluccio at nearby Alanno, the winery sits atop a hill overlooking the Rome-Pescara *autostrada* near Scafa beside the Via Tiburtina, exactly 200 kilometers from Rome. Scali, formerly a textile manufacturer, recently directed his financial resources and exceptional drive into his new venture, which he is determined to make into a leader among Italian wineries that work exclusively with their own grapes. He is expanding vineyard capacity to produce about 700,000 bottles a year, double the 1979 figure, with an eventual goal of 1 million bottles a year.

Despite the recentness of planting, the wines from 1975 were already exemplary. The 1977 and 1978 vintages produced wines of excellent tone, and the 1979 vintage was extraordinary, especially for the red Montepulciano. The Trebbiano, which is 100 percent Toscano, shows Alberton's northern touch with white wines. Scali and Alberton are not stopping at the DOC level. They used Montepulciano grapes to make a sparkling white wine by the charmat method and a Recioto Amarone–style red. Both, as far as I know, are unique in the Abruzzi and reflect the dynamic imagination of the owner and the talent of the wine-maker.

"We have enormous possibilities here," said Scali, "and I'm not speaking of ourselves alone, but other wineries as well. We're encouraging others to follow our lead when we do something successfully, because by working together we can generate more impact than any of us could alone."

Scafa, in the valley of the Pescara River some 30 kilometers inland from Pescara, was known for the quality of its wines when the Romans founded a town called Interprominius. The chalky clay soil here is enriched in places by gypsum, which is reputed to give the wines greater harmony and fragrance. The zone, as one of those privileged places, will certainly be the object of quests for individual recognition one of these days. Among Scali's manifold programs to upgrade the zone's image is an *enoteca* in the twelfth-century Castello Caracciolo, the family castle, a project of restoration that was begun in 1979. Scali planned to display the Abruzzi's finer wines there, along with bottles from other parts of Italy, all exclusively estate-bottled.

The trend in the Abruzzi, as elsewhere, is toward thoroughly modern methods of winemaking on a relatively large scale, exemplified by the better cooperatives and such private enterprises as Duchi di Castelluccio and Rino Moretti's new Meridiana at Caldari above the seaside town of Ortona. Meridiana's wines from 1978 were introduced locally in 1979, even before the winemaking facilities were completely finished. Some new large wineries need a shakedown vintage or two before they begin to hit their stride, but Moretti, by now very comfortable with Montepulciano and Trebbiano, coasted into his new venture as a seasoned pro and made Meridiana an overnight success.

"Winemaking, as an applied science, is largely a matter of technique," said Moretti, an articulate progressive who somehow manages not to sound chauvinistic when he states that Italy now has the best grapes, the best winemaking facilities, the best oenologists, and, overall, the best wines on earth. "Combine all that with the least effective system of promotion and sales of any major wine nation, and you can understand how Italy can sell in the United States three times as much wine as France does and make less money at it. The French consider themselves individualists, but they can't touch us Italians," said Moretti. "Imagine what could be done if each producer were to put a token amount, a few lire per bottle, into a promotional fund to improve the image of our wine internationally, as the French have done through their SOPEXA. But do you think that will ever happen? Don't count on it. In Italy, it's every man for himself."

The Rugged Individualists: Valentini and Pepe

The Abruzzi harbors some truly rugged individualists, devotees of artisanal winemaking who scoff at such concepts as cold fermentation, pasteurization, sterile filtration, and so on, and continue to produce wine and sell it on a personal basis. Some do so out of economic necessity because they cannot afford the new equipment or the time to learn new techniques, and they resolutely refuse to take part in cooperative ventures. A few others persist out of a studied conviction that theirs is the only way to make wine that is *naturale, genuino,* and *di carattere.*

An outspoken exponent of this philosophy is Edoardo Valentini, who studied to be a lawyer like his father, quickly decided that law was not for him, and opted for agriculture instead. So, as a young man with a degree in jurisprudence and a distaste for city life, he moved into the family *palazzo* in the pretty country town of Loreto Aprutino, a place previously used for weekend retreats and summer holidays, and against his family's wishes set himself up as a farmer. Valentini, however, is not an ordinary farmer. He lives in one of the most imposing homes in town, directly in front of the town castle, with a terrace affording views on clear days across the rolling hills of Aprutino to the snow-capped peaks of the Maiella. The interior has touches of nineteenth-century elegance interspersed with clutters of magazines and books.

"I'm a compulsive reader," Valentini explained, "and my favorite subject is oenology. I've read every work I know of on the subject, everything, including the tracts on modern technology. And you know who my favorite is, the one I most often turn to? Columella. That's right, the Roman. Do you know that almost everything that's happening in oenology today was known to some extent by Columella. The secrets were there nearly two thousand years ago."

Valentini, bearded and wearing a plain short-sleeved shirt, baggy safari-style trousers, and boots, folded his arms and leaned against the wall of his terrace as he explained how he attains wines that have been hailed as artisan masterpieces.

The key is selection. From 125 acres in Montepulciano and Trebbiano d'Abruzzo (not Toscano, he insists), Valentini selects only the grapes of optimum quality to be made into wine in the cellars of his home. The rest are sold to other producers. Valentini grows enough grapes to make some 350,000 bottles of wine a year, but he chooses to work with only enough to make about 20,000, and then only in good years. From the weak vintages of 1972 and 1976, he made just enough to keep his barrels filled. ("If you don't, they dry out," he explained). But that wine was sold off in demijohns. Even in good years, the wine that ends up in bottles is subjected to his most exacting chemical and sensory control and only the best ends up in bottles. His few pieces of modern equipment are labor-saving devices, such as an electric crusher and a pump. Otherwise, his is a traditional operation all the way, with normal fermentation and barrel age for both Montepulciano and Trebbiano, though the white wine is not aged in wood as long as the red is.

Because other Abruzzi winemakers are more skilled with red than white wine, Valentini's Montepulciano might have some competition in the quality field. But the Trebbiano is in a class by itself, unquestionably the finest wine of that name I have tasted. The 1974 Trebbiano d'Abruzzo, drunk in 1979, had everything a dry white wine should have plus the elegance, breed, and strength of character that even some of the finest lack. I would not hesitate to compare it to the white wines of Puligny Montrachet.

"I could have a profitable operation if I chose to mass-produce wine from my grapes," said Valentini. "But no thanks. You've got to love it to go through what I do to make my kind of wine, but I just wouldn't have it any other way. It's hard work and it doesn't pay, but wine is my way of committing myself."

It is also his *divertimento*, a recurring amusement that Valentini shares with his vineyard-cellar crew every time a barrel is ready. "We start about five A.M. by tapping the barrel and sometimes we go on through the whole day and night and well into the next day before we're finished. It's all done with a siphon tube directly from barrel to bottle and it's essential that it be done in one continuous operation and that no more than a half-minute pass from when the bottle is full until it's corked (with a simple hand-lever apparatus). It's crazy, I know," said Valentini. "We eat and drink and take turns napping and working. By the time we're done we're exhausted and dizzy, but it's a great *festa* and everybody looks forward to the next one."

Another idiosyncrasy is the black bottles that Valentini uses for all his wine, red and white. He buys them exclusively from the Vetreria Dego of Savona in Liguria at ridiculous expense. They resemble in shape Burgundy and Barolo bottles, except that they are heavier and darker.

"Light is the enemy of wine," said Valentini, "but, of course, I'm talking about live wine and not the sterilized kind usually found in commerce. The black bottles keep light out and allow the wine to live longer. They're especially important for white wine. And, by the way, I think white wine, dry white wine racked and treated naturally, can be made to last up to ten years keeping its qualities intact. Pasteurization is an expediency that inhibits the wine's natural development."

Corks and labels are also extravagances. The labels, based on a bookplate illustration from the 1500s and designed by Valentini, depict a man in medieval garb holding a sign bearing the wine's name, with a row of vines and a mountain in the background. "The man is me," explained Valentini, "and the mountain is the Maiella."

Although he does not make it himself, Valentini keeps a small barrel of Vin Cotto (cooked wine) in his cellar as a traditional offering of hospitality in the Abruzzi, even though almost nobody makes it anymore. He gave me my first taste of a wine that is made by cooking down must into a syrupy consistency in which the sugar is heavily concentrated. Then fresh must is added and fermented out to about 18° to 20° of alcohol, a process that resembles one of the steps in making Marsala. This Vin Cotto was singular, deep brown, rather dry, with a slight burned-caramel taste and a touch of acidity that made it an excellent *digestivo*.

Emidio Pepe may be even more of a purist than Valentini. He crushes his grapes by foot and, as far as I could see, possesses not a single piece of modern equipment in his rustic winery adjacent to his newly built house at Torano Nuovo in the province of Teramo. Pepe, who produces about 40,000 bottles a year, two-thirds Montepulciano, the rest Trebbiano, is a believer in bottle age. He uses no barrels, only glass-lined vats, and once the wines are fermented, racked, and settled, he puts them in bottles carefully piled horizontally in his aging rooms. Then, before selling them, he transfers the contents of each bottle to another, leaving any sediment behind.

"I want to keep my wine young as long as possible," he explained, and that is why, using artisanal methods, he avoids the inevitable contact with air that barrels and large storage vats imply. Like Valentini, Pepe believes that Trebbiano, when fermented in a natural way followed by three months in vat and then into bottle with no filtration or stabilization, can be made to last from good vintages. From weak vintages, he makes wine "the way it turns out," and sells it for what he thinks it is worth. For example, in 1976 when the Trebbiano developed only 10° alcohol, he made a *frizzante* that was so appreciated that he ended up

Emidio Pepe

selling it for the same price as wine from better years. By Abruzzi standards Pepe's wines are expensive, but considering the work behind each bottle they are by no means out of line.

Pepe works the land with the help of his wife and a hired hand. He adamantly refuses to add anything to the wine apart from the absolute minimum of sulfur that is simply unavoidable in a commercial wine. He develops his own fermentation yeasts by picking 10 kilograms or so of grapes and letting them sit for ten days before the harvest.

Pepe, who started bottling wine in 1964 from vineyards that his father used for bulk wines, has stuck stubbornly to his philosophy of total naturalness, to such an extent that other Abruzzesi, from local farmers to progressive oenologists regard him, as did his father at first, as a fanatic. A self-taught winemaker, Pepe accepts the fortunes of each vintage. He considers consistency in wine from year to year not only undesirable but dishonest, and he wastes no words in criticizing producers who achieve such results. Still, he is not in the least stuffy or old-fashioned in his life-style. He lives in a spacious modern house, drives a new car, wears clothes that might be described as trendy. His sales techniques are hardly slick, but by 1979 he had arranged to ship some wine to the United States. He was encouraged by the results of a tasting by the Friends of Wine Club of Chicago in 1979, in which his Montepulciano from 1970 was ranked first out of ten red wines tasted (nine Italian), including a host of Barolos, a Brunello di Montalcino, and a California Nebbiolo (which finished last). Little things like that mean a lot to as dedicated a winemaker as Emidio Pepe.

The Abruzzi's Special Zones

By now, patterns of quality winemaking in the Abruzzi have developed to the point that select zones can be singled out. A leading area, especially for Montepulciano, is in the province of Teramo in the hills between the Vibrata and Tronto rivers, south of the border of the Marches and west of Alba Adriatica on the coast. Emidio Pepe, Dino Illuminati, Antonio Scialletti, and Barone Cornacchio are leading names there. To the south, around Giulianova and Roseto degli Abruzzi are the towns of Mosciano Sant'Angelo, Morro d'Oro, and Notaresco, where the Casal Thaulero cooperative dominates production.

In the province of Pescara, Loreto Aprutino, Città Sant'Angelo, and Scafa are outstanding. Valentini, Duchi di Castelluccio, and Nestore Bosco are respected names.

The province of Chieti in the south is a major source of table grapes (the Abruzzi ranks second behind Apulia in their production). The area is also noted for its blending wines, but there is new emphasis on bottled wines from such special areas as Caldari, Poggio Fiorito, and Miglianico. The Cantina Sociale di Tollo and Consorzio Vino d'Abruzzo at Ortona are large-scale cooperatives. Independent producers with good reputations are Meridiana and Gaetano Petrosemolo.

L'Aquila, the region's capital, includes most of the high mountains in its province that covers the western half of the Abruzzi and is more noted for ski resorts and wildlife than wine. Traditionally, Montepulciano was turned into rosé here, apparently because grapes could not always develop the strength and pigmentation required for robust reds. Still, there are valleys where Montepulciano and Trebbiano thrive, most conspicuously the Valtirino around the town of Ofena, where Janni Vittorio, the leading winery of L'Aquila, has its vineyards. Another good winery in the province is Di Prospero at Pratola Peligna.

L'Aquila, at more than 2,000 feet above sea level, is named after the eagle given it as a symbol by Emperor Friedrich II of Hohenstaufen in 1240. An attractively austere city of massive stone ramparts, it has a magic number, 99, that recurs in many of its ancient structures and symbols.

Montepulciano and Trebbiano monopolize the region's oenology to the point that no other wine of real importance, at least commercially, is made here. Sangiovese is used almost exclusively for mixing with Montepulciano; I know of no place where it dominates a wine. Moscato is grown in various parts of the region, most notably along the Pescara River valley, but it seems to be declining in favor. Although some high points in the region seem amply suited to northerly vines, only scattered attempts to make wine from them have been noted. Still, some experimentation with new vines has been underway. A French hybrid known as Sejve Villard 12.375 has been used to make white wine in the Peligna valley in the province of L'Aquila. At Pratola Peligna, Santoro Colella has been producing wine from northerly grapes — Traminer, Riesling Renano, Pinot Grigio, and Veltliner, among them — though on a limited scale.

Vin Cotto production seems to be approaching extinction at an even greater rate than the region's wolves, who still now and then wander away from the game reserves long enough to plunder a few sheep and gain some notice in the nation's newspapers, but just often enough to keep the myth alive.

The Cooking: A Life-and-Death Matter

Abruzzi cooking divides neatly into two categories — land and sea — with obvious geographical delineations. Food from the land is nutritious, tasty, often piquant, served in portions to keep outdoors-oriented people strong and happy. Regional *gourmandise* is epitomized by *la panarda*, a feast of epic dimensions. Although served to celebrate important events and holidays, it is taken quite seriously by the Abruzzesi. Outsiders have been known to balk after the initial couple of dozen opening dishes have been served. One such was Edoardo Scarfoglio, a journalist from Naples who during a tour of the region at the beginning of the century was invited to take part in a *panarda*. After digging into the opening rounds with relish, unaware of what was still to come, Scarfoglio announced contentedly that he was full. His hosts suddenly turned silent and stared at the writer until finally an old man at the head of the table arose, left the room, and quickly returned with a rifle. Pointing it at Scarfoglio, he said: "Eat or I'll shoot you." Scarfoglio ate.

La panarda is rarely as challenging now as it was in the good old days; today, twenty-five or thirty dishes will do where once upon a time the number could run to twice that many. The specialties involved are too numerous to list, but you could be certain to find excellent cured and cooked hams among them, along with sausages and salami, often enlivened with pimentos and other sharply flavored ingredients. Pasta dishes would certainly include *maccheroni alla chitarra,* so called because its rectangular noodles are formed by passing the rolled dough through the strings of an instrument that resembles a guitar, and *scrippelle,* a crêpe layered into a lasagnalike timbale with various meats and vegetables and cheese. There are also *gnocchi* and soups dominated by vegetables and flavored with herbs. Pork and mutton pie vie as the most popular meats, depending largely on the locale. In high pasture areas, grilled and roast lamb is popular, and everywhere *porchetta* and other pork preparations are popular. Chicken, turkey, veal, and trout can also be special here. *La panarda,* if you find it (restaurants rarely even attempt it), will be washed down by Montepulciano, either red or Cerasuolo or both, also in formidable quantity. Good inland food can be found at the Tre Marie in L'Aquila, the Centrale in Teramo, and Tatobbe in Penne, among other places.

Seafood is similar in type to that found all along the Adriatic, simply grilled, fried, baked, or boiled and served with that touch of herbs, oil, and occasionally a light sauce that leave the fish the protagonist. Fish soups and chowders, however, may be strongly flavored with peppers, garlic, herbs, including saffron, which is grown in certain places in the Abruzzi. Young Trebbiano is the obvious regional choice with seafood, which is invariably fresh at such noted seaside restaurants as La Nave at Francavilla, Beccaceci in Giulianova, and Guerino in Pescara.

The Vintages

	Montepulciano	Trebbiano
1979	Excellent	Excellent
1978	Excellent	Excellent
1977	Excellent	Excellent
1976	Fair	Poor
1975	Excellent	Excellent
1974	Exceptional	Excellent
1973	Excellent	Very good
1972	Fair	Poor
1971	Fair	Good
1970	Fair	Good
1969	Poor	—
1968	Great	—

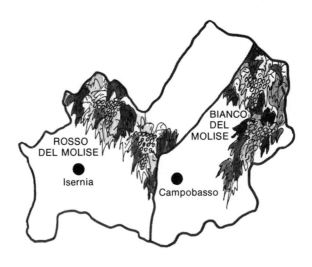

ROSSO
DEL MOLISE

Isernia

BIANCO
DEL
MOLISE

Campobasso

MOLISE

PROVINCES

CAMPOBASSO, Isernia

POPULATION

333,000

AREA

1,334 square miles

AVERAGE WINE PRODUCTION

40 million liters

WINES

Aglianico · Barbera · Bianco del Molise · Bombino Bianco · Montepulciano · Moscato · Ramitello · Rosato del Molise · Rosso del Molise · San Barbato · Sangiovese · Trebbiano

The Forgotten Region

MOLISE has been an independent region since 1963, but it is still often thought of as an appendix of the Abruzzi. More often than not its agricultural production, like its other statistics, are lumped into the sum of its neighbor to the north in what is still referred to as Abruzzo e Molise. Well, Molise, Italy's forgotten region, may be a land of modest means and modest aspirations, but it is not as desolate as some people make it out to be.

I tried in Rome to get some facts and figures about Molise's wine production, but the only information I could obtain came from a taxi driver, a friendly sort who hailed from near Campobasso. "Oh my God," he exclaimed, when I told him I was planning a wine tour of his home region, "you won't find anything worthwhile there. If you like wine, why don't you go up to Piedmont?" It turned out the driver was a tee-totaler, a condition which he attributed to "unfortunate experiences as a youth." Molise is the only region without a DOC wine, and the little advance knowledge I could gather about the place from bits and pieces scrounged out of literature on Abruzzo e Molise seemed to bear out the taxi driver's warning.

As one drives in from the Abruzzi, northwestern Molise does not make a bad initial impression, at least in terms of mountain scenery. It is a bit too high there for commercial production, but there is no lack of neat little vineyards for home winemaking. In fact, as I was to learn in Campobasso, of the region's 53,000 farms, 34,800 have vineyards, so simple country wine is not difficult to find.

Funds from the Cassa per il Mezzogiorno have modernized the two main cities, Campobasso and Isernia, almost overnight (at a rate that, if it continues, by the year 2000 may find the entire urban population of southern Italy living in prefabricated boxes), and linked them with fast roads. New factories around the towns and along the river valleys have played a role in reducing the farm population to 50 percent of the total and leaving the country villages largely to widows in black and old men who still move about on donkeys.

Funds for vine cultivation have been scarcer here than elsewhere because Molise has never shown a clear-cut aptitude for quality wine. It has no solid tradition, no colorful history; until recently it had not so much as a labeled bottle to show for its oenological prowess. Still, as I learned in an inspired briefing at the office of the Regional Assessor of Agriculture, the situation is by no means hopeless.

"We see certain advantages in starting from scratch," said Paolo Dalena, an official who obligingly provided literature, documents, and figures to show that there is indeed something happening in the world of Molise wine. Among other points, Molise's average production surpasses Liguria's and Valle d'Aosta's, and has even outstripped Basilicata's some years. "This is a young, forward-looking region, whose only fault is that it was late getting started," said Dalena. "We've got a program to develop two DOC wines based on grape varieties found to be best suited to Molise's climate and geographical conditions by a team led by Michele Vitagliano of Bari, one of Italy's most respected experts in the field."

Rosso del Molise will consist of Montepulciano at 75 to 80 percent with Trebbiano Toscano or possibly other red varieties included, depending on the location. Bianco del Molise will consist of Bombino Bianco at 65 to 70 percent and other light grapes as suggested by the experts for each area. In addition, quality table wines will be encouraged, the reds from Montepulciano, Aglianico, and Barbera, and the whites from Malvasia del Chianti, Bombino Bianco, and Moscato Bianco.

The zones to be included in the production of DOC wines have been determined. And, with the limited funds available, vines are being planted and cooperatives are being developed. After a thorough study of terrain and meteorological conditions, Vitagliano concluded that the Adriatic side of Molise has some localities with good to excellent prospects for quality wine, comparable to such privileged zones as Campania's Avellino hills and Basilicata's Vulture.

Dalena explained that the program was aimed at obtaining maximum quality — and quantity — through the most rational types of vine cultivation in each zone. The coastal area of Campobasso province is considered the most important. "We're trying to avoid the errors older regions are still working to overcome," said Dalena. "In the past we often copied Apulia, but now we're going to build our own image by doing things in a scientific way. We want wine of moderate alcoholic grade with more aroma than the stronger wines of southern regions."

On paper, the plan seemed promising, certainly ambitious, though the total commitment to cooperatives could prove to be as unfruitful as it has been in other regions. In 1978, Molise's cooperatives had the facilities to produce 40 percent of the wine, but they worked at only two-thirds capacity, meaning that three-quarters of the region's wine was being produced by independents who could expect no more for any effort to upgrade quality than lukewarm moral support.

Anyone who ventures a qualitative assessment of the work of Italian cooperatives these days risks being labeled a wine snob, capitalist pig, and worse. Nonetheless, I submit that the overwhelming majority of *cantine sociali,* however admirable their purposes, have not lived up to expectations. Many would be commercial failures were it not for the generous subsidies, incentives, and guarantees provided by regional, federal, and Common Market programs. Granted, some cooperatives produce excellent wines that rank with the best of their type, but they are the exception, not the rule. Many suffer from what *Civiltà del Bere* once described as "congenital weaknesses" — poor planning, inexperience, lack of organization, difficulty in selling their products. With the sort of support given a cooperative, *Civiltà del Bere* speculated, "a private concern would easily be launched into orbit; the cooperative, on the other hand, barely manages to keep afloat."

The cooperative movement, particularly in undeveloped regions such as Molise, is designed to be the instrument of viticultural and oenological development. But valid as the idea may be, the result is too often a flop. By providing modest financial support and incentives to the private sector — with strings attached, of course — some regions might achieve their aims of developing vineyards and providing employment and security to cultivators, spend less money, and come up with better wine. Granted, there is a need for everyday wine at everyday prices, but at the rate at which the cooperatives have been turning it out the nation runs the risk of being flooded with mediocre wine of little market value, while neglecting the high-quality wine that certain private producers (some of whom barely break even or operate at a loss) and a chosen few cooperatives contribute to raising the image and the value of Italian wine in general.

An Idea Whose Time Had Come

In Molise neither the cooperatives nor private wineries have been developed to the point that valid comparisons between products of the two can be made. To sample the wine of one cooperative and the private producer who asserts that he was the first of Molise to sell wine in labeled bottles, I spent an afternoon driving through much of the province of Campobasso, first to Guglionesi, a short distance from the Adriatic city of Termoli, and then back down to Gambatesa through the arid hill country bordering Apulia. The trip was instructive and rewarding. Indications are that Molise has a future in the field of quality wine production that can be equated to that of neighboring Abruzzi and northern Apulia.

The Cantina Valbiferno di Guglionesi is the largest of Molise's cooperatives and the most promising, highlighted by the fact that its president is Michele Vittorino Monte, Regional Assessor of Agriculture. Housed in a pair of low-slung red buildings surrounded by asphalt in the middle of the flat Biferno valley, the winery lacks the sort of appearance that warrants depiction on a label, but it did appear to meet the contemporary requirements of size and function. I was greeted there by Donato Bagordo, an oenologist from Locorotondo in Apulia, wearing jeans and a denim jacket as he supervised the early stages of the 1979 vintage, the fourth for the cooperative.

Bagordo, an amiable pragmatist not about to get excited about the glories of cooperative winemaking, was nonetheless encouraged about the quality of the current vintage and confident that his bottled and labeled wines would find a growing market. While others in Molise talked about a great year, Bagordo would concede only that 1979 looked "very good at this stage, not abundant." He expected to process some 7.5 million liters of wine in 1979, 30 percent more than the previous year and five times as much as in the initial 1976 vintage. "We've got more members and more new vines coming into production," he explained. The Cantina Valbiferno has been producing about 80 percent red wine and the rest white, but Bagordo expected the split to even out eventually because the Biferno valley seems to have a predilection for white.

Tasted straight from the vat, the white and red wines from the 1978 vintage were impressive, clearly above average cooperative wines. Cantina Valbiferno is obviously designed to be Molise's model winery and leading experimental station. From the looks of things, it is well on the way to success. Bagordo, who has an assistant and a staff of viticultural advisers, can also count on advice from Professors Vitagliano and Carmine Liuni of Bari. The Molise region has been developing cooperatives at Campomarino (second in importance), Macchia d'Isernia, Valtappino, San Zenone, Monte Roduni, and Montenero di Bisaccia, all of which will eventually sell wine in bottles as well as bulk.

Many private wineries are small in scale, and only a few sell wine in bottles. Among those who do are Majo Morante and Giulio Silvio at Campomarino, Petrella in the Biferno valley, and Serra Meccaglia and Francesco d'Alessandro at Gambatesa.

Francesco d'Alessandro planted specialized vineyards in 1971 in the Piano della Noce below Gambatesa, and by 1975 he was selling what he believed to be the first bottled and labeled wine of Molise. He makes a Rosso and Rosato from Montepulciano and Sangiovese and a Bianco from Trebbiano Toscano and Bombino Bianco, all sold under the estate name Sanbarbato. D'Alessandro was almost certainly the first producer of Molise to export wine to the United States — a small but possibly significant shipment in 1979.

Following the advice of an oenologist from Ortona in the Abruzzi, D'Alessandro set up a modern winemaking facility and plunged ahead. "The main problem was in getting farmers to adjust to the new concepts of cultivation we follow (using the low-arbor type of *tendone* rather than the traditional head-trained *alberello* method) and to making wine in an up-to-date way," said D'Alessandro. He shrugged modestly at the suggestion that he showed pioneer spirit, replying that making and selling high-quality wine in Molise was merely an idea whose time had come.

The wines of Sanbarbato are convincing, well made and attractively packaged, worthy of being sold nationally and abroad. Other private wineries have also begun to produce Bianco, Rosso, and Rosato, following various formulas; some were also making varietals under the names Montepulciano, Moscato, Sangiovese, Trebbiano, Barbera, and Bombino Bianco. Majo Morante uses the name Ramitello for his wines.

The choice of bottles available from the region now range into double figures. With the emerging cooperative products due out soon, it appears that Molise, at long last, is about to appear as a separate entity on Italy's wine map.

The Vintages

Vintage ratings have not been established in Molise, though among recent harvests 1979, 1977, and 1975 were very good to excellent; 1978 varied from fair to good; and 1976 was generally poor.

SOLOPACA

Benevento

TAURASI

Caserta

GRECO DI TUFO

Avellino

Naples

FIANO DI AVELLINO

ISCHIA

Salerno

CAPRI

LACRYMA CHRISTI
DEL VESUVIO

CAMPANIA

PROVINCES

NAPLES, Avellino, Benevento, Caserta, Salerno

POPULATION

4,760,000

AREA

5,214 square miles

AVERAGE WINE PRODUCTION

310 million liters

DOC WINES

Capri (Bianco, Rosso) · *Fiano di Avellino* · *Greco di Tufo* · *Ischia (Bianco, Rosso)* · *Solopaca (Bianco, Rosso)* · *Taurasi* · *Vesuvio–Lacryma Christi del Vesuvio (Bianco, Rosso, Rosato)*

OTHER WINES

Aglianichello · *Aglianico* · *Alburno* · *Alta Sele* · *Asprino* · *Barbera d'Avellino* · *Barbera del Sannio* · *Biancolella* · *Calitto* · *Cilento* · *Corbara* · *Don Alfonso* · *Epomeo* · *Episcopio* · *Falerno* · *Falernum* · *Gragnano* · *Hirpinia (Irpinia)* · *Lacrimarosa d'Irpinia* · *Lettere* · *Montonico* · *Pannarano* · *Per'e Palummo* · *Procida* · *Ravello* · *Sangioioso* · *Sangiovese* · *Tintiglia* · *Tintore* · *Trebbiano*

A Bit Part in the Histrionics

CAMPANIA has two faces. Everybody knows the one that looks toward the sea (if not in person, at least from pictures), the images of Naples, Vesuvius, Capri, Pompeii, Herculaneum, Sorrento, Amalfi, Ischia, the face that sings "O Sole Mio" with tears in its eyes and then puts on the harlequin getup to masquerade as a clown. But few are well acquainted with the face on the other side of Vesuvius, the one that looks toward the mountain country of Benevento, Caserta, Avellino, the fertile valleys of Campania Felix, the face with the open smile.

The Romans, who preferred these lush fields to their own countryside, kept the fruit, nuts, vegetables, and grain flowing north to the capital along the Appian Way. Even today, parts of Latium have a lean and hungry look while the interior of Campania, as always, is green and flourishing. The Romans came south for wine, too, to the hills of Falernum and Abellinum and the black slopes of Vesuvius, where the vines were draped over the branches of trees and yielded grapes full of sugar and sunshine. They appreciated more profoundly than modern people do that this was a privileged place.

Today, Campania produces much less wine than does Latium, a fact that would surely make Cicero, Horace, and Virgil scratch their wise heads in wonder. Why viticulture in Campania fell upon hard times is difficult to fathom. Perhaps it has something to do with the decline of Naples, which not so very long ago was a world capital, a city that never recovered its self-respect after the fall of the Kingdom of the Two Sicilies in the course of Italy's unification. Well, whatever the reason, only a few wines of genuine interest can be found in Campania today, and most come from the other side of Vesuvius.

Precisely at what is now the border of Campania and Latium, the Appian Way veers inland toward Capua, the chief city under the Romans, and the Via Domiziana splits off to follow the Tyrrhenian coast to Naples, leaving the traveler with a choice. The Appian Way leads to

Avellino and Campania's greatest wines, the Domiziana to those places where wine plays a bit part in the histrionics of day-to-day existence. Seeing that the normal progression begins with the lightweight wines and works up, the obvious first choice is the Domiziana, saving the best for later.

Before going anywhere, though, one for the road seems in order, for between the fork of the two Roman ways lie some of the modern vineyards of Ager Falernus, home of Falernum and Falerno. As mentioned earlier (Latium), the grapes and the wine are not the same as they were in Roman times. Still, something must remain in the soil and the sunlight revered by the ancients. Possibly the finest of the modern wines of the name Falerno in Campania is that of Michele Moio of Mondragone. Made from the Aglianico grape, it is a full-bodied red wine that ages admirably.

After one curves east on the Domiziana, past the remains of the Greek city of Cumae and the Phlegrean Fields where sulfurous gases spout from the earth in a setting that undoubtedly inspired some of the early apprehensions of hell, Naples comes into view across the bay with Vesuvius as a backdrop in what at first glance looks like paradise. Well, apart from the setting, there is little that could be considered heavenly about Naples today. What remains of its former dignity has been subjected to a pitiless onslaught of urban degeneration that has kept the city constantly on the brink of chaos. And yet, though it takes a measure of courage even to go there and a stout sense of humor to feel at ease in the place, Naples has something irresistible about it. Vincenzo Buonassisi, one of Italy's most astute chroniclers of food, wine, and humanity, provided insights into the city when he wrote:

There are many ways of arriving in Naples, though I am not so much referring to your mode of transportation as to the sort of ideas you might be carrying in your head. You might be thinking of the endless drama of life in the city, today as always: the poverty, the tragic pattern of building, the tragic pollution of that fabulous sea. You might show up with *Funiculi Funiculà* in your heart and find sweetness destroyed, mistrust rooted in the imaginative schemes of thieves and swindlers (in Naples even the tricks played on unfortunate strangers can become little works of art). The literature of every era is filled with both rapturous and alarming tales, but that is all the more reason Naples has its unique and different charm. You feel it the moment you establish a rapport — so true, so close, so human that it seems to have all the power of love.

Buonassisi gives two rules to follow if you want to get the most out of the city: "The first is to establish human contact. If you look a Neapolitan straight in the eye he will never cheat you. Second, put your faith in the natural flow of things; follow the philosophy of the Greeks and accept the world as it is."

The city still offers some fascinating historical sites to attract outsiders, along with the endless drama, but hardly anybody comes to Naples expressly to eat or drink anymore. It is difficult to imagine that this was once a capital of *gourmandise,* the city where, they say, not only the pizza but the crêpe was invented, the first cookbook was written, and where some of the most lavish feasts of all time were proffered. Perhaps the most extravagant were thrown by the Roman consul Lucullus in the Castello d'Ovo with ships arriving from the Orient and Africa with the makings of the ultimate in exotic dishes (a platter containing two thousand parrots' tongues, for instance). Those were the days.

Naples currently has not so much as a Michelin-starred restaurant. It can be risky to eat seafood from the Gulf. Old-timers even complain that the pizza is nothing like what it used to be. The habitual wine of the city used to be Asprino, a light white from Asprino grapes grown a short way to the north in the countryside around Aversa. The vines were supposedly brought from Champagne during one of the French dominions. Served ice-cold, Asprino was appreciated for its sharp astringency due to its high degree of fixed acidity. It resembled, as the name suggests, aspirin. Nowadays, the real thing is difficult to find and the substitutes may well require aspirin to alleviate the aftereffects.

Cashing In on Capri

From Naples' waterfront, ferries and hovercraft leave regularly for Capri, the fabled isle where people used to go to get away from it all. But quiet days in Capri are a thing of the past. Capri cashed in on its famous name and was awarded DOC for red and white wines in 1977, years after the island's most respected producer proclaimed his disgust with patterns of winemaking there and declared his irrevocable decision to close his cantina.

Marchese Ettore Patrizi continued to sell grapes from his vineyards on the isle, but his last wine was bottled from the 1971 vintage. Mario Soldati, in his first volume of *Vino a Vino,* described him as "the only one who still makes true wine of Capri: what I mean is the only one who makes it on Capri, and with grapes all harvested on Capri."

That Marchese Patrizi, who for years ran the winery founded by his father in 1909, refused to consider resumption even when DOC was introduced, shows the depth of his defiance. Patrizi made a white wine called Bianco Acqua (white water) that was noted as light and refreshing in the flower of its youth, and a red with enough depth and sturdiness to take a few years of aging. The wines were widely respected not only for their innate goodness but for the integrity and competence shown by Patrizi in making them.

DOC permits the use of grapes grown on the slopes of Vesuvius as well as on the island, confirming the reality that Capri itself, on the bit of vineyard space left between the rocks and the hotels, could never produce enough wine to meet visitors' needs. In the old days, according to Soldati, wines called Capri originated in such far-flung places as Sicily and Apulia and even on the high seas in the holds of cargo ships (they were made from water, mashed dates, or the fruit of the carob tree, sugar, and alcohol, he speculated).

Today, even though wine called Capri need not be from Capri, DOC has set limits on production. The Bianco is made from Falanghina and Greco grapes at a maximum of 50 percent each with the possible addition of Biancolella at up to 20 percent. The Rosso is from Piedirosso at 80 percent or more, with Tintora and Barbera making up the difference. The white must have at least 11° alcohol, the red 11.5°. Both are suited to casual summer meals.

Ischia: An Aura of Authenticity

Ischia, the other fabled island in the Gulf of Naples, has a significant number of vineyards and a notable production of wine (all, in theory at least, from the place). As much as 15 million liters have been produced in some years, more than enough to supply visiting tourists and still have plenty left over to send across the water to Naples and beyond. Only about a quarter of production is DOC, which consists of Ischia Bianco, Ischia Bianco *superiore,* and Ischia Rosso.

Though not as romanticized as Capri, Ischia, ringed by a road around its central crater of Monte Epomeo, whose slopes are draped with vines, has an invitingly agrarian air about it that lends an aura of authenticity to the wines. Whitewashed farm dwellings, some carved into the tufa, often have an arbor of grapevines for shade and braided clusters of cherry tomatoes hanging neatly along the walls in the fall to be used in sauces in the winter. Donkeys are still employed to haul in the grapes, as well as sticks of vine and olive prunings to fuel the wood stoves. In the off season it is possible to forget that Ischia is an international resort, at least in those places where hotels have not yet arrived.

The island's winemaking tradition is firmly established (its wines were referred to at least as long ago as 1596) and well organized (Ischia was the third DOC zone of Italy in 1966). The island's chief grape varieties are apparently unique: the light Forastera and Biancolella and the dark Guarnaccia. The volcanic soil and ample sunshine of Ischia would seem to favor quality, but maybe it is a bit too hot and sunny, or perhaps those native vines leave something to be desired, or it might be that the summer beach crowd is not discriminating enough to demand anything better, but somehow the overwhelming majority of the island's wines are disappointingly ordinary.

Exceptions should be made for the wines of Perrazzo, whose Bianco *superiore* has more depth and character than any other I have tasted, and D'Ambra Vini d'Ischia, part of the Winefood group. D'Ambra, whose founder, Salvatore D'Ambra, was the leading force behind DOC recognition and wide distribution, is still the best-known name in Ischian wine. In addition to the DOC types, Perrazzo produces red, white, and rosé wines called Don Alfonso, and D'Ambra produces the white Biancolella and Forastera and the red Per'e Palummo (the local name for Piedirosso), all good-quality table wines.

Ischia Bianco consists of Forastera grapes at 65 percent, Biancolella at 20 percent, and other varieties at 15 percent. A delicately dry strawgolden wine of 11°, it is designed for immediate consumption. Ischia Bianco *superiore* is made from grapes grown in a restricted part of the island under a somewhat different formula: Forastera at 50 percent, Biancolella at 40 percent, San Lunardo at 10 percent. With 12° alcohol, more body, and a distinct aroma, the *superiore* tends to gain character with a few months of bottle age. Both whites are best suited to seafood.

Ischia Rosso, from Guarnaccia at 50 percent, Piedirosso at 40 percent, and Barbera at 10 percent, has medium body and a hint of tannin, a wine that can take a few years of aging. When well made, it can be a good accompaniment to poultry and light meats.

Among the minor wines of Ischia are Epomeo Bianco and Rosso,

Calitto Bianco and Rosso, and the red Tintiglia and Tintore. Procida, Ischia's neighbor, is the forgotten island in the Gulf, home of fishermen, sailors, and a few winemakers. Procida Bianco, Rosso, and Rosato can match the wines of Ischia, and Aglianichello, from the noble Aglianico grape with a bit of Barbera included, can be the most pleasing red wine of the islands, though it is rarely found away from Procida. It tends to be rather strong with a vein of light sweetness. Wines called Procida are also made on the mainland around Monte di Procida and Bacoli.

The Southern Coast: Occasional Magic

Skipping across the Gulf to the Sorrentine peninsula and following the often tortuous route through the coastal hills from Vesuvius to Sorrento, Positano, Amalfi, Ravello, and Salerno, one finds so many terraced vineyards and so many unclassified wines that the only way to get to know them is to go there and bask and hope that the magic of the place will find its way into the carafe on your table. If not, at least the scenery will be unforgettable. If you stick close to the Tyrrhenian coast, you will not cross another DOC zone until you reach the Savuto River valley, deep in Calabria, but that does not mean that you will not find good wines, some indeed on par with those already classified. A few deserve honorary mention, and some have a chance of being formally recognized someday.

Just south of Pompeii, in the hills back of Castellamare di Stabia, a red wine from Aglianico and Piedirosso grapes is usually called Gragnano, from the town of that name. A good related version of the wine can be found at the village of Lettere, where Antonio Pentangelo serves it with local dishes at his restaurant, La Canonica. Around Sorrento, Massalubrense, and Positano, white, red, and rosé wines are made which, if you are lucky about where you go to try them, can prove to be of more than routine interest.

The Corniche, the road from Sorrento to Salerno, is one of the world's most scenic drives, winding precariously through a landscape that qualifies for all the superlatives habitually heaped upon it. The rugged Amalfi coast has remained largely intact over recent decades; villages, churches, villas, orchards, gardens, and vineyards have a well-kept appearance. Tourism has brought prosperity to the Amalfitani, but from the looks of things life has not changed all that much.

Here, with few exceptions, you eat fish and drink white wine, cool, light, unimposing, good because it has not been forced to travel. The most noted wines of the coast come from vineyards around the village of Ravello, with its villas, flowers, narrow streets, passageways, and unmatchable views, where the Bianco, Rosso, and Rosato known as Gran Caruso have an international following. Sound wines that travel well, you may find the Gran Caruso trio in New York or London, but you may never enjoy them more than right here at home. The place is the family hotel and restaurant, the Caruso Belvedere, where the food and the setting are elegant and the hospitality as warm as the Campanian sunshine. Gran Caruso Bianco is made from San Nicola, Bianca Tenera, and other light grapes and the Rosso and Rosato mainly from Per'e Palummo.

Another worthy producer in Ravello is P. Vuilleumier, a long-established family winery, whose Bianco, Rosso, and Rosato are sold under the name Episcopio. The Rosso from good vintages is aged in oak casks and has been known to keep well for fifteen to twenty years.

After Salerno, the coastline suddenly turns flat and there are lonely sand beaches as far as Paestum, the ancient Greek city with its pillared temples, so grand and solitary amidst the low brush and cypresses. The hills back of the coast on either side of the Sele River produce wines of interest, usually reds, rather robust, dry, sometimes better than you might expect to find in an area largely ignored by those who determine oenological worth. Among the names are Alburno, Monti Alburni, Alto Sele, Basso Sele, and Cilento. The Campanian stalwarts, Aglianico and Piedirosso, are occasionally supplemented by such outsiders as Barbera, Sangiovese, and Primitivo di Gioia from Apulia. The Cantina Sociale di Cilento at Rutino makes a fine Rosso di Cilento. Other good wines in the area include a full-bodied Barbera di San Lorenzo and a sharp, strong Rosso di Castellabate. Good red wines from the hills above Battipaglia are often sold under the name Corbara.

Lacryma Christi del Vesuvio: Tears and Laughter

Vesuvius, Naples' symbol and Campania's point of reference, is also the nation's most ostentatious wine zone. Although the volcano's slopes have been noted for at least two millennia for their distinctive wines, DOC went into effect in late 1979 under the two-tiered appellation of Vesuvio and Lacryma Christi del Vesuvio. Wines that carry the latter name are stronger and, in theory, more qualified.

With a name like Christ's Tear there would have to be a legend, of course; there are several. The popular version is that the Archangel Lucifer, cast from heaven, desperately grabbed a piece of it with his fingernails as he fell and placed it on earth as the Gulf of Naples and environs. Noticing the loss, the Lord wept, and where each of his tears fell the first vines grew on earth. This tale probably drew inspiration from a pagan legend that had Bacchus shedding tears with similar results. The Roman Columella noted the quality of wines of the "celebrated Vesuvian hills." Scholars credit the name Lacryma Christi and the survival of Vesuvian wines to monks who fastidiously cared for the vines on the slopes during the Middle Ages while saving the remnants of Latin culture and agriculture.

Although a number of Italian wines continue to be called Lacryma Christi, Lacrima, and so on (with variations in spelling), the only DOC wines of the name are the Bianco, Rosso, and Rosato of Vesuvio. But because the tears have been so widely shed, so to speak, and the name applied to so many wines, usually white and often sweet and sparkling, it was decided that Vesuvio could not have exclusive rights to the name. DOC may help to raise the quality standards of Vesuvian wines, which have not always been exemplary in recent times, though there have been conspicuous exceptions such as Mastroberardino of Atripalda and Saviano of Ottaviano.

The Vesuvio DOC territory extends through twelve communities, most lying along the southern face of the mountain in the communities of Ercolano, Torre del Greco, Torre Annunziata, and Boscotrecase. Vesuvio Rosso and Rosato are both made from Piedirosso and Olivella grapes (here commonly known as Palombina and Sciascianoso) with Aglianico permitted at up to 20 percent. The basic Vesuvio Rosso and Rosato must have 10.5° alcohol, the Lacryma Christi Rosso 12°, and the Lacryma Christi Rosato 12.5°. The red, ruby and dry, can be a fairly hearty wine that can take a few years of aging. The Rosato, of a rather pronounced rose color, is sturdy and adaptable. Vesuvio Bianco is made from Coda di Volpe (known locally as Caprettona) and Verdeca grapes at a minimum of 80 percent between them, with the possible addition of Falanghina and Greco. Pale straw in color, dry and acidulous, it must have at least 11° alcohol. When it has 12° or more it may be called Lacryma Christi. From the base white wine a natural *spumante* and fortified *liquoroso* can be made.

From the lip of the crater of Vesuvius, if you care to climb that high, on a clear day you can see across to the mountains in the provinces of Caserta, Benevento, and Avellino, and, in between, the fertile valleys treasured by the Romans. Leaving behind seaside Campania with its beauty and its blemishes, its laughter and its tears, you can coast down the eastern side of Vesuvius and soon sense the difference as you roll through the land the Romans called *felix,* the face with the open smile. Whatever delights and surprises the wines of the islands and coastal zones provided, the true gems of Campanian oenology lie ahead. All, conveniently enough, are to be found in the town of Atripalda, which is adjacent but by no means part of Avellino, and all in an old family winery behind an arched doorway with only an inconspicuous sign carved in stone to indicate the name: Casa Vinicola Mastroberardino.

Emancipating the South

The wine world is filled with people who like to draw neat lines between the types of wine that come from different places. Some even go so far as to submit that there is such a thing as, for example, a "typical Italian" or "typical French" wine. In Italy, distinctions are often drawn between "northern" and "southern" wines, the implication usually being that the northerners are naturally superior. I would direct any such misguided souls to the brothers Antonio and Walter Mastroberardino, administrators of a winery that ranks as outstanding, not only in Campania or in southern Italy or, indeed, in all of Italy, but anywhere in the world today. All that would be needed to sweep away the cobwebs from prejudiced minds would be two or three glasses of the finer Mastroberardino wines, which in speaking for themselves also put in a good word for their southern brothers.

Antonio and Walter and their late brother Angelo Mastroberardino, like their father, grandfather and great-grandfather before them, have probably done more than anyone else has to emancipate the quality wines of the south. They have also managed to sway some skeptical non-Italians, though in a limited way, for wines of the quality of Mastroberardino inevitably come in small doses.

Although the winery was officially founded in 1878, when registered with the Chamber of Commerce of Avellino by Michele Mastroberardino, great grandfather of the present owners, winemaking in the family actually started much earlier, probably around 1720. Believed to be the region's oldest continuing winery, it began its operations at the foot of a hill called Civita that the Romans esteemed for its wine. Mastroberardino was also among the first in Campania to bottle and export, but perhaps its greatest contribution to oenology has been the preservation and enhancement of the great wine tradition of the hills of Avellino. When other wineries opted for volume through more productive grape varieties and more efficient concepts of vinification, the Mastroberardinos decided to continue doing their best with what they had, knowing that which they had was superior to anything else around.

"Greco, Fiano, and Aglianico were the great grapes of antiquity in Campania," said Antonio Mastroberardino. "But now Greco and Fiano, as they were then, can be found only around Avellino. They're what are known as archaeological vines. If we hadn't saved them, they wouldn't exist. Even Aglianico, brought by the Greeks to Lucania and transferred into Campania, is not as widespread as it might be."

The Mastroberardino efforts were later joined by the Scuola Enologica di Avellino and its founder, Francesco De Sanctis. These archaeological vines produce the three great wines of Campania — Greco di Tufo, Fiano di Avellino, and Taurasi. Here and there you may find other bottles of those DOC wines, but not often and never of the quality of Mastroberardino. The Oenological School is the only other noted producer. This supremacy, acknowledged by Antonio Mastroberardino without a trace of vanity, is now taken for granted by connoisseurs, too, which explains why the wines are priced at about the same levels as their few peers from the north.

Antonio Mastroberardino, who took his degree in chemistry and then studied briefly in France, is acknowledged as one of the grand masters of Italian winemaking today. "The schools of oenology are a good place to start," he said, "but practical experience is much more important." He drew nearly all his useful experience in Atripalda in what qualifies as an almost quaint winery, far from the scholastic currents of Conegliano, San Michele, and Alba. Still, many budding oenologists of the north could learn a few things from Tonino Mastroberardino, especially about how to give a wine those touches that result in what is variously referred to as class, personality, character. Whatever you want to call it, it is often the element lacking in those modern wines that may be virtually flawless but are somehow not very interesting.

One of Mastroberardino's personal practices is giving a bit of barrel age to nearly all his wines: red, rosé, and even white. "White wines here are naturally a little hard and sharp when young," he explained.

"Six months, never more than a year, of barrel age takes the rough edges off and gives them balance and tone."

Greco di Tufo and Fiano di Avellino are extraordinary white wines from special vines whose grapes have been vinified by a man who seems

Antonio Mastroberardino

to believe in perfection. Mastroberardino uses horizontal presses and cold fermentation, but he shies away from some other modern conveniences and lets the wines achieve a natural stability through barrel and bottle age that puts each in a class by itself. They are both so excellent that it is difficult to give one or the other the nod of supremacy, though Mastroberardino himself confesses that if pressed to choose he would pick Fiano by a shade.

Fiano is a corruption of Apiano, a name given the grape by Romans in reference to its attraction to bees ("bee" is *apis* in Latin). Though the DOC production zone completely surrounds Avellino and Atripalda,

Fiano vineyards are sparse and the vine rather unproductive and the yield of wine from grapes is also low because only the choice must is used — about half the weight of the grape. DOC, bestowed on Fiano only recently, requires a minimum of 11.5° alcohol, though it may range as high as 13° in some years. It is light straw in color with elegant body and texture, its bouquet is distinguished by the scent of pears and toasted hazelnuts, and its dry flavor has extraordinary finesse. Mastroberardino noted that as the wine grows older the odor of pear diminishes and the hazelnuts become more pronounced.

Greco di Tufo comes from a small zone due north of Avellino and southwest of Benevento, its epicenter in the town of Tufo. The Greco grape is of very ancient origin, supposedly brought from Thessalonica to Magna Grecia long before the birth of Christ. Praised by writers of various epochs, from the Roman to the present, Greco is not nearly as widely cultivated as it once was. Greco di Tufo can include 20 percent of Coda di Volpe grapes, which enrich its body and increase its capacity to age. DOC calls for a minimum of 11.5° alcohol, but it can approach 14° from some vintages. This strength is noticeable in bouquet and flavor, though always in harmony with the other elements. Dry and delicate, its aroma hints at bitter almond, which also grows more prominent with age.

Both Greco and Fiano can be served with seafood, though not if it has an aggressively flavored sauce. It seems a shame somehow to share their uniqueness with anything else. The first glass or two of either should be taken as *aperitivo,* and then the rest might go with a white fish baked or grilled and dressed with a light sauce or simply olive oil and lightly flavored herbs.

The town of Taurasi lies at the center of the zone in the Sannio hills northeast of Avellino, stretching as far north as Benevento. Taurasi is so much wine that it is routinely praised in the same breath with the noblest reds of Tuscany, Piedmont, Burgundy. It has even been called the Barolo of the south, a term which, if flattering, is also misleading because Taurasi is every bit its own thing, the ultimate expression of the antique nobility of the Aglianico grape. (The name Aglianico comes from Hellenico, as the vine was called after the Greek era in Campania and Basilicata.) In the hills of Avellino it develops its own style, which differs markedly from the Aglianico of other places.

Mastroberardino explained that the hills, at 1,000 to 2,000 feet above sea level, are cooler and damper than the other classic Aglianico zone,

Monte Vulture in Basilicata, and that therefore the vine has developed hearty individual traits that differentiate it from other Aglianicos. Although DOC allows for the use of Piedirosso, Sangiovese, and Barbera at up to 30 percent, he prefers to keep the wine a thoroughbred. It must have 12° alcohol, but often goes higher. With four years of aging Taurasi may be called *riserva*. From such exceptional vintages as 1968, 1961, and 1958, Taurasi can stand with the greatest aged reds anywhere, maintaining its full aroma, ruby-garnet color, and robust elegance long after lesser wines have faded.

These three are the pride of Mastroberardino, though similar care is taken with the other wines, the Lacryma Christi del Vesuvio, a pale pink called Lacrimarosa, and even with Sangioioso, red and white wines made for everyday drinking from the second selection of grapes for the other wines. Lacrimarosa, made from dark grapes into a wine with pale copper-rose reflections, is really closer in character to the great whites than to most rosés. The Mastroberardinos are so pleased with it that they plan to propose it for DOC.

As might be expected, Mastroberardino makes the finest Lacryma Christi del Vesuvio, though the most interesting of the three Lacryma types the winery makes — the Bianco *amabile,* a lightly sweet dessert wine — is not covered by DOC. "Ironically, the historical Lacryma Christi was *amabile,*" said Mastroberardino. "The monks certainly made it that way and we did the same, to respect tradition. But the DOC discipline excludes it. If I'd made too much of a fuss over the point, it might have delayed the whole Vesuvio DOC approval, which was already delayed enough, so I decided to request an amendment later."

Lacryma Christi *amabile* is the only Mastroberardino wine that gets no barrel age. To retain its exquisite light sweetness and fruity bouquet, it is bottled in January after the harvest and gently pasteurized to preserve its delicacy. It is best to drink soon after bottling. "I don't believe in pasteurization as a rule," said Mastroberardino, "but in this case it is justified."

Another tradition the Mastroberardinos have been quietly maintaining is the local system of separate roles for grape growers and winemakers. "We've had plenty of opportunity to buy land and have our own vineyards," said Mastroberardino, "but our feeling is that it is better to maintain relations with the individual cultivator who works his own land. If you hire people to work your land, they don't have the same pride as they would have in working their own. Our grape suppliers know what our standards are and we work together to meet them, but always by placing our confidence in the farmer. We don't support the principle that industry is the answer to the problems of the Mezzogiorno, and we do what we can to keep people on the land."

Mastroberardino produces about 70,000 bottles a year, maintaining the comfortable dimensions of a winery that is neither large nor small but totally directed toward quality. Some 400,000 bottles a year are the prestigious wines, and 300,000 Sangioioso. Instead of expanding, Mastroberardino hopes to concentrate production in a single winery rather than the present two. The winery on the edge of Atripalda that once belonged to an uncle is used for pressing and storage, but Antonio Mastroberardino wants to move everything into the main winery in the center of town.

To do so, the plant will have to be expanded into an adjacent lot that happens to be zoned as a historical monument because there is a Roman wall there. The Mastroberardinos had presented plans that would preserve the wall and they were hoping for a positive reply to their bid. "After all we've done for the heritage of this zone, I should think we'd be due that small concession that will actually make the wall more visible," said Antonio Mastroberardino. "We're the last people around here who would ever destroy a bit of history."

Solopaca and the Wines of Hirpinia

The remaining DOC zone of Campania, Solopaca, lies in the Sannio hills in the province of Benevento, northwest of the city and south of the border of Molise. Though not well known, the Rosso and Bianco of Solopaca show promise, particularly the red. Conditions of soil, altitude, and climate in the zone resemble those around Avellino, though the countryside is more rugged and wooded, noted as the legendary meeting place of the witches of Benevento, whose memory lives on in the city's Strega liqueur.

Solopaca Rosso is made from Sangiovese (here often incorrectly called Montepulciano) at 45 to 60 percent with Piedirosso, Aglianico, Sciascianoso, and other local dark varieties into a smooth, perfumed wine that can take a few years of age. The Bianco, from Trebbiano Toscano, Malvasia di Candia, with some Malvasia Toscana and Coda di Volpe permitted, is of no great interest, though it can be sound enough when very young. La Vinicola Ocone at Ponte makes both types.

The provinces of Benevento and Avellino also have a number of minor wines with good reputations. Wines called Aglianico can, in isolated cases, be of excellent quality. Barbera d'Avellino and Barbera del Sannio are sometimes rounder and fuller than the Barberas of Piedmont. Red wines from the Montonico grape can be assertive, strong and full of flavor, good with hearty country food. Pannarano is another good red wine made from Aglianico and Aglianichello grapes with some Sangiovese.

The hills of Hirpinia or Irpinia, from the Sabine *hirpus* for wolf, lie to the north and east of Avellino, an area rich in woods, water, and country wine. Red, white, and rosé wines there often carry the area name. The whites come from Coda di Volpe with some Malvasia, Greco, and Trebbiano, and the reds and rosés from various grapes, among them Sanginoso, Olivella, Aglianico, Sangiovese, Piedirosso, and Barbera. Moves are afoot to organize production of the wines of Hirpinia and seek official recognition.

The Pristine Pizza and the Ubiquitous Tomato

Whether or not the world's first pizza was made in Naples — or Sicily or Rome or somewhere else — really does not matter; Naples gave it its present basic form and its worldwide fame. The classic *pizza napoletana* was made from hard-wheat flour with freshly made *pizzaiola* — tomatoes cooked with onions, garlic, basil, and olive oil — and topped with real *mozzarella* cheese (from buffalo milk), grated Parmesan, oregano, black pepper, and baked in an open dome-shaped oven heated by a wood fire. The variations on pizza that have followed, especially in America, the sausages, peppers, anchovies, olives, and hundreds of other toppings, may be tasty and valid innovations, but are never, to my taste, quite the equal of the classic pizza in its pristine form with its simple but unbeatable combination of flavors, colors, and textures. Alas, the pristine pizza scarcely exists anymore. Even at the city's most renowned *pizzerie* you may end up with only a pale imitation, the dough from refined flour, the mozzarella from cow's milk, and the *pizzaiola*, heaven forbid, from a can.

If you pick your restaurant carefully, however, you can still eat well in Campania and even savor the tastes of bygone days. The tomato is so ubiquitous in Campanian cooking that you might think it originated here and not in faraway America. As a flavoring, tomato is nearly always supported by garlic, onion, herbs, and pimento, its sauces enlivening all sorts of dishes: on pastas such as the spiral-formed *fusilli* or the ear-shaped *orecchiette,* with fish, or even on steak (*bistecca alla pizzaiola*).

Fresh vegetables, as full of flavor as you would imagine from this fertile volcanic soil, are prepared in imaginative ways, or simply employed in the salads that appear so often on the tables of Campania that the people are sometimes called *mangiafogli* (leafeaters). The most famous vegetable dish is *parmigiana di melanzane,* eggplant baked with tomato sauce, *mozzarella,* Parmesan; there are local variations, one that includes hard-boiled eggs and another chocolate. Needless to say, it is a dish that defies you to find a wine to go with it. It is wise to stick with something unpresumptuous, possibly a rosé. And if you have the ill fortune of being served a *parmigiana di melanzane* with chocolate, it might be better to forgo the wine and order a soft drink.

At the Ristorante Barone in the center of Avellino, the pizza is among the finest of Campania and the cooking has an authentic touch that seems out of keeping somehow with the glassed-in environment. The pasta is freshly made each morning: *fusilli, linguine, bucatini,* and the whole-wheat *orecchiette* served with turnip greens and hot pimento and oil, an exquisite dish. After grilled lamb and garden-fresh vegetables, a slice of local *provola* cheese is recommended to go with the Taurasi.

The favorite Neapolitan way of preparing seafood is deep fried, though soups, chowders, grilled and baked fish, and poached mussels, clams, crayfish, and squid are also popular. The *zuppa di pesce* at La Misenetta, 25 kilometers from Naples at Bacoli, is a meal in itself. For seafood at its finest, there is the Antico Francischiello da Peppino at Massalubrense on the Sorrentine peninsula.

The Vintages

	Ischia Bianco, Rosso	Lacryma Christi del Vesuvio
1979	Exceptional	Fair to good
1978	Good	Excellent
1977	Excellent	Excellent

	Ischia Bianco, Rosso	Lacryma Christi del Vesuvio
1976	Fair	Fair
1975	Excellent	Good
1974	Good	Excellent
1973	Excellent	Good
1972	Good	Fair
1971	Good	Good
1970	Excellent	Good

	Greco di Tufo, Fiano di Avellino	Taurasi
1979	Great	Fair
1978	Excellent	Excellent
1977	Excellent	Excellent
1976	Fair	Fair
1975	Good to excellent	Excellent
1974	Excellent	Good
1973	Excellent	Excellent
1972	Good	Good
1971	Excellent	Excellent
1970	Excellent	Excellent
1969	—	Good
1968	—	Great

(Previous outstanding vintages: 1961, 1958)

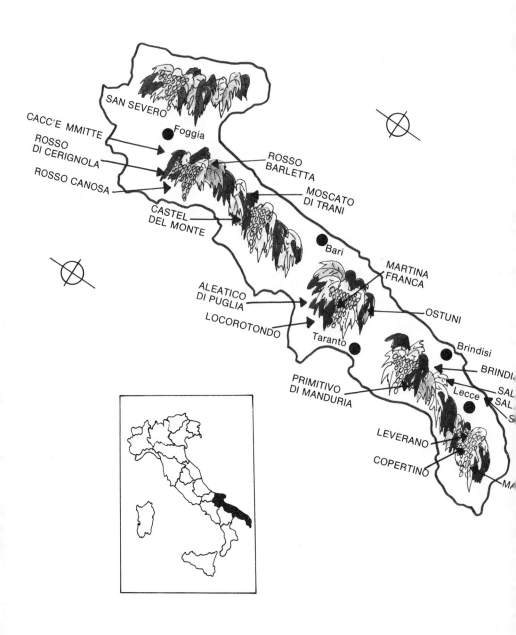

SAN SEVERO

Foggia

CACC'E MMITTE

ROSSO
DI CERIGNOLA

ROSSO
BARLETTA

ROSSO CANOSA

MOSCATO
DI TRANI

CASTEL
DEL MONTE

Bari

MARTINA
FRANCA

ALEATICO
DI PUGLIA

OSTUNI

LOCOROTONDO

Taranto

Brindisi

BRINDI

PRIMITIVO
DI MANDURIA

SAL
SAL

Lecce

S

LEVERANO

COPERTINO

MA

APULIA

PROVINCES

BARI, Brindisi, Foggia, Lecce, Taranto

POPULATION

4,000,000

AREA

7,469 square miles

AVERAGE WINE PRODUCTION

930 million liters

DOC WINES

Aleatico di Puglia · Brindisi (Rosso, Rosato) · Cacc'e Mmitte di Lucera · Castel del Monte (Bianco, Rosso, Rosato) · Copertino (Rosso, Rosato) · Leverano (Bianco, Rosso, Rosato) · Locorotondo · Martina Franca · Matino (Rosso, Rosato) · Moscato di Trani · Ostuni (Bianco, Ottavianello) · Primitivo di Manduria · Rosso Barletta · Rosso Canosa · Rosso di Cerignola · Salice Salentino (Rosso, Rosato) · San Severo (Bianco, Rosso, Rosato) · Squinzano (Rosso, Rosato)

OTHER WINES

Albino · Apulia · Bianco del Salento · Don Carmelo · Doxi Vecchio · Favonio · Five Roses · Lacrima di Terra d'Otranto · Malbec · Messapia · Mitrano · Negrino · Portulano · Primitivo di Gioia · Rosa del Golfo · Rosato del Salento · Rosso del Salento · Torre Quarto · Torre Saracena · Ursi

A Land of Revelations

SINCE all of Apulia is virtually a vineyard, the only challenge it poses to the traveler in quest of wine is in deciding where to begin wandering through it. The most methodical approach might be from the north, with an eventual goal of the heel of the boot, nearly 400 kilometers along a straight line but perhaps double that with all the zigzagging involved in taking a close look at the chief points of oenological interest. These comprise eighteen DOC zones, one of which (Aleatico di Puglia) covers the region. Despite the number, which equals Latium for second behind Piedmont, Apulia produces only about 20 million liters of DOC wine a year — between 2 and 3 percent of its total production.

Apulia no longer leads the nation in volume of production. From a peak of 1.27 billion liters in 1967 — a record for an Italian region — volume hit a low of 632 million liters in 1977, though the average remains close to 930 million liters, about the same as Sicily and somewhat less than Emilia-Romagna and the Veneto. Still, Apulia, whose land mass is longer from end to end and overall more nearly horizontal than any other region's, probably has the heaviest concentration of grapevines of any territory of significant size on earth. Much of its production is of table grapes, of which Apulia provides more than half the national total.

The decline in wine production has resulted from an about-face in regional policy over the last decade. The traditional role of furnishing *vino da taglio* to other regions and nations has been deliberately downgraded, while a new image of quality has been projected through lighter, fruitier, fresher table wines and more refined dessert wines. This has involved an overhaul of epic dimensions that has revolutionized the attitudes of the region's wine industry along with the products. Regional agricultural officials envision a further reduction in output to about 700 million liters a year. Though the transformation is not yet complete, and may never be, progress has been remarkable, even if the emphasis has been overwhelmingly on the development of cooperatives, where quality is not always as evident as it is in the private sector. The range of Apulian bottled wine goes well beyond the scope of what I had imagined before I began the grand tour of the region's wineries. The main problem at the moment is in making these products better known and appreciated, especially at home. Only about 35 percent of Apulian wines are consumed by Apulians, who actually drink more beer than wine.

Apulia is a land of revelations which, whether they have been lying there waiting to be noticed through the ages or are spontaneously contemporary, invariably stand alone. The cities and towns have a way of revealing the high points of their histories individualistically, peaks that somehow never occurred simultaneously with those of their neighbors. Thus in an area of a few hundred square miles lie Brindisi, with its Roman columns at the end of the Appian Way; Gallipoli and Taranto, which were thoroughly Greek; Lecce, a triumph of baroque; Ostuni, with its whitewashed appearance scarcely altered since the time of the Illyrians; Martina Franca, a masterpiece of architecture that might be described as a bit of everybody's but most of all its own; and Alberobello, with hundreds of the most intriguing of all the region's buildings, the *trulli,* the cone-shaped stone dwellings whose prehistoric origins remain an exquisite mystery.

There is more. Throughout Apulia you will find sterling examples of Doric, Romanesque, Gothic, Renaissance architecture, and reminders of the various adventurers over time who found the open, rolling contours a breeze to conquer but not so easy to retain. After the Samnites and Illyrians came the Greeks, who left the most lasting impression, followed by Romans, and, later still, by Goths and Visigoths, Longobards, Saracens, Byzantines, Swabians, Normans, Angevins, Spaniards, and various species of crusaders, mercenaries, and strivers after fortunes who could not resist the temptations of this sunny land.

Today, of course, Apulia shares with its neighbors the stigma of being considered poor and underprivileged, another neglected place wilting in the heat of summer. Misconceptions of this sort die hard, which is one reason that Apulian wines have not registered the impact they deserve either nationwide or worldwide. Northern Italians and non-Italians still tend to think of Apulian wines as sunbaked, despite increasing evidence to the contrary on the market. Such prejudices fail to recognize that much of Apulia is not particularly hot and that even where it is very hot, new concepts of vine growing, harvesting, and vinification are creating wines of superior tone.

Apulian blending wines have consisted of two basic types: the strong, heavy, dense, usually red, that are used to give alcohol, body, and color to weaker wines, and the neutral whites that are best suited as bases for vermouth. Most strong red types have originated in the Salento peninsula south of a line between Brindisi and Taranto; most neutral whites came from north of that line. Apulia can still be split neatly into two viticultural sectors with the same line of division, though the difference in styles between the wines of the south and the wines of the north is no longer so uncompromisingly black and white.

The north (the northernmost point of the region lies at the same latitude as Rome) has all of Apulia's heights, including the modest mountain ranges known as the Daunia and the Murge and the hills of the Gargano promontory, the spur of the Italian boot. Climate ranges from rather cool in the interior to rather warm along the coast. Parts of some DOC zones in the northern interior — Castel del Monte and Canosa among them — would fall into the second category of the world's climatic regions for grapevines on a scale ascending from coolest to hottest, corresponding to such places as Washington State's Yakima Valley and Asti in Piedmont. The north is somewhat protected from the prevailing hot winds from Africa in the summer, which are blocked by the southernmost Apennines in Campania and Basilicata. Growers in Castel del Monte have requested that the alcohol for their DOC Rosato be lowered from 11.5° to 11° because many seasons are too cool for the grapes to develop enough sugars to attain the higher grade.

The south, the plain of the Salento peninsula, is not only low in altitude but directly in the path of the *scirocco,* the hot breeze that originates in the Sahara and picks up humidity as it crosses the Mediterranean. The Salento falls into the fourth and fifth climatic zones for viticulture, like Fresno, California, and coastal Campania. Very hot, but not quite torrid, thanks to the moderating influence of the sea, Salento is a center of robust red wines and rosés of bold character that when made by skilled producers no longer need have that cooked taste that has long turned connoisseurs away from them.

San Severo and Cacc'e Mmitte

Northern Apulia is flanked by the Daunia range of the Apennines and the Gargano massif, the peninsula whose rocky coastline and wooded hills have a rugged beauty atypical of this thoroughly agrarian region. Between the flanks lies the broad plain of the Capitanata, whose name — from the Spanish *capitanos* who once ruled here — is more romantic than the setting of placid grainfields and vineyards surrounding the cities of San Severo, Lucera, and the provincial capital of Foggia. The Capitanata produces lots of wine, little of distinction, though here and there an oenological gem can be located. San Severo is the northernmost DOC zone of Apulia and second to Castel del Monte in volume of production.

San Severo's traditional wine was white, made from nearly equal parts of Bombino Bianco and Trebbiano Toscano with some Malvasia Bianca and Verdeca permitted. Light in color, aroma, flavor, and alcohol (11° minimum), the Bianco when young is satisfactory with fish. A *spumante* is also permitted.

San Severo Rosso and Rosato are the outgrowth of the more recent introduction of Montepulciano d'Abruzzo and Sangiovese vines into Apulia, a combination that has delivered impressive results elsewhere along the Adriatic but has yet to prove itself here. Montepulciano dominates the formula, with Sangiovese included at a maximum of 30 percent. The Rosso is rather robust and deep in color; even the Rosato is full. Both must have at least 11.5° alcohol.

Although 3.6 million liters of San Severo DOC wine have been declared from some vintages, the name is not well known outside Apulia. Bottles are available from D'Alfonso Del Sordo and Riforma Fondiaria, whose full name also includes Centrale Cantina Cooperativa di Puglia, Lucania e Molise. A winery known as Federico II makes a good San Severo Bianco.

Cacc'e Mmitte di Lucera, whose DOC zone lies directly south of San Severo centered in Lucera, with its Angevin castle and cathedral, is a name to reckon with. Unfortunately, the same cannot be said for the wine. The name means "drink and refill" in one interpretation of the dialect. Cacc'e Mmitte is made from a mind-boggling combination of grapes — the local Uva di Troia (also called Summarello) at 35 to 60 percent, with Montepulciano, Sangiovese, and Malvasia Nera (alone or combined) at 25 to 35 percent, and Trebbiano Toscano, Bombino Bianco, and Malvasia Bianca (again alone or combined) at 15 to 30 percent. It is difficult to define a Cacc'e Mmitte style, though DOC calls for a red wine of fairly dark ruby color, intense aroma, full and harmonious flavor with "typical aftertaste" and at least 11.5° of alcohol. But with all those different light and dark grapes developing in different manners according to the season, it is difficult to predict how Cacc'e Mmitte will turn out each year. Normally, it is not a wine to age. Producers include Riforma Fondiaria and Lorenzo Carapelle.

Rosso di Cerignola is related to Cacc'e Mmitte in composition and geography but enjoys certain advantages over its colorfully named neighbor. For instance, it may contain all dark grapes — Uva di Troia, Negroamaro, Sangiovese, Montepulciano, and Malbec — because the use of the light Trebbiano Toscano is optional. Rosso di Cerignola can develop into a wine of good body and balance with some aging potential. The *riserva*, which must have 13° of alcohol and be aged two years in barrel, shows finesse after several years in bottle. Giuseppe Strippoli of Bari, a producer of numerous select wines of Apulia, makes a fine Rosso di Cerignola, most bottles of which are sold in Milan, where his relatives distribute them in their restaurants and through other outlets.

Strange Names: Malbec, Cabernet, I.M.6,0,13

Perhaps the finest wines of Foggia province are neither DOC nor Apulian in nature. The Torre Quarto Rosso produced by the Cirillo Farrusi family at its estate at Quarto outside Cerignola is a wine full of character made from Malbec, oddly enough, for that nearly always plays a bit part in Bordeaux and behind the Cabernets and Merlots of northeastern Italy. But here it shines as a protagonist with a bit of Uva di Troia to back it up. Thoroughly aged in wood, it develops slowly into a warm, well-rounded wine of impressive bouquet, its basic ruby taking on orange tints as it passes a decade, which it can do with grace. The Cirillo Farrusi brothers — Michele, Fabrizio, and Emmanuele — run the estate founded in 1847 by the Ducs de la Rochefoucauld, on what was believed to once have been the largest agricultural holding in Europe. Torre Quarto Rosé, from the same grapes as the red, takes a few years of aging as well. The Cirillo Farrusi break the French lineage with their Torre Quarto Bianco, from Bombino Bianco, Trebbiano, and Greco, a pale, dry, refreshing white.

The boldest innovator in the area, and possibly in all of Apulia, is Attilio Simonini of Foggia, who has proved that such unfamiliar vines as Cabernet Franc, Pinot Bianco, Pinot Nero, Chardonnay, and even the hybrid I.M.6,0,13 of Riesling and Pinot (which seems to be grown only in the Veneto, Friuli, and here) can thrive in northern Apulia. Simonini, who applies the estate name of Favonio to his wines, serves as a model for what other winemakers in the zone could achieve through individual initiative. His wines, in addition to being unique, are outstanding by any measure. The Cabernet Franc, Pinot Bianco, and Chardonnay are most distinguished. The Cabernet is comparable to fine wines of that name from the Veneto, where Simonini was born. The Pinot Bianco and I.M.6,0,13 have the crisp fruitiness usually associated with cold-climate whites, and the Chardonnay, produced in minute quantities, has few peers in Italy. Amazingly, they grow on the low plain east of Foggia in an area so dry that it must be irrigated (using a drip system) throughout the summer. Simonini's secret seems to be in his selection of clones and his knack for harvesting at the perfect moment, which results in wines that show no trace of hot climate.

Links in the Chain: Barletta, Trani, and Canosa

The chain of DOC zones continues unbroken into the province of Bari, the regional capital and chief seaport and one of the most accomplished cities of Italy's south. Along the coast and extending into the province of Foggia is the zone of Rosso Barletta around the historically important seaport known in recent times as a commercial center for wine. Rosso Barletta, even with DOC behind it, is an everyday wine, though it can be a good one. Based on Uva di Troia, it may include Montepulciano, Sangiovese, and Malbec at a maximum of 30 percent between them. When it has 12° alcohol and at least two years of age, it may be labeled *invecchiato*. Giuseppe Strippoli and the Fattoria Torricciola produce good versions of Rosso Barletta.

The Cantina Sociale di Barletta is the largest producer of Rosso Barletta. The cooperative makes a portion of select wine for bottling and sells most of the rest in larger bottles or bulk. Barletta's Cantina Sperimentale has been operating for more than a century as the chief research station for wine in southeastern Italy. Working closely with the faculty of the highly respected agricultural institute of Bari, the Cantina Sperimentale has been the focal point of much of the recent oenological progress of the southern mainland.

Moscato di Trani is a rich dessert wine that carries the name of the picturesque old port city with its handsome Cathedral of San Nicolà Pellegrino, whose façade often appears on labels. The DOC zone extends from the Adriatic coast across the entire width of Apulia to the border of Basilicata. Moscato di Trani, like other Muscat wines, has a long and sometimes glorious history that certainly dates to the Middle Ages and probably well before. But in recent times the name Trani has been ingloriously applied by the Milanese to the coarse bar wines that came from Apulia. These days, however, the term *Trani* is no longer often heard in Milan.

Moscato di Trani is made from the Moscato Reale grape, as it is known locally, with a 15 percent addition of other light grapes permitted, into two types of wine. The *dolce naturale* has a full Moscato aroma with sweet and velvety flavor. It must have at least 15° alcohol with 13° developed. A *liquoroso* version is stronger — 18° alcohol with 16° developed — and sweeter. These wines, of deep golden to amber color, have been improved considerably lately, thanks to the efforts of the Cantina Sperimentale of Barletta and DOC supervision, and are starting to find markets outside the region. Botta produces the finest Moscato di Trani, an excellent natural dessert wine. The so-called Golden, bottled by Rivera, is a good example of the *liquoroso*. Other producers are Gennaro Marasciulo and Nuova Vinicola Picardi. Barletta and Trani have long been the main departure points for Apulian wines going north to Venice, Trieste, Genoa, and Sète in France.

A new DOC, Rosso Canosa, is made from Ulva di Troia at 75 percent with Montepulciano and/or Sangiovese grown in a limited area around the hill town whose Roman name was Canusium. Though Rosso Canosa has not had much time to prove its worthiness, the Murge hills where its vines grow have patches of choice terrain. When young, Rosso Canosa is bright and refreshing. The *riserva,* of 13° alcohol and two years of aging, can be a wine of some distinction. Giuseppe Strippoli has selected wine from Canosa for years. Some local producers now have bottles on the market as well.

Pioneer Spirit in Castel del Monte

Castel del Monte is considered the primary zone of quality wine of Apulia's north, its reputation enhanced by the studied techniques and intelligent promotion of Rivera, a winery owned by the De Corato family of Andria. The name and symbol of the zone come from the striking

Swabian castle built about 1200 on a gentle rise by Friedrich II of Hohenstaufen. Its octagonal form distinguishes it as a singular monument to Frederick's genius, strength, and originality. The emperor, who may have been inspired by buildings he saw during his travels in the Near East, used the castle mainly as a base for his favorite sport — hunting with falcons.

The hills of Castel del Monte, though not steep, are stony and barren, with vineyards and olive groves concentrated in those channels where soil blown by wind and washed by water has accumulated over the millennia. It is a stark landscape worked by farmers who now usually live in nearby villages and use the *trulli* where their peasant ancestors lived for ages as storage sheds for tools and crops and as temporary shelters from sun, rain, and wind. Vines, most of them head-trained in the *alberello* form, yield rather meagerly by Apulian standards, a factor reflected favorably in the quality of grapes and wine. Castel del Monte produces more DOC wine than any other zone of Apulia; peak production was 4.36 million liters in 1978, a hardly staggering figure.

Of the three Castel del Monte types, Rosato prevails, known throughout Italy for its bold pink color behind a bright red label with the name Rivera in white script climbing it diagonally. Not that Rivera, whose

Carlo De Corato at Castel del Monte

name is taken from the locality of the winery, has exclusive rights to the Castel del Monte appellation; it is just that that family winery alone, with a little luck, some ingenuity, and a lot of work, has succeeded in making the wine famous. Sebastiano De Corato, the pioneer of this success, related in his amiably sophisticated manner how it all came about.

"In the old days we sold wine in bulk, mainly to northerners, as all of us Apulians then seemed destined to do forever," he recalled. "Most of what we made was rosé and much of that went to Alto Adige to be sold as local wine. Well, one day I got to thinking philosophically about the fate of my wine, which I thought showed rather good quality despite its total lack of status, and I decided, innocently enough, to put it to a little test. So I bought four prestigious rosés, three from northern Italy and one from France, and presented them blind, along with my own, to an expert friend of mine. He chose mine as best, which frankly stunned me. It also opened my eyes. I said to myself, if that's the case, why not bottle it and sell it directly? That's easier said than done, naturally, but in the long run it worked."

Italians, like other wine drinkers, are not easy to convince of the virtues of a good rosé, but gradually over twenty-five years Rivera has consolidated its position as one of the best and best-selling pink wines in the country. Just recently, it has started to make progress abroad, primarily in West Germany, but also in Britain and the United States.

The DOC formula for Castel del Monte Rosato calls for Bombino Nero grapes at 65 percent minimum with Montepulciano and Uva di Troia making up the difference. But Rivera, after thorough experimentation, has chosen to use only Bombino Nero in a wine noted for its exceptional fruit-acid balance. The fresh musts are left on the skins for a few hours after crushing, long enough to give the wine that bright pink that is almost a Rivera trademark. Then they are drawn off the skins before the cold fermentation begins.

Castel del Monte Rosso, on the other hand, is based on Uva di Troia for at least 65 percent with Bombino Nero, Montepulciano, and Sangiovese. Castel del Monte may be the only DOC zone of Italy whose Rosso and Rosato have clear-cut differences in grape composition. Carlo De Corato, Sebastiano's son, explained why.

"Bombino Nero, here at least, is a natural rosé grape, because of the peculiar way it develops," he said. "Even when ripe, most grapes on the clusters are purple, but some are still green. And it's these green grapes that seem to give the wine its freshness, which is really its outstanding attribute. Most of our Bombino Nero is planted at high altitudes (between one thousand and two thousand feet) because it comes out better in a cooler climate. Lately, though, growers here have had a problem bringing them to the required 11.5° alcohol because there's been a gradual shift in climate over recent decades and summers are cooler than before. So we've asked to have the minimum lowered to 11°. We've also been perfecting cultivation methods in our vineyards and those we have under contract, and this has led to a constant qualitative improvement."

The red wine grapes are grown at below one thousand feet, where they have little trouble reaching the 12°, or 12.5° for *riserva,* which requires three years of aging. Rivera Rosso is a solid table wine with the robustness to stand up to roasts and cheeses. The *riserva,* made in minute quantities, is called Il Falcone (in honor of Frederick's falcons), a wine that takes at least seven years to round into form after aging in casks of Slavonian oak. The De Coratos let the Montepulciano grape dominate Il Falcone, despite the regulations, reasoning that DOC was not designed to stand in the way of quality and that Montepulciano makes a decidedly nobler wine.

Castel del Monte Bianco is made from a grape called Pampanino or Pampanuto for at least 65 percent with Trebbiano Toscano and Giallo, Bombino Bianco, and Palumbo for the rest. It is a dry, fresh table wine that is best well chilled. The De Corato strategy is to emphasize the Bianco and Rosso in the United States initially, and follow up with the Rosato and possibly even Il Falcone. This may fit the recent U.S. pattern of favoring clean, fairly neutral whites and unimposing reds from Italy, but in this case one could hope that the rosé and Il Falcone will not be far behind, because they show Rivera and Castel del Monte at its finest.

The class of Rivera wines, beyond their commercial success in Italy, has led to some unexpected recognition for the De Coratos. A few years ago, Sebastiano De Corato, attending a wine function in Milan, was introduced as "Marchese" De Corato by a master of ceremonies who apparently was misled by the "De" which often precedes noble last names, or by De Corato's genteel manner, or by the aristocratic Rivera wines (or a combination of those factors). De Corato did not have a chance to correct the error then, thinking it was just a temporary slip, but afterward whenever the De Coratos were cited in print, as they often have been lately, the "Marchese" invariably preceded the name.

"It was just one of those silly things that got out of hand," his son Carlo related. "At first my father seemed a little embarrassed, but he didn't want to make an issue of it either. And then it became a sort of 'in' joke with us. After all, we didn't start it, and we certainly would never use the title ourselves, but if other people want to call us Marchesi, that's their business."

Rivera is a bigger name in Italy than is Castel del Monte, but the De Coratos have not deliberately created that situation either. "We want to build the Castel del Monte name nationally and internationally," said Carlo De Corato, "and we've been helping and encouraging other producers to bring up the general quality level, especially private producers because, let's face it, quality is best achieved through direct responsibility."

But for the moment at least, Rivera, which produces about 1 million liters of DOC wine a year, slightly more than half of it rosé, is the big name. Vini Chiddo at Bitonto makes a Castel del Monte Rosso that ages magnificently. A bottle from 1968 drunk in 1979 was still deep ruby in color with little of the customary garnet and orange tints aged reds develop, and it still had a fine measure of fruit. Evidently, Chiddo's production is limited, for bottles are not often seen in Italy. The Riforma Fondiaria cooperative at Andria is the only other producer of important size. Rivera also makes unclassified table wines that are sold in bulk, and it has increased bottling facilities to the point where it can put out DOC Locorotondo and Moscato di Trani under its name.

Locorotondo and Martina: White Wine and "Trulli"

Between Castel del Monte and Alberobello, some 50 kilometers to the southeast, there is a gap in the succession of DOC zones but no apparent lapse in wine production. Here, around the pretty towns of Altamura, Gioia del Colle, Acquaviva delle Fonti, Conversano, and Turi, vineyards and olive groves dominate the gently rolling landscape as elsewhere, each plot delineated by walls of stones piled one by one as they were extracted from the earth and held together by nature's own mortar, water turning to mud the gathering dirt and drifting sands of time. The flatter stones were used to make *trulli* from a circular base to a conical roof whose symmetry resulted from the primitive skill of achieving a balance based on the force of gravity. These curious structures abound throughout central Apulia, becoming so prevalent at Alberobello, the capital of the *trulli* with some thousand clumped together like white beehives gleaming in the sun, that the town has an otherworldly air, like Disneyland, almost too cute to believe.

All through the Itria valley from Alberobello past Locorotondo to Martina Franca, the *trulli* are surrounded by rows of vines neatly trained into bushes in the rust-colored soil. In the past, this area where the provinces of Bari, Taranto, and Brindisi meet was the leading center of neutral whites that went into vermouth. The wines, described by color as *bianco acqua* (water white), *paglierino* (straw), and *verdolino* (light green), seldom went into a bottle on their own. But today, though neutral whites are still in demand for blending in the north, some growers here are adding prestige to their profits by bottling the two most distinguished dry white DOC wines of Apulia: Locorotondo and Martina Franca, which is also known as simply Martina.

There is no essential difference between Locorotondo and Martina, apart from their separate zones of origin. Each is made from Verdeca at 50 to 65 percent, with Bianco di Alessano for most of the rest, with the possible inclusion at up to 5 percent of Fiano, Bombino, and Malvasia Toscana. Each has a minimum of 11° alcohol and each may become *spumante*. The Locorotondo zone extends from the province of Bari into the province of Brindisi at Cisternino. Martina's extends from the province of Taranto north to surround Alberobello in the province of Bari.

Here, for once, it can be stated emphatically that the finest wine of the area is made by a cooperative: the Cantina Sociale di Locorotondo. Its superior tone is apparently due to select picking of grapes and to a slow, temperature controlled fermentation in stainless steel, followed by a brief stay in oaken casks to round it out and give it character. Best to drink within a year or two, the Locorotondo of the Cantina Sociale is a superb fish wine, among the most pleasing of the type in Italy. The Locorotondo produced by Leone de Castris of Salice Salentino and another bottled (but not produced) by Rivera are also recommended.

Martina Franca, all in white with its carved stone portals and ironwork balconies, its narrow winding streets with cobblestones worn to a sheen by centuries of footsteps, its record of independence, and its knack for keeping it all a secret from international tourists, is a charmed place that deserves a special wine. The bottled DOC wine of Vinicola Miali, Lippolis, Giuseppe Strippoli, and Riforma Fondiaria are all commendable products that can be enjoyed elsewhere, though surely the best place to sip Martina Franca's wines — not only the Bianco but also the Rosso and

Rosato — is on the spot. At Le Terrazze, in the Spanish style with white arcades and a view over the fairyland of the Itria valley, the food and wine, both in carafe and bottle, are up to the occasion. The *orecchiette* are homemade and delicious, though the most intriguing pasta is the *spaghetti alla Val d'Itria*, created by owner-cook Iolanda Margiotta, with a sauce of fresh tuna, black olives, capers, and mushrooms. Skewers of grilled lamb or thrush in gelatin call for the fine local red or rosé.

Vinicola Miali, on the edge of Martina Franca, is a family winery run by Martino and Francesco Miali, who produce Martina and an Aglianico dei Colli Lucani (from grapes grown in Basilicata), a robust red called Apulia, and a tasty rosé. The Rosato is made from the wine of Martina blended with Aglianico, which is drawn off the skins a few hours after fermentation begins. Apulia is one of the most impressive red wines of the region, distinguished by its smooth, robust, perfumed elegance and exceptional longevity. The Miali brothers make it from a combination of three different varieties grown in different places: Primitivo, Negro-amaro, and Malvasia Nera.

Ostuni and Brindisi, the Gateway to Greece

Ostuni, another splendor of ancient Apulian civilization, is the center of a DOC zone that extends along the Adriatic north of Brindisi inland to the towns of Ceglie Messapico, San Michele Salentino, and San Vito dei Normanni. Both its red and white wines are unique because their main grapes are grown only here. The Bianco consists of Impigno at 50 to 85 percent complemented by Francavilla. Verdeca and Bianco d'Alessano may be included at no more than 10 percent. Fresh, delicate, pleasing when young, Ostuni Bianco is recommended with seafood. The red wine is known as Ostuni Ottavianello after the Ottavianello grape, which may be mixed with no more than 15 percent of Negroamaro, Malvasia Nera, Notar Domenico, and Sussumariello. A fairly light, all-purpose red of cherry to light ruby color, it is best to drink inside four or five years. It goes with a whole range of foods, especially lamb and poultry.

Brindisi, the seaport that since antiquity has served as Italy's gateway to Greece, has recently been granted a DOC of its own, extending from the city inland to Mesagne on either side of the Appian Way. Brindisi Rosso and Rosato are both made from Negroamaro with the addition of

Malvasia Nera di Brindisi, Sussumariello, Montepulciano, and Sangiovese (though the latter may not surpass 10 percent). The Rosso develops a fairly deep ruby color, intense aroma, and dry and smoothly balanced flavor. When it has 12.5° of alcohol and two years of age it may be labeled *riserva*. Brindisi Rosato has a coral color and lightly fruity, delicate flavor marked by a slightly bitter bite.

A number of good wines have been produced in the Brindisi-Mesagne area for years. Because 1979 was the first vintage in which the Brindisi appellation was permitted, it remained to be seen whether some name wines in the zone would become DOC. In terms of grape composition, many seemed to qualify. They include Messapia, a red produced by Ubaldo Zanzarella at Mesagne; Mitrano Rosso and Rosato produced by the Cantina Sociale di Mitrano and by Antonio Tarantini (whose Castel Mitrano Rosso may be the outstanding wine of the zone); the Torre Saracena of Casa Vinicola Teodoro Caiulo, a winery owned by Nicola De Gregorio; and Don Carmelo Rosso and Rosato made by pop singer Albano Carrisi at Cellino San Marco.

Primitivo: Have Punch, Will Travel

The Salento peninsula, Italy's high heel, has long raised the levels of red wines from points north. It still does, always without credit and sometimes surreptitiously, though these days some of the homegrown products are beginning to stand tall on their own. The most potent elevators of northern reds have been wines from the Primitivo or Primativo grape, whose vines are reputedly the most diffused of Apulia but whose name rarely shows up on a label. Primitivo refers to early (not primitive), because it is the earliest maturing red wine grape of Europe, if not the world. It is also exceptionally laden with sugar. Some years its grapes register as much as 32 Brix, which converts to a knockout punch of 18.4° alcohol. When the grapes are slightly raisined, it can climb even higher.

Primitivo's attraction both to growers in the Salento and to northern blenders was that grapes picked in August could be completely transformed into dark, strong, dense wine ready to travel as the harvest got underway up north. The Primitivo pattern continues, even though growers were given the right a few years ago to make DOC wines from the grape in a large area whose center is the walled town of Manduria, in the province of Taranto. So far, only one producer, Giovanni Soloperto, has taken the initiative to produce and sell wines under the Primitivo di Manduria appellation. The rest — and there seem to be hundreds though the number has decreased of late — continue to put their wines into the pipelines north.

Primitivo, almost certainly of Greek origin, is apparently related to the Zinfandel grape so admired in California. There, in the hot central valleys, it makes a wine considered useful only for blending, but in cooler climes, such as the Napa Valley, with a bit of aging it reaches its own heights of full-blooded distinction. As far as I could learn, Italians have not tried growing it in a genuinely cool place. Evidently as far north as it has gone so far is Gioia del Colle, halfway between Bari and Taranto, which, if cooler than Manduria, hardly qualifies as a test of the vine's heartiness. After phylloxera wiped out Primitivo in the Salento peninsula, growers had to bring the vine back from Gioia, where it survived as Primitivo di Gioia.

Giovanni Soloperto, a veteran cultivator who started making wine from his grapes in 1969, said he was not aware of Primitivo's Zinfandel connection, if indeed it exists, but he was intrigued by the idea that Americans (and perhaps other people too) appreciate big wines like Zinfandel, have a sweet tooth, and are getting more conscientious about natural foods, because he thinks he has just the drink for them.

"Primitivo can be made into several types of wine — *secco, amabile, dolce* — with varying degrees of alcoholic strength, body, etcetera," said Soloperto. "But my taste and experience lead me to conclude that it is best when made from fully mature grapes that have just begun to shrivel on the vine into a dessert wine with as much natural alcohol and as much natural sugar as any fortified wine, such as Porto. If I read the barometer correctly, tastes are swinging back toward sweet wines, and I'm convinced that we growers of Primitivo, with a little private initiative, could put a product on the market that would involve less time, less work, and less contrivance, and be as good as any fortified wine around. And it would cost less and be better for your health."

Soloperto outlined his program for a new winery that could put 2 million bottles of sweet Primitivo on the market annually in a short time. The hitch, however, was that an investor was needed, because Soloperto and his fellow Mandurians lacked the cash to build and acquire the equipment needed to prepare and bottle that much wine. At first glance, Soloperto's seemed not so wild a scheme. If he finds his investor and can convince his fellow cultivators to take part ("That's no problem," he said; "even in Salento, money talks"), he might be remembered someday as the man who rescued Primitivo di Manduria. Already he deserves a special nod as the only producer-bottler of the DOC wine.

His production of about 100,000 liters a year of Primitivo is in three styles. The dry wine of 14° is made from grapes picked earliest, a very good table wine but, as Soloperto ruminated, "That 14 degrees scares people. It's obviously not an everyday wine." The medium-range Primitivo of 17° alcohol with 16° developed is reminiscent of some northern wines made with semi-dried grapes, Sfursat of the Valtellina or Amarone. Its robust power and depth are underlined by a distinct sweet vein that makes it a match for game, strong cheeses, liver pâtés; it also makes good casual sipping. The *dolce naturale* of 20° is what Soloperto thinks producers should concentrate on. It has 16° of natural alcohol and 4° left over as sugar. DOC permits *liquoroso secco* and *liquoroso dolce naturale*, which are fortified, but Soloperto does not produce those types.

The Soloperto plan might help to end the steady decline in Primitivo production of recent years. Growers are getting old, and some have retired. Also the vine is an extremely modest yielder when properly cared for. Responsible growers use the head-trained *alberello* rather than the more productive *tendone*, in which vines are trained high and horizontally. But the Primitivo vine offers advantages. It thrives in poor, stony, crusty soil. It needs no water during the summer and very little care other than an annual pruning and a binding up of the new shoots during the season. At present, most growers harvest in early August to have the wine ready to go by late September, but by waiting until late August or early September they could have the 32–33 Brix needed for the 20° dessert wine.

In Soloperto's view, the wine would carry a price justifiably well above that of most dry table wine but under such classic dessert wines as port and Marsala. "This is a wine of which you'd buy a few bottles a year and keep on the shelf," he said. "A unique, natural wine."

Soloperto makes Primitivo only of grapes from his own vineyards, though he buys grapes to make Rosso, Rosato, and Bianco del Salento, dry table wines of 11° to 13° alcohol. Non-DOC wines called either Primitivo or Manduria appear on the market from time to time in Italy, usually bottled somewhere else. The Manduria of Giuseppe Strippoli is noteworthy. Azienda Vinicola Amanda of Sava had a Rosso di Sava on the market that, although made from Primitivo grapes in the DOC zone, was not labeled as Primitivo di Manduria. Some Rosso di Sava has been exported to the United States.

Space-Age Winery in Salice Salentino

Salice Salentino, a dusty town on the broad plain west of Lecce, is typified by low-slung, block-shaped buildings of whitewashed plaster with only a window or two opening onto the street. It is perhaps more Greek or Spanish in appearance, if you consider stereotypes, than Italian. But as in other sleepy southern towns, there is more there than meets the eye; behind the plain façades are bright and cheerful interiors opening onto courtyards and patios lush with potted plants, flowers, and climbing vines. Here, as in many parts of Italy, it is considered imprudent to be ostentatious about your means.

Leone De Castris, the largest private winery of Apulia, fits the pattern. You could drive past on the Via Senatore De Castris without noticing it, for only a red awning and a wrought-iron sign mark the entrance. But through the door lies another world: well-appointed offices and reception rooms with paintings, diplomas, and framed messages on the walls (most having to do with wine), and beyond that a spacious plant as lavishly up-to-date as I have seen anywhere (including California). Any lingering suspicion I had that Apulian winemaking was still behind the times vanished. At Leone De Castris the winemaking process is fully computerized. There is a lab worthy of a chemical factory; every imaginable piece of modern equipment; a tasting room with space-age spittoons; employee educational and recreational facilities, including a library, basketball and tennis courts, a bar and restaurant, and a nursery. And the entire layout is scanned by an intercom television system. If there is anything modest about Antica Azienda Agricola Vitivinicola Leone De Castris, it might be the owner himself.

His calling card reads "Conte Dottore Avvocato Salvatore Leone De Castris, Cavaliere del Lavoro," but despite the profusion of titles, the man himself seems relatively free of airs. Though he once practiced law and taught at a university, Salvatore Leone De Castris now devotes his time to managing his winery, working on a scale that while grand is completely subject to his personal surveillance. He runs the operation, which has been in the family for centuries, from a small, dimly lit office that he shares with his father, Piero, from whom he bought the business

*Salvatore Leone De Castris (right) with father Piero
and son Piernicola*

several years ago but who remains as his active partner. In contrast with
the antique furnishings is the electronic gear used for frequent exchanges
of messages with employees or to check on the details of the plant, which
has storage capacity of 20 million liters and produces some 11 million
liters of wine a year. It has 75 permanent employees, 500 part-time
workers, and collects its grapes from a network of 150 salaried growers
who work either the Leone De Castris family land or their own.

The wines are headed by Salice Salentino DOC, red from Negroamaro
with the possible addition of Malvasia Nera di Brindisi at up to 20 percent. Full-bodied and deep ruby in color, with 12.5° or more alcohol, it
ages for a decade or more into a velvety, warm wine. It may be called
riserva after two years. Red and rosé called Maïana, after the family
property where vines surround a castle, also qualify as Salice Salentino
DOC.

The Leone De Castris name is best known abroad, at least in America,
for a rosé called Five Roses. Created in the 1930s, it may have been the

first rosé bottled and sold in Italy. After the war, American officers stationed in the area showed a fondness for it, prompting the family to export it to the United States. Five Roses has such extraordinary aging capacity for a rosé that it is usually sold only after several years in bottle. Other Leone De Castris products are the dry, white Albino and Locorotondo DOC; a red dessert wine known as Negrino, from the Malvasia Nera grape; red, white, and pink table wines known as Ursi; and a Leone De Castris rosé.

Leone De Castris has done more to build Salento's reputation in Italy and abroad than has any other winery. About a quarter of production is exported, not only to Europe and North America but to Nigeria, Mexico, Hong Kong, and some Arab countries as well.

As Salvatore Leone De Castris explained it: "Until just recently, the wines of Salento, with their special body, strength, and tone were considered the finest blending wines of their type in Italy. The climate and iron-rich soil here result in uncommonly big wines that need to be carefully controlled as table wines. In this sense, we have benefited not only from the technological transformation of production but also from harvesting grapes at the proper point of maturity. At last, the wines of Salento have begun to be esteemed as excellent table wines, several distinguished by DOC."

The Harvest: No Time for Nostalgia

In Salento, as Leone De Castris maintains, you usually dine better in a private home with a good cook than in a restaurant. Thus forewarned, I accepted his invitation to lunch. The good cook, in this case, was his wife, Marisa, with a little help from the local bakery, which provided a selection of breads that might have made a meal in itself.

Later, with *espresso* on the terrace of their ornate *palazzo* (behind an unmarked wooden door in the center of Salice), three generations of the Leone De Castris family talked about wine from viewpoints varying with age and experience. From an enlightening conversation, I recall most clearly the words of Marisa Leone De Castris, who does not participate but obviously keeps abreast of the winery's activities. She talked about the vintage which was underway at the moment.

"Modern winemaking offers undeniable advantages to producers, cultivators, and consumers," she said, "but it also has victims, as all things seem to. One of them is the harvest. I remember when I was a girl what a great event the *vendemmia* was. We skipped school and everybody, family and friends, picked grapes — not for money but for the fun of it. It was a marvelous *festa* that went on for days and nights. But now everybody is so careful and businesslike about it. You pick at the exact moment, meet your daily quota, and rush the grapes to the winery where the machines take over. Nowadays people talk about harvesting grapes as they do grain or other crops. It's not a family affair anymore. That's gone, and so, I'm afraid, is the joy of the occasion."

Her reference was to Salento, but it could have been about most areas of Italy where the *civiltà contadina,* the country way of life with its quaint customs and little pleasures, is fading fast. True, the *vendemmia* in the old days had to do with donkey carts and teams of oxen, foot stomping and hand presses, musty cellars and leaky wooden vats and barrels. And even in good years coming up with a good wine required more than a little luck. It is also true that farming in the good old days often carried with it social implications that are no longer acceptable: absentee landlords, sharecropping, poverty, ignorance. But it does seem a shame that the progress that has made country people financially better off, more sophisticated, more aware of their rights to health, education, and welfare, seems to have contributed so little to their pursuit of happiness. Instead of gaining a sense of dignity, country life too often seems to have been losing it, which is one reason why it is so difficult to convince a youth to stay on the land. And, sadly, the vintage, once a national celebration, is now little more than an annual routine. Many Italian country people seem to be looking forward to the day when machines will pick their grapes for them.

Salento's Multitude of New DOCs

The Salento peninsula is emerging at an ever-increasing pace as an area of prestige wine production, reflected in the recent multitude of DOC zones. The province of Lecce has four new DOCs — Copertino, Leverano, Salice Salentino, and Squinzano — and Matino, which dates to 1971. Squinzano, northwest of Lecce, has Rosso and Rosato, both based on Negroamaro with the possible addition of Malvasia Nera at 30 percent and Sangiovese at a maximum of 15 percent. Like other red wines of the peninsula, it has robust character, plenty of size and depth and aging capacity, with at least 12.5° of alcohol, 13° in the *riserva,* which must be aged two years. Squinzano Rosato ranges from light ruby to light cherry in color with a refined, smooth flavor, and delicately fruity aroma. Giuseppe Strippoli and the Casa Vinicola ed Olearia Renna are recommended producers.

Copertino, from the town of that name, is basically the same: Negroamaro with 30 percent of Malvasia Nera plus Montepulciano and Sangiovese in Rosso and Rosato. The Rosso *riserva*, of at least 12.5° alcohol, must be aged two years. The Rosato by tradition is made into a rather light wine in Copertino, often with a salmon pink color and a somewhat herbaceous and slightly bitter undertone. Barone Fabio Bacile di Castiglione makes very good versions of both.

Leverano, newest of the region's DOC zones, is just a few kilometers from Copertino in the plain southwest of Lecce. It enjoys the distinction of having the only DOC white of the Salento peninsula, full-blossomed wine from Malvasia Bianca with Bombino Bianco or Trebbiano Toscano included at a maximum of 35 percent. Deep straw yellow, aromatic, it is soft, as Malvasia wines tend to be, though basically dry. Leverano's Rosso and Rosato are virtually identical to the other DOC wines of Salento in composition and style.

Matino is Apulia's southernmost zone, covering an area around the town of that name and extending through the range of low hills known as the Murge Salentino to the coast of the Ionian Sea near the ancient Greek city of Gallipoli. Matino's Rosso and Rosato are, once again, based on Negroamaro with the usual supporting cast. Considering the similarity in the wines made throughout the heel of the boot, with the exception of Primitivo di Manduria, it would seem only natural to unite the Rosso and Rosato of Salento under a single DOC appellation with possible subdenominations by community. Evidently such a plan has not even been considered, though non-DOC table wines of the peninsula are recognized as Rosso, Rosato, and Bianco del Salento.

Several good wines made in the Salento have been selling under special names, though in some cases they could qualify as DOC. Niccolò Coppola at Alezio makes two red wines, Doxi Vecchio and Lacrima di Terra d'Otranto, both from Negroamaro and Malvasia Nera, each from different vineyards. Giuseppe Calò, also at Alezio, makes a prized red Portulano and a pink Rosa del Golfo, that ranks with the finest rosés I've tasted, a match for the elite Tavels and the better pink wines of Merlot, Pinot Nero, and Lagrein. Rosa del Golfo gets its cherry pink hue and exquisite delicacy as a result of the ancient *lacrima* or teardrop system of vinification, which uses the musts of uncrushed grapes.

Apulia's regionwide DOC classification, Aleatico di Puglia, is red dessert wine made from the Aleatico di Puglia grape with Negroamaro, Malvasia Nera, and Primitivo permitted at 15 percent maximum. Aleatico is made into two types: *dolce naturale* and *liquoroso dolce naturale*. The difference is in the degrees of sweetness and alcohol. The first has at least 15° natural alcohol and the second can be fortified to reach 18.5° or more. Both are garnet with violet tints, and both may be aged almost indefinitely (after three years they qualify as *riserva*). The *dolce naturale* is medium sweet, smooth and warm, the *liquoroso* is richer and stronger. Despite the regionwide status, only a small amount of Aleatico di Puglia is produced and bottles are rarely found in commerce in Italy. The only producer I know of is Botta at Trani, whose *dolce naturale* is excellent.

The Cooking: From "Cavatieddi" to "Gniummerieddi"

Despite what some people might tell you, you can dine well in Apulian restaurants, even if the food is sometimes less painstakingly prepared than it once was. Fish, meat (especially lamb and kid), and fresh vegetables, herbs, and spices abound here. Though you will find spaghetti on every menu, *orecchiette* are the most typical of Apulian pastas, served in dozens of different ways. *Cavatelli*, or *cavatieddi*, rolled by hand and dressed with *ricotta*, rue, and grated *pecorino*, are an ancient specialty to be found in traditional restaurants. Then there are *ciceri e trii* (chickpea and *tagliatelle* soup), and *troccoli* (noodles cut with a stringed instrument somewhat like the Abruzzi's *maccheroni alla chitarra*), and a simple but delicious soup of fava beans, wild chicory, onions, and olive oil that supposedly dates to the time of Aristophanes.

Among other fixtures of Apulian cooking are the *gniummerieddi* of Martina Franca (the innards of lamb or kid cooked in a sort of pudding with pecorino, lard, lemon, and parsley), *capriata* (a vegetable stew enlivened by pimento), and *la tortiera pugliese* (rice, scalloped potatoes, zucchini, and peppers in a casserole). Apulians have a natural touch with fish, showing a favoritism for squid, octopus, oysters, and mussels. The latter figure in a dish called *tielli* with potatoes, anchovies, breadcrumbs, and herbs, though there are other ingredients for *tielli* as well.

Among Apulia's good restaurants, Da Tommaso at Palese on the coast just north of Bari is unbeatable for seafood. If the sea is too rough for fishing, owner Sebastiano Basile will serve meat instead, for he insists on absolute freshness. In Bari, La Pignata offers traditional dishes in an elegant setting. For good traditional food and wine in rustic surroundings, the Ostello di Federico adjacent to Castel del Monte and the Fagiano da Gastone at Selva di Fasano are recommended. Pizzomunno la Punta del Mondo at Vieste on the extreme tip of the Gargano promontory prepares everything well and serves it on a peaceful garden terrace in the summer.

The Vintages

	Castel del Monte	Locorotondo, Martina
1979	Good	Exceptional
1978	Very good	Excellent
1977	Excellent	Excellent
1976	Fair to good	Fair to good
1975	Excellent	Excellent
1974	Excellent	Excellent
1973	Excellent	Fair
1972	Good	—
1971	Good	—
1970	Good	—
1969	Excellent	—
1968	Exceptional	—

Salento red wines

1979	Excellent
1978	Good
1977	Very good
1976	Good
1975	Excellent
1974	Excellent
1973	Good
1972	Good
1971	Exceptional
1970	Excellent

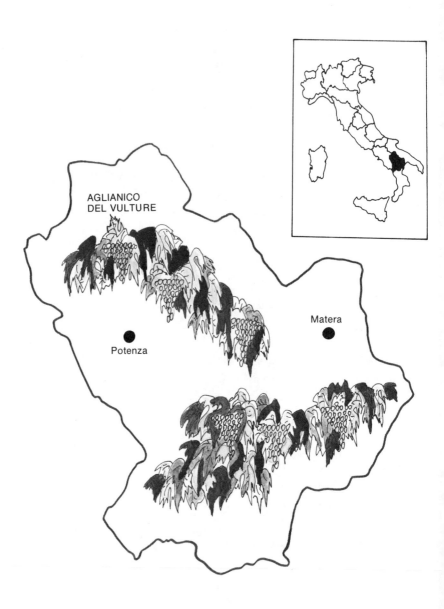

AGLIANICO
DEL VULTURE

Potenza

Matera

BASILICATA

PROVINCES

POTENZA, Matera

POPULATION

550,000

AREA

3,856 square miles

AVERAGE WINE PRODUCTION

50 million liters

DOC WINE

Aglianico del Vulture

OTHER WINES

Aglianico dei Colli Lucani · Aglianico di Matera · Aglianico Rosato ·
Asprino · Malvasia · Metapontum · Montepulciano · Moscato

Extracting Good Things from the Stones

WEDGED compactly between Campania, Apulia, and Calabria with only a couple of meager outlets to the sea, Basilicata stoically resists an active role in what is sometimes billed as Italy's dynamic new south. On the map, at least, it might appear to be the heart of the southern mainland, but on close examination Basilicata is too old, too poor, too tired to pump lifeblood into anything, a neglected collection of well-worn stones whose chief appeal seems to be to archaeologists.

The Greek stamp remains on Basilicata, even in its name, which was attributed to a governor, Basilikos. The Roman influence can also be seen here and there and heard in the region's alternate name, Lucania, which was bestowed by the Emperor Augustus. But in places it seems that life has not changed its pattern profoundly since the Stone Age and that the dominant ancient culture was that of the Oscan tribes from the mountains rather than the more urbane Greek or Roman.

Basilicata was never a favored place. Indeed, it is still so economically deprived that much of the male population has gone north to the factories of Turin, Milan, Germany, and Belgium, leaving their women and children behind to make do with a periodic transfer of money. The Cassa per il Mezzogiorno has provided some new roads, factories, opportunities, but Basilicata has remained for the most part solemnly attached to its rudimentary but time-proven forms of agriculture: the cultivation of vines, olives, fruit, and nuts, and the raising of pork and mutton.

If largely ignored, Basilicata is still capable of surprising the rare outsider who lingers there on his way to somewhere else. Perhaps the biggest shock is the climate; though the bit of lowland in the coastal regions is hot enough for citrus, the interior is cold, typified by the capital, Potenza, at 2,700 feet above sea level, whose temperatures many days of the year are lower than Bolzano's. A more pleasant surprise is the warmth that lies behind the rather forbidding exterior, expressed in the generosity of a people who through the ages have mastered the magic of extracting good things from the stones.

One such product of the stones is Basilicata's lone DOC wine, Aglianico del Vulture, whose heritage dates to when the Greeks noted that their native vines fared so well in southern Italy that they referred to their colonies collectively as Enotria. The vine that came to be called Aglianico (through Hellenico) found a chosen land on the volcanic slopes of Monte Vulture, an oasis of water and plant life that broods over the desolate northern interior of Basilicata like the bird of prey that shares its name. But the haunting image cast by the dark green mountain from afar dissipates as you approach it, after turning off the Naples–Bari *autostrada* and rolling into Melfi, the first whitewashed town of the range.

The Aglianico del Vulture zone could be rated as productive only by humble regional standards. Erosion has depleted the hillside topsoil, forcing the vine roots to work their way down through the rocky substrata to attain that resilience that results in grapes with all the more strength of character for knowing what it is to struggle. Significantly, the best grapes come from fragmented plots at heights of up to 2,200 feet, around Rionero and Barile on the southeastern slopes of the mountain. Vineyards in the more fertile lower sectors of the zone render greater quantities of grapes per hectare and wines of less distinction. Inevitably, most new planting — though there has not been all that much — has been in the lower zones, such as Venosa, where Horace was born and where Winefood recently planted a large tract of Aglianico vineyards. In the tough upper reaches, vines have been decreasing because no younger generation of growers has emerged to replace the old. This attrition, a problem nearly everywhere in Italy, is felt more acutely in areas such as this, where the population has been declining.

DOC defines three types of Aglianico del Vulture: the young, the old (both dry), and the sparkling (sweet). The latter is largely of regional interest, a natural *spumante* with at least 11.5° alcohol and enough residual sugar to make it *amabile*. Young, dry Aglianico can be a worthy table wine when it goes on sale after a year of aging. But the prestige products are the *vecchio* (aged three years, at least two in barrel) and the *riserva* (aged five years, at least two in barrel). Deep, smooth, robust wines of at least 12.5° alcohol, they approach a peak of elegance after six to ten years and have been known to age gracefully for two decades or more.

With its long history and recent illustrious record for quality and longevity, Aglianico del Vulture could very well rank among the classic red wines of Italy, but so far its appreciators are a limited few who have had the privilege of tasting wine from the better producers in the better years. Like other big wines of the south, Aglianico has long contributed anonymously to the stature of northerly reds. It still does, but less so because it has managed to establish an identity through DOC and the diligent efforts of a few writers and merchants who have extolled its virtues to a wider public.

Still, its status would certainly be greater if its potential markets were not so distant and if its producers could organize a modest campaign to promote its name and facilitate its distribution. Instead, intramural rivalry has prevented Aglianico from presenting a serious challenge to the few wines of Europe that stand in its class.

Local production of Aglianico is carried out by a cooperative whose wines are sold in bulk (mostly to northerners) and by a half dozen or so private producers, among them Fratelli D'Angelo, Armando Martino, Paternoster, Botte, Sasso, and Fratelli Napolitano, all of whom are based either in Rionero or Barile. Winefood's new operation was not yet producing DOC wine. Wines sold under the name Aglianico del Vulture are also bottled in Apulia and Lombardy (Brescia), among other places.

Basilicata has always produced wine grapes, but only in recent times have wineries in the region taken over a significant part of the commercial production, which was and still often is carried out in Apulia. Even today, DOC regulations for Aglianico del Vulture specify that the grapes may be vinified in the Apulian communities of Barletta, Trani, and Canosa, where once upon a time nearly all the Aglianico of Vulture was made.

The elite names in Aglianico at the moment are Martino, Paternoster, Napolitano, and D'Angelo, each with their partisans in Basilicata and beyond. All are small wineries that purchase select grapes from growers and make from them both excellent aged Aglianico and the more popularly priced Aglianico *spumante*, as well as rosé, Malvasia, and Moscato.

Gold Medals and Giveaway Prices

Donato D'Angelo is a young graduate of Conegliano whose winemaking skills have drawn attention to his family's Aglianico with gold medals at Pramaggiore in the Veneto and the Douja d'Or of Asti in Piedmont, as well as in regional competition. Still, he has trouble selling the 100,000 to 150,000 bottles from good vintages at prices that by northern standards are giveaways.

"My family has tried to organize a consortium, not only to control the standards but to promote our wines as a unit," said D'Angelo, whose soft-spoken manner fails to conceal his intensity. "But the others don't want it. So it's everyone for himself."

Fratelli D'Angelo has exported a small amount of Aglianico to the United States while looking for new markets in Italy, particularly in prestigious shops and restaurants. But the problem is that the D'Angelos are winemakers, not traveling salesmen, and they have not been able effectively to reach the sort of consumer who would appreciate the quality of their Aglianico and pay a justified price for it — that is, consumers who still for the most part live in cities of the north.

In Basilicata, the current market is for light, dry table wines and lightly sweet sparkling wines, not too strong, not too heavy, and not too high in price. D'Angelo continues to produce such wines largely to sustain production costs of the aged Aglianico. The winery, run by two generations

Donato D'Angelo (left) with growers

of brothers, Rocco and Pasquale, the elder, and Donato and Lucio, is a busy operation that occupies a newly expanded building on the edge of Rionero.

Fratelli D'Angelo buys most of its grapes in the vicinity from reliable growers who follow traditional methods of pruning low and training the new growth onto cane poles set tepee-style around the trunk. Although they have always been able to obtain satisfactory grapes in good years, they are considering buying land and planting vines of their own to compensate for the gradual diminution of vineyards on the steep hills. "There's no question that the grapes are superior here when the season is favorable," said Donato D'Angelo. "The practice has been to maintain separate roles between winemaker and cultivator, but that seems destined to change out of necessity."

D'Angelo, who has updated the vinification process at the winery with new fermentation vats and stainless steel tanks for making the white and sparkling wines, takes issue with his former mentors in the Veneto who favor reducing the use of barrels or even doing away with them. "Wood is essential to aged Aglianico," he said as we tasted a succession of vintages from 1978 back to 1973. "Aglianico has a sharpness and ample tannin when it's young that mellows with a year and a half in barrel while taking on that hint of oak that adds to its elegance. Bottle age is essential in developing bouquet and rounding out the flavor.

"Up north, everybody's talking about young wines and light fermentation," D'Angelo continued. "We can do it with Aglianico, especially in years when the natural alcohol is low, which happens frequently enough here because this is as harsh a climate as you'll find in Piedmont or the Veneto. But the *vecchio* and *riserva* are what I'm aiming at, despite the cost and the tying up of capital for five years or more, because I simply can't accept anything less. I believe in all sincerity that Aglianico is a great wine. How great, I don't know. I'll leave that to experts and consumers to judge."

The 1973, an exceptional vintage, had a bright ruby-garnet color and full bouquet with a rich complexity of flavors in which the austere dryness was counterbalanced by an almond-caramel sort of bitter undertone and plenty of fruit along with the light tannin and that hint of oak. It was superb by 1979, and indications were that its prime still lies ahead. For parallels, only the Taurasi of Mastroberardino comes to mind. The only relation this Aglianico bore to other great wines — from Cabernet, Merlot, Pinot Noir, Nebbiolo, Sangiovese — was in breeding, in its unquestionable nobility. D'Angelo's 1974 and 1975 Aglianico were similar but clearly younger, though apparently almost as full of possibility. The 1977 and 1978 from the barrel were impressive and 1979 produced Aglianico of excellent tone, a vintage to compare with 1973.

The Cooking: Ancient, Exotic, and Hot

Aglianico's smoothness contrasts with the strong seasoning of regional cooking, highlighted by the tang of garlic, capers, nutmeg, and mountain herbs, the relentless piquancy of ginger and all manner of peppers, especially red-hot pimento. You can eat most enjoyable meals in Basilicata if you like homegrown produce and country cooking with all the simplicity of antiquity, and, of course, if you can take the heat. Preserved pork products are the pride of Basilicata, so famous that certain types of sausage, now imitated elsewhere, are known throughout Italy as *lucaniche*, or *luganighe* following the local pronunciation. *Prosciutto* can be exquisite, as can *soppressata, coppa,* and lean, tender *salame,* all enhanced by curing in the well-ventilated mountain environment.

Perhaps because of its lack of tourist traffic, Basilicata has no restaurants of more than local renown, so their survival depends on the loyalty of a regular clientele. This may be the surest indication of authenticity one could ask for, a sign that what you will be served is bound to be typical. I went with Donato D'Angelo to La Pergola in Rionero, a tidy, small-town *trattoria* where the wholesome cooking and friendly service are a matter of family pride. Our object was to match a 1975 Aglianico with some suitable local dishes. The mission could not have been described as a total success, though both the wine and the food showed extremely well on their own.

From La Pergola's own *prosciutto* and *salame,* we proceeded to a *pasta e fagioli* laced with *piccante,* a pepper sauce that would not have been out of place in North Africa. It should have been resisted for the wine's sake but was not. More *piccante* on a plate of *cavatelli* with tomato sauce and grated *pecorino,* and the wine seemed compromised for the nonce. But tender charcoal-grilled lamb and veal took away the burning sensation, and by the time grilled *scamorza* cheese was served with some crisp aqua-green olives, our palates were back in form to savor the Aglianico, which by then had had a chance to breathe. A wedge of soft *pecorino* and the wine took command, bringing nods of approval even from its producer, who was by then putting it through another in the endless series of organoleptic examinations that conscientious wine-makers apply with the detachment of laboratory technicians, all the time speculating on whether the 1975 vintage would turn out as well as the 1973 had.

If the family had made it that day, we would no doubt have opted as a meat course for *cutturieddu*, lamb stew flavored with tomato, onion, rosemary, celery, and bay leaf, considered the ideal match for an aged Aglianico. Actually, a wine of this class can be put up against nearly any dish of meat, poultry, game, or cheese and more than hold its own.

The sounds of Basilicata's food specialties are every bit as exotic as their flavors. There are pastas called *minuich* and *strangulapreuti*; stuffed artichokes are known as *ciaudedda*; a stew of lamb's innards, soft cheese, and *prosciutto* is *cazmarr*; and there are snails called *pecorelle* cooked in tomato sauce flavored with garlic, pepper, and oregano. For digestive purposes, Basilicata also has a bitter liqueur called Amaro Lucano, which is better known in Italy than is Aglianico del Vulture.

Other Wines, from Asprino to Metapontum

The Aglianico vine is cultivated elsewhere in Basilicata, notably in the area bordering Apulia in the province of Matera, but it rarely reaches the heights it attains around Monte Vulture. The Aglianico dei Colli Lucani, produced and bottled by Vinicola Miali of Martina Franca in Apulia, is perhaps the best, capable of long aging from certain vintages. Aglianico del Matera, the best of which comes from the Val Bradano, is consumed for the most part in the region's second city whose Citta Vecchia atop a hill facing the Murge mountains is one of the most striking sites of Basilicata, a village carved from stone and webbed by a labyrinth of narrow streets.

Malvasia and Moscato are also cultivated in various parts of the region. The Moscato is always sweet, often sparkling, sometimes surprisingly good at the end of a meal. Malvasia ranges from *amabile* to bone-dry. Its tendency to maderize makes it a wine to drink on the spot soon after it is ready, though it may also be kept as an apéritif or dessert wine when maderization is desirable. Some of the better Moscatos and Malvasias are produced in the Vulture area, though they can also be found elsewhere, more often than not straight from the barrel. There is some talk of eventually proposing the Malvasia of Vulture for DOC, though the general level will have to be improved markedly.

The one other wine that regularly finds its way out of the region is Asprino, which is similar to the wine of that name that once reigned in Naples. In fact, nearly all the Asprino of Basilicata winds up in Naples, where it is said to be every bit the equal of its counterpart from Aversa, though this could not be considered the ultimate in praise. The best Asprino of Basilicata is made around the town of Ruoti in the province of Potenza.

Though almost deprived of a maritime climate (the region has about 25 kilometers of seafront on the Tyrrhenian and maybe 35 kilometers on the Ionian), Basilicata exploits what little there is of hot terrain for citrus and other sunny products. The area around Metaponto, the Greek Ionian colony of Metapontion founded in 700 B.C., is sometimes alluded to rather lamely as Basilicata's "California." The plains there have shown some of the promise for viticulture already realized in adjacent sections of Apulia. The Cantina Sociale del Metapontino makes a Metapontum Bianco of Malvasia Bianca, Trebbiano, and Moscato di Terracina that is dry and pleasantly perfumed, and a Metapontum Rosso of Sangiovese, Negroamaro, and Malvasia Nera of sound quality. Just recently, the cooperative has also been producing a Montepulciano with the depth and body to merit serious consideration among the quality red wines of southeastern Italy.

The Vintages

Aglianico del Vulture

1979	Exceptional	1971	Good
1978	Very good	1970	Good
1977	Excellent	1969	Excellent
1976	Fair	1968	Good
1975	Excellent		(Previous superior
1974	Excellent		vintages: 1965,
1973	Exceptional		1954, 1951)
1972	Poor		

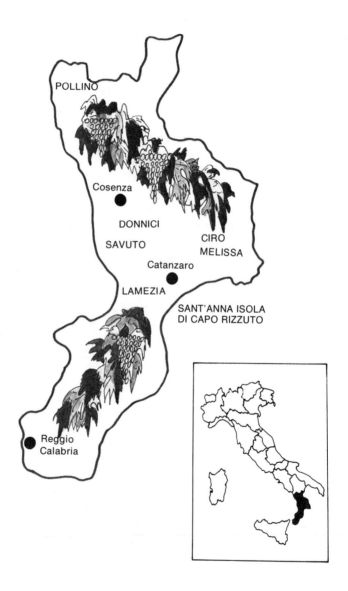

POLLINO

Cosenza

DONNICI

SAVUTO

CIRO
MELISSA

Catanzaro

LAMEZIA

SANT'ANNA ISOLA
DI CAPO RIZZUTO

Reggio
Calabria

CALABRIA

PROVINCES

CATANZARO, Cosenza, Reggio di Calabria

POPULATION

2,050,000

AREA

5,823 square miles

AVERAGE WINE PRODUCTION

105 million liters

DOC WINES

Cirò (Bianco, Rosso, Rosato) · Donnici · Lamezia · Melissa (Bianco, Rosso) · Pollino · Sant'Anna Isola di Capo Rizzuto · Savuto

OTHER WINES

Bianco d'Enotria · Calabria · Esaro · Greco di Bianco · Greco di Gerace · Lametino · Malvasia · Mantonico · Moscato · Nicastro · Pellaro · Sambiase · Squillace · Verbicaro

Enotria Revisited

WHAT the Greeks called Enotria, at least in the beginning, was a part of the Salento peninsula where the Enotri people dwelled. But when the name came to apply to the land of wine, the Greeks probably had in mind Calabria, an early and long a favored part of Magna Grecia, where life was filled with pleasures. Indeed, the city of Sybaris with its Temple of Dionysus and its voluptuous life-style became so influential that its citizens went elsewhere to found colonies and spread the good word. Today, Calabria and Calabrians scarcely hint at this sybaritic heritage. A gorgeously wild region, the toe of the Italian boot is mostly mountain and seacoast with not much arable land in between. Calabria is still rather poor and still rather secluded by distance and geography from the mainstream of Italian life.

Some names and places correspond to those of ancient Greece. There are Crotone (Kroton), home of Pythagoras; and Scilla, the legendary Scylla at the top of the Straits of Messina, where, as Homer's *Odyssey* relates, ships often foundered in the tricky currents; and the Sila Greca, the mountains whose forests provided wood for Greek boat builders. But the remnants of Hellenic civilization are not as visible here as they are in other regions, such as Sicily and Campania, even though Calabria was noted as the most Greek of the colonies and evidently had, at one point at least, the most elevated standard of living.

Links between the wines of Calabria today and those of Magna Grecia are noted more for their propaganda value than for any real similarity in taste. Still, it is maintained that Greco, the mainstay of most of the region's white wines, was brought here by the Greeks. And possibly Gaglioppo, which is the source of nearly all the region's red and rosé wines and the cultivation of which is almost exclusively Calabrian, had roots in Hellas as well. Calabria has only one wine whose name has national and by now international standing, Cirò, which claims direct descent from what promoters freely refer to as "the oldest wine in the world," Krimisa or Cremissa or Crimissa, supposed to have been used to toast returning Calabrian athletes after their triumph in one of the early Olympiads. Even if that is true, it is difficult to determine how Krimisa became the oldest wine in the world.

Calabria now has seven DOC zones, though for years Cirò alone represented the region, and even now the others are for the most part known and appreciated at home. In recent years, DOC has represented only about 2 percent of regional production, partly because a lot of potential DOC wine is not declared but instead is sold in bulk — a surer market than bottles here. Calabria has some excellent non-DOC wines, both dessert and tables wines, one of which — Greco di Gerace — is considered great by its limited few admirers. Calabria has always shipped away some *vino da taglio*, too, but in quantities that do not begin to approach the outflow from some other southern regions. For the most part, oenological patterns evolved independently here, and Calabria's grapes and wines have little to do with those of its neighbors.

Pollino: Memories of Alpine Wines

The range known as the Monti Pollino, which picks up where the Lucanian Apennines leave off in Basilicata and walls off Calabria from the rest of peninsular Italy, offers an immediate taste of the region's individualistic wines to travelers approaching from the north. Pollino, DOC since 1975, is a sturdy red mountain wine from Gaglioppo at 60 percent or more with Greco Nero and three light varieties —Malvasia Bianca, Mantonico Bianco, and Guarnaccia Bianca — permitted at 20 percent between them. Color can vary from a bright ruby to a light cherry, virtually a rosé. When the alcohol is 12.5° or more and after two years of aging, Pollino may be labeled *superiore*.

Vines are head-trained close to the ground here to soak up the heat, which is not excessive because many vineyards are 1,500 feet or more above sea level. Though generally stronger, Pollino bears a striking resemblance to some wines of nothern Italy's Alpine areas, a certain ethereal fragrance and a delicacy in body that makes it most pleasant to drink when young and cool. The village of Frascineto is reputed to have the finest wines of the Monti Pollino, though production is concentrated in the Cantina Sociale Vini del Pollino, which draws its grapes from all over the zone.

Frascineto and Civita, on the eastern edge of the zone in the province of Cosenza, overlook the plains of Sibari, the modern name of Sybaris, only traces of which have been found in the alluvial soil. Near where the ancient city stood is the nondescript little town of Sibari, surrounded by orange groves, a place that has become oriented toward tourism lately because of the proximity of the Ionian Sea.

The coast, a garden of the Greeks, is one of the few agriculturally prosperous sections of Calabria, source of citrus, olives, grain, and a major share of the region's wine. Following the coast southeast from Sibari past the medieval city of Rossano and parks of giant, centuries-old olive trees, you soon arrive in the zone of Cirò. The vineyards extend from the peninsula of Punta Alice back into the softly terraced hills around the villages of Cirò, Crucoli, and Melissa in the province of Catanzaro. Most wineries are situated unobtrusively in the flat seaside town of Cirò Marina, on the site of the Krimisa of antiquity, today a collection of rectangular buildings whose pastels gleam in the Mediterranean sun.

Cirò: Improved but Unproven

Cirò remains the prime DOC wine of Calabria, though actual production is only a fraction of the potential. Most Cirò is made by about a dozen producers, none of whom work on a particularly large scale. Of its three types — Bianco, Rosso, and Rosato — Rosso is the most respected and the most heavily produced. Made almost exclusively of Gaglioppo (though the light Greco and Trebbiano Toscano may be included at a maximum of 5 percent between them), the red is a strong, sometimes distinguished wine of medium ruby turning toward rust with age. From some vintages, Cirò Rosso ages exceedingly well. Wine from a specified area around Cirò and Cirò Marina may be called Classico. When subjected to three years of aging, Cirò Rosso may be designated as *riserva,* which must have at least 13.5° alcohol and often has more. With age, it mellows to a soft warmth with fine bouquet and subtle flavors marked by a hint of sweetness set off against a suggestion of bitterness. The younger red and the Rosato, which comes from the same grapes, are frank, fruity table wines.

Cirò Bianco, though not highly esteemed by Italian connoisseurs, has shown marked improvement in recent years from those producers who have introduced the new technology for white wine. One such is Vincenzo Ippolito, a family winery in the center of Cirò Marina run by brothers Salvatore and Antonio Ippolito, whose views on wine are decidedly avant-garde.

Salvatore Ippolito does not concur in the least with the idea that only the Rosso is to be taken seriously among the three types of Cirò. "That's what I'd call an outdated opinion," he said thoughtfully. "I think our Bianco has special character and marked flavor all its own. It's a lovely sipping wine, and few whites go better with *gamberi* [prawns]."

He agreed, however, that cold fermentation of the select free-run musts, a fairly recent innovation, has made all the difference. The Ippolito Cirò Bianco from the 1978 vintage lived up to its producer's estimation and maybe even went a bit beyond it. It had the sort of tone and harmony that, indeed, deserve another review by the experts, for dry white wines of this class are by no means common.

The Ippolito brothers, like a few other cultivator-producers of Cirò, have also upgraded the quality of their red and rosé wines through a change in method of training vines. "The historical problem with Cirò Rosso was low fixed acids," said Salvatore Ippolito. "Through experimentation it was discovered that the traditional head-training here was the cause, because grapes were too close to the ground and developed prematurely. So we switched to cordon. Now the grapes mature more slowly, develop similar degrees of sugar, and have adequate fixed acids."

Another habitual error, according to the Ippolito brothers, was barrel aging. "There's a saying in Calabria that wines, like women, age too quickly," said Salvatore Ippolito. "Well, we've managed to solve the problem with wine anyway by eliminating barrels, which in this climate are simply not suitable because they invite oxidation. We now do all our processing in stainless steel and glass-lined cement vats. The wines retain their fruit and bouquet better this way and it has lessened the tendency to maderization, which can be excessive here. Gaglioppo is a noble grape that ages with the best of them, but the question of aging is very different here from what it is in Piedmont or Bordeaux."

Despite the improvements, Cirò from Ippolito and other qualified producers is not sweeping any markets. The Ippolito wines move well in Calabria, Naples, Rome, but northern markets have been slow and exports are still very limited, though the names Ippolito, Librandi, Fratelli Antonio, Caruso, Cirovin, Caparra & Siciliani, and Scala are known in the United States.

Antonio (left) and Salvatore Ippolito

The Ippolito brothers recalled that their father, Vincenzo, namesake of the winery that has been in operation since 1845, was probably the first to bottle Cirò and certainly the first to promote it nationally. Not that Cirò lacked admirers through the ages. One, Norman Douglas, wrote in 1907: "This wine of Cirò, for instance, is purest nectar."

"Papa was a plucky sort," said Antonio Ippolito, smiling at the memory. "Every time he went somewhere, first on the train, and later in a Topolino [Fiat's original compact car], he'd fill up a suitcase with bottles of Cirò, and whenever the occasion presented itself, he'd pop open a bottle and offer it around. It worked in its little way, because he was always getting orders and shipping off a few cases here and there."

"Yes," said his brother, "but you know Cirò still isn't proven. It needs nationwide promotion. Our small-scale wineries can't afford it on our own, so we've been trying to get some backing from the region, but those things come about slowly here."

The consortium of some twenty active members has obviously not been successful in persuading local wineries to produce DOC Cirò. If statistics I have come across are to be trusted, out of a possible production of some 20 million to 25 million liters a year (if all registered vineyards were used), production of DOC Cirò reached a peak of 2.83 million liters in 1975 and has tended to diminish since. As the region's only "established" wine, Cirò does not seem to offer much incentive to producers in newly emerged and emerging zones to make DOC wine.

Vincenzo Ippolito, with about 1 million bottles a year from some 250 acres of vineyards in the Classico area, is among the largest producers of DOC Cirò. Another widely praised winemaker is Antonio Cataldo Librandi, whose aged Classico is often found in good restaurants and shops in Italy.

Melissa and Sant'Anna, New DOCs

The town of Melissa lies within the Cirò DOC domain, but not the Classico area, which may be one reason why growers there and in communities to the south requested (and were recently granted) an appellation of their own. The new DOC of Melissa includes a Rosso and Bianco almost identical to those of Cirò and a Rosso *superiore* that needs 13° of alcohol and must be aged at least two years. The zone is large, extending along the coast from Melissa nearly to Crotone and back into the low hills. The largest producer in the area is the Cantina Sociale di Torre Melissa. In addition to DOC Melissa and Cirò, it makes a white, primarily of Greco and Malvasia, known as Bianco d'Enotria, and red and white table wines known as Calanco. The Cantina Sociale Val di Neto at Scandale makes Rosso and Bianco wines that seem to qualify as Melissa DOC. They are among the finest table wines of the Ionian coast.

The area between Crotone and Isola di Capo Rizzuto (despite the name, it is not an island but a town) is the home of another new DOC: Sant'Anna Isola di Capo Rizzuto. The name, like the ingredients, is somewhat long-winded. The wine is made from Gaglioppo at 40 to 60 percent and Nocera, Nerello Mascalese, Nerello Cappuccio, Malvasia Nera, Malvasia Bianca, and Greco Bianco, alone or combined at 40 to 60 percent (except that the light grapes cannot make up more than 35 percent of the total). Light ruby to roseate in color, Sant'Anna Isola di Capo Rizzuto is noted for its youthful freshness and easy drinkability. Minimum alcohol is 12°. A wine known as Sant'Anna Bianco from the same area is not included in DOC. It is produced by the Sant'Anna Cantina Sociale at Isola di Capo Rizzuto.

The Sila: Vast Forests, Vanishing Folklore

Though neat sociological conclusions have a way of backfiring in Italy, Calabria does have a fairly clean split between life on the coast and life in the mountains, for in this region there is plenty of coast and plenty of mountain and precious little else. It is debatable which section is physically more attractive; Calabria can still claim to be unspoiled, though less so as oil refineries, power plants, and sprawling factories are constructed to make life better here.

The region is governed from Catanzaro, which sits on a hill overlooking the sea and is the second largest city. The largest is Reggio di Calabria, on the coast near the tip of the toe across from Sicily, capital of the southernmost province. The third provincial capital is Cosenza, a mountain city at the edge of the Sila massifs.

From Crotone, a fast road now crosses the mountains to Cosenza between the Sila Grande and the Sila Piccola. With its great sweeps of woodland in fir, pine, beech, and chestnut and large lakes formed by the damming of rivers, the Sila offers some of the grandest mountain scenery in the nation. Sometimes referred to as "Italy's great woods" or even "little Switzerland," the Sila has added tourism to its traditional economies of lumbering and grazing, so some towns on the massif now have a prosperous look, though not many years ago life could be pretty grim in a place that might have snow on the ground for four or five months a year. The people of the Sila, who used to wear their local costumes regularly, now seem to put them on only for special occasions when encouraged by the tourist boards. For even in this rustic upland, television and the onslaught of tourism, which fills the new hotels, campgrounds, and trailer parks in the warm months, make folklore seem hopelessly camp.

Calabrian mountain people favor red wines which seem to be light in style though some can pack an unexpected wallop. Three mountain wines have gained DOC status — Pollino, from the north, Donnici, from the hills south of Cosenza, and Savuto, from the valley of the river of that name between the provinces of Cosenza and Catanzaro. Donnici and Savuto have points in common. Both are still considered local wines with growing reputations in the region but only rarely are they seen anywhere else. They are based on Gaglioppo and, though sometimes strong, they are light, bright, and easy to drink.

Donnici and Savuto in a Changing World

Donnici, from a town a few kilometers south of Cosenza whose DOC zone touches the city limits, is the favorite table wine of the western Sila. Most is still sold by the demijohn. Only two producers bottle the wine, the Cantina Sociale di Donnici and the private firm of Pasquale Bozzo.

The Bozzo winery at Donnici Inferiore, where Pasquale Bozzo took over from his father, Antonio, a few years ago and has since renovated the cellars, is an example of what an optimist with a measure of courage expressed in a calculated financial gamble can do to put a wine on the map. Bozzo, who in two years of selling Donnici in labeled bottles has already pioneered markets outside Calabria and even overseas, is convinced that as Donnici makes a name for itself its success will help to change the dismal pattern here of migration from farm to city.

"Already there's been a return to the land," said Pasquale Bozzo as he pointed on a map to the areas considered privileged in the Donnici zone. "DOC came in here in 1975 and with that as motivation, our cantina was transformed and expanded to handle not only grapes from our family vineyards (ten acres in the community of Aprigliano), but also those of other growers." Bozzo's recent annual production of DOC Donnici has been about 30,000 liters. The winery also produces a dry Rosato and Bianco and a Malvasia *amabile* that is impressively perfumed. Bozzo has steadily increased production of all these wines.

The return to the land, like its abandonment, is perhaps not so dramatic around Donnici as it has been in other places, for Cosenza is only ten minutes away on a municipal bus, meaning that farmers could easily commute if they happened to prefer city to country life. But growers, spurred by increasing grape prices, are planting new vines and reworking the old in the conviction that Donnici's fortunes are turning upward. Its vineyards are among the highest of any DOC zone of Italy, ranging from 1,100 to 2,200 feet above sea level. All head-trained low vines on steep hillsides, they require manual care and they do not yield prolifically. "But it's worthwhile," Bozzo explained, "because prices for the select grapes are among the highest in Italy, so here vines are more profitable than other types of agriculture."

Pasquale (left) and Antonio Bozzo

Gaglioppo, which is used at 65 percent (along with Greco Nero at 15 percent, Malvasia Bianca at 15 percent, and Mantonico Bianco at 5 percent), matures late here, in late October, and usually comes out with 13° to 13.5° alcohol. The strength, however, is not apparent in the wine, of a bright cherry-ruby hue, fragrant, fruity, soft, with no complexity. It takes a bit of aging, though not in wood, and is best to drink within one to five years after the harvest. DOC seems to permit a Rosato as well, though it is simply a lighter version of the Rosso.

Pasquale Bozzo, the fourth generation of winemakers in the family, has invested so much in his modernized winery that his father, Antonio, who built a sterling reputation locally, still seems to have reservations about his son's ambitious pursuits. "I never even considered bottling wine," said the father, with a modest smile and shrug. "But the world is changing. People seem to like to drink wine from somewhere else nowadays."

The Bozzo Donnici, which has found a ready market among the hotels of the Sila, has also been introduced in cities to the north. And just recently, Pasquale Bozzo had a label and information sheet done in English before shipping some wine to the United States. "I think there's a market there; anyway, it's worth a try," said Pasquale Bozzo. "Maybe so," said his father. "I've heard that a lot of Calabresi live there."

Savuto is adjacent to Donnici, its DOC zone following the Savuto River to the Tyrrhenian coastal town of Amantea. Though similar to Donnici, it has a more intricate formula: Gaglioppo (also known as Magliocco or Arvino) at 35 to 45 percent with Greco Nero, Nerello Cappuccio, Magliocco Canino, and Sangiovese, alone or combined at 30 to 40 percent (though Sangiovese cannot exceed 10 percent of the total) and Malvasia Bianca and Pecorino, alone or combined, at a maximum of 25 percent. As interpreted by some producers, that combination can make a delightfully tasty wine, whether Rosso or Rosato (which is only a shade lighter), when served fresh. Savuto may be called *superiore* if it has 12.5° alcohol and two years' aging. Much Savuto is sold by the demijohn by small-scale producers, though some can be found in commerce, notably from the G. B. Longo winery at Marina di Cleto.

The Cooking: A Middle Ground of Vegetables and Pasta

Calabria, naturally, has two basic forms of cooking, meat in the interior and fish on the coast, with a comfortable middle ground provided by vegetables and pasta, which thrive everywhere. In the mountains the basic diet has not changed much, even if a growing share of the fare tends to come from packages. Pasta and vegetables laced with pimento, herbs, and spices are the foundations upon which mountain people constructed their meals, adding pork, lamb, sausages, and sharp *pecorino* and mild *ricotta* when times were good. Soups of various vegetables and pasta cooked to a thick consistency have provided an inexpensive and substantial nourishment against the cold.

Like most everything else in Calabria, pasta has its unique styles and names. *Suffrittu* is a hearty sauce based on a combination of pork innards, wine, and herbs and used to dress various types of noodles. *Sagne chine* is a type of *lasagne* that includes meat, cheese, vegetables, and mushrooms, a meal in itself. Around Cosenza, where snails are appreciated, they are the base of a hot sauce used on pasta and known as *perciatelli e lumache*. *Schiaffetoni* are pasta tubes each individually stuffed with a meat-cheese filling and baked in the oven. Among meat dishes, in addition to pork (which is used in every style imaginable) and grilled lamb and kid, there are more elaborate preparations, such as *murseddu*, a meat pie, and *mursiellu alla catanzarese*, a rich stew with ingredients similar to *suffrittu*.

On the coast, fish shares the limelight with vegetables. Peppers, tomatoes, garlic, onions, olives, and eggplant are put together in countless ways. Perhaps the most renowned eggplant dish of Calabria is *melanzane a polpetta*, a stew that includes eggs and bread crumbs and plenty of garlic and pepper. Calabrians also take advantage of ample supplies of olive oil to preserve foods. Eggplants, artichokes, onions, peppers, and mushrooms *sott'olio* keep Calabrian tables bright during the winter. Another special preserve of Calabria is *mùstica*, newborn anchovies in oil.

The most noted seafood preparations of the region are *zuppa di pesce*, fish soup made in an infinite number of ways, always piquant, and *pesce spada*, the swordfish of Bagnara on the Calabrian Riviera. Until not long ago they were harpooned on the high seas by the town's fishermen, but lately they have been caught in more conventional ways. In Bagnara, swordfish is often prepared with lemon, peppers, capers, parsley, garlic, oil, and herbs in a delicious stew. Here you may also taste *alalonga*, a small tuna whose tender, light meat is especially prized.

Lamezia and Calabria's Good Non-DOCs

The Tyrrhenian coastal plain south of the Savuto River is the home of a new DOC wine, Lamezia, whose character is somewhat different from that of other Calabrian reds because of the predominance of Greco Nero, which is used at 40 to 70 percent. Nerello Mascalese and Nerello Cappuccio figure at 20 to 30 percent, along with Gaglioppo at 10 to 25 percent. The DOC zone, named for the spa town of Lamezia, covers several nearby communities in the plains and low hills due west of Catanzaro. Both the DOC red and the non-DOC whites of Lamezia, including a semisweet Lametino, have sound reputations in Calabria. Production seems to be centered in the Opera Sila cooperative at Sambiase, which also produces table wines sold under the names Sambiase and Calabria Rosso, Rosato, and Bianco.

The town of Nicastro, above Lamezia, is also noted for its wines, a red made chiefly from Gaglioppo, a dry white from Malvasia Bianca, and an *abboccato* white from a grape called Annarella, among others. Across from Lamezia and Nicastro, on the western side of the narrowest section of the Calabrian peninsula, is the town of Squillace, whose white wines from Greco Bianco grapes are fragile but excellent when drunk on the spot with seafood.

Among the many non-DOC wines of Calabria, three have been recognized as *vino da tavola a denominazione geografica*, which means they will probably qualify as *vini tipici* when that category comes into effect in Italy. Two, Esaro and Verbicaro, are in the northwestern part of the region in the province of Cosenza. Esaro, both Bianco (from Malvasia, Greco, and Guarnaccia) and Rosso (from Gaglioppo, Greco Nero, and Nerello), is produced by the Cantina Sociale Casella at Tarsia and the Istituto Professionale di Stato Todaro, an agricultural school at Cosenza. Verbicaro Bianco and Rosso, from the same grapes as Esaro, is produced by the Cantina Sociale San Giuseppe at Verbicaro.

The other special *vino da tavola*, the generous red Pellaro, is made from Alicante grapes at the tip of the Calabrian peninsula around the Pellaro promontory south of Reggio di Calabria. A robust, deep ruby wine that can be strong, it is especially recommended with wild boar, which is still hunted on the rugged slopes of Aspromonte, the mountain that dominates southern Calabria and has the region's highest peak, Altomonte, at 6,417 feet. Producers of good Pellaro are Vincenzo Oliva, Pasquale Scaramozzino, and Cristoforo Pastorino.

Greco di Gerace: Sweet and Rare

Calabrians rival Sicilians as Italy's foremost makers of sweets, with a tempting range of desserts and pastries often based on fresh and candied fruits, nuts, and raisins. They also have the wines to go with them, many from Moscato and Malvasia, a few from Greco and Mantonico, which stand in a class by themselves.

I first tasted the Greco di Gerace of Umberto Ceratti about ten years ago and noted at the time that it was among the finest dessert wines of Italy, with velvety richness that demand to be savored in small sips. It ranks with a certain few Picolits and a half dozen other rarities at the head of the list of sweet wines. Despite its 17° to 19° of alcohol, Greco di Gerace is delicate, flowery, perfumed, perhaps best in its early, golden years. Ceratti, whose vineyards are at Caraffa di Bianco in the southeastern part of the toe, makes only a tiny amount of it each year of semi-dried Greco grapes from vines purposely held to minuscule yields in the scorched earth of the low hills above the seaside town of Bianco. From recent vintages, Ceratti's Greco di Gerace has been classified as Greco di

Bianco, a geographical appellation that is scheduled to become Calabria's next DOC. The Cacib cooperative at Bianco also produces and distributes a Greco di Bianco.

Ceratti's Greco is almost impossible to find. Trimani in Rome and a few other shops and restaurants in Italy come up with a few bottles now and then, naturally at high prices. Ceratti also makes a semisweet Mantonico, which becomes drier and increasingly amber with age. It is close to Sherry in style.

The Vintages

	Cirò	Donnici, Savuto, Pollino
1979	Excellent	Exceptional
1978	Excellent	Excellent
1977	Good	Good
1976	Fair	Fair
1975	Good	(No records
1974	Excellent	kept before
1973	Excellent	DOC in 1975)
1972	Fair	
1971	Exceptional	
1970	Exceptional	
1969	Good	
1968	Excellent	

VERMENTINO
DI GALLURA

MOSCATO
DI SORSO
SENNORI

Sassari

CANNONAU
DI SARDEGNA

MONICA
DI SARDEGNA

MALVASIA
DI BOSA

MOSCATO
DI SARDEGNA

Nuoro

MANDROLISAI

VERNACCIA
DI ORISTANO

CAMPIDANO
DI TERRALBA

GIRO
DI CAGLIARI

MALVASIA
DI CAGLIARI

MONICA
DI CAGLIARI

MOSCATO
DI CAGLIARI

Cagliari

NASCO
DI CAGLIARI

NURAGUS
DI CAGLIARI

CARIGNANO
DEL SULICIS

SARDINIA

PROVINCES
CAGLIARI, Nuoro, Oristano, Sassari

POPULATION
1,500,000

AREA
9,196 square miles

AVERAGE WINE PRODUCTION
250 million liters

DOC WINES
Campidano di Terralba · Cannonau di Sardegna (Rosso, Rosato) · Carignano del Sulcis (Rosso, Rosato) · Girò di Cagliari · Malvasia di Bosa · Malvasia di Cagliari · Mandrolisai (Rosso, Rosato) · Monica di Cagliari · Monica di Sardegna · Moscato di Cagliari · Moscato di Sardegna · Moscato di Sorso-Sennori · Nasco di Cagliari · Nuragus di Cagliari · Vermentino di Gallura · Vernaccia di Oristano

OTHER WINES
Abbaia · Aghiloia · Anghelu Ruju · Aragosta · Bianco di Dorgali · Gregu Nieddu · I Piani · Is Arenas · Jerzu · Malvasia di Planargia · Nieddera · Nuraghe Majore · Perda Rubia · Rosato di Dorgali · Rosato di Villasanta · Rosé di Alghero · Rosso di Montesanto · Rosso Giogantinu · Sangiovese di Arborea · Thaòra · Torbato Secco di Alghero · Trebbiano di Arborea · Vermentino di Alghero

Cracking the Outer Shell

MORE than just an island, Sardinia is a world apart, though that highly unoriginal observation is less valid today than it once was. For it is true that you can walk the streets of Cagliari or even Nuoro, in the heart of what is often described as the "savage" Barbagia, and feel that you are in just another Italian city with all the stereotypes that have become so rapidly and thoroughly ingrained in modern Italian life. Or you can park yourself on a beach on the Costa Smeralda or some other resort and be subjected to all the privileges or abuses, depending on how you look at it, that go with the concept of international tourism.

No, these days it takes longer to sense Sardinia's uniqueness. It might involve getting out of the cities, away from the beaches, off the main roads to feel the full effect. But Sardinia, for all its recent concessions to contemporaneity, is still different, not only from other parts of Italy but from any place anywhere, even Corsica, which is just a hop across the Bocche di Bonifacio to the north.

Sardinia's outer shell, as Sardinians themselves may tell you, is hard to crack. Outsiders, starting with the Cretans, came to conquer, and some seemed to succeed. Phoenicians, Carthaginians, Romans, Byzantines, Pisans, Genoese, and Spaniards all managed to establish possession before the House of Savoy made the island Italian once and for all. Those peoples and more left their marks here. But through it all, at least until recently, Sardinian ways endured: the austere, proud, uncompromising spirit, quietly expressed in the will of the shepherd or, if metaphorically, in the stoicism of the *nuraghi*, those enigmatic stone towers that are still seen everywhere on the island and whose prehistoric origins have never been definitely explained.

You may have heard how the ancient Greeks came to call the island Ichnusa, from *ikhnos*, or footprint, which indeed describes its shape. Supposedly the gods, as they were nearing the end of their task of creating the earth, had a lump of soil left over and one of them plopped it into the middle of the Mediterranean and stomped it down with his foot. Sardinians like to relate this tale, perhaps because its irony seems to fit with the island's sometimes downtrodden fortunes. If you wonder why Sardinians do not always take quickly to strangers, consider the intruders in the island's past. And yet, despite what they might tell you, Sardinians, if not as malleable and spontaneous as Italians in other regions, seem to make up for any initial coolness with a special sense of hospitality that seems all the more authentic for its inherent dignity. Sardinia has long been known for its bandits and kidnappers, but even the rogues were often admired for their Robin-Hood-style conduct and rough-hewn aplomb.

Casual observers may quickly draw conclusions about Sardinia to add to the superficialities already written about the island. But before I continue with mine, a stroke of native insight might help to set the tone. Enzo Biondo, who in addition to being an oenologist, biologist, and administrator of one of the island's most successful wine cooperatives is also a student of Sardinian history, folkways, and mores. He recently published a book whose contents range well beyond the main subject, Sardinian wine. After some forty years as a Sardinian, Biondo, by his own admission, is still trying to get to know the place.

Enzo Biondo

"Every time I go somewhere, I discover something, learn something new," he said. "Every locality has its own dialect, its own customs, its own wine, its own food. Just as an example, take the breads. There must be as many types of bread as there are towns in Sardinia. But the only way to find out about them is to go there and taste them. And that applies to everything else about the island. Why? Because Sardinians are closed people who confide in their family and friends and not in strangers. Every Sardinian has his own idea of what Sardinia is. Maybe that's why there are so few writers here. It isn't in the Sardinian's nature to talk about himself and his ways to others."

Biondo's wisdom also applies to wine. Many Sardinian vines and the style of wine that comes from them are peculiar to the island. Nowadays, winemaking is largely up-to-date and centered in cooperatives. Grape varieties from outside have been introduced, but their acceptance has been slow and unsteady, and, interestingly, the native varieties have not only survived but prevailed. They still provide their own inimitable tastes of Sardinia.

Raw Power, Sunny Dispositions

Some vines of Sardinia have familiar names: Malvasia, Moscato, Vermentino, and Vernaccia, for instance. But there is little familiar about their flavors, which decidedly do not correspond to wines of those names from other places. Other major varieties include Cannonau, Girò, Monica, Nasco, and Nuragus. The first four are believed to have come from Spain, and Nuragus may have been brought to Sardinia by the Phoenicians. The range of Sardinian wines is well distributed among dry, semi-sweet, and sweet. The climate here has always been conducive to wines of raw power and sunny dispositions, though there is something to the notion that the strength of Sardinian wines is tempered by a delicacy, a subtlety that makes them less overbearing than other wines from hot places.

The second largest island in the Mediterranean after Sicily, Sardinia lies as close to France, Spain, Algeria, and Tunisia as it does to many parts of Italy. Its position in midsea and its climate, like its personality, make it difficult to classify. Though it is usually identified with the south statistically, some observers place it in central Italy. The northern part of the island is level with southern Latium and is much closer to Rome, and even Genoa, than to Palermo. Sardinians can be somewhat noncommittal on that point, preferring to let their region stand by itself in splendid isolation. Although Sardinia is approachable from any direction, the heaviest maritime traffic, at least during the tourist season, is along the eight-hour ferry route from Civitavecchia to Olbia on the edge of the Costa Smeralda.

Sardinia's capital and busiest port of call is Cagliari, on the gulf at the southern end, a city of 250,000 that dominates trends without leaning too heavily on the island's time-honored soul. Cagliari thrives not only because of its well-protected harbor but also because it is hard by the Campidano, the region's richest and flattest agricultural area and the center of heaviest wine production. With sixteen DOCs, some rather recent, Sardinia ranks as an already important producer of quality wine with a record of steady, rational growth.

Lucio Salis, who documents and promotes the region's wines from his office in the Chamber of Commerce of Cagliari, described the current status. "Unlike in mainland Italy, in Sardinia the *cantine sociali* tend to produce most of the better-quality wine. Of course, there are exceptions, most notably Sella & Mosca of Alghero. And there are numerous small but excellent independent producers. But, all in all, I think you'd have to rate the cooperative movement a success here, with many good to excellent wines on the market and more to come. The groundwork has been laid for a promising future."

Although the wine names are often strange, the DOC structure in Sardinia is orderly. A regionwide consortium of DOC wine producers grants a neck label to qualified wines depicting a black and white ribbon with the words *"Prodotto di Qualità — Sardegna."*

All but two wines — Campidano di Terralba and Mandrolisai — are varietal wines identified by a place name. Campidano di Terralba is a red wine from the Bovale grape, and Mandrolisai consists of Rosso and Rosato from a mixture of Muristellu with Cannonau, Monica, and Girò. There are three regionwide categories: Cannonau di Sardegna, Monica di Sardegna, and Moscato di Sardegna, which took effect in 1980. Cagliari has six classifications: Girò, Malvasia, Monica, Moscato, Nasco, and Nuragus, all with the appendage "di Cagliari." Then there are Carignano del Sulcis, Malvasia di Bosa, Moscato di Sorso-Sennori, Vermentino di Gallura, and Vernaccia di Oristano.

The province of Cagliari produces an overwhelming share of the wine, though many gems of Sardinian viticulture come from more remote parts of the island. Vernaccia di Oristano is the Sardinian answer to Sherry, though Malvasia di Bosa can be even more distinctive with an inimitable aroma that is reputed to derive from the potassium-rich chalk soil of the Planargia. Vermentino di Gallura, and specifically the Vermentino of Monti and Berchidda, ranks among the island's primary dry whites. Torbato di Alghero, made exclusively by Sella & Mosca, is one of the most impressive wines of its type anywhere. Cannonau, which can be grown in various parts of the island, reaches its greatest heights in the southeastern hills below Nuoro, around Capo Ferrato and the towns of Dorgali and Oliena. A robust giant, Sardinians rightfully advance it as their representative among the great red wines of Italy.

The Wines of Cagliari

Of Sardinia's sixteen DOC wines, Nuragus di Cagliari is far and away the most prominent, with nearly 20 million liters in 1978, easily surpassing production of all other DOC wines combined. Possibly the grandest thing about Nuragus is its history. The vine, apparently of Phoenician origin, eventually acquired the Roman name of the island's most characteristic monuments, the *nuraghi*. Its DOC zone covers much of the province of Cagliari, extending into the provinces of Oristano and Nuoro.

It is made from Nuragus grapes at 80 to 90 percent, supplemented by Trebbiano (either the Tuscan or Romagnan subvarieties), Vermentino, Clairette, and Semidano. Pale, dry, and light, with a minimum of 11° alcohol, it has an acidic vein that makes it well suited to accompany fish. Among the many producers of Nuragus, the Cantina Sociale Marmilla at Sanluri stands out with an especially crisp, clean, well-made wine. The Cantina Sociale di Dolianova, which uses the brand name Parteolla, and the Cantina Sociale di Mogoro also produce good Nuragus.

All the other DOC wines of Cagliari fall into the dessert or, perhaps just as often, *aperitivo* categories. Often made from very ripe or semi-dried grapes, they are all produced in strictly limited quantity. Malvasia di Cagliari is made from Malvasia grapes alone, though 5 percent of other varieties may be planted in the vineyards to favor pollination. A vine of ancient standing on the island, Malvasia is grown throughout the province of Cagliari and in part of Oristano, but not much wine is made and what is produced is treasured. It is usually dry, though it may also be sweet or somewhere in between, but in any case Malvasia is a golden-amber color, darkening with age, finely scented with a bitter undertone that hints at toasted almonds. Malvasia di Cagliari *secco* and *dolce* must each have at least 14° alcohol with more residual sugar in the *dolce*. The *liquoroso* versions, fortified with alcohol, come in three types with at least 17.5° alcohol: *dolce, secco,* and *dry,* which is bone-dry. When aged two years, Malvasia di Cagliari may be labeled *riserva*. The Cantina Sociale Marmilla makes an excellent Malvasia *secco*.

Moscato, introduced in Sardinia in Roman times, is invariably sweet, fragrant, smooth, and deep golden in color. Moscato di Cagliari, from roughly the same area as the Malvasia, may be *dolce naturale,* which has at least 15° alcohol, though usually about 3° remains undeveloped as residual sugar. The *liquoroso* has at least 17.5°. When aged a year, Moscato di Cagliari may be labeled *riserva*. The private winery Vini Classici di Sardegna at Pirri makes a fine Moscato.

Monica di Cagliari is a 100 percent varietal made from semi-dried grapes into strong and usually sweet wine (the more popular Monica di Sardegna, however, is usually dry and lighter in alcohol). Most Monica di Cagliari is made into either *dolce naturale,* of 15.5° alcohol with residual sugar at 4° or more, or *secco,* which has at least 15° alcohol but no more than .8° residual sugar. There are also a *liquoroso dolce naturale* of at least 17.5° and a *liquoroso dry*. When aged at least two years, the *liquoroso* types may be called *riserva*. Whatever the style, Monica di Cagliari tends to be soft and smooth and delicately perfumed with a brilliant ruby color taking on orange tones with age.

The red Girò di Cagliari and white Nasco di Cagliari are rare and becoming rarer because of the modest yields of their vines, most of which were planted long ago. Average annual production of Nasco has been about 20,000 liters in recent years, and Girò is about half that. Girò follows the same pattern as the other dessert wines with *dolce* and *secco* versions of 14.5° and *liquoroso dolce naturale* and *liquoroso secco* at 17.5°. Light ruby, delicate and warm with a pleasant grapy aroma, Girò may be labeled *riserva* after two years of aging, at least one in barrel.

Nasco di Cagliari, made from semi-dried grapes, is the most delicate of the dessert wines of Cagliari in aroma, flavor, and color. Straw yellow and finely scented, it is probably best as a fairly dry *aperitivo*. Again there are *dolce naturale* and *secco, liquoroso dolce naturale* and *liquoroso secco* with alcohol levels similar to the others. With two years of aging,

Nasco qualifies as *riserva*. Vini Classici di Sardegna makes a minuscule amount of fine Girò. For Nasco the cooperatives of Dolianova and Marmilla are recommended.

Cantina Sociale Marmilla: Image and Price

The Cantina Sociale Marmilla at Sanluri is one of the biggest cooperatives of Sardinia and one of the best. Its stature has been built by Enzo Biondo, who sees no reason why a cooperative cannot be as efficient, profitable, and quality-oriented as a private winery. Marmilla is one of twenty-two Sardinian subregions whose significance, though seldom cited nowadays, has roots deep in history. A hilly area at the northern edge of the Campidano, it has been noted as the island's breadbasket since the Romans brought slaves here to grow grain and cereals.

"The Marmilla had no wine tradition," said Biondo. "The first vines were planted here only seventy or eighty years ago, and it's still virgin territory. That's actually an advantage, because the calcareous subsoil is being exploited for the first time and the wines have bouquet, delicate character, and distinct flavors that wines from lower and flatter sections of the Campidano don't have."

The cooperative, whose 2,000 members work some 13,000 acres of vines, nearly all on hillsides, has increased its capacity from 1.3 million liters in 1953 to 31.6 million liters in 1979, though only a fraction of the annual production is in DOC wines. Biondo, however, is determined to build DOC to 80 percent and work exclusively with the quality wines that are now sold in labeled bottles in six types: the DOC Nuragus di Cagliari, Monica di Sardegna, and Cannonau di Sardegna, and non-DOC Nasco Marmilla, Malvasia di Sardegna, and Rosato di Villasanta. The cooperative's strong points are Nuragus and Malvasia and the robust and dry red Cannonau and Monica, which are purposely harvested and vinified to have no more than 13° alcohol and ample finesse, even when young. All the bottled wines are at a quality level that would be exemplary anywhere — Piedmont, the Veneto, France, California.

Marmilla has been increasing sales in Sardinia and mainland Italy (from Rome north), while cautiously trying markets in Germany, Belgium, Holland, Britain, and even France. Biondo wants to enter the U.S. market as well, but so far he has found American importers to be more concerned about bargain prices than quality. "We had a bid to sell quite a lot of wine at seven hundred lire a bottle," said Biondo. "I refused, of course, because that price doesn't cover costs, though I suspect the bidder went somewhere else and got a wine at that price. Frankly, I find that approach not only condescending but shortsighted. The only way it will change, though, is if we Italians determine the true value of our wine and hold out for just prices. Otherwise, foreign buyers, particularly Americans, I believe, will continue to turn to France for quality and Italy for quantity, knowing that there's always someone here who will meet their offer. Unfortunately, many people in the wine trade, Italians included, have no more taste in wine than they have business principles. No, when Marmilla wines go to America, they'll go proudly and at a fair price. And in the long run, everyone will be better off, producer, middlemen, and consumer alike."

Our conversation was interrupted by a telephone call from a wine dealer in northern Italy. During a lively discussion about whether the previously agreed price on an upcoming shipment held, I overheard Biondo say, "Look, if we sold it for that, we'd be under mineral water." The previously agreed price held. Then, as though nothing had intervened, Biondo picked up the thread of his argument.

"Making good wine is difficult enough, even if Italian conditions provide fewer obstacles than do those of most other countries," he said. "But the real challenge, in Italy at least, is selling wine. And here in Sardinia, which is thought of as a hot southern source of blending wine, even though much of the island has a temperate climate, the problems are multiplied. You can have a magnificent wine, but if you don't have the image behind it, and the price, nobody will believe it."

Carignano, Terralba, and Mandrolisai

Three recent DOC wines of Sardinia are still scarcely known quantities outside their immediate zones. Carignano del Sulcis, Campidano di Terralba (or simply Terralba), and Mandrolisai, all reds, seem to represent the latest direction in Sardinian viniculture, toward dry table wines that are not exaggerated in alcoholic strength.

Carignano del Sulcis includes a robust Rosso and a tasty Rosato. Its vineyards are mainly on the island of Sant'Antioco, known to the Carthaginians as Sulcis, though the zone also includes sections of the southeastern corner of the main island. Carignano is the Carignan vine prominent in southern France, though it apparently arrived here from Spain, for the locals still call it Uva di Spagna. Mixed with no more than 15 percent of Monica, Alicante, and Pascale, it makes a full-bodied red with at least 11.5° alcohol, though an *invecchiato* version, aged at least a year, is often headier and more robust, well suited to roast meat and game. The Rosato is a lighter version from the same grapes. The Cantina Sociale di Sant'Antioco makes an excellent Carignano called Sardus Pater. The cooperatives at Santadi and Calasetta also make good Carignano.

Campidano di Terralba, from the northwestern part of the Campidano near Oristano, is a red that can at times be as light in color and body as a rosé, though its alcohol often goes higher than the 11.5° prescribed by DOC. Made from the Bovale grape at 80 percent or more, it may include Pascale, Greco Nero, and Monica. A good table wine, it is produced principally by the Cantina Sociale del Campidano at Terralba, which also makes a non-DOC red wine called Gregu Nieddu, dialect for Greco Nero, its chief grape. In the flatland of Arborea just to the north of Terralba, Sangiovese and Trebbiano wines are made, though those Tuscan natives have not made much headway anywhere else on the island.

Mandrolisai, which became DOC in 1979, takes its name from the subregion at the center of the island in the foothills of the Gennargentu mountain range in the province of Nuoro. Made from Muristellu (or Muristeddu) at up to 65 percent, with Cannonau, Monica, and Girò, it becomes a bright ruby wine of generous body, acquiring some finesse with age. There is also a Rosato from the same grapes, of a full rosé color and fresh aroma and flavor. Its chief producer is the Cantina Sociale del Mandrolisai at Sorgono.

Vernaccia di Oristano: Sherry with a Sardinian Twist

Vernaccia di Oristano, the most Sardinian wine, is appreciated on the island as a beverage for all hours. It is also known in certain circles as Italy's answer to Sherry, to which it indeed bears a striking resemblance even if it has traits all its own and time-proven techniques behind it.

The DOC zone is in the flatlands to the north of Oristano, stretching from the mouth of the Tirso River along the Stagno di Cabras, a lagoon with rich fishing grounds, inland as far as Milis, Tramatza, and Zerfaliu. Vines are head-trained close to the ground in the alluvial soil of the Tirso plain to give the grapes the sustenance to make wines that benefit from years, even decades, of aging. In this environment they also develop the all-important yeast, whose scientific name is *Saccharomyces rouxii,* which form a white veil on the surface of the wine that is known in Jerez de la Frontera as *flor*.

Where this Vernaccia vine originated is uncertain, though it has been cultivated for so long in Sardinia, and in particular here around Oristano, that it is considered indigenous. It seems to be dissimilar from other varieties called Vernaccia, including those of San Gimignano in Tuscany and Serrapetrona in the Marches. Nor does it bear any strong resemblance to the Palomino grape of Jerez. Legend has it that Vernaccia was bestowed upon the people of Oristano by Santa Giustina, the vines springing from the tears the saint shed over the sorry condition of that malaria-ridden city.

The process of making Vernaccia di Oristano, though it has twists of its own that are distinctly different from the *solera* system of Sherry, also has enough in common with its Spanish cousin to lead to the conclusion that the basics arrived here from Spain. Spanish dominion was strongest here in western Sardinia, where the looks of the towns, like their names, often have more than a hint of Iberia about them. An essential difference between Vernaccia di Oristano and Sherry is that Vernaccia is not as a rule "educated" by older wine. Also the regular versions of Vernaccia and the *superiore* and *riserva* are not fortified (though the *liquoroso* types are). Still, the best Vernaccia can stand comparison with some of the finest Fino, Amontillado, and Manzanilla Sherries in class.

The Vernaccia harvest takes place in September when the tiny grapes are so ripe that their skins often rupture, and hence they must be collected in earthenware vessels. After crushing and pressing, the must is separated from the dregs and placed in small barrels with narrow staves, which induce evaporation and increase the alcohol content. The barrels are stored in airy ground-floor *magazzini* whose brick walls have plenty of openings to let in air and sun, as in Spanish *bodegas*.

The production of Vernaccia seems to defy all the normal rules of winemaking. The casks are open on top and never filled to the brim so that air and sunshine can work on the yeasts and induce a thick *flor*. In most wines, air feeds the so-called *Acetobacter* bacteria that would turn it to vinegar if not controlled, but in Vernaccia and sherry the air and sunshine instead work their magic on the *Saccharomyces rouxii,* which metabolize the ethyl alcohol, acetic acids, residual sugar, and glycerol, leaving the wine dry. For the first year or more Vernaccia is murky, but after two it can be ready to bottle and sell with at least 15° alcohol.

Better Vernaccia has at least three years of age and 15.5° alcohol, when it can be labeled *superiore*. The treasured *riserva* must have 16° and four years of age, after which it may be kept for decades.

Some Sardinians still drink Vernaccia with their meals, though that practice is considered eccentric these days, even though the wine can go famously with certain *antipasti* and fish dishes, including the famous *bottarga originaria,* mullet or tuna eggs dried in the sun, a specialty of Oristano. These days, however, Vernaccia's price prohibits its use as a table wine. It shines as a well-chilled *aperitivo* because of its subtle, persistent bouquet and very dry flavor, smoothly balanced between acidic and bitter.

DOC permits *liquoroso dolce* and *liquoroso dry* versions of Vernaccia, fortified and close in style to the Spanish Olorosos and Creams in the dessert-wine field. To my taste, though, the dry, unfortified *superiore* and *riserva* are not only the most typical but the most important Vernaccias. Superb wines are made by Fratelli Contini at Cabras, Josto Puddu at San Vero Milis, Silvio Carta at Baratili San Pietro, and Sella & Mosca, whose Vernaccia from vineyards at Baratili San Pietro is called Is Arenas. The Cantina Sociale della Vernaccia at Oristano is the largest producer, with a very good wine sold as Sardinian Gold. Contini and Giuseppe Cossu also make good red wines called Nieddera from vines in the Tirso valley.

Malvasia di Bosa, a Drop of Liquid Gold

Above the plain of Oristano, spotted with lagoons, vineyards, and crumbled *nuraghi,* the coast becomes rugged and the road north to Alghero veers inland past sleepy towns whose appearances, like their names, leave no doubt that the Catalans passed through here. Above San Leonardo de Siete Fuentes are Tresnuraghes and Magomadas in the hills of the Planargia, home of a wine whose esteem has totally eclipsed its availability. Some praise Malvasia di Bosa in hushed tones, fearing perhaps that too much acclaim would not only spoil its exquisite country aspect but exhaust its meager supply. Others have not been able to resist shouting. Adriano Ravegnani in *I cento vini d'Italia* proclaimed Malvasia di Bosa "the gem of Sardinian viniculture," adding: "I consider it one of the greatest wines of all the world. Its liquid is liquid gold." Nearly one hundred fifty years earlier, one Goffredo Casalis had written: "It bears comparison to the most famous wines of southern Europe, and if it has that improvement in goodness that only time can give, it will be superior to all."

Bosa, a quiet fishing port with a smattering of small hotels, straddles the Temo River in a pretty green valley dominated by the Castello di Serravalle. The Malvasia Sarda vines grow in small plots scattered through the Planargia hills south of Bosa around Modolo, Tresnuraghes, and Magomadas, an area of steep but not excessively lofty rises at center stage of an amphitheater of mountains flanked by Monte Mannu to the north and Monte Ferru to the south and opening onto the sea.

Malvasia Sarda was believed to have been brought directly to Sardinia by Greeks from the Peloponnesus who came here under the Byzantines. The vine is sometimes called Malmasia or Malmazia here, a corruption of the name of the Greek town of Monembasia, where the vine known in other languages as Malvoisie, Malvagia, and Malmsey originated. People here tout their Malvasia as superior to any other vine of the name, quite a claim because it is unquestionably one of the largest, most diffuse, and most varied families of southern European vines, though not every wine of those names is related.

Producers here are not otherwise given to boasting, but rather, as quietly dignified country people, they go about creating their Malvasia in highly individualistic ways and doling it out in samples to those *intenditori* who venture here in search of it. But the price — 5,000, 6,000, 8,000 lire, sometimes more — is hardly in line with that of a country wine.

"No, certainly not," said Gilberto Arru, a determined young man who guides his father in making and selling Malvasia. "But it's not just a question of prestige. Here, low *alberello* vines yield anywhere from one thousand to an absolute maximum of four thousand liters of wine from a hectare, as low as you'll find anywhere. The vines are worked by hand and the wine is made by artisans who all try to give it a personal touch to differentiate their wine from the others'. In other words, you're dealing with a very special wine made in minute quantities. The price of a bottle is justified by the work behind it and the goodness, at least from the better producers. Believe me, nobody's getting rich off Malvasia."

Gilberto Arru and his father, Emilio, invited me into the family home in the center of Magomadas, where, seated at the dining room table, we tasted the 1977 and 1976 vintages against one of the vaunted Vernaccias of Oristano. Emilio Arru beamed when I agreed with his son that the Malvasias of both years were clearly superior to the Vernaccia. The younger wine had a paler golden-amber hue than the older wine, marked

Gilberto Arru

by a delicate but distinctive bouquet and flavor that while dry was round
and velvety in texture thanks to ample glycerol. Still somewhat fruity, it
was deliciously suave. No denying it, a grand wine that probably surpassed anything I had sampled from the Malvasia family to date.

Satisfied with that judgment, Gilberto Arru, who went away to live
and work in Cagliari but still calls Magomadas home, talked about the
failings of the local Malvasia and how he and anyone willing to follow
his ideas or at least listen to them were going to improve its quality
further and build its reputation as one of Italy's great wines of the type.

"The most obvious flaw is that the wine has been officially recognized
as Malvasia di Bosa DOC," said Arru, "because some people have more
political clout than others. Well, we don't go along with it. We call our
wine Malvasia di Planargia, a denomination that more accurately reflects
the geography of the better vineyards and one that we'll stick with, DOC
or not."

Another failing, according to Arru, is inadequate exploitation of the
land. "By using the choicest plots in these hills, those in chalky, potassium-rich soil and facing south, quality production could be increased

several times over," he said. "But instead, many slopes are abandoned or covered with olive trees, a low-profit crop. Unfortunately, some new vineyards have been planted in cordon-trained vines, a mistake here because, though they produce more, the quality rarely equals that of grapes from head-trained vines."

The third shortcoming is vinification techniques, said Arru, who considers them at least ten years behind the times. "Malvasia here demands manual cultivation and artisanal methods. But some of what is passed off as artisanal, unfortunately, is just plain backward. A more rational, uniform approach by winemakers guided by expert oenologists would make for more consistent quality. Surprisingly, though, despite the age-old and often irrational methods employed, you almost never get a really bad Malvasia here. But there could be so much more excellent wine. It's a shame to see a Malvasia poorly made or aged too long in barrels. There's a trend here to cut back barrel aging to a minimum, certainly less than the two years required by Malvasia di Bosa DOC, because one of the beauties of Malvasia is its delicately fruity scent and flavor, qualities that diminish with age. I'm convinced the wine is at its best from a year to two or three after the harvest. And that view is backed by expert opinion."

Malvasia di Bosa may also be made into the usual range of types for the so-called dessert wines of Sardinia, even though the traditional and still-prevalent style of Malvasia is decidedly dry. The better Malvasias are either *secco* or *dolce naturale,* which is mildly sweet, each with about 16° alcohol, sometimes a bit more. They are best when served at cellar temperature, though some prefer them well chilled as *aperitivo.* The *liquoroso,* whether *dolce naturale, secco,* or *dry,* must have 17.5° alcohol.

Gilberto Arru's intensity and idealism, which he expresses not only verbally but in thoughtful articles in wine and food publications, go well beyond those of most producers in the zone. Many current producers are middle-aged or older, though Arru pointed out that some younger people have joined the ranks recently and more will follow as the wine's prestige grows. Arru's standards are high and his goals are challenging, but the Malvasia of Bosa and Planargia is already a proven quantity in Sardinia and its quality deserves wider exaltation. If only there were a little more available.

Emilio and Gilberto Arru are among the few small-scale producers who sell their wine in labeled bottles. Another highly regarded producer is Salvatore Deriu Mocci of Bosa. There are others, too, who will consent to part with a bottle or two if they know you have come all the way to Bosa, Modolo, Tresnuraghes, or Magomadas to buy it.

Sella & Mosca: Grandiose and Progressive

The newly improved coastal road from Bosa to Alghero provides those vistas of mountain and sea that Sardinia is famous for, without so much as a village to interrupt the natural splendor. Alghero, with its Catalan Gothic buildings and Spanish dialect, is sometimes referred to as Sardinia's "Barcelonetta." Fishing port and holiday resort, Alghero is also noted as the home of Sella & Mosca, long the leading name in Sardinian wine.

In wine terminology, estate seems to carry the connotation of a relatively small-scale property that grows its own grapes and makes and bottles its own wine; a comforting concept that calls up visions of châteaux, villas, and farms surrounded by vines, it carries more than a little weight among appreciators of fine wine. Sella & Mosca does not fit the limited dimensions of that mold, but it qualifies in every other sense as a wine estate. It is not only one of the most grandiose but one of the most progressive of Europe.

Founded by two enterprising Piedmontese — Emilio Sella, an engineer, and Edgardo Mosca, a lawyer — the firm has come a long way in its eighty years of existence, most of them as a pioneer in the field of Sardinian high-quality wine. The place has changed since Sella and Mosca started clearing swamps and brushland in the plains north of Alghero and planting vines.

Today, Sella & Mosca is a model of large-scale agricultural efficiency, if not exactly a storybook estate. Approached from Alghero along the road that leads to Sassari and Porto Torres across the gently rolling hills, the first vines of the estate at I Piani can be seen near the stream called the Serra Sette Ortas, and they look as though they might go on forever. In all, Sella & Mosca possesses some 650 hectares (about 1,600 acres) of vineyards that render the equivalent of about 6 million standard bottles of wine a year, all estate-bottled.

Though known for such Sardinian classics as Vernaccia, Malvasia, Monica, Nasco, Moscato, and Cannonau (both dry and a sweet version called Anghelu Ruju), Sella & Mosca has been orienting an increasing portion of its production toward youth and freshness in three wines: Vermentino di Alghero, Torbato Secco di Alghero, and Rosé di Alghero. This policy, being pursued under Mario Consorte, the firm's astute director, is based on national and international market trends recorded through the late 1970s. The company has invested heavily in new vines while expanding and revitalizing a plant that has practically doubled its production capacity in a few years.

Sella & Mosca has been around so long with such a sound line of products that it makes no difference if most of its wines are not DOC. The vineyards of I Piani could produce only the regionwide classifications of Monica, Cannonau, and Moscato, but by now the firm's wines, which range through most colors, flavors, and degrees of dryness and sweetness, have been confirmed throughout Italy and to a growing extent abroad. Besides those already named, there are the white Aragosta (from Vermentino) and Nuraghe Majore (from Clairette) and the red I Piani (from Carignano).

Sella & Mosca has been putting increased emphasis on a unique white, Torbato Secco di Alghero, which to my taste is one of the better wines of its type in Italy. The Torbato vine, which came from Spain more than three centuries ago, has been used for both dry and dessert wines by the firm. Torbato Secco is the result of thoroughly avant-garde techniques of viticulture (new vineyards were converted from *alberello* to *tendone* training, which spreads the foliage on arbors) and oenology (horizontal presses, cold fermentation, etcetera) in a fresh, clean, and tautly fruity wine that is now well promoted in Italy, as are the other young wines, Vermentino and Rosé. Production of Torbato has quadrupled in the last decade to more than 200,000 bottles, and that has not been enough to meet the demand. Of a pale straw yellow color with hints of green, Torbato's fragrance is outstanding and its dryness is balanced by a hint of bitter that makes it refreshing as a well-chilled *aperitivo*. It is considered the white par excellence with a lobster dish of Alghero known as *aragosta alla catalana*.

Wines of the North: Moscato and Vermentino

Sassari, Sardinia's second city, administers the northernmost province that crosses the island to Olbia and includes the Costa Smeralda on the Gallura peninsula, the tip of the island across the straits from Corsica. The millionaires' playground image is rather recent here and does not fit all that snugly with the otherwise rustic nature of the place. The rocky coast is spotted with fishing villages and the interior mountains are cloaked in the shimmering green of cork oaks. Tempio Pausania is the hub of Italy's cork industry, still an important livelihood in the hill country.

Sassari is on the edge of a small but qualitatively significant DOC zone, Moscato di Sorso-Sennori, named for the nearby towns that lie along the scenic road to Castel Sardo. Made in quantities similar to Malvasia di Bosa, Moscato di Sorso-Sennori is considered the finest Muscat of Sardinia with notable aroma and finesse. The basic wine is deep golden yellow with 15° alcohol. Although a *liquoroso* is defined under DOC, local admirers disdain the addition of extra alcohol as tampering with the already sterling character.

Sardinia's newest DOC, to be instituted with the 1980 vintage, is Moscato di Sardegna, a lightly sweet *spumante* to be produced at various parts of the island.

The Vermentino di Gallura DOC zone is vast, covering much of the northeastern corner of the island from the lovely port of Santa Teresa in Gallura down the eastern coast to Olbia and Budoni, and inland as far as Ozieri. Despite the expanse, DOC production is only about 300,000 liters a year, though increasing with the demand on the island for dry whites.

Within the DOC zone, the finest Vermentino is reputed to come from two cooperatives, the Cantina Sociale Cooperativa Giogantinu at Berchidda and the Cantina Sociale del Vermentino at Monti. Oddly, at last check, neither carried *denominazione di origine controllata* on their Vermentino labels. The Berchidda wine is full-flavored, deep straw yellow in color, both slightly sweet and bitter. A lighter, subtler, and more attractive wine is the S'éleme of the Monti cooperative, of a pale straw green and delicate fragrance and flavor — an excellent fish wine. That cooperative also makes a stronger Vermentino called Aghiloia, which is dry, though its alcohol can mount to 15° or more.

Under DOC, Vermentino di Gallura must have at least 12° alcohol and be made from Vermentino grapes at 95 percent. The *superiore* must have 14° or more; it is considered a reasonably good white for aging, though I cannot see how time would do much for it beyond a couple of years.

Both the Berchidda and Monti cooperatives make good red wines that include a dose of Vermentino for lightness. The Berchidda wine called Rosso Giogantinu is made principally of Pascale grapes. At Monti, Abbaia, which is based on Malaga and Pascale grapes, is particularly refreshing when young. The Monti cooperative also makes a rosé called Thaòra from the same grapes.

Some good wines called Vermentino may also come from outside the DOC area. Sella & Mosca's Vermentino di Alghero compares favorably with any other wine of the name.

Cannonau: Sardinian Dynamite

Eastern Sardinia, from the province of Nuoro south, is a land of high mountains, lonely moors, the lair of the legendary bandits and the contemporary kidnappers, the abode of shepherds, and the realm of Cannonau. That name has explosive resonance and the firepower to back it up. (The vine supposedly arrived here from Seville as Canonazo and is still sometimes spelled Canonau.) The adjectives strike you as you size it up: rich, deep, powerful, enormous; or, as the humorist at a small café in Oliena put it, *dinamite sarda,* Sardinian dynamite. But as you sniff it and roll it around the tongue — when you manage to find a well-made dry Cannonau, which is not always easy in the Barbagia — it soon becomes apparent that there is more to Cannonau than just oomph. Like other giants of Italian oenology, it can have a genteel side, a streak of finesse not lost in a grandeur that defies measure by ordinary standards.

The chronic problem with Cannonau has been its lack of inhibition, its tendency, when production is not purposely restrained, to run away from its makers. Its alcohol can easily surmount the limits of table wine and range into the forbidden land of the sweet. Forbidden? Well, only in the sense that even if there is a market for them at home, strong red dessert wines are not currently in much favor elsewhere, though there are exceptions such as Porto.

Cannonau di Sardegna can come in many styles, too many for my taste. DOC, in its islandwide classification, calls for Cannonau grapes at 90 percent or more, with the possible inclusion of Bovale Grande, Bovale Sardo, Carignano, Pascale di Cagliari, Monica, or (strange as it seems) Vernaccia di San Gimignano, though that light grape may not make up more than 5 percent of the total. The basic Cannonau may be either dry or lightly sweet, with at least 13.5° alcohol, and be aged at least a year in barrels of oak or chestnut. Sometimes aged a few years longer, sometimes not, it is often served cool on its home grounds. It may also be made into a Rosato with the same alcoholic minimum. When aged at least three years, Cannonau di Sardegna may be labeled *riserva*. The *superiore* versions of at least 15° are *naturale secco, naturale amabile,* and *naturale dolce*. The *liquoroso naturale dolce* has at least 16° and the *liquoroso secco* 18°. Cannonau from the areas of Capo Ferrato and Oliena may cite those names as subdenominations.

Sardinians have advanced Cannonau as their great red wine, comparing it to everything from Romanée-Conti to Taurasi with stops in between in the Langhe, Montalcino, and other revered places. Possibly the closest wines to it in character are the *passito* types from semi-dried grapes, specifically Amarone and Sfursat, though that analogy is rather lame in that Cannonau grapes need no drying to make wines of Amarone levels of strength and beyond. There is also some resemblance between Cannonau and Primitivo di Manduria or some of the larger Zinfandels of California, or even Aglianico del Vulture, but if it comes down to a final judgment, there is really nothing quite like it.

The trend among Sardinian producers who think in terms of national and international markets is to full-bodied, dry, balanced wines whose alcohol is contained within the limits of 15°. Sella & Mosca has a good dry Cannonau di Alghero of about 12.5°, and the Cantina Sociale Marmilla has managed to hold alcohol under 13° in its Cannonau Marmilla, though at those levels the right to DOC is sacrificed. Some devotees insist that Cannonau cannot be kept too low in alcohol without losing other qualities.

Indeed, in some places considered elite for Cannonau — Capo Ferrato near the southeastern corner of the island and the towns of Oliena and Dorgali in the vicinity of Nuoro — it is difficult to find a Cannonau of less than 15°. Fratelli Deiana at Oliena make a Cannonau of close to 18°, which, though considered dry, is dry like a fortified Porto. It makes a fine after-dinner drink. Another highly respected Cannonau has been sold under the name Perda Rubia for years by its producer, Commendatore Mario Mereu of Tortolì. Dry and generous with about 15°, Perda Rubia is one of the outstanding examples of the breed.

Much production of Cannonau is now concentrated in three cooperatives: the Cantina Sociale di Jerzu, whose wine is often called Jerzu; the Cantina Sociale di Oliena, whose wine is often called Oliena; and the Cantina Sociale di Dorgali, which has been selling Rosso, Rosato, and Bianco di Dorgali, all made from Cannonau grapes. Though Cannonau is one of Sardinia's most widely diffused vines, the production of DOC wine has been fluctuating between 750,000 and 1.3 million liters annually. In other words, only a fraction of the grapes that could be used for DOC wine are. The Cantina Sociale Bonnanaro near Sassari has an excellent dry Rosso di Montesanto, from Cannonau with Girò and Nieddu Mannu grapes.

The people of Dorgali, bless them, have been slow to exploit the many attractive things about their town. It dominates one of the most dramatic coastal settings of the island, overlooking the Gulf of Orosei, where the last seals of the Mediterranean live in the Grotta dei Bue Marino. Nearby is the site of Serra Orios, a whole city of *nuraghi*. Dorgali also has a winery full of Cannonau, a stock of nearly 3 million liters in the months following the harvest, much of it to be sold as non-DOC wine at non-DOC prices.

There, at the end of a tour led by Santino Spanu, the cooperative's young secretary, I tasted a 1978 Cannonau that had been resting less than a year in oak barrels. Absolute splendor. A red wine with everything winemakers in other places dream about but are lucky to achieve once every decade or two. Granted, it lacked the tannic austerity that distinguishes some of the world's acknowledged great red wines, but that, to me, is only attractive in big wines from great years that can balance the wood, acids, and tannins with a handsome measure of fruit and alcohol. This 1978 had harmony and breed all its own, though at a shade over 15° it was, as the man said back at Oliena, Sardinian dynamite. Assuredly not a wine for milquetoasts.

"If it weren't for DOC, we'd bottle it now," said Spanu, "because barrels can't do anything more for it. Cannonau from great years like 1978 needs no more than six to eight months in barrel to round into form. From lesser years it needs none at all. That's one reason why we sell a lot of Cannonau as *vino da tavola* and why we even ferment it off the skins and make a white wine, because it's excellent young and anyway we don't have enough barrels to age more than six hundred thousand liters of Cannonau at a time. We make a little *riserva* mainly because there have been signs of a demand, but in my view *riserva* is unnecessary. Cannonau ages best in bottle."

Demand for bottles is a new and not firmly established tendency at a cooperative that started out in 1958 with an eye on the blending wine market. It succeeded in that way at selling off its annual production. But just recently it switched directions and now sells an ever-increasing portion of its Cannonau as DOC or at least superior *vino da tavola*.

"The base quality had always been there," said Spanu. "That's never been a problem with Cannonau around Dorgali, even when it was considered a country wine and was not well known." A vine of modest yields in the hills here, it was traditionally head-trained, though lately some members of the cooperative have been experimenting with a type of low cordon training with obvious labor-saving advantages, though that has yet to equal the results of *alberello*.

The Cooking: Suckling Pig and Music Paper

The vineyards of Cannonau run through the foothills of the Barbagia mountains around the peaks of the Monti Gennargentu, where the cooking is noted as the tastiest and most authentic of the island. Restaurants here are simple as a rule, rustic and inviting, especially in the months when a fire is going constantly in the hearth and suckling pigs and lambs roast slowly on heavy spits leaned vertically against the mantle and turned every now and then to let all sides cook evenly. One of the best such country restaurants is situated halfway between Dorgali and Oliena amidst brush-covered hills.

Su Gologone, a hotel and restaurant complex, occupies a series of white buildings with arcades, terraces, and loggias sprawled attractively over a knoll near the source of a stream called the Gologone. The interior plaster, beams, antique furnishings, bright murals, hand-woven tapestries, copper pots, and painted crockery set the tone for a memorable meal. That begins when a bottle of cool Cannonau and a plate heaped with sheets of *pane carasau* are placed in front of you. *Pane carasau*, also known as *carta di musica* or music paper, is as crisp and almost as slender as a potato chip, something like a *tortilla* but even more brittle, another one of those things you can't stop eating.

Paschetta Palimodde, the hostess, observing that I was new to the area, suggested a sampling of local specialties. "*Ci penso io*," she said with a smile, so I left it to her. Sampling indeed. The *antipasti* with the music paper bread would have made a fine meal: tender local *prosciutto* and *salame*, huge black olives, and two or three tasty pork products whose names I did not catch. Then came the most Sardinian of pastas, *malloreddus*, a type of *gnocchi* flavored by saffron and covered with tomato sauce, and *ravioli* stuffed with fresh *pecorino* cheese and wild herbs and greens.

At Su Gologone, a clear division of labor was evident, with women busily making pasta, preparing plates, and waiting on tables, and men languidly tending to the fire and spits, a task that required an occasional poke at the burning logs and a twist of the spits about every quarter-hour. They had that touch, though, because the *porceddu* was as tender as suckling pig can be and the lamb was its equal. And as if they were not enough, some delicious sausages were also heaped on the plate. The mixed vegetables included a new one on me, something called *melanzane spagnola* (Spanish eggplant), which resembled a cross between a regular eggplant and a cucumber. With that I bowed out, passing up the island's favorite dessert, *sebadas,* a pastry with cheese and bitter honey from bees who take the nectar from a plant known as *corbezzolo,* which my dictionary tells me is the strawberry tree (arbutus).

Sardinians generally prefer meat to seafood, they say, and as evidence, even along the coast few restaurants offer seafood exclusively. The land-based diet consists of a head-spinning array of pastas, pastries, stews, game, poultry, cheeses, and especially breads. I doubt that any other place this size in the world has such a variety of breads with exotic names like *coccoi, cozzula, tanconi, lotture, muddizzosu, pan'e simbula.* Even the music-paper bread has at least four names: *pane carasau, carta di musica, pistocco,* and *fresa.* And when softened and served with tomatoes, cheese, and eggs, it is known as *pane frattau.* Sardinia's sheep-milk cheese is famous, both when soft, mild, and used in pasta fillings or eaten alone and when hard and sharp and used for grating.

Despite its underemphasis, seafood in Sardinia can be outstanding, fresh and available in great variety. Lobsters are splendid, as are the popular *dentice* and *orata* (different species of Mediterranean sea bream), and tuna. Around Oristano, gray mullet and eel are special, and *bottarga,* the dried fish eggs that are more refined from mullet than tuna, are the local answer to caviar, though because they are dried they have a more pungent flavor. Two excellent restaurants at opposite ends of the island that provide the best in seafood, other typical Sardinian dishes, and well-chosen wines are Dal Corsaro in Cagliari and Da Franco at Palau, near the Costa Smeralda.

The Vintages

	DOC wines of Cagliari	Vernaccia di Oristano
1979	Excellent	Excellent
1978	Fair to good	Good
1977	Excellent	Excellent
1976	Fair to good	Fair
1975	Good	Excellent
1974	Good	Excellent
1973	Excellent	Good
1972	Exceptional	Excellent
1971	Fair	Excellent
1970	Excellent	Excellent
		(Previous great vintages: 1959 and 1958)

Cannonau di Sardegna

1979	Excellent
1978	Exceptional
1977	Good
1976	Fair to good
1975	Fair
1974	Good
1973	Good
1972	Excellent
1971	Fair
1970	Good

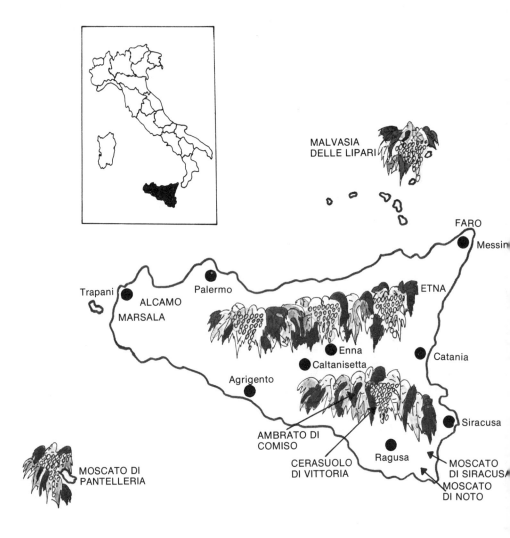

MALVASIA
DELLE LIPARI

FARO

Messin

Trapani

Palermo

ETNA

ALCAMO

MARSALA

Enna

Catania

Caltanisetta

Agrigento

AMBRATO DI
COMISO

Siracusa

MOSCATO DI
PANTELLERIA

CERASUOLO
DI VITTORIA

Ragusa

MOSCATO
DI SIRACUSA

MOSCATO
DI NOTO

SICILY

PROVINCES

PALERMO, Agrigento, Caltanissetta, Catania, Enna, Messina, Ragusa, Siracusa, Trapani

POPULATION

4,900,000

AREA

9,831 square miles

AVERAGE WINE PRODUCTION

930 million liters

DOC WINES

Alcamo · Cerasuolo di Vittoria · Etna (Bianco, Rosso, Rosato) · Faro · Malvasia delle Lipari · Marsala · Moscato di Noto · Moscato di Pantelleria · Moscato di Siracusa

OTHER WINES

Ala · Ambrato di Comiso · Bianco di Sicilia · Bonera · Capo Bianco · Capo Rosso · Carboj · Cariddi · Casalgismondo · Corbera · Corvo · Damaschino · Eloro · Flaming · Fontana Calda · Luparello · Mamertino · Meligauro · Nero d'Avola · Normanno · Pachino · Partinico · Perpetuo · Regaleali · Ribera · Rincione · Rocche di Rao · Rosato di Sicilia · Rosso di Sicilia · Segesta · Settesoli · Solunto · Solicchiato · Steri · Stravecchio di Sicilia · Torre Salsa · Trebbiano · Valle del Belice · Valledolmo · Velvety · Villa Fontane

New Day on an Old Island

APPROACHED from certain angles, the new Sicily does indeed look rather new. From across the straits where the frequent ferries from Calabria will one day be replaced by a long bridge, Messina gleams in the foreground of a majestic panorama that sweeps south from the island of Stromboli past the lighthouse at Torre Faro to the snows of Etna, itself just a youth, geologically speaking, and still growing.

The twenty-minute sally across the straits from Villa San Giovanni to Messina hardly gives you time enough to brace for an entry into the novel world of Sicily, so close to the Italian mainland and so far away in spirit. But when that bridge is finished (which from the looks of things will still be quite some time), they say that Sicily will cease to be an island unto itself. Still, some Sicilians seem to be looking forward to this historic link.

On close examination, Messina, with its wide streets and square blocks of recent buildings, does not ooze old-world charm. (It was rudely deprived of that by an earthquake in 1908.) But it does have other attractions: plenty of sunshine, beaches, mountains, views across the water, fresh fish, and fine local wines. From Messina you can get on one *autostrada* and be in Catania in an hour or on another and be in Palermo in two. But even in those sophisticated metropolises, remnants of the past are often encased ingloriously between structures of reinforced concrete and glass. Sometimes it looks as though Sicilians are trying to forget their past. Well, it must be conceded that between the high points of their history there were plenty of lows, and not all of them so distant.

Few places on earth have been so meddled with by foreigners with such little regard for the fortunes of the inhabitants. Even when the occupiers were not cruel, and some were not, the shifts of fate from one cultural extreme to the other left Sicilians with little choice but to formulate their own sets of credos and myths, their own sense of values, their own codes of morality and honor, and unique skills in the art of self-defense.

Wine, too, has had to roll with the punches. A Sicilian legend says that the first grapevine was brought here by Bacchus, who squeezed the first wine from its grapes at the foot of Etna. Life in Sicily has been anything but wine and roses since. After the Greeks brought viniculture to enviable levels, the Romans came and planted grain, neglecting all but a chosen few wines. The Arabs banned wine altogether for religious reasons, but a few faithless in their midst managed surreptitiously to keep the tradition alive. And so it went through the ages as one by one came hordes of barbarians, Saracens, Normans, the Holy Roman Empire, Aragonese, Bourbons, and finally Garibaldi with the "Thousand" who made the port of Marsala their starting point on the way to putting Italy back together. What man did not lay asunder, nature did; earthquakes, drought, and phylloxera took their toll in the vineyards. Though wine survived, not long ago things were in a sorry state indeed.

On my first visit to Sicily in the mid-1960s, I recall a certain difficulty in acquiring good local wines. There were the reds and whites of Corvo, good even then, and perhaps a precious few other dry table wines around, but they were not much in evidence. More than once I sat down to a meal of fine fresh seafood, ordered a dry white wine, and ended up sulking over a bottle of something amber-rust in color with alcohol ranging upward from 16° and flavor somewhere between sweet, sour, bitter, smoky, musty, and flat. To complete the insult, it was usually served at room temperature. Even when mixed with three parts of cold mineral water, such derelicts were beyond salvation. My luck with red wines was scarcely better.

Part of the problem was that Sicilians are not avid wine drinkers. Even as late as the 1960s, the concept of table wines — light, dry, easy to drink — was still foreign here. Sicily has always been among the leading regions in volume of production (finally hitting the top in 1979), but Sicilians drink less wine per capita than any other Italians — 54 liters a year, a shade over half the national average and a barrel less than the 136 liters the citizens of Valle d'Aosta put away. Even today a lot of Sicilian wine is quickly gone and forgotten, bound northward to the blending vats of Piedmont and the Midi.

But a new day has dawned for Sicilian wine, and one result is that you can now find what qualifies admirably as table wine anywhere in

Sicily you care to venture. Its value is no longer measured in degrees of alcohol, and a growing portion of production is bottled and sent abroad with a Q for quality prominent on its label. The Q is the regional mark of approval bestowed by the Istituto Regionale della Vite e del Vino, which has supervised what is sometimes referred to as "the great leap forward" in Sicilian winemaking, the transformation of the region's wine industry in less than two decades into one of the most technologically advanced of Europe.

As in other southern regions, Sicily has banked its fortunes on cooperatives. By 1978 there were 110 *cantine sociali* producing some 80 percent of Sicilian wine. But what the regional government proudly termed the "miracle of cooperation," others labeled a "disaster," pointing out that the glut of medium-grade wine in Sicily by 1980 was undercutting rather than building the value of the region's products on world markets. Though some cooperatives made good, even excellent, wine, many operated as little more than wine factories with mounting problems about where to sell their supplies. Most of the outstanding wine of Sicily was being produced by private wineries and Corvo, which works on the principle of a private firm though it is financially controlled by the region. By 1979, less than 5 percent of Sicilian wine was DOC.

Messina's Rarities: Mamertino, Faro, Malvasia delle Lipari

Many wines of the old Sicily were gladly bidden good riddance, but some antiques were just too valuable to be swept out in the housecleaning. A few have been dusted off and returned to a respectable position. Marsala is one, a wine whose image was so smeared that its producers almost forgot what a glorious beverage it was; only recently have they got around to restoring some of its former glitter. There are others as well, none so well known as Marsala but some even older, such as Messina's Mamertino, one of the few Sicilian wines treasured by the Romans.

Julius Caesar had no trouble procuring enough Mamertino to celebrate his third election as Consul of Rome, but modern-day searchers would have a harder time of it. Made from Catarratto, Inzolia, and Grillo, the three classic vines for Sicilian white wines, with a little Pedro Jimenez thrown in for accent, it can occasionally be found in the area of Castroreale and Furnari near the city of Milazzo. The color of old gold with a pronounced aroma of raisins, it is best as a lightly *amabile*, soft, smooth dessert wine. A drier version makes a good *aperitivo*.

Messina's proudest modern wine is Faro, which is DOC and could be a sleeper candidate for the honor of best dry red wine of the island, if it were not almost as hard to come by as Mamertino. Grown north of Messina through the hills behind the lighthouse (*faro*) at the top of the straits, it is made from Nerello Mascalese, Nocera, and Nerello Cappuccio grapes with up to 15 percent of Calabrese, Gaglioppo, and Sangiovese permitted. With at least 12° alcohol and often more than 13°, it can be an elegant wine of exceptional character after moderate aging, when its bright ruby takes on brick-red reflections and the sharp aroma and flavor of its youth begin to soften. Spinasanta of Messina produces the only Faro I know of in commerce. That private winery also makes a little Mamertino and table wines, a white Capo Bianco, a red Capo Rosso, and Cariddi in white, red, and rosé.

Sicily is a constellation of islands and islets within the sphere of the main island, which the Greeks called Trinarchia because of its triangular shape. Sicily's main island is the largest in the Mediterranean. The region is not only the largest of Italy but the most spread out. More than 430 kilometers (mostly water) separate its northernmost point, Stromboli, from its southernmost point, Lampedusa, which lies between Malta and the Tunisian coast well south of Tunis.

North of Messina are the Lipari or Aeolian Islands, as the Greeks called them after Aeolus, god of the winds. An archipelago of seven isles and numerous islets, their familiar landmark is the volcano Stromboli, which lies well off from the rest. Reachable by boat from Messina, Milazzo, or Naples, the Lipari Islands are a target for vacationers who like to really get away from it all. The clear water here is reputed to have marine life rarely seen anywhere else in the Mediterranean and the black lava and rust-colored soil of the sun-scorched slopes produce a Malvasia that also stands by itself.

Malvasia delle Lipari, though DOC, is not often found off the island, except at the occasional *enoteca* or restaurant that picked up a bottle or two out of curiosity. It is made from Malvasia grapes, though Corinto Nero must be included at 5 to 8 percent of the total. Here the vines are trained onto pergolas and sometimes dried on mats after being picked. The freshly harvested grapes are pressed into a light-bodied wine of ample color and flavor with at least 11.5° alcohol. The semi-dried grapes make wine of much greater strength, a *dolce naturale* or *passito* of 18° minimum and a *liquoroso* of 20° minimum.

Though Malvasia delle Lipari may be grown on the various islands, the best reputedly comes from Salina, where Nino Lo Schiavo produces a subtly perfumed, lightly sweet wine that is most pleasing with dessert. The few vineyards of Stromboli also make prized Malvasia, though to taste it you would probably have to sail there.

A *di rigore* stop on the isle of Lipari is the restaurant Filippino, where Filippo Bernardi and his family provide seafood freshly caught by their own crew of fishermen and wine from their own vineyards. The Malvasia is excellent. The *zuppa di pesce* here has been hailed as the greatest of the Tyrrhenian, and the *maccheruna* (homemade *maccheroni*) and *risotto nero con i calamaretti* (blackened by the squid's ink) are also worthy of Filippino's reputation.

Etna: The Master of the Mountain

Any complete tour of Sicily involves a great deal of skipping from place to place, island-hopping, and even the ascent of mountains. The eastern side of the region, the provinces of Messina, Catania, Enna, Siracusa, and Ragusa, produces only about one-eighth of Sicilian wine, but significantly there are more DOC zones in those five provinces than in the four western provinces of heaviest production, Trapani, Palermo, Agrigento, and Caltanissetta. The DOC wines of eastern Sicily are scarce commodities with special status, none more special, at least symbolically, than Etna with its Bianco, Rosso, and Rosato.

Etna dominates the face of eastern Sicily, so massive that the route around it covers 140 kilometers and so tall that it can be seen from as far as 250 kilometers away. Its frequent eruptions make good newspaper copy. But, as the inhabitants of its would-be Pompeiis point out, despite the "threat" their mountain is not a killer, though its lava flows have destroyed towns, including Catania. On balance, though, the people who live around it love their mountain, especially those who till its fertile black soil.

It was here, at what is now the village of Nasso, near Taormina, where Bacchus was supposed to have made that first wine, though these days few vines are seen around Taormina, apparently because the land is so valuable that only speculators with an eye on the tourist trade can afford to buy. Most vineyards of Etna lie higher up the slopes at altitudes of 1,300 to 2,500 feet, along an arc around the eastern side of the mountain that runs from Randazzo on the north to Biancavilla on the south. The best vineyards are around the town of Milo on the estate of Barone di

Villagrande, which has been in the family since the eighteenth century, when Emperor Charles VI, a Hapsburg, was also king of Sicily.

On my Esso map, Milo looked like a five-minute drive from the Giarre turnoff of the Messina–Catania *autostrada,* but it turned out to be somewhat longer. The Etna road climbs quickly away from the citrus, almond, and olive groves of the coastal plain and winds through a series of ramshackle towns past farms and villas flanked by gnarled, low-cut vines that step up the slopes on terraces walled by chunks of cinder piled neatly, the black earth interspersed occasionally with broom and cactus. Along the road, which often narrows to a single lane and only now and then is favored by a sign, graffitists had been busy. Obviously delighted by the bold effect of white paint on black walls, they splashed their messages, mostly political and identified with party initials and symbols, at every convenient vantage point: crosses, hammers and sickles, flaming torches, warnings, threats, and promises, crude and humorless, signs of the times. After Sant'Alfio the road cuts through woods of pine and chestnut and across empty spaces where recent lava flows have cleared all vegetation. Here and there along the way there are hand-lettered signs advertising *vino padronale* at competitive prices, though whether all would qualify as Etna is difficult to say.

Milo, at nearly 2,000 feet, is well below the 10,959-foot summit, but already you breathe mountain air and sense mountain altitudes. Whatever it looks like on the map, Milo is a long way from the coast. The estate of Barone di Villagrande lies a short way south of town along the road to Zafferana, a small billboard indicating the stony, tree-lined lane that leads to the cellars and villa, all in the color of volcanic ash. With the snowy hulk of Etna looming behind and a theater of Mediterranean views opening across the water to Reggio di Calabria and Aspromonte, this is an incomparable setting for a wine estate, the one that perhaps more than any other has upheld the noble tradition of winemaking in Sicily.

Carmelo Nicolosi Asmundo, Barone di Villagrande, is tall, lean, naturally genteel, and modest in appraising his wines. He submits that they are indeed good but might be better and he characterizes his own role in their production as the efforts of an enthusiastic dabbler in the art. Others have hailed him as the master of the mountain, a pioneer in producing quality wine of the type in Sicily and in proving its worth, not only to people in other places but, even more important, also to his fellow Sicilians. Other good wine is now produced here, but Etna is a

Carmelo Nicolosi Asmundo

southern pillar of Italian wine today erected on the strength of Barone di Villagrande.

The Baron likes to give credit to the mountain. "It's just about ideal," he said of his 75 acres of vineland. "The earth is rich in phosphorus and iron, exposure to the sun is complete, and the altitude favors a moderate climate in which the grapes ripen with a balance in sugars and acids. And there's something more as well, a chemistry that we like to say derives from the force of the volcano."

Etna was the first DOC zone of Sicily in 1968, though its production has never been large and still rarely surpasses 1.5 million bottles a year. Barone di Villagrande has been approaching 100,000 bottles in good years, exclusively in Etna's DOC wines. The Rosso and Rosato (which is called Gattopardo) are made from Nerello Mascalese at 80 percent or more with the possibility of Nerello Cappuccio at no more than 20 percent and local light grapes at no more than 10 percent. They must have at least 12.5° alcohol. The rosé is to drink young, but the red is kept two or three years, most of the time in large old barrels in the Villagrande cellars, before going on sale. The Rosso can age extremely well, certainly a decade from some vintages, though from others it is best to consume within three to five years of the harvest.

Etna Bianco consists of Carricante grapes at 60 percent or more with Catarratto at a maximum of 40 percent, and the possibility of Trebbiano, Minnella Bianca, and other local light grapes at no more than 15 percent. It must have 11.5°. Etna Bianco *superiore*, for which only the wine of Villagrande qualifies, must be made from no less than 80 percent Carricante grapes and have 12° of alcohol. A fine, balanced white with the delicately fruity aroma of Carricante, it is excellent with fish and is best well chilled.

Nicolosi's youngest son, Carlo, a professor of agricultural science at the University of Catania, introduced the new equipment for white wine and rosé in 1977, a move his father now proudly credits with bringing a marked improvement in quality. Carlo Nicolosi has also been converting the vineyards gradually from head-trained to cordon. And he has touched up the procedures for Rosso too. "We still consider the vinification to be traditional," said his father, "though I must confess the context of that term traditional has been stretched some in recent years."

Barone Nicolosi, who has been forced by an injury to limit his activities, is content that the winery is in good hands. "I learned the techniques from my father and then later I went ahead and made modifications of my own," he said. "That's how most family wine operations evolve. This time I think the advancement from one generation to the next has been more significant. I think with Carlo in charge, our wines will express the natural qualifications of Etna better than ever before."

Other producers of Etna include the Cantina Sociale di Torrepalino at Solicchiata, a commendable cooperative, and Etnea Vini of Catania.

The Moscato of Siracusa and Noto: Sweet but Short

Catania, one of the hottest and most modern cities of the Italian south, was the home of Vincenzo Bellini, whose opera *La Norma* inspired a dish called *pasta con la Norma*, spaghetti dressed with a sauce of tomato, eggplant, basil, *ricotta*, garlic, and oil. Catania is also the capital of sweets and ices, for which Sicily is justly glorified. The masterpiece of Sicilian desserts is *cassata*, which can be made in many ways, even frozen, but it reaches its pinnacle as a work of art in the pastry shops of Catania. The triumphant range of Sicilian desserts explains why so many noted wines of the island were, and still are, sweet.

From Catania the road south to Siracusa hugs the seacoast for a way and then winds through hills covered with subtropical vegetation on the peninsula of Augusta. An immense power plant and chemical factories are the present-day introductions to ancient Syracuse, providing to visitors arriving from the north not so much as a hint that just ahead lies the city that once rivaled Athens as a center of Greek civilization. Still, the old town and the remains of the city where Archimedes lived and dreamed are among the wonders of Sicily.

Though vineyards are evident through the low hills west of the city, a wine shop in the center could offer plenty of Corvo, Chianti, and Valpolicella but not a drop of anything called Moscato di Siracusa. There had been some a couple of months earlier, they said, but when that was sold they had not been able to get any more. Anyway, there was not much demand, because people seem to want table wines these days. Records of the national DOC committee backed the shopkeeper. No Moscato di Siracusa was officially declared from the 1978 vintage.

For the record, Moscato di Siracusa can be made from Moscato Bianco grapes grown only in the community of Siracusa. It is supposed to be golden yellow with amber tints, delicately perfumed, sweet and smooth with 16.5° alcohol at minimum. It has been written that the Moscato here is similar to wines called Pollio or Biblino in ancient times, praised by the Greek poet Hesiod in the eighth century B.C. and later by Pliny.

It has also been reported that some producers still make the wine from semi-dried grapes fermented in amphorae as did the ancients. The only winery I know of with Moscato di Siracusa in commerce is the Casa Vinicola Aretusa, which also produces a white called Val d'Anapo Ambra and, according to Mario Soldati, has experimented successfully with Nebbiolo, though evidently that is not widely available either.

Moscato di Noto, another DOC wine, whose zone covers the southeastern corner of the Sicilian triangle inland from Capo Passero, is almost as rare, though the national committee reported that 3,900 liters were officially declared in 1978. Noto is the southernmost DOC zone of Italy, though the island of Pantelleria, home of Moscato di Pantelleria, is almost as southerly and possibly even hotter.

The leading producer of Moscato di Noto is the Cantina Sperimentale di Noto, the experimental center where Professor Paolo Fici, one of the most respected oenologists in Sicily today, carries out his research within the walls of a former Capuchin monastery. The basic Moscato di Noto is a still wine called *naturale* of at least 13° alcohol made from Moscato

Bianco into a lightly sweet straw-yellow wine of fine aroma. A *spumante* is also allowed, refermented from the *naturale*. Served well chilled, the *naturale* and *spumante* are fine light dessert wines. A *liquoroso* of at least 16° is made by arresting the fermentation by the addition of wine alcohol, leaving the wine even more fragrant and sweeter than the *naturale*, with scents of almonds and oranges, so they say, from the plants that often alternate with vines in this handsome agricultural country.

Moscato is one of several varieties of vines grown in the sunbaked hills around Noto, which was rebuilt in baroque after being destroyed by an earthquake in the eighteenth century. Avola, Rosolino, and Pachino are other centers with a noted avocation for vines despite the torrid heat of summer. Most vines here are trained in extremely low *alberello*, the trunks cut at just a few inches above the ground. This method is well suited to the highly alcoholic blending wines that still seem the *raison d'être* of local viticulture, though by 1980, with French markets for Italian wine drying up and northern Italian producers demanding abolition of legislation that forces them to use concentrates and strong musts instead of sugar, the future of *vino da taglio* seemed very much in doubt.

Whether or not this southernmost point of Italian wine grape production will survive depends on the adjustment to modern needs. Cooperative winemaking has not been introduced to the province of Siracusa, though some private wineries have begun to make quality white wines from Albanello, Catarratto, Grillo, and Inzolia, and reds and rosés from Calabrese, Nero d'Avola, Frappato di Vittoria, Nerello Mascalese, and even Barbera, Sangiovese, and Nebbiolo. Few bottled wines were in evidence locally, though products by the names of Eloro, Nero d'Avola, and Pachino have been noted. Undoubtedly, most of the wine and musts made here are being employed by Sicilian wineries that buy grapes from different parts of the region and by wineries in the north.

One example of how good the local table wine can be is Luparello, which might be classified as either a light red or a dark rosé. From the estate of Michele Cricole, a native of Noto and professor of maritime law in Rome, the wine is rich though dry, with a suggestion of both bitter and sweet in its flavor. It is made from Calabrese grapes alone, fermented briefly on the skins and then aged for two years in oak casks. A new winery, Cricole's has a capacity of 1.5 million liters from 120 acres of vines. Professor Cricole, who has found markets for his wine in Catania, Rome, and Milan, is one of the few producers in the zone who sell all wine in labeled bottles.

The cooking in this southeastern corner of Sicily is known for its tastes of sea and sun expressed in innumerable variations on fresh fish and fresh vegetables. There is the most Sicilian *caponata*, a stew based on eggplant, and *peperonata*, which is based on peppers, brilliant in their colors and flavors. At Porto Palo, near the tip of Capo Passero, the Trattoria dei Due Mari, run by Carmen, who has a classic Greek profile and a country sense of hospitality, is a simple setting for gracious seaside dining. Spaghetti here is dressed with tomatoes and fried eggplant or zucchini. The assortment of grilled fish is called *purpetti di milinciani,* and with that Carmen offers stuffed peppers, tomatoes, or eggplant flavored with wild herbs and olive oil. At Al Sorcio in Donnalucata the specialty is *sardi a linguata,* breaded sardines grilled over the coals, and a few kilometers farther along the coast at Marina di Ragusa is the most lauded restaurant of the area, Alberto il Mago del Pesce, where Alberto Mattei shows his wizardry with fish dishes ranging from *zuppa di pesce* to *spigola* (sea bass) baked in paper.

Ambrato, Cerasuolo, and the Colonel's Arsenal

In the adjacent province of Ragusa, vineyards are much less evident than they were in Siracusa. The road from Noto and Ispica is flanked by interminable stone walls as it climbs hills dramatically eroded and sometimes barren save for cactus and sagebrush, past Modica, at the foot of a yawning canyon, and Ragusa, whose new city dominates one hill and its old city, Ibla, another. Winding down from the high plateau into the valley of the Ippari River, the road reaches Comiso and Vittoria, homes of the only important wines of the province.

Ambrato di Comiso, Sicily's latest candidate for DOC, is an oddity, a sweet white wine made from the pulp of dark grapes. White? Well, closer to amber, as its name implies, somewhere between *abboccato* and *amabile* and ranging from 13° to 17° alcohol. Although the precise terms of its DOC had not been defined by 1980, wine of the name is made from Calabrese, Frappato di Vittoria, Nerello Mascalese, and Damaschino grapes. It has a pronounced scent of esters, velvety texture, a hint of bitterness, and a tendency to become drier with age. It is not an easy wine to make, so very little is available.

Cerasuolo di Vittoria is the one established DOC wine of the province, a strong rosé, also known as Frappato, with an uncanny capacity for aging. It is made from Calabrese at 60 percent and Frappato di Vittoria at 40 percent, with the possibility of a slight addition of Grosso Nero or Nero Mascalese. It must have at least 13° alcohol, though it can easily approach 15°. Dry, but full and round, it is delicately perfumed and when served at cellar temperature makes a fine accompaniment to poultry and rabbit.

The commanding figure in Cerasuolo production is Giuseppe Coria, a retired army officer who has turned his attention and sense of discipline to making wine and writing about it. Still addressed as "Colonello," Coria has written three books on Italian wine, including an encyclopedia, while reshaping his family farm into a model estate. The colonel calls his Cerasuolo Stravecchio Siciliano when it is well aged — as much as forty years, when it becomes similar to very old Sherry. That is just one in an arsenal of special wines made on his estate of 20 acres: dry red Villa Fontane that also ages magnificently, Moscato di Villa Fontane, and Bianco Dolce di Villa Fontane (which is called Solicchiato when thoroughly aged), for a total of 20,000 bottles between them.

Coria's most intriguing product is Perpetuo, which derives from an ancient Sicilian custom related to the Spanish *solera*. The principle is simple enough. From an old barrel of wine, a small quantity is drawn off each year and replaced with an equal quantity of new wine, resulting in a perpetual wine. But in practice it is successful only with the right kind of wine under the right kind of conditions. Coria uses the Stravecchio Siciliano for his Perpetuo, and, though the few bottles that he releases each year are nearly impossible to acquire, some who have tasted it have pronounced it splendid and, like the colonel, one of a kind.

Regaleali, a Question of Scale

Enna and Caltanissetta are the forgotten cities of Sicily's mountainous interior, an area of vast panoramas across green hills topped by walled towns with castles that date to Greek, Roman, and Arab times. Enna, at more than 3,000 feet above sea level, is known as both the belly button and the *belvedere* of Sicily because of its central position with views in all directions. The province of Enna produces very little wine compared with other provinces of Sicily, and what is made remains for the most part obscure, though it is difficult to imagine how wines called Flaming and Velvety, both red and both made near the town of Piazza Armerina, could remain obscure for long. East of Piazza Armerina,

around the reservoir of Ogliastro, the Azienda Malaricotta produces red
and white wines called Casalgismondo, with excellent reputations in
the province. The white is good with the fresh-water eels of Ogliastro
and the red is recommended with lamb and the excellent *pecorino* cheese
from the nearby mountains.

Caltanissetta, which lies 35 kilometers west of Enna along a scenic
mountain road, is a center of increasing wine production, some of it in
the high-quality field where the name Regaleali stands out.

Regaleali Bianco, Rosso, and Rosato, from the estate of Conte Tasca
d'Almerita at Vallelunga, were once esteemed by Italians from points
north as the insider's Sicilian estate wines. Perhaps they were seduced
by the noble name, the rustic farm buildings depicted on the label, and,
above all, the quality into thinking Regaleali was a small-scale outfit.
Well, most insiders now know that Regaleali is not small-scale and
though the wines have always been blessedly free of anything that could
be identified as a "southern" taste, some connoisseurs have remarked on
an ever-so-subtle slippage in quality over the last decade or so as the
size of the operation grew and the name became well known.

That slippage may be nothing more than the imaginations of those
who believe that only small estates make superb wine. It is hard to be
objective about such things, though I must admit that Regaleali, which
is not DOC, no longer stands head and shoulders over most other Sicilian dry wines as it did not long ago. It is, however, still among the best
on the market and might even be as good as it was in the early 1970s
when I made its acquaintance. I suspect that more than anything else
it is a matter of competition catching up.

Regaleali Bianco, probably the best of the three types, is made from
Catarratto and Inzolia with a little Sauvignon, pale straw, crisp, fresh,
fruitier than whites from vineyards in low coastal zones that sometimes
have more than a hint of that "baked" taste. Regaleali Bianco grapes
come from vineyards at 1,300 to 2,000 feet above sea level, in other
words, from a climate that compares with some of the temperate zones
of central and northern Italy. Its fruit and acids balance admirably with
about 12.5° alcohol.

Regaleali Rosso, from Perricone, Nero d'Avola, and Calabrese, is
robust, dry, with plenty of depth and increasing smoothness as it ages,
a big wine that excels with roast meat. The Rosato has uncommon class
in the genre; made from the same grapes as the red, it too can age a bit.
Both have about 13°, sometimes slightly more, of alcohol.

Most wine produced in the province of Caltanissetta comes from the hills and plains back of the coastal town of Gela toward Butera and Riesi. Some good wines, red, white, and rosé, are made there, though so far none is well known.

From the Folkloristic to the Futuristic

The old Sicily is not always so easy to spot anymore, not even here along the back roads through the center of the island. Occasionally, you may still see a donkey pulling a cart, a *carretta,* with wood carvings on its sides, peasant art of the highest order, and you may even see a farmer drinking wine from a little barrel, a *carrateddu,* that once upon a time every *contadino* toted with him into the fields to quench his thirst. But these days you are more likely to see a *carretta* or a *carrateddu* in museums or antique shops than in the countryside. That Sicilians are not heavy drinkers does not mean that wine has not played an important role in the history of the island, in the art, the literature, and the folklore. As Alfredo Ferruzza, author, journalist, native son, once noted: "In Sicily, since the beginning of time, wine has been a sign of contradiction: either all good or all bad, rarely and sporadically anything in between."

As examples, Ferruzza quoted two proverbs: "He who has a vineyard has the mange" and "He who has a good vineyard has bread, wine, and wood." The sayings, said Ferruzza, "represent the opposite sides of a two-faced bust in its two visions of vines and wine — an image that is faithful to the courses and recourses of Sicilian history."

The Sicilian love of the land is legend, though because of circumstances of history, from a feudal system that evolved into oppressively secret networks of land control by the silent lords that survived even the reforms of Napoleon, the Risorgimento, and Mussolini, many poor people were deprived of their humble dream of owning a home in the country surrounded by a vineyard. Still the belief prevailed that the only genuine wine was made by one's own hands, as expressed in the saying: "*È megghiu stari sulu a la tò vigna, ca la vigna d'autri cunsari.*" (It's better to stand alone in your own vineyard than to tend the vineyards of others.)

As you move across the island from east to west, the new world of Sicilian viticulture becomes ever more assertive. In the back country, promiscuous culture is still a reality, rows of vines amidst groves of olives, almonds, pistachios, tangerines, lemons, and fields of grain. But in western Sicily, in the provinces of Palermo, Agrigento, and especially Trapani, the great leap forward has transformed the face of the land. Great stretches of vineyards have been planted, though few people stand alone in them, for here the cooperative movement is the prevailing force. But the transformation has not been as smooth as anticipated. Beneath a rather slick surface lie some vexing problems.

The changes began in the 1950s, when the Istituto Regionale della Vite e del Vino was created by the regional government to pull Sicily out of the dark ages of viniculture and into the realm of the futuristic. At that point it was a question of economic survival. The initial funds could be found through the Cassa per il Mezzogiorno and Common Market, regional, and provincial development programs. The mission was launched inconspicuously with a census of vineyard and winery conditions, the first priority being the determination of vines best suited to modern winemaking and Sicilian conditions and reduction or elimination of the others. Preference was given to such light varieties as Catarratto, Inzolia, Grillo, Grecanico, Trebbiano Toscano, and Damaschino, and, among the dark varieties, Nerello Mascalese, Calabrese, Frappato, Perricone, Barbera, and Sangiovese.

Obviously, the *alberello* or low-bush training long favored in Sicily produced grapes with excessive sugar and inadequate acids, so cordon and low-arbor *tendone* systems have been substituted in many areas, especially of low altitude. It was also found that hillside vineyards, with what had been taken for granted to be natural advantages of drainage and cooler conditions for quality wines, were not as suitable in areas of light rainfall (especially western Sicily) as were vineyards in heavy soil in the plains. Dams were constructed to provide irrigation to dry places.

The advent of DOC in the 1960s encouraged Sicilians gradually to deemphasize blending wines and to aim more production at the high-quality bottled-wine market. New cooperatives were constructed and given the latest in equipment and professional direction, with greater attention given to all phases of making and selling wine. A system was devised under which grape prices were guaranteed by the region, which has intervened to keep them from going below set minimums. The regional government also began its ambitious program of selecting the best quality wines from all sources, public and private, and awarding them the Q, that unique seal of approval in Italian wine.

In the last twenty years, Sicily has probably achieved more profound progress in viticulture and oenology than has any other region. Its facilities, its techniques, its potential place it in the avant-garde of winemaking worldwide. But however commendable the aims and amazing the achievement, there is no suppressing the uneasy feeling in Sicily that something is wrong. It seems that for every case of excellent wine that leaves the island with a Q proudly stamped on each bottle, there is a demijohn, a barrel, perhaps even a vat full of wine back home with no clear destination. By 1980, after record harvests in Italy and France, the demand for blending wine suddenly ceased. Even medium-quality table wines, whether bottled or in bulk, were often selling at cost or less on an excruciatingly slow market. There was simply much more wine around than anyone knew what to do with, a surplus of crisis proportions. But why?

Looking back, it now seems clear that the Sicilian program was based on two principles that did not work out the way they might have. One was that the world market for medium-grade table wine would continue to increase at a spiraling rate. (In fact, after starting out that way in the early 1970s, the pace lapsed to a fitful upward trend.) The other was the conviction that cooperatives can compete efficiently and profitably in the high-quality field. (As has already been mentioned, most have not, and it seems increasingly clear that, given the current concepts of operation and financing, most cannot.) By 1980, Sicilian officials were talking about cutting back output and reexamining the cooperative movement with new emphasis on elevating quality. Once again, it had come down to a question of economic survival.

Corvo, Something to Crow About

Casa Vinicola Duca di Salaparuta was once, as the name suggests, the holding of a nobleman. In 1824, Edoardo Alliata di Villafranca, Duca di Salaparuta, founded a winery beneath his castle at Casteldaccia, 18 kilometers east of Palermo, overlooking the sea. Heeding suggestions from some of the leading figures in French oenology of the day, he was soon making wines considered among the foremost of Sicily. He baptized them Corvo, Italian for crow, after a local legend in which an old man who was bothered by one of the birds was given a stick by the villagers to do away with it. The deed done, the grateful hermit planted the stick in the ground and it became a flourishing vine. The Salaparuta tradition was enriched by Edoardo Alliata's son, Enrico, whose wines were widely known and honored well into this century.

A glance at the labels with their crests, crowns, and medallions garnered over time might suggest that little has changed, that in the cellars of their castle the Dukes of Salaparuta are still making wine among the foremost of Sicily. The truth is, though, that all that remain from the old days are the noble emblems and the name, for a few years after Enrico Alliata's death in 1946, the trademark was sold to a public holding company with capital put up by the region of Sicily. A new winery was built along the Palermo-Messina road 50 meters from the sea. It was later expanded, and the best talent obtainable was hired to relaunch the name. Corvo has since given the region something to crow about.

Unlike the other publicly backed wineries of Sicily, Corvo is not a cooperative. Instead, it was set up with a board of directors answerable to the owners, the region primarily, and run exactly like a private winery, though not one of ordinary dimensions. By 1980, Corvo was pushing its annual production toward 8 million bottles in six basic types — the traditional dry Corvo Rosso and Bianco, the white Colomba Platino, the Sherry-type Stravecchio di Sicilia, a cherry-flavored *liquoroso* wine called Ala, and, just recently, Corvo Spumante in brut and demi-sec. About half of Corvo's total production is sold outside Italy.

No Corvo wines are DOC, for a fundamental reason. Grapes are acquired from a network of growers in many parts of the island, coastal and interior, high and low, mostly in the central and western provinces. There is simply no standard way of determining the geographical origin of the grapes used in each year's wine and no chance of official delimitation, but Corvo does not seem to need DOC anyway.

Casa Vinicola Duca di Salaparuta, whose president is Silvio Ruffino and new director is Benedetto Migliore, is the best-known name in Sicilian wine today, both in Italy and abroad, with a reputation for unerringly consistent quality in wines that fit comfortably the descriptions "modern" and "widely appealing." The impetus for this quality was provided by Ezio Rivella, who designed the winemaking facilities and remains an adviser, though the current operation is directed by Franco Giacosa, who like Rivella learned the craft at the family farm in the Langhe, studied at Alba, and headed south to make a career.

"My greatest satisfaction," said Giacosa, whose articulation is still unmistakably Piedmontese, "is to take bottles of Corvo home to my father

Franco Giacosa

and friends. At first they were sort of smug . . . you know how Piedmontese are about wine. But now they put it to the test. Every time. The whole tasting routine. And they always say, 'Hmmm, not bad, not bad.' When somebody from Alba says that about a wine from somewhere else, that's lofty praise indeed."

Giacosa is an advocate of the intrinsic advantages of Sicily's climate and terrain, especially for white wines made in the Corvo manner. "We almost never have a bad year," he said, "because by selecting grapes from different altitudes, from near sea level to as high as seven hundred or eight hundred meters, we can balance the components and control the quality year in and year out." The still whites and *spumante* are made from Inzolia, Trebbiano, Catarratto, and Albanello grapes selected to convert into natural alcohol of 11.5° to 12°. Only free-run must is used, about 50 percent of the weight of the grapes. Interestingly, the original

Duca di Salaparuta, using the best know-how of the time, followed the same principle and even named his white wine Prima Goccia (first drop) in honor of it. Corvo Bianco is still called Prima Goccia, a straw-yellow, perfumed, delicately fruity, and nicely balanced wine that is the strong point of the company's production, the best-seller. The other dry white, Colomba Platino, so called for its platinum color, is leaner and more acidulous, excellent with fish. The *spumante* types, both made by charmat, are increasingly in demand in Sicily and the few other places in Italy where they are available.

Giacosa places his Corvo Rosso in a "league with fine Chianti," which is a pretty fair assessment, even if the wines represent completely different bloodlines. Made from Calabrese, Nerello Mascalese, and Perricone, Corvo Rosso's vinification begins with the relatively recent Blachère system of maceration that results in wines ready to drink earlier than those made in traditional ways. Still, with strength of 12.5° to 13° and ample body, Corvo Rosso needs some barrel age. Giacosa, who recalled a "lively discussion" with Professor Luciano Usseglio-Tomasset, the wood adversary from his alma mater, said he still believed that six to eight months in casks was an absolute minimum and that some vintages needed two to three years to strike the desired balance. Still, the Corvo trend is toward a wine to drink sooner than before, starting at about three years after the harvest and retaining its attributes for up to a decade.

Stravecchio di Sicilia and Ala, both traditional products of the winery, are not widely distributed though they are appreciated by those who know them. Corvo Bianco became one of the most popular Italian white wines in the United States in the late 1970s. With the supply of Corvo Rosso also increasing, sales in that country were approaching 2 million bottles a year by 1980. West Germany and Britain followed.

"A few years ago, we were approached by foreign importers who wanted made-to-measure wines, light, *frizzante,* and, naturally, low-priced," said Giacosa. "But we said no, and our sales since have justified our insistence on quality. I think other wineries would be well advised to follow suit and not fall into the cheap-wine trap. Because once you're in it, it's nearly impossible to get out."

Palermo, Cosmopolitan Crossroads

Palermo, with its busy port and fine location snuggled within the semicircle of hills known as the Conca d'Oro, bears reminders of the score or more of peoples who strayed into this crossroads of civilization and decided to stay awhile. The mix, both historical and contemporary, is outwardly apparent in the building and the ethnic makeup of the citizenry, features that contribute to a cosmopolitan air about the place that does not fit neatly into the grooves of southern Italian stereotypes. Yes, poverty persists, and somewhere behind the scenes lurks the Mafia, though these days, as a local newspaper reporter confided, "you can't tell who is and who isn't, because everybody with even the most tenuous link to an influential person in this town acts like a *mafioso.*"

Well, some force has accomplished what might be described as urban renewal, which has made Palermo into a relatively comfortable modern city that has almost, but not quite, succeeded in draining itself of local color. Splashes of that remain in the Vucciria, the central market area surrounded by a labyrinth of narrow streets where washing hangs between the buildings like banners blowing in the breeze. There, in the *trattorie* and *osterie,* some just holes in the wall, when well directed you can dine well and cheaply on typical fare such as celery soup and *pasta con le sarde* (with sardines), the pride of Sicilian *minestre,* and on other simple dishes based on that morning's choices at the fish and vegetable stalls. At the other extreme is the Charleston, which the food guides agree is the region's ranking restaurant. Its reputation is based on traditional Sicilian dishes, a brilliant range, elegantly prepared and served with appropriate wines.

A new and different place to sample Sicilian foods and wines together is La Cannata, an *osteria-trattoria-enoteca* within the walls of an old manor house with a terrace opening onto an orange grove. Created by Franca Colonna Romano, author, television personality, and tireless defender of the good things in Sicilian life, La Cannata is a little monument to the island's heritage of food and drink. Here you can help yourself to typical specialties that load the tables in a colorful array. The breads (Franca Colonna Romano has written a book on them) and cheeses are worth the price of the menu, and the wines represent the best of Sicily and other regions.

The countryside around Palermo has plenty of vineyards, though the only classified ones contribute to the DOC wines of Marsala and Alcamo, which are centered in the province of Trapani. The valley of the Jato River, which flows through Palermo from above the cathedral town of Monreale, is a source of much of what Palermo considers local wines, some of them worthy of recognition. The hills around Corleone have been noted for ages for their wines; the Fattoria Rocche di Rao is one of several producers of good red and white wines there. In the southeastern hills of the province, almost adjacent to the vineyards of Regaleali, the Fontana Murata winery makes excellent Rosso, Rosato, and Bianco that take the name of the town of Valledolmo. Some white wines of Partinico, west of Palermo, have been distributed in the United States. In Palermo, the firm of Solunto Vini Pregiati makes good wines called Solunto, though the grapes often come from the province of Trapani.

Agrigento: Lambrusco in the Land of the Leopard

When you consider that the provinces of Agrigento, Palermo, and Caltanissetta between them produce about a third of a billion liters of wine a year and that not one of them has a DOC it can call its own, something would seem to be amiss. True, many of the wines and musts are used for blending, but a significant and increasing portion has been turned into good-quality table wine, exemplified by Corvo and Regaleali, though the list of qualified producers does not stop there.

The lack of recognition is most striking in Agrigento, whose production approaches 200 million liters some years, ranking the province second in volume to Trapani in Sicily and sixth or seventh nationally. Among the multitude are several wines of distinction to which some sort of official nod would by now seem due. When the *vino tipico* category takes effect in Italy, much of the current *vino da tavola* of Agrigento should be classified as Bianco, Rosso, and Rosato di Sicilia within the Common Market category of VQPRD. But in the meantime, the wines of Agrigento have been rather ungraciously neglected.

The province's vineyards are strung out in an almost unbroken chain through hills and valleys oriented toward the sea from Menfi on the northwest to Licata on the southeast. Though hot and dry and exposed to the *scirocco* through the summer, producers have quickly applied new techniques and perhaps even more importantly a new philosophy about grape growing and winemaking that have resulted in a net improvement in quality over the last decade. Experts are particularly impressed by certain red wines of the province, though white wines, too, can certainly vie with many DOCs in quality. Here cooperatives account for a major share of production.

Two outstanding cooperatives are Enocarboj at Sciacca (whose wines carry the trade name Carboj in Bianco, Rosso, and Rosato di Sciacca and Trebbiano di Sicilia), and Settesoli of Menfi, with Settesoli Bianco, Damaschino, and Bonera. Other cooperatives with good products are Terra di Sicilia (Ribera Bianco and Rosso); La Vite, which uses the trade name Corbera (Bianco Verdolino, Rosso Rubino, and Rosé della Valle del Belice); Grappolo d'Oro (Fontana Calda Bianco and Rosso); Torre Salsa (Bianco, Rosso, and Rosato di Sicilia and Meligauro Bianco and Rosato). At Palma di Montechiaro, the small Cantina Sociale del Gattopardo calls its wines Gattopardo in homage to the late Giuseppe Tomasi di Lampedusa, author of *Il Gattopardo* (*The Leopard*).

The land of *The Leopard* has changed in the more than two decades since it was written. One can only shudder at what the nostalgic Lampedusa might have to say about his home today. Palma di Montechiaro is a new town and Agrigento a new city, a crest of high rises looming over the Valley of the Temples, which is still the most splendid remnant of the ancient Greeks in Italy.

The wines of Agrigento are decidedly new. The good ones are not exclusively cooperative products nor are they necessarily prepared from native varieties. The most bizarre exceptions to the norm are made in the Comarco di Naro, a fertile valley due east of Agrigento, by Giuseppe Camilleri, a professor of oenology whose wines, called Steri, are convincing evidence that Agrigento has a vital share of that elusive factor called quality.

Camilleri, a big man whose ingenious drive is not apparent in his easygoing manner, bought some 65 acres in the Comarco di Naro in 1966, land that had been part of those tracts that were carry-overs from the days of the great feudal holdings of southern Sicily. Camilleri put in vines and trained them not in the usual *alberello* but the arbored *tendone* and built a winery with stainless steel tanks, casks of Slavonian oak, and plenty of shiny equipment that piqued the curiosity of local farmers. "They waited until the results came in," Camilleri recalled, "and when they tasted it, that set off a chain reaction. Everybody started planting vines and talking about quality wine. Almond and olive trees were removed and grain fields replaced by vines trained in *tendone*." Camilleri continued his own operation, which he has expanded to a capacity of 1.5 million liters, while helping to found the Cantina Ciccobriglio at nearby Naro, a small cooperative that he directs.

Camilleri, not one to fall into line, decided to do some experimenting with his vines, selecting, of all things, Lambrusco Salamino on a hunch that the rich soil here would suit it perfectly. He also planted Barbera. Both these strange northerners came in with what he termed "surprisingly good results." Camilleri produces three wines under the name Steri, from the Latin *hosterium,* a place where guests gather.

The Steri Bianco, from Trebbiano, Inzolia, and Vernaccia di San Gimignano, is light straw with clean, fresh aroma and flavor. Steri Rosso is made from Nero d'Avola at 50 percent, Barbera at 40 percent, and Lambrusco at 10 percent, a bright ruby wine, warm, soft, with a trace of tannin in its full body. Steri *riserva speciale* stands apart from all other wines of Sicily for its extraordinary aroma and flavor that derive from Lambrusco Salamino at 60 percent with Barbera at 30 percent and Nero d'Avola. A still wine of deep ruby-vermilion color, it is soft, dense, full of aroma and flavor, rich in extracts, and strong (13° to 14°). Perhaps the closest things to it are some Barberas of the Oltrepò Pavese, but really there is nothing quite like it, certainly not in the Lambrusco zones of Emilia. The wines should develop finesse as the vines grow older, for they still have a somewhat raw texture and a touch of aggressiveness.

Camilleri is delighted with the success of not only the wine but the vines. He noted that both Lambrusco and Barbera thrive here, yield prolifically, and provide healthy grapes full of sugar in wines that mature to optimum drinkability in about two years.

Alcamo: Banking on Neutrality

Looking across its wide open spaces, it is hard to think of the province of Trapani as choice vineland. Bleached by the sun and battered by hot winds from Africa, which lies just over the horizon across the Sicilian Channel, conditions are torrid and arid (rainfall averages about 20 inches a year). Yet Trapani has more vines than any other province of Italy and vies with Ravenna in Romagna as the leader in production of wine grapes and wine. About half of Sicily's wine is made here and roughly 95 percent of the island's DOC wine is produced here under three names: Marsala, Moscato di Pantelleria, and Bianco Alcamo or Alcamo. If any more evidence is needed that the region has banked its future on Trapani, nearly two-thirds of Sicily's cooperative wineries are located here. There are also a number of large and diversified private firms.

The province has two basic levels of vineland, the high and the low, with the heaviest concentrations in the coastal plains around Castelvetrano, Mazara del Vallo, Marsala, and Trapani. Vines in the reddish, iron-rich soil here are predominately in light varieties: Catarratto, Inzolia, Grillo, with some Trebbiano, Damaschino, and Grecanico. They are employed in two basic styles of wine: the heavy and rich, as represented by Marsala, and the light and neutral, as represented by Alcamo. On the island of Pantelleria, Zibibbo dominates in the heavy and rich Moscato di Pantelleria.

The town of Alcamo is the axis of a hilly DOC zone that extends on the west from Castellammare del Golfo to Calatafimi and east into the province of Palermo as far as San Cipriello and Camporeale. Production of Alcamo has been increasing, reaching 5.7 million liters in 1978, though that figure hardly reflects the grand expectations held for this wine. Sicilians have boosted Alcamo as their answer to the world demand for neutral whites, but so far it has failed to fire many imaginations in other lands.

The Alcamo area has long been noted as a supplier of blending wines for light vermouth. The basic character has not changed drastically, for Catarratto has that sort of lack of personality that can be a desirable quality in certain white wines. Alcamo consists of at least 80 percent Catarratto in the Lucido subvariety, with Damaschino, Grecanico, and Trebbiano for the difference. Minimum alcohol is 11.5°. The techniques introduced here over the last decade have markedly improved the quality of Alcamo as a table wine that is light, dry, fairly crisp but at the same time rather soft; in short, a smooth and easy wine to drink well chilled. Some producers have managed to give it a touch of personality and even a hint of fragrance, though fruitiness is not one of its long suits. The Cantina Sociale Paladino at Alcamo and the Cantina Sociale Aurora at Salemi work well on a fairly large scale. Their Alcamo is among the better cooperative products of Sicily. Among private producers, two stand out, Comte Hugues Bernard de la Gatinais, originally of Brittany, and Pietro Papè, Principe di Valdina.

De la Gatinais calls his wine Rapitalà, after a stream that runs through the property near Camporeale in the province of Palermo. Rapitalà is made from free-run must, cold fermented, a good example of the new white wine of Sicily. By now it is almost as well known in Milan as it is in Palermo, for the count's northern distributor has been an active promoter.

Pietro Papè produces a fine Alcamo at his Tenuta Rincione near Calatafimi, but the prince calls his premier products Rincione, non-DOC white and rosé. Rincione Bianco Secco is only a shade different from Alcamo in that it uses Catarratto at 50 percent and Inzolia and Trebbiano at 25 percent each, a formula that gives the wine its fruit and finesse. The Rincione Rosato comes from Nero d'Avola at 50 percent with Nerello Mascalese, Vernaccia Nera, and Trebbiano for the rest, a fresh rosé of delicate fragrance.

Washing the Egg off Marsala's Face

West of Calatafimi and the nearby Greek temple of Segesta, splendid in its solitude, the hills that taper toward the sea support an awesome sweep of vines. If not exactly a garden of Eden, the landscape does have the functional appeal of well-kept farmland. On the horizon to the north above Trapani is the mountain of Erice with the ancient town at its summit, and across the water lie the Egadi Islands. To the southwest is the port of Marsala, known to the Arabs as Marsa el Allah; from afar it still seems to have a trace of Araby about it.

Marsala, a small and rather drab city, has a busy port and a burgeoning industrial center along the waterfront, most of the activity there concentrated on the processing of wine and related beverages. This is another place where the word *industry* is aptly applied to the making of wine. As an indication of the scope, the port of Marsala handles some 300 million liters of wine a year (nearly all outbound), second in the Mediterranean after Séte in southern France (where the movement is nearly all inbound).

Mere mention of the name Marsala to serious wine drinkers can provoke all manner of negative reactions, one of the printable being "You call that stuff wine?" The answer to that is yes and no, with perhaps more emphasis on the negative than the positive. Marsala might be loosely evaluated in three classes: the good, the bad, and the gooey. The last can be dispensed with quickly, for most Marsala that meets the description has flavorings that qualify it as Marsala *speciale* and disqualify it as DOC and as what any discriminating palate would accept as wine.

As a recent convert to Marsala — good, nay, excellent Marsala — I risk sounding like a missionary of a very unpopular faith. Oh well, good Marsala needs a few apostles to spread the word if it is ever to carry off its revival, now that some responsible producers have determined to wash the egg (not to mention cream, coffee, banana, strawberry, and chocolate syrup) off its face.

The instigator of my conversion was Giacomo Rallo, who believes in letting the Marsala of his family firm, Diego Rallo & Figli, speak for itself. Of the several Rallo types, the one that did the most talking was a *vergine* which, as could be deduced from its identification, is the purest of the Marsala family, which also includes some other reputable members, mostly in the *superiore* category. Some of the rest of the clan, after generations of inbreeding, have some rather grotesque features.

Marsala was originated by a merchant from Liverpool, John Woodhouse, who found the wines of western Sicily to his liking, and to preserve them on the voyage back to England added about 2 gallons of alcohol to each of the 60 pipes (elongated 100-gallon barrels). This procedure, which the English had learned through their experience with wines of the Iberian peninsula, was a grand success. Marsala soon became so fashionable back home that Woodhouse founded a winery–blending center at the tuna fishing port of Cannozzo and established the basic principles of Marsala production, still followed to a great extent today. Woodhouse was soon joined by other Englishmen and, somewhat later, by Sicilians.

The English presence in Marsala was later credited with facilitating Garibaldi's landing there with the "Thousand" in 1860. Because British ships were in port taking on wine, so one story goes, Bourbon forces declined to fire on Garibaldi's steamers for fear of hitting a British vessel and drawing England's wrath, though there are several versions to that bit of history. In the late nineteenth century, Marsala's fame spread from England through the rest of the Western world. By 1900, some 4 million liters of Marsala were exported, an astounding figure for those days. Over the years variations were improvised and different types were devised to suit a wide range of tastes.

The original Marsala grape was Grillo, which is still considered the best, though today Catarratto in subvarieties known as Lucido and Opaco is more often used with Inzolia, a table grape, also permitted at 15 percent. Grapes for DOC Marsala come from the province of Trapani and parts of Palermo and Agrigento. Only a minor share of Trapani's grape production, usually from older plants and generally head-trained and not irrigated, is used in Marsala. The vines render small, golden-yellow grapes naturally loaded with sugar when picked in late August and early September. Marsala's basic character depends upon oxidation of the grapes on the vine before they are harvested, which gives the *rancio* taste, which typifies Marsala, Sherry, and other wines of the genre. The base wine must have at least 12° natural alcohol, though it usually has 2° to 4° more.

Each winery makes some of the grapes into wine and converts another portion into what are called *sifone* (or *mistella*) and *cotto* (or *calamich*). *Sifone* is a blend of sweet wine from semi-dried grapes and wine alcohol known as *buon gusto*. *Cotto* is must, usually from Catarratto grapes, reduced for about twenty-four hours in copper cauldrons under fire or steam to a thick, syrupy consistency with its sugars caramelized. Together, *sifone* and *cotto* are called *concia*, a concoction that varies somewhat in degree of alcohol and sweetness. The *concia* gives Marsala its nuances which are, to say the least, confounding.

There are four basic categories of Marsala, three DOC and the *speciale*. Within each are what remains of the old commercial classifications.

★ Marsala *fine* must have 17° alcohol and at least four months of aging. Made with more *cotto* than *sifone,* it is considered the common grade. It was traditionally known as Italy Particular (IP) or Italia, among other things.

★ Marsala *superiore* must have 18° alcohol and two years of aging. Depending on the producer and the blend, it may have different degrees of dryness or sweetness. The range includes the traditional products known as Superior Old Marsala (SOM), London Particular (LP), and Garibaldi Dolce (GD). In the past, the most highly prized Marsala, especially in England, was usually in the *superiore* category.

★ Marsala *vergine* must have 18° alcohol and at least five years of age. It is dry to very dry natural wine that does not include *sifone* or *cotto*. Different producers have different styles of developing its ultimate elegance, sometimes through *solera,* like Sherry, sometimes through other means. This is now considered the finest and most prestigious Marsala.

★ Marsala *speciale* of 18° and six months of aging is the subject of some controversy over status, though recent rulings determined it was not to be considered DOC wine. Once popular, the special types have been declining slightly in flavor.

From Grandmother's Cupboard to the Lips of Connoisseurs

Marsala enjoyed wide esteem in the nineteenth century, especially in England. It also reached peaks of favor in this century. When export fell off due to international disruptions, the Italian market picked up the slack. Production reached 25 million liters in 1936, 35 million in 1942, and an all-time high of 45 million in 1960. But tastes were changing, and it soon began to look as though Marsala had had its day.

Despite legislation in 1930 and 1950 that officially determined the zone and rules of production, Marsala's credibility and reputation deteriorated. The special contrivances were partly to blame, but rampant competition had made Marsala of every type cheap, not only in price but in substance. By the mid-1960s, not many arbiters of taste took the wine seriously. As Cyril Ray noted in *The Wines of Italy* in 1966: ". . . although it is rather out of fashion in England nowadays as an aperitif or dessert wine, in Regency and Victorian times it rivalled Madeira." Nonetheless, its production continued at reasonable levels of volume because Marsala has always had a role in the kitchen, in desserts, in grandmother's cupboard. Much Marsala is still assembled and distributed by Piedmontese firms and, in fact, in Piedmont it has long been considered virtually a regional product, a tonic and base of the fabled zabaglione.

DOC, introduced in 1969, was a big step on the road back, but Marsala still has a long way to go. Lately the revival has shown signs of accelerating, thanks to the push given it by a few producers who have determined not to cut corners in bringing Marsala back to the lips of connoisseurs as one of the finest wines of its type in the world.

Among the revivalists, Diego Rallo & Figli stands out. Founded by Diego Rallo in 1860, the firm is now run by a directorate of brothers and cousins, two Giacomos, Enrico, and Tony. The elder Giacomo, an attorney who handles international dealings, seems to enjoy applying his youthful energy to the challenge of rebuilding the image.

"The first consideration in any meaningful discussion of Marsala today is that it is by definition costly," said Rallo. And just in case I doubted it, he took me on a tour of the winery, a large walled-in complex like the others but with a bit less of the factory appearance than many Marsala firms. Among the old-world fixtures at Diego Rallo & Figli is the barrel shop where coopers put together containers that are put to plenty of use here.

First, Giacomo Rallo explained how the *cotto* and *sifone* are made, complex processes that involve aging. For the *sifone,* racking and aerating are used to bring the sweetness and alcohol content of the wine to desired levels. Rallo makes superb Garibaldi Dolce and Extra Dry, both in the *superiore* category, but the *vergine* is the prima donna with a beauty all its own.

Vergine refers to its untampered state, though this Marsala, too, is developed through a series of intricate maneuvers. The base wine of 14° to 16° is made from free-run must fermented off the skins in a process known here as *pesta-imbotta.* Then the wine is racked and stored for years in barrels, piled row upon row almost up to the high rafters. This barrel aging was often neglected in the price-war days but is now considered indispensable to the making of a fine Marsala.

The keys to the flavor of Marsala *vergine* are the *lieviti,* whose literal translation is yeasts, but which refers in producers' jargon to the well-aged wines cultured for blending. "It has often been said that Marsala is made by the *solera* method like Sherry," said Rallo, "but that is true only in a few wineries, not ours. Instead, we develop the *lieviti* through barrel aging and evaporation into different degrees of strength, color, density, and flavor. Some *lieviti* are seventeen or eighteen years old, others younger."

Rallo had some 400,000 liters of *lieviti* aging in barrels. We tasted one seven years old and one of about seventeen. The older wine was, as Rallo said, almost decrepit but curiously tasty. "*Solera* is the luck of the barrel," said Rallo, but *lieviti* are the handiwork of man. Each achieves approximately the same end, but the *lieviti* can be more exactly controlled. It takes inordinate skill to use just the right amounts of each *lievito* to keep a general consistency in the product from year to year."

The talent behind Rallo's consistency is Francesco Agate, the company oenologist, who backs his judgments by consulting with the Rallo family and other experts during the blending. The process takes place after the base wine is three or four years old. Then, before it is sold (after at least five years), it is subjected to stabilization through repeated clarification, filtration, and cold treatments. In short, Marsala *vergine* has to be expensive.

Marsala in the dry range is noted primarily as an *aperitivo* and the sweet as a dessert wine. Differences of opinion occur over serving temperatures. In Italy, both types are generally served cool but not chilled. They are both suited to casual sipping. The *vergine* has an unexpected affinity for cheese, especially cheese with plenty of flavor such as Parmesan, Sicilian *pecorino,* and above all Lombardian Gorgonzola. Rallo Marsala *vergine* and a still soft and creamy Gorgonzola should have made Garibaldi happy (even if he did have a sweet tooth) because they constitute one of the most convincing arguments yet for the cause of national unity.

A few other Marsala firms make excellent wines. The largest is Florio, controlled by Cinzano, with its Marsala *superiore* called ACI. The region of Sicily has been promoting Marsala as the most honored wine of the island, understandably, for DOC production is nearly 40 million liters a year, far more than any other classified wine of Sicily. Another boost has come from writers, critics, and people in the wine and restaurant businesses who have recently "rediscovered" fine Marsala and praised it to their publics.

Still, there is no excess of first-rate Marsala available, though there seems to be plenty of second-rate wine of the name in Italy and abroad. Stricter self-discipline is obviously needed by individual producers under the guidance of the Marsala consortium, and regional and national wine authorities. There has been some talk of limiting Marsala sales to bottles only and restricting bottling and commercialization of Marsala to producers in the DOC zone, measures that might help control quality. Ultimately, though, as the word is spread, Marsala will have to speak for itself.

Like other large wineries of the area, Diego Rallo & Figli produces and bottles wines other than Marsala, some well known abroad. Red and white Segesta and white Bell'Agio are distributed in the United States. Red and white Normanno and Etna DOC are sold mostly in Italy. All are dry table wines sold at competitive prices. The Normanno Bianco is an especially good fish wine, which accounts for its high standing in Sicily. Rallo has also been producing *spumante,* both brut and demi-sec, by the charmat method.

Cooperatives in the province of Trapani have also been emphasizing dry table wines, especially white, low in alcohol (10.5° to 11°), from free-run must. Kept fresh and crisp by cold fermentation, these wines, often referred to locally as *verdelli* because of their greenish tints, are most competitive in terms of quality and price, though some have had trouble establishing markets.

Pantelleria: Enduring Myths, Disturbing Realities

From Trapani, boats leave daily for the island of Pantelleria, a seven-hour voyage into the Sicilian Channel to the "black pearl of the Mediterranean." Nearer Tunisia than the main island of Sicily, Pantelleria is off by itself in letter and spirit, the farthest outpost of Italian commercial winemaking. It is not the southernmost point of Italy, a distinction reserved for Lampedusa in the Pelagian Islands, but if Lampedusa has wine — as in all probability it has — the fact is certainly not publicized.

Pantelleria is an extreme in a nation of extremes, 32 square miles of volcanic residue spewed forth from Monte Grande, the 3,200-foot-high crater at the center of the mass. Over time, a productive mixture of powdery sand, ash, and pebbles has been collected among the stone walls that delineate the arable land from the edge of the sea back to where the rubble and brush take over in the hills. Some 80 percent of the island's 9,000 inhabitants manages to earn a living off the land, by growing peaches, almonds, olives, and the two leading crops, capers and grapes.

Among the walls grow the vines of Zibibbo, in the Muscat family, which produce a superb table grape known as Moscatellone and a wine called Moscato di Pantelleria, one of the most admired dessert wines of Italy. The vines are trained low across the ash-gray soil, crouching as if to duck the winds that whip through here with a fury off the Sahara.

Pantelleria is an island of enduring myths and disturbing realities. The mythology lingers in many facets of life, including an almost mystical attitude toward the island's vines and wines. They say Zibibbo was brought here by the Phoenicians along with the cult of the goddess Tanit, whose worship entailed, among other things, human sacrifices. During Greek dominion, according to the legend, Pantelleria at one point fell from favor with the gods, but Tanit managed to restore Apollo's interest in the island by taking him some of its sweet wine in place of his daily ambrosia. The sun god liked it so much that he has smiled on Pantelleria ever since.

The disturbing realities also involve vines and wines. The island has about 10,000 acres of vines, though Zibibbo is not very productive and in its own way is as challenging to work as any, rivaling even those vines that grow at the opposite extreme of Italy, in the Alps. Some years the grapes do not develop sufficiently to meet DOC requirements, and because Moscato does not convert very satisfactorily into lightweight table wine, which in any case is unprofitable to make, growers are sometimes left with little to show for their year's effort. Hence interest in vine cultivation has been waning while vines diminish in number. Some vineland has been claimed by construction along the coast. And only unusual longevity has kept some other vines productive. When the old plants give out, new ones are not likely to take their place.

Even when the grapes are healthy, production of Moscato di Pantelleria is limited. A peak was reached in 1976 when nearly 2 million liters were made, but the average is just over 1 million liters. Even that quantity is hard to sell, because Moscato di Pantelleria is costly, especially the Moscato Passito, which is pressed from semi-dried grapes. The market for the exquisite Pantelleria wine is often undermined by cheaper competition. Plenty of unclassified Moscato is made in Italy, much of it in Marsala; if rarely equal to the Moscato di Pantelleria in class, its lower price is decisive with consumers.

There are two base categories, Moscato di Pantelleria and Moscato Passito di Pantelleria, the first made from ripe grapes and the second from semi-dried or *passito* grapes. The first has four versions: *naturale* (lightly sweet, fragrant, of at least 12.5° alcohol), *naturalmente dolce* (naturally sweet with at least 17.5° alcohol, some left in residual sugar), *spumante* (the sparkling version of the *naturale*), and *liquoroso* (the *naturale* or *naturalmente dolce* fortified with wine alcohol).

The Passito has three versions: *naturalmente dolce* (of at least 14°), *liquoroso* (fortified to at least 21.5° with at least 15° developed and the rest sugar), and *extra* (the superior product that must have at least 23.9° and 15.5° developed, be aged a year, and be bottled on Pantelleria).

Most Moscato Passito *extra*, some 600,000 bottles a year, is produced by the Agricoltori Associati of Pantelleria, a cooperative that groups about a thousand registered grape growers. The winery makes as much as 8 million liters in good years, most of it not DOC, in red and white table wines, blending wines, and musts. The cooperative sells its still Moscato and Moscato Passito under the brand name Tanit and the Moscato *spumante* under the name Solimano. There are also some good private producers of Moscato and other wines on the island, among them Fortunato Errera, Leonardo Minardi, and F. Maccotta.

The Tanit Passito *extra* is smooth, rich, deliciously fragrant, a special wine that merits a special price comfortably above that of many other Sicilian dessert wines. Vito Valenza, the cooperative's director, charged in 1979 that the terms Moscato and Pantelleria had been "contrabanded" by producers and bottlers elsewhere who had no right to the names. He complained that appeals to Sicilian, Italian, and Common Market officials had not put a stop to the unethical practices, and that authorities had not responded to suggestions that all wine labeled Moscato di Pantelleria be vinified and bottled on the island from grapes grown there. "If this continues," said Valenza, "the future of Moscato di Pantelleria must be considered doubtful."

Though the true Moscato di Pantelleria, and particularly Tanit Passito *extra,* has developed a following in Italy, sales have not been adequate to prompt an upturn in the wine's fortunes. As Fiorino Perletto, a Piedmontese who serves as the cooperative's chief oenologist, explains: "The only satisfactory way to make the Passito is from grapes dried in the sun, a traditional, painstaking process that doesn't permit innovations, simplifications, or expedients." The only concession to streamlined techniques, according to Perletto, is in the making of *spumante,* which is nonetheless accomplished through natural fermentation.

On Pantelleria, as in so many other places in Italy north and south, mechanized cultivation of vines is a practical impossibility. They must be tended vineyard by vineyard, plant by plant, by the knowing hands of man, as they have been for millennia, since the Greeks and the Phoenicians came to this dark and mystical island in the sun and created nectars for the gods.

The Vintages

	Etna Bianco, Rosso	Corvo Bianco, Rosso
1979	Excellent	Excellent
1978	Good	Good
1977	Exceptional, scarce	Exceptional
1976	Fair	Good
1975	Excellent	Excellent
1974	Good	Excellent
1973	Good	Good to excellent
1972	Fair	Good to excellent
1971	Fair	Excellent
1970	Excellent	Excellent

INDEX